Revenue Statistics 2024

HEALTH TAXES IN OECD COUNTRIES

1965-2023

OECD
BETTER POLICIES FOR BETTER LIVES

Please cite this publication as:
OECD (2024), *Revenue Statistics 2024: Health Taxes in OECD Countries*, OECD Publishing, Paris, https://doi.org/10.1787/c87a3da5-en.

ISBN 978-92-64-42218-6 (print)
ISBN 978-92-64-50157-7 (PDF)
ISBN 978-92-64-84367-7 (HTML)
ISBN 978-92-64-46708-8 (epub)

Revenue Statistics
ISSN 2522-7696 (print)
ISSN 2522-770X (online)

Photo credits: Cover © some of the graphic elements in the main cover illustration were adapted from Freepik.com.

Corrigenda to OECD publications may be found at: https://www.oecd.org/en/publications/support/corrigenda.html.

Foreword

This annual publication provides internationally comparative data on tax levels and tax structures in member countries of the Organisation for Economic Cooperation and Development (OECD). The taxes imposed in each country are presented in a standardised framework based upon the OECD classification of taxes and its Interpretative Guide as contained in Annex A to this Report. The data for the Report has, for the most part, been provided by Delegates to Working Party No.2 (WP2) on Tax Policy Analysis and Tax Statistics of the Committee on Fiscal Affairs. The OECD acknowledges the co-operation of the International Monetary Fund, whose classification of tax revenues in the *Government Finance Statistics Manual 2014* is in many respects similar to that of the OECD. The most important of the other classifications currently in use is the System of National Accounts (henceforth referred to as SNA) and the European System of Integrated Economic Accounts of EU member states (henceforth referred to as ESA), which is primarily an elaboration of the SNA, though differing from it in certain respects. Subject to a few exceptions, SNA/ESA figures can be reconciled with the figures in the present Report, since SNA criteria and definitions have been adopted unless the contrary is specifically indicated.

The material is organised in six chapters. Chapter 1 summarises tax revenue trends over the past six decades, with a focus on the ratio of tax revenues to GDP, tax structures and taxes by level of government. It also discusses the treatment of non-wastable tax credits and provides information on financing of social security-type benefits. This year's issue also carries in Chapter 2 a special feature on "Health taxes in OECD countries". Chapter 3 contains a set of comparative statistical tables for years 1965-2023. Chapter 4 provides country tables with tax revenue and tax-to-GDP ratios broken down by selected tax categories and by level of government for years between 1990 and 2022. Two memorandum tables show how countries finance their social benefits and report taxes and social security contributions paid by general government as a percentage of GDP. Chapter 5, only available online, provides statistical tables with a detailed breakdown of tax revenues by country between 1965 and 2022. A further two memorandum tables show how countries finance their social benefits and report taxes and social security contributions paid by general government in national currency. Chapter 6, which is also only available online, attributes tax revenues to general government by the following sub-sectors: central, state, local and social security funds. It contains tables that provide a detailed breakdown of tax revenues by country between 1975 and 2022. Because of space limitations, Chapters 4, 5 and 6 show data for selected years between 1965 and 2022; data for the years not shown are available online.

Revenue Statistics 2024 has been produced by the OECD's Centre for Tax Policy and Administration (CTPA). The authors of this edition were Alexander Pick, Nicolás Miranda and Michael Sharratt. The special feature was written by Alexander Pick. The authors would like to thank colleagues in the OECD for their invaluable comments and practical support in finalising the publication, including Bert Brys, Stéphane Buydens, Céline Colin, Kurt Van Dender, Rebekka Hviid Kanstrup, Sabine Laudage Teles, Alexandra Le Cam, Michael Sicsic and Jingjing Xia in CTPA. Stephanie Coic in the Development Co-operation Directorate designed the cover. The authors would also like to thank WP2 delegates and their colleagues working in national administrations for their input and comments.

In Memoriam

This edition of *Revenue Statistics* is dedicated to the memory of Christian Valenduc, who died on 1 October 2024. Christian served as Chair of Working Party No. 2 (WP2) on Tax Policy and Statistics as well as the WP2 delegate for Belgium. Christian was an outstanding colleague who made a profound contribution to the OECD's work on tax.

Table of contents

FIGURES

TABLES

Executive summary

In 2023, the average tax-to-GDP ratio of OECD countries declined by 0.1 percentage points (p.p.) to 33.9%. This was the second year in a row that the average tax-to-GDP ratio has declined slightly, although it remained above the level in 2019, prior to a challenging period for public finances in OECD countries that has included the COVID-19 pandemic, Russia's illegal invasion of Ukraine and the highest level of inflation in OECD countries for 30 years. OECD countries continued to use tax policy to ease cost-of-living challenges in 2023 amid growing spending pressures related to long-term challenges such as climate change and population ageing, which will require higher revenues.

In this publication, taxes are defined as compulsory, unrequited payments to the general government or to a supranational authority. They are unrequited in that the benefits provided by governments to taxpayers are not normally allocated in proportion to their payments. Taxes are classified according to their base: income, profits and capital gains; payroll; property; goods and services; and other taxes. Compulsory social security contributions paid to general government are also treated as taxes. Revenues are analysed by level of government: federal or central; state; local; and social security funds. Detailed information on the classification of taxes is set out in the Interpretative Guide in Annex A.

Tax levels in 2023

Across OECD countries, tax-to-GDP ratios ranged from 17.7% in Mexico to 43.8% in France in 2023. Between 2022 and 2023, the OECD average tax-to-GDP ratio declined from 34.0% to 33.9%.

- In 2023, tax-to-GDP ratios increased from the previous year in 18 of the 36 countries for which preliminary data is available, declined in 17 countries and remained unchanged in one.
- The largest increase in 2023 was observed in Luxembourg, whose tax-to-GDP ratio rose by 2.7 p.p. due to higher revenues as a share of GDP from personal income tax (PIT) and social security contributions. The second-largest increase was in Colombia, where tax revenues rose by 2.6 p.p. as a result of higher revenues from corporate income tax (CIT).
- The largest declines in the tax-to-GDP ratio in 2023 occurred in Chile and Korea (of 3.2 p.p. and 3.1 p.p. respectively). In both cases, this was primarily due to a decline in income tax revenues. The United States and Israel also recorded declines in their tax-to-GDP ratio larger than 2 p.p.

Over the longer term, 29 OECD countries reported higher tax-to-GDP ratios in 2023 than in 2010, with the largest increases in Japan (8.2 p.p.), the Slovak Republic (7.6 p.p.) and Greece (7.5 p.p.). Among the remaining nine countries, Ireland's tax-to-GDP ratio was 5.8 p.p. lower in 2023 than in 2010 while Hungary's was 2.6 p.p. lower.

Tax structures in 2022

In 2022, the latest year for which final tax revenue data is available for all OECD countries, social security contributions accounted for the largest share of tax revenues in the OECD, at just under one-quarter (24.8%), on average, while revenues from PIT accounted for the second-largest share, at 23.6%. VAT accounted for just over one-fifth of total revenues (20.8%), with other consumption taxes generating a further 10.8%. CIT accounted for 12.0% of total tax revenues in 2022, with property taxes (5.3%) and residual taxes accounting for the remainder.

Between 2021 and 2022, the average share of income tax revenues (PIT and CIT combined) in total tax revenues increased by 1.4 p.p. to 36.5%, with the share of CIT in total tax revenues increasing over this period while the share of PIT declined. In 2022, the average share of social security contributions in the OECD average tax structure fell by 0.8 p.p. while the share of tax revenues from taxes on goods and services decreased by 0.4 p.p.

Changes by level of government

On average, subnational governments received a lower share of tax revenues in 2022 than in 2021. The central government's average share of revenues rose from 53.5% to 53.7% of general government revenue in federal countries and from 63.6% to 64.6% in unitary countries between 2021 and 2022. In federal countries, 17.8% of tax revenues were received at state level and 7.3% at local government level on average in 2022. At state level, the average share of tax revenues ranged from 1.9% in Austria to 38.9% in Canada, while at local government level it ranged from 1.8% in Mexico to 15.8% in Switzerland. In unitary countries, the share of local government revenues was 10.3% on average, ranging from 0.6% in Estonia to 35.1% in Sweden.

Health taxes in OECD countries

The Special Feature in this publication examines revenues from health taxes in OECD countries. Health taxes, defined by the World Health Organisation as 'taxes levied on products that have a negative public health impact', have emerged as a major focus of policy makers in public finances and health over the past two decades. This reflects the capacity of health taxes to meet two objectives: not only do they generate a modest but stable source of revenues to finance public spending but they have also been shown to be a cost-effective means of reducing consumption of unhealthy products and thus improving health outcomes. Although taxes on alcohol and tobacco are present in all OECD countries, taxes on sugar-sweetened beverages (SSBs) are relatively new and have not yet been implemented by all countries.

The Special Features uses granular data provided by countries for this edition of *Revenue Statistics* to examine revenues from excise taxes on alcohol, tobacco and SSBs between 2000 and 2022. Revenue data is a key input for designing and monitoring the effectiveness of health taxes, although revenue trends should be interpreted with caution as it may be difficult to clearly identify the underlying drivers. International comparison of revenue levels should also take into account differences in consumption patterns between countries.

On average across OECD countries, revenues from these three health taxes amounted to 0.74% of GDP and accounted for 2.24% of total tax revenues in 2022. In 27 of the 38 OECD countries, revenues from excise taxes on tobacco were the principal source of health tax revenues in that year. Revenues from health excise taxes have declined as a proportion of GDP between 2000 and 2022 on average across the OECD (especially since 2010), with the largest decline observed for excise taxes on alcohol.

1 Tax revenue trends 1965-2023

Chapter 1 provides information on trends in tax revenues in OECD countries, including changes in tax-to-GDP ratios, tax structures, taxes by level of government, non-wastable tax credits and financing of social security-type benefits.

Revenue Statistics 2024 presents detailed internationally comparable data on tax revenues of OECD countries for all levels of government. The latest edition provides final data on tax revenues for the period from 1965 up to 2022, a year marked by Russia's illegal invasion of Ukraine and the highest levels of inflation in OECD countries for over three decades. In addition, provisional estimates of tax revenues in 2023 are included for almost all OECD countries.[1] OECD countries continued to use tax policy to ease cost-of-living challenges in 2023 amid growing spending pressures related to long-term challenges such as climate change and population ageing, which will require higher revenues (OECD, 2024[1]), (OECD, 2024[2]).

Box 1.1. Revenue Statistics in OECD countries – Definitions & classifications

In *Revenue Statistics 2024*, taxes are defined as compulsory, unrequited payments to the general government or to a supranational authority. Taxes are unrequited in the sense that benefits provided by government are not normally in proportion to their payments.

In the OECD classification, taxes are classified by the base of the tax:

- Income and profits (heading 1000)
- Compulsory social security contributions paid to general government that are treated as taxes (heading 2000)
- Payroll and workforce (heading 3000)
- Property (heading 4000)
- Goods and services (heading 5000)
- Other (heading 6000)

Greater detail on the tax concepts, the classification of taxes and the accrual basis of reporting is set out in the OECD Interpretative Guide in Annex A of *Revenue Statistics 2024*.

All the averages presented in this summary are unweighted.

Tax-to-GDP ratios

Tax ratios for 2023 (provisional data)

According to provisional data provided by OECD countries for this report, tax revenues as a percentage of GDP (i.e. the tax-to-GDP ratio) were 33.9% on average in 2023, a decrease of 0.1 percentage points (p.p.) of GDP relative to 2022. This was the second consecutive small decline in the OECD's tax-to-GDP ratio following a drop of 0.04 p.p. in 2022.

The tax-to-GDP ratio increased in 18 of the 36 countries for which a full set of preliminary data for 2023 are available, declined in 17 and remained the same in one. However, the declines were larger than the increases on average (-1.4 p.p. versus 1.1 p.p.). The largest increases occurred in Luxembourg (2.7 p.p.), Colombia (2.6 p.p.) and Türkiye (2.5 p.p.). The largest decline in 2023 occurred in Chile, whose tax-to-GDP ratio fell by 3.2 p.p., while declines also exceeded 2.0 p.p. in Korea (3.1 p.p.), Israel (3.0 p.p.) and the United States (2.4 p.p.).

Figure 1.1. Trends in tax-to-GDP ratios, 1965-2023p

Percentage of GDP

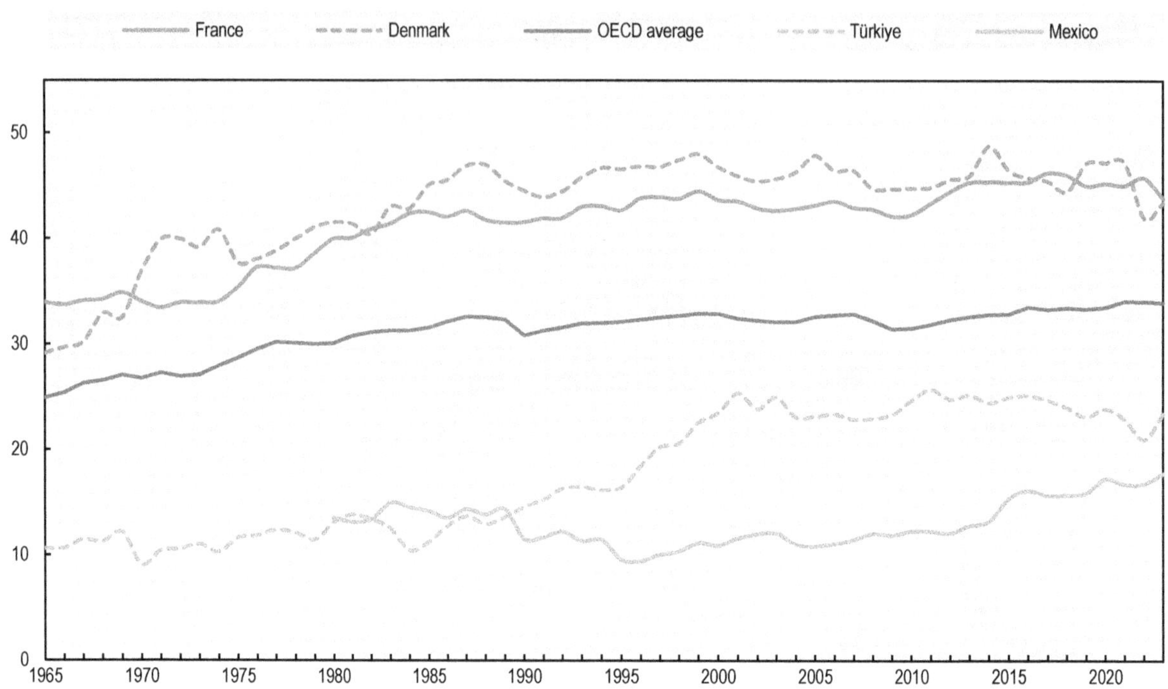

Notes: Data for 2023 are preliminary. The OECD average in 2023 is calculated by applying the unweighted average percentage change for 2023 in the 36 countries providing data for that year to the overall average tax-to-GDP ratio in 2022.
The 2016 OECD average tax-to-GDP ratio includes the one-off revenues from stability contributions in Iceland. Excluding these revenues, the OECD average tax-to-GDP ratio in 2016 would have been 33.1%.
Source: Table 3.1.

StatLink https://stat.link/mvfquo

Tax-to-GDP ratios varied considerably across OECD countries in 2023 (Table 1.1). Key observations include:

- France had the highest tax-to-GDP ratio among OECD countries for the second consecutive year in 2023, at 43.8%. Denmark had the second-highest tax-to-GDP ratio (43.4%) while Mexico had the lowest tax-to-GDP ratio (17.7%).
- Luxembourg observed the largest increase in its tax-to-GDP ratio in 2023, of 2.7 p.p. This was largely due to a 1.2 p.p. increase in revenues from personal income tax (PIT) and a 0.8 p.p. increase in social security contributions (Figure 1.2).
- The increase in Colombia's tax-to-GDP ratio (of 2.6 p.p.) was due to a 2.2 p.p. increase in revenues from corporate income tax (CIT), while the 2.5 p.p. increase in Türkiye was due to a 1.6 p.p. increase in taxes from goods and services and a rise of 1.1 p.p. in social security contributions.
- Chile observed the largest fall in the tax-to-GDP ratio across OECD countries between 2022 and 2023, with a drop of 3.2 p.p. that was primarily due to a decline in revenues from taxes on income and profits.
- The next-largest decline was observed in Korea (3.1 p.p.), where PIT revenues fell by 0.8 p.p., CIT revenues fell by 1.2 p.p. and revenues from taxes on goods and services fell by 0.7 p.p.

Table 1.1. Revenue Statistics: Key figures

	Tax revenue as % of GDP				Tax revenue as % of total tax revenue in 2022						
	2023p	2022	2021	2000	1100 Taxes on income, individuals (PIT)	1200 Taxes on income, corporates (CIT)	2000 Social security contributions (SSC)	4000 Taxes on property	5111 Value added taxes	Other consumption taxes[3]	All other taxes[4]
Australia	..	29.4	29.2	30.4	40.4	21.8	0.0	9.3	11.5	12.3	4.7
Austria[1]	42.7	43.2	43.4	42.3	22.3	7.9	34.1	1.4	18.4	8.5	7.4
Belgium[1]	42.6	42.4	42.1	43.8	28.2	9.2	30.4	7.7	15.3	9.1	0.0
Canada	34.8	33.8	34.8	34.7	36.4	13.9	14.0	10.4	13.4	8.4	3.6
Chile	20.6	23.8	22.3	18.7	10.5	23.7	4.1	5.5	39.0	8.8	8.3
Colombia	22.2	19.7	19.2	15.7	7.0	25.4	8.3	7.8	31.8	13.0	6.7
Costa Rica	24.9	25.2	24.8	21.1	6.1	10.5	34.8	2.0	19.4	13.1	14.0
Czechia	33.7	33.2	33.7	32.2	9.2	12.9	45.9	0.5	22.9	8.6	0.0
Denmark[1]	43.4	41.9	47.2	46.8	55.8	7.9	0.2	4.1	22.0	8.4	1.7
Estonia	33.5	32.6	33.5	31.1	19.2	5.0	34.8	0.5	27.9	12.6	0.0
Finland	42.4	43.2	43.2	45.8	29.9	7.0	27.6	3.3	21.7	10.3	0.1
France[1]	43.8	45.8	45.1	43.7	21.2	6.2	32.4	8.1	16.4	9.7	6.1
Germany	38.1	39.6	39.8	36.4	26.9	6.0	36.9	2.8	18.9	8.5	0.0
Greece	39.8	41.2	40.0	33.4	13.6	6.0	29.6	6.6	21.9	21.4	0.9
Hungary	34.2	35.1	33.8	38.5	15.2	4.7	28.0	2.3	28.9	18.6	2.4
Iceland	35.9	35.2	34.8	35.9	39.9	7.4	8.5	5.6	23.7	9.0	5.9
Ireland	21.9	20.3	20.0	30.8	31.3	21.5	15.1	4.7	18.2	8.3	0.9
Israel	29.8	32.8	32.3	34.0	22.0	13.1	15.3	12.3	22.5	9.9	4.9
Italy	42.8	42.8	42.5	40.5	25.5	6.7	30.5	5.7	16.5	11.2	3.9
Japan	..	34.4	33.9	25.3	18.8	13.7	38.5	7.9	15.1	5.8	0.2
Korea	28.9	32.0	29.8	20.9	20.5	16.8	25.6	11.9	15.3	7.4	2.5
Latvia	31.9	30.8	30.7	29.0	19.2	3.3	30.6	2.5	30.8	13.6	0.0
Lithuania[1]	32.6	31.6	31.9	30.8	24.0	7.4	31.1	0.9	26.5	10.1	0.0
Luxembourg[1]	40.9	38.3	38.2	37.0	27.1	11.5	27.8	9.7	15.8	8.1	0.1
Mexico	17.7	16.8	16.7	10.9	21.6	23.0	13.8	2.1	24.7	8.1	6.8
Netherlands	38.5	38.1	38.3	36.9	20.3	12.5	32.9	3.9	18.6	11.5	0.3
New Zealand	34.0	33.1	34.5	32.5	41.6	13.7	0.0	5.8	30.3	5.7	2.9
Norway	41.4	43.4	41.3	41.8	18.7	42.3	17.3	2.2	15.0	4.5	0.1
Poland[1]	35.1	34.4	36.7	32.9	13.1	8.1	37.1	3.4	21.1	15.4	1.8
Portugal	35.8	36.0	35.2	30.9	19.4	9.3	28.3	4.3	26.0	12.2	0.5
Slovak Republic	35.5	35.0	35.4	33.6	10.7	10.4	41.6	1.2	22.0	13.3	0.8
Slovenia[1]	36.9	37.4	38.3	37.7	13.8	6.2	42.8	1.6	21.9	13.4	0.1
Spain	37.3	37.6	37.8	33.0	24.1	7.2	34.1	6.9	18.6	9.0	0.0
Sweden	41.4	42.5	42.8	50.0	28.0	8.0	20.8	2.2	22.1	6.6	12.2
Switzerland[1]	27.1	26.9	28.0	27.0	31.0	11.9	24.8	8.1	11.6	8.3	4.3
Türkiye	23.5	20.9	22.9	23.5	11.3	16.1	24.4	3.5	24.0	19.6	1.1
United Kingdom	35.3	35.4	34.2	32.7	28.6	9.2	19.9	11.3	20.7	9.9	0.4
United States	25.2	27.6	26.7	28.3	44.0	7.4	21.9	10.4	0.0	16.3	0.1
OECD Average[2]	**33.9**	**34.0**	**34.1**	**32.9**	**23.6**	**12.0**	**24.8**	**5.3**	**20.8**	**10.8**	**2.8**

.. Not available

1. The total tax revenue has been reduced by the amount of any capital transfer that represents uncollected taxes.
2. The provisional average for 2023 is calculated by applying the unweighted average percentage change for 2023 in the 36 countries providing data for that year to the overall average tax-to-GDP ratio in 2022.
3. Calculated as 5000 Taxes on goods and services less 5111 Value added taxes.
4. Includes 1300 Unallocable between personal and corporate income tax, 3000 Taxes on payroll and workforce and 6000 Other taxes.

Figure 1.2. Changes in tax-to-GDP ratios, 2022-23p and 2010-23p

Percentage points

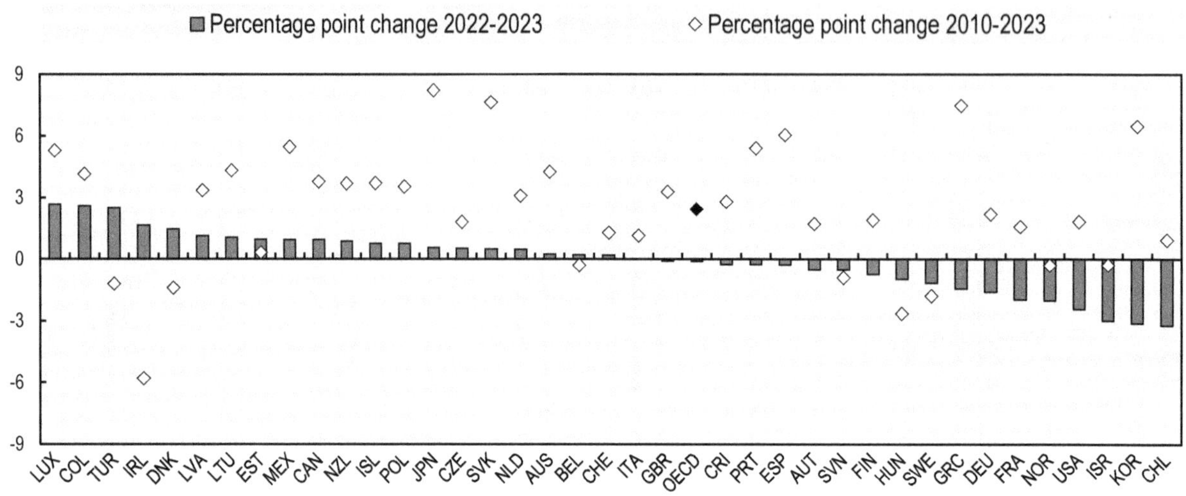

Note: Preliminary data for 2023 is not available for Australia and Japan. For these countries, the comparison shows data for 2021-2022 and 2010-2022.
Source: Secretariat calculations based on Table 3.1.

StatLink https://stat.link/a7jsin

The OECD average tax-to-GDP ratio was higher in 2023 than in 2010, when it was 31.5%. The tax-to-GDP ratio increased in 29 countries over this period (including data for 2022 in the cases of Australia and Japan) (Figure 1.2). The largest increases were seen in Japan (8.2 p.p.), the Slovak Republic (7.6%) and Greece (7.5 p.p.); increases of over 5 p.p. were also observed in Korea, Spain, Mexico, Portugal and Luxembourg. In the remaining nine countries, the tax-to-GDP ratio decreased between 2010 and 2023. The largest fall occurred in Ireland, from 27.7% in 2010 to 21.9% in 2023, largely due to an exceptional GDP increase in 2015. The next largest drop occurred in Hungary (2.6 p.p.).

Changes in the tax-to-GDP ratio are driven by the relative changes in nominal tax revenues and nominal GDP (Box 1.2). From one year to the next, if tax revenues rise by more than GDP (or fall by less than GDP), the tax-to-GDP ratio will increase. Conversely, if tax revenues rise by less than GDP, or fall further, the tax-to-GDP ratio will fall. Therefore, a higher tax-to-GDP ratio does not necessarily mean that the amount of tax revenues has increased in nominal, or even real, terms.

In 2023, nominal tax revenues increased from the previous year in 31 out of the 36 OECD countries for which data is available, while nominal GDP increased in 33 out of 36 countries. In Denmark and Ireland, tax revenues rose in nominal terms while GDP shrunk, while the opposite was the case in the United States, Israel, Korea and Chile (Figure 1.3). In Norway, tax revenues and GDP both declined in nominal terms in 2023 relative to the previous year; its tax-to-GDP ratio declined because the decline in revenues was larger than the decline in GDP.

Changes between 2021 and 2022 are shown for Australia and Japan in Figure 1.3 because the tax-to-GDP ratio is not available in 2023. Australia's tax-to-GDP ratio rose by 0.2 p.p. between 2021 and 2022 while Japan's rose by 0.6 p.p. with nominal tax revenues increasing by more than GDP in both countries.

Box 1.2. Methodology: the tax-to-GDP ratio

The tax-to-GDP ratios shown in *Revenue Statistics 2024* express aggregate tax revenues as a percentage of GDP. The value of this ratio depends on its denominator (GDP) as well as its numerator (tax revenues). The denominator – GDP – is subject to historical revision.

The numerator (tax revenues)

- For the numerator, the OECD Secretariat uses revenue figures that are submitted annually by correspondents from national Ministries of Finance, Tax Administrations or National Statistics Offices. Although provisional figures for most countries become available with a lag of about six months, there is a lag of around one and a half years before finalised data is available. Final revenue data for 2022 were received during the period May-August 2024.
- In 35 OECD countries, the reporting year coincides with the calendar year. Three countries – Australia, Japan and New Zealand – have different reporting years. Reporting year 2022 spans Q2/2022-Q1/2023 in Japan and Q3/2022-Q2/2023 in Australia and New Zealand (Q = quarter).

The denominator (GDP)

- For the denominator, the GDP figures used for *Revenue Statistics 2024* are the most recently available in October 2024. At that point, GDP figures for 2023 were available for all OECD countries.
- Using these GDP figures ensures a maximum of consistency and international comparability for the tax-to-GDP ratios reported.
- The GDP figures are based on the OECD Annual National Accounts (ANA – SNA) for the 35 OECD countries where the calendar year is the same as the reporting year.
- Where the reporting year differs from the calendar year, annual GDP estimates are obtained by aggregating quarterly GDP estimates provided by the OECD Statistics Directorate for those quarters corresponding to each country's fiscal (tax) year.

The average shown in this publication is an unweighted average of all countries for which data is available. The provisional average for 2023 is calculated by applying the unweighted average percentage change for 2023 in the 36 countries providing data for that year to the overall average tax-to-GDP ratio for all OECD countries in 2022.

Figure 1.3. Relative changes in nominal tax revenues and nominal GDP, 2022-23p

Percent

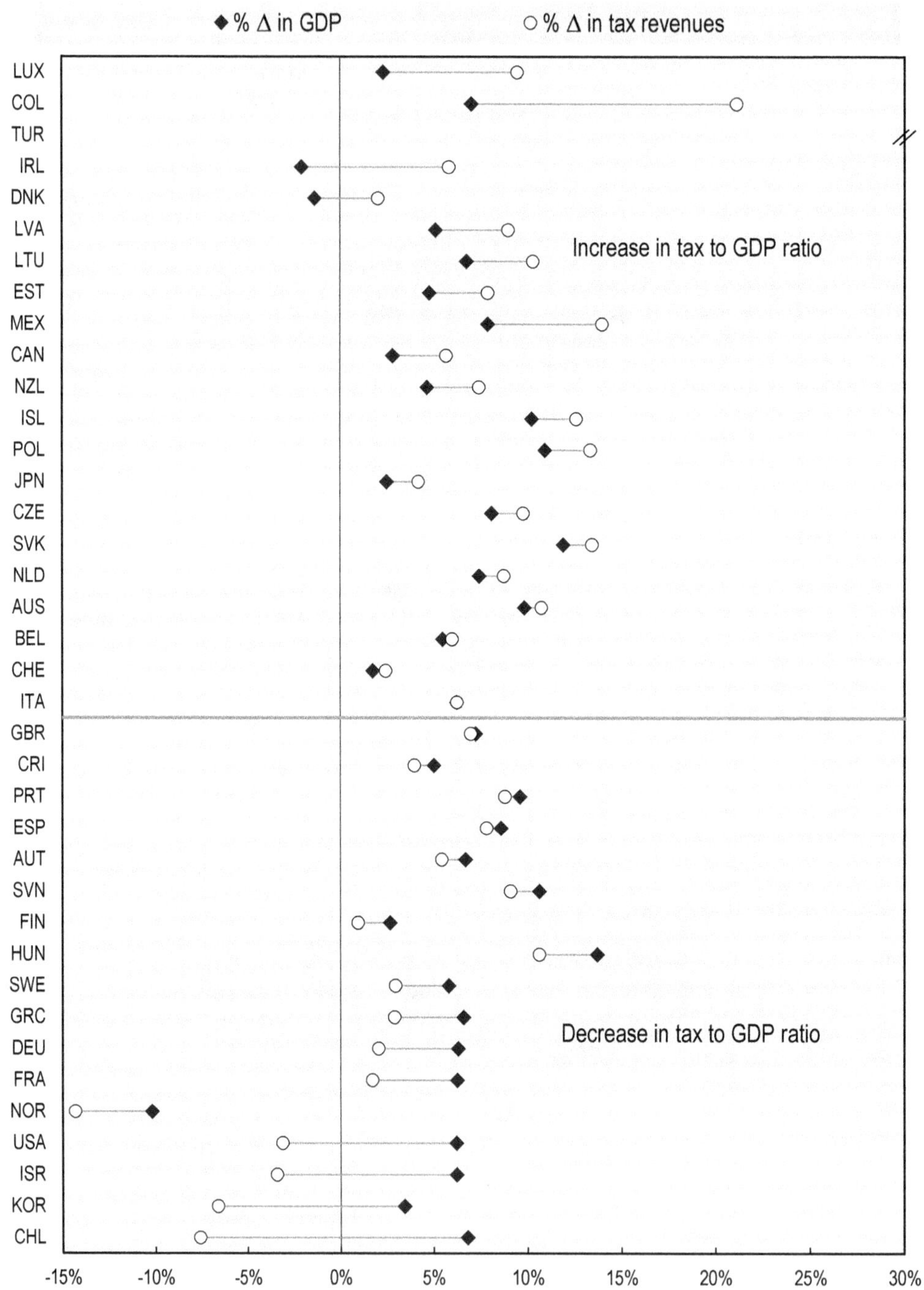

Note: In Türkiye, nominal tax revenues increased by 96% in 2023 while nominal GDP rose by 75%. Data for Australia and Japan show the change between 2021 and 2022 as preliminary data for 2023 was not available for these countries.

Source: Secretariat calculations based on Chapter 4 (tax revenues) and Table 3.19 (GDP).

StatLink https://stat.link/ebpo3h

Figure 1.4. Tax-to-GDP ratios in 2022 and 2023p

Percent of GDP

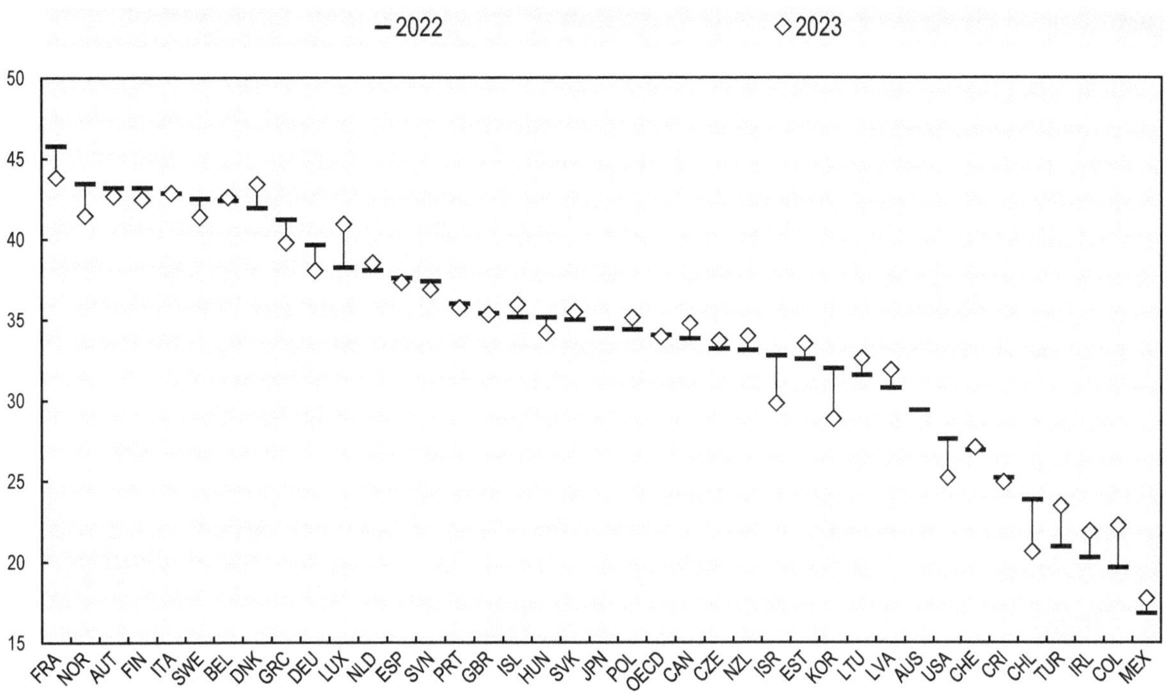

Note: Preliminary data for 2023 were not available for Australia and Japan.
Source: Secretariat calculations based on Table 3.1

StatLink https://stat.link/de0ysv

Tax-to-GDP ratios for 2022 (final data)

The latest year for which tax-to-GDP ratios are based on final data and available for all OECD countries is 2022 (Figure 1.4). These data show that tax ratios varied considerably across countries:

- In 2022, France had the highest tax-to-GDP ratio (45.8%), followed by Norway (43.4%). Seven other countries had tax-to-GDP ratios above 40% (Austria, Finland, Italy, Sweden, Belgium, Denmark and Greece).
- Mexico had the lowest ratio at 16.8%, followed by Colombia (19.7%), Ireland (20.3%), Türkiye (20.9%) and Chile (23.8%). Four other countries had ratios below 30% in 2022: Australia, the United States, Switzerland and Costa Rica.
- The tax-to-GDP ratio in the OECD area as a whole (unweighted average) was 34.0% in 2022, unchanged from 2021.
- Relative to 2021, the tax-to-GDP ratio rose in 21 countries and fell in 17.
- The largest increases in the tax-to-GDP ratio were in Korea (2.2 p.p.) and Norway (2.1 p.p.). Chile, Hungary, United Kingdom and Greece were the only other countries where the increase exceeded 1.0 p.p.
- The largest declines occurred in Denmark (5.3 p.p.) and Poland (2.3 p.p.).

As concerns the average tax-to-GDP for OECD countries, a 0.6 p.p. increase in revenues from CIT between 2021 and 2022 was offset by declines of 0.3 p.p. in revenues from excises, of 0.2 p.p. in social security contributions and of 0.1 p.p. in revenues from PIT (Table 1.2).

Table 1.2. Average tax structure in OECD countries, selected years (unweighted average as % of GDP)

	1965	1990	2000	2007	2010	2015	2020	2021	2022
Total tax revenue	24.9	30.9	32.9	32.9	31.5	32.9	33.5	34.1	34.0
1000 Taxes on income, profits and capital gains	8.7	11.5	11.4	11.7	10.2	10.9	11.3	11.9	12.3
of which:									
1100 Taxes on income, profits and capital gains of individuals	6.8	9.3	8.5	7.8	7.2	7.8	8.3	8.3	8.2
1200 Taxes on income, profits and capital gains of corporates	2.1	2.4	3.1	3.6	2.7	2.8	2.8	3.3	3.9
2000 Social security contributions (SSC)	4.5	7.1	8.4	8.2	8.6	8.8	9.2	9.0	8.7
3000 Taxes on payroll and workforce	0.3	0.4	0.4	0.4	0.4	0.4	0.5	0.5	0.5
4000 Taxes on property	1.9	1.7	1.7	1.7	1.6	1.8	1.9	1.9	1.8
5000 Taxes on goods and services	9.4	9.9	10.8	10.7	10.5	10.8	10.6	10.7	10.6
of which:									
5111 Value added taxes	0.7	5.1	6.3	6.5	6.3	6.5	6.7	6.9	7.0
5121 Excises	3.5	2.5	2.9	2.7	2.7	2.6	2.3	2.2	1.9
6000 Other Taxes	0.1	0.4	0.2	0.2	0.2	0.2	0.2	0.1	0.2

Note: Percentage share of major tax categories in GDP. Data are included from 1965 onwards for Australia, Austria, Belgium, Canada, Denmark, Finland, France, Germany, Greece, Iceland, Ireland, Italy, Japan, Luxembourg, the Netherlands, New Zealand, Norway, Portugal, Spain, Sweden, Switzerland, Türkiye, United Kingdom and United States; from 1972 for Korea; from 1980 for Mexico; from 1990 for Chile, Colombia and Costa Rica; from 1991 for Hungary and Poland; from 1993 for Czechia and from 1995 for Estonia, Israel, Latvia, Lithuania, the Slovak Republic and Slovenia.
Source: OECD (2024), "Revenue Statistics: Comparative tables", *OECD Tax Statistics (database).*

Tax ratio changes between 1965 and 2022

Between 1965 and 2022, the average tax-to-GDP ratio in OECD countries increased from 24.9% to 34.0%, an increase of 9.2 p.p. (Figure 1.1). Before the first oil shock (1973 to 1974), strong, almost uninterrupted income growth enabled tax levels to rise in all OECD countries. In part, tax levels rose automatically through the effect of fiscal drag on PIT schedules. From 1975 to 1985, the average tax-to-GDP ratio in OECD countries increased by 2.9 p.p. After the mid-1970s, the combination of slower real income growth and higher levels of unemployment apparently limited the revenue raising capacity of governments. But during and after the deep recession that followed the second oil shock (1980), tax levels in European countries rose further to finance higher spending on social security and rein in budget deficits.

After the mid-1980s, most OECD countries substantially reduced the statutory rates of their personal and corporate income tax, although the negative revenue impact was often offset by reducing or abolishing tax reliefs. By 1999, the average OECD tax-to-GDP ratio had risen to 32.9%, the highest recorded level at that time. It fell back slightly between 2001 and 2004 then rebounded between 2005 and 2007 before falling back during the Global Financial Crisis in 2008 and 2009. The tax-to-GDP ratio increased in all but two years between 2010 and 2022[2] despite the impact of the COVID-19 pandemic in 2020-21. For more detailed analysis of the long-term evolution of tax revenues, please see the Special Feature in the 2023 edition of this report, which examines the buoyancy of tax revenues in OECD countries between 1980 and 2021 (OECD, 2023[3]).

The OECD average tax-to-GDP ratio conceals great variety between countries. In 1965, tax-to-GDP ratios in OECD countries ranged from 10.6% in Türkiye to 33.9% in France. By 2022, the corresponding range was from 16.8% in Mexico to 45.8% in France. The trend towards higher tax levels over this period reflects the need to finance a significant increase in public sector outlays in almost all OECD countries.

Tax structures

Tax structures are measured by the share of major taxes in total tax revenues. In 2022, the tax structures of OECD countries varied. Eighteen countries raised the largest part of their revenues from income taxes (both corporate and personal), eleven countries raised the largest part of their revenues from social security contributions, and nine countries raised the largest part of their revenues from consumption taxes (including VAT). Taxes on property and payroll taxes played a smaller role in the revenue systems of OECD countries in 2022, both on average and in most countries (Figure 1.5).

Figure 1.5. Tax structures in 2022 (as % of total tax revenue)

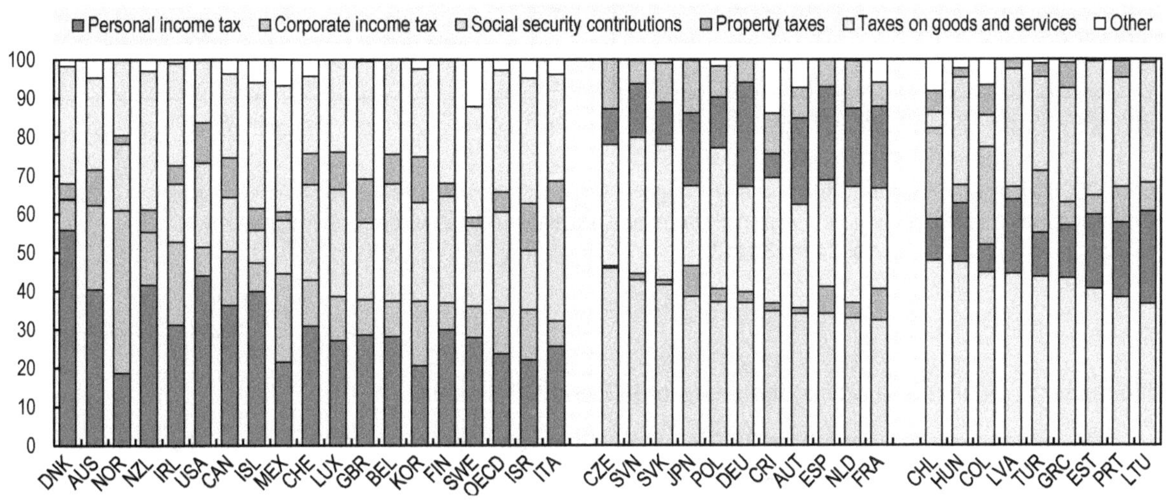

Note: Countries are grouped and ranked by those where income tax revenues (personal and corporate) form the highest share of total tax revenues, followed by those where social security contributions, or taxes on goods and services, form the highest share.
Source: Secretariat calculations based on data in Chapter 4.

StatLink https://stat.link/48coed

While the level of tax revenues has generally been rising on average in the OECD, the tax structure (or 'tax mix') has been remarkably stable over time. Nevertheless, several trends have emerged up to 2022 – the latest year for which data is available for all 38 OECD countries. These trends are discussed below.

Taxes on income and profits

On average, in 2022, OECD countries collected 36.5% of their tax revenues through taxes on income and profits (PIT and CIT taken together). Taxes on personal and corporate incomes remained the most important source of revenues to finance public spending in 18 OECD countries; in ten of these – Australia, Canada, Denmark, Iceland, Ireland, Mexico, New Zealand, Norway, Switzerland and the United States – the share of income taxes in the tax mix exceeded 40% in 2022.

Figure 1.6. Trends in tax structures (1965-2022, as % of total tax revenue)

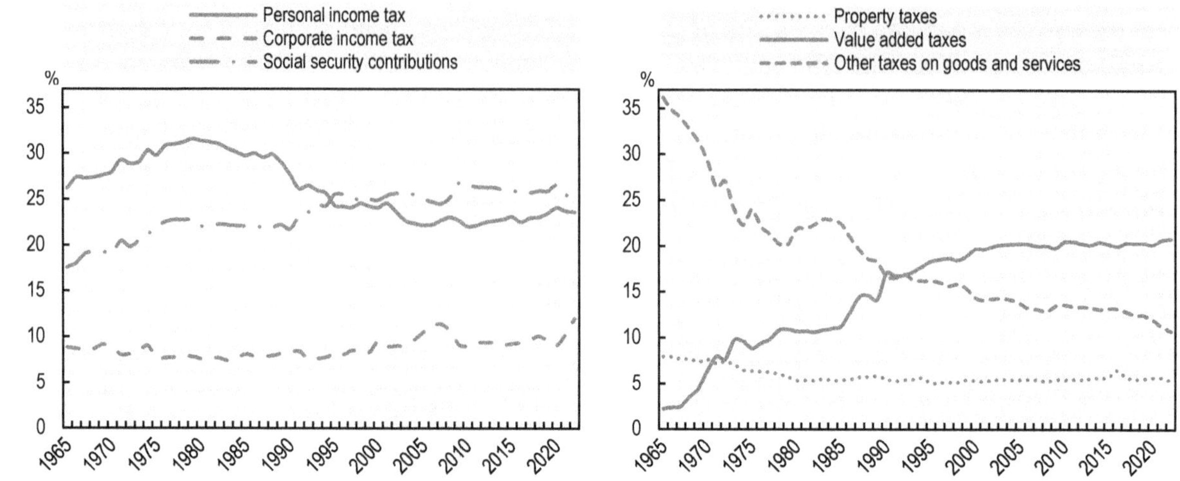

Note: The OECD average tax revenue in 2016 from main categories includes the one-off revenues from stability contributions in Iceland. This predominately affects the average revenues from property taxes, as a percentage of total tax revenues, in that year only.
Source: Secretariat calculations based on Tables 3.8 to 3.14.

StatLink https://stat.link/d8jage

Within taxes on income and profits, the share of PIT and CIT varies:

- Revenues from PIT generated 23.6% of total taxes on average in 2022 compared with around 30% in the 1980s. About two percentage points of this reduction can be attributed to the impact on the average of a number of relatively recent entrants to the OECD from Eastern Europe and Latin America, for which tax revenue data is only available from the 1990s onwards. These countries tend to have relatively low PIT revenues and high revenues from social security contributions or CIT, but this impact is only observed in the data after 1990.
- The variation in the share of PIT revenues between countries is considerable. In 2022, it ranged from 6.1% in Costa Rica to 44.0% in the United States and 55.8% in Denmark (Figure 1.5).
- CIT revenues represented between 8% and 9% of total tax revenues on average throughout the period from 1965 to 2003. They then increased to 11.3% in 2007 before dropping to 9.0% in 2010 after the Global Financial Crisis. They remained between 9.0% and 10.0% of total tax revenues until they increased to 10.3% in 2021 and 12.0% in 2022.
- The share of CIT in total tax revenues in 2022 varied considerably across countries, from less than 6% (Estonia, Hungary and Latvia) to over 20% in Ireland (21.5%), Australia (21.8%), Mexico (23.0%), Chile (23.7%), Colombia (25.4%) and Norway (42.3%). Apart from the spread in statutory CIT rates, these differences are partly explained by institutional and country-specific factors, including:
    - the degree to which firms are incorporated;
    - the breadth of the CIT base; for example, some narrowing may occur as a consequence of generous depreciation schemes and tax incentives:
    - the degree of cyclicality of the corporate tax system, for which one of the important elements is loss-offset provisions:
    - the extent of reliance upon tax revenues from the exploitation of oil and/or mineral deposits; or
    - other instruments to postpone the taxation of earned profits.

Social security contributions

Social security contributions accounted for 24.8% of total tax revenues on average across OECD countries in 2022. They exceeded 40% in Czechia, Slovenia and the Slovak Republic (45.9%, 42.8% and 41.6%, respectively). Australia and New Zealand do not levy social security contributions.

There was wide variation across OECD countries in the relative proportions of social security contributions paid by employees and employers in 2022 (Figure 1.7):

- Nine OECD countries (Chile, Greece, Hungary, Israel, Lithuania, Luxembourg, Poland, Slovenia and Switzerland) raised more revenues from employee social security contributions while the rest raised more from employer social security contributions.
- The highest share of employee social security contributions was in Lithuania, at 23.8% of total tax revenues. Employee social security contributions also amounted to over 15% of total revenues in Germany, Greece, Hungary, Japan, Poland and Slovenia. Denmark had the lowest share, at 0.1% of total revenues. Apart from Denmark, only Chile and Estonia had revenues from employee social security contributions of less than 5% of total revenues.
- The highest share of employer social security contributions in total tax revenues was in Estonia, at 31.8%. Employer social security contributions also exceeded 25% of total tax revenues in Czechia (28.3%) and Spain (25.2%). Denmark and Chile had the lowest shares, at 0.1% and 0.2% of total revenues respectively.
- The highest share of self-employed or non-employed social security contributions was in Czechia (8.4%), followed by the Netherlands and Poland, at 7.5% and 7.4% of total revenues respectively.

Figure 1.7. Composition of social security contributions, as % of total social security contributions, 2022

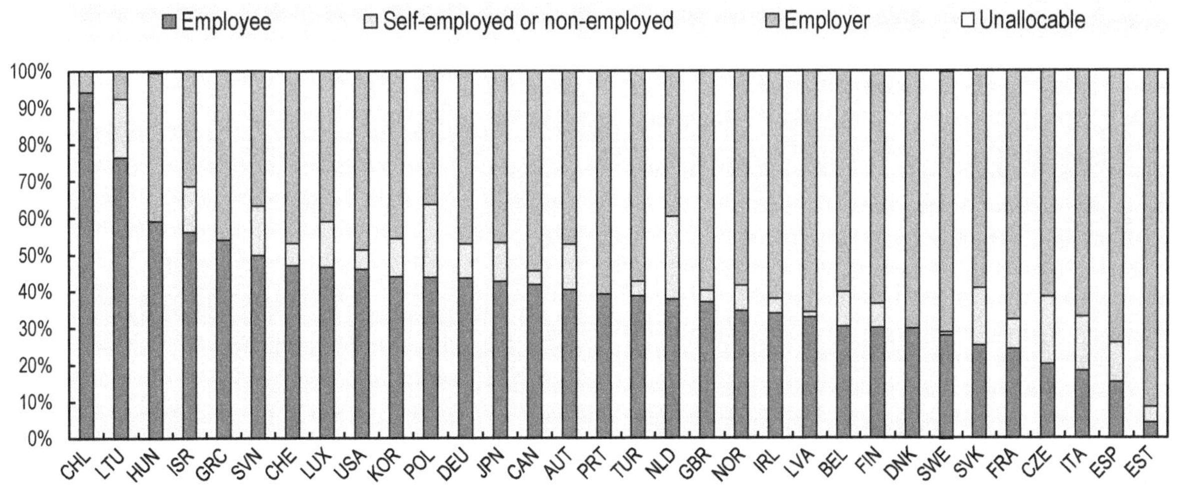

Note: Australia, Costa Rica, Colombia, Iceland, Mexico, and New Zealand are not included in Figure 1.7. Although Colombia, Costa Rica, Iceland and Mexico collect social security contributions, disaggregated data is not available. New Zealand and Australia do not levy social security contributions.
Source: Secretariat calculations based on data in Chapter 4.

StatLink https://stat.link/ev3780

Property taxes

Between 1965 and 2022, the share of taxes on property fell from 7.9% to 5.3% of total tax revenues on average across the OECD (Figure 1.6). In Canada, Israel, Korea, the United Kingdom and the United States, property tax revenues amounted to more than 10% of total tax revenues in 2022. By contrast, property taxes accounted for less than 1% of total tax revenues in Czechia, Estonia and Lithuania.

Consumption taxes

- The share of taxes on consumption (general consumption taxes plus specific consumption taxes) fell from 38.4% to 31.5% between 1965 and 2022 (Figure 1.6).
- During this period, the composition of taxes on goods and services changed. A fast-growing revenue source has been general consumption taxes, especially VAT, which is imposed in 37 of 38 OECD countries.[3]
- General consumption taxes accounted for 21.4% of total tax revenues in 2022, compared with only 13.3% in the mid-1970s. In 2022, the vast majority of this was from VAT (20.8% of total tax revenues).
- The increased importance of VAT has counteracted the diminishing share of specific consumption taxes, such as excises and customs duties.
- Between 1975 and 2022, the share of specific taxes on consumption (mostly on tobacco, alcohol and fuels, as well as some environmentally-related taxes) more than halved, from 17.7% to 8.2% of total revenues. In 2022, excises were the largest single category of total revenues under this heading, accounting for 5.7% of total revenues (Figure 1.8). The Special Feature in Chapter 2 of this report examines trends in revenues from excises on alcohol, tobacco and sugar-sweetened beverages, which are commonly referred to as 'health taxes'.
- Rates of taxes on imported goods were considerably reduced across all OECD countries, reflecting a global trend to remove trade barriers.
- Nevertheless, Hungary, Latvia, Slovenia, Slovak Republic and Poland (between 10%-13%), Greece (15.6%) and Türkiye (18.8%) still collected more than 10% of their tax revenues through taxes on specific goods and services in 2022.

Figure 1.8. Share of general consumption tax revenues (left panel) and specific consumption revenues (right panel) as % of total revenues, 1975-2022

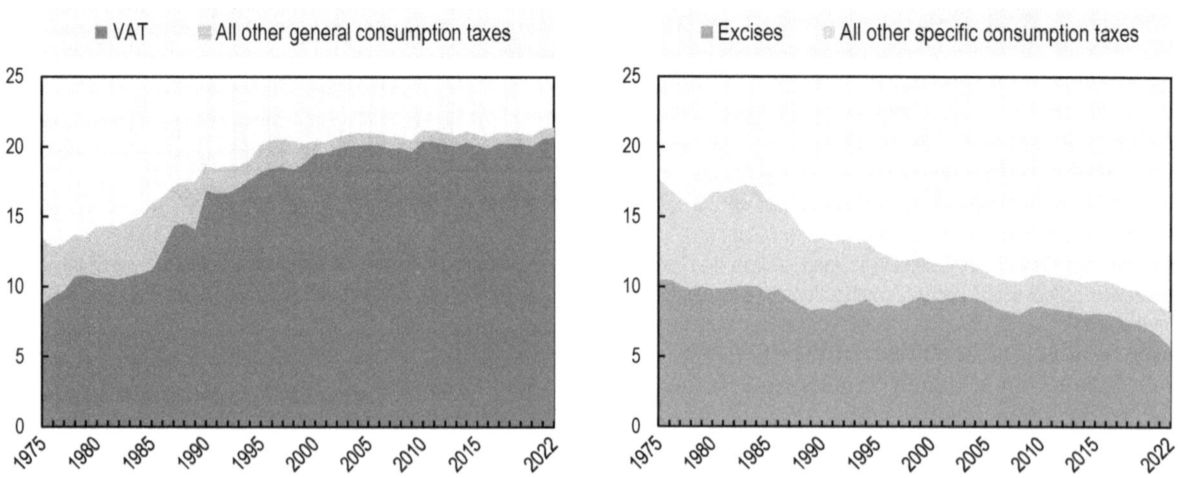

Note: The unweighted average for each year includes all countries which report revenue in the categories shown in that year. The OECD averages for 2016 include the one-off revenues from stability contributions in Iceland.
Source: Secretariat calculations based on Chapter 4.

StatLink https://stat.link/zmth3v

Taxes by level of government

This section discusses the share of tax revenues attributed to the various sub-sectors of general government in 2022. The different sub-sectors are:

- Central government
- State government (federal and regional countries only)
- Local government
- Social security funds
- Supranational authorities (EU countries only)

The guidelines for attributing revenues to different levels of government are based on the final version of the 2008 System of National Accounts. These guidelines are discussed in the special feature S.1 in the 2011 edition of *Revenue Statistics*.

Revenues of sub-national government in federal and unitary countries

Eight OECD countries have a federal structure. Among these countries, central government received 53.7% of total revenues on average in 2022. The second-highest share of revenues on average was received by social security funds, which are a sub-sector of general government, at 21.0% of total revenues, followed by 17.8% at the state level and 7.3% at the local level (Table 1.3).

Within countries with a federal structure, there was considerable variation around these averages:

- In 2022, the share of central government receipts in the eight federal OECD countries ranged from 28.9% in Germany to 80.0% in Mexico and 81.6% in Australia.
- In 2022, the share of the states ranged from 1.9% in Austria and 4.4% in Mexico to 38.9% in Canada. The share of local government varied from 1.8% in Mexico to 13.1% in the United States and 15.8% in Switzerland.
- Between 1975 and 2022, the share of central government revenues declined by over 12 p.p. in Belgium and by more than 5 p.p. in Spain.
- The share of central government revenues increased in Austria by just under 14 p.p. over the same period. There was little change in Australia.
- Of the seven federal countries with social security funds, five increased the share of revenue between 1975 and 2022. The exceptions were Canada and Mexico, where the share declined between 1975 (1980 for Mexico due to data availability) and 2022.

Colombia and Spain, which are classified as regional rather than unitary countries because of their highly decentralised political structure, have very different revenue compositions by level of government. In Colombia, the share of central government receipts was 75.2% in 2022, with regional governments receiving 4.8% of total revenues and local governments receiving 11.8%. In Spain, the share of central government receipts in 2022 was 42.5% compared with 15.1% for regional government and 8.2% for local government.

Table 1.3. Attribution of tax revenues to sub-sectors of general government as % of total tax revenue, federal countries

Per cent

	Supranational			Central government			State or Regional government			Local government			Social Security Funds		
	1975	1995	2022	1975	1995	2022	1975	1995	2022	1975	1995	2022	1975	1995	2022
Federal countries															
Australia	..	..	..	80.1	77.5	81.6	15.7	19.0	15.5	4.2	3.4	2.9	0.0	0.0	0.0
Austria[1]	..	0.4	0.5	51.7	64.7	65.6	10.6	1.8	1.9	12.4	4.1	3.0	25.3	29.0	29.0
Belgium[1]	1.4	1.0	1.2	65.3	60.1	52.5	..	1.8	10.1	4.4	4.8	4.5	28.8	32.2	31.7
Canada	..	..	..	47.6	39.1	42.9	32.5	37.1	38.9	9.9	9.8	8.6	10.0	14.0	9.6
Germany	1.2	0.6	0.7	33.5	31.4	28.9	22.3	21.6	24.7	9.0	7.4	8.9	34.0	39.0	36.9
Mexico	..	..	..	..	73.9	80.0	..	2.8	4.4	..	1.5	1.8	..	21.8	13.8
Switzerland[1]	..	..	..	30.7	31.7	33.8	27.0	24.0	25.6	20.3	17.5	15.8	22.0	26.8	24.8
United States	..	..	..	45.4	41.4	44.1	19.5	20.0	20.9	14.7	13.3	13.1	20.5	25.2	21.9
Unweighted average	1.3	0.7	0.8	50.6	52.5	53.7	21.3	16.0	17.8	10.7	7.7	7.3	20.1	23.5	21.0
Regional countries															
Colombia[2]	..	..	..	..	63.2	75.2	..	5.5	4.8	..	8.6	11.8	..	22.7	8.3
Spain[2]	..	0.8	0.8	48.2	51.1	42.5	..	5.0	15.1	4.3	8.6	8.2	47.5	34.6	33.4

.. Not available

1. The total tax revenue has been reduced by the amount of any capital transfer that represents uncollected taxes.

2. Colombia and Spain are not constitutionally federal countries but both have a highly decentralised political structure, with high autonomy of their territorial entities.

The remaining twenty-eight OECD countries have a unitary structure (Table 1.4). In these countries, an average of 64.6% of revenues were derived at the central level in 2022, with social security funds accounting for 24.6%. A further 10.3% of revenues was raised by local government.

Among unitary OECD countries:

- The share of central government receipts varied from 31.1% in France to 93.6% in New Zealand in 2022.
- The local government share ranged from 0.6% in Estonia to 35.1% in Sweden.
- Between 1975 and 2022, there were increases in the local government share in excess of 5 p.p. in six countries: France, Iceland, Italy, Korea, Portugal and Sweden. Decreases of 5 p.p. or more occurred in three countries: Ireland, Norway and the United Kingdom.
- Between 1975 and 2022, there were increases in the share of social security funds of 10 p.p. or more in France and Korea and corresponding decreases in Italy and Norway.

Table 1.4. Attribution of tax revenues to sub-sectors of general government as % of total tax revenue, unitary countries

Per cent

	Supranational			Central government			State or Regional government			Local government			Social Security Funds		
	1975	1995	2022	1975	1995	2022	1975	1995	2022	1975	1995	2022	1975	1995	2022
Unitary countries															
Chile	..	..	..	..	89.9	89.9	..	..	..	..	6.5	6.9	..	3.6	3.2
Costa Rica	..	..	..	..	65.5	61.4	..	..	..	..	1.6	2.7	..	33.0	35.9
Czechia	..	..	0.5	..	57.7	52.5	..	..	..	..	0.9	1.0	..	41.4	45.9
Denmark[1]	1.0	0.5	0.4	69.5	68.2	73.1	..	..	..	29.4	31.3	26.5	0.1	0.0	0.0
Estonia	..	..	0.8	..	84.3	82.5	..	..	..	..	0.8	0.6	..	14.9	16.0
Finland	..	0.4	0.5	56.0	46.6	48.8	..	..	..	23.5	22.3	23.0	20.4	30.8	27.6
France[1]	0.7	0.7	0.6	51.2	42.6	31.1	..	..	..	7.6	10.9	14.4	40.6	45.7	54.0
Greece	..	0.6	0.6	67.1	66.3	67.2	..	..	..	3.4	2.0	2.3	29.5	31.0	29.8
Hungary	..	..	0.5	..	63.8	67.5	..	..	..	..	2.5	4.7	..	33.6	27.4
Iceland	..	..	..	81.3	79.2	72.5	..	..	..	18.7	20.8	27.5	0.0	0.0	0.0
Ireland	2.3	1.5	0.8	77.4	83.1	84.1	..	..	..	7.3	2.7	1.6	13.1	12.7	13.5
Israel	..	..	..	..	79.0	76.5	..	..	..	..	7.1	8.2	..	13.9	15.3
Italy	..	0.4	0.6	53.2	62.7	58.0	..	..	..	0.9	5.4	10.9	45.9	31.5	30.5
Japan	..	..	..	45.5	41.2	39.0	..	..	..	25.6	25.2	22.5	29.0	33.6	38.5
Korea	..	..	..	89.0	69.2	57.3	..	..	..	10.1	18.7	17.2	0.9	12.1	25.6
Latvia	..	..	0.8	..	43.5	53.2	..	..	..	..	19.5	16.4	..	36.9	29.6
Lithuania[1]	..	..	1.0	..	71.7	66.9	..	..	..	..	2.3	1.0	..	26.1	31.1
Luxembourg[1]	0.8	0.4	1.2	63.6	66.4	68.2	..	..	..	6.7	6.5	3.6	29.0	26.6	27.0
Netherlands	1.5	1.3	1.3	58.9	56.0	62.6	..	..	..	1.2	3.1	3.2	38.4	39.5	32.9
New Zealand	..	..	..	92.3	94.7	93.6	..	..	..	7.7	5.3	6.4	0.0	0.0	0.0
Norway	..	..	..	50.6	57.9	89.7	..	..	..	22.4	19.9	10.3	27.0	22.3	0.0
Poland[1]	..	..	0.8	..	61.2	50.0	..	..	..	..	8.5	11.8	..	30.3	37.3
Portugal	..	0.8	0.6	65.4	68.6	65.1	..	..	..	0.0	9.0	7.1	34.6	21.6	27.2
Slovak Republic	..	..	0.5	..	62.6	57.2	..	..	..	..	1.3	1.9	..	36.1	40.4
Slovenia[1]	..	..	0.5	..	50.6	48.6	..	..	..	..	6.2	8.5	..	43.2	42.4
Sweden	..	0.4	0.4	51.3	46.9	52.5	..	..	..	29.2	30.9	35.1	19.5	21.8	12.1
Türkiye	..	..	..	..	75.1	65.8	..	..	..	..	12.8	9.7	..	12.1	24.4
United Kingdom	1.0	1.0	..	70.5	77.5	75.2	..	..	..	11.1	3.7	4.9	17.5	17.8	19.9
Unweighted average	1.2	0.7	0.7	65.2	65.4	64.6	..	..	..	12.8	10.3	10.3	21.6	24.0	24.6

.. Not available

1. The total tax revenue has been reduced by the amount of any capital transfer that represents uncollected taxes.

Composition of central and sub-central government revenues

Figure 1.9 shows revenues from each major category of tax revenue for central and sub-central governments. For federal and regional countries, the sub-central level includes revenues received by both state and local governments. Figure 1.9 demonstrates that:

- Central government revenues in almost all OECD countries are predominantly derived from taxes on income and on goods and services, with a negligible share from property taxes.
- Property taxes provide a much larger share of revenues at the subnational level, and account for over 90% of revenues in four countries: Israel, Ireland, Greece and the United Kingdom.
- By contrast, the share of income taxes and taxes on goods and services is generally lower at the sub-central level, although over 90% of sub-central revenues in Finland, Luxembourg and Sweden was derived from income taxes in 2022.

Figure 1.9. Composition of revenues of federal or central government (left) and sub-national government (right), 2022

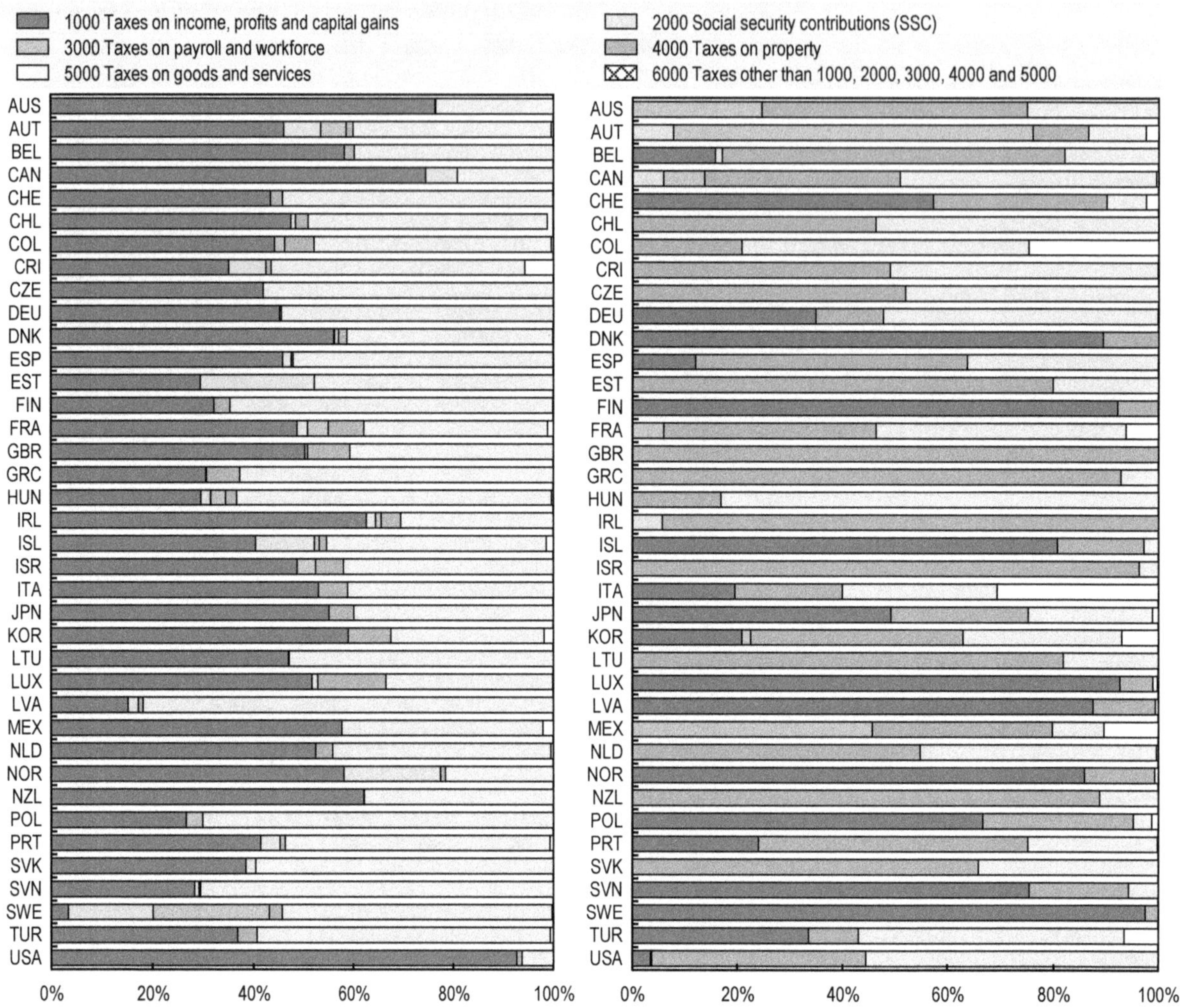

Note: The left-hand panel (a) refers to only those taxes that are classified as central government taxes. Social security contributions paid to social security funds are excluded. The right-hand panel (b) refers only to those taxes that are classified as sub-central taxes (local and [where relevant] state taxes). Social security contributions paid to social security funds are excluded.
Source: Secretariat calculations based on Tables 3.16 to 3.18.

StatLink https://stat.link/96jnlo

Revenues paid to a supranational authority

The 22 member states of the European Union (EU) that are also members of the OECD collect taxes on behalf of the EU, as did the United Kingdom prior to 2020. These taxes primarily consist of customs duties and contributions to the Single Resolution Fund (SRF).[4] Both taxes are collected on behalf of the EU by national tax administrations and are included in the total tax figures under headings 5123 and 5126 at the SUPRA level of government. In addition, they are shown as a memorandum item separately from the main figures since they represent a tax imposed by the EU and collected by national administrations.[5]

Table 1.5 shows the level of taxes collected on behalf of supranational governments in EU countries that are also OECD members, divided into countries in the Euro area and other EU member countries.

Table 1.5. Levies collected on behalf of the European Union, as % of GDP

Per cent

	2000	2005	2010	2015	2018	2019	2020	2021	2022	2023p
Euro area										
Austria, total supranational	0.2	0.1	0.1	0.2	0.2	0.2	0.2	0.2	0.2	0.2
of which: Customs duties	0.2	0.1	0.1	0.1	0.1	0.1	0.1	0.1	0.1	0.1
of which: SRF contributions	..	..	..	0.1	0.1	0.0	0.1	0.1	0.1	0.1
Belgium, total supranational	0.4	0.4	0.4	0.4	0.4	0.4	0.4	0.4	0.5	0.4
of which: Customs duties	0.4	0.4	0.3	0.3	0.4	0.4	0.3	0.3	0.4	0.3
of which: SRF contributions	..	..	..	0.1	0.1	0.1	0.1	0.1	0.1	0.1
Estonia, total supranational	..	0.2	0.2	0.2	0.2	0.2	0.2	0.2	0.3	0.1
of which: Customs duties	..	0.2	0.2	0.2	0.2	0.2	0.2	0.2	0.2	0.1
of which: SRF contributions	..	..	..	..	0.0	0.0	0.0	0.0	0.0	0.0
Finland, total supranational	0.1	0.1	0.1	0.1	0.1	0.2	0.2	0.2	0.2	0.2
of which: Customs duties	0.1	0.1	0.1	0.1	0.1	0.1	0.1	0.1	0.1	0.1
of which: SRF contributions	..	..	..	0.0	0.0	0.1	0.1	0.1	0.1	0.1
France, total supranational	0.1	0.1	0.1	0.1	0.2	0.2	0.2	0.2	0.3	0.2
of which: Customs duties	0.1	0.1	0.1	0.1	0.1	0.1	0.1	0.1	0.1	0.1
of which: SRF contributions	..	..	..	0.0	0.1	0.1	0.1	0.1	0.2	0.1
Germany, total supranational	0.2	0.2	0.2	0.2	0.2	0.2	0.2	0.2	0.3	0.2
of which: Customs duties	0.2	0.1	0.2	0.2	0.2	0.1	0.1	0.1	0.2	0.1
of which: SRF contributions	..	..	..	0.1	0.1	0.1	0.1	0.1	0.1	0.1
Greece, total supranational	0.2	0.1	0.1	0.2	0.2	0.2	0.2	0.2	0.3	0.2
of which: Customs duties	0.1	0.1	0.1	0.1	0.1	0.2	0.2	0.2	0.2	0.2
of which: SRF contributions	..	..	..	0.1	0.1	0.0	0.1	0.1	0.1	0.0
Ireland, total supranational	0.2	0.1	0.1	0.1	0.1	0.1	0.1	0.2	0.2	0.2
of which: Customs duties	0.2	0.1	0.1	0.1	0.1	0.1	0.1	0.1	0.1	0.1
of which: SRF contributions[1]	..	..	..	..	0.0	0.0	0.0	0.0	0.0	0.1
Italy, total supranational	0.1	0.1	0.1	0.3	0.2	0.2	0.2	0.2	0.3	0.2
of which: Customs duties	0.1	0.1	0.1	0.1	0.1	0.1	0.1	0.1	0.2	0.1
of which: SRF contributions[2]	..	..	..	0.1	0.1	0.0	0.1	0.1	0.1	0.1
Lithuania, total supranational	..	0.2	0.2	0.3	0.3	0.3	0.3	0.3	0.3	0.2
of which: Customs duties	..	0.2	0.2	0.3	0.3	0.2	0.3	0.3	0.3	0.2
of which: SRF contributions	..	..	..	0.0	0.0	0.0	0.0	0.0	0.0	0.0
Latvia, total supranational	..	0.2	0.1	0.2	0.2	0.2	0.2	0.2	0.2	0.2
of which: Customs duties	..	0.2	0.1	0.2	0.2	0.2	0.2	0.2	0.2	0.1
of which: SRF contributions	..	..	..	0.0	0.0	0.0	0.0	0.0	0.0	0.0
Luxembourg, total supranational	0.1	0.1	0.0	0.1	0.3	0.3	0.3	0.4	0.4	0.3
of which: Customs duties	0.1	0.1	0.0	0.0	0.0	0.0	0.0	0.0	0.0	0.0
of which: SRF contributions	..	..	..	0.1	0.2	0.2	0.3	0.3	0.4	0.3
Netherlands, total supranational	0.4	0.3	0.3	0.4	0.4	0.4	0.4	0.5	0.5	0.4
of which: Customs duties	0.3	0.2	0.3	0.3	0.3	0.3	0.3	0.3	0.4	0.3
of which: SRF contributions	..	..	..	0.1	0.1	0.1	0.1	0.1	0.1	0.1
Portugal, total supranational	0.2	0.1	0.1	0.1	0.2	0.2	0.2	0.2	0.2	0.2
of which: Customs duties	0.2	0.1	0.1	0.1	0.1	0.1	0.1	0.1	0.2	0.1
of which: SRF contributions	..	..	..	..	0.1	0.1	0.1	0.1	0.1	0.0
Slovak Republic, total supranational	..	0.1	0.2	0.1	0.2	0.2	0.1	0.2	0.2	0.2
of which: Customs duties	..	0.1	0.2	0.1	0.2	0.1	0.1	0.1	0.1	0.1
of which: SRF contributions	..	..	..	..	0.0	0.0	0.0	0.0	0.0	0.0
Slovenia, total supranational	..	0.1	0.2	0.2	0.1	0.1	0.2	0.2	0.2	0.1
of which: Customs duties	..	0.1	0.2	0.1	0.1	0.1	0.1	0.2	0.2	0.1
of which: SRF contributions	..	..	..	0.0	0.0	0.0	0.0	0.0	0.0	0.0
Spain, total supranational	0.2	0.2	0.1	0.2	0.2	0.2	0.2	0.2	0.3	0.2

of which: Customs duties	0.1	0.2	0.1	0.2	0.2	0.2	0.1	0.2	0.2	0.2
of which: SRF contributions	..	..	..	0.1	0.1	0.1	0.1	0.1	0.1	0.1
Non-euro area										
Czechia, total supranational	..	0.2	0.2	0.2	0.2	0.1	0.1	0.2	0.2	0.1
of which: Customs duties	..	0.2	0.2	0.2	0.2	0.1	0.1	0.2	0.2	0.1
Denmark, total supranational	0.2	0.2	0.2	0.2	0.1	0.1	0.1	0.1	0.2	0.1
of which: Customs duties	0.2	0.2	0.2	0.2	0.1	0.1	0.1	0.1	0.2	0.1
Hungary, total supranational	..	0.1	0.1	0.1	0.1	0.1	0.1	0.1	0.2	0.1
of which: Customs duties	..	0.1	0.1	0.1	0.1	0.1	0.1	0.1	0.2	0.1
Poland, total supranational	..	0.1	0.1	0.2	0.2	0.2	0.2	0.2	0.3	0.2
of which: Customs duties	..	0.1	0.1	0.2	0.2	0.2	0.2	0.2	0.3	0.2
Sweden, total supranational	0.2	0.2	0.2	0.1	0.1	0.1	0.1	0.1	0.2	0.1
of which: Customs duties	0.1	0.1	0.2	0.1	0.1	0.1	0.1	0.1	0.2	0.1
United Kingdom, total supranational[3]	0.2	0.2	0.2	0.2	0.2	0.1	0.1	..	..	..
of which: Customs duties	0.2	0.1	0.2	0.2	0.2	0.1	0.1	..	..	..

.. Not available

Note: SRF figures may differ slightly from those published on the SRB website. These differences are primarily due to timing. Details on these revenues for each country can be found in Chapters 4 and 5.

1. In 2016, the figure includes the 2016 payment of 99.12 million euros and also a payment of 75.89 million euros which was due in Quarter 4 of 2015 but was paid in Quarter 1 of 2016. The figures in this table were reported by the Central Statistics Office and are gross amounts and therefore due to adjustments will differ from the figures reported on the SRB website, which are net figures.

2. The "Bank contribution to the unique European Resolution Fund" amount includes not only the European but also the National Resolution Fund, as required by the Eurostat classification.

3. Supranational taxes reported by the United Kingdom are reported until 2020 in *Revenue Statistics*. From 2021, at the end of the Brexit transition period, this came to an end and taxes subsequently introduced by the United Kingdom are reflected in the appropriate tax category at the national or subnational levels of government, as appropriate.

Source: *Revenue Statistics 2023*, supplemented by discussions with delegates.

In 2022, the combined total of payments collected for the EU was highest in Belgium and the Netherlands (both 0.5% of GDP). All other EU countries that are also members of the OECD collected revenues on behalf of the EU equivalent to 0.2% of GDP or higher. In all countries except Finland, France and Luxembourg, customs duties were the primary source of these revenues.

Non-wastable tax credits

OECD countries apply two kinds of tax credits to income taxes (both personal and corporate):

- Non-payable or wastable tax credits are those that can only ever be used to reduce or eliminate a tax liability. They cannot be paid out to either taxpayers or non-taxpayers as a benefit. They are, therefore, the same as a tax allowance or relief.
- Payable or non-wastable tax credits can be divided into two parts. One part is used to reduce or eliminate a tax liability in the same way as a wastable tax credit. The other part can be paid directly to recipients as a benefit payment when the value of the benefit exceeds the tax liability.

The OECD methodology for classifying non-wastable tax credits is set out in paragraphs 25 and 26 of the Interpretative Guide. These state that only the part of a non-wastable tax credit that is used to reduce or eliminate a taxpayer's tax liability should be subtracted in the reporting of tax revenues. This is referred to as the 'tax expenditure component' of the credit. In contrast, the part of the tax credit that exceeds the taxpayer's tax liability and is paid to that taxpayer is treated as an expenditure item and not subtracted in the reporting of tax revenues. This part is referred to as the 'transfer component'.

Table 1.6. Effect of alternative treatments of non-wastable tax credits, 2022

	Non-wastable tax credits in billions of national currency			Total tax revenue in billions of national currency			Total tax revenue as a percentage of GDP		
	Total value	Transfer component	Tax expenditure component	Net basis	Split basis (per current guidance)	Gross basis	Net basis	Split basis (per current guidance)	Gross basis
Australia	11.9	8.3	3.6	744.9	753.2	756.8	29.1	29.4	29.5
Austria[1, 2]	0.4	0.2	0.2	192.9	193.1	193.3	43.1	43.2	43.2
Belgium[2]	1.2	0.3	0.9	234.5	234.9	235.8	42.3	42.4	42.5
Canada[3]	21.9	19.2	2.8	932.6	951.8	954.5	33.1	33.8	33.9
Chile[4]	352.8	250.4	102.4	62901.4	63151.8	63254.2	23.8	23.9	24.0
Czechia	42.1	12.9	29.2	2326.7	2339.6	2368.8	33.0	33.2	33.6
Denmark[2]	2.3	0.1	2.1	1192.6	1192.7	1194.8	41.9	41.9	42.0
France[2]	23.5	13.2	10.3	1202.4	1215.5	1225.9	45.3	45.8	46.2
Germany	51.8	18.6	33.2	1518.5	1537.0	1570.3	39.2	39.6	40.5
Iceland	11.6	10.9	0.7	1354.5	1365.4	1366.1	34.9	35.2	35.2
Ireland	0.4	0.0	0.4	..	105.5	105.9	..	20.3	20.3
Israel	1.9	1.9	0.0	579.2	581.1	581.1	32.7	32.8	32.8
Italy	6.6	2.1	4.5	838.7	840.8	845.3	42.7	42.8	43.1
Luxembourg[2, 5]	0.4	..	..	..	..	29.7	..	..	38.3
Mexico	43.2	0.1	43.1	4948.2	4948.3	4991.4	16.8	16.8	16.9
New Zealand	2.9	1.4	1.6	129.4	130.8	132.3	32.8	33.1	33.5
Norway	3.5	2.7	0.8	2476.7	2479.5	2480.3	43.4	43.4	43.5
Slovak Republic[5]	0.5	..	..	..	..	38.4	..	..	35.0
Spain	3.2	1.9	1.3	504.2	506.1	507.4	37.4	37.6	37.7
United Kingdom[6]	18.0	14.2	3.8	873.4	887.6	891.5	34.9	35.4	35.6
United States	452.5	324.2	128.3	6782.9	7107.1	7235.4	26.3	27.6	28.1

.. Not available

Note: In *Revenue Statistics* the tax revenue data are reported on a split basis, unless indicated otherwise.

1. The children's tax credit is not regarded as a tax credit in *Revenue Statistics* and is treated entirely as an expenditure provision.
2. The total tax revenue has been reduced by the amount of any capital transfer that represents uncollected taxes.
3. Some non-wastable tax credits cannot be split into the transfer and tax expenditure components. Their total values have been added to the transfer component.
4. In *Revenue Statistics*, the tax revenue data for Chile are reported on a net basis.
5. In *Revenue Statistics*, the tax revenue data for Luxembourg and Slovak Republic are reported on a gross basis.
6. Please note that the non-wastable tax credit data for the United Kingdom is on a cash basis and includes estimates in some years. Please see the footnotes in the table for the United Kingdom in Chapter 5 for more information.

Table 1.6 provides information on non-wastable tax credits in 2022 for those countries reporting them in *Revenue Statistics 2024* (it may be that some countries with non-wastable tax credits do not report them and thus do not appear in the table). It shows the amount of the non-wastable tax credits and their two components together with the results of using the figures to calculate tax revenue values and the associated tax-to-GDP ratios. Table 1.6 also shows two alternative treatments for non-wastable tax credits:

- The 'net basis', which treats non-wastable tax credits entirely as tax provisions, so that the full value of the tax credit reduces reported tax revenues, as shown in columns 4 and 7.
- The 'gross basis' is the opposite, treating non-wastable tax credits entirely as expenditure provisions, with neither the transfer component nor the tax expenditure component deducted from tax revenues, as shown in columns 6 and 9. This is the approach followed by the GFSM and the SNA.

Table 1.6 shows that, with a few exceptions, the choice of method for reporting non-wastable tax credits has only a small impact on the ratio of total tax revenues to GDP. For countries with available data, the difference between the ratios on a net basis and on a gross basis only exceeds one percentage point for Germany and the United States, and is between half a percentage point and one percentage point for Canada, Czechia, France, New Zealand and the United Kingdom.

Financing of social security-type benefits in OECD countries

A memorandum item[6] in *Revenue Statistics 2024* describes the financing of social security-type benefits in OECD countries. Unlike social assistance benefits, which are funded from general government revenues, social security-type benefits are funded via contributions to social security funds or to private insurance schemes, or by other earmarked sources of funding. These sources of financing include:

- Earmarked financing from tax revenues:
    1. Social security contributions (category 2000 in the OECD classification)
    2. Other taxes earmarked for social security-type benefits
- Earmarked financing from non-tax revenues:
    3. Voluntary contributions to the government (VCG)
    4. Compulsory contributions to the private sector (CCPS)

Figure 1.10 shows the relative contribution of each of these sources to financing for social security-type benefits in OECD countries, based on data provided by countries for inclusion in the memorandum item.

Figure 1.10. Composition of earmarked financing for social security-type benefits, 2022

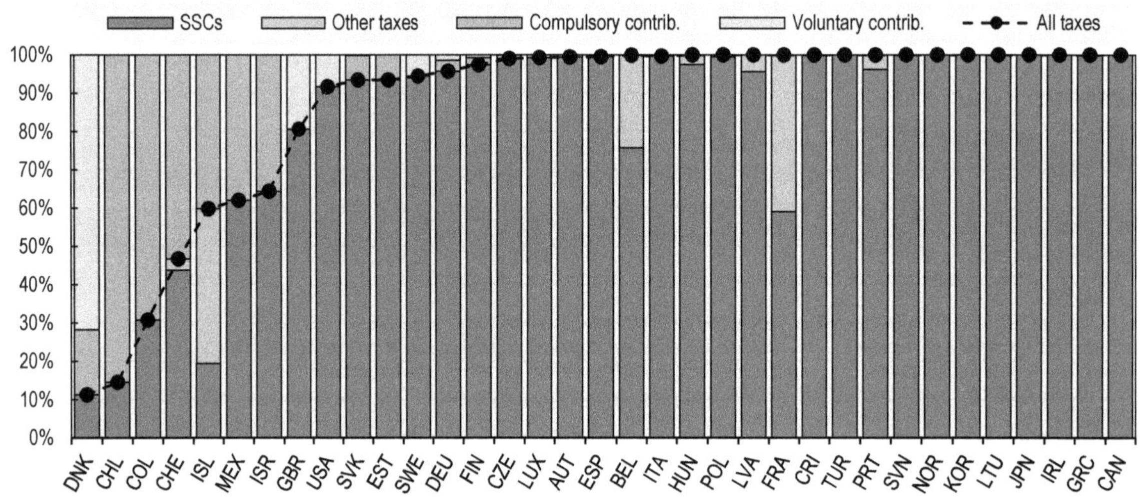

Note: Two countries (Australia and New Zealand) provide social benefits via social assistance rather than via social security, so are not included in the table. In addition, the Netherlands is not included in the figure as complete data on mandatory contributions was not available in *Revenue Statistics*. The figures for Denmark should be interpreted with care as the level of social security-type benefits is very small compared to the level of social assistance benefits. Further, there may be borderline issues in some countries when distinguishing between quasi-compulsory and voluntary schemes.
Source: Secretariat calculations based on chapter 4

StatLink https://stat.link/nl6cgu

Taxes represent the largest source of earmarked financing for social security-type benefits, predominantly via social security contributions. Together, social security contributions and other earmarked taxes account for over 90% of the financing of social security-type benefits in 27 of the 35 OECD countries that provide this level of data (including 10 countries where they account for 100%). In the remaining eight OECD countries that provide this data, six countries report that compulsory contributions to the private sector play a significant role in financing social-security type benefits, including Chile (where they account for 85.5%), Colombia (69.3%) and Switzerland (53.2%). Voluntary contributions accounted for a significant share of funding in only a few countries, notably the United Kingdom (19.4%) and Denmark (71.8%).

Figure 1.11 shows tax-to-GDP ratios (as in Table 1.1 and Figure 1.4) both *exclusive* of earmarked funding for social security-type benefits (i.e. tax-to-GDP ratios *less* social security contributions and other earmarked taxes) and *inclusive* of all non-tax earmarked financing for social security-type benefits (i.e. tax-to-GDP ratios – including social security contributions and other earmarked taxes – *plus* compulsory contributions to the private sector and voluntary contributions to government).

The countries with the largest share of social security-type schemes financed by non-tax earmarked contributions are Switzerland (8.1% of GDP), Iceland and Chile (6.1% and 5.8% respectively), which materially affects their rankings:

- Switzerland has a relatively low tax-to-GDP ratio among OECD countries, at 26.9%, but its combined ratio is just below halfway in the OECD distribution.
- Iceland has a tax-to-GDP ratio of 35.2%, in the top-third of OECD countries, and a combined ratio of 41.3%, which is the ninth-highest in the OECD.
- Chile has the fifth-lowest tax-to-GDP ratio at 23.8% and the eighth-lowest combined ratio at 29.6%.

Figure 1.11. Tax-to-GDP ratios and earmarked social security financing (% of GDP, 2022)

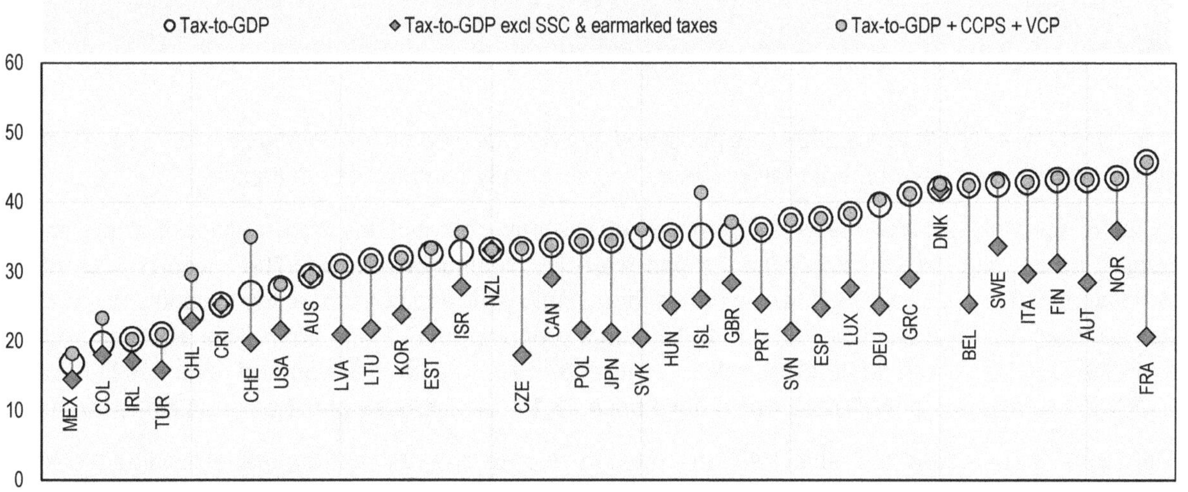

Note: The Netherlands are not included in the figure as complete data on social security financing in the Netherlands were not available.
Source: Secretariat calculations based on data in Chapter 4.

StatLink https://stat.link/5c3kn7

Excluding earmarked financing for social security benefits from the tax-to-GDP ratio does not affect Australia and New Zealand, where benefits are funded out of general taxation. Figure 1.11 highlights that the largest share of earmarked funding for social security-type benefits is seen in France, at 25.1% of GDP, as indicated by the difference between the highest and lowest points on the figure. Belgium, the Slovak Republic and Slovenia have the next highest shares, at between 15% and 17% of GDP.

References

OECD (2024), *OECD Economic Outlook, Volume 2024 Issue 1*, OECD Publishing, Paris, https://doi.org/10.1787/69a0c310-en. [2]

OECD (2024), *Tax Policy Reforms 2024: OECD and Selected Partner Economies*, OECD Publishing, Paris, https://doi.org/10.1787/c3686f5e-en. [1]

OECD (2023), *Revenue Statistics 2023: Tax Revenue Buoyancy in OECD Countries*, OECD Publishing, Paris, https://doi.org/10.1787/9d0453d5-en. [3]

OECD (2022), *Revenue Statistics 2022: The Impact of COVID-19 on OECD Tax Revenues*, OECD Publishing, Paris, https://doi.org/10.1787/8a691b03-en. [5]

OECD (2021), *Revenue Statistics 2021: The Initial Impact of COVID-19 on OECD Tax Revenues*, OECD Publishing, Paris, https://doi.org/10.1787/6e87f932-en. [4]

Notes

[1] At the time *Revenue Statistics 2024* was published, provisional data on tax revenues in 2023 for Australia was not available nor were provisional figures on social security contributions in Japan.

[2] In 2016, Iceland received revenues from one-off stability contributions from entities that previously operated as commercial or savings banks and were concluding operations. The revenue from these contributions led to unusually high tax revenues for a single year and consequently, Iceland's tax-to-GDP ratio rose from 35.1% in 2015 to 50.3% in 2016 before dropping to 37.1% in 2017. This led to an artificial high in the OECD average tax-to-GDP ratio in 2016 of 33.5%. Without these one-off revenues in Iceland, the OECD average tax-to-GDP ratio would have been 33.1%, an increase of 0.2 p.p. relative to 2015.

[3] The terms "value-added tax" and "VAT" are used to refer to any national tax that embodies the basic features of a value-added tax by whatever name or acronym it is known e.g. "Goods and Services Tax" ("GST").

[4] The Single Resolution Fund (SRF) has been in place since 2015. Countries in the Eurozone are required to make SRF contributions under the Single Resolution Mechanism (Regulation (EU) No 806/2014). Contributions are paid on an ex-ante basis and contributions are transferred from the national authorities to the SRF. So far, contributions have been collected for the years 2015 to 2023.

[5] In addition, EU civil servants pay income taxes and social security contributions directly to the EU. These revenues are not included in the data for total tax revenues in this publication as they are not paid to or collected by a national government. However, for the four countries with the highest number of EU civil servants (Belgium, Luxembourg, Italy and Germany), a memorandum account at the end of the respective country table in Chapter 5 provides information on the scale of these payments.

[6] The financing of social security-type benefits is shown in Table 4.77 on a comparable basis (percentage of GDP) and in Table 5.39 on a national currency basis.

2 Health taxes in OECD countries

Chapter 2, the Special Feature of this report, examines the growing prominence of health taxes in OECD countries and their importance within the revenue mix. Using detailed *Revenue Statistics* data on excise taxes on alcohol, tobacco and sugar-sweetened beverages, the chapter investigates how these revenues evolved in the period from 2000 to 2022.

Introduction

Over the past 20 years, OECD countries have reconceptualised existing taxes and introduced new taxes in response to a growing awareness of the impact that taxation can have on health outcomes. The concept of 'health taxes' has emerged to describe fiscal instruments whose purpose is not only to generate public revenues but also to reduce consumption of products that can have harmful effects on the health of consumers and society at large. This two-fold impact makes health taxes of interest both to fiscal policymakers and health policymakers in OECD countries and beyond.

The purpose of this Special Feature is to track recent trends in revenues from health taxes in OECD countries, benefitting from the granular data provided by countries for this edition of *Revenue Statistics*. In so doing, the report (and accompanying *Revenue Statistics* database) addresses a specific constraint on the analysis of health taxes, namely the absence of comprehensive and standardised data on revenues from health taxes over time that facilitates monitoring and benchmarking within and across countries. The objective of the Special Feature is not to carry out in-depth analysis, derive specific conclusions or present policy recommendations concerning the design of health taxes but rather to enhance the evidence base for specialists working in this area.

The chapter is structured as follows. The first section defines health taxes and outlines their emergence as a tool for fiscal and health policy in OECD countries. The second section explains the importance of analysing revenues from health taxes while acknowledging the limitations of this analysis. The third section uses *Revenue Statistics* data to track trends in revenues from health taxes across OECD countries. A fourth section concludes.

Defining health taxes

This Special Feature adheres to the World Health Organisation definition of 'health taxes', namely '[T]axes levied on products that have a negative public health impact' (World Health Organization, 2024[1]). The classification of taxes in this chapter follows that set out in the OECD's Interpretative Guide, whose definition of taxes is consistent with that of the System of National Accounts: compulsory, unrequited payments to the general government or to a supranational authority.

Health taxes are generally levied in the form of excise duties, which (unlike other general goods and services taxes) are levied only on specific goods. Although excise taxes are generally levied on producers rather than consumers, they nevertheless change the price of the product for consumers if producers pass on the taxes. In the case of health taxes, excise taxes can be levied directly on the component that creates negative health effects (e.g. alcohol volume or grams of sugar, salt or saturated fat) or on the product that contains the component that is harmful to consumers' health (e.g. per litre of soft drink or alcoholic beverage or per pack of cigarettes). They can also be levied when these components or products are used as inputs in the production process.

Excise duties apply to goods regardless of whether they are produced domestically or imported, and they do not apply to exported products. Excise taxes interact with customs duties as well as the value-added tax (VAT); although this chapter focuses on revenues from excise taxes rather than customs duties and VAT, Box 2.1 provides additional detail on this interaction.

Since the Interpretative Guide classifies taxes according to their base, it does not include a specific category for 'health taxes'. However, detailed data on tax revenues provided by countries through the *Revenue Statistics* initiative and classified according to the Interpretative Guide allows for the identification of different tax types that fall under this definition. As was the case with the Special Feature on environmental taxation in the 2019 edition of the report (OECD, 2019[2]), this chapter demonstrates the value of harmonised data in providing a comprehensive and internationally comparable view of revenues from taxes that have in common a specific policy objective of growing importance to OECD countries.

Notwithstanding the potential breadth of the WHO definition of health taxes,[1] this chapter will focus on excise taxes on alcohol, tobacco and sugar-sweetened beverages (SSBs)[2]. Of these three types of health tax, taxes on alcohol and tobacco predate the term 'health taxes' by many centuries, over which time they have been implemented worldwide. Taxes on SSBs, on the other hand, are a relatively recent innovation and are less common globally, although this is changing rapidly. All OECD countries tax alcohol and tobacco while an increasing number tax SSBs, although data is only available for 12 countries in this chapter (OECD, 2022[3]).[3]

The emergence of 'health taxes' as a concept first arose from developments not in tax policy but in the health sector (Lauer et al., 2022[4]). The effectiveness of what were sometimes referred to as 'sin taxes' on tobacco and alcohol as health interventions became a topic of interest when policy makers began to take a more comprehensive view of public health systems. Amid widespread evidence that taxation was a cost-effective mechanism for improving health outcomes by reducing the consumption of harmful goods (and encouraged by broader fiscal challenges in the wake of the Global Financial Crisis), policy makers focused on the taxation of SSBs to improve nutritional outcomes and tackle rapid growth in the prevalence of obesity (Lauer et al., 2022[4]).

Health taxes thus have two principal purposes. On the one hand, they have been shown to generate a modest but stable source of revenues to finance public spending (Lauer et al., 2022[4]). On the other, they aim to reduce consumption of unhealthy goods for public health purposes. A tension exists within these objectives, namely that lower consumption of a specific good (ceteris paribus) entails a reduction in revenues. Although the design of health taxes is beyond the scope of this chapter,[4] factors that may influence the rate at which policy makers set health taxes as they balance these objectives will be influenced (inter alia) by the elasticity of demand with respect to prices of the different products and the externalities and internalities associated with consumption of the product.

The question of elasticities demonstrates how the dual impact of health taxes can influence the design of health taxes. If demand for a product is inelastic (i.e. demand diminishes relatively little in response to prices), governments may be able to increase tax rates on that product to generate higher revenues without significantly reducing demand (absent an increase in cross-border shopping, smuggling or illegal production, as discussed below). However, this same inelasticity would imply that health taxes would have to be increased significantly before they trigger a strong demand response.

In practice, demand for alcohol and tobacco has generally been found to be relatively inelastic with respect to prices, while demand for SSBs is more elastic (Burton et al., 2024[5]). However, elasticity estimates for the different taxes vary in countries at different incomes levels, as well as across different income groups; elasticities tend to be higher among low-income individuals, implying their consumption declines more in response to increased prices (Fuchs, 2019[6]).

Meanwhile, policymakers may want to set rates that account for the adverse impact of certain products on consumers and society. In the case of health taxes, internalities can be understood as the harm individuals inflict upon themselves on account of their failure to recognise the adverse short- and long-term consequences of consuming these products. Externalities, meanwhile, include the economic costs[5] for society but not taken into account by smokers. They may include costs for the smokers themselves as well as costs for individuals, such as the impact of passive smoking or the emotional burden of caring for or losing a loved one due to illness (DeCicca, Kenkel and Lovenheim, 2022[7]).

Setting excise rates to reflect the full range of externalities is very complicated. Some of the external costs are already priced into social insurance mechanisms and it is challenging to value in monetary terms the lives of (for example) smokers and second-hand smokers that are lost as a result of smoking. Instead of seeking precise external cost estimates, simpler approaches include tax level targets or smoking reduction goals. Taxes account for at least 60% of the purchase price of a pack of cigarettes in almost all OECD countries, while the World Health Organisation recommends this proportion be at least 75% (OECD, 2022[3]).

The concept of health taxes thus brings together old and new taxes on a wide range of products under a similar logic that recognises the impact of these instruments on consumer behaviour, health outcomes and public finances. These impacts are likely to span a range of timeframes, including from a fiscal perspective: a tax may not generate significant revenues in the short term but may achieve long-term savings for the government on the basis that healthier lifestyles would reduce public health costs over time.

Box 2.1. Excises and other health taxes

Excise taxes, classified under category 5121 of the Interpretative Guide (Annex A), are taxes levied as a product specific unit tax on a predefined limited range of goods. Excises are often levied on nonessential or luxury goods, alcoholic beverages and tobacco products, as well as on energy products. Excises may be imposed at any stage of production or distribution and are usually assessed as a specific charge per unit based on characteristics by reference to the value, weight, strength, or quantity of the product. However, excises are not the only taxes imposed on these products, which will also be subject to value-added tax (VAT), customs and other import duties. Australia and New Zealand, for example, levy 'excise-equivalent customs duties' on alcohol and tobacco that are included in this analysis.[6]

Value-added tax (VAT) is a general consumption tax, which cannot be classified as a health tax. It is therefore not discussed in this chapter. It is, however, important to bear in mind how VAT interacts with excises and the impact this may have on government revenues as well as on the health-related objectives. In most cases, excise duties are part of the VAT base because a VAT is generally levied on the total value of the products, inclusive of excise duties.

In these situations, an increase in excise duties will also increase the VAT burden and revenue on the targeted products. The higher the rate of VAT, the greater the impact of (the increase in) excise duty that has to be paid. On the other hand, if health taxes reduce demand for a certain good, this will reduce revenues from both excises and VAT. The close relationship between VAT and excises implies that health taxes and VAT should ideally be evaluated jointly. For instance, applying a reduced VAT rate on SSBs may partly offset the impact of excises on the same products and would undermine the coherence of tax and health policy.[7]

Meanwhile, the customs duties that countries apply to imports of harmful products also generate revenues for the government and affect the prices of these goods at the border. This chapter does not cover customs duties in its data and analysis but these revenues can be significant.

Like other excise duties, health taxes are usually levied at the producer level and not on final consumers. This reduces the administrative burden and the risk of non-compliance but creates opportunities for suppliers to manipulate the tax base and affect prices, thereby undermining the effectiveness of health taxes in reaching its health objectives.

Why track revenues from health taxes (and reasons for caution)

The recognition that health taxes have the capacity to generate revenues and improve health outcomes – and that these impacts may occur over different timeframes – entails trade-offs that policy makers must manage. Although revenues from health taxes are only part of the equation, high-quality and standardised revenue data is an essential input for understanding the role of health taxes in public finances and for evaluating their effectiveness. Nonetheless, revenue trends need to be treated with caution.

Although (as will be discussed below) revenues from health taxes amount to a relatively small proportion of GDP and are a small component of the overall tax mix in OECD countries, a reduction in revenues from these taxes where these previously represented a steady source of income for the government may have adverse consequences for the financing of public services. Over the longer term, a reduction in health revenues may be offset by future savings in health expenditure or higher revenues from a more productive population if the health tax succeeds in improving a specific health outcome or outcomes.

Revenue data is a key input for designing and monitoring the effectiveness of health taxes. The revenue impact of a health tax will reflect a range of design aspects, including tax rates, the tax structure, and the tax base. Health tax revenues will not only depend on the design of the health taxes but also on the levels of consumption (e.g. smoking prevalence) and other economic elements (e.g. extent of cross-border shopping). While health tax revenues on their own do not allow to infer whether a health tax is designed effectively, they constitute an important variable to assess a country's health tax policy.

Despite the importance of tracking revenues from health taxes, analysing this data requires caution. A decline in revenues from a health tax on a specific product might be a sign of success if the purpose of the tax were to deter individuals from consuming that product. However, the positive health impact will be diminished if consumers switch to a cheaper product that is a close substitute which is not taxed in the same way and itself has adverse health impacts, such as from cigarettes to vaping.

Another factor that may not be apparent from the revenue data is the extent to which a health tax is passed on to consumers. As mentioned above, excises are generally applied at the producer level; the extent to which retailers pass on the health tax to consumers through higher prices will affect the impact on revenues and health outcomes. Numerous factors affect the extent of 'pass-through', including the structure of the industry, the possibility of tax avoidance and the specific design of the tax (Belloni and Sassi, 2022[8]). If producers absorb a higher excise tax within their profit margin, the increase in the rate may not lead to the intended decline in consumption.

The impact of health taxes on revenues (and health outcomes) will be affected by individuals who cross international borders to buy a specific product in response to differences in prices between the two jurisdictions that may be related to lower tax rates. Attesting to the potential scale of this phenomenon, (Hillion, 2024[9]) estimates that border closures related to the COVID-19 pandemic increased domestic tobacco sales in France by 9.5%, compared to the counterfactual if borders had stayed open. An analogous phenomenon may occur within countries where neighbouring sub-national jurisdictions impose health taxes at different rates (Bollinger and Sexton, 2023[10]).

In addition to legal transactions, revenues may also be affected if products are smuggled across borders to avoid taxes. Illicit production and sale of a particular good within a country's borders will also result in foregone revenues as well as (potentially) worse health outcomes if the product is sub-standard.

Trends in revenues from health taxes in OECD countries

This section shows trends in health tax revenues across OECD countries. As explained in Box 2.2, this data was submitted by delegates for this edition of *Revenue Statistics*. It covers the period from 2000 up to 2022, the most recent year for which final *Revenue Statistics* data is available for all OECD countries. Figures 2.1-2.3 show revenues from taxes on alcohol, tobacco and SSBs as a percentage of GDP and total government revenues (i.e. their weight within the tax mix) in 2022 as well as trends in revenues from health taxes since 2000. Table 2.A.1. sets out which countries are included in the respective graphs.

As noted above, the results shown in this section need to be interpreted with caution. First of all, these results only include revenues from excises. Notably, they do not include taxes on imports of alcohol, tobacco and SSBs, which means they may understate the taxes levied on these products. Moreover, there are challenges with the comparability of the data that are explained further in Box 2.2.

Box 2.2. Data on health tax revenues: availability and comparability challenges

While there is a clear rationale for tracking revenues from health taxes, comparing revenues from health taxes across countries and over time has been challenging in the absence of a centralised repository for data on health taxes.

The revenue data for excise taxes shown in this chapter was provided as part of the data submission for this edition of *Revenue Statistics.* OECD countries are not required to report revenues from specific excises but provided significantly more-granular data on revenues from health taxes to inform this Special Feature, meaning that the results shown in this chapter have not been published previously here or elsewhere.

Although data has been provided by all countries, countries may not have been able to provide data on all revenues from health taxes. This might be because some health taxes are collected at a sub-national level and not reported to *Revenue Statistics* with sufficient granularity to be included in the analysis. This is the case for the United States, for example, which taxes alcohol and tobacco at a federal, state and local level but only taxes SSBs at a local level; the disaggregation of revenues from SSBs at local level is not available for this analysis.

Differences in how OECD countries label or the extent to which they report revenues from health taxes limits the comparability of revenues from health taxes across countries. Even within the categories chosen for analysis in this Special Feature – alcohol, tobacco and SSBs – there are differences and gaps across countries that limit the comparability of this data.

For example, OECD countries often may not differentiate between taxes on different alcohol products when reporting revenues. Some might report a single figure for revenues from taxes on alcohol while others will specify revenues from taxes on certain specific alcohol products – wine, beer or spirits for example – but not others.

The variance is greatest in the domain of SSBs. As noted above, although many OECD countries have introduced taxes on SSBs, the breadth of coverage differs significantly and not all countries report revenues from SSBs on a disaggregated basis, notably in cases where the taxes are implemented sub-nationally.

Further challenges may arise depending on which level of government has responsibility for excises. If a sub-national government has responsibility, issues such as missing data and differences in classification may be magnified considerably.

Secondly, caution is required when comparing revenues across countries for reasons that extend beyond these data challenges. Relatively high (low) revenues from a specific health tax may indicate that consumption of that product is relatively high (low) rather than that product being taxed more or less effectively. As an example of how prevalence varies across OECD countries, the proportion of individuals aged 15 and over that smoke daily ranges from 7.2% in Iceland to 28.0% in Türkiye according to (OECD, 2023[11]). In addition, it should not be assumed that a higher (lower) level of revenues from health taxes in a country or countries is a result of higher (lower) tax rates.

A range of other factors may affect the revenue trends shown in the graphs. For example, a decline in revenues might attest to the success of a tax whose principal objective is to reduce consumption of a specific product but it may also (for example) be a consequence of an increase in the number of consumers acquiring the product abroad. Depending on the denominator, the decline may also be a result of economic growth (when considering revenues as a share of GDP) or increases in revenues from another tax or taxes (when considering revenues as a share of total tax revenues).

Revenues from health taxes across OECD countries in 2022

Figure 2.1 shows the breakdown of revenues from excise taxes on alcohol, tobacco and SSBs across OECD countries as a percentage of GDP (Panel A) and as a share of total government revenues (Panel B) in 2022. For both indicators, there is wide variation across OECD countries in terms of the overall weight of health taxes. Annex Figures 2.A.1 and 2.A.2. show the disaggregation of revenues from the different excise taxes by product in 2022 both as a share of GDP and percentage of total tax revenues.

Total revenues from the three health excise taxes ranged from 0.19% of GDP in the United States to 1.42% in Latvia, while they ranged from 0.70% of total tax revenues in the United States to 4.62% in Latvia and 4.74% in Türkiye. On average across OECD countries, the health excise taxes on tobacco, alcohol and SSBs equated to 0.74% of GDP and generated 2.24% of total tax revenues in 2022.

In 27 of the 38 OECD countries, revenues from excise taxes on tobacco were the principal source of health tax revenues, exceeding 50% of total revenues in 25 of these. As a percentage of GDP, revenues from tobacco taxes ranged from 1.15% in Luxembourg to 0.05% in Costa Rica. As a proportion of total tax revenues, they ranged from 3.0% or more in Türkiye and Luxembourg to 0.20% in Costa Rica.

In the remaining countries, excise taxes on alcohol were the next-largest source of revenues in 2022. Revenues from excises alcohol ranged from above 0.6% of GDP in Latvia, Estonia, Lithuania and Iceland to 0.1% in Switzerland. As a proportion of total tax revenues, they ranged from above 2% in Latvia, Colombia, Lithuania and Estonia to below 0.2% in Switzerland, Austria and Italy.

Revenues from excises on SSBs in the 12 countries for which data for 2022 is available ranged from 0.69% of total tax revenues in Mexico to less than 0.05% of total revenues in France, the United Kingdom and Ireland. As a share of GDP, they exceeded 0.1% in Mexico and Costa Rica, at 0.12% and 0.11% respectively.

Figure 2.1. Level and structure of health taxes in the OECD in 2022

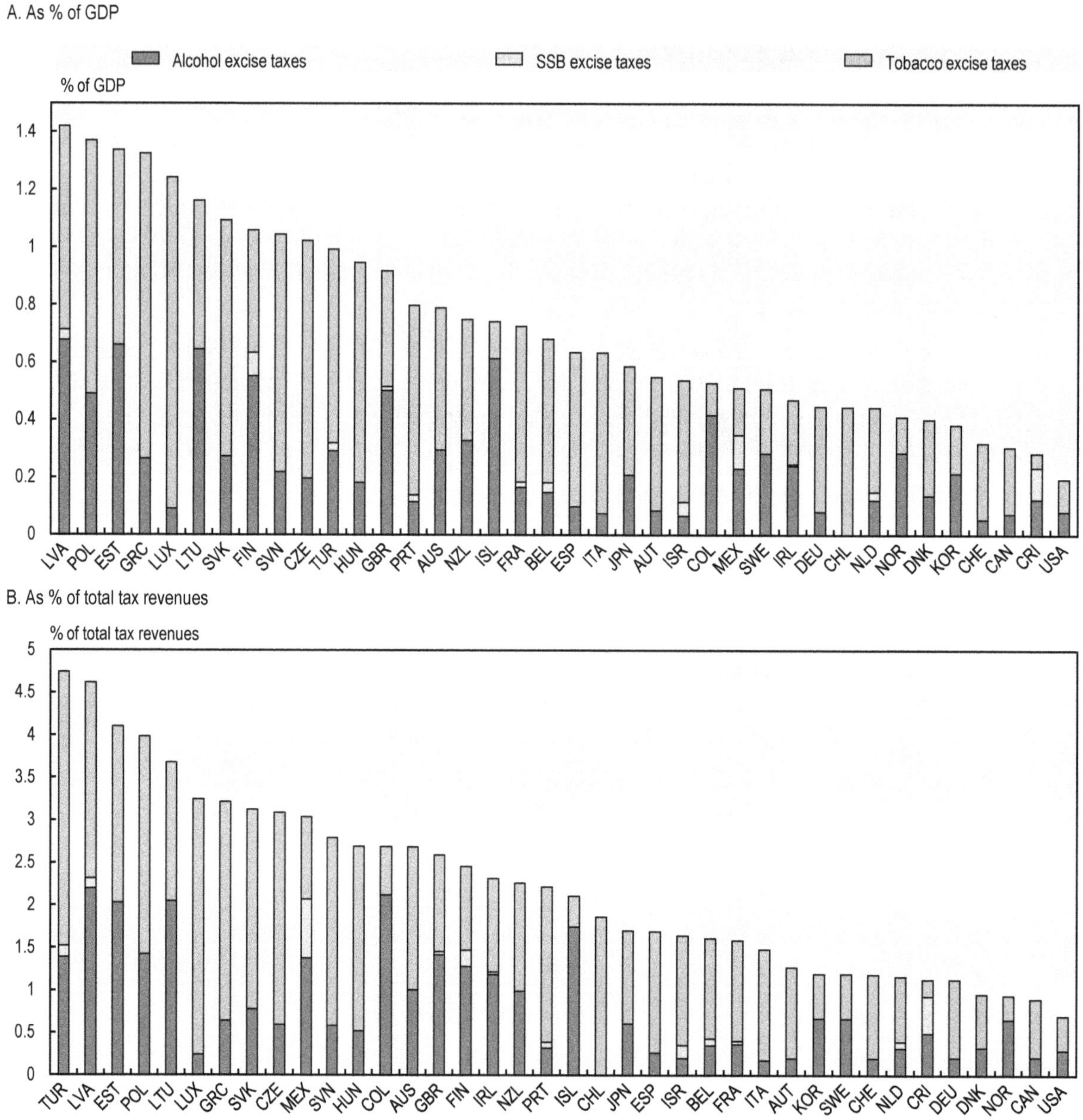

Note: Health excise tax revenue is the sum of reported tax revenue collected from excise taxes levied on tobacco, alcohol and SSBs (category 5121) for all reporting countries and years. The OECD average for health excise tax revenue is calculated based on 38 countries for tobacco, 37 countries for alcohol and 12 countries for SSBs (Annex Table 2.A.1.shows a list of reporting countries).
Source: Authors' calculations based on data provided to *OECD Revenue Statistics 2024* for all countries and years.

StatLink https://stat.link/5try73

Long-term trends in health tax revenues

Figure 2.2 shows trends in revenues from total health taxes across the three categories on average across OECD countries from 2000 to 2022 as a share of GDP. Revenues from health excise taxes have declined as a proportion of GDP over this period on average across the OECD (especially since 2010) due to declines in revenues from excise taxes on alcohol and tobacco. Although a full analysis of these revenue trends is beyond the scope of this chapter, the declines have coincided with significant changes in both the consumption and the taxation of tobacco and alcohol over this period.

According to (OECD, 2023[11]), the proportion of the population aged 15 and over that smokes daily has fallen sharply across the OECD on average, from 20.6% in 2011 to 15.9% in 2021, with 32 of the 37 countries for which data is available observing a decline. Meanwhile, average alcohol consumption in OECD countries fell from 8.9 litres per person in 2011 to 8.6 litres per person in 2021, declining in 23 countries over this period.

According to the biennial *Consumption Tax Trends* publication, which tracks excise rates on various tobacco and alcohol products, there has been an upwards trend in excise tax rates across the OECD since 2000.[8] However, these rates are expressed in units of currency, meaning that inflation may have eroded the real value of excise duties and caused them to fall as a proportion of GDP in some countries. As with other taxes, indexing health excises is an important means of ensuring their effectiveness as a mechanism for both generating revenues and reducing consumption (OECD, 2024[12]).

Revenues from tobacco taxes, which is the largest source of revenues from health taxes among the three categories across the time period, declined from 0.57% of GDP in 2000 to 0.47% in 2022. Revenues from tobacco excises demonstrate the greatest degree of volatility over this period, with a notable increase in revenues from 2007 to 2011 declining in most years from 2012 onwards. The aforementioned trend for higher excise rates was particularly pronounced for tobacco products; for example, the excise rate on cigarettes doubled in nominal terms between 2012 and 2022 in all but three of the 30 countries for which data for 2012 is available, and it increased by more than 200% in ten countries.

On average across OECD countries, the largest decline (in relative and absolute terms) across the three excise types occurred in revenues from excises on alcohol, which declined steadily from 0.40% of GDP in 2000 to 0.26% in 2022. Revenues from SSBs have been stable as a share of GDP (at around 0.05%) during the period under analysis despite the gradual expansion of SSBs over time.

Figure 2.3 shows the changes in health tax revenues between 2000 and 2022 as a share of GDP by OECD country. Panel A shows changes in combined health tax revenues across individual countries while Panels B, C and D show changes in each of the three health taxes under consideration over this period. For each Figure, countries are ranked according to the level of revenues in 2022 in descending order, left to right.

Figure 2.2. OECD average revenues from the three difference categories of health taxes, 2000-2022

Percentage of GDP

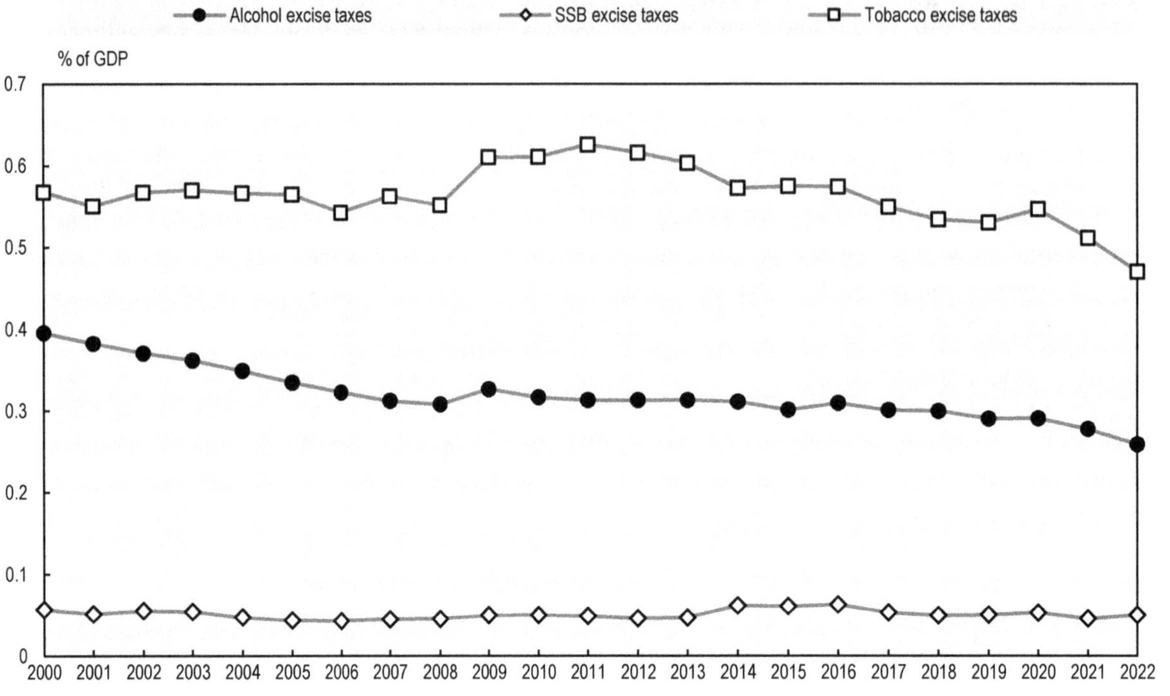

Note: Tax revenue from excise taxes levied on tobacco, alcohol and SSBs (category 5121) are included for all reporting countries and years. The OECD average is computed using countries reporting positive excise taxes. See Table 2.A.1 for a list of reporting countries in 2000, 2010 and 2022.
Source: Authors' calculations based on data provided to *OECD Revenue Statistics 2024* for all countries and years.

StatLink https://stat.link/02g8bt

Combined health tax revenues fell between 2000 and 2022 as a share of GDP in all but five countries: Czechia, Slovenia, Mexico, Switzerland and Costa Rica. In Czechia and Slovenia, the increases (of 0.01 p.p. and 0.21 p.p., respectively) were due to an increase in excise revenues from tobacco. Switzerland observed increases in revenues from tobacco and alcohol excises (of 0.26 p.p. and 0.05 p.p., respectively) while revenues from tobacco and SSBs increased slightly in Costa Rica. In Mexico, revenues increased as a share of GDP in all three categories (it introduced excises on SSBs in 2014).

Declines of 0.5% of GDP or more in health tax revenues as a percentage of GDP occurred in Ireland (1.29 p.p.), Luxembourg (0.75 p.p.), Norway (0.70 p.p.) and Denmark (0.51 p.p.). In Ireland, excise revenues from both tobacco and alcohol declined by 0.73 p.p. and 0.56 p.p. respectively. In Norway, there was a 0.33 p.p. decline in revenues from tobacco excises, a 0.30 p.p. decline in excises in alcohol and a 0.07 p.p. decline in revenues from excises on SSBs, while in Denmark revenues from tobacco excises declined by 0.31 p.p. and from excises on alcohol by 0.20 p.p. The decline in Luxembourg was largely due to a 0.73 p.p. decline in revenues from excises on tobacco between 2000 and 2022.

Across the three categories, 31 countries observed a decline in revenues from excises on alcohol as a share of GDP between 2000 and 2022, while 22 observed a decline in revenues from excises on tobacco. Of the eleven countries that reported revenues from excise taxes on SSBs in 2022 to *OECD Revenue Statistics* for this edition of the report, only two countries (Belgium and Netherlands) reported a decline in revenues from this category between 2000 and 2022. Relatively large increases in revenues from SSBs as a share of GDP were observed in Mexico and Costa Rica (due to the implementation of excises on SSBs), although even in these countries the level is low relative to revenues from excises on alcohol and tobacco. Revenues from excises on SSBs declined sharply in Norway because the SSB excise tax was repealed in 2021.

Figure 2.3. Changes in the level of revenues from the different health taxes between 2000 and 2022 by OECD country

Percentage of GDP

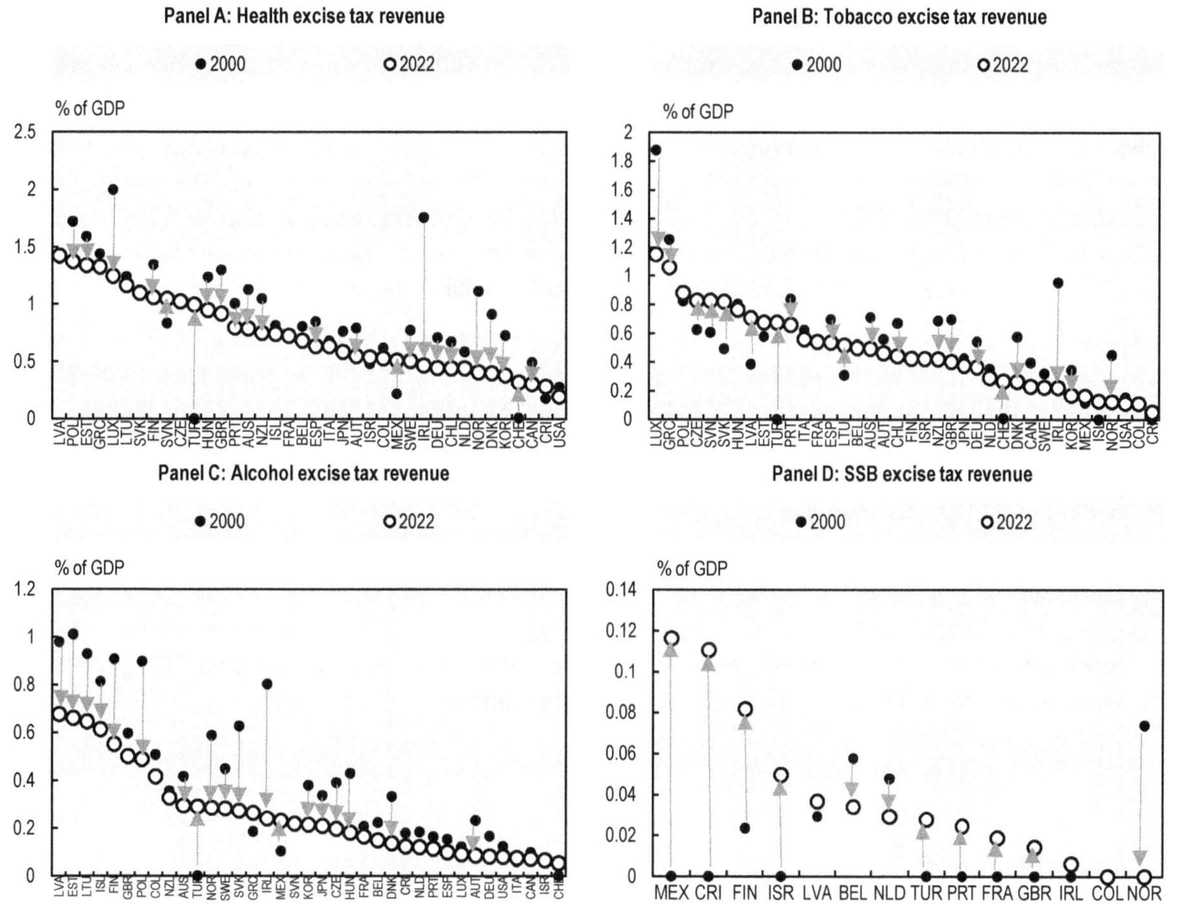

Note: Health excise tax revenue is the sum of reported tax revenue collected from excise taxes levied on tobacco, alcohol and SSBs. The estimates of total health excise tax revenue raised are based on data reported by the countries (see Table 2.A.1 in the annex for a list of reporting countries). The OECD average is based on 37 OECD countries reporting at least one health excise tax revenue in 2000 (excluding Türkiye due an absence of data). Health excise tax revenue data are sourced from *OECD Revenue Statistics* (category 5121) for the 37 OECD countries displayed.
Source: Authors' calculations based on data provided to *OECD Revenue Statistics 2024* for all countries and years.

StatLink https://stat.link/c4ikhd

Conclusion

Health taxes have emerged as a potentially valuable tool for policymakers in public finance and health alike thanks to their capacity to generate revenues and improve health outcomes in OECD. This chapter shows revenues from health taxes (exclusively those levied through excises) on alcohol and tobacco products as well as SSBs across the OECD between 2000 and 2022 based on data provided by OECD countries for *Revenue Statistics OECD 2024*.

The chapter provides data on revenues from health excise taxes in OECD countries that is unique in terms of its granularity, comprehensiveness and comparability. Detailed and comparable data on revenues from health taxes is important to understand their impact and effectiveness as well as to enhance the design of these instruments. However, this data needs to be interpreted with caution due to the range and complexity of factors that may explain changes and trends in health tax revenues, as well as differences in the level of revenues from health taxes across countries.

As shown in this chapter, revenues from health excise taxes equate to a relatively small proportion of GDP and account for a relatively small share of total tax revenues. On average across OECD countries, health excise taxes amounted to 0.74% of GDP and generated 2.24% of total tax revenues in 2022. Taxes on tobacco generated the largest amount of revenues out of the three categories on average across the OECD, followed by taxes on alcohol. Excise taxes on SSBs remain relatively small.

Revenues from tobacco and alcohol have declined as a share of GDP in almost all OECD countries since 2000, resulting in a steady overall decline in total revenues from health taxes as a share of GDP on average. Over this period, consumption of alcohol and tobacco has declined on average across OECD countries while (nominal) excise rates have trended upwards. Revenues from taxes on SSBs have remained at a very similar level across this timeframe, although this data does not capture all the SSBs implemented in OECD countries due to reporting issues.

Revenue Statistics will continue to work with OECD countries (and some non-OECD countries) to enhance the granularity and comprehensiveness of data on revenues from health taxes as a basis for enhancements in policy making and cross-country analysis. In time, data on excise revenues could be complemented by information on revenues from customs duties on alcohol, tobacco and SSBs, which also generate revenues for the government and influence consumption.

References

Australian Taxation Office (2024), *Tobacco and excise*, https://www.ato.gov.au/businesses-and-organisations/gst-excise-and-indirect-taxes/tobacco-and-excise. [16]

Bollinger, B. and S. Sexton (2023), "Local excise taxes, sticky prices, and spillovers: evidence from Berkeley's soda tax", *Quantitative Marketing and Economics (QME)*, Vol. 21(2)/June, pp. 281-331, https://doi.org/10.1007/s11129-023-09263-y. [10]

Burton, R. et al. (2024), "The relationship between the price and demand of alcohol, tobacco, unhealthy food, sugar-sweetened beverages, and gambling: an umbrella review of systematic reviews", *BMC Public Health*, Vol. 24, https://doi.org/10.1186/s12889-024-18599-3. [5]

Crosetto, P. and L. Muller (2024), *Label or Taxes: Why Not Both? Testing Nutritional Mixed Policies in the Lab*, https://doi.org/10.2139/ssrn.4744950. [13]

DeCicca, P., D. Kenkel and M. Lovenheim (2022), "The Economics of Tobacco Regulation: A Comprehensive Review", *J Econ Lit*, Vol. Sep/60(3), pp. 883-970, https://doi.org/10.1257/jel.20201482. [7]

Fuchs, A. (2019), *Is Tobacco Taxation Regressive? Evidence on Public Health, Domestic Resource Mobilization, and Equity Improvements*, https://doi.org/10.1596/31575. [6]

Goodchild, M., N. Nargis and E. Tursan d'Espaignet (2018), "Global economic cost of smoking-attributable diseases", *Tob Control*, Vol. 27(1), pp. 58-64, https://doi.org/10.1136/tobaccocontrol-2016-053305. [15]

Hillion, M. (2024), *Une évaluation des achats transfrontaliers de tabac et des pertes fiscales associées en France*, Insee. [9]

Lauer, J. et al. (eds.) (2022), *Health taxes : policy and practice*, World Scientific Publishing Europe Ltd, Singapore, https://doi.org/10.1142/q0365. [4]

Lauer, J. et al. (eds.) (2022), *Supply-side responses to health taxes*, World Scientific Publishing Europe Ltd. [8]

New Zealand Customs Service (2024), *https://www.customs.govt.nz/about-us/news/important-notices/new-excise-duty-and-levy-rates-for-alcohol-from-1-july-2024/.* [14]

OECD (2024), *Tobacco Taxation in Latin America and the Caribbean: A Call for Tobacco Tax Reform*, OECD Publishing, Paris, https://doi.org/10.1787/080cd662-en. [12]

OECD (2023), *Health at a Glance 2023: OECD Indicators*, OECD Publishing, Paris, https://doi.org/10.1787/7a7afb35-en. [11]

OECD (2022), *Consumption Tax Trends 2022: VAT/GST and Excise, Core Design Features and Trends*, OECD Publishing, Paris, https://doi.org/10.1787/6525a942-en. [3]

OECD (2019), *Revenue Statistics 2019*, OECD Publishing, Paris, https://doi.org/10.1787/0bbc27da-en. [2]

World Health Organization (2024), *https://www.who.int/data/gho/data/themes/health-taxes#:~:text=Health%20taxes%20are%20excise%20taxes,%2Dsweetened%20beverages%20(SSBs).*. [1]

World Health Organization (2023), *Global report on the use of sugar-sweetened beverage taxes, 2023*, Geneva: World Health Organization. [17]

Annex 2.A. Additional information on health tax data

Annex Table 2.A.1. Overview on health tax reporting OECD countries in 2000, 2010 and 2022

	2000			2010			2022		
	Tobacco	Alcohol	SSBs	Tobacco	Alcohol	SSBs	Tobacco	Alcohol	SSBs
AUS	✓	✓	×	✓	✓	×	✓	✓	×
AUT	✓	✓	×	✓	✓	×	✓	✓	×
BEL	✓	✓	✓	✓	✓	✓	✓	✓	✓
CAN	✓	✓	×	✓	✓	×	✓	✓	×
CHE	✓	✓	×	✓	✓	×	✓	✓	×
CHL [1]	✓	×	×	✓	×	×	✓	×	×
COL	✓	✓	×	✓	✓	×	✓	✓	×
CRI	×	✓	×	×	✓	✓	✓	✓	✓
CZE	✓	✓	×	✓	✓	×	✓	✓	×
DEU	✓	✓	×	✓	✓	×	✓	✓	×
DNK	✓	✓	×	✓	✓	×	✓	✓	×
ESP	✓	✓	×	✓	✓	×	✓	✓	×
EST	✓	✓	×	✓	✓	×	✓	✓	×
FIN	✓	✓	✓	✓	✓	✓	✓	✓	✓
FRA	✓	✓	×	✓	✓	×	✓	✓	✓
GBR	✓	✓	×	✓	✓	×	✓	✓	✓
GRC	✓	✓	×	✓	✓	×	✓	✓	×
HUN	✓	✓	×	✓	✓	×	✓	✓	×
IRL	✓	✓	×	✓	✓	×	✓	✓	✓
ISL	×	✓	×	✓	✓	×	✓	✓	×
ISR	✓	×	×	✓	×	×	✓	✓	✓
ITA	✓	✓	×	✓	✓	×	✓	✓	×
JPN	✓	✓	×	✓	✓	×	✓	✓	×
KOR [2]	✓	✓	×	✓	✓	×	✓	✓	×
LTU	✓	✓	×	✓	✓	×	✓	✓	×
LUX	✓	✓	×	✓	✓	×	✓	✓	×
LVA	✓	✓	✓	✓	✓	✓	✓	✓	✓
MEX	✓	✓	×	✓	✓	×	✓	✓	✓
NLD	✓	✓	✓	✓	✓	✓	✓	✓	✓
NOR [3]	✓	✓	✓	✓	✓	✓	✓	✓	×
NZL	✓	✓	×	✓	✓	×	✓	✓	×
POL	✓	✓	×	✓	✓	×	✓	✓	×
PRT	✓	✓	×	✓	✓	×	✓	✓	✓
SVK	✓	✓	×	✓	✓	×	✓	✓	×
SVN	✓	✓	×	✓	✓	×	✓	✓	×
SWE	✓	✓	×	✓	✓	×	✓	✓	×
TUR	×	×	×	✓	✓	✓	✓	✓	✓
USA	✓	✓	×	✓	✓	×	✓	✓	×
# countries	**35**	**35**	**5**	**37**	**36**	**7**	**38**	**37**	**11**

Notes: This table provides an overview on the reporting of health excise tax revenue by country for the years 2000, 2010 and 2022. All data is reported in *OECD Revenue Statistics* (category 5121), except for data for Türkiye prior to 2018, which is sourced from the national government's "General Budget" annual publications starting in 2009 that provide identical data as in Revenue Statistics for the overlapping years. The following OECD countries currently have a SSB excise tax in place but do not report a separate SSB excise tax revenue category in *OECD Revenue Statistics* (and are therefore not included in this Special Feature): Canada (sub-national), Hungary, Poland, Spain (sub-national), United States of America (sub-national).

[1] A special case applies to Chile, as it levies an indirect tax on alcohol and SSBs, respectively, classified as "Tasas especiales del impuesto al valor agregado" (or "VAT special rates") under official tax revenue reports; hence, revenue raised from this tax are not classified under the "5121-Excise" category in *OECD Revenue Statistics* and thus not included in the displayed figures.

[2] Korea levies a "special consumption tax on tobacco excise" but due to a lack of disaggregation, it is not included in the figures displayed.

[3] Norway reports SSB excise tax revenue *OECD Revenue Statistics* until 2021 as the tax was repealed in that year.

Source: *OECD Revenue Statistics 2024*

Annex Figure 2.A.1. Level of health, tobacco, alcohol and SSB excise tax revenue by OECD country, 2022

Percentage of GDP

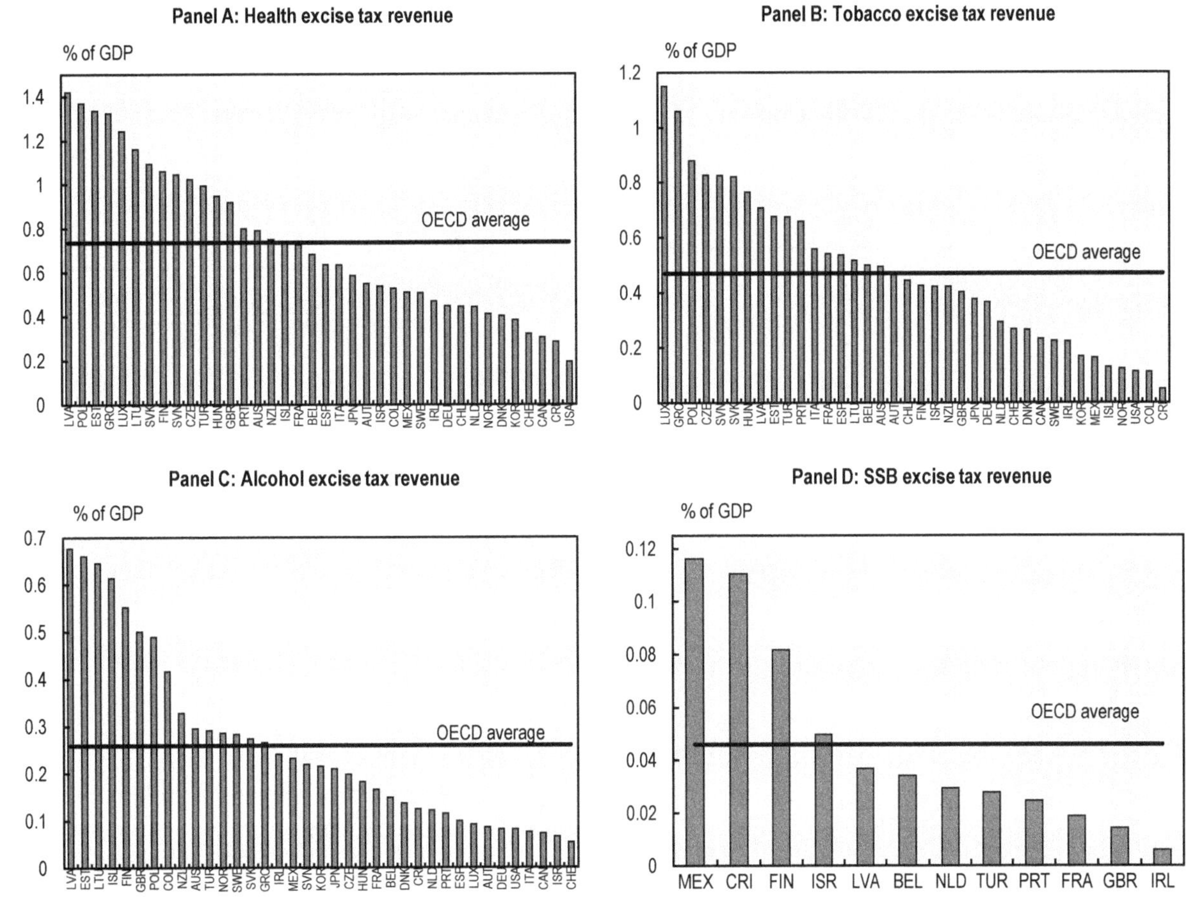

Note: Health excise tax revenue (Panel A) is the sum of reported tax revenue collected from excise taxes levied on tobacco (Panel B), alcohol (Panel C) and SSBs (Panel D). The estimates of health excise tax revenues are based on data reported by the countries. The OECD average for health excise tax revenues is calculated based on 38 countries for total health excise tax revenue, 38 countries for tobacco, 37 countries for alcohol and 12 countries for SSB (Annex Table 2.A.1. provides a list of reporting countries). Health excise tax revenue data are sourced from *OECD Revenue Statistics* (category 5121) for all OECD countries in 2022.
Source: Authors' calculations based on *OECD Revenue Statistics 2024*.

StatLink https://stat.link/t6oe0y

Annex Figure 2.A.2. Share of health, tobacco, alcohol and SSB excise tax revenue by OECD country, 2022

Percentage of total tax revenues

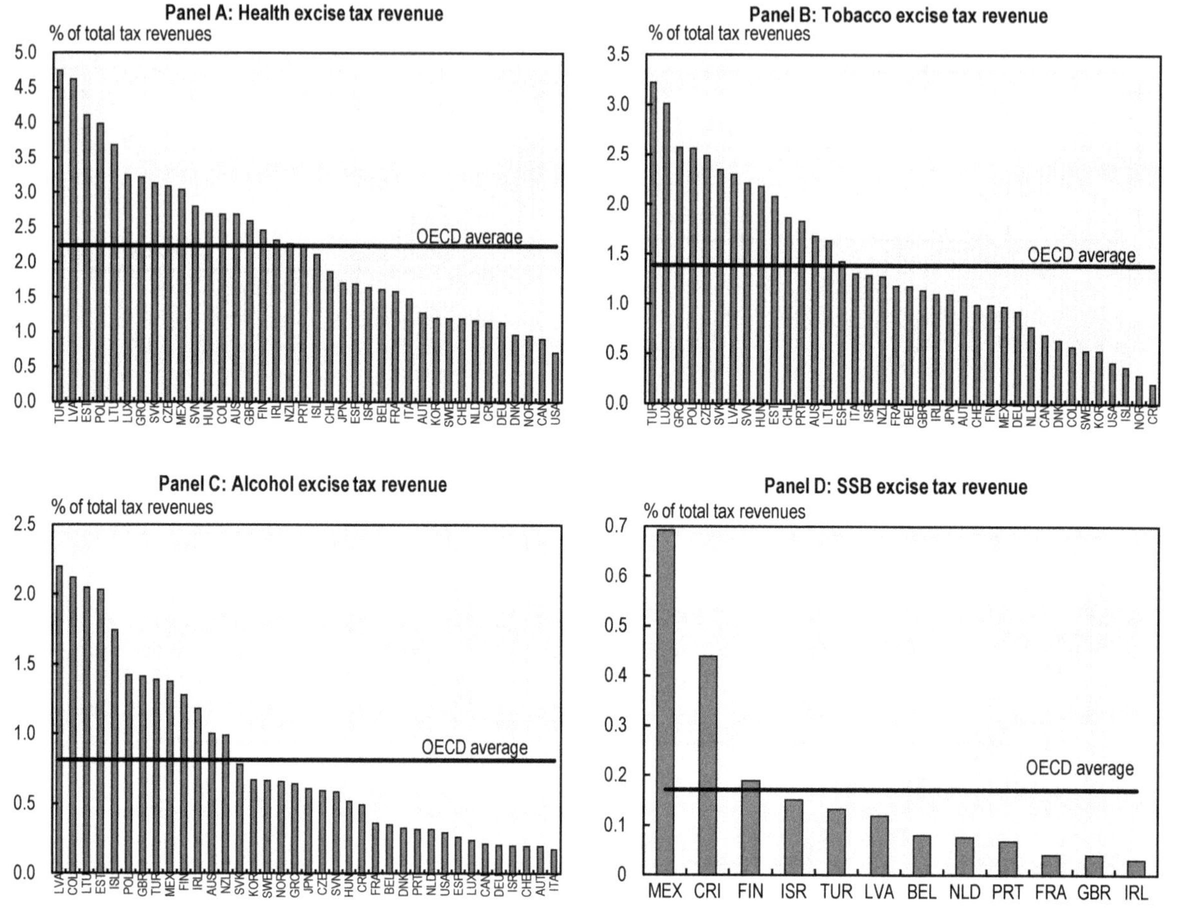

Note: Health excise tax revenue (Panel A) is the sum of reported tax revenue collected from excise taxes levied on tobacco (Panel B), alcohol (Panel C) and SSBs (Panel D). The estimates of health excise tax revenues are based on data reported by the countries. The OECD average for health excise tax revenues is calculated based on 38 countries for total health excise tax revenue, 38 countries for tobacco, 37 countries for alcohol and 12 countries for SSBs (Annex Table 2.A.1. provides a list of reporting countries). Health excise tax revenue data are sourced from *OECD Revenue Statistics* (category 5121) for all OECD countries in 2022.

Source: Authors' calculations based on *OECD Revenue Statistics 2024*.

StatLink https://stat.link/216s8n

Notes

[1] The definition could reasonably be extended to include (for example) products that damage the environment, given the impact of pollution on people's health.

[2] For the purposes of this study, the definition of SSBs follows that of the World Health Organisation: '[A]ll types of beverages containing free sugars, and these include carbonated or non-carbonated beverages, fruit/vegetable juices and drinks, liquid and powder concentrates, flavoured water, energy and sports drinks, ready-to-drink tea, ready-to-drink coffee and flavoured milk drinks.' (World Health Organization, 2023[17]) However, it should be noted that products taxed as SSBs in OECD countries may use artificial sweeteners rather than sugar. For the purposes of this chapter, such products are still counted as SSBs, even though the title is not strictly accurate.

[3] In addition to the 12 countries discussed in this chapter, the following countries implement taxes on SSBs but do not report a separate SSB excise tax revenue category to *OECD Revenue Statistics* and are therefore not included in this Special Feature: Canada (at sub-national level), Hungary, Poland, Spain (sub-national) and United States (sub-national). Norway is one of the countries for which revenues on SSBs are included in the chapter but data is not shown for 2022 as its SSB excise tax was abolished in 2021.

[4] Please consult Chapter 3 of (OECD, 2022[3]) for a broader exploration of this topic.

[5] According to (Goodchild, Nargis and Tursan d'Espaignet, 2018[15]), the economic costs of smoking-attributable diseases was equivalent to 2.2% of GDP on average across high-income countries in 2012.

[6] Please consult (Australian Taxation Office, 2024[16]) for additional information on the excise-equivalent customs duties in Australia and (New Zealand Customs Service, 2024[14])for New Zealand.

[7] Chile levies an indirect tax on alcohol and SSBs, respectively, which are classified as "Tasas especiales del impuesto al valor agregado" (or "VAT special rates"); revenue raised from this tax are not classified as an excise in *Revenue Statistics* and thus not included in this chapter.

[8] Please refer to (OECD, 2022[3]) and previous editions of the same report for data on excise rates for *(inter alia)* cigarettes, cigars, rolling tobacco for cigarettes, beer, still wine, sparkling wine and other alcoholic beverages.

3 Tax levels and tax structures, 1965-2023

Chapter 3 provides an overview of tax levels and tax structures in OECD countries.

In all the following tables, the symbol (..) indicates not available or not applicable. The main series in this chapter cover a selection of years between 1990 and 2023. A complete series is available online. Data for 1955 and 1960 (for nineteen OECD countries) are provided in Part V of the 1998 edition of this Report.

The Gross Domestic Product (GDP) figures are based on the 2008 System of National Accounts (SNA) for all OECD countries.

Box 3.1. Treatment of capital transfers

Footnotes to Tables 3.1 to 3.18 refer to the treatment of the capital transfers that some countries make to account for taxes that have been assessed but not collected. The capital transfer has been subtracted directly from the specific taxes to which they relate, except for France, where the capital transfer has been allocated between tax headings in proportion to their tax revenues at the level of government against which these transfers were recorded.

Countries reporting capital transfers include:

- Austria from 2020 to 2022
- Belgium from 1995
- Denmark from 1971
- France from 1992
- Lithuania from 1999
- Luxembourg from 2013
- Poland from 1995
- Slovenia from 1995
- Switzerland from 1990

Table 3.1. Total tax revenue as % of GDP

	1965	1990	2000	2007	2010	2015	2020	2021	2022	2023p
Australia	20.6	28.1	30.4	29.4	25.1	27.8	28.3	29.2	29.4	..
Austria[1]	33.5	39.3	42.3	40.5	41.0	43.1	42.1	43.4	43.2	42.7
Belgium[1]	30.8	41.4	43.8	42.9	42.9	44.1	42.2	42.1	42.4	42.6
Canada	25.0	35.1	34.7	32.5	31.0	32.8	34.5	34.8	33.8	34.8
Chile	..	16.8	18.7	22.8	19.7	20.5	19.3	22.3	23.8	20.6
Colombia	..	11.3	15.7	19.3	18.1	19.9	18.8	19.2	19.7	22.2
Costa Rica	..	22.4	21.1	23.1	22.1	22.9	22.6	24.8	25.2	24.9
Czechia	..	..	32.2	34.1	31.9	32.9	34.0	33.7	33.2	33.7
Denmark[1]	29.1	44.6	46.8	46.5	44.8	46.5	47.2	47.2	41.9	43.4
Estonia	..	..	31.1	31.0	33.2	32.7	32.8	33.5	32.6	33.5
Finland	30.0	42.9	45.8	41.4	40.6	43.5	41.8	43.2	43.2	42.4
France[1]	33.9	41.5	43.7	42.9	42.2	45.4	45.2	45.1	45.8	43.8
Germany	31.7	34.8	36.4	35.7	35.9	38.1	38.7	39.8	39.6	38.1
Greece	17.1	25.2	33.4	31.8	32.3	36.9	39.5	40.0	41.2	39.8
Hungary	..	..	38.5	39.2	36.8	38.7	36.0	33.8	35.1	34.2
Iceland	25.7	30.5	35.9	38.4	32.2	35.1	36.2	34.8	35.2	35.9
Ireland	24.5	32.4	30.8	30.8	27.7	22.3	19.4	20.0	20.3	21.9
Israel	..	..	34.0	33.2	30.1	31.0	29.6	32.3	32.8	29.8
Italy	24.6	36.3	40.5	41.6	41.7	43.0	42.6	42.5	42.8	42.8
Japan	17.3	27.7	25.3	27.2	26.2	30.2	32.9	33.9	34.4	..
Korea	..	18.6	20.9	23.7	22.4	23.7	27.7	29.8	32.0	28.9
Latvia	..	..	29.0	28.2	28.5	29.8	31.1	30.7	30.8	31.9
Lithuania[1]	..	..	30.8	30.1	28.3	28.9	31.2	31.9	31.6	32.6
Luxembourg[1]	27.3	34.7	37.0	35.7	35.7	34.8	38.3	38.2	38.3	40.9
Mexico	..	11.5	10.9	11.5	12.3	15.4	17.2	16.7	16.8	17.7
Netherlands	30.4	39.6	36.9	35.5	35.4	36.5	39.0	38.3	38.1	38.5
New Zealand	24.5	36.2	32.5	33.9	30.3	31.5	33.7	34.5	33.1	34.0
Norway	29.4	40.4	41.8	42.0	41.7	38.3	38.7	41.3	43.4	41.4
Poland[1]	..	..	32.9	34.6	31.6	32.5	35.6	36.7	34.4	35.1
Portugal	15.7	26.5	30.9	31.8	30.4	34.4	35.2	35.2	36.0	35.8
Slovak Republic	..	..	33.6	29.2	27.9	32.5	34.8	35.4	35.0	35.5
Slovenia[1]	..	..	37.7	38.0	37.8	37.3	37.6	38.3	37.4	36.9
Spain	14.3	31.5	33.0	36.4	31.3	33.8	36.8	37.8	37.6	37.3
Sweden	31.0	48.8	50.0	45.0	43.1	42.9	42.6	42.8	42.5	41.4
Switzerland[1]	16.0	23.2	27.0	25.5	25.8	27.0	27.9	28.0	26.9	27.1
Türkiye	10.6	14.5	23.5	22.9	24.7	25.0	23.9	22.9	20.9	23.5
United Kingdom	30.1	32.9	32.7	33.0	32.0	31.9	32.8	34.2	35.4	35.3
United States	23.6	26.0	28.3	26.7	23.4	26.1	25.6	26.7	27.6	25.2
OECD Average[2]	**24.9**	**30.9**	**32.9**	**32.9**	**31.5**	**32.9**	**33.5**	**34.1**	**34.0**	**33.9**

.. Not available

Note: Full time series can be accessed at http://data-explorer.oecd.org/s/nb.

1. The capital transfers were subtracted directly from the specific taxes to which they relate, except for France, where the capital transfers have been allocated between tax headings in proportion to the reported tax revenue.
2. Calculated by applying the unweighted average percentage change for 2023 in the 36 countries providing data for that year to the overall average tax to GDP ratio in 2022.

Table 3.2. Total tax revenue in billions of US dollars at market exchange rates

	1965	1990	2000	2007	2010	2015	2020	2021	2022	2023p
Australia	5.6	90.8	117.4	290.5	346.4	344.3	423.9	490.7	511.2	..
Austria[1]	..	68.6	83.4	157.8	160.7	164.7	183.2	207.9	203.4	220.2
Belgium[1]	..	89.4	103.8	202.1	206.4	204.0	222.1	252.8	247.3	269.2
Canada	14.2	210.2	259.9	477.3	501.5	510.9	570.7	698.6	731.3	745.1
Chile	..	5.8	14.6	39.4	42.8	49.7	49.0	70.4	72.0	69.2
Colombia	..	5.1	14.7	39.8	51.8	58.4	50.8	61.1	67.9	80.9
Costa Rica	..	1.3	3.2	6.2	8.3	13.0	14.1	16.1	17.4	21.6
Czechia	..	..	20.0	64.9	67.4	62.3	85.5	97.9	100.2	115.7
Denmark[1]	3.0	61.6	76.8	148.9	144.4	140.3	168.0	193.0	168.6	176.6
Estonia	..	..	1.8	7.0	6.5	7.6	10.4	12.5	12.5	13.8
Finland	..	49.6	57.7	106.1	101.2	102.1	113.8	128.1	121.7	126.2
France[1]	..	550.7	594.3	1 139.9	1 117.7	1 108.0	1 197.9	1 336.7	1 280.0	1 337.1
Germany	..	577.4	708.5	1 222.8	1 219.4	1 277.6	1 502.7	1 702.0	1 618.6	1 696.3
Greece	..	14.6	43.6	101.4	96.0	72.3	74.5	86.0	89.7	94.8
Hungary	..	..	18.2	55.0	48.7	48.4	56.6	61.5	62.2	72.6
Iceland	0.1	2.0	3.2	8.3	4.4	6.2	7.8	9.0	10.1	11.1
Ireland	0.7	15.6	30.8	83.3	61.5	67.6	84.6	106.5	111.1	120.7
Israel	..	..	46.4	61.4	72.1	94.2	122.2	159.1	173.0	153.1
Italy	..	336.6	464.7	919.9	890.8	789.0	808.0	915.0	885.4	966.1
Japan	17.1	919.7	1 225.1	1 281.1	1 544.3	1 386.1	1 649.2	1 632.0	1 464.3	..
Korea	..	52.6	120.6	278.2	255.9	348.0	456.2	541.2	535.3	494.2
Latvia	..	..	1.8	8.8	6.8	8.1	10.7	12.1	12.4	13.9
Lithuania[1]	..	..	3.8	12.0	10.5	12.0	17.8	21.3	22.4	25.4
Luxembourg[1]	..	4.7	7.9	18.4	20.0	20.9	28.2	32.7	31.2	35.1
Mexico	..	36.3	81.1	126.5	135.8	186.4	193.1	219.6	245.9	317.5
Netherlands	..	132.6	154.1	302.8	302.1	283.3	363.9	403.5	398.4	444.7
New Zealand	1.4	16.1	17.4	46.0	47.0	56.8	78.2	84.1	81.6	86.3
Norway	2.4	48.5	71.7	169.0	179.9	148.8	142.3	208.1	257.9	201.1
Poland[1]	..	..	56.6	148.6	150.3	154.9	213.2	250.0	237.1	285.0
Portugal	..	18.8	36.7	76.6	72.3	68.6	80.5	89.9	91.9	102.7
Slovak Republic	..	..	9.8	25.3	25.4	28.9	37.1	42.0	40.5	47.1
Slovenia[1]	..	..	6.6	18.3	18.2	16.1	20.2	23.7	22.5	25.2
Spain	..	131.6	197.8	536.7	444.9	404.6	470.9	546.6	533.0	590.0
Sweden	7.7	127.7	131.5	220.6	212.6	215.3	232.1	272.5	246.5	242.0
Switzerland[1]	2.6	61.6	75.5	125.4	154.6	187.1	207.1	228.0	220.2	239.8
Türkiye	1.3	30.2	64.4	155.8	191.6	215.7	171.9	187.9	190.0	259.6
United Kingdom	30.6	359.3	543.9	1 018.9	796.5	934.2	885.2	1075.2	1 094.1	1 180.2
United States	167.0	1 552.4	2 900.5	3 868.6	3 517.1	4 772.7	5 452.2	6 301.7	7 107.1	6 887.4
OECD Average	**19.5**	**192.1**	**220.3**	**357.1**	**348.3**	**383.4**	**433.0**	**494.1**	**508.3**	**..**

.. Not available

Note: Full time series can be accessed at http://data-explorer.oecd.org/s/nb.

1. The capital transfers were subtracted directly from the specific taxes to which they relate, except for France, where the capital transfers have been allocated between tax headings in proportion to the reported tax revenue.

Table 3.3. Tax revenue of main headings as % of GDP, 2022

	1000 Income & profits	2000 Social security	3000 Payroll	4000 Property	5000 Goods and services[3]	6000 Others	Memorandum item: supranational revenues
Australia	18.3	0.0	1.4	2.7	7.0	0.0	..
Austria[1]	13.4	14.7	2.7	0.6	11.6	0.2	0.2
Belgium[1]	15.9	12.9	0.0	3.3	10.4	0.0	0.5
Canada	17.5	4.7	0.7	3.5	7.4	0.0	..
Chile	10.4	1.0	0.0	1.3	11.4	-0.3	..
Colombia	6.5	1.6	0.3	1.5	8.8	0.9	..
Costa Rica	5.4	8.8	1.4	0.5	8.2	0.9	..
Czechia	7.3	15.2	0.0	0.2	10.5	0.0	0.2
Denmark[1]	27.1	0.1	0.3	1.7	12.8	0.0	0.2
Estonia	7.9	11.3	0.0	0.2	13.2	0.0	0.3
Finland	15.9	11.9	0.0	1.4	13.8	0.0	0.2
France[1]	12.5	14.8	2.0	3.7	11.9	0.8	0.3
Germany	13.1	14.6	0.0	1.1	10.8	0.0	0.3
Greece	8.5	12.2	0.0	2.7	17.8	0.0	0.3
Hungary	7.0	9.8	0.7	0.8	16.7	0.1	0.2
Iceland	18.1	3.0	0.3	2.0	11.5	0.4	..
Ireland	10.7	3.1	0.2	1.0	5.4	0.0	0.2
Israel	12.2	5.0	0.9	4.0	10.6	0.0	..
Italy	14.0	13.1	0.0	2.5	11.8	1.4	0.3
Japan	11.2	13.3	0.0	2.7	7.2	0.1	..
Korea	11.9	8.2	0.1	3.8	7.3	0.7	..
Latvia	6.9	9.4	0.0	0.8	13.7	0.0	0.2
Lithuania[1]	9.9	9.8	0.0	0.3	11.5	0.0	0.3
Luxembourg[1]	14.8	10.6	0.0	3.7	9.1	0.0	0.4
Mexico	7.7	2.3	0.5	0.4	5.5	0.4	..
Netherlands	12.5	12.5	0.0	1.5	11.5	0.1	0.5
New Zealand	19.3	0.0	0.0	1.9	11.9	0.0	..
Norway	26.5	7.5	0.0	1.0	8.5	0.0	..
Poland[1]	7.3	12.8	0.6	1.2	12.6	0.0	0.3
Portugal	10.3	10.2	0.0	1.5	13.8	0.2	0.2
Slovak Republic	7.7	14.5	0.0	0.4	12.3	0.0	0.2
Slovenia[1]	7.5	16.0	0.0	0.6	13.2	0.0	0.2
Spain	11.8	12.8	0.0	2.6	10.4	0.0	0.3
Sweden	15.3	8.8	5.1	0.9	12.2	0.1	0.2
Switzerland[1]	12.5	6.7	0.0	2.2	5.4	0.1	..
Türkiye	5.8	5.1	0.0	0.7	9.1	0.2	..
United Kingdom[2]	13.4	7.1	0.1	4.0	10.8	0.0	..
United States	14.2	6.0	0.0	2.9	4.5	0.0	..
OECD Average	**12.3**	**8.7**	**0.5**	**1.8**	**10.6**	**0.2**	**0.3**

.. Not available

1. The capital transfers were subtracted directly from the specific taxes to which they relate, except for France, where the capital transfers have been allocated between tax headings in proportion to the reported tax revenue.
2. Supranational taxes reported by the United Kingdom are reported until 2020 in Revenue Statistics. From 2021, at the end of the Brexit transition period, this came to an end and taxes subsequently introduced by the United Kingdom are reflected in the appropriate tax category at the national or subnational levels of government, as appropriate.
3. The figures in category 5000 include supranational revenues, which are also presented separately under the Supranational heading.

Table 3.4. Tax revenue of main headings as % of total tax revenue, 2022

	1000 Income & profits	2000 Social security	3000 Payroll	4000 Property	5000 Goods and services[3]	6000 Others	Memorandum item: supranational revenues
Australia	62.3	0.0	4.7	9.3	23.8	0.0	..
Austria[1]	30.9	34.1	6.3	1.4	26.9	0.4	0.5
Belgium[1]	37.4	30.4	0.0	7.7	24.5	0.0	1.2
Canada	51.6	14.0	2.2	10.4	21.7	0.1	..
Chile	43.7	4.1	0.0	5.5	47.8	-1.1	..
Colombia	33.2	8.3	1.5	7.8	44.8	4.4	..
Costa Rica	21.5	34.8	5.7	2.0	32.6	3.5	..
Czechia	22.0	45.9	0.0	0.5	31.5	0.0	0.5
Denmark[1]	64.6	0.2	0.6	4.1	30.4	0.1	0.4
Estonia	24.2	34.8	0.0	0.5	40.5	0.0	0.8
Finland	36.9	27.6	0.0	3.3	32.0	0.1	0.5
France[1]	27.4	32.4	4.3	8.1	26.1	1.8	0.6
Germany	32.9	36.9	0.0	2.8	27.3	0.0	0.7
Greece	20.5	29.6	0.0	6.6	43.3	0.0	0.6
Hungary	19.9	28.0	2.0	2.3	47.5	0.3	0.5
Iceland	51.5	8.5	0.7	5.6	32.7	1.0	..
Ireland	52.8	15.1	0.9	4.7	26.4	0.0	0.8
Israel	37.2	15.3	2.8	12.3	32.4	0.0	..
Italy	32.8	30.5	0.0	5.7	27.6	3.3	0.6
Japan	32.5	38.5	0.0	7.9	20.8	0.2	..
Korea	37.4	25.6	0.3	11.9	22.7	2.2	..
Latvia	22.5	30.6	0.0	2.5	44.4	0.0	0.8
Lithuania[1]	31.4	31.1	0.0	0.9	36.6	0.0	1.0
Luxembourg[1]	38.6	27.8	0.0	9.7	23.9	0.1	1.2
Mexico	46.1	13.8	2.9	2.1	32.8	2.3	..
Netherlands	32.7	32.9	0.0	3.9	30.1	0.3	1.3
New Zealand	58.2	0.0	0.0	5.8	36.0	0.0	..
Norway	60.9	17.3	0.1	2.2	19.5	0.0	..
Poland[1]	21.2	37.1	1.6	3.4	36.5	0.1	0.8
Portugal	28.6	28.3	0.0	4.3	38.3	0.5	0.6
Slovak Republic	22.0	41.6	0.0	1.2	35.2	0.0	0.5
Slovenia[1]	20.1	42.8	0.1	1.6	35.3	0.0	0.5
Spain	31.4	34.1	0.0	6.9	27.6	0.0	0.8
Sweden	36.0	20.8	12.1	2.2	28.8	0.1	0.4
Switzerland[1]	46.6	24.8	0.0	8.1	19.9	0.6	..
Türkiye	27.5	24.4	0.0	3.5	43.6	1.1	..
United Kingdom[2]	37.8	19.9	0.4	11.3	30.6	0.0	..
United States	51.4	21.9	0.1	10.4	16.3	0.0	..
OECD Average	**36.5**	**24.8**	**1.3**	**5.3**	**31.5**	**0.6**	**0.7**

.. Not available

1. The capital transfers were subtracted directly from the specific taxes to which they relate, except for France, where the capital transfers have been allocated between tax headings in proportion to the reported tax revenue.
2. Supranational taxes reported by the United Kingdom are reported until 2020 in Revenue Statistics. From 2021, at the end of the Brexit transition period, this came to an end and taxes subsequently introduced by the United Kingdom are reflected in the appropriate tax category at the national or subnational levels of government, as appropriate.
3. The figures in category 5000 include supranational revenues, which are also presented separately under the Supranational heading.

Table 3.5. Tax revenue of main headings as % of GDP, 2023p

	1000 Income & profits	2000 Social security	3000 Payroll	4000 Property	5000 Goods and services[3]	6000 Others	Memorandum item: supranational revenues
Australia	..	..	..	..	..	..	..
Austria[1]	12.9	14.8	2.7	0.5	11.6	0.2	0.2
Belgium[1]	15.8	13.2	0.0	3.1	10.5	0.0	0.4
Canada	17.9	5.2	0.8	3.4	7.5	0.0	..
Chile	7.2	1.2	0.0	1.3	11.2	-0.3	..
Colombia	8.9	1.6	0.3	1.6	8.8	1.0	..
Costa Rica	5.3	8.9	1.5	0.5	8.3	0.5	..
Czechia	8.0	15.2	0.0	0.2	10.4	0.0	0.1
Denmark[1]	29.0	0.1	0.3	1.7	12.3	0.1	0.1
Estonia	8.1	12.0	0.0	0.2	13.2	0.0	0.1
Finland	15.5	12.3	0.0	1.4	13.2	0.0	0.2
France[1]	11.7	14.6	1.9	3.5	11.3	0.9	0.2
Germany	12.4	14.7	0.0	0.9	10.1	0.0	0.2
Greece	9.5	11.5	0.0	2.8	16.0	0.0	0.2
Hungary	7.5	9.6	0.6	0.7	15.6	0.2	0.1
Iceland	18.7	3.0	0.3	2.0	11.6	0.4	..
Ireland	11.6	3.4	0.2	1.0	5.7	0.0	0.2
Israel	11.0	5.0	0.9	3.2	9.6	0.0	..
Italy	14.7	12.7	0.0	2.2	11.9	1.4	0.2
Japan	10.4	..	0.0	2.6	6.8	0.1	..
Korea	9.9	8.4	0.1	3.3	6.5	0.6	..
Latvia	7.6	10.2	0.0	0.7	13.4	0.0	0.2
Lithuania[1]	10.6	10.4	0.0	0.3	11.3	0.0	0.2
Luxembourg[1]	16.6	11.5	0.0	3.5	9.3	0.0	0.3
Mexico	7.9	2.4	0.5	0.3	6.2	0.4	..
Netherlands	13.8	12.1	0.0	1.2	11.3	0.1	0.4
New Zealand	19.9	0.0	0.0	2.0	12.0	0.0	..
Norway	21.4	9.2	0.1	1.2	9.6	0.0	..
Poland[1]	6.9	13.4	0.5	1.1	11.0	2.1	0.2
Portugal	10.4	10.4	0.0	1.4	13.3	0.2	0.2
Slovak Republic	7.7	15.1	0.0	0.4	12.4	0.0	0.2
Slovenia[1]	7.5	15.8	0.0	0.6	12.9	0.0	0.1
Spain	12.0	12.9	0.0	2.3	10.0	0.0	0.2
Sweden	14.6	8.9	5.3	0.8	11.7	0.0	0.1
Switzerland[1]	12.7	6.7	0.0	2.2	5.4	0.1	..
Türkiye	5.6	6.2	0.0	0.7	10.7	0.2	..
United Kingdom[2]	14.2	6.7	0.1	3.7	10.6	0.0	..
United States	12.1	6.1	0.0	2.8	4.2	0.0	..

.. Not available

1. The capital transfers were subtracted directly from the specific taxes to which they relate, except for France, where the capital transfers have been allocated between tax headings in proportion to the reported tax revenue.
2. Supranational taxes reported by the United Kingdom are reported until 2020 in Revenue Statistics. From 2021, at the end of the Brexit transition period, this came to an end and taxes subsequently introduced by the United Kingdom are reflected in the appropriate tax category at the national or subnational levels of government, as appropriate.
3. The figures in category 5000 include supranational revenues, which are also presented separately under the Supranational heading.

Table 3.6. Tax revenue of main headings as % of total tax revenue, 2023p

	1000 Income & profits	2000 Social security	3000 Payroll	4000 Property	5000 Goods and services[3]	6000 Others	Memorandum item: supranational revenues
Australia	..	..	..	..	..	..	..
Austria[1]	30.3	34.8	6.3	1.1	27.2	0.4	0.4
Belgium[1]	37.1	31.0	0.0	7.4	24.6	0.0	0.9
Canada	51.3	14.9	2.2	9.9	21.6	0.1	..
Chile	35.2	5.6	0.0	6.5	54.2	-1.5	..
Colombia	40.1	7.3	1.4	7.4	39.5	4.3	..
Costa Rica	21.2	35.7	5.9	1.9	33.4	1.9	..
Czechia	23.6	45.2	0.0	0.5	30.7	0.0	0.4
Denmark[1]	66.9	0.2	0.6	3.8	28.3	0.1	0.3
Estonia	24.3	35.8	0.0	0.5	39.5	0.0	0.4
Finland	36.6	28.9	0.0	3.3	31.1	0.1	0.4
France[1]	26.8	33.2	4.4	7.9	25.7	1.9	0.5
Germany	32.5	38.5	0.0	2.5	26.5	0.0	0.5
Greece	24.0	28.8	0.0	7.1	40.1	0.0	0.5
Hungary	21.9	28.0	1.7	2.2	45.7	0.6	0.4
Iceland	52.0	8.3	0.8	5.6	32.3	1.0	..
Ireland	52.8	15.6	0.9	4.6	26.1	0.0	0.8
Israel	37.1	16.7	3.1	10.9	32.3	0.0	..
Italy	34.2	29.6	0.0	5.3	27.7	3.2	0.5
Japan	..	..	..	..	..	..	..
Korea	34.2	29.2	0.3	11.5	22.6	2.0	..
Latvia	23.9	31.9	0.0	2.3	42.0	0.0	0.5
Lithuania[1]	32.5	31.9	0.0	0.9	34.7	0.0	0.5
Luxembourg[1]	40.5	28.0	0.0	8.6	22.8	0.1	0.8
Mexico	44.6	13.5	3.0	1.7	35.2	2.0	..
Netherlands	35.8	31.4	0.0	3.2	29.2	0.3	1.0
New Zealand	58.6	0.0	0.0	6.0	35.4	0.0	..
Norway	51.6	22.2	0.1	2.9	23.2	0.0	..
Poland[1]	19.7	38.1	1.6	3.2	31.4	6.0	0.5
Portugal	29.2	29.1	0.0	4.0	37.3	0.5	0.4
Slovak Republic	21.6	42.4	0.0	1.2	34.8	0.0	0.4
Slovenia[1]	20.4	42.9	0.1	1.5	35.1	0.0	0.4
Spain	32.3	34.7	0.0	6.2	26.8	0.0	0.7
Sweden	35.3	21.4	12.8	2.0	28.4	0.1	0.3
Switzerland[1]	46.7	24.7	0.0	8.1	20.0	0.5	..
Türkiye	24.0	26.5	0.0	3.0	45.6	0.9	..
United Kingdom[2]	40.1	19.0	0.4	10.5	30.0	0.0	..
United States	48.1	24.0	0.1	11.0	16.8	0.0	..

.. Not available

1. The capital transfers were subtracted directly from the specific taxes to which they relate, except for France, where the capital transfers have been allocated between tax headings in proportion to the reported tax revenue.
2. Supranational taxes reported by the United Kingdom are reported until 2020 in Revenue Statistics. From 2021, at the end of the Brexit transition period, this came to an end and taxes subsequently introduced by the United Kingdom are reflected in the appropriate tax category at the national or subnational levels of government, as appropriate.
3. The figures in category 5000 include supranational revenues, which are also presented separately under the Supranational heading.

Table 3.7. Taxes on income and profits (1000) as % of GDP and as % of total tax revenue

	% of GDP					% of total tax revenue				
	1990	2000	2010	2021	2022	1990	2000	2010	2021	2022
Australia	16.0	17.6	14.3	17.9	18.3	57.1	57.9	56.7	61.5	62.3
Austria[1]	10.0	12.0	11.5	12.8	13.4	25.5	28.3	28.1	29.5	30.9
Belgium[1]	15.3	16.9	14.7	15.0	15.9	36.9	38.6	34.2	35.7	37.4
Canada	17.0	17.4	14.5	18.0	17.5	48.6	50.1	46.6	51.6	51.6
Chile	3.9	4.4	7.5	8.5	10.4	23.2	23.3	38.2	38.3	43.7
Colombia	3.4	3.6	4.8	6.1	6.5	29.9	23.2	26.6	32.0	33.2
Costa Rica	2.3	2.8	3.8	5.1	5.4	10.0	13.2	17.1	20.6	21.5
Czechia	..	7.3	6.4	7.0	7.3	..	22.8	20.2	20.8	22.0
Denmark[1]	27.2	28.7	27.6	31.4	27.1	61.1	61.4	61.7	66.4	64.6
Estonia	..	7.7	6.6	8.4	7.9	..	24.8	19.8	24.9	24.2
Finland	16.8	19.7	14.4	15.6	15.9	39.2	43.1	35.5	36.1	36.9
France[1]	6.7	10.8	9.6	11.7	12.5	16.1	24.8	22.7	26.1	27.4
Germany	11.3	11.0	10.1	12.8	13.1	32.4	30.1	28.0	32.2	32.9
Greece	5.0	9.0	7.1	8.4	8.5	19.9	26.8	22.0	20.9	20.5
Hungary	..	9.4	7.6	5.5	7.0	..	24.3	20.7	16.2	19.9
Iceland	9.0	14.3	14.3	17.4	18.1	29.7	39.9	44.3	50.0	51.5
Ireland	12.3	13.4	11.1	10.0	10.7	38.0	43.6	40.1	49.7	52.8
Israel	..	13.4	8.7	11.5	12.2	..	39.4	29.0	35.6	37.2
Italy	13.2	13.4	13.6	13.5	14.0	36.5	33.2	32.7	31.8	32.8
Japan	13.9	8.8	7.9	10.8	11.2	50.2	34.8	30.2	31.9	32.5
Korea	6.1	6.0	6.3	9.9	11.9	32.8	28.8	28.0	33.2	37.4
Latvia	..	7.0	7.1	6.9	6.9	..	24.1	25.0	22.4	22.5
Lithuania[1]	..	8.3	4.6	9.5	9.9	..	27.0	16.2	29.8	31.4
Luxembourg[1]	13.9	13.5	12.9	14.6	14.8	40.2	36.5	36.2	38.3	38.6
Mexico	3.9	3.9	4.9	7.1	7.7	34.0	36.0	39.8	42.7	46.1
Netherlands	12.8	9.6	9.9	12.1	12.5	32.3	25.9	27.9	31.6	32.7
New Zealand	21.6	19.5	16.3	20.2	19.3	59.6	60.0	53.8	58.6	58.2
Norway	14.2	18.9	19.7	20.4	26.5	35.0	45.2	47.2	49.3	60.9
Poland[1]	..	6.7	6.3	8.0	7.3	..	20.4	20.1	21.7	21.2
Portugal	6.8	9.1	8.1	9.3	10.3	25.7	29.4	26.7	26.5	28.6
Slovak Republic	..	6.9	5.2	7.7	7.7	..	20.5	18.8	21.6	22.0
Slovenia[1]	..	6.8	7.4	7.9	7.5	..	18.0	19.6	20.6	20.1
Spain	9.7	9.3	8.7	11.3	11.8	30.6	28.1	28.0	29.8	31.4
Sweden	20.3	21.4	15.4	15.7	15.3	41.6	42.7	35.7	36.7	36.0
Switzerland[1]	10.8	11.8	11.8	13.4	12.5	46.8	43.8	45.7	47.7	46.6
Türkiye	4.9	6.9	5.3	5.5	5.8	33.5	29.5	21.3	23.9	27.5
United Kingdom	12.9	12.9	12.0	12.9	13.4	39.3	39.6	37.4	37.7	37.8
United States	11.8	14.2	9.9	13.2	14.2	45.2	50.1	42.3	49.5	51.4
OECD Average	**11.5**	**11.4**	**10.2**	**11.9**	**12.3**	**36.2**	**33.9**	**32.2**	**35.1**	**36.5**

.. Not available

Note: Full time series can be accessed at http://data-explorer.oecd.org/s/nb.

1. The capital transfers were subtracted directly from the specific taxes to which they relate, except for France, where the capital transfers have been allocated between tax headings in proportion to the reported tax revenue.

Table 3.8. Taxes on personal income (1100) as % of GDP and as % of total tax revenue

	% of GDP					% of total tax revenue				
	1990	2000	2010	2021	2022	1990	2000	2010	2021	2022
Australia	12.1	11.4	9.7	11.4	11.9	43.0	37.7	38.7	39.0	40.4
Austria[1]	8.2	9.3	9.2	9.7	9.6	21.0	22.0	22.4	22.4	22.3
Belgium[1]	13.2	13.8	12.1	11.3	11.9	32.0	31.4	28.2	26.8	28.2
Canada	14.3	12.8	10.9	12.6	12.3	40.8	36.8	35.0	36.3	36.4
Chile	0.9	1.4	1.3	2.4	2.5	5.6	7.6	6.8	10.8	10.5
Colombia	0.2	0.8	1.0	1.3	1.4	1.8	4.9	5.3	6.9	7.0
Costa Rica	..	..	1.0	1.5	1.5	..	..	4.6	6.2	6.1
Czechia	..	4.2	3.3	3.2	3.0	..	12.9	10.2	9.4	9.2
Denmark[1]	24.1	24.6	23.3	24.9	23.4	54.2	52.6	52.0	52.7	55.8
Estonia	..	6.8	5.3	6.8	6.3	..	22.0	15.9	20.4	19.2
Finland	14.9	14.0	12.0	12.9	12.9	34.7	30.6	29.5	29.8	29.9
France[1]	4.4	7.9	7.6	9.3	9.7	10.7	18.1	17.9	20.7	21.2
Germany	9.6	9.2	8.6	10.5	10.7	27.6	25.3	23.9	26.3	26.9
Greece	3.6	4.3	4.0	6.0	5.6	14.1	13.0	12.4	14.9	13.6
Hungary	..	7.2	6.4	4.1	5.3	..	18.6	17.4	12.1	15.2
Iceland	8.2	12.5	11.7	14.4	14.0	26.9	34.8	36.4	41.4	39.9
Ireland	10.7	9.8	8.8	6.5	6.3	33.1	31.9	31.6	32.7	31.3
Israel	..	9.8	5.4	7.1	7.2	..	28.9	17.9	22.0	22.0
Italy	9.5	10.1	11.2	11.0	10.9	26.3	24.8	26.9	25.9	25.5
Japan	7.7	5.3	4.9	6.4	6.5	27.8	21.0	18.6	18.9	18.8
Korea	3.7	3.1	3.2	6.1	6.6	20.0	14.6	14.2	20.4	20.5
Latvia	..	5.5	6.2	6.0	5.9	..	18.8	21.6	19.6	19.2
Lithuania[1]	..	7.6	3.6	7.5	7.6	..	24.8	12.7	23.4	24.0
Luxembourg[1]	8.3	6.8	7.4	10.1	10.4	24.1	18.5	20.9	26.5	27.1
Mexico	..	..	2.2	3.5	3.6	..	..	18.3	21.1	21.6
Netherlands	9.8	5.6	7.6	8.3	7.7	24.7	15.1	21.5	21.8	20.3
New Zealand	17.4	14.0	11.4	14.1	13.8	48.0	43.1	37.7	40.9	41.6
Norway	10.5	10.1	9.9	10.6	8.1	26.1	24.2	23.7	25.7	18.7
Poland[1]	..	4.3	4.4	5.3	4.5	..	13.2	13.9	14.6	13.1
Portugal	4.2	5.3	5.4	6.9	7.0	15.9	17.0	17.7	19.7	19.4
Slovak Republic	..	3.3	2.6	3.8	3.8	..	9.9	9.3	10.6	10.7
Slovenia[1]	..	5.5	5.6	5.4	5.2	..	14.6	14.7	14.1	13.8
Spain	6.9	6.4	6.9	8.6	9.1	21.7	19.3	22.1	22.8	24.1
Sweden	18.8	17.7	12.1	12.4	11.9	38.5	35.4	28.1	28.9	28.0
Switzerland[1]	7.5	7.9	8.2	8.5	8.3	32.3	29.4	31.8	30.3	31.0
Türkiye	3.9	5.2	3.5	3.0	2.4	26.8	22.2	14.0	13.2	11.3
United Kingdom	9.7	9.5	9.1	10.0	10.1	29.4	29.0	28.5	29.1	28.6
United States	9.8	11.9	8.1	11.6	12.1	37.7	42.2	34.8	43.3	44.0
OECD Average	**9.3**	**8.5**	**7.2**	**8.3**	**8.2**	**27.6**	**24.1**	**22.0**	**23.7**	**23.6**

.. Not available

Note: Full time series can be accessed at http://data-explorer.oecd.org/s/nb.

1. The capital transfers were subtracted directly from the specific taxes to which they relate, except for France, where the capital transfers have been allocated between tax headings in proportion to the reported tax revenue.

Table 3.9. Taxes on corporate income (1200) as % of GDP and as % of total tax revenue

	% of GDP					% of total tax revenue				
	1990	2000	2010	2021	2022	1990	2000	2010	2021	2022
Australia	4.0	6.1	4.5	6.6	6.4	14.1	20.2	17.9	22.5	21.8
Austria[1]	1.4	1.9	1.9	2.8	3.4	3.6	4.6	4.6	6.4	7.9
Belgium[1]	2.0	3.1	2.5	3.7	3.9	4.8	7.2	5.9	8.9	9.2
Canada	2.5	4.2	3.2	4.9	4.7	7.0	12.2	10.5	14.1	13.9
Chile	2.1	2.1	4.0	3.8	5.6	12.4	11.2	20.4	17.1	23.7
Colombia	1.6	2.6	3.8	4.6	5.0	13.9	16.7	20.7	23.8	25.4
Costa Rica	..	..	2.3	2.4	2.7	..	..	10.3	9.7	10.5
Czechia	..	3.2	3.2	3.8	4.3	..	9.9	10.0	11.4	12.9
Denmark[1]	1.6	3.2	2.3	4.0	3.3	3.6	6.8	5.2	8.4	7.9
Estonia	..	0.9	1.3	1.5	1.6	..	2.8	4.0	4.6	5.0
Finland	1.9	5.7	2.4	2.7	3.0	4.5	12.5	6.0	6.3	7.0
France[1]	2.2	2.9	2.0	2.4	2.8	5.3	6.7	4.8	5.3	6.2
Germany	1.7	1.8	1.5	2.3	2.4	4.8	4.8	4.2	5.8	6.0
Greece	1.4	4.0	2.6	2.0	2.5	5.5	11.9	7.9	5.0	6.0
Hungary	..	2.2	1.2	1.4	1.7	..	5.7	3.3	4.1	4.7
Iceland	0.8	1.2	0.9	2.0	2.6	2.8	3.3	2.7	5.7	7.4
Ireland	1.6	3.6	2.4	3.4	4.3	4.9	11.7	8.5	17.0	21.5
Israel	..	3.2	2.6	3.5	4.3	..	9.5	8.6	11.0	13.1
Italy	3.6	2.8	2.3	1.9	2.9	10.0	6.9	5.5	4.4	6.7
Japan	6.2	3.5	3.0	4.4	4.7	22.4	13.7	11.6	13.1	13.7
Korea	2.4	3.0	3.1	3.8	5.4	12.8	14.1	13.8	12.8	16.8
Latvia	..	1.5	1.0	0.9	1.0	..	5.3	3.4	2.8	3.3
Lithuania[1]	..	0.7	1.0	2.1	2.3	..	2.2	3.5	6.4	7.4
Luxembourg[1]	5.6	6.7	5.4	4.5	4.4	16.1	18.0	15.3	11.8	11.5
Mexico	..	..	1.8	3.4	3.9	..	..	14.4	20.2	23.0
Netherlands	3.0	4.0	2.3	3.7	4.7	7.5	10.9	6.4	9.8	12.5
New Zealand	2.3	4.0	3.7	5.4	4.5	6.5	12.4	12.2	15.7	13.7
Norway	3.6	8.8	9.8	9.8	18.4	9.0	21.0	23.5	23.6	42.3
Poland[1]	..	2.4	2.0	2.6	2.8	..	7.3	6.2	7.1	8.1
Portugal	2.1	3.7	2.7	2.4	3.3	8.0	11.9	9.0	6.8	9.3
Slovak Republic	..	2.6	2.4	3.6	3.7	..	7.6	8.7	10.2	10.4
Slovenia[1]	..	1.1	1.8	2.5	2.3	..	3.0	4.9	6.5	6.2
Spain	2.8	2.9	1.8	2.6	2.7	8.8	8.8	5.9	7.0	7.2
Sweden	1.5	3.6	3.3	3.3	3.4	3.1	7.3	7.6	7.8	8.0
Switzerland[1]	1.7	2.4	2.6	3.1	3.2	7.3	8.8	10.1	10.9	11.9
Türkiye	1.0	1.7	1.8	2.5	3.4	6.7	7.3	7.3	10.7	16.1
United Kingdom	3.3	3.5	2.8	2.9	3.3	9.9	10.6	8.9	8.6	9.2
United States	2.0	2.2	1.8	1.7	2.0	7.5	7.9	7.5	6.2	7.4
OECD Average	**2.4**	**3.1**	**2.7**	**3.3**	**3.9**	**8.3**	**9.5**	**9.0**	**10.3**	**12.0**

.. Not available

Note: Full time series can be accessed at http://data-explorer.oecd.org/s/nb.

1. The capital transfers were subtracted directly from the specific taxes to which they relate, except for France, where the capital transfers have been allocated between tax headings in proportion to the reported tax revenue.

Table 3.10. Social security contributions (2000) as % of GDP and as % of total tax revenue

	% of GDP					% of total tax revenue				
	1990	2000	2010	2021	2022	1990	2000	2010	2021	2022
Australia	0.0	0.0	0.0	0.0	0.0	0.0	0.0	0.0	0.0	0.0
Austria[1]	12.9	14.3	14.0	15.4	14.7	32.9	33.8	34.2	35.4	34.1
Belgium[1]	13.7	13.5	13.9	12.9	12.9	33.2	30.8	32.4	30.7	30.4
Canada	4.3	4.7	4.6	4.8	4.7	12.1	13.6	14.9	13.8	14.0
Chile	1.5	1.4	1.3	1.2	1.0	9.0	7.3	6.8	5.3	4.1
Colombia	0.9	2.6	2.1	1.8	1.6	7.9	16.3	11.7	9.5	8.3
Costa Rica	6.5	6.4	7.3	8.9	8.8	28.9	30.4	33.1	36.0	34.8
Czechia	..	14.2	14.3	15.9	15.2	..	44.3	44.8	47.3	45.9
Denmark[1]	0.0	0.6	0.1	0.1	0.1	0.0	1.4	0.3	0.2	0.2
Estonia	..	10.9	12.7	11.6	11.3	..	35.1	38.4	34.7	34.8
Finland	11.0	11.5	12.0	12.0	11.9	25.6	25.2	29.7	27.9	27.6
France[1]	18.3	15.6	16.0	14.7	14.8	44.1	35.8	37.9	32.7	32.4
Germany	13.0	14.2	13.8	14.8	14.6	37.5	39.0	38.5	37.1	36.9
Greece	7.6	10.1	11.0	12.9	12.2	30.2	30.3	34.2	32.2	29.6
Hungary	..	11.3	11.6	10.5	9.8	..	29.4	31.4	31.0	28.0
Iceland	1.0	2.8	3.8	3.0	3.0	3.1	7.7	11.7	8.5	8.5
Ireland	4.6	3.7	5.1	3.1	3.1	14.1	11.9	18.2	15.3	15.1
Israel	..	5.0	5.1	5.0	5.0	..	14.6	16.8	15.5	15.3
Italy	11.9	11.6	13.0	13.2	13.1	32.9	28.5	31.1	31.1	30.5
Japan	7.3	8.9	10.8	13.3	13.3	26.5	35.2	41.1	39.2	38.5
Korea	1.9	3.5	5.2	7.8	8.2	10.1	16.7	23.3	26.2	25.6
Latvia	..	9.7	8.6	9.6	9.4	..	33.5	30.1	31.1	30.6
Lithuania[1]	..	9.9	11.6	10.1	9.8	..	32.2	41.1	31.8	31.1
Luxembourg[1]	9.6	9.7	10.3	10.6	10.6	27.5	26.1	29.0	27.7	27.8
Mexico	1.9	2.0	2.0	2.3	2.3	16.8	18.0	16.2	13.7	13.8
Netherlands	14.8	14.3	12.9	12.6	12.5	37.4	38.7	36.3	33.0	32.9
New Zealand	0.0	0.0	0.0	0.0	0.0	0.0	0.0	0.0	0.0	0.0
Norway	10.6	8.8	9.3	9.3	7.5	26.2	21.0	22.3	22.5	17.3
Poland[1]	..	12.9	10.9	13.0	12.8	..	39.2	34.4	35.3	37.1
Portugal	7.2	7.9	8.6	10.4	10.2	27.2	25.6	28.4	29.6	28.3
Slovak Republic	..	13.9	11.9	15.2	14.5	..	41.4	42.6	43.0	41.6
Slovenia[1]	..	14.9	15.8	16.4	16.0	..	39.6	41.8	42.8	42.8
Spain	11.2	11.5	11.9	13.4	12.8	35.4	34.9	37.9	35.4	34.1
Sweden	13.3	12.7	10.8	9.0	8.8	27.2	25.5	25.1	21.0	20.8
Switzerland[1]	5.4	6.5	6.1	6.8	6.7	23.3	24.2	23.7	24.2	24.8
Türkiye	2.9	4.4	6.1	6.6	5.1	19.7	18.7	24.9	28.9	24.4
United Kingdom	5.6	5.5	6.1	6.8	7.1	17.0	16.8	18.9	20.0	19.9
United States	6.7	6.7	6.1	6.1	6.0	25.6	23.6	26.1	22.7	21.9
OECD Average	**7.1**	**8.4**	**8.6**	**9.0**	**8.7**	**21.8**	**24.9**	**26.6**	**25.6**	**24.8**

.. Not available

Note: Full time series can be accessed at http://data-explorer.oecd.org/s/nb.

1. The capital transfers were subtracted directly from the specific taxes to which they relate, except for France, where the capital transfers have been allocated between tax headings in proportion to the reported tax revenue.

Table 3.11. Taxes on payroll and workforce (3000) as % of GDP and as % of total tax revenue

	% of GDP					% of total tax revenue				
	1990	2000	2010	2021	2022	1990	2000	2010	2021	2022
Australia	1.7	1.4	1.3	1.3	1.4	6.1	4.5	5.2	4.3	4.7
Austria[1]	2.4	2.7	2.8	2.8	2.7	6.0	6.4	6.9	6.5	6.3
Belgium[1]	0.0	0.0	0.0	0.0	0.0	0.0	0.0	0.0	0.0	0.0
Canada	0.8	0.7	0.6	0.8	0.7	2.3	2.1	2.1	2.2	2.2
Chile	0.0	0.0	0.0	0.0	0.0	0.0	0.0	0.0	0.0	0.0
Colombia	0.0	0.7	0.7	0.3	0.3	0.0	4.2	4.1	1.7	1.5
Costa Rica	1.4	1.3	1.3	1.4	1.4	6.4	6.3	5.9	5.7	5.7
Czechia	..	0.0	0.0	0.0	0.0	..	0.0	0.0	0.0	0.0
Denmark[1]	0.3	0.2	0.2	0.3	0.3	0.7	0.4	0.5	0.5	0.6
Estonia	..	0.0	0.0	0.0	0.0	..	0.0	0.0	0.0	0.0
Finland	0.0	0.0	0.0	0.0	0.0	0.0	0.0	0.0	0.0	0.0
France[1]	0.8	1.1	1.4	1.9	2.0	1.9	2.5	3.4	4.2	4.3
Germany	0.0	0.0	0.0	0.0	0.0	0.0	0.0	0.0	0.0	0.0
Greece	0.2	0.0	0.0	0.0	0.0	0.7	0.0	0.0	0.0	0.0
Hungary	..	1.4	0.4	1.1	0.7	..	3.6	1.1	3.2	2.0
Iceland	1.1	0.0	0.2	0.3	0.3	3.5	0.1	0.5	0.8	0.7
Ireland	0.4	0.0	0.2	0.2	0.2	1.3	0.0	0.7	0.9	0.9
Israel	..	1.2	1.1	1.0	0.9	..	3.6	3.8	3.1	2.8
Italy	0.1	0.0	0.0	0.0	0.0	0.3	0.0	0.0	0.0	0.0
Japan	0.0	0.0	0.0	0.0	0.0	0.0	0.0	0.0	0.0	0.0
Korea	0.1	0.0	0.1	0.1	0.1	0.4	0.2	0.2	0.3	0.3
Latvia	..	0.0	0.0	0.0	0.0	..	0.0	0.1	0.0	0.0
Lithuania[1]	..	0.0	0.0	0.0	0.0	..	0.0	0.0	0.0	0.0
Luxembourg[1]	0.0	0.0	0.0	0.0	0.0	0.0	0.0	0.0	0.0	0.0
Mexico	0.2	0.2	0.3	0.4	0.5	1.8	1.5	2.2	2.6	2.9
Netherlands	0.0	0.0	0.0	0.0	0.0	0.0	0.0	0.0	0.0	0.0
New Zealand	0.0	0.0	0.0	0.0	0.0	0.0	0.0	0.0	0.0	0.0
Norway	0.0	0.0	0.0	0.1	0.0	0.0	0.0	0.0	0.1	0.1
Poland[1]	..	0.2	0.3	0.6	0.6	..	0.7	0.8	1.5	1.6
Portugal	0.0	0.0	0.0	0.0	0.0	0.0	0.0	0.0	0.0	0.0
Slovak Republic	..	0.0	0.0	0.0	0.0	..	0.0	0.0	0.0	0.0
Slovenia[1]	..	1.5	0.1	0.0	0.0	..	4.1	0.2	0.1	0.1
Spain	0.0	0.0	0.0	0.0	0.0	0.0	0.0	0.0	0.0	0.0
Sweden	1.2	2.1	3.0	5.1	5.1	2.5	4.2	7.0	12.0	12.1
Switzerland[1]	0.0	0.0	0.0	0.0	0.0	0.0	0.0	0.0	0.0	0.0
Türkiye	0.0	0.0	0.0	0.0	0.0	0.0	0.0	0.0	0.0	0.0
United Kingdom	0.0	0.0	0.0	0.1	0.1	0.0	0.0	0.0	0.4	0.4
United States	0.0	0.0	0.0	0.0	0.0	0.0	0.0	0.1	0.1	0.1
OECD Average	**0.4**	**0.4**	**0.4**	**0.5**	**0.5**	**1.2**	**1.2**	**1.2**	**1.3**	**1.3**

.. Not available

Note: Full time series can be accessed at http://data-explorer.oecd.org/s/nb.

1. The capital transfers were subtracted directly from the specific taxes to which they relate, except for France, where the capital transfers have been allocated between tax headings in proportion to the reported tax revenue.

Table 3.12. Taxes on property (4000) as % of GDP and as % of total tax revenue

	% of GDP					% of total tax revenue				
	1990	2000	2010	2021	2022	1990	2000	2010	2021	2022
Australia	2.5	2.7	2.4	3.2	2.7	9.0	8.8	9.4	10.9	9.3
Austria[1]	1.1	0.6	0.5	0.6	0.6	2.7	1.3	1.3	1.5	1.4
Belgium[1]	1.6	2.1	3.1	3.5	3.3	3.8	4.7	7.2	8.4	7.7
Canada	3.5	3.3	3.8	3.9	3.5	10.0	9.5	12.3	11.2	10.4
Chile	1.0	1.3	0.8	1.2	1.3	6.2	7.0	4.0	5.4	5.5
Colombia	0.2	1.0	1.6	1.7	1.5	2.2	6.6	8.7	9.0	7.8
Costa Rica	0.3	0.2	0.3	0.5	0.5	1.3	0.9	1.5	2.1	2.0
Czechia	..	0.5	0.4	0.2	0.2	..	1.4	1.3	0.6	0.5
Denmark[1]	1.9	1.6	1.8	1.8	1.7	4.3	3.3	4.1	3.9	4.1
Estonia	..	0.4	0.3	0.2	0.2	..	1.2	1.0	0.6	0.5
Finland	1.1	1.1	1.1	1.5	1.4	2.4	2.4	2.7	3.5	3.3
France[1]	2.6	3.0	3.5	3.9	3.7	6.3	6.8	8.4	8.6	8.1
Germany	1.2	0.8	0.8	1.2	1.1	3.4	2.3	2.3	3.1	2.8
Greece	1.2	2.6	1.7	2.9	2.7	4.6	7.7	5.2	7.3	6.6
Hungary	..	0.7	1.1	0.9	0.8	..	1.7	3.1	2.6	2.3
Iceland	2.6	2.4	2.1	2.1	2.0	8.4	6.6	6.5	5.9	5.6
Ireland	1.5	1.8	1.4	1.1	1.0	4.6	5.7	5.1	5.4	4.7
Israel	..	3.2	3.4	3.9	4.0	..	9.5	11.1	12.1	12.3
Italy	0.8	1.9	2.0	2.5	2.5	2.3	4.6	4.8	5.8	5.7
Japan	2.6	2.7	2.6	2.7	2.7	9.4	10.5	9.7	7.9	7.9
Korea	2.2	2.6	2.5	4.5	3.8	11.8	12.4	11.3	15.1	11.9
Latvia	..	1.1	0.9	0.9	0.8	..	3.8	3.0	2.9	2.5
Lithuania[1]	..	0.5	0.4	0.3	0.3	..	1.5	1.3	0.9	0.9
Luxembourg[1]	2.9	4.0	2.5	4.0	3.7	8.4	10.7	7.0	10.5	9.7
Mexico	0.2	0.2	0.3	0.3	0.4	1.9	1.8	2.3	2.0	2.1
Netherlands	1.4	1.9	1.4	1.6	1.5	3.7	5.3	3.8	4.1	3.9
New Zealand	2.5	1.7	2.0	1.9	1.9	6.8	5.3	6.6	5.6	5.8
Norway	1.2	0.9	1.1	1.1	1.0	2.9	2.2	2.6	2.7	2.2
Poland[1]	..	1.4	1.3	1.3	1.2	..	4.3	4.2	3.5	3.4
Portugal	0.7	1.1	1.1	1.5	1.5	2.7	3.7	3.7	4.4	4.3
Slovak Republic	..	0.6	0.4	0.5	0.4	..	1.8	1.4	1.3	1.2
Slovenia[1]	..	0.6	0.6	0.6	0.6	..	1.7	1.6	1.6	1.6
Spain	1.7	2.1	2.1	2.8	2.6	5.5	6.5	6.6	7.3	6.9
Sweden	1.7	1.7	1.0	1.0	0.9	3.5	3.3	2.4	2.2	2.2
Switzerland[1]	2.1	2.6	2.0	2.2	2.2	8.9	9.7	7.7	8.0	8.1
Türkiye	0.3	0.7	1.0	1.0	0.7	2.3	3.2	4.1	4.2	3.5
United Kingdom	2.7	3.7	3.8	3.9	4.0	8.2	11.4	12.0	11.5	11.3
United States	3.1	2.9	3.1	2.9	2.9	11.7	10.3	13.5	11.0	10.4
OECD Average	**1.7**	**1.7**	**1.6**	**1.9**	**1.8**	**5.5**	**5.3**	**5.4**	**5.6**	**5.3**

.. Not available

Note: Full time series can be accessed at http://data-explorer.oecd.org/s/nb.

1. The capital transfers were subtracted directly from the specific taxes to which they relate, except for France, where the capital transfers have been allocated between tax headings in proportion to the reported tax revenue.

Table 3.13. Taxes on goods and services (5000) as % of GDP and as % of total tax revenue

	% of GDP					% of total tax revenue				
	1990	2000	2010	2021	2022	1990	2000	2010	2021	2022
Australia	7.8	8.7	7.2	6.8	7.0	27.8	28.8	28.8	23.3	23.8
Austria[1]	12.4	12.4	11.7	11.6	11.6	31.5	29.3	28.7	26.7	26.9
Belgium[1]	10.8	11.3	11.2	10.6	10.4	26.1	25.9	26.1	25.2	24.5
Canada	9.1	8.4	7.4	7.4	7.4	25.8	24.2	24.0	21.2	21.7
Chile	10.6	11.9	10.1	11.8	11.4	62.9	63.8	51.3	53.1	47.8
Colombia	6.1	7.3	8.2	8.3	8.8	53.8	46.3	45.1	43.4	44.8
Costa Rica	10.2	9.9	8.9	8.7	8.2	45.5	46.7	40.3	34.8	32.6
Czechia	..	10.1	10.8	10.5	10.5	..	31.5	33.8	31.3	31.5
Denmark[1]	15.1	15.7	14.9	13.6	12.8	34.0	33.5	33.4	28.9	30.4
Estonia	..	12.1	13.5	13.3	13.2	..	38.8	40.7	39.8	40.5
Finland	14.0	13.4	13.0	14.0	13.8	32.5	29.2	32.0	32.4	32.0
France[1]	11.8	11.5	11.2	12.2	11.9	28.4	26.3	26.5	27.1	26.1
Germany	9.3	10.4	11.2	11.0	10.8	26.7	28.5	31.2	27.5	27.3
Greece	11.2	11.8	12.5	15.9	17.8	44.5	35.2	38.6	39.6	43.3
Hungary	..	15.6	15.9	15.9	16.7	..	40.6	43.3	47.1	47.5
Iceland	15.6	16.3	11.5	11.7	11.5	51.3	45.3	35.8	33.6	32.7
Ireland	13.6	11.9	9.9	5.8	5.4	41.9	38.8	35.8	28.7	26.4
Israel	..	11.2	11.8	10.9	10.6	..	32.9	39.2	33.7	32.4
Italy	10.2	11.4	11.1	12.0	11.8	28.0	28.2	26.6	28.3	27.6
Japan	3.8	4.9	4.9	7.0	7.2	13.7	19.3	18.7	20.8	20.8
Korea	8.2	8.0	7.5	6.9	7.3	44.3	38.4	33.7	23.1	22.7
Latvia	..	11.2	11.9	13.4	13.7	..	38.6	41.8	43.6	44.4
Lithuania[1]	..	12.1	11.7	12.0	11.5	..	39.4	41.4	37.5	36.6
Luxembourg[1]	8.2	9.8	9.9	8.9	9.1	23.6	26.6	27.6	23.3	23.9
Mexico	5.1	4.6	4.7	6.2	5.5	44.0	41.7	38.0	37.0	32.8
Netherlands	10.5	10.9	11.2	11.8	11.5	26.4	29.7	31.5	30.9	30.1
New Zealand	12.1	11.3	12.0	12.4	11.9	33.6	34.7	39.6	35.9	36.0
Norway	14.5	13.3	11.7	10.5	8.5	35.9	31.7	27.9	25.4	19.5
Poland[1]	..	11.6	12.7	13.9	12.6	..	35.3	40.3	37.9	36.5
Portugal	11.7	12.7	12.4	13.7	13.8	44.2	41.0	40.8	39.0	38.3
Slovak Republic	..	12.2	10.4	12.1	12.3	..	36.3	37.2	34.1	35.2
Slovenia[1]	..	13.8	13.9	13.3	13.2	..	36.6	36.8	34.9	35.3
Spain	9.0	10.1	8.6	10.4	10.4	28.4	30.6	27.5	27.4	27.6
Sweden	12.2	12.1	12.8	11.9	12.2	25.0	24.2	29.7	27.9	28.8
Switzerland[1]	4.8	6.0	5.8	5.5	5.4	20.9	22.2	22.5	19.6	19.9
Türkiye	4.1	9.9	11.8	9.6	9.1	27.9	42.0	47.7	41.9	43.6
United Kingdom	10.2	10.5	10.2	10.4	10.8	31.0	32.2	31.7	30.4	30.6
United States	4.5	4.5	4.2	4.5	4.5	17.5	16.0	18.1	16.7	16.3
OECD Average	**9.9**	**10.8**	**10.5**	**10.7**	**10.6**	**33.7**	**33.9**	**34.0**	**31.9**	**31.5**

.. Not available

Note: Full time series can be accessed at http://data-explorer.oecd.org/s/nb.

1. The capital transfers were subtracted directly from the specific taxes to which they relate, except for France, where the capital transfers have been allocated between tax headings in proportion to the reported tax revenue.

Table 3.14. Value added taxes (5111) as % of GDP and as % of total tax revenue

	% of GDP					% of total tax revenue				
	1990	2000	2010	2021	2022	1990	2000	2010	2021	2022
Australia	0.0	3.4	3.3	3.2	3.4	0.0	11.1	13.1	11.1	11.5
Austria[1]	8.2	7.9	7.7	7.6	8.0	20.8	18.7	18.7	17.5	18.4
Belgium[1]	6.8	7.1	7.0	6.7	6.5	16.4	16.1	16.2	16.0	15.3
Canada	0.0	3.2	4.2	4.6	4.5	0.0	9.2	13.7	13.2	13.4
Chile	6.3	7.8	7.6	9.5	9.3	37.4	41.8	38.5	42.6	39.0
Colombia	2.6	4.3	5.3	5.9	6.2	22.6	27.6	29.3	30.5	31.8
Costa Rica	4.1	4.8	4.6	5.1	4.9	18.1	22.8	21.0	20.4	19.4
Czechia	..	5.9	6.5	7.3	7.6	..	18.3	20.5	21.8	22.9
Denmark[1]	8.4	9.1	9.3	9.5	9.2	18.9	19.5	20.8	20.1	22.0
Estonia	..	8.4	8.5	9.1	9.1	..	27.1	25.7	27.3	27.9
Finland	8.3	8.0	8.3	9.4	9.4	19.3	17.4	20.4	21.7	21.7
France[1]	7.7	7.3	6.8	7.4	7.5	18.4	16.6	16.0	16.3	16.4
Germany	5.8	6.7	7.0	7.2	7.5	16.6	18.4	19.6	18.1	18.9
Greece	6.2	6.3	7.1	8.4	9.0	24.6	18.9	22.0	20.9	21.9
Hungary	..	8.7	8.5	9.9	10.1	..	22.5	23.0	29.3	28.9
Iceland	8.7	10.2	7.4	8.5	8.3	28.4	28.5	22.8	24.4	23.7
Ireland	6.6	7.0	6.0	3.7	3.7	20.4	22.9	21.7	18.5	18.2
Israel	..	7.2	7.3	7.5	7.4	..	21.0	24.3	23.2	22.5
Italy	5.3	6.2	6.1	6.6	7.1	14.7	15.4	14.5	15.6	16.5
Japan	1.2	2.3	2.5	5.1	5.2	4.4	9.1	9.6	14.9	15.1
Korea	3.5	3.6	3.9	4.3	4.9	18.7	17.0	17.5	14.4	15.3
Latvia	..	6.9	6.6	8.6	9.5	..	23.9	23.3	28.1	30.8
Lithuania[1]	..	7.5	7.8	8.3	8.4	..	24.4	27.5	26.0	26.5
Luxembourg[1]	4.2	4.9	6.2	5.7	6.1	12.1	13.2	17.3	14.9	15.8
Mexico	3.0	2.7	3.6	4.2	4.1	26.1	24.7	29.4	25.2	24.7
Netherlands	6.5	6.4	6.6	7.3	7.1	16.5	17.3	18.7	19.2	18.6
New Zealand	8.1	8.1	9.3	10.1	10.0	22.4	24.9	30.7	29.3	30.3
Norway	7.6	8.2	7.7	7.8	6.5	18.7	19.7	18.5	19.0	15.0
Poland[1]	..	6.9	7.6	8.6	7.3	..	21.0	24.2	23.3	21.1
Portugal	5.2	7.6	7.5	8.9	9.4	19.6	24.5	24.8	25.2	26.0
Slovak Republic	..	6.8	6.1	7.5	7.7	..	20.4	21.8	21.1	22.0
Slovenia[1]	..	8.5	8.1	8.2	8.2	..	22.7	21.3	21.5	21.9
Spain	5.0	5.8	5.2	6.8	7.0	15.7	17.6	16.5	18.1	18.6
Sweden	7.3	8.2	9.1	9.1	9.4	14.9	16.4	21.1	21.4	22.1
Switzerland[1]	2.7	3.5	3.3	3.2	3.1	11.5	13.0	12.7	11.3	11.6
Türkiye	2.7	5.7	5.4	5.3	5.0	18.3	24.2	21.7	23.2	24.0
United Kingdom	5.5	5.9	6.1	6.9	7.3	16.9	18.1	18.9	20.2	20.7
United States	0.0	0.0	0.0	0.0	0.0	0.0	0.0	0.0	0.0	0.0
OECD Average	**5.1**	**6.3**	**6.3**	**6.9**	**7.0**	**17.0**	**19.6**	**20.5**	**20.7**	**20.8**

.. Not available

Note: Full time series can be accessed at http://data-explorer.oecd.org/s/nb.

1. The capital transfers were subtracted directly from the specific taxes to which they relate, except for France, where the capital transfers have been allocated between tax headings in proportion to the reported tax revenue.

Table 3.15. Tax revenues of sub-sectors of general government as % of GDP

	Supranational			Central government			State or Regional government			Local government			Social Security Funds		
	1975	1995	2022	1975	1995	2022	1975	1995	2022	1975	1995	2022	1975	1995	2022
Federal countries															
Australia	..	..	..	20.3	21.9	24.0	4.0	5.4	4.6	1.1	1.0	0.9	0.0	0.0	0.0
Austria[1]	..	0.2	0.2	18.8	26.7	28.3	3.9	0.7	0.8	4.5	1.7	1.3	9.2	12.0	12.5
Belgium[1]	0.6	0.4	0.5	25.4	25.8	22.2	..	0.8	4.3	1.7	2.0	1.9	11.2	13.8	13.4
Canada	..	..	..	14.8	13.5	14.5	10.1	12.8	13.2	3.1	3.4	2.9	3.1	4.8	3.2
Germany	0.4	0.2	0.3	11.5	11.4	11.5	7.6	7.9	9.8	3.1	2.7	3.5	11.7	14.1	14.6
Mexico	..	..	..	..	7.1	13.4	..	0.3	0.7	..	0.1	0.3	..	2.1	2.3
Switzerland[1]	..	..	..	6.7	7.9	9.1	5.9	6.0	6.9	4.4	4.4	4.2	4.8	6.7	6.7
United States	..	..	..	11.2	11.0	12.2	4.8	5.3	5.8	3.6	3.5	3.6	5.0	6.7	6.0
Unweighted average	0.5	0.3	0.3	15.5	15.7	16.9	6.0	4.9	5.8	3.1	2.4	2.3	6.4	7.5	7.4
Regional countries															
Colombia[2]	..	..	..	..	10.1	14.8	..	0.9	0.9	..	1.4	2.3	..	3.6	1.6
Spain[2]	..	0.2	0.3	8.6	16.0	16.0	..	1.6	5.7	0.8	2.7	3.1	8.5	10.8	12.5
Unitary countries															
Chile	..	..	..	..	16.3	21.4	..	..	..	..	1.2	1.6	..	0.7	0.8
Costa Rica	..	..	..	..	12.4	15.5	..	..	..	..	0.3	0.7	..	6.2	9.0
Czechia	..	..	0.2	..	19.8	17.4	..	..	..	..	0.3	0.3	..	14.2	15.2
Denmark[1]	0.4	0.2	0.2	26.2	31.8	30.7	..	..	..	11.1	14.6	11.1	0.0	0.0	0.0
Estonia	..	..	0.3	..	29.5	26.9	..	..	..	..	0.3	0.2	..	5.2	5.2
Finland	..	0.2	0.2	20.3	20.7	21.1	..	..	..	8.5	9.9	9.9	7.4	13.7	11.9
France[1]	0.2	0.3	0.3	18.1	18.2	14.2	..	..	..	2.7	4.7	6.6	14.3	19.5	24.7
Greece	..	0.2	0.3	12.5	18.8	27.7	..	..	..	0.6	0.6	0.9	5.5	8.8	12.3
Hungary	..	..	0.2	..	26.0	23.7	..	..	..	..	1.0	1.7	..	13.7	9.6
Iceland	..	..	..	24.0	24.3	25.5	..	..	..	5.5	6.4	9.7	0.0	0.0	0.0
Ireland	0.6	0.5	0.2	21.6	26.4	17.0	..	..	..	2.0	0.8	0.3	3.6	4.0	2.7
Israel	..	..	..	..	26.8	25.1	..	..	..	..	2.4	2.7	..	4.7	5.0
Italy	..	0.1	0.3	13.0	24.1	24.8	..	..	..	0.2	2.1	4.7	11.2	12.1	13.1
Japan	..	..	..	9.0	10.5	13.4	..	..	..	5.1	6.4	7.7	5.7	8.5	13.3
Korea	..	..	..	13.2	13.0	18.3	..	..	..	1.5	3.5	5.5	0.1	2.3	8.2
Latvia	..	..	0.2	..	12.9	16.4	..	..	..	..	5.8	5.1	..	11.0	9.1
Lithuania[1]	..	..	0.3	..	19.8	21.1	..	..	..	..	0.6	0.3	..	7.2	9.8
Luxembourg[1]	0.2	0.2	0.4	20.7	23.9	26.1	..	..	..	2.2	2.3	1.4	9.4	9.6	10.3
Netherlands	0.6	0.5	0.5	22.2	20.8	23.8	..	..	..	0.4	1.2	1.2	14.5	14.7	12.5
New Zealand	..	..	..	27.7	33.7	31.0	..	..	..	2.3	1.9	2.1	0.0	0.0	0.0
Norway	..	..	..	19.7	22.9	39.0	..	..	..	8.7	7.9	4.5	10.5	8.8	0.0
Poland[1]	..	..	0.3	..	22.4	17.2	..	..	..	..	3.1	4.1	..	11.1	12.8
Portugal	..	0.2	0.2	12.3	20.0	23.5	..	..	..	0.0	2.6	2.5	6.5	6.3	9.8
Slovak Republic	..	..	0.2	..	24.7	20.0	..	..	..	..	0.5	0.6	..	14.2	14.1
Slovenia[1]	..	..	0.2	..	19.8	18.2	..	..	..	..	2.4	3.2	..	16.9	15.9
Sweden	..	0.2	0.2	19.7	21.2	22.3	..	..	..	11.2	14.0	14.9	7.5	9.8	5.1
Türkiye	..	..	..	..	12.3	13.8	..	..	..	..	2.1	2.0	..	2.0	5.1
United Kingdom	0.3	0.3	..	24.1	22.7	26.6	..	..	..	3.8	1.1	1.7	6.0	5.2	7.1
Unweighted average	0.4	0.3	0.2	19.0	21.3	22.2	..	..	..	4.1	3.6	3.8	6.4	8.2	8.7

.. Not available

1. The capital transfers were subtracted directly from the specific taxes to which they relate, except for France, where the capital transfers have been allocated between tax headings in proportion to the reported tax revenue.

2. Colombia and Spain are not constitutionally federal countries, but both have a highly decentralised political structure, with high autonomy of their territorial entities.

Table 3.16. Main central government taxes as % of total tax revenues of central government, 2022

	1000 Income & profits	2000 Social security[3]	3000 Payroll	4000 Property	5000 Goods and services	6000 Others
Federal countries						
Australia	76.3	0.0	0.2	0.0	23.5	0.0
Austria[1]	46.0	7.4	5.2	1.4	39.5	0.5
Belgium[1]	58.2	0.0	0.0	2.1	39.7	0.0
Canada	74.4	6.5	0.0	0.0	19.1	0.0
Germany	45.2	0.0	0.0	0.4	54.5	0.0
Mexico	57.6	0.0	0.0	0.0	40.2	2.1
Switzerland[1]	43.4	0.0	0.0	2.4	54.1	0.1
United States	92.8	0.0	0.0	1.0	6.2	0.0
Unweighted average	61.7	1.7	0.7	0.9	34.6	0.3
Regional countries						
Colombia[2]	44.2	0.0	2.0	5.8	47.6	0.4
Spain[2]	45.8	1.7	0.0	0.4	52.0	0.1
Unitary countries						
Chile	48.6	1.0	0.0	2.6	49.1	-1.3
Costa Rica	35.1	7.4	0.0	1.0	50.8	5.7
Czechia	41.9	0.0	0.0	0.0	58.0	0.0
Denmark[1]	56.0	0.2	0.8	1.8	41.1	0.2
Estonia	29.4	22.7	0.0	0.0	47.9	0.0
Finland	32.1	0.0	0.0	3.2	64.5	0.2
France[1]	48.7	2.1	4.2	7.4	36.6	1.2
Greece	30.5	0.1	0.0	6.7	62.7	0.0
Hungary	29.5	2.0	3.0	2.2	62.9	0.4
Iceland	40.4	11.7	1.0	1.4	44.1	1.4
Ireland	62.7	1.8	1.1	3.9	30.4	0.0
Israel	48.7	0.0	3.7	5.7	42.0	0.0
Italy	52.9	0.0	0.0	6.0	41.1	0.0
Japan	55.0	0.0	0.0	5.2	39.8	0.0
Korea	59.0	0.0	0.0	8.6	30.6	1.8
Latvia	15.2	2.0	0.1	0.9	81.9	0.0
Lithuania[1]	46.9	0.0	0.0	0.1	53.0	0.0
Luxembourg[1]	51.6	1.1	0.0	13.8	33.3	0.1
Netherlands	52.3	0.0	0.0	3.4	43.7	0.5
New Zealand	62.2	0.0	0.0	0.1	37.7	0.0
Norway	58.1	19.3	0.1	0.9	21.6	0.0
Poland[1]	26.6	0.0	3.2	0.0	70.2	0.0
Portugal	41.4	3.9	0.0	1.0	53.0	0.7
Slovak Republic	38.4	2.0	0.0	0.0	59.6	0.0
Slovenia[1]	28.2	0.9	0.3	0.0	70.6	0.0
Sweden	3.5	16.6	23.0	2.6	54.1	0.3
Türkiye	36.8	0.0	0.0	3.9	58.7	0.7
United Kingdom	50.2	0.0	0.5	8.6	40.6	0.0
Unweighted average	42.2	3.4	1.5	3.3	49.3	0.4

Note: Excluding social security contributions accruing to social security funds.
1. The capital transfers were subtracted directly from the specific taxes to which they relate, except for France, where the capital transfers have been allocated between tax headings in proportion to the reported tax revenue.
2. Colombia and Spain are not constitutionally federal countries, but both have a highly decentralised political structure, with high autonomy of their territorial entities.
3. These comprise only social security contributions accruing to central government.

Table 3.17. Main state government taxes as % of total tax revenues of state government, 2022

	1000 Income & profits	2000 Social security	3000 Payroll	4000 Property	5000 Goods and services	6000 Others
Federal countries						
Australia	0.0	0.0	29.1	41.1	29.7	0.0
Austria[1, 2]	39.2	11.1	32.8	1.3	12.7	2.8
Belgium[1, 2]	46.7	1.2	0.0	37.7	14.4	0.0
Canada	50.6	4.3	5.6	5.1	34.4	0.0
Germany[2]	50.8	0.0	0.0	7.4	41.8	0.0
Mexico	0.0	0.0	64.5	15.4	13.4	6.6
Switzerland[1]	75.6	0.0	0.0	17.7	5.9	0.8
United States	46.2	0.0	0.2	3.2	50.3	0.0
Unweighted average	38.6	2.1	16.5	16.1	25.3	1.3
Regional countries						
Colombia[3]	0.0	0.0	0.0	0.0	70.8	29.2
Spain[2, 3]	68.1	0.0	0.0	22.0	9.9	0.0
Unitary countries						
Chile	..	..	..	..	..	..
Costa Rica	..	..	..	..	..	..
Czechia	..	..	..	..	..	..
Denmark	..	..	..	..	..	..
Estonia	..	..	..	..	..	..
Finland	..	..	..	..	..	..
France	..	..	..	..	..	..
Greece	..	..	..	..	..	..
Hungary	..	..	..	..	..	..
Iceland	..	..	..	..	..	..
Ireland	..	..	..	..	..	..
Israel	..	..	..	..	..	..
Italy	..	..	..	..	..	..
Japan	..	..	..	..	..	..
Korea	..	..	..	..	..	..
Latvia	..	..	..	..	..	..
Lithuania	..	..	..	..	..	..
Luxembourg	..	..	..	..	..	..
Netherlands	..	..	..	..	..	..
New Zealand	..	..	..	..	..	..
Norway	..	..	..	..	..	..
Poland	..	..	..	..	..	..
Portugal	..	..	..	..	..	..
Slovak Republic	..	..	..	..	..	..
Slovenia	..	..	..	..	..	..
Sweden	..	..	..	..	..	..
Türkiye	..	..	..	..	..	..
United Kingdom	..	..	..	..	..	..
Unweighted average	..	..	..	..	..	..

.. Not available

1. The capital transfers were subtracted directly from the specific taxes to which they relate.
2. Payments to the European Union are excluded from these comparisons.
3. Colombia and Spain are not constitutionally federal countries, but both have a highly decentralised political structure, with high autonomy of their territorial entities.

Table 3.18. Main local government taxes as % of total tax revenues of local government, 2022

	1000 Income & profits	2000 Social security	3000 Payroll	4000 Property	5000 Goods and services	6000 Others
Federal countries						
Australia	0.0	0.0	0.0	100.0	0.0	0.0
Austria[1, 2]	0.0	3.8	73.7	13.9	7.0	1.5
Belgium[1, 2]	34.7	0.2	0.0	58.1	7.0	0.0
Canada	0.0	0.0	0.0	96.9	1.9	1.3
Germany[2]	82.7	0.0	0.0	10.1	7.0	0.3
Mexico	0.0	0.0	0.0	79.2	1.5	19.3
Switzerland[1]	79.9	0.0	0.0	17.3	0.8	1.9
United States	6.5	0.0	0.0	70.4	23.0	0.0
Unweighted average	25.5	0.5	9.2	55.7	6.0	3.0
Regional countries						
Colombia[3]	0.0	0.0	0.0	29.2	47.9	22.9
Spain[2, 3]	19.2	0.0	0.0	41.5	39.3	0.0
Unitary countries						
Chile	0.0	0.0	0.0	46.3	53.7	0.0
Costa Rica	0.0	0.0	0.0	49.1	50.9	0.1
Czechia[2]	0.0	0.0	0.0	51.9	48.1	0.0
Denmark[1, 2]	89.5	0.0	0.0	10.5	0.0	0.0
Estonia[2]	0.0	0.0	0.0	79.9	20.1	0.0
Finland[2]	92.3	0.0	0.0	7.7	0.0	0.0
France[1, 2]	0.0	0.0	6.0	40.4	47.5	6.1
Greece[2]	0.0	0.0	0.0	93.0	7.0	0.0
Hungary[2]	0.0	0.0	0.0	16.9	83.1	0.0
Iceland	80.7	0.0	0.0	16.5	2.8	0.0
Ireland[2]	0.0	5.7	0.0	94.3	0.0	0.0
Israel	0.0	0.0	0.0	96.4	3.6	0.0
Italy[2]	19.5	0.0	0.0	20.5	29.4	30.6
Japan	49.2	0.0	0.0	26.0	23.7	1.1
Korea	20.8	0.0	1.7	40.5	30.1	6.9
Latvia[2]	87.5	0.0	0.0	11.9	0.6	0.0
Lithuania[1]	0.0	0.0	0.0	81.8	18.2	0.0
Luxembourg[1, 2]	92.8	0.0	0.0	6.2	0.9	0.1
Netherlands[2]	0.0	0.0	0.0	54.8	44.9	0.4
New Zealand	0.0	0.0	0.0	88.9	11.1	0.0
Norway	85.9	0.0	0.0	13.5	0.7	0.0
Poland[1, 2]	66.7	0.0	0.0	28.6	3.5	1.2
Portugal[2]	23.9	0.0	0.0	51.2	24.7	0.2
Slovak Republic[2]	0.0	0.0	0.0	65.9	34.1	0.0
Slovenia[1, 2]	75.4	0.0	0.0	19.0	5.6	0.0
Sweden[2]	97.5	0.0	0.0	2.5	0.0	0.0
Türkiye	33.5	0.0	0.0	9.5	50.5	6.4
United Kingdom[2]	0.0	0.0	0.0	100.0	0.0	0.0
Unweighted average	32.7	0.2	0.3	43.7	21.2	1.9

1. The capital transfers were subtracted directly from the specific taxes to which they relate, except for France, where the capital transfers have been allocated between tax headings in proportion to the reported tax revenue.
2. Payments to the European Union are excluded from these comparisons.
3. Colombia and Spain are not constitutionally federal countries, but both have a highly decentralised political structure, with high autonomy of their territorial entities.

Table 3.19. Gross domestic product for tax reporting years at market prices, in billions of national currency

		1965	1990	2000	2007	2010	2015	2020	2021	2022	2023p
Australia[1]	AUD	24.4	415.3	707.4	1 179.6	1 418.7	1 658.9	2 088.9	2 333.2	2 562.1	2 670.3
Austria	EUR	18.5	137.5	213.6	284.0	295.9	344.3	380.9	405.2	447.2	477.2
Belgium	EUR	20.9	170.1	256.4	343.6	363.1	416.7	460.5	508.1	554.2	584.7
Canada	CAD	61.2	696.1	1 125.5	1 577.7	1 666.0	1 990.4	2 220.5	2 517.1	2 813.3	2 892.1
Chile	CLP	..	10 594.8	42 215.0	90 159.5	110 777.9	158 622.9	201 257.7	239 562.0	263 842.7	281 870.3
Colombia	COP	..	22 731.4	195 108.6	428 506.0	544 060.0	804 692.0	998 471.0	1192 634.0	1 469 791.0	1 572 658.4
Costa Rica[2]	CRC	..	525.3	4 627.1	13 889.1	19 802.0	30 171.9	36 495.2	40 326.6	44 810.0	47 059.3
Czechia	CZK	..	736.4	2 399.7	3 856.6	4 033.0	4 651.8	5 828.3	6 307.8	7 049.9	7 618.6
Denmark	DKK	71.5	855.4	1 326.0	1 743.1	1 812.9	2 030.2	2 326.6	2 567.5	2 844.2	2 804.7
Estonia	EUR	..	..	6.2	16.4	14.7	21.0	27.9	31.4	36.4	38.2
Finland	EUR	4.5	91.0	136.4	187.1	188.1	211.4	238.0	250.7	267.7	274.9
France	EUR	76.0	1 044.0	1 473.5	1 937.9	1 996.1	2 201.4	2 318.3	2 508.1	2 655.4	2 822.5
Germany	EUR	234.8	1 306.7	2 109.1	2 499.6	2 564.4	3 026.2	3 403.7	3 617.5	3 876.8	4 122.2
Greece	EUR	0.7	45.5	141.2	232.7	224.1	176.4	165.0	181.5	206.6	220.3
Hungary	HUF	..	..	13 324.1	25 741.9	27 485.1	34 965.2	48 444.5	55 205.0	65 951.7	74 992.0
Iceland	ISK	0.2	377.0	709.6	1 387.0	1 681.0	2 310.8	2 929.2	3 276.0	3 882.8	4 279.0
Ireland	EUR	1.3	37.9	108.5	197.1	167.4	272.5	382.2	449.2	520.9	510.0
Israel	ILS	..	125.1	556.6	758.8	896.2	1 179.5	1 422.4	1 591.2	1 772.8	1 883.6
Italy	EUR	22.4	730.9	1 241.5	1 614.8	1 611.3	1 655.4	1 661.2	1 821.9	1 962.8	2 085.4
Japan[1]	JPY	35 751.0	472 523.8	537 614.3	538 485.4	504 873.8	540 740.9	538 825.7	554 834.2	568 649.5	596 458.9
Korea[3]	KRW	831.4	200 556.2	651 634.4	1 089 660.2	1 322 611.2	1 658 020.4	1 940 726.2	2 080 198.5	2 161 773.9	2 236 329.5
Latvia	EUR	..	..	6.9	22.7	18.1	24.6	30.1	33.3	38.4	40.3
Lithuania	EUR	..	..	13.4	29.0	28.0	37.3	49.9	56.5	67.4	72.0
Luxembourg	EUR	1.0	10.6	23.0	37.6	42.4	54.1	64.5	72.4	77.5	79.3
Mexico	MXN	..	885.5	7 016.6	12 046.8	13 968.1	19 228.6	24 081.8	26 619.1	29 452.8	31 768.3
Netherlands	EUR	35.7	263.4	452.2	622.8	643.0	699.2	816.5	891.6	993.8	1067.6
New Zealand[1]	NZD	4.1	75.9	122.2	188.8	205.7	258.7	342.7	364.1	394.9	413.3
Norway	NOK	57.2	749.9	1 509.1	2 360.2	2 605.4	3 130.2	3 461.6	4 323.9	5 708.2	5 126.5
Poland	PLN	..	62.7	748.5	1 187.5	1 434.4	1 798.5	2 337.7	2 631.3	3 074.8	3 410.1
Portugal	EUR	0.6	56.0	128.4	175.5	179.6	179.7	200.5	216.1	242.3	265.5
Slovak Republic	EUR	..	10.0	31.7	63.2	68.8	80.1	93.4	100.2	109.8	122.8
Slovenia	EUR	..	0.9	18.9	35.1	36.4	38.9	47.0	52.3	57.0	63.1
Spain	EUR	8.7	328.7	647.9	1 075.5	1 072.7	1 078.1	1 119.0	1 222.3	1 346.4	1 461.9
Sweden	SEK	129.1	1 547.6	2 408.8	3 312.2	3 551.5	4 231.7	5 021.0	5 464.9	5 865.2	6 206.5
Switzerland	CHF	70.1	369.2	471.5	589.1	624.5	668.0	696.6	743.3	781.5	795.1
Türkiye	TRY	0.0	0.5	171.5	887.7	1 167.7	2 350.9	5 048.6	7 256.1	15 011.8	26 276.3
United Kingdom	GBP	36.4	615.7	1 100.8	1 544.6	1 608.6	1 916.5	2 104.3	2 284.1	2 506.0	2 687.2
United States	USD	709.0	5 963.1	10 251.0	14 474.2	15 049.0	18 295.0	21 323.0	23 594.0	25 744.1	27 348.0

.. Not available

1. GDP is fiscal year. The year Y is calculated as the sum of: Q2(Y) to Q1(Y+1) for Japan; and Q3(Y) to Q2(Y+1) for Australia and New Zealand.
2. The GDP shown for 1990 in Costa Rica is taken from the IMF (World Economic Outlook Database, accessed in October 2024). The GDP for all other years is taken from the OECD National Accounts.
3. The GDP shown for 2023 in Korea is taken from the OECD National Accounts, accessed in October 2024, and is a provisional value.

Source: OECD National Accounts, accessed in October 2024.

Table 3.20. Exchange rates used, national currency per US dollar at market exchange rates

		1965	1990	2000	2007	2010	2015	2020	2021	2022	2023p
Australia	AUD	0.9	1.3	1.8	1.2	1.0	1.3	1.4	1.4	1.5	1.5
Austria	EUR	..	0.8	1.1	0.7	0.8	0.9	0.9	0.8	0.9	0.9
Belgium	EUR	..	0.8	1.1	0.7	0.8	0.9	0.9	0.8	0.9	0.9
Canada	CAD	1.1	1.2	1.5	1.1	1.0	1.3	1.3	1.3	1.3	1.3
Chile	CLP	0.0	304.9	539.6	522.5	510.2	654.1	792.7	759.0	873.3	840.1
Colombia	COP	10.5	502.3	2 087.9	2 077.8	1 899.0	2 741.8	3 693.3	3 744.2	4 256.2	4 326.0
Costa Rica	CRC	6.6	91.6	308.2	516.6	525.8	534.6	584.9	620.8	647.1	544.1
Czechia	CZK	..	..	38.6	20.3	19.1	24.6	23.2	21.7	23.4	22.2
Denmark	DKK	6.9	6.2	8.1	5.4	5.6	6.7	6.5	6.3	7.1	6.9
Estonia	EUR	..	0.8	1.1	0.7	0.8	0.9	0.9	0.8	0.9	0.9
Finland	EUR	..	0.8	1.1	0.7	0.8	0.9	0.9	0.8	0.9	0.9
France	EUR	..	0.8	1.1	0.7	0.8	0.9	0.9	0.8	0.9	0.9
Germany	EUR	..	0.8	1.1	0.7	0.8	0.9	0.9	0.8	0.9	0.9
Greece	EUR	..	0.8	1.1	0.7	0.8	0.9	0.9	0.8	0.9	0.9
Hungary	HUF	..	63.2	282.2	183.6	207.9	279.3	308.0	303.1	372.6	353.1
Iceland	ISK	0.4	58.3	78.6	64.1	122.2	131.9	135.4	127.0	135.3	137.9
Ireland	EUR	0.5	0.8	1.1	0.7	0.8	0.9	0.9	0.8	0.9	0.9
Israel	ILS	0.0	2.0	4.1	4.1	3.7	3.9	3.4	3.2	3.4	3.7
Italy	EUR	..	0.8	1.1	0.7	0.8	0.9	0.9	0.8	0.9	0.9
Japan	JPY	360.0	142.3	111.2	114.2	85.8	118.0	107.5	115.2	133.7	140.5
Korea	KRW	266.3	707.8	1 130.4	929.4	1 156.5	1 131.0	1 180.3	1 144.0	1 291.4	1 305.7
Latvia	EUR	..	0.8	1.1	0.7	0.8	0.9	0.9	0.8	0.9	0.9
Lithuania	EUR	..	0.8	1.1	0.7	0.8	0.9	0.9	0.8	0.9	0.9
Luxembourg	EUR	..	0.8	1.1	0.7	0.8	0.9	0.9	0.8	0.9	0.9
Mexico	MXN	0.0	2.8	9.5	10.9	12.6	15.8	21.5	20.3	20.1	17.8
Netherlands	EUR	..	0.8	1.1	0.7	0.8	0.9	0.9	0.8	0.9	0.9
New Zealand	NZD	0.7	1.7	2.3	1.4	1.3	1.4	1.5	1.5	1.6	1.6
Norway	NOK	7.1	6.3	8.8	5.9	6.0	8.1	9.4	8.6	9.6	10.6
Poland	PLN	0.0	1.0	4.3	2.8	3.0	3.8	3.9	3.9	4.5	4.2
Portugal	EUR	..	0.8	1.1	0.7	0.8	0.9	0.9	0.8	0.9	0.9
Slovak Republic	EUR	..	0.8	1.1	0.7	0.8	0.9	0.9	0.8	0.9	0.9
Slovenia	EUR	..	0.8	1.1	0.7	0.8	0.9	0.9	0.8	0.9	0.9
Spain	EUR	..	0.8	1.1	0.7	0.8	0.9	0.9	0.8	0.9	0.9
Sweden	SEK	5.2	5.9	9.2	6.8	7.2	8.4	9.2	8.6	10.1	10.6
Switzerland	CHF	4.4	1.4	1.7	1.2	1.0	1.0	0.9	0.9	1.0	0.9
Türkiye	TRY	0.0	0.0	0.6	1.3	1.5	2.7	7.0	8.9	16.5	23.7
United Kingdom	GBP	0.4	0.6	0.7	0.5	0.6	0.7	0.8	0.7	0.8	0.8
United States	USD	1.0	1.0	1.0	1.0	1.0	1.0	1.0	1.0	1.0	1.0

.. Not available
Source: OECD Financial indicators data.

4 Country tables, 1990-2022

Chapter 4 provides a summary of tax revenues by category and by level of government for each OECD country.

Tax revenue and % of GDP by selected tax category and by level of government

In all the following tables, the symbol (..) indicates not available or not applicable. The main series in this chapter cover a selection of years between 1990 and 2022. A complete series is available online. Data for 1955 and 1960 (for nineteen OECD countries) are provided in Part V of the 1998 edition of this Report.

Gross Domestic Product (GDP) figures are based on the 2008 System of National Accounts (SNA) for all OECD countries.

Box 4.1. Treatment of capital transfers

Some tables refer to the treatment of the capital transfers that some countries make to account for taxes that have been assessed but not collected. The capital transfer has been subtracted directly from the specific taxes to which they relate, except for France, where the capital transfer has been allocated between tax headings in proportion to their tax revenues at the level of government against which these transfers were recorded.

Countries reporting capital transfers include:

- Austria from 2020 to 2022
- Belgium from 1995
- Denmark from 1971
- France from 1992
- Lithuania from 1999
- Luxembourg from 2013
- Poland from 1995
- Slovenia from 1995
- Switzerland from 1990

Table 4.1. Australia, tax revenue and % of GDP by selected tax category

	Billion AUD					% of GDP				
	1990	2000	2010	2021	2022	1990	2000	2010	2021	2022
Total tax revenue	116.5	214.8	356.7	680.3	753.2	28.1	30.4	25.1	29.2	29.4
1000 Taxes on income, profits and capital gains	66.5	124.4	202.2	418.3	468.9	16.0	17.6	14.3	17.9	18.3
1100 Of individuals	50.1	81.0	138.2	265.4	304.6	12.1	11.4	9.7	11.4	11.9
1200 Corporate	16.5	43.4	64.0	153.0	164.3	4.0	6.1	4.5	6.6	6.4
1300 Unallocable between 1100 and 1200	0.0	0.0	0.0	0.0	0.0	0.0	0.0	0.0	0.0	0.0
2000 Social security contributions	0.0	0.0	0.0	0.0	0.0	0.0	0.0	0.0	0.0	0.0
2100 Employees	0.0	0.0	0.0	0.0	0.0	0.0	0.0	0.0	0.0	0.0
2200 Employers	0.0	0.0	0.0	0.0	0.0	0.0	0.0	0.0	0.0	0.0
2300 Self-employed or non-employed	0.0	0.0	0.0	0.0	0.0	0.0	0.0	0.0	0.0	0.0
2400 Unallocable between 2100, 2200 and 2300	0.0	0.0	0.0	0.0	0.0	0.0	0.0	0.0	0.0	0.0
3000 Taxes on payroll and workforce	7.1	9.6	18.5	29.4	35.3	1.7	1.4	1.3	1.3	1.4
4000 Taxes on property	10.4	18.8	33.5	74.2	69.9	2.5	2.7	2.4	3.2	2.7
4100 Recurrent taxes on immovable property	6.1	9.1	19.9	36.5	40.2	1.5	1.3	1.4	1.6	1.6
4200 Recurrent taxes on net wealth	0.0	0.0	0.0	0.0	0.0	0.0	0.0	0.0	0.0	0.0
4300 Estate, inheritance and gift taxes	0.0	0.0	0.0	0.0	0.0	0.0	0.0	0.0	0.0	0.0
4400 Taxes on financial and capital transactions	4.3	9.8	13.6	37.6	29.7	1.0	1.4	1.0	1.6	1.2
4500 Non-recurrent taxes	0.0	0.0	0.0	0.0	0.0	0.0	0.0	0.0	0.0	0.0
4600 Other recurrent taxes on property	0.0	0.0	0.0	0.0	0.0	0.0	0.0	0.0	0.0	0.0
5000 Taxes on goods and services	32.4	61.9	102.6	158.4	179.1	7.8	8.7	7.2	6.8	7.0
5100 Taxes on production, sale, transfer, etc	27.2	56.2	90.8	134.8	152.4	6.6	7.9	6.4	5.8	5.9
5110 General taxes	9.4	25.8	48.1	77.7	88.6	2.3	3.7	3.4	3.3	3.5
5111 Value added taxes	0.0	23.9	46.9	75.6	86.3	0.0	3.4	3.3	3.2	3.4
5120 Taxes on specific goods and services	17.8	30.3	42.7	57.1	63.8	4.3	4.3	3.0	2.4	2.5
5121 Excises	12.0	19.8	26.7	23.7	27.6	2.9	2.8	1.9	1.0	1.1
5200 Taxes on use of goods and perform activities	5.2	5.7	11.7	23.6	26.7	1.3	0.8	0.8	1.0	1.0
5300 Unallocable between 5100 and 5200	0.0	0.0	0.0	0.0	0.0	0.0	0.0	0.0	0.0	0.0
6000 Other taxes	0.0	0.0	0.0	0.0	0.0	0.0	0.0	0.0	0.0	0.0
Non-wastable tax credits										
Non-wastable tax credits against 1000	..	0.2	6.7	11.0	11.9	..	0.0	0.5	0.5	0.5
Transfer component	..	0.0	4.4	7.4	8.3	..	0.0	0.3	0.3	0.3
Tax expenditure component	..	0.2	2.4	3.6	3.6	..	0.0	0.2	0.2	0.1

.. Not available

Note: More detailed country data and country notes are available in Chapter 5 "Detailed country tables". Full time series can be accessed at http://data-explorer.oecd.org/s/nb.

Source: Australian Bureau of Statistics.

Table 4.2. Australia, tax revenue and % of GDP by level of government and main taxes

	Billion AUD					% of GDP				
	1990	2000	2010	2021	2022	1990	2000	2010	2021	2022
Federal or Central government										
Total tax revenue	92.6	175.7	285.9	546.9	614.5	22.3	24.8	20.2	23.4	24.0
1000 Taxes on income, profits and capital gains	66.5	124.4	202.2	418.3	468.9	16.0	17.6	14.3	17.9	18.3
2000 Social security contributions	0.0	0.0	0.0	0.0	0.0	0.0	0.0	0.0	0.0	0.0
3000 Taxes on payroll and workforce	1.3	0.1	0.5	1.1	1.2	0.3	0.0	0.0	0.0	0.0
4000 Taxes on property	0.2	0.0	0.0	0.0	0.0	0.1	0.0	0.0	0.0	0.0
5000 Taxes on goods and services	24.5	51.1	83.2	127.5	144.4	5.9	7.2	5.9	5.5	5.6
6000 Other taxes	0.0	0.0	0.0	0.0	0.0	0.0	0.0	0.0	0.0	0.0
State/Regional										
Total tax revenue	19.7	32.7	58.4	112.4	116.9	4.7	4.6	4.1	4.8	4.6
1000 Taxes on income, profits and capital gains	0.0	0.0	0.0	0.0	0.0	0.0	0.0	0.0	0.0	0.0
2000 Social security contributions	0.0	0.0	0.0	0.0	0.0	0.0	0.0	0.0	0.0	0.0
3000 Taxes on payroll and workforce	5.8	9.5	18.0	28.3	34.1	1.4	1.3	1.3	1.2	1.3
4000 Taxes on property	6.0	12.4	21.0	53.2	48.1	1.4	1.8	1.5	2.3	1.9
5000 Taxes on goods and services	7.9	10.8	19.3	30.9	34.7	1.9	1.5	1.4	1.3	1.4
6000 Other taxes	0.0	0.0	0.0	0.0	0.0	0.0	0.0	0.0	0.0	0.0
Local government										
Total tax revenue	4.2	6.4	12.4	20.9	21.8	1.0	0.9	0.9	0.9	0.9
1000 Taxes on income, profits and capital gains	0.0	0.0	0.0	0.0	0.0	0.0	0.0	0.0	0.0	0.0
2000 Social security contributions	0.0	0.0	0.0	0.0	0.0	0.0	0.0	0.0	0.0	0.0
3000 Taxes on payroll and workforce	0.0	0.0	0.0	0.0	0.0	0.0	0.0	0.0	0.0	0.0
4000 Taxes on property	4.2	6.4	12.4	20.9	21.8	1.0	0.9	0.9	0.9	0.9
5000 Taxes on goods and services	0.0	0.0	0.0	0.0	0.0	0.0	0.0	0.0	0.0	0.0
6000 Other taxes	0.0	0.0	0.0	0.0	0.0	0.0	0.0	0.0	0.0	0.0
Social Security Funds										
Total tax revenue	0.0	0.0	0.0	0.0	0.0	0.0	0.0	0.0	0.0	0.0
1000 Taxes on income, profits and capital gains	0.0	0.0	0.0	0.0	0.0	0.0	0.0	0.0	0.0	0.0
2000 Social security contributions	0.0	0.0	0.0	0.0	0.0	0.0	0.0	0.0	0.0	0.0
3000 Taxes on payroll and workforce	0.0	0.0	0.0	0.0	0.0	0.0	0.0	0.0	0.0	0.0
4000 Taxes on property	0.0	0.0	0.0	0.0	0.0	0.0	0.0	0.0	0.0	0.0
5000 Taxes on goods and services	0.0	0.0	0.0	0.0	0.0	0.0	0.0	0.0	0.0	0.0
6000 Other taxes	0.0	0.0	0.0	0.0	0.0	0.0	0.0	0.0	0.0	0.0

Note: More detailed country data and country notes are available in Chapter 6 "Tax revenues by sub-sectors of general government". Full time series can be accessed at http://data-explorer.oecd.org/s/nb.

Source: Australian Bureau of Statistics.

Table 4.3. Austria, tax revenue and % of GDP by selected tax category

	Billion EUR					% of GDP				
	1990	2000	2010	2021	2022	1990	2000	2010	2021	2022
Total tax revenue	54.0	90.3	121.2	175.8	193.1	39.3	42.3	41.0	43.4	43.2
1000 Taxes on income, profits and capital gains	13.8	25.6	34.0	51.9	59.7	10.0	12.0	11.5	12.8	13.4
1100 Of individuals	11.3	19.9	27.1	39.4	43.0	8.2	9.3	9.2	9.7	9.6
1200 Corporate	1.9	4.2	5.5	11.2	15.3	1.4	1.9	1.9	2.8	3.4
1300 Unallocable between 1100 and 1200	0.5	1.5	1.4	1.3	1.4	0.4	0.7	0.5	0.3	0.3
2000 Social security contributions	17.8	30.5	41.4	62.3	65.9	12.9	14.3	14.0	15.4	14.7
2100 Employees	7.5	12.5	16.8	25.0	26.6	5.5	5.8	5.7	6.2	5.9
2200 Employers	8.8	14.7	19.4	29.2	31.1	6.4	6.9	6.6	7.2	6.9
2300 Self-employed or non-employed	0.0	0.0	0.0	0.0	0.0	0.0	0.0	0.0	0.0	0.0
2400 Unallocable between 2100, 2200 and 2300	0.0	0.0	0.0	0.0	0.0	0.0	0.0	0.0	0.0	0.0
3000 Taxes on payroll and workforce	3.3	5.8	8.4	11.3	12.1	2.4	2.7	2.8	2.8	2.7
4000 Taxes on property	1.5	1.2	1.6	2.6	2.6	1.1	0.6	0.5	0.6	0.6
4100 Recurrent taxes on immovable property	0.4	0.5	0.7	0.9	0.9	0.3	0.2	0.2	0.2	0.2
4200 Recurrent taxes on net wealth	0.6	0.0	0.0	0.0	0.0	0.5	0.0	0.0	0.0	0.0
4300 Estate, inheritance and gift taxes	0.1	0.1	0.0	0.0	0.0	0.1	0.1	0.0	0.0	0.0
4400 Taxes on financial and capital transactions	0.4	0.6	0.8	1.7	1.7	0.3	0.3	0.3	0.4	0.4
4500 Non-recurrent taxes	0.0	0.0	0.0	0.0	0.0	0.0	0.0	0.0	0.0	0.0
4600 Other recurrent taxes on property	0.0	0.0	0.0	0.0	0.0	0.0	0.0	0.0	0.0	0.0
5000 Taxes on goods and services	17.0	26.5	34.7	47.0	52.0	12.4	12.4	11.7	11.6	11.6
5100 Taxes on production, sale, transfer, etc	16.2	24.6	32.1	42.9	47.6	11.8	11.5	10.9	10.6	10.6
5110 General taxes	11.2	16.9	22.7	30.8	35.7	8.2	7.9	7.7	7.6	8.0
5111 Value added taxes	11.2	16.9	22.7	30.8	35.6	8.2	7.9	7.7	7.6	8.0
5120 Taxes on specific goods and services	4.9	7.7	9.4	12.0	11.8	3.5	3.6	3.2	3.0	2.6
5121 Excises	3.3	5.5	6.9	8.0	7.5	2.4	2.6	2.3	2.0	1.7
5200 Taxes on use of goods and perform activities	0.9	1.9	2.6	4.1	4.4	0.6	0.9	0.9	1.0	1.0
5300 Unallocable between 5100 and 5200	0.0	0.0	0.0	0.0	0.0	0.0	0.0	0.0	0.0	0.0
6000 Other taxes	0.7	0.8	1.1	0.7	0.8	0.5	0.4	0.4	0.2	0.2
Non-wastable tax credits										
Non-wastable tax credits against 1000	..	0.7	0.7	0.3	0.4	..	0.3	0.2	0.1	0.1
Transfer component	..	0.1	0.2	0.1	0.2	..	0.0	0.1	0.0	0.0
Tax expenditure component	..	0.6	0.4	0.2	0.2	..	0.3	0.1	0.0	0.0
Revenues collected on behalf of the EU										
Revenues collected on behalf of the EU, total	..	0.4	0.3	0.8	1.0	..	0.2	0.1	0.2	0.2
Customs duties	..	0.4	0.3	0.5	0.7	..	0.2	0.1	0.1	0.1
SRF contributions	..	..	..	0.3	0.4	..	..	..	0.1	0.1

.. Not available

Note: The total tax revenue has been reduced by the amount of any capital transfer that represents uncollected taxes. The capital transfers were subtracted directly from the specific taxes to which they relate. Therefore, the tax revenue amounts are different to those reported in the detailed country data available in Chapter 5 "Detailed country tables".

More detailed country data and country notes are available in Chapter 5 "Detailed country tables". Full time series can be accessed at http://data-explorer.oecd.org/s/nb.

Source: Statistics Austria.

Table 4.4. Austria, tax revenue and % of GDP by level of government and main taxes

	Billion EUR					% of GDP				
	1990	2000	2010	2021	2022	1990	2000	2010	2021	2022
Federal or Central government										
Total tax revenue	27.2	60.5	80.7	113.5	126.7	19.8	28.3	27.3	28.0	28.3
1000 Taxes on income, profits and capital gains	8.6	24.9	33.1	50.5	58.3	6.2	11.7	11.2	12.5	13.0
2000 Social security contributions	2.4	5.1	6.3	8.9	9.3	1.7	2.4	2.1	2.2	2.1
3000 Taxes on payroll and workforce	2.6	3.9	5.8	6.3	6.6	1.9	1.8	1.9	1.6	1.5
4000 Taxes on property	0.9	0.7	0.9	1.7	1.8	0.6	0.3	0.3	0.4	0.4
5000 Taxes on goods and services	12.3	25.3	33.7	45.5	50.1	8.9	11.8	11.4	11.2	11.2
6000 Other taxes	0.5	0.6	0.9	0.6	0.6	0.4	0.3	0.3	0.1	0.1
State/Regional										
Total tax revenue	5.8	1.4	2.0	3.5	3.7	4.2	0.7	0.7	0.9	0.8
1000 Taxes on income, profits and capital gains	2.8	0.6	0.9	1.4	1.5	2.0	0.3	0.3	0.3	0.3
2000 Social security contributions	0.2	0.4	0.5	0.4	0.4	0.2	0.2	0.2	0.1	0.1
3000 Taxes on payroll and workforce	0.0	0.1	0.2	1.1	1.2	0.0	0.1	0.1	0.3	0.3
4000 Taxes on property	0.1	0.0	0.0	0.0	0.0	0.0	0.0	0.0	0.0	0.0
5000 Taxes on goods and services	2.7	0.2	0.3	0.4	0.5	2.0	0.1	0.1	0.1	0.1
6000 Other taxes	0.0	0.1	0.1	0.1	0.1	0.0	0.0	0.0	0.0	0.0
Local government										
Total tax revenue	6.1	3.2	3.8	5.3	5.8	4.4	1.5	1.3	1.3	1.3
1000 Taxes on income, profits and capital gains	2.4	0.0	0.0	0.0	0.0	1.8	0.0	0.0	0.0	0.0
2000 Social security contributions	0.2	0.3	0.3	0.2	0.2	0.1	0.1	0.1	0.1	0.0
3000 Taxes on payroll and workforce	0.7	1.8	2.4	3.9	4.3	0.5	0.8	0.8	1.0	1.0
4000 Taxes on property	0.5	0.5	0.6	0.8	0.8	0.4	0.2	0.2	0.2	0.2
5000 Taxes on goods and services	2.1	0.6	0.4	0.3	0.4	1.5	0.3	0.1	0.1	0.1
6000 Other taxes	0.2	0.1	0.1	0.1	0.1	0.1	0.0	0.0	0.0	0.0
Social Security Funds										
Total tax revenue	15.0	24.8	34.4	52.7	55.9	10.9	11.6	11.6	13.0	12.5
1000 Taxes on income, profits and capital gains	0.0	0.0	0.0	0.0	0.0	0.0	0.0	0.0	0.0	0.0
2000 Social security contributions	15.0	24.8	34.4	52.7	55.9	10.9	11.6	11.6	13.0	12.5
3000 Taxes on payroll and workforce	0.0	0.0	0.0	0.0	0.0	0.0	0.0	0.0	0.0	0.0
4000 Taxes on property	0.0	0.0	0.0	0.0	0.0	0.0	0.0	0.0	0.0	0.0
5000 Taxes on goods and services	0.0	0.0	0.0	0.0	0.0	0.0	0.0	0.0	0.0	0.0
6000 Other taxes	0.0	0.0	0.0	0.0	0.0	0.0	0.0	0.0	0.0	0.0

Note: The total tax revenue has been reduced by the amount of any capital transfer that represents uncollected taxes. The capital transfers were subtracted directly from the specific taxes to which they relate. Therefore, the tax revenue amounts are different to those reported in the detailed country data available in Chapter 6 "Tax revenues by sub-sectors of general government".

More detailed country data and country notes are available in Chapter 6 "Tax revenues by sub-sectors of general government". Full time series can be accessed at http://data-explorer.oecd.org/s/nb.

Source: Statistics Austria.

Table 4.5. Belgium, tax revenue and % of GDP by selected tax category

	Billion EUR					% of GDP				
	1990	2000	2010	2021	2022	1990	2000	2010	2021	2022
Total tax revenue	70.4	112.4	155.7	213.7	234.9	41.4	43.8	42.9	42.1	42.4
1000 Taxes on income, profits and capital gains	26.0	43.4	53.2	76.3	87.9	15.3	16.9	14.7	15.0	15.9
1100 Of individuals	22.5	35.3	44.0	57.2	66.2	13.2	13.8	12.1	11.3	11.9
1200 Corporate	3.4	8.1	9.2	19.0	21.7	2.0	3.1	2.5	3.7	3.9
1300 Unallocable between 1100 and 1200	0.0	0.1	0.0	0.1	0.1	0.0	0.0	0.0	0.0	0.0
2000 Social security contributions	23.4	34.6	50.5	65.5	71.4	13.7	13.5	13.9	12.9	12.9
2100 Employees	7.2	10.9	15.0	19.8	21.6	4.2	4.3	4.1	3.9	3.9
2200 Employers	14.7	20.8	30.9	39.3	43.0	8.6	8.1	8.5	7.7	7.8
2300 Self-employed or non-employed	0.0	0.0	0.0	0.0	0.0	0.0	0.0	0.0	0.0	0.0
2400 Unallocable between 2100, 2200 and 2300	0.0	0.0	0.0	0.0	0.0	0.0	0.0	0.0	0.0	0.0
3000 Taxes on payroll and workforce	0.0	0.0	0.0	0.0	0.0	0.0	0.0	0.0	0.0	0.0
4000 Taxes on property	2.7	5.3	11.3	18.0	18.0	1.6	2.1	3.1	3.5	3.3
4100 Recurrent taxes on immovable property	0.6	1.2	4.6	6.2	6.7	0.4	0.5	1.3	1.2	1.2
4200 Recurrent taxes on net wealth	0.0	0.1	0.2	1.0	1.1	0.0	0.0	0.1	0.2	0.2
4300 Estate, inheritance and gift taxes	0.5	1.1	2.3	3.7	3.6	0.3	0.4	0.6	0.7	0.6
4400 Taxes on financial and capital transactions	1.5	2.7	3.5	5.9	5.6	0.9	1.0	1.0	1.2	1.0
4500 Non-recurrent taxes	0.0	0.0	0.0	0.0	0.0	0.0	0.0	0.0	0.0	0.0
4600 Other recurrent taxes on property	0.1	0.2	0.3	0.7	0.8	0.1	0.1	0.1	0.1	0.1
5000 Taxes on goods and services	18.4	29.1	40.7	53.9	57.5	10.8	11.3	11.2	10.6	10.4
5100 Taxes on production, sale, transfer, etc	17.4	27.0	38.3	51.1	54.3	10.2	10.5	10.5	10.1	9.8
5110 General taxes	11.6	18.2	25.5	34.6	36.3	6.8	7.1	7.0	6.8	6.6
5111 Value added taxes	11.5	18.1	25.3	34.3	36.0	6.8	7.1	7.0	6.7	6.5
5120 Taxes on specific goods and services	5.8	8.7	12.8	16.4	18.0	3.4	3.4	3.5	3.2	3.3
5121 Excises	3.5	5.7	7.8	9.9	10.0	2.0	2.2	2.1	1.9	1.8
5200 Taxes on use of goods and perform activities	1.0	2.1	2.4	2.8	3.1	0.6	0.8	0.7	0.6	0.6
5300 Unallocable between 5100 and 5200	0.0	0.0	0.0	0.0	0.0	0.0	0.0	0.0	0.0	0.0
6000 Other taxes	0.0	0.0	0.0	-0.0	0.0	0.0	0.0	0.0	-0.0	0.0
Non-wastable tax credits										
Non-wastable tax credits against 1000	..	..	1.0	1.1	1.2	..	..	0.3	0.2	0.2
Transfer component	..	..	0.4	0.3	0.3	..	..	0.1	0.1	0.1
Tax expenditure component	..	..	0.6	0.8	0.9	..	..	0.2	0.2	0.2
Revenues collected on behalf of the EU										
Revenues collected on behalf of the EU, total	0.9	1.0	1.3	2.0	2.7	0.6	0.4	0.4	0.4	0.5
Customs duties	..	1.0	1.2	1.6	2.3	..	0.4	0.3	0.3	0.4
SRF contributions	..	..	..	0.3	0.4	..	..	..	0.1	0.1

.. Not available

Note: The total tax revenue has been reduced by the amount of any capital transfer that represents uncollected taxes. The capital transfers were subtracted directly from the specific taxes to which they relate. Therefore, the tax revenue amounts are different to those reported in the detailed country data available in Chapter 5 "Detailed country tables".

More detailed country data and country notes are available in Chapter 5 "Detailed country tables". Full time series can be accessed at http://data-explorer.oecd.org/s/nb.

Source: Institute for National Accounts; Federal Ministry of Finance.

Table 4.6. Belgium, tax revenue and % of GDP by level of government and main taxes

	Billion EUR					% of GDP				
	1990	2000	2010	2021	2022	1990	2000	2010	2021	2022
Federal or Central government										
Total tax revenue	42.5	69.4	87.8	111.9	123.2	25.0	27.1	24.2	22.0	22.2
1000 Taxes on income, profits and capital gains	23.9	39.6	49.3	62.8	71.8	14.0	15.4	13.6	12.4	12.9
2000 Social security contributions	0.9	1.3	2.5	0.1	0.1	0.5	0.5	0.7	0.0	0.0
3000 Taxes on payroll and workforce	0.0	0.0	0.0	0.0	0.0	0.0	0.0	0.0	0.0	0.0
4000 Taxes on property	1.1	2.3	0.9	2.6	2.5	0.6	0.9	0.3	0.5	0.5
5000 Taxes on goods and services	16.7	26.3	35.0	46.5	48.9	9.8	10.2	9.7	9.1	8.8
6000 Other taxes	0.0	0.0	0.0	0.0	0.0	0.0	0.0	0.0	0.0	0.0
State/Regional										
Total tax revenue	1.2	2.4	8.1	21.8	23.8	0.7	1.0	2.2	4.3	4.3
1000 Taxes on income, profits and capital gains	0.0	0.1	0.0	9.1	11.1	0.0	0.0	0.0	1.8	2.0
2000 Social security contributions	0.0	0.0	0.0	0.3	0.3	0.0	0.0	0.0	0.1	0.1
3000 Taxes on payroll and workforce	0.0	0.0	0.0	0.0	0.0	0.0	0.0	0.0	0.0	0.0
4000 Taxes on property	0.9	1.9	5.6	9.3	9.0	0.5	0.7	1.5	1.8	1.6
5000 Taxes on goods and services	0.2	0.5	2.4	3.1	3.4	0.1	0.2	0.7	0.6	0.6
6000 Other taxes	0.0	0.0	0.0	-0.0	0.0	0.0	0.0	0.0	-0.0	0.0
Local government										
Total tax revenue	3.1	4.6	7.9	9.5	10.6	1.8	1.8	2.2	1.9	1.9
1000 Taxes on income, profits and capital gains	2.1	3.1	2.9	3.1	3.7	1.2	1.2	0.8	0.6	0.7
2000 Social security contributions	0.1	0.0	0.0	0.0	0.0	0.1	0.0	0.0	0.0	0.0
3000 Taxes on payroll and workforce	0.0	0.0	0.0	0.0	0.0	0.0	0.0	0.0	0.0	0.0
4000 Taxes on property	0.6	1.0	4.4	5.8	6.2	0.3	0.4	1.2	1.1	1.1
5000 Taxes on goods and services	0.3	0.4	0.6	0.7	0.7	0.2	0.2	0.2	0.1	0.1
6000 Other taxes	0.0	0.0	0.0	0.0	0.0	0.0	0.0	0.0	0.0	0.0
Social Security Funds										
Total tax revenue	22.7	34.9	50.7	68.6	74.5	13.4	13.6	14.0	13.5	13.4
1000 Taxes on income, profits and capital gains	0.0	0.6	1.0	1.3	1.3	0.0	0.2	0.3	0.3	0.2
2000 Social security contributions	22.4	33.3	48.0	65.2	71.1	13.2	13.0	13.2	12.8	12.8
3000 Taxes on payroll and workforce	0.0	0.0	0.0	0.0	0.0	0.0	0.0	0.0	0.0	0.0
4000 Taxes on property	0.1	0.2	0.3	0.3	0.3	0.1	0.1	0.1	0.1	0.1
5000 Taxes on goods and services	0.2	0.8	1.3	1.8	1.7	0.1	0.3	0.4	0.3	0.3
6000 Other taxes	0.0	0.0	0.0	0.0	0.0	0.0	0.0	0.0	0.0	0.0

Note: The total tax revenue has been reduced by the amount of any capital transfer that represents uncollected taxes. The capital transfers were subtracted directly from the specific taxes to which they relate. Therefore, the tax revenue amounts are different to those reported in the detailed country data available in Chapter 6 "Tax revenues by sub-sectors of general government".

More detailed country data and country notes are available in Chapter 6 "Tax revenues by sub-sectors of general government". Full time series can be accessed at http://data-explorer.oecd.org/s/nb.

Source: Institute for National Accounts; Federal Ministry of Finance.

Table 4.7. Canada, tax revenue and % of GDP by selected tax category

	Billion CAD					% of GDP				
	1990	2000	2010	2021	2022	1990	2000	2010	2021	2022
Total tax revenue	244.2	390.2	516.6	875.9	951.8	35.1	34.7	31.0	34.8	33.8
1000 Taxes on income, profits and capital gains	118.6	195.3	241.0	451.8	490.9	17.0	17.4	14.5	18.0	17.5
1100 Of individuals	99.7	143.7	180.9	318.0	346.2	14.3	12.8	10.9	12.6	12.3
1200 Corporate	17.2	47.6	54.1	123.3	132.0	2.5	4.2	3.2	4.9	4.7
1300 Unallocable between 1100 and 1200	1.7	4.0	6.0	10.5	12.7	0.2	0.4	0.4	0.4	0.5
2000 Social security contributions	29.7	53.1	76.8	120.9	133.6	4.3	4.7	4.6	4.8	4.7
2100 Employees	10.6	21.4	30.6	50.5	55.8	1.5	1.9	1.8	2.0	2.0
2200 Employers	18.4	30.3	43.5	65.8	72.7	2.7	2.7	2.6	2.6	2.6
2300 Self-employed or non-employed	0.0	0.0	0.0	0.0	0.0	0.0	0.0	0.0	0.0	0.0
2400 Unallocable between 2100, 2200 and 2300	0.0	0.0	0.0	0.0	0.0	0.0	0.0	0.0	0.0	0.0
3000 Taxes on payroll and workforce	5.5	8.0	10.8	18.9	20.7	0.8	0.7	0.6	0.8	0.7
4000 Taxes on property	24.5	37.2	63.7	98.0	98.5	3.5	3.3	3.8	3.9	3.5
4100 Recurrent taxes on immovable property	20.2	30.2	51.7	73.5	74.7	2.9	2.7	3.1	2.9	2.7
4200 Recurrent taxes on net wealth	1.9	4.2	1.5	0.5	0.6	0.3	0.4	0.1	0.0	0.0
4300 Estate, inheritance and gift taxes	0.0	0.0	0.2	0.4	0.5	0.0	0.0	0.0	0.0	0.0
4400 Taxes on financial and capital transactions	0.0	0.0	3.1	12.3	10.8	0.0	0.0	0.2	0.5	0.4
4500 Non-recurrent taxes	0.0	0.0	0.0	0.0	0.0	0.0	0.0	0.0	0.0	0.0
4600 Other recurrent taxes on property	0.0	0.0	0.0	0.0	0.0	0.0	0.0	0.0	0.0	0.0
5000 Taxes on goods and services	63.1	94.5	123.8	185.3	207.0	9.1	8.4	7.4	7.4	7.4
5100 Taxes on production, sale, transfer, etc	59.6	88.9	116.2	172.0	192.9	8.6	7.9	7.0	6.8	6.9
5110 General taxes	34.5	55.3	72.1	117.0	129.1	5.0	4.9	4.3	4.6	4.6
5111 Value added taxes	0.0	35.9	70.7	115.4	127.2	0.0	3.2	4.2	4.6	4.5
5120 Taxes on specific goods and services	25.2	33.6	44.0	55.0	63.7	3.6	3.0	2.6	2.2	2.3
5121 Excises	14.5	18.4	23.3	29.9	31.7	2.1	1.6	1.4	1.2	1.1
5200 Taxes on use of goods and perform activities	3.5	5.6	7.6	13.3	14.1	0.5	0.5	0.5	0.5	0.5
5300 Unallocable between 5100 and 5200	0.0	0.0	0.0	0.0	0.0	0.0	0.0	0.0	0.0	0.0
6000 Other taxes	2.9	2.2	0.6	1.0	1.1	0.4	0.2	0.0	0.0	0.0
Non-wastable tax credits										
Non-wastable tax credits against 1000	..	3.4	11.1	18.8	21.9	..	0.3	0.7	0.7	0.8
Transfer component	..	3.1	10.2	16.5	19.2	..	0.3	0.6	0.7	0.7
Tax expenditure component	..	0.3	0.9	2.3	2.8	..	0.0	0.1	0.1	0.1

.. Not available

Note: More detailed country data and country notes are available in Chapter 5 "Detailed country tables". Full time series can be accessed at http://data-explorer.oecd.org/s/nb.

Source: Statistics Canada.

Table 4.8. Canada, tax revenue and % of GDP by level of government and main taxes

	Billion CAD					% of GDP				
	1990	2000	2010	2021	2022	1990	2000	2010	2021	2022
Federal or Central government										
Total tax revenue	101.7	184.4	212.8	373.9	407.9	14.6	16.4	12.8	14.9	14.5
1000 Taxes on income, profits and capital gains	73.6	126.3	148.7	280.1	303.5	10.6	11.2	8.9	11.1	10.8
2000 Social security contributions	0.0	18.8	17.9	24.0	26.4	0.0	1.7	1.1	1.0	0.9
3000 Taxes on payroll and workforce	0.0	0.0	0.0	0.0	0.0	0.0	0.0	0.0	0.0	0.0
4000 Taxes on property	0.0	0.0	0.0	0.0	0.0	0.0	0.0	0.0	0.0	0.0
5000 Taxes on goods and services	28.1	39.4	46.2	69.8	78.0	4.0	3.5	2.8	2.8	2.8
6000 Other taxes	0.0	0.0	0.0	0.0	0.0	0.0	0.0	0.0	0.0	0.0
State/Regional										
Total tax revenue	89.3	148.2	201.1	339.1	370.5	12.8	13.2	12.1	13.5	13.2
1000 Taxes on income, profits and capital gains	44.9	69.0	92.2	171.7	187.4	6.5	6.1	5.5	6.8	6.7
2000 Social security contributions	0.0	8.3	11.7	14.5	15.9	0.0	0.7	0.7	0.6	0.6
3000 Taxes on payroll and workforce	5.5	8.0	10.8	18.9	20.7	0.8	0.7	0.6	0.8	0.7
4000 Taxes on property	4.2	8.4	9.8	19.9	19.0	0.6	0.7	0.6	0.8	0.7
5000 Taxes on goods and services	34.6	54.5	76.7	114.1	127.4	5.0	4.8	4.6	4.5	4.5
6000 Other taxes	0.0	0.0	0.0	0.0	0.0	0.0	0.0	0.0	0.0	0.0
Local government										
Total tax revenue	23.5	31.5	55.4	80.4	82.1	3.4	2.8	3.3	3.2	2.9
1000 Taxes on income, profits and capital gains	0.0	0.0	0.0	0.0	0.0	0.0	0.0	0.0	0.0	0.0
2000 Social security contributions	0.0	0.0	0.0	0.0	0.0	0.0	0.0	0.0	0.0	0.0
3000 Taxes on payroll and workforce	0.0	0.0	0.0	0.0	0.0	0.0	0.0	0.0	0.0	0.0
4000 Taxes on property	20.3	28.8	53.9	78.0	79.5	2.9	2.6	3.2	3.1	2.8
5000 Taxes on goods and services	0.4	0.6	0.9	1.4	1.5	0.1	0.1	0.1	0.1	0.1
6000 Other taxes	2.9	2.2	0.6	1.0	1.1	0.4	0.2	0.0	0.0	0.0
Social Security Funds										
Total tax revenue	29.7	26.0	47.2	82.5	91.3	4.3	2.3	2.8	3.3	3.2
1000 Taxes on income, profits and capital gains	0.0	0.0	0.0	0.0	0.0	0.0	0.0	0.0	0.0	0.0
2000 Social security contributions	29.7	26.0	47.2	82.5	91.3	4.3	2.3	2.8	3.3	3.2
3000 Taxes on payroll and workforce	0.0	0.0	0.0	0.0	0.0	0.0	0.0	0.0	0.0	0.0
4000 Taxes on property	0.0	0.0	0.0	0.0	0.0	0.0	0.0	0.0	0.0	0.0
5000 Taxes on goods and services	0.0	0.0	0.0	0.0	0.0	0.0	0.0	0.0	0.0	0.0
6000 Other taxes	0.0	0.0	0.0	0.0	0.0	0.0	0.0	0.0	0.0	0.0

Note: More detailed country data and country notes are available in Chapter 6 "Tax revenues by sub-sectors of general government". Full time series can be accessed at http://data-explorer.oecd.org/s/nb.
Source: Statistics Canada.

Table 4.9. Chile, tax revenue and % of GDP by selected tax category

	Billion CLP					% of GDP				
	1990	2000	2010	2021	2022	1990	2000	2010	2021	2022
Total tax revenue	1 777.2	7 902.0	21 815.4	53 463.3	62 901.4	16.8	18.7	19.7	22.3	23.8
1000 Taxes on income, profits and capital gains	413.0	1 841.6	8 329.1	20 456.9	27 491.9	3.9	4.4	7.5	8.5	10.4
1100 Of individuals	99.2	604.1	1 492.8	5 780.4	6 626.6	0.9	1.4	1.3	2.4	2.5
1200 Corporate	219.6	882.9	4 448.7	9 145.9	14 900.6	2.1	2.1	4.0	3.8	5.6
1300 Unallocable between 1100 and 1200	94.2	354.6	2 387.5	5530.6	5 964.7	0.9	0.8	2.2	2.3	2.3
2000 Social security contributions	159.6	576.8	1 494.0	2 815.1	2 585.4	1.5	1.4	1.3	1.2	1.0
2100 Employees	154.0	553.9	1 433.2	2 686.0	2 435.4	1.5	1.3	1.3	1.1	0.9
2200 Employers	5.5	22.8	60.8	129.1	150.0	0.1	0.1	0.1	0.1	0.1
2300 Self-employed or non-employed	0.0	0.0	0.0	0.0	0.0	0.0	0.0	0.0	0.0	0.0
2400 Unallocable between 2100, 2200 and 2300	0.0	0.0	0.0	0.0	0.0	0.0	0.0	0.0	0.0	0.0
3000 Taxes on payroll and workforce	0.0	0.0	0.0	0.0	0.0	0.0	0.0	0.0	0.0	0.0
4000 Taxes on property	109.3	554.0	867.9	2 885.1	3 466.2	1.0	1.3	0.8	1.2	1.3
4100 Recurrent taxes on immovable property	60.0	302.2	631.7	2 002.4	2 284.3	0.6	0.7	0.6	0.8	0.9
4200 Recurrent taxes on net wealth	0.0	0.0	0.0	0.0	0.0	0.0	0.0	0.0	0.0	0.0
4300 Estate, inheritance and gift taxes	3.4	10.9	39.3	291.8	416.2	0.0	0.0	0.0	0.1	0.2
4400 Taxes on financial and capital transactions	45.9	240.9	196.9	590.8	765.7	0.4	0.6	0.2	0.2	0.3
4500 Non-recurrent taxes	0.0	0.0	0.0	0.0	0.0	0.0	0.0	0.0	0.0	0.0
4600 Other recurrent taxes on property	0.0	0.0	0.0	0.0	0.0	0.0	0.0	0.0	0.0	0.0
5000 Taxes on goods and services	1 118.7	5 041.8	11 185.2	28 368.6	30 080.5	10.6	11.9	10.1	11.8	11.4
5100 Taxes on production, sale, transfer, etc	1 074.0	4 789.8	10 532.9	26 628.0	28 078.7	10.1	11.3	9.5	11.1	10.6
5110 General taxes	664.4	3 306.4	8 399.9	22 785.9	24 515.2	6.3	7.8	7.6	9.5	9.3
5111 Value added taxes	664.4	3 306.4	8 399.9	22 785.9	24 515.2	6.3	7.8	7.6	9.5	9.3
5120 Taxes on specific goods and services	409.6	1 483.5	2 133.0	3 842.1	3 563.4	3.9	3.5	1.9	1.6	1.4
5121 Excises	166.0	816.2	1 561.2	2 799.0	2 331.1	1.6	1.9	1.4	1.2	0.9
5200 Taxes on use of goods and perform activities	44.7	251.9	652.3	1 740.6	2 001.8	0.4	0.6	0.6	0.7	0.8
5300 Unallocable between 5100 and 5200	0.0	0.0	0.0	0.0	0.0	0.0	0.0	0.0	0.0	0.0
6000 Other taxes	-23.4	-112.2	-60.7	-1062.4	-722.6	-0.2	-0.3	-0.1	-0.4	-0.3
Non-wastable tax credits										
Non-wastable tax credits against 1000	0.0	0.0	0.0	279.4	352.8	0.0	0.0	0.0	0.1	0.1
Transfer component	..	..	..	215.8	250.4	..	..	..	0.1	0.1
Tax expenditure component	..	..	..	63.5	102.4	..	..	..	0.0	0.0

.. Not available

Note: More detailed country data and country notes are available in Chapter 5 "Detailed country tables". Full time series can be accessed at http://data-explorer.oecd.org/s/nb.

Source: Servicio de Impuestos internos (Chile's Tax Service).

Table 4.10. Chile, tax revenue and % of GDP by level of government and main taxes

	Billion CLP					% of GDP				
	1990	2000	2010	2021	2022	1990	2000	2010	2021	2022
Federal or Central government										
Total tax revenue	1 579.7	6 936.8	19 214.8	47 410.5	56 529.2	14.9	16.4	17.3	19.8	21.4
1000 Taxes on income, profits and capital gains	413.0	1 841.6	8 329.1	20 456.9	27 491.9	3.9	4.4	7.5	8.5	10.4
2000 Social security contributions	66.7	232.7	371.4	511.5	548.6	0.6	0.6	0.3	0.2	0.2
3000 Taxes on payroll and workforce	0.0	0.0	0.0	0.0	0.0	0.0	0.0	0.0	0.0	0.0
4000 Taxes on property	59.7	255.4	244.6	1187.2	1456.8	0.6	0.6	0.2	0.5	0.6
5000 Taxes on goods and services	1 063.7	4 719.3	10 330.4	26 317.2	27 754.6	10.0	11.2	9.3	11.0	10.5
6000 Other taxes	-23.4	-112.2	-60.7	-1062.4	-722.6	-0.2	-0.3	-0.1	-0.4	-0.3
State/Regional										
Total tax revenue	..	..	..	..	..	..	..	..	..	..
1000 Taxes on income, profits and capital gains	..	..	..	..	..	..	..	..	..	..
2000 Social security contributions	..	..	..	..	..	..	..	..	..	..
3000 Taxes on payroll and workforce	..	..	..	..	..	..	..	..	..	..
4000 Taxes on property	..	..	..	..	..	..	..	..	..	..
5000 Taxes on goods and services	..	..	..	..	..	..	..	..	..	..
6000 Other taxes	..	..	..	..	..	..	..	..	..	..
Local government										
Total tax revenue	104.7	621.2	1 478.0	3 749.3	4 335.4	1.0	1.5	1.3	1.6	1.6
1000 Taxes on income, profits and capital gains	0.0	0.0	0.0	0.0	0.0	0.0	0.0	0.0	0.0	0.0
2000 Social security contributions	0.0	0.0	0.0	0.0	0.0	0.0	0.0	0.0	0.0	0.0
3000 Taxes on payroll and workforce	0.0	0.0	0.0	0.0	0.0	0.0	0.0	0.0	0.0	0.0
4000 Taxes on property	49.6	298.7	623.3	1 697.9	2 009.4	0.5	0.7	0.6	0.7	0.8
5000 Taxes on goods and services	55.0	322.5	854.8	2 051.4	2 325.9	0.5	0.8	0.8	0.9	0.9
6000 Other taxes	0.0	0.0	0.0	0.0	0.0	0.0	0.0	0.0	0.0	0.0
Social Security Funds										
Total tax revenue	92.8	344.0	1 122.6	2 303.6	2 036.9	0.9	0.8	1.0	1.0	0.8
1000 Taxes on income, profits and capital gains	0.0	0.0	0.0	0.0	0.0	0.0	0.0	0.0	0.0	0.0
2000 Social security contributions	92.8	344.0	1 122.6	2 303.6	2 036.9	0.9	0.8	1.0	1.0	0.8
3000 Taxes on payroll and workforce	0.0	0.0	0.0	0.0	0.0	0.0	0.0	0.0	0.0	0.0
4000 Taxes on property	0.0	0.0	0.0	0.0	0.0	0.0	0.0	0.0	0.0	0.0
5000 Taxes on goods and services	0.0	0.0	0.0	0.0	0.0	0.0	0.0	0.0	0.0	0.0
6000 Other taxes	0.0	0.0	0.0	0.0	0.0	0.0	0.0	0.0	0.0	0.0

.. Not available

Note: More detailed country data and country notes are available in Chapter 6 "Tax revenues by sub-sectors of general government". Full time series can be accessed at http://data-explorer.oecd.org/s/nb.

Source: Servicio de Impuestos internos (Chile's Tax Service).

Table 4.11. Colombia, tax revenue and % of GDP by selected tax category

	Billion COP					% of GDP				
	1990	2000	2010	2021	2022	1990	2000	2010	2021	2022
Total tax revenue	2 579.4	30 598.6	98 455.3	228 906.8	288 842.3	11.3	15.7	18.1	19.2	19.7
1000 Taxes on income, profits and capital gains	771.7	7 103.5	26 218.9	73 222.9	95 911.1	3.4	3.6	4.8	6.1	6.5
1100 Of individuals	47.2	1 499.3	5 192.4	15 825.3	20 356.5	0.2	0.8	1.0	1.3	1.4
1200 Corporate	359.8	5 119.8	20 405.2	54 442.5	73 300.9	1.6	2.6	3.8	4.6	5.0
1300 Unallocable between 1100 and 1200	364.7	484.4	621.3	2 955.1	2 253.7	1.6	0.2	0.1	0.2	0.2
2000 Social security contributions	203.6	4 989.0	11 478.1	21 674.0	23 908.5	0.9	2.6	2.1	1.8	1.6
2100 Employees	..	..	..	..	..	..	..	..	..	..
2200 Employers	..	..	..	..	..	..	..	..	..	..
2300 Self-employed or non-employed	..	..	..	..	..	..	..	..	..	..
2400 Unallocable between 2100, 2200 and 2300	203.6	4 989.0	11 478.1	21 674.0	23 908.5	0.9	2.6	2.1	1.8	1.6
3000 Taxes on payroll and workforce	0.0	1 286.8	4 022.5	3 927.1	4 422.0	0.0	0.7	0.7	0.3	0.3
4000 Taxes on property	56.2	2 027.7	8 535.2	20 652.6	22 525.1	0.2	1.0	1.6	1.7	1.5
4100 Recurrent taxes on immovable property	56.2	991.1	3 338.9	9 643.7	9 937.0	0.2	0.5	0.6	0.8	0.7
4200 Recurrent taxes on net wealth	0.0	0.0	1 970.5	1032.1	73.1	0.0	0.0	0.4	0.1	0.0
4300 Estate, inheritance and gift taxes	0.0	0.0	0.0	0.0	0.0	0.0	0.0	0.0	0.0	0.0
4400 Taxes on financial and capital transactions	0.0	1 036.6	3 225.8	9 831.2	12 281.8	0.0	0.5	0.6	0.8	0.8
4500 Non-recurrent taxes	0.0	0.0	0.0	0.0	0.0	0.0	0.0	0.0	0.0	0.0
4600 Other recurrent taxes on property	0.0	0.0	0.0	0.0	0.0	0.0	0.0	0.0	0.0	0.0
5000 Taxes on goods and services	1 388.7	14 180.5	44 411.6	99 258.0	129 331.9	6.1	7.3	8.2	8.3	8.8
5100 Taxes on production, sale, transfer, etc	1 388.7	14 048.7	44 038.1	97 214.9	127 046.4	6.1	7.2	8.1	8.2	8.6
5110 General taxes	672.4	9 585.9	33 333.8	80 093.9	105 084.1	3.0	4.9	6.1	6.7	7.1
5111 Value added taxes	583.1	8 445.8	28 811.7	69 883.4	91 723.3	2.6	4.3	5.3	5.9	6.2
5120 Taxes on specific goods and services	716.3	4 462.8	10 704.3	17 121.0	21 962.3	3.2	2.3	2.0	1.4	1.5
5121 Excises	404.7	2 718.7	6 052.3	12 906.4	15 703.7	1.8	1.4	1.1	1.1	1.1
5200 Taxes on use of goods and perform activities	0.0	131.8	373.6	2 043.1	2 285.6	0.0	0.1	0.1	0.2	0.2
5300 Unallocable between 5100 and 5200	0.0	0.0	0.0	0.0	0.0	0.0	0.0	0.0	0.0	0.0
6000 Other taxes	159.3	1 011.2	3 789.0	10 172.3	12 743.6	0.7	0.5	0.7	0.9	0.9
Non-wastable tax credits										
Non-wastable tax credits against 1000	..	..	..	..	..	..	..	..	..	..
Transfer component	..	..	..	..	..	..	..	..	..	..
Tax expenditure component	..	..	..	..	..	..	..	..	..	..

.. Not available

Note: More detailed country data and country notes are available in Chapter 5 "Detailed country tables". Full time series can be accessed at http://data-explorer.oecd.org/s/nb.

Source: Dirección de Impuestos y Aduanas Nacionales de Colombia, Ministerio de Hacienda y Crédito Público y Banco Central de Colombia. (National Tax and Customs Administration, Ministry of Finance and Public Credit and Central Bank of Colombia).

Table 4.12. Colombia, tax revenue and % of GDP by level of government and main taxes

	Billion COP					% of GDP				
	1990	2000	2010	2021	2022	1990	2000	2010	2021	2022
Federal or Central government										
Total tax revenue	1 885.9	21 016.3	71 304.3	166 725.8	217 075.6	8.3	10.8	13.1	14.0	14.8
1000 Taxes on income, profits and capital gains	771.7	7 103.5	26 218.9	73 222.9	95 911.1	3.4	3.6	4.8	6.1	6.5
2000 Social security contributions	0.0	0.0	0.0	0.0	0.0	0.0	0.0	0.0	0.0	0.0
3000 Taxes on payroll and workforce	0.0	1 286.8	4 022.5	3 927.1	4 422.0	0.0	0.7	0.7	0.3	0.3
4000 Taxes on property	0.0	1 036.6	5 196.3	11 008.8	12 588.1	0.0	0.5	1.0	0.9	0.9
5000 Taxes on goods and services	1 035.9	11 108.6	35 382.9	78 060.1	103 231.3	4.6	5.7	6.5	6.5	7.0
6000 Other taxes	78.3	480.8	483.8	506.9	923.1	0.3	0.2	0.1	0.0	0.1
State/Regional										
Total tax revenue	263.4	1723.2	4781.3	11699.6	13 871.0	1.2	0.9	0.9	1.0	0.9
1000 Taxes on income, profits and capital gains	0.0	0.0	0.0	0.0	0.0	0.0	0.0	0.0	0.0	0.0
2000 Social security contributions	0.0	0.0	0.0	0.0	0.0	0.0	0.0	0.0	0.0	0.0
3000 Taxes on payroll and workforce	0.0	0.0	0.0	0.0	0.0	0.0	0.0	0.0	0.0	0.0
4000 Taxes on property	0.0	0.0	0.0	0.0	0.0	0.0	0.0	0.0	0.0	0.0
5000 Taxes on goods and services	263.4	1 481.7	3 406.3	8 435.8	9 817.1	1.2	0.8	0.6	0.7	0.7
6000 Other taxes	0.0	241.5	1 375.0	3 263.7	4 053.9	0.0	0.1	0.3	0.3	0.3
Local government										
Total tax revenue	226.5	2 870.1	10 891.7	28 807.5	33 987.2	1.0	1.5	2.0	2.4	2.3
1000 Taxes on income, profits and capital gains	0.0	0.0	0.0	0.0	0.0	0.0	0.0	0.0	0.0	0.0
2000 Social security contributions	0.0	0.0	0.0	0.0	0.0	0.0	0.0	0.0	0.0	0.0
3000 Taxes on payroll and workforce	0.0	0.0	0.0	0.0	0.0	0.0	0.0	0.0	0.0	0.0
4000 Taxes on property	56.2	991.1	3 338.9	9 643.7	9 937.0	0.2	0.5	0.6	0.8	0.7
5000 Taxes on goods and services	89.3	1 590.1	5 622.5	12 762.1	16 283.6	0.4	0.8	1.0	1.1	1.1
6000 Other taxes	81.0	288.9	1 930.3	6 401.7	7 766.6	0.4	0.1	0.4	0.5	0.5
Social Security Funds										
Total tax revenue	203.6	4 989.0	11 478.1	21 674.0	23 908.5	0.9	2.6	2.1	1.8	1.6
1000 Taxes on income, profits and capital gains	0.0	0.0	0.0	0.0	0.0	0.0	0.0	0.0	0.0	0.0
2000 Social security contributions	203.6	4 989.0	11 478.1	21 674.0	23 908.5	0.9	2.6	2.1	1.8	1.6
3000 Taxes on payroll and workforce	0.0	0.0	0.0	0.0	0.0	0.0	0.0	0.0	0.0	0.0
4000 Taxes on property	0.0	0.0	0.0	0.0	0.0	0.0	0.0	0.0	0.0	0.0
5000 Taxes on goods and services	0.0	0.0	0.0	0.0	0.0	0.0	0.0	0.0	0.0	0.0
6000 Other taxes	0.0	0.0	0.0	0.0	0.0	0.0	0.0	0.0	0.0	0.0

Note: More detailed country data and country notes are available in Chapter 6 "Tax revenues by sub-sectors of general government". Full time series can be accessed at http://data-explorer.oecd.org/s/nb.

Source: Dirección de Impuestos y Aduanas Nacionales de Colombia, Ministerio de Hacienda y Crédito Público y Banco Central de Colombia. (National Tax and Customs Administration, Ministry of Finance and Public Credit and Central Bank of Colombia).

Table 4.13. Costa Rica, tax revenue and % of GDP by selected tax category

	Billion CRC					% of GDP				
	1990	2000	2010	2021	2022	1990	2000	2010	2021	2022
Total tax revenue	117.7	978.1	4 382.4	10 019.3	11 286.0	22.4	21.1	22.1	24.8	25.2
1000 Taxes on income, profits and capital gains	11.8	128.8	748.1	2 063.8	2 430.2	2.3	2.8	3.8	5.1	5.4
1100 Of individuals	..	..	202.8	622.8	691.3	..	..	1.0	1.5	1.5
1200 Corporate	..	..	450.3	970.5	1188.8	..	..	2.3	2.4	2.7
1300 Unallocable between 1100 and 1200	11.8	128.8	94.9	470.5	550.1	2.3	2.8	0.5	1.2	1.2
2000 Social security contributions	34.0	297.1	1 450.5	3 605.7	3 925.7	6.5	6.4	7.3	8.9	8.8
2100 Employees	..	..	..	..	..	..	..	..	..	..
2200 Employers	3.4	37.3	207.2	389.2	412.9	0.7	0.8	1.0	1.0	0.9
2300 Self-employed or non-employed	..	..	..	..	..	..	..	..	..	..
2400 Unallocable between 2100, 2200 and 2300	30.5	259.8	1 243.3	3 216.5	3 512.8	5.8	5.6	6.3	8.0	7.8
3000 Taxes on payroll and workforce	7.6	61.8	260.7	569.3	639.7	1.4	1.3	1.3	1.4	1.4
4000 Taxes on property	1.6	8.4	63.7	208.5	220.7	0.3	0.2	0.3	0.5	0.5
4100 Recurrent taxes on immovable property	1.2	5.4	49.0	150.3	154.9	0.2	0.1	0.2	0.4	0.3
4200 Recurrent taxes on net wealth	0.0	0.0	0.0	0.0	0.0	0.0	0.0	0.0	0.0	0.0
4300 Estate, inheritance and gift taxes	0.0	0.0	0.0	0.0	0.0	0.0	0.0	0.0	0.0	0.0
4400 Taxes on financial and capital transactions	0.4	3.0	14.7	58.2	65.8	0.1	0.1	0.1	0.1	0.1
4500 Non-recurrent taxes	0.0	0.0	0.0	0.0	0.0	0.0	0.0	0.0	0.0	0.0
4600 Other recurrent taxes on property	0.0	0.0	0.0	0.0	0.0	0.0	0.0	0.0	0.0	0.0
5000 Taxes on goods and services	53.5	456.9	1 766.9	3 488.5	3 674.7	10.2	9.9	8.9	8.7	8.2
5100 Taxes on production, sale, transfer, etc	49.9	425.7	1 600.3	3 150.4	3 330.8	9.5	9.2	8.1	7.8	7.4
5110 General taxes	21.3	222.8	920.3	2 065.6	2 217.7	4.1	4.8	4.6	5.1	4.9
5111 Value added taxes	21.3	222.8	920.3	2 040.0	2 193.2	4.1	4.8	4.6	5.1	4.9
5120 Taxes on specific goods and services	28.5	202.9	680.0	1084.8	1 113.0	5.4	4.4	3.4	2.7	2.5
5121 Excises	11.1	157.2	523.6	863.1	883.1	2.1	3.4	2.6	2.1	2.0
5200 Taxes on use of goods and perform activities	3.6	31.1	166.6	338.1	344.0	0.7	0.7	0.8	0.8	0.8
5300 Unallocable between 5100 and 5200	0.0	0.0	0.0	0.0	0.0	0.0	0.0	0.0	0.0	0.0
6000 Other taxes	9.3	25.2	92.5	83.3	394.9	1.8	0.5	0.5	0.2	0.9
Non-wastable tax credits										
Non-wastable tax credits against 1000	..	..	..	..	..	..	..	..	..	..
Transfer component	..	..	..	..	..	..	..	..	..	..
Tax expenditure component	..	..	..	..	..	..	..	..	..	..

.. Not available

Note: More detailed country data and country notes are available in Chapter 5 "Detailed country tables". Full time series can be accessed at http://data-explorer.oecd.org/s/nb.

Source: Secretaría Técnica de la Autoridad Presupuestaria, Ministerio de Finanzas y Contraloría General de la República (Technical Secretary of the Budgeting Authority, Ministry of Finance and National General Comptroller).

Table 4.14. Costa Rica, tax revenue and % of GDP by level of government and main taxes

	Billion CRC					% of GDP				
	1990	2000	2010	2021	2022	1990	2000	2010	2021	2022
Federal or Central government										
Total tax revenue	75.0	619.3	2 616.6	6 016.8	6 931.1	14.3	13.4	13.2	14.9	15.5
1000 Taxes on income, profits and capital gains	11.8	128.8	748.1	2 063.8	2 430.2	2.3	2.8	3.8	5.1	5.4
2000 Social security contributions	1.3	18.7	61.2	469.2	515.7	0.3	0.4	0.3	1.2	1.2
3000 Taxes on payroll and workforce	0.0	0.0	0.0	0.0	0.0	0.0	0.0	0.0	0.0	0.0
4000 Taxes on property	0.4	3.0	18.3	63.3	71.0	0.1	0.1	0.1	0.2	0.2
5000 Taxes on goods and services	52.2	444.9	1 696.6	3 337.3	3 519.5	9.9	9.6	8.6	8.3	7.9
6000 Other taxes	9.3	24.0	92.5	83.2	394.7	1.8	0.5	0.5	0.2	0.9
State/Regional										
Total tax revenue	..	..	..	..	..	..	..	..	..	..
1000 Taxes on income, profits and capital gains	..	..	..	..	..	..	..	..	..	..
2000 Social security contributions	..	..	..	..	..	..	..	..	..	..
3000 Taxes on payroll and workforce	..	..	..	..	..	..	..	..	..	..
4000 Taxes on property	..	..	..	..	..	..	..	..	..	..
5000 Taxes on goods and services	..	..	..	..	..	..	..	..	..	..
6000 Other taxes	..	..	..	..	..	..	..	..	..	..
Local government										
Total tax revenue	2.5	18.6	115.8	296.6	305.2	0.5	0.4	0.6	0.7	0.7
1000 Taxes on income, profits and capital gains	0.0	0.0	0.0	0.0	0.0	0.0	0.0	0.0	0.0	0.0
2000 Social security contributions	0.0	0.0	0.0	0.0	0.0	0.0	0.0	0.0	0.0	0.0
3000 Taxes on payroll and workforce	0.0	0.0	0.0	0.0	0.0	0.0	0.0	0.0	0.0	0.0
4000 Taxes on property	1.2	5.4	45.4	145.2	149.7	0.2	0.1	0.2	0.4	0.3
5000 Taxes on goods and services	1.3	12.0	70.3	151.3	155.2	0.2	0.3	0.4	0.4	0.3
6000 Other taxes	0.0	1.2	0.0	0.1	0.2	0.0	0.0	0.0	0.0	0.0
Social Security Funds										
Total tax revenue	40.2	340.2	1 650.0	3 705.9	4 049.7	7.7	7.4	8.3	9.2	9.0
1000 Taxes on income, profits and capital gains	0.0	0.0	0.0	0.0	0.0	0.0	0.0	0.0	0.0	0.0
2000 Social security contributions	32.6	278.4	1 389.3	3 136.5	3 410.0	6.2	6.0	7.0	7.8	7.6
3000 Taxes on payroll and workforce	7.6	61.8	260.7	569.3	639.7	1.4	1.3	1.3	1.4	1.4
4000 Taxes on property	0.0	0.0	0.0	0.0	0.0	0.0	0.0	0.0	0.0	0.0
5000 Taxes on goods and services	0.0	0.0	0.0	0.0	0.0	0.0	0.0	0.0	0.0	0.0
6000 Other taxes	0.0	0.0	0.0	0.0	0.0	0.0	0.0	0.0	0.0	0.0

.. Not available

Note: More detailed country data and country notes are available in Chapter 6 "Tax revenues by sub-sectors of general government". Full time series can be accessed at http://data-explorer.oecd.org/s/nb.

Source: Secretaría Técnica de la Autoridad Presupuestaria, Ministerio de Finanzas y Contraloría General de la República (Technical Secretary of the Budgeting Authority, Ministry of Finance and National General Comptroller).

Table 4.15. Czechia, tax revenue and % of GDP by selected tax category

	Billion CZK					% of GDP				
	1990	2000	2010	2021	2022	1990	2000	2010	2021	2022
Total tax revenue	..	771.6	1 286.9	2 122.8	2 339.6	..	32.2	31.9	33.7	33.2
1000 Taxes on income, profits and capital gains	..	175.8	259.9	441.1	515.4	..	7.3	6.4	7.0	7.3
1100 Of individuals	..	99.7	131.7	198.8	214.1	..	4.2	3.3	3.2	3.0
1200 Corporate	..	76.2	128.2	242.4	301.2	..	3.2	3.2	3.8	4.3
1300 Unallocable between 1100 and 1200	..	0.0	0.0	0.0	0.0	..	0.0	0.0	0.0	0.0
2000 Social security contributions	..	341.5	576.0	1004.8	1 074.2	..	14.2	14.3	15.9	15.2
2100 Employees	..	77.3	116.8	201.0	215.2	..	3.2	2.9	3.2	3.1
2200 Employers	..	220.2	363.1	618.3	661.3	..	9.2	9.0	9.8	9.4
2300 Self-employed or non-employed	..	0.0	0.0	0.0	0.0	..	0.0	0.0	0.0	0.0
2400 Unallocable between 2100, 2200 and 2300	..	0.0	0.0	0.0	0.0	..	0.0	0.0	0.0	0.0
3000 Taxes on payroll and workforce	..	0.0	0.0	0.0	0.0	..	0.0	0.0	0.0	0.0
4000 Taxes on property	..	10.9	16.4	11.9	12.5	..	0.5	0.4	0.2	0.2
4100 Recurrent taxes on immovable property	..	4.5	8.8	11.9	12.4	..	0.2	0.2	0.2	0.2
4200 Recurrent taxes on net wealth	..	0.0	0.0	0.0	0.0	..	0.0	0.0	0.0	0.0
4300 Estate, inheritance and gift taxes	..	0.6	0.2	0.0	0.0	..	0.0	0.0	0.0	0.0
4400 Taxes on financial and capital transactions	..	5.8	7.4	0.1	0.1	..	0.2	0.2	0.0	0.0
4500 Non-recurrent taxes	..	0.0	0.0	0.0	0.0	..	0.0	0.0	0.0	0.0
4600 Other recurrent taxes on property	..	0.0	0.0	0.0	0.0	..	0.0	0.0	0.0	0.0
5000 Taxes on goods and services	..	243.0	434.4	664.7	737.3	..	10.1	10.8	10.5	10.5
5100 Taxes on production, sale, transfer, etc	..	226.4	408.6	636.0	708.7	..	9.4	10.1	10.1	10.1
5110 General taxes	..	141.2	263.5	463.5	536.9	..	5.9	6.5	7.3	7.6
5111 Value added taxes	..	141.2	263.5	463.5	536.9	..	5.9	6.5	7.3	7.6
5120 Taxes on specific goods and services	..	85.1	145.2	172.5	171.8	..	3.5	3.6	2.7	2.4
5121 Excises	..	71.4	138.4	161.6	158.7	..	3.0	3.4	2.6	2.3
5200 Taxes on use of goods and perform activities	..	16.6	25.7	28.7	28.7	..	0.7	0.6	0.5	0.4
5300 Unallocable between 5100 and 5200	..	0.0	0.0	0.0	0.0	..	0.0	0.0	0.0	0.0
6000 Other taxes	..	0.4	0.1	0.2	0.2	..	0.0	0.0	0.0	0.0
Non-wastable tax credits										
Non-wastable tax credits against 1000	..	0.0	25.7	41.1	42.1	..	0.0	0.6	0.7	0.6
Transfer component	..	..	7.8	12.0	12.9	..	..	0.2	0.2	0.2
Tax expenditure component	..	..	17.9	29.2	29.2	..	..	0.4	0.5	0.4
Revenues collected on behalf of the EU										
Revenues collected on behalf of the EU, total	..	..	6.6	10.7	12.7	..	..	0.2	0.2	0.2
Customs duties	..	..	6.6	10.7	12.7	..	..	0.2	0.2	0.2
SRF contributions	..	..	..	..	..	..	..	..	..	..

.. Not available

Note: More detailed country data and country notes are available in Chapter 5 "Detailed country tables". Full time series can be accessed at http://data-explorer.oecd.org/s/nb.

Source: Ministry of Finance, Tax Analyses Department.

Table 4.16. Czechia, tax revenue and % of GDP by level of government and main taxes

	Billion CZK					% of GDP				
	1990	2000	2010	2021	2022	1990	2000	2010	2021	2022
Federal or Central government										
Total tax revenue	..	423.4	687.3	1 087.2	1 228.8	..	17.6	17.0	17.2	17.4
1000 Taxes on income, profits and capital gains	..	175.8	259.9	441.1	515.4	..	7.3	6.4	7.0	7.3
2000 Social security contributions	..	0.0	0.0	0.0	0.0	..	0.0	0.0	0.0	0.0
3000 Taxes on payroll and workforce	..	0.0	0.0	0.0	0.0	..	0.0	0.0	0.0	0.0
4000 Taxes on property	..	6.4	7.6	0.1	0.1	..	0.3	0.2	0.0	0.0
5000 Taxes on goods and services	..	241.0	419.6	645.8	713.1	..	10.0	10.4	10.2	10.1
6000 Other taxes	..	0.1	0.1	0.2	0.2	..	0.0	0.0	0.0	0.0
State/Regional										
Total tax revenue	..	..	..	..	..	..	..	..	..	..
1000 Taxes on income, profits and capital gains	..	..	..	..	..	..	..	..	..	..
2000 Social security contributions	..	..	..	..	..	..	..	..	..	..
3000 Taxes on payroll and workforce	..	..	..	..	..	..	..	..	..	..
4000 Taxes on property	..	..	..	..	..	..	..	..	..	..
5000 Taxes on goods and services	..	..	..	..	..	..	..	..	..	..
6000 Other taxes	..	..	..	..	..	..	..	..	..	..
Local government										
Total tax revenue	..	6.7	17.0	20.1	23.9	..	0.3	0.4	0.3	0.3
1000 Taxes on income, profits and capital gains	..	0.0	0.0	0.0	0.0	..	0.0	0.0	0.0	0.0
2000 Social security contributions	..	0.0	0.0	0.0	0.0	..	0.0	0.0	0.0	0.0
3000 Taxes on payroll and workforce	..	0.0	0.0	0.0	0.0	..	0.0	0.0	0.0	0.0
4000 Taxes on property	..	4.5	8.7	11.8	12.4	..	0.2	0.2	0.2	0.2
5000 Taxes on goods and services	..	2.0	8.2	8.3	11.5	..	0.1	0.2	0.1	0.2
6000 Other taxes	..	0.3	0.0	0.0	0.0	..	0.0	0.0	0.0	0.0
Social Security Funds										
Total tax revenue	..	341.5	576.0	1004.8	1 074.2	..	14.2	14.3	15.9	15.2
1000 Taxes on income, profits and capital gains	..	0.0	0.0	0.0	0.0	..	0.0	0.0	0.0	0.0
2000 Social security contributions	..	341.5	576.0	1004.8	1 074.2	..	14.2	14.3	15.9	15.2
3000 Taxes on payroll and workforce	..	0.0	0.0	0.0	0.0	..	0.0	0.0	0.0	0.0
4000 Taxes on property	..	0.0	0.0	0.0	0.0	..	0.0	0.0	0.0	0.0
5000 Taxes on goods and services	..	0.0	0.0	0.0	0.0	..	0.0	0.0	0.0	0.0
6000 Other taxes	..	0.0	0.0	0.0	0.0	..	0.0	0.0	0.0	0.0

.. Not available

Note: More detailed country data and country notes are available in Chapter 6 "Tax revenues by sub-sectors of general government". Full time series can be accessed at http://data-explorer.oecd.org/s/nb.

Source: Ministry of Finance, Tax Analyses Department.

Table 4.17. Denmark, tax revenue and % of GDP by selected tax category

	Billion DKK					% of GDP				
	1990	2000	2010	2021	2022	1990	2000	2010	2021	2022
Total tax revenue	381.1	620.5	812.1	1 213.1	1 192.7	44.6	46.8	44.8	47.2	41.9
1000 Taxes on income, profits and capital gains	232.7	380.8	501.0	805.4	770.7	27.2	28.7	27.6	31.4	27.1
1100 Of individuals	206.5	326.2	421.9	639.9	665.3	24.1	24.6	23.3	24.9	23.4
1200 Corporate	13.6	42.3	42.6	102.1	94.3	1.6	3.2	2.3	4.0	3.3
1300 Unallocable between 1100 and 1200	12.6	12.4	36.5	63.4	11.2	1.5	0.9	2.0	2.5	0.4
2000 Social security contributions	0.1	8.5	2.3	2.5	2.3	0.0	0.6	0.1	0.1	0.1
2100 Employees	0.1	8.2	0.9	0.7	0.7	0.0	0.6	0.0	0.0	0.0
2200 Employers	0.0	0.2	1.4	1.8	1.6	0.0	0.0	0.1	0.1	0.1
2300 Self-employed or non-employed	0.0	0.0	0.0	0.0	0.0	0.0	0.0	0.0	0.0	0.0
2400 Unallocable between 2100, 2200 and 2300	0.0	0.0	0.0	0.0	0.0	0.0	0.0	0.0	0.0	0.0
3000 Taxes on payroll and workforce	2.5	2.3	4.2	6.7	7.1	0.3	0.2	0.2	0.3	0.3
4000 Taxes on property	16.2	20.7	33.5	47.1	48.4	1.9	1.6	1.8	1.8	1.7
4100 Recurrent taxes on immovable property	8.9	13.6	24.2	32.4	33.1	1.0	1.0	1.3	1.3	1.2
4200 Recurrent taxes on net wealth	0.9	0.0	0.0	0.0	0.0	0.1	0.0	0.0	0.0	0.0
4300 Estate, inheritance and gift taxes	2.2	2.9	3.6	6.1	7.4	0.3	0.2	0.2	0.2	0.3
4400 Taxes on financial and capital transactions	4.2	4.2	5.7	8.6	8.0	0.5	0.3	0.3	0.3	0.3
4500 Non-recurrent taxes	0.0	0.0	0.0	0.0	0.0	0.0	0.0	0.0	0.0	0.0
4600 Other recurrent taxes on property	0.0	0.0	0.0	0.0	0.0	0.0	0.0	0.0	0.0	0.0
5000 Taxes on goods and services	129.5	207.8	270.9	350.2	362.7	15.1	15.7	14.9	13.6	12.8
5100 Taxes on production, sale, transfer, etc	123.5	196.9	251.3	326.4	338.6	14.4	14.9	13.9	12.7	11.9
5110 General taxes	80.5	120.9	169.0	243.8	262.1	9.4	9.1	9.3	9.5	9.2
5111 Value added taxes	72.0	120.9	169.0	243.8	262.1	8.4	9.1	9.3	9.5	9.2
5120 Taxes on specific goods and services	43.0	76.0	82.3	82.5	76.5	5.0	5.7	4.5	3.2	2.7
5121 Excises	38.4	68.8	73.6	73.8	66.7	4.5	5.2	4.1	2.9	2.3
5200 Taxes on use of goods and perform activities	4.4	7.5	14.7	13.8	13.5	0.5	0.6	0.8	0.5	0.5
5300 Unallocable between 5100 and 5200	1.6	3.4	4.9	10.0	10.6	0.2	0.3	0.3	0.4	0.4
6000 Other taxes	0.0	0.4	0.2	1.3	1.4	0.0	0.0	0.0	0.1	0.0
Non-wastable tax credits										
Non-wastable tax credits against 1000	..	..	5.0	3.0	2.3	..	..	0.3	0.1	0.1
Transfer component	..	..	0.2	0.2	0.1	..	..	0.0	0.0	0.0
Tax expenditure component	..	..	4.7	2.9	2.1	..	..	0.3	0.1	0.1
Revenues collected on behalf of the EU										
Revenues collected on behalf of the EU, total	2.7	2.6	3.3	3.7	4.6	0.3	0.2	0.2	0.1	0.2
Customs duties	0.0	2.3	3.2	3.7	4.6	0.0	0.2	0.2	0.1	0.2
SRF contributions	..	..	..	..	..	..	..	..	..	..

.. Not available

Note: More detailed country data and country notes are available in Chapter 5 "Detailed country tables". Full time series can be accessed at http://data-explorer.oecd.org/s/nb.

The total tax revenue has been reduced by the amount of any capital transfer that represents uncollected taxes. The capital transfers were subtracted directly from the specific taxes to which they relate. Therefore, the tax revenue amounts are different to those reported in the detailed country data available in Chapter 5 "Detailed country tables".

Source: Statistics Denmark.

Table 4.18. Denmark, tax revenue and % of GDP by level of government and main taxes

	Billion DKK					% of GDP				
	1990	2000	2010	2021	2022	1990	2000	2010	2021	2022
Federal or Central government										
Total tax revenue	260.6	419.1	590.6	897.6	871.9	30.5	31.6	32.6	35.0	30.7
1000 Taxes on income, profits and capital gains	123.8	202.7	307.9	526.7	488.1	14.5	15.3	17.0	20.5	17.2
2000 Social security contributions	0.1	1.4	1.4	1.7	1.8	0.0	0.1	0.1	0.1	0.1
3000 Taxes on payroll and workforce	2.5	2.3	4.2	6.7	7.1	0.3	0.2	0.2	0.3	0.3
4000 Taxes on property	7.4	7.2	9.4	14.7	15.4	0.9	0.5	0.5	0.6	0.5
5000 Taxes on goods and services	126.8	205.1	267.6	346.5	358.1	14.8	15.5	14.8	13.5	12.6
6000 Other taxes	0.0	0.4	0.2	1.3	1.4	0.0	0.0	0.0	0.1	0.0
State/Regional										
Total tax revenue	..	..	..	..	..	..	..	..	..	..
1000 Taxes on income, profits and capital gains	..	..	..	..	..	..	..	..	..	..
2000 Social security contributions	..	..	..	..	..	..	..	..	..	..
3000 Taxes on payroll and workforce	..	..	..	..	..	..	..	..	..	..
4000 Taxes on property	..	..	..	..	..	..	..	..	..	..
5000 Taxes on goods and services	..	..	..	..	..	..	..	..	..	..
6000 Other taxes	..	..	..	..	..	..	..	..	..	..
Local government										
Total tax revenue	117.8	191.7	217.3	311.1	315.7	13.8	14.5	12.0	12.1	11.1
1000 Taxes on income, profits and capital gains	108.9	178.1	193.1	278.6	282.6	12.7	13.4	10.7	10.9	9.9
2000 Social security contributions	0.0	0.0	0.0	0.0	0.0	0.0	0.0	0.0	0.0	0.0
3000 Taxes on payroll and workforce	0.0	0.0	0.0	0.0	0.0	0.0	0.0	0.0	0.0	0.0
4000 Taxes on property	8.9	13.6	24.2	32.4	33.1	1.0	1.0	1.3	1.3	1.2
5000 Taxes on goods and services	0.0	0.0	0.0	0.0	0.0	0.0	0.0	0.0	0.0	0.0
6000 Other taxes	0.0	0.0	0.0	0.0	0.0	0.0	0.0	0.0	0.0	0.0
Social Security Funds										
Total tax revenue	0.0	7.1	0.9	0.8	0.5	0.0	0.5	0.1	0.0	0.0
1000 Taxes on income, profits and capital gains	0.0	0.0	0.0	0.0	0.0	0.0	0.0	0.0	0.0	0.0
2000 Social security contributions	0.0	7.1	0.9	0.8	0.5	0.0	0.5	0.1	0.0	0.0
3000 Taxes on payroll and workforce	0.0	0.0	0.0	0.0	0.0	0.0	0.0	0.0	0.0	0.0
4000 Taxes on property	0.0	0.0	0.0	0.0	0.0	0.0	0.0	0.0	0.0	0.0
5000 Taxes on goods and services	0.0	0.0	0.0	0.0	0.0	0.0	0.0	0.0	0.0	0.0
6000 Other taxes	0.0	0.0	0.0	0.0	0.0	0.0	0.0	0.0	0.0	0.0

.. Not available

Note: More detailed country data and country notes are available in Chapter 6 "Tax revenues by sub-sectors of general government". Full time series can be accessed at http://data-explorer.oecd.org/s/nb.

The total tax revenue has been reduced by the amount of any capital transfer that represents uncollected taxes. The capital transfers were subtracted directly from the specific taxes to which they relate. Therefore, the tax revenue amounts are different to those reported in the detailed country data available in Chapter 6 "Tax revenues by sub-sectors of general government".

Source: Statistics Denmark.

Table 4.19. Estonia, tax revenue and % of GDP by selected tax category

	Billion EUR					% of GDP				
	1990	2000	2010	2021	2022	1990	2000	2010	2021	2022
Total tax revenue	..	1.9	4.9	10.5	11.9	..	31.1	33.2	33.5	32.6
1000 Taxes on income, profits and capital gains	..	0.5	1.0	2.6	2.9	..	7.7	6.6	8.4	7.9
1100 Of individuals	..	0.4	0.8	2.1	2.3	..	6.8	5.3	6.8	6.3
1200 Corporate	..	0.1	0.2	0.5	0.6	..	0.9	1.3	1.5	1.6
1300 Unallocable between 1100 and 1200	..	0.0	0.0	0.0	0.0	..	0.0	0.0	0.0	0.0
2000 Social security contributions	..	0.7	1.9	3.7	4.1	..	10.9	12.7	11.6	11.3
2100 Employees	..	0.0	0.1	0.2	0.2	..	0.0	0.8	0.5	0.5
2200 Employers	..	0.7	1.7	3.3	3.8	..	10.7	11.8	10.4	10.3
2300 Self-employed or non-employed	..	0.0	0.0	0.0	0.0	..	0.0	0.0	0.0	0.0
2400 Unallocable between 2100, 2200 and 2300	..	0.0	0.0	0.0	0.0	..	0.0	0.0	0.0	0.0
3000 Taxes on payroll and workforce	..	0.0	0.0	0.0	0.0	..	0.0	0.0	0.0	0.0
4000 Taxes on property	..	0.0	0.1	0.1	0.1	..	0.4	0.3	0.2	0.2
4100 Recurrent taxes on immovable property	..	0.0	0.1	0.1	0.1	..	0.4	0.3	0.2	0.2
4200 Recurrent taxes on net wealth	..	0.0	0.0	0.0	0.0	..	0.0	0.0	0.0	0.0
4300 Estate, inheritance and gift taxes	..	0.0	0.0	0.0	0.0	..	0.0	0.0	0.0	0.0
4400 Taxes on financial and capital transactions	..	0.0	0.0	0.0	0.0	..	0.0	0.0	0.0	0.0
4500 Non-recurrent taxes	..	0.0	0.0	0.0	0.0	..	0.0	0.0	0.0	0.0
4600 Other recurrent taxes on property	..	0.0	0.0	0.0	0.0	..	0.0	0.0	0.0	0.0
5000 Taxes on goods and services	..	0.7	2.0	4.2	4.8	..	12.1	13.5	13.3	13.2
5100 Taxes on production, sale, transfer, etc	..	0.7	1.9	4.0	4.5	..	11.7	13.1	12.7	12.3
5110 General taxes	..	0.5	1.3	2.9	3.3	..	8.4	8.6	9.1	9.1
5111 Value added taxes	..	0.5	1.3	2.9	3.3	..	8.4	8.5	9.1	9.1
5120 Taxes on specific goods and services	..	0.2	0.7	1.1	1.2	..	3.3	4.6	3.6	3.2
5121 Excises	..	0.2	0.6	1.0	1.0	..	3.0	4.2	3.1	2.7
5200 Taxes on use of goods and perform activities	..	0.0	0.1	0.2	0.3	..	0.4	0.4	0.6	0.9
5300 Unallocable between 5100 and 5200	..	0.0	0.0	0.0	0.0	..	0.0	0.0	0.0	0.0
6000 Other taxes	..	0.0	0.0	0.0	0.0	..	0.0	0.0	0.0	0.0
Non-wastable tax credits										
Non-wastable tax credits against 1000	..	..	..	..	..	..	..	..	..	..
Transfer component	..	..	..	..	..	..	..	..	..	..
Tax expenditure component	..	..	..	..	..	..	..	..	..	..
Revenues collected on behalf of the EU										
Revenues collected on behalf of the EU, total	..	..	0.0	0.1	0.1	..	..	0.2	0.2	0.3
Customs duties	..	..	0.0	0.1	0.1	..	..	0.2	0.2	0.2
SRF contributions	..	..	..	0.0	0.0	..	..	..	0.0	0.0

.. Not available

Note: More detailed country data and country notes are available in Chapter 5 "Detailed country tables". Full time series can be accessed at http://data-explorer.oecd.org/s/nb.

Source: Statistics Estonia.

Table 4.20. Estonia, tax revenue and % of GDP by level of government and main taxes

	Billion EUR					% of GDP				
	1990	2000	2010	2021	2022	1990	2000	2010	2021	2022
Federal or Central government										
Total tax revenue	..	1.6	3.9	8.7	9.8	..	26.3	26.7	27.5	26.9
1000 Taxes on income, profits and capital gains	..	0.5	1.0	2.6	2.9	..	7.7	6.6	8.4	7.9
2000 Social security contributions	..	0.4	1.0	1.9	2.2	..	6.6	6.8	6.1	6.1
3000 Taxes on payroll and workforce	..	0.0	0.0	0.0	0.0	..	0.0	0.0	0.0	0.0
4000 Taxes on property	..	0.0	0.0	0.0	0.0	..	0.0	0.0	0.0	0.0
5000 Taxes on goods and services	..	0.7	2.0	4.1	4.7	..	12.0	13.2	13.1	12.9
6000 Other taxes	..	0.0	0.0	0.0	0.0	..	0.0	0.0	0.0	0.0
State/Regional										
Total tax revenue	..	..	..	..	..	..	..	..	..	..
1000 Taxes on income, profits and capital gains	..	..	..	..	..	..	..	..	..	..
2000 Social security contributions	..	..	..	..	..	..	..	..	..	..
3000 Taxes on payroll and workforce	..	..	..	..	..	..	..	..	..	..
4000 Taxes on property	..	..	..	..	..	..	..	..	..	..
5000 Taxes on goods and services	..	..	..	..	..	..	..	..	..	..
6000 Other taxes	..	..	..	..	..	..	..	..	..	..
Local government										
Total tax revenue	..	0.0	0.1	0.1	0.1	..	0.5	0.5	0.2	0.2
1000 Taxes on income, profits and capital gains	..	0.0	0.0	0.0	0.0	..	0.0	0.0	0.0	0.0
2000 Social security contributions	..	0.0	0.0	0.0	0.0	..	0.0	0.0	0.0	0.0
3000 Taxes on payroll and workforce	..	0.0	0.0	0.0	0.0	..	0.0	0.0	0.0	0.0
4000 Taxes on property	..	0.0	0.1	0.1	0.1	..	0.4	0.3	0.2	0.2
5000 Taxes on goods and services	..	0.0	0.0	0.0	0.0	..	0.1	0.1	0.0	0.0
6000 Other taxes	..	0.0	0.0	0.0	0.0	..	0.0	0.0	0.0	0.0
Social Security Funds										
Total tax revenue	..	0.3	0.9	1.7	1.9	..	4.3	5.9	5.5	5.2
1000 Taxes on income, profits and capital gains	..	0.0	0.0	0.0	0.0	..	0.0	0.0	0.0	0.0
2000 Social security contributions	..	0.3	0.9	1.7	1.9	..	4.3	5.9	5.5	5.2
3000 Taxes on payroll and workforce	..	0.0	0.0	0.0	0.0	..	0.0	0.0	0.0	0.0
4000 Taxes on property	..	0.0	0.0	0.0	0.0	..	0.0	0.0	0.0	0.0
5000 Taxes on goods and services	..	0.0	0.0	0.0	0.0	..	0.0	0.0	0.0	0.0
6000 Other taxes	..	0.0	0.0	0.0	0.0	..	0.0	0.0	0.0	0.0

.. Not available

Note: More detailed country data and country notes are available in Chapter 6 "Tax revenues by sub-sectors of general government". Full time series can be accessed at http://data-explorer.oecd.org/s/nb.

Source: Statistics Estonia.

Table 4.21. Finland, tax revenue and % of GDP by selected tax category

	Billion EUR					% of GDP				
	1990	2000	2010	2021	2022	1990	2000	2010	2021	2022
Total tax revenue	39.1	62.4	76.3	108.3	115.6	42.9	45.8	40.6	43.2	43.2
1000 Taxes on income, profits and capital gains	15.3	26.9	27.1	39.1	42.7	16.8	19.7	14.4	15.6	15.9
1100 Of individuals	13.6	19.1	22.5	32.3	34.6	14.9	14.0	12.0	12.9	12.9
1200 Corporate	1.8	7.8	4.6	6.8	8.1	1.9	5.7	2.4	2.7	3.0
1300 Unallocable between 1100 and 1200	0.0	0.0	0.0	0.0	0.0	0.0	0.0	0.0	0.0	0.0
2000 Social security contributions	10.0	15.8	22.6	30.2	32.0	11.0	11.5	12.0	12.0	11.9
2100 Employees	1.2	2.9	4.7	9.1	9.6	1.3	2.1	2.5	3.6	3.6
2200 Employers	8.1	11.6	16.0	18.9	20.3	8.9	8.5	8.5	7.5	7.6
2300 Self-employed or non-employed	0.0	0.0	0.0	0.0	0.0	0.0	0.0	0.0	0.0	0.0
2400 Unallocable between 2100, 2200 and 2300	0.0	0.0	0.0	0.0	0.0	0.0	0.0	0.0	0.0	0.0
3000 Taxes on payroll and workforce	0.0	0.0	0.0	0.0	0.0	0.0	0.0	0.0	0.0	0.0
4000 Taxes on property	1.0	1.5	2.1	3.8	3.9	1.1	1.1	1.1	1.5	1.4
4100 Recurrent taxes on immovable property	0.1	0.6	1.2	2.0	2.0	0.1	0.4	0.6	0.8	0.8
4200 Recurrent taxes on net wealth	0.0	0.2	0.0	0.0	0.0	0.0	0.1	0.0	0.0	0.0
4300 Estate, inheritance and gift taxes	0.1	0.4	0.4	0.8	0.9	0.2	0.3	0.2	0.3	0.3
4400 Taxes on financial and capital transactions	0.7	0.4	0.5	1.0	0.9	0.8	0.3	0.3	0.4	0.3
4500 Non-recurrent taxes	0.0	0.0	0.0	0.0	0.0	0.0	0.0	0.0	0.0	0.0
4600 Other recurrent taxes on property	0.0	0.0	0.0	0.0	0.0	0.0	0.0	0.0	0.0	0.0
5000 Taxes on goods and services	12.7	18.2	24.4	35.1	37.0	14.0	13.4	13.0	14.0	13.8
5100 Taxes on production, sale, transfer, etc	12.6	17.8	23.6	33.7	35.3	13.8	13.0	12.6	13.4	13.2
5110 General taxes	7.5	10.9	15.5	23.6	25.1	8.3	8.0	8.3	9.4	9.4
5111 Value added taxes	7.5	10.9	15.5	23.6	25.1	8.3	8.0	8.3	9.4	9.4
5120 Taxes on specific goods and services	5.0	6.9	8.1	10.1	10.3	5.5	5.1	4.3	4.0	3.8
5121 Excises	3.8	5.6	6.3	7.8	7.9	4.2	4.1	3.3	3.1	2.9
5200 Taxes on use of goods and perform activities	0.2	0.4	0.8	1.4	1.7	0.2	0.3	0.4	0.6	0.6
5300 Unallocable between 5100 and 5200	0.0	0.0	0.0	0.0	0.0	0.0	0.0	0.0	0.0	0.0
6000 Other taxes	0.1	0.0	0.1	0.1	0.1	0.1	0.0	0.0	0.0	0.0
Non-wastable tax credits										
Non-wastable tax credits against 1000	..	..	..	..	..	..	..	..	..	..
Transfer component	..	..	..	..	..	..	..	..	..	..
Tax expenditure component	..	..	..	..	..	..	..	..	..	..
Revenues collected on behalf of the EU										
Revenues collected on behalf of the EU, total	..	0.1	0.2	0.5	0.6	..	0.1	0.1	0.2	0.2
Customs duties	..	0.1	0.2	0.2	0.3	..	0.1	0.1	0.1	0.1
SRF contributions	..	..	..	0.3	0.3	..	..	..	0.1	0.1

.. Not available

Note: More detailed country data and country notes are available in Chapter 5 "Detailed country tables". Full time series can be accessed at http://data-explorer.oecd.org/s/nb.

Source: Statistics Finland, basing on data from State Treasury, Tax Administration, Finnish Customs, Finnish Transport and Communication Agency, Financial Stability Authority and Financial Supervisory Authority. Supplementary information from unpublished sources.

Table 4.22. Finland, tax revenue and % of GDP by level of government and main taxes

	Billion EUR					% of GDP				
	1990	2000	2010	2021	2022	1990	2000	2010	2021	2022
Federal or Central government										
Total tax revenue	20.7	33.1	35.0	51.8	56.4	22.7	24.2	18.6	20.7	21.1
1000 Taxes on income, profits and capital gains	7.0	14.0	9.8	15.2	18.1	7.7	10.3	5.2	6.1	6.8
2000 Social security contributions	0.0	0.0	0.0	0.0	0.0	0.0	0.0	0.0	0.0	0.0
3000 Taxes on payroll and workforce	0.0	0.0	0.0	0.0	0.0	0.0	0.0	0.0	0.0	0.0
4000 Taxes on property	0.9	0.9	0.9	1.8	1.8	1.0	0.7	0.5	0.7	0.7
5000 Taxes on goods and services	12.7	18.1	24.3	34.6	36.4	14.0	13.2	12.9	13.8	13.6
6000 Other taxes	0.1	0.0	0.1	0.1	0.1	0.1	0.0	0.0	0.0	0.0
State/Regional										
Total tax revenue	..	..	..	..	..	..	..	..	..	..
1000 Taxes on income, profits and capital gains	..	..	..	..	..	..	..	..	..	..
2000 Social security contributions	..	..	..	..	..	..	..	..	..	..
3000 Taxes on payroll and workforce	..	..	..	..	..	..	..	..	..	..
4000 Taxes on property	..	..	..	..	..	..	..	..	..	..
5000 Taxes on goods and services	..	..	..	..	..	..	..	..	..	..
6000 Other taxes	..	..	..	..	..	..	..	..	..	..
Local government										
Total tax revenue	8.4	13.5	18.5	25.8	26.6	9.2	9.9	9.8	10.3	9.9
1000 Taxes on income, profits and capital gains	8.3	12.9	17.3	23.9	24.5	9.1	9.4	9.2	9.5	9.2
2000 Social security contributions	0.0	0.0	0.0	0.0	0.0	0.0	0.0	0.0	0.0	0.0
3000 Taxes on payroll and workforce	0.0	0.0	0.0	0.0	0.0	0.0	0.0	0.0	0.0	0.0
4000 Taxes on property	0.1	0.6	1.2	2.0	2.0	0.1	0.4	0.6	0.8	0.8
5000 Taxes on goods and services	0.0	0.0	0.0	0.0	0.0	0.0	0.0	0.0	0.0	0.0
6000 Other taxes	0.0	0.0	0.0	0.0	0.0	0.0	0.0	0.0	0.0	0.0
Social Security Funds										
Total tax revenue	10.0	15.8	22.6	30.2	32.0	11.0	11.5	12.0	12.0	11.9
1000 Taxes on income, profits and capital gains	0.0	0.0	0.0	0.0	0.0	0.0	0.0	0.0	0.0	0.0
2000 Social security contributions	10.0	15.8	22.6	30.2	32.0	11.0	11.5	12.0	12.0	11.9
3000 Taxes on payroll and workforce	0.0	0.0	0.0	0.0	0.0	0.0	0.0	0.0	0.0	0.0
4000 Taxes on property	0.0	0.0	0.0	0.0	0.0	0.0	0.0	0.0	0.0	0.0
5000 Taxes on goods and services	0.0	0.0	0.0	0.0	0.0	0.0	0.0	0.0	0.0	0.0
6000 Other taxes	0.0	0.0	0.0	0.0	0.0	0.0	0.0	0.0	0.0	0.0

.. Not available

Note: More detailed country data and country notes are available in Chapter 6 "Tax revenues by sub-sectors of general government". Full time series can be accessed at http://data-explorer.oecd.org/s/nb.

Source: Statistics Finland, basing on data from State Treasury, Tax Administration, Finnish Customs, Finnish Transport and Communication Agency, Financial Stability Authority and Financial Supervisory Authority. Supplementary information from unpublished sources.

Table 4.23. France, tax revenue and % of GDP by selected tax category

	Billion EUR					% of GDP				
	1990	2000	2010	2021	2022	1990	2000	2010	2021	2022
Total tax revenue	433.8	643.4	843.1	1 130.1	1 215.5	41.5	43.7	42.2	45.1	45.8
1000 Taxes on income, profits and capital gains	69.6	159.5	191.3	294.5	333.1	6.7	10.8	9.6	11.7	12.5
1100 Of individuals	46.3	116.3	150.8	234.3	257.5	4.4	7.9	7.6	9.3	9.7
1200 Corporate	23.1	43.1	40.5	60.2	75.5	2.2	2.9	2.0	2.4	2.8
1300 Unallocable between 1100 and 1200	0.3	0.0	0.0	0.0	0.0	0.0	0.0	0.0	0.0	0.0
2000 Social security contributions	191.1	230.2	319.8	369.2	393.3	18.3	15.6	16.0	14.7	14.8
2100 Employees	57.3	57.3	76.9	89.1	95.0	5.5	3.9	3.9	3.6	3.6
2200 Employers	118.1	158.3	217.3	251.6	266.5	11.3	10.7	10.9	10.0	10.0
2300 Self-employed or non-employed	0.0	0.0	0.0	0.0	0.0	0.0	0.0	0.0	0.0	0.0
2400 Unallocable between 2100, 2200 and 2300	0.0	0.0	0.0	0.0	0.0	0.0	0.0	0.0	0.0	0.0
3000 Taxes on payroll and workforce	8.3	16.1	28.4	47.1	51.9	0.8	1.1	1.4	1.9	2.0
4000 Taxes on property	27.4	44.1	70.8	97.5	98.3	2.6	3.0	3.5	3.9	3.7
4100 Recurrent taxes on immovable property	14.8	27.4	47.7	52.0	51.8	1.4	1.9	2.4	2.1	2.0
4200 Recurrent taxes on net wealth	2.6	2.4	4.4	2.0	2.3	0.3	0.2	0.2	0.1	0.1
4300 Estate, inheritance and gift taxes	4.1	6.9	7.7	19.0	19.0	0.4	0.5	0.4	0.8	0.7
4400 Taxes on financial and capital transactions	5.9	7.4	11.0	24.5	25.3	0.6	0.5	0.6	1.0	1.0
4500 Non-recurrent taxes	0.0	0.0	0.0	0.0	0.0	0.0	0.0	0.0	0.0	0.0
4600 Other recurrent taxes on property	0.0	0.0	0.0	0.0	0.0	0.0	0.0	0.0	0.0	0.0
5000 Taxes on goods and services	123.2	169.2	223.1	305.8	317.2	11.8	11.5	11.2	12.2	11.9
5100 Taxes on production, sale, transfer, etc	119.2	163.1	215.2	295.4	309.3	11.4	11.1	10.8	11.8	11.6
5110 General taxes	81.3	109.7	150.5	196.3	212.8	7.8	7.4	7.5	7.8	8.0
5111 Value added taxes	80.0	106.9	135.1	184.7	198.9	7.7	7.3	6.8	7.4	7.5
5120 Taxes on specific goods and services	37.9	53.4	64.7	99.1	96.5	3.6	3.6	3.2	4.0	3.6
5121 Excises	26.8	39.7	45.9	65.7	59.4	2.6	2.7	2.3	2.6	2.2
5200 Taxes on use of goods and perform activities	4.0	6.2	7.9	10.4	7.9	0.4	0.4	0.4	0.4	0.3
5300 Unallocable between 5100 and 5200	0.0	0.0	0.0	0.0	0.0	0.0	0.0	0.0	0.0	0.0
6000 Other taxes	14.1	24.4	9.7	16.1	21.8	1.3	1.7	0.5	0.6	0.8
Non-wastable tax credits										
Non-wastable tax credits against 1000	..	0.5	17.4	22.6	23.5	..	0.0	0.9	0.9	0.9
Transfer component	..	..	10.8	13.8	13.2	..	..	0.5	0.6	0.5
Tax expenditure component	..	..	6.6	8.8	10.3	..	..	0.3	0.4	0.4
Revenues collected on behalf of the EU										
Revenues collected on behalf of the EU, total	2.6	1.9	2.0	5.5	6.9	0.2	0.1	0.1	0.2	0.3
Customs duties	..	1.5	1.8	2.1	2.3	..	0.1	0.1	0.1	0.1
SRF contributions	..	..	..	3.3	4.7	..	..	..	0.1	0.2

.. Not available

Note: More detailed country data and country notes are available in Chapter 5 "Detailed country tables". Full time series can be accessed at http://data-explorer.oecd.org/s/nb.

The total tax revenue has been reduced by the amount of any capital transfer that represents uncollected taxes. The capital transfer has been allocated between tax headings in proportion to the reported tax revenue. Therefore, the tax revenue amounts are different to those reported in the detailed country data available in Chapter 5 "Detailed country tables".

Source: National accounts for France, Insee.

Table 4.24. France, tax revenue and % of GDP by level of government and main taxes

	Billion EUR					% of GDP				
	1990	2000	2010	2021	2022	1990	2000	2010	2021	2022
Federal or Central government										
Total tax revenue	200.1	271.4	303.1	348.0	377.4	19.2	18.4	15.2	13.9	14.2
1000 Taxes on income, profits and capital gains	69.6	94.8	99.6	157.8	183.6	6.7	6.4	5.0	6.3	6.9
2000 Social security contributions	3.2	5.4	7.6	8.0	7.8	0.3	0.4	0.4	0.3	0.3
3000 Taxes on payroll and workforce	6.2	11.6	5.4	13.9	15.7	0.6	0.8	0.3	0.6	0.6
4000 Taxes on property	8.6	11.4	13.4	30.0	27.8	0.8	0.8	0.7	1.2	1.0
5000 Taxes on goods and services	112.1	145.2	169.6	137.5	138.0	10.7	9.9	8.5	5.5	5.2
6000 Other taxes	0.4	3.1	7.4	0.8	4.4	0.0	0.2	0.4	0.0	0.2
State/Regional										
Total tax revenue	..	..	..	..	..	..	..	..	..	..
1000 Taxes on income, profits and capital gains	..	..	..	..	..	..	..	..	..	..
2000 Social security contributions	..	..	..	..	..	..	..	..	..	..
3000 Taxes on payroll and workforce	..	..	..	..	..	..	..	..	..	..
4000 Taxes on property	..	..	..	..	..	..	..	..	..	..
5000 Taxes on goods and services	..	..	..	..	..	..	..	..	..	..
6000 Other taxes	..	..	..	..	..	..	..	..	..	..
Local government										
Total tax revenue	40.2	64.7	89.2	163.7	174.6	3.9	4.4	4.5	6.5	6.6
1000 Taxes on income, profits and capital gains	0.0	0.0	0.1	0.0	0.0	0.0	0.0	0.0	0.0	0.0
2000 Social security contributions	0.0	0.0	0.0	0.0	0.0	0.0	0.0	0.0	0.0	0.0
3000 Taxes on payroll and workforce	1.7	3.9	7.5	9.7	10.5	0.2	0.3	0.4	0.4	0.4
4000 Taxes on property	18.8	32.7	57.4	67.4	70.5	1.8	2.2	2.9	2.7	2.7
5000 Taxes on goods and services	6.0	7.1	22.4	76.8	82.9	0.6	0.5	1.1	3.1	3.1
6000 Other taxes	13.7	21.0	1.9	9.8	10.6	1.3	1.4	0.1	0.4	0.4
Social Security Funds										
Total tax revenue	190.9	305.4	448.8	612.9	656.5	18.3	20.7	22.5	24.4	24.7
1000 Taxes on income, profits and capital gains	0.0	64.7	91.6	136.6	149.4	0.0	4.4	4.6	5.4	5.6
2000 Social security contributions	187.9	224.8	312.2	361.2	385.4	18.0	15.3	15.6	14.4	14.5
3000 Taxes on payroll and workforce	0.4	0.6	15.5	23.6	25.6	0.0	0.0	0.8	0.9	1.0
4000 Taxes on property	0.0	0.0	0.0	0.0	0.0	0.0	0.0	0.0	0.0	0.0
5000 Taxes on goods and services	2.5	15.0	29.0	86.1	89.3	0.2	1.0	1.5	3.4	3.4
6000 Other taxes	0.0	0.3	0.5	5.5	6.7	0.0	0.0	0.0	0.2	0.3

.. Not available

Note: More detailed country data and country notes are available in Chapter 6 "Tax revenues by sub-sectors of general government". Full time series can be accessed at http://data-explorer.oecd.org/s/nb.

The total tax revenue has been reduced by the amount of any capital transfer that represents uncollected taxes. The capital transfer has been allocated between tax headings in proportion to the reported tax revenue. Therefore, the tax revenue amounts are different to those reported in the detailed country data available in Chapter 6 "Tax revenues by sub-sectors of general government".

Source: National accounts for France, Insee.

Table 4.25. Germany, tax revenue and % of GDP by selected tax category

	Billion EUR					% of GDP				
	1990	2000	2010	2021	2022	1990	2000	2010	2021	2022
Total tax revenue	454.8	767.0	919.8	1 439.1	1 537.0	34.8	36.4	35.9	39.8	39.6
1000 Taxes on income, profits and capital gains	147.3	231.2	257.8	463.3	506.0	11.3	11.0	10.1	12.8	13.1
1100 Of individuals	125.3	194.2	219.4	379.1	413.4	9.6	9.2	8.6	10.5	10.7
1200 Corporate	22.0	37.1	38.4	84.2	92.6	1.7	1.8	1.5	2.3	2.4
1300 Unallocable between 1100 and 1200	0.0	0.0	0.0	0.0	0.0	0.0	0.0	0.0	0.0	0.0
2000 Social security contributions	170.4	299.4	354.3	534.4	567.1	13.0	14.2	13.8	14.8	14.6
2100 Employees	73.6	131.6	152.8	229.1	246.4	5.6	6.2	6.0	6.3	6.4
2200 Employers	86.7	147.4	165.5	253.5	266.7	6.6	7.0	6.5	7.0	6.9
2300 Self-employed or non-employed	0.0	0.0	0.0	0.0	0.0	0.0	0.0	0.0	0.0	0.0
2400 Unallocable between 2100, 2200 and 2300	0.0	0.0	0.0	0.0	0.0	0.0	0.0	0.0	0.0	0.0
3000 Taxes on payroll and workforce	0.0	0.0	0.0	0.0	0.0	0.0	0.0	0.0	0.0	0.0
4000 Taxes on property	15.3	17.5	21.0	44.8	43.2	1.2	0.8	0.8	1.2	1.1
4100 Recurrent taxes on immovable property	4.5	8.8	11.3	15.0	15.3	0.3	0.4	0.4	0.4	0.4
4200 Recurrent taxes on net wealth	6.2	0.4	0.0	1.8	1.6	0.5	0.0	0.0	0.0	0.0
4300 Estate, inheritance and gift taxes	1.5	3.0	4.4	9.8	9.2	0.1	0.1	0.2	0.3	0.2
4400 Taxes on financial and capital transactions	3.1	5.2	5.3	18.3	17.1	0.2	0.2	0.2	0.5	0.4
4500 Non-recurrent taxes	0.0	0.0	0.0	0.0	0.0	0.0	0.0	0.0	0.0	0.0
4600 Other recurrent taxes on property	0.0	0.0	0.0	0.0	0.0	0.0	0.0	0.0	0.0	0.0
5000 Taxes on goods and services	121.6	218.7	286.6	396.3	420.3	9.3	10.4	11.2	11.0	10.8
5100 Taxes on production, sale, transfer, etc	117.2	211.4	269.9	375.5	389.2	9.0	10.0	10.5	10.4	10.0
5110 General taxes	75.5	140.9	180.5	260.7	290.0	5.8	6.7	7.0	7.2	7.5
5111 Value added taxes	75.5	140.9	180.5	260.7	290.0	5.8	6.7	7.0	7.2	7.5
5120 Taxes on specific goods and services	41.7	70.6	89.0	114.6	98.9	3.2	3.3	3.5	3.2	2.6
5121 Excises	31.2	57.2	72.2	87.9	67.6	2.4	2.7	2.8	2.4	1.7
5200 Taxes on use of goods and perform activities	4.4	7.2	16.7	20.8	31.2	0.3	0.3	0.7	0.6	0.8
5300 Unallocable between 5100 and 5200	0.0	0.0	0.0	0.0	0.0	0.0	0.0	0.0	0.0	0.0
6000 Other taxes	0.2	0.2	0.1	0.3	0.4	0.0	0.0	0.0	0.0	0.0
Non-wastable tax credits										
Non-wastable tax credits against 1000	..	39.3	46.3	52.1	51.8	..	1.9	1.8	1.4	1.3
Transfer component	..	..	17.7	19.2	18.6	..	..	0.7	0.5	0.5
Tax expenditure component	..	..	28.6	32.9	33.2	..	..	1.1	0.9	0.9
Revenues collected on behalf of the EU										
Revenues collected on behalf of the EU, total	4.1	3.7	4.2	7.8	10.1	0.3	0.2	0.2	0.2	0.3
Customs duties	3.7	3.4	4.2	5.3	6.7	0.3	0.2	0.2	0.1	0.2
SRF contributions	..	..	..	2.5	3.4	..	..	..	0.1	0.1

.. Not available

Note: More detailed country data and country notes are available in Chapter 5 "Detailed country tables". Full time series can be accessed at http://data-explorer.oecd.org/s/nb.

Source: Finanzbericht, Bonn; Tax Statistics. Unpublished estimates by the Ministry of Finance.

Table 4.26. Germany, tax revenue and % of GDP by level of government and main taxes

	Billion EUR					% of GDP				
	1990	2000	2010	2021	2022	1990	2000	2010	2021	2022
Federal or Central government										
Total tax revenue	143.9	234.8	291.8	419.7	444.3	11.0	11.1	11.4	11.6	11.5
1000 Taxes on income, profits and capital gains	58.2	97.9	104.5	184.3	200.6	4.5	4.6	4.1	5.1	5.2
2000 Social security contributions	0.0	0.0	0.0	0.0	0.0	0.0	0.0	0.0	0.0	0.0
3000 Taxes on payroll and workforce	0.0	0.0	0.0	0.0	0.0	0.0	0.0	0.0	0.0	0.0
4000 Taxes on property	1.2	0.0	0.0	1.8	1.6	0.1	0.0	0.0	0.0	0.0
5000 Taxes on goods and services	84.6	136.9	187.3	233.6	242.1	6.5	6.5	7.3	6.5	6.2
6000 Other taxes	0.0	0.0	0.0	0.0	0.0	0.0	0.0	0.0	0.0	0.0
State/Regional										
Total tax revenue	97.8	172.1	199.4	352.0	379.4	7.5	8.2	7.8	9.7	9.8
1000 Taxes on income, profits and capital gains	58.2	88.9	97.6	177.6	192.8	4.5	4.2	3.8	4.9	5.0
2000 Social security contributions	0.0	0.0	0.0	0.0	0.0	0.0	0.0	0.0	0.0	0.0
3000 Taxes on payroll and workforce	0.0	0.0	0.0	0.0	0.0	0.0	0.0	0.0	0.0	0.0
4000 Taxes on property	7.0	8.5	11.0	29.6	27.9	0.5	0.4	0.4	0.8	0.7
5000 Taxes on goods and services	32.6	74.6	90.8	144.8	158.7	2.5	3.5	3.5	4.0	4.1
6000 Other taxes	0.0	0.0	0.0	0.0	0.0	0.0	0.0	0.0	0.0	0.0
Local government										
Total tax revenue	38.4	57.0	70.0	125.2	136.1	2.9	2.7	2.7	3.5	3.5
1000 Taxes on income, profits and capital gains	30.9	44.4	55.7	101.4	112.5	2.4	2.1	2.2	2.8	2.9
2000 Social security contributions	0.0	0.0	0.0	0.0	0.0	0.0	0.0	0.0	0.0	0.0
3000 Taxes on payroll and workforce	0.0	0.0	0.0	0.0	0.0	0.0	0.0	0.0	0.0	0.0
4000 Taxes on property	7.2	9.0	10.0	13.4	13.7	0.5	0.4	0.4	0.4	0.4
5000 Taxes on goods and services	0.3	3.4	4.3	10.1	9.5	0.0	0.2	0.2	0.3	0.2
6000 Other taxes	0.2	0.1	0.1	0.3	0.4	0.0	0.0	0.0	0.0	0.0
Social Security Funds										
Total tax revenue	170.4	299.4	354.3	534.4	567.1	13.0	14.2	13.8	14.8	14.6
1000 Taxes on income, profits and capital gains	0.0	0.0	0.0	0.0	0.0	0.0	0.0	0.0	0.0	0.0
2000 Social security contributions	170.4	299.4	354.3	534.4	567.1	13.0	14.2	13.8	14.8	14.6
3000 Taxes on payroll and workforce	0.0	0.0	0.0	0.0	0.0	0.0	0.0	0.0	0.0	0.0
4000 Taxes on property	0.0	0.0	0.0	0.0	0.0	0.0	0.0	0.0	0.0	0.0
5000 Taxes on goods and services	0.0	0.0	0.0	0.0	0.0	0.0	0.0	0.0	0.0	0.0
6000 Other taxes	0.0	0.0	0.0	0.0	0.0	0.0	0.0	0.0	0.0	0.0

Note: More detailed country data and country notes are available in Chapter 6 "Tax revenues by sub-sectors of general government". Full time series can be accessed at http://data-explorer.oecd.org/s/nb.

Source: Finanzbericht, Bonn; Tax Statistics. Unpublished estimates by the Ministry of Finance.

Table 4.27. Greece, tax revenue and % of GDP by selected tax category

	Billion EUR					% of GDP				
	1990	2000	2010	2021	2022	1990	2000	2010	2021	2022
Total tax revenue	11.5	47.2	72.4	72.7	85.2	25.2	33.4	32.3	40.0	41.2
1000 Taxes on income, profits and capital gains	2.3	12.7	16.0	15.2	17.5	5.0	9.0	7.1	8.4	8.5
1100 Of individuals	1.6	6.1	9.0	10.8	11.5	3.6	4.3	4.0	6.0	5.6
1200 Corporate	0.6	5.6	5.7	3.6	5.1	1.4	4.0	2.6	2.0	2.5
1300 Unallocable between 1100 and 1200	0.0	0.9	1.2	0.7	0.8	0.1	0.6	0.5	0.4	0.4
2000 Social security contributions	3.5	14.3	24.7	23.4	25.2	7.6	10.1	11.0	12.9	12.2
2100 Employees	1.7	7.6	13.3	12.2	13.6	3.8	5.4	5.9	6.7	6.6
2200 Employers	1.7	6.7	11.5	11.2	11.6	3.8	4.7	5.1	6.2	5.6
2300 Self-employed or non-employed	0.0	0.0	0.0	0.0	0.0	0.0	0.0	0.0	0.0	0.0
2400 Unallocable between 2100, 2200 and 2300	0.0	0.0	0.0	0.0	0.0	0.0	0.0	0.0	0.0	0.0
3000 Taxes on payroll and workforce	0.1	0.0	0.0	0.0	0.0	0.2	0.0	0.0	0.0	0.0
4000 Taxes on property	0.5	3.6	3.7	5.3	5.7	1.2	2.6	1.7	2.9	2.7
4100 Recurrent taxes on immovable property	0.0	0.4	0.6	3.2	3.2	0.0	0.3	0.2	1.8	1.5
4200 Recurrent taxes on net wealth	0.0	0.7	1.3	1.2	1.3	0.0	0.5	0.6	0.6	0.6
4300 Estate, inheritance and gift taxes	0.1	0.4	0.2	0.2	0.2	0.3	0.3	0.1	0.1	0.1
4400 Taxes on financial and capital transactions	0.4	2.0	1.1	0.7	0.9	0.8	1.4	0.5	0.4	0.5
4500 Non-recurrent taxes	0.0	0.0	0.0	0.0	0.0	0.0	0.0	0.0	0.0	0.0
4600 Other recurrent taxes on property	0.0	0.1	0.6	0.0	0.0	0.0	0.1	0.3	0.0	0.0
5000 Taxes on goods and services	5.1	16.6	28.0	28.8	36.8	11.2	11.8	12.5	15.9	17.8
5100 Taxes on production, sale, transfer, etc	4.9	14.8	25.5	24.6	32.2	10.7	10.5	11.4	13.5	15.6
5110 General taxes	3.0	9.2	16.5	15.3	18.9	6.7	6.5	7.4	8.4	9.1
5111 Value added taxes	2.8	8.9	16.0	15.2	18.6	6.2	6.3	7.1	8.4	9.0
5120 Taxes on specific goods and services	1.8	5.5	8.9	9.2	13.3	3.9	3.9	4.0	5.1	6.4
5121 Excises	1.4	4.1	7.6	7.5	7.8	3.0	2.9	3.4	4.1	3.8
5200 Taxes on use of goods and perform activities	0.2	1.3	1.7	3.6	4.0	0.5	0.9	0.8	2.0	1.9
5300 Unallocable between 5100 and 5200	0.0	0.5	0.8	0.7	0.7	0.0	0.4	0.4	0.4	0.3
6000 Other taxes	0.0	0.0	0.0	0.0	0.0	0.0	0.0	0.0	0.0	0.0
Non-wastable tax credits										
Non-wastable tax credits against 1000	..	..	..	..	..	..	..	..	..	..
Transfer component	..	..	..	..	..	..	..	..	..	..
Tax expenditure component	..	..	..	..	..	..	..	..	..	..
Revenues collected on behalf of the EU										
Revenues collected on behalf of the EU, total	0.1	0.2	0.3	0.4	0.6	0.2	0.2	0.1	0.2	0.3
Customs duties	0.1	0.2	0.3	0.3	0.4	0.2	0.1	0.1	0.2	0.2
SRF contributions	..	..	..	0.1	0.1	..	..	..	0.1	0.1

.. Not available

Note: More detailed country data and country notes are available in Chapter 5 "Detailed country tables". Full time series can be accessed at http://data-explorer.oecd.org/s/nb.

Source: Ministry of Finance, General Accounting Office, Directorate of General Government Budget in collaboration with the National Statistical Authority (ELSTAT).

Table 4.28. Greece, tax revenue and % of GDP by level of government and main taxes

	Billion EUR					% of GDP				
	1990	2000	2010	2021	2022	1990	2000	2010	2021	2022
Federal or Central government										
Total tax revenue	7.8	31.9	46.5	47.1	57.2	17.1	22.6	20.7	25.9	27.7
1000 Taxes on income, profits and capital gains	2.3	12.7	15.9	15.2	17.5	5.0	9.0	7.1	8.4	8.4
2000 Social security contributions	0.0	0.7	1.3	0.1	0.1	0.1	0.5	0.6	0.0	0.0
3000 Taxes on payroll and workforce	0.0	0.0	0.0	0.0	0.0	0.0	0.0	0.0	0.0	0.0
4000 Taxes on property	0.5	2.6	2.1	3.7	3.8	1.2	1.8	0.9	2.0	1.9
5000 Taxes on goods and services	4.9	16.0	27.1	28.2	35.9	10.9	11.3	12.1	15.5	17.4
6000 Other taxes	0.0	0.0	0.0	0.0	0.0	0.0	0.0	0.0	0.0	0.0
State/Regional										
Total tax revenue	..	..	..	..	..	..	..	..	..	..
1000 Taxes on income, profits and capital gains	..	..	..	..	..	..	..	..	..	..
2000 Social security contributions	..	..	..	..	..	..	..	..	..	..
3000 Taxes on payroll and workforce	..	..	..	..	..	..	..	..	..	..
4000 Taxes on property	..	..	..	..	..	..	..	..	..	..
5000 Taxes on goods and services	..	..	..	..	..	..	..	..	..	..
6000 Other taxes	..	..	..	..	..	..	..	..	..	..
Local government										
Total tax revenue	0.1	1.0	1.7	1.7	2.0	0.3	0.7	0.8	0.9	0.9
1000 Taxes on income, profits and capital gains	0.0	0.0	0.0	0.0	0.0	0.0	0.0	0.0	0.0	0.0
2000 Social security contributions	0.0	0.0	0.0	0.0	0.0	0.0	0.0	0.0	0.0	0.0
3000 Taxes on payroll and workforce	0.1	0.0	0.0	0.0	0.0	0.2	0.0	0.0	0.0	0.0
4000 Taxes on property	0.0	0.8	1.5	1.6	1.8	0.0	0.6	0.7	0.9	0.9
5000 Taxes on goods and services	0.1	0.2	0.2	0.1	0.1	0.1	0.1	0.1	0.1	0.1
6000 Other taxes	0.0	0.0	0.0	0.0	0.0	0.0	0.0	0.0	0.0	0.0
Social Security Funds										
Total tax revenue	3.4	14.1	24.0	23.5	25.4	7.5	10.0	10.7	13.0	12.3
1000 Taxes on income, profits and capital gains	0.0	0.0	0.0	0.0	0.0	0.0	0.0	0.0	0.0	0.0
2000 Social security contributions	3.4	13.6	23.4	23.4	25.1	7.5	9.6	10.5	12.9	12.2
3000 Taxes on payroll and workforce	0.0	0.0	0.0	0.0	0.0	0.0	0.0	0.0	0.0	0.0
4000 Taxes on property	0.0	0.2	0.1	0.0	0.0	0.0	0.1	0.1	0.0	0.0
5000 Taxes on goods and services	0.0	0.3	0.4	0.2	0.3	0.0	0.2	0.2	0.1	0.1
6000 Other taxes	0.0	0.0	0.0	0.0	0.0	0.0	0.0	0.0	0.0	0.0

.. Not available

Note: More detailed country data and country notes are available in Chapter 6 "Tax revenues by sub-sectors of general government". Full time series can be accessed at http://data-explorer.oecd.org/s/nb.

Source: Ministry of Finance, General Accounting Office, Directorate of General Government Budget in collaboration with the National Statistical Authority (ELSTAT).

Table 4.29. Hungary, tax revenue and % of GDP by selected tax category

	Billion HUF					% of GDP				
	1990	2000	2010	2021	2022	1990	2000	2010	2021	2022
Total tax revenue	..	5 132.6	10 121.7	18 646.4	23 181.3	..	38.5	36.8	33.8	35.1
1000 Taxes on income, profits and capital gains	..	1 247.4	2 093.8	3 011.8	4 618.4	..	9.4	7.6	5.5	7.0
1100 Of individuals	..	954.7	1 764.1	2 255.0	3 524.5	..	7.2	6.4	4.1	5.3
1200 Corporate	..	292.7	329.7	756.9	1093.9	..	2.2	1.2	1.4	1.7
1300 Unallocable between 1100 and 1200	..	0.0	0.0	0.0	0.0	..	0.0	0.0	0.0	0.0
2000 Social security contributions	..	1 506.8	3 179.5	5 781.5	6 481.8	..	11.3	11.6	10.5	9.8
2100 Employees	..	275.3	1 112.6	3 165.8	3 829.8	..	2.1	4.0	5.7	5.8
2200 Employers	..	1 213.2	2 043.8	2 585.7	2 619.4	..	9.1	7.4	4.7	4.0
2300 Self-employed or non-employed	..	0.0	0.0	0.0	0.0	..	0.0	0.0	0.0	0.0
2400 Unallocable between 2100, 2200 and 2300	..	17.4	23.2	30.0	32.7	..	0.1	0.1	0.1	0.0
3000 Taxes on payroll and workforce	..	183.4	113.7	598.8	472.4	..	1.4	0.4	1.1	0.7
4000 Taxes on property	..	89.0	312.1	482.7	531.9	..	0.7	1.1	0.9	0.8
4100 Recurrent taxes on immovable property	..	30.8	92.5	236.0	238.1	..	0.2	0.3	0.4	0.4
4200 Recurrent taxes on net wealth	..	0.0	135.7	52.3	66.7	..	0.0	0.5	0.1	0.1
4300 Estate, inheritance and gift taxes	..	5.5	6.3	9.1	11.4	..	0.0	0.0	0.0	0.0
4400 Taxes on financial and capital transactions	..	52.8	77.6	185.3	215.8	..	0.4	0.3	0.3	0.3
4500 Non-recurrent taxes	..	0.0	0.0	0.0	0.0	..	0.0	0.0	0.0	0.0
4600 Other recurrent taxes on property	..	0.0	0.0	0.0	0.0	..	0.0	0.0	0.0	0.0
5000 Taxes on goods and services	..	2 081.4	4 383.9	8 790.4	11 002.0	..	15.6	15.9	15.9	16.7
5100 Taxes on production, sale, transfer, etc	..	2 052.7	4 272.3	8 550.6	10 716.2	..	15.4	15.5	15.5	16.2
5110 General taxes	..	1 340.6	3 010.8	6 420.3	7 796.7	..	10.1	11.0	11.6	11.8
5111 Value added taxes	..	1 153.7	2 325.6	5 460.2	6 691.2	..	8.7	8.5	9.9	10.1
5120 Taxes on specific goods and services	..	712.1	1 261.5	2 130.4	2 919.5	..	5.3	4.6	3.9	4.4
5121 Excises	..	533.5	929.9	1 352.1	1 389.6	..	4.0	3.4	2.4	2.1
5200 Taxes on use of goods and perform activities	..	28.7	111.6	239.8	285.9	..	0.2	0.4	0.4	0.4
5300 Unallocable between 5100 and 5200	..	0.0	0.0	0.0	0.0	..	0.0	0.0	0.0	0.0
6000 Other taxes	..	24.5	38.7	-18.8	74.6	..	0.2	0.1	-0.0	0.1
Non-wastable tax credits										
Non-wastable tax credits against 1000	..	..	..	..	..	..	..	..	..	..
Transfer component	..	..	..	..	..	..	..	..	..	..
Tax expenditure component	..	..	..	..	..	..	..	..	..	..
Revenues collected on behalf of the EU										
Revenues collected on behalf of the EU, total	..	..	25.7	72.8	104.9	..	..	0.1	0.1	0.2
Customs duties	..	..	25.0	72.8	104.9	..	..	0.1	0.1	0.2
SRF contributions	..	..	..	..	..	..	..	..	..	..

.. Not available

Note: More detailed country data and country notes are available in Chapter 5 "Detailed country tables". Full time series can be accessed at http://data-explorer.oecd.org/s/nb.

Source: Ministry of Finance, Economic Department.

Table 4.30. Hungary, tax revenue and % of GDP by level of government and main taxes

	Billion HUF					% of GDP				
	1990	2000	2010	2021	2022	1990	2000	2010	2021	2022
Federal or Central government										
Total tax revenue	..	3 308.0	6 379.4	11 966.0	15 641.7	..	24.8	23.2	21.7	23.7
1000 Taxes on income, profits and capital gains	..	1 230.8	2 064.3	3 011.7	4 618.4	..	9.2	7.5	5.5	7.0
2000 Social security contributions	..	136.6	182.0	253.6	307.5	..	1.0	0.7	0.5	0.5
3000 Taxes on payroll and workforce	..	15.4	103.1	590.2	463.5	..	0.1	0.4	1.1	0.7
4000 Taxes on property	..	29.1	182.8	300.8	347.3	..	0.2	0.7	0.5	0.5
5000 Taxes on goods and services	..	1 878.6	3 808.5	7 834.9	9 841.0	..	14.1	13.9	14.2	14.9
6000 Other taxes	..	17.5	38.7	-25.2	64.0	..	0.1	0.1	-0.0	0.1
State/Regional										
Total tax revenue	..	..	..	..	..	..	..	..	..	..
1000 Taxes on income, profits and capital gains	..	..	..	..	..	..	..	..	..	..
2000 Social security contributions	..	..	..	..	..	..	..	..	..	..
3000 Taxes on payroll and workforce	..	..	..	..	..	..	..	..	..	..
4000 Taxes on property	..	..	..	..	..	..	..	..	..	..
5000 Taxes on goods and services	..	..	..	..	..	..	..	..	..	..
6000 Other taxes	..	..	..	..	..	..	..	..	..	..
Local government										
Total tax revenue	..	266.0	652.2	944.8	1092.6	..	2.0	2.4	1.7	1.7
1000 Taxes on income, profits and capital gains	..	2.2	0.1	0.0	0.0	..	0.0	0.0	0.0	0.0
2000 Social security contributions	..	0.0	0.0	0.0	0.0	..	0.0	0.0	0.0	0.0
3000 Taxes on payroll and workforce	..	1.2	1.2	0.0	0.0	..	0.0	0.0	0.0	0.0
4000 Taxes on property	..	59.9	129.3	181.8	184.6	..	0.4	0.5	0.3	0.3
5000 Taxes on goods and services	..	202.8	521.6	763.0	907.9	..	1.5	1.9	1.4	1.4
6000 Other taxes	..	0.0	0.0	0.0	0.0	..	0.0	0.0	0.0	0.0
Social Security Funds										
Total tax revenue	..	1 558.6	3 064.5	5 662.7	6 342.2	..	11.7	11.1	10.3	9.6
1000 Taxes on income, profits and capital gains	..	14.5	29.4	0.2	-0.0	..	0.1	0.1	0.0	-0.0
2000 Social security contributions	..	1 370.2	2 997.5	5 527.8	6 174.4	..	10.3	10.9	10.0	9.4
3000 Taxes on payroll and workforce	..	166.9	9.4	8.6	8.9	..	1.3	0.0	0.0	0.0
4000 Taxes on property	..	0.0	0.0	0.0	0.0	..	0.0	0.0	0.0	0.0
5000 Taxes on goods and services	..	0.0	28.1	119.8	148.3	..	0.0	0.1	0.2	0.2
6000 Other taxes	..	7.0	0.0	6.4	10.6	..	0.1	0.0	0.0	0.0

.. Not available

Note: More detailed country data and country notes are available in Chapter 6 "Tax revenues by sub-sectors of general government". Full time series can be accessed at http://data-explorer.oecd.org/s/nb.

Source: Ministry of Finance, Economic Department.

Table 4.31. Iceland, tax revenue and % of GDP by selected tax category

	Billion ISK					% of GDP				
	1990	2000	2010	2021	2022	1990	2000	2010	2021	2022
Total tax revenue	114.9	254.6	541.6	1 140.0	1 365.4	30.5	35.9	32.2	34.8	35.2
1000 Taxes on income, profits and capital gains	34.1	101.5	239.7	569.6	703.0	9.0	14.3	14.3	17.4	18.1
1100 Of individuals	30.9	88.5	197.3	471.9	545.1	8.2	12.5	11.7	14.4	14.0
1200 Corporate	3.2	8.4	14.6	65.5	100.9	0.8	1.2	0.9	2.0	2.6
1300 Unallocable between 1100 and 1200	0.0	4.6	27.7	32.3	56.9	0.0	0.7	1.7	1.0	1.5
2000 Social security contributions	3.6	19.7	63.6	97.4	115.6	1.0	2.8	3.8	3.0	3.0
2100 Employees	0.3	..	..	..	..	0.1	..	..	..	..
2200 Employers	3.3	..	..	..	..	0.9	..	..	..	..
2300 Self-employed or non-employed	0.0	..	..	..	..	0.0	..	..	..	..
2400 Unallocable between 2100, 2200 and 2300	0.0	19.7	63.6	97.4	115.6	0.0	2.8	3.8	3.0	3.0
3000 Taxes on payroll and workforce	4.1	0.2	2.8	9.2	10.0	1.1	0.0	0.2	0.3	0.3
4000 Taxes on property	9.7	16.8	35.4	67.8	76.2	2.6	2.4	2.1	2.1	2.0
4100 Recurrent taxes on immovable property	4.1	10.1	28.5	58.2	62.4	1.1	1.4	1.7	1.8	1.6
4200 Recurrent taxes on net wealth	2.4	5.2	3.8	0.0	0.0	0.6	0.7	0.2	0.0	0.0
4300 Estate, inheritance and gift taxes	0.2	0.8	2.6	8.4	12.2	0.1	0.1	0.2	0.3	0.3
4400 Taxes on financial and capital transactions	2.9	0.0	0.0	0.0	0.0	0.8	0.0	0.0	0.0	0.0
4500 Non-recurrent taxes	0.0	0.0	0.0	0.0	0.0	0.0	0.0	0.0	0.0	0.0
4600 Other recurrent taxes on property	0.0	0.7	0.3	0.6	0.8	0.0	0.1	0.0	0.0	0.0
5000 Taxes on goods and services	58.9	115.4	194.1	382.8	446.5	15.6	16.3	11.5	11.7	11.5
5100 Taxes on production, sale, transfer, etc	56.6	103.8	183.0	361.4	419.4	15.0	14.6	10.9	11.0	10.8
5110 General taxes	37.1	75.8	126.4	284.5	329.6	9.8	10.7	7.5	8.7	8.5
5111 Value added taxes	32.7	72.7	123.7	277.8	323.5	8.7	10.2	7.4	8.5	8.3
5120 Taxes on specific goods and services	19.5	28.0	56.6	76.8	89.9	5.2	3.9	3.4	2.3	2.3
5121 Excises	2.3	23.6	46.7	66.6	77.1	0.6	3.3	2.8	2.0	2.0
5200 Taxes on use of goods and perform activities	2.4	11.6	11.1	21.4	27.1	0.6	1.6	0.7	0.7	0.7
5300 Unallocable between 5100 and 5200	0.0	0.0	0.0	0.0	0.0	0.0	0.0	0.0	0.0	0.0
6000 Other taxes	4.5	1.0	6.0	13.3	14.2	1.2	0.1	0.4	0.4	0.4
Non-wastable tax credits										
Non-wastable tax credits against 1000	..	..	..	10.4	11.6	..	..	..	0.3	0.3
Transfer component	..	..	..	9.7	10.9	..	..	..	0.3	0.3
Tax expenditure component	..	..	..	0.7	0.7	..	..	..	0.0	0.0

.. Not available

Note: More detailed country data and country notes are available in Chapter 5 "Detailed country tables". Full time series can be accessed at http://data-explorer.oecd.org/s/nb.

Source: Statistics Iceland.

Table 4.32. Iceland, tax revenue and % of GDP by level of government and main taxes

	Billion ISK					% of GDP				
	1990	2000	2010	2021	2022	1990	2000	2010	2021	2022
Federal or Central government										
Total tax revenue	91.6	195.1	403.6	798.9	990.0	24.3	27.5	24.0	24.4	25.5
1000 Taxes on income, profits and capital gains	19.9	55.5	132.9	295.6	400.1	5.3	7.8	7.9	9.0	10.3
2000 Social security contributions	3.6	19.7	63.6	97.4	115.6	1.0	2.8	3.8	3.0	3.0
3000 Taxes on payroll and workforce	4.1	0.2	2.8	9.2	10.0	1.1	0.0	0.2	0.3	0.3
4000 Taxes on property	6.0	6.7	7.0	9.8	14.0	1.6	0.9	0.4	0.3	0.4
5000 Taxes on goods and services	57.7	112.0	191.3	373.6	436.1	15.3	15.8	11.4	11.4	11.2
6000 Other taxes	0.4	1.0	6.0	13.3	14.2	0.1	0.1	0.4	0.4	0.4
State/Regional										
Total tax revenue	..	..	..	..	..	..	..	..	..	..
1000 Taxes on income, profits and capital gains	..	..	..	..	..	..	..	..	..	..
2000 Social security contributions	..	..	..	..	..	..	..	..	..	..
3000 Taxes on payroll and workforce	..	..	..	..	..	..	..	..	..	..
4000 Taxes on property	..	..	..	..	..	..	..	..	..	..
5000 Taxes on goods and services	..	..	..	..	..	..	..	..	..	..
6000 Other taxes	..	..	..	..	..	..	..	..	..	..
Local government										
Total tax revenue	23.3	59.4	138.0	341.1	375.4	6.2	8.4	8.2	10.4	9.7
1000 Taxes on income, profits and capital gains	14.2	46.0	106.8	274.0	302.9	3.8	6.5	6.4	8.4	7.8
2000 Social security contributions	0.0	0.0	0.0	0.0	0.0	0.0	0.0	0.0	0.0	0.0
3000 Taxes on payroll and workforce	0.0	0.0	0.0	0.0	0.0	0.0	0.0	0.0	0.0	0.0
4000 Taxes on property	3.7	10.1	28.4	57.9	62.1	1.0	1.4	1.7	1.8	1.6
5000 Taxes on goods and services	1.2	3.3	2.8	9.1	10.4	0.3	0.5	0.2	0.3	0.3
6000 Other taxes	4.1	0.0	0.0	0.0	0.0	1.1	0.0	0.0	0.0	0.0
Social Security Funds										
Total tax revenue	0.0	0.0	0.0	0.0	0.0	0.0	0.0	0.0	0.0	0.0
1000 Taxes on income, profits and capital gains	0.0	0.0	0.0	0.0	0.0	0.0	0.0	0.0	0.0	0.0
2000 Social security contributions	0.0	0.0	0.0	0.0	0.0	0.0	0.0	0.0	0.0	0.0
3000 Taxes on payroll and workforce	0.0	0.0	0.0	0.0	0.0	0.0	0.0	0.0	0.0	0.0
4000 Taxes on property	0.0	0.0	0.0	0.0	0.0	0.0	0.0	0.0	0.0	0.0
5000 Taxes on goods and services	0.0	0.0	0.0	0.0	0.0	0.0	0.0	0.0	0.0	0.0
6000 Other taxes	0.0	0.0	0.0	0.0	0.0	0.0	0.0	0.0	0.0	0.0

.. Not available

Note: More detailed country data and country notes are available in Chapter 5 "Detailed country tables". Full time series can be accessed at http://data-explorer.oecd.org/s/nb.

Source: Statistics Iceland.

Table 4.33. Ireland, tax revenue and % of GDP by selected tax category

	Billion EUR					% of GDP				
	1990	2000	2010	2021	2022	1990	2000	2010	2021	2022
Total tax revenue	12.3	33.4	46.4	90.0	105.5	32.4	30.8	27.7	20.0	20.3
1000 Taxes on income, profits and capital gains	4.7	14.6	18.6	44.7	55.7	12.3	13.4	11.1	10.0	10.7
1100 Of individuals	4.1	10.6	14.7	29.4	33.0	10.7	9.8	8.8	6.5	6.3
1200 Corporate	0.6	3.9	3.9	15.3	22.6	1.6	3.6	2.4	3.4	4.3
1300 Unallocable between 1100 and 1200	0.0	0.0	0.0	0.0	0.0	0.0	0.0	0.0	0.0	0.0
2000 Social security contributions	1.7	4.0	8.5	13.8	16.0	4.6	3.7	5.1	3.1	3.1
2100 Employees	0.6	1.0	3.2	4.2	5.4	1.5	0.9	1.9	0.9	1.0
2200 Employers	1.1	2.8	4.9	8.9	9.9	2.9	2.6	2.9	2.0	1.9
2300 Self-employed or non-employed	0.0	0.0	0.0	0.0	0.0	0.0	0.0	0.0	0.0	0.0
2400 Unallocable between 2100, 2200 and 2300	0.0	0.0	0.0	0.0	0.0	0.0	0.0	0.0	0.0	0.0
3000 Taxes on payroll and workforce	0.2	0.0	0.3	0.8	1.0	0.4	0.0	0.2	0.2	0.2
4000 Taxes on property	0.6	1.9	2.4	4.8	5.0	1.5	1.8	1.4	1.1	1.0
4100 Recurrent taxes on immovable property	0.3	0.6	1.3	1.7	2.1	0.8	0.5	0.8	0.4	0.4
4200 Recurrent taxes on net wealth	0.0	0.0	0.0	0.0	0.0	0.0	0.0	0.0	0.0	0.0
4300 Estate, inheritance and gift taxes	0.0	0.2	0.2	0.6	0.6	0.1	0.2	0.1	0.1	0.1
4400 Taxes on financial and capital transactions	0.2	1.1	0.8	2.6	2.3	0.6	1.0	0.5	0.6	0.4
4500 Non-recurrent taxes	0.0	0.0	0.0	0.0	0.0	0.0	0.0	0.0	0.0	0.0
4600 Other recurrent taxes on property	0.0	0.0	0.0	0.0	0.0	0.0	0.0	0.0	0.0	0.0
5000 Taxes on goods and services	5.1	12.9	16.6	25.8	27.9	13.6	11.9	9.9	5.8	5.4
5100 Taxes on production, sale, transfer, etc	4.9	12.4	15.3	23.8	26.2	13.0	11.4	9.1	5.3	5.0
5110 General taxes	2.5	7.6	10.1	16.6	19.2	6.6	7.0	6.0	3.7	3.7
5111 Value added taxes	2.5	7.6	10.1	16.6	19.2	6.6	7.0	6.0	3.7	3.7
5120 Taxes on specific goods and services	2.4	4.7	5.3	7.2	7.0	6.4	4.4	3.1	1.6	1.3
5121 Excises	2.1	4.4	4.9	5.9	5.6	5.5	4.1	2.9	1.3	1.1
5200 Taxes on use of goods and perform activities	0.2	0.6	1.3	2.0	1.7	0.5	0.5	0.8	0.4	0.3
5300 Unallocable between 5100 and 5200	0.0	0.0	0.0	0.0	0.0	0.0	0.0	0.0	0.0	0.0
6000 Other taxes	0.0	0.0	0.0	0.0	0.0	0.0	0.0	0.0	0.0	0.0
Non-wastable tax credits										
Non-wastable tax credits against 1000	..	..	1.1	0.4	0.4	..	..	0.6	0.1	0.1
Transfer component	..	..	0.0	0.0	0.0	..	..	0.0	0.0	0.0
Tax expenditure component	..	..	1.1	0.4	0.4	..	..	0.6	0.1	0.1
Revenues collected on behalf of the EU										
Revenues collected on behalf of the EU, total	0.2	0.2	0.2	0.7	0.9	0.5	0.2	0.1	0.2	0.2
Customs duties	0.1	0.2	0.2	0.5	0.6	0.4	0.2	0.1	0.1	0.1
SRF contributions	..	..	..	0.2	0.3	..	..	..	0.0	0.0

.. Not available

Note: More detailed country data and country notes are available in Chapter 5 "Detailed country tables". Full time series can be accessed at http://data-explorer.oecd.org/s/nb.

Source: Annual Report of the Revenue Commissioners, Financial Accounts and National Income and Expenditure Accounts.

Table 4.34. Ireland, tax revenue and % of GDP by level of government and main taxes

	Billion EUR					% of GDP				
	1990	2000	2010	2021	2022	1990	2000	2010	2021	2022
Federal or Central government										
Total tax revenue	10.1	28.7	37.9	75.9	88.8	26.7	26.5	22.6	16.9	17.0
1000 Taxes on income, profits and capital gains	4.7	14.6	18.6	44.7	55.7	12.3	13.4	11.1	10.0	10.7
2000 Social security contributions	0.1	0.1	1.5	1.5	1.6	0.2	0.1	0.9	0.3	0.3
3000 Taxes on payroll and workforce	0.2	0.0	0.3	0.8	1.0	0.4	0.0	0.2	0.2	0.2
4000 Taxes on property	0.3	1.3	1.1	3.7	3.5	0.7	1.2	0.6	0.8	0.7
5000 Taxes on goods and services	5.0	12.7	16.4	25.1	27.0	13.1	11.7	9.8	5.6	5.2
6000 Other taxes	0.0	0.0	0.0	0.0	0.0	0.0	0.0	0.0	0.0	0.0
State/Regional										
Total tax revenue	..	..	..	..	..	..	..	..	..	..
1000 Taxes on income, profits and capital gains	..	..	..	..	..	..	..	..	..	..
2000 Social security contributions	..	..	..	..	..	..	..	..	..	..
3000 Taxes on payroll and workforce	..	..	..	..	..	..	..	..	..	..
4000 Taxes on property	..	..	..	..	..	..	..	..	..	..
5000 Taxes on goods and services	..	..	..	..	..	..	..	..	..	..
6000 Other taxes	..	..	..	..	..	..	..	..	..	..
Local government										
Total tax revenue	0.3	0.7	1.5	1.2	1.6	0.9	0.6	0.9	0.3	0.3
1000 Taxes on income, profits and capital gains	0.0	0.0	0.0	0.0	0.0	0.0	0.0	0.0	0.0	0.0
2000 Social security contributions	0.0	0.1	0.2	0.1	0.1	0.1	0.1	0.1	0.0	0.0
3000 Taxes on payroll and workforce	0.0	0.0	0.0	0.0	0.0	0.0	0.0	0.0	0.0	0.0
4000 Taxes on property	0.3	0.6	1.3	1.1	1.6	0.8	0.5	0.8	0.2	0.3
5000 Taxes on goods and services	0.0	0.0	0.0	0.0	0.0	0.0	0.0	0.0	0.0	0.0
6000 Other taxes	0.0	0.0	0.0	0.0	0.0	0.0	0.0	0.0	0.0	0.0
Social Security Funds										
Total tax revenue	1.6	3.8	6.7	12.2	14.2	4.3	3.5	4.0	2.7	2.7
1000 Taxes on income, profits and capital gains	0.0	0.0	0.0	0.0	0.0	0.0	0.0	0.0	0.0	0.0
2000 Social security contributions	1.6	3.8	6.7	12.2	14.2	4.3	3.5	4.0	2.7	2.7
3000 Taxes on payroll and workforce	0.0	0.0	0.0	0.0	0.0	0.0	0.0	0.0	0.0	0.0
4000 Taxes on property	0.0	0.0	0.0	0.0	0.0	0.0	0.0	0.0	0.0	0.0
5000 Taxes on goods and services	0.0	0.0	0.0	0.0	0.0	0.0	0.0	0.0	0.0	0.0
6000 Other taxes	0.0	0.0	0.0	0.0	0.0	0.0	0.0	0.0	0.0	0.0

.. Not available

Note: More detailed country data and country notes are available in Chapter 6 "Tax revenues by sub-sectors of general government". Full time series can be accessed at http://data-explorer.oecd.org/s/nb.

Source: Annual Report of the Revenue Commissioners, Financial Accounts and National Income and Expenditure Accounts.

Table 4.35. Israel, tax revenue and % of GDP by selected tax category

	Billion ILS					% of GDP				
	1990	2000	2010	2021	2022	1990	2000	2010	2021	2022
Total tax revenue	..	189.3	269.7	514.0	581.1	..	34.0	30.1	32.3	32.8
1000 Taxes on income, profits and capital gains	..	74.6	78.3	182.9	216.4	..	13.4	8.7	11.5	12.2
1100 Of individuals	..	54.8	48.2	113.2	127.9	..	9.8	5.4	7.1	7.2
1200 Corporate	..	18.0	23.1	56.5	76.2	..	3.2	2.6	3.5	4.3
1300 Unallocable between 1100 and 1200	..	1.8	6.9	13.2	12.3	..	0.3	0.8	0.8	0.7
2000 Social security contributions	..	27.6	45.3	79.6	88.8	..	5.0	5.1	5.0	5.0
2100 Employees	..	15.8	27.8	44.4	49.9	..	2.8	3.1	2.8	2.8
2200 Employers	..	8.2	11.4	24.7	27.8	..	1.5	1.3	1.6	1.6
2300 Self-employed or non-employed	..	0.0	0.0	0.0	0.0	..	0.0	0.0	0.0	0.0
2400 Unallocable between 2100, 2200 and 2300	..	0.0	0.0	0.0	0.0	..	0.0	0.0	0.0	0.0
3000 Taxes on payroll and workforce	..	6.8	10.3	16.1	16.3	..	1.2	1.1	1.0	0.9
4000 Taxes on property	..	18.0	30.0	62.0	71.4	..	3.2	3.4	3.9	4.0
4100 Recurrent taxes on immovable property	..	11.3	18.8	29.0	31.5	..	2.0	2.1	1.8	1.8
4200 Recurrent taxes on net wealth	..	0.0	0.0	0.0	0.0	..	0.0	0.0	0.0	0.0
4300 Estate, inheritance and gift taxes	..	0.0	0.0	0.0	0.0	..	0.0	0.0	0.0	0.0
4400 Taxes on financial and capital transactions	..	3.2	4.1	12.6	14.4	..	0.6	0.5	0.8	0.8
4500 Non-recurrent taxes	..	0.0	0.0	0.0	0.0	..	0.0	0.0	0.0	0.0
4600 Other recurrent taxes on property	..	0.0	0.0	0.0	0.0	..	0.0	0.0	0.0	0.0
5000 Taxes on goods and services	..	62.3	105.8	173.4	188.3	..	11.2	11.8	10.9	10.6
5100 Taxes on production, sale, transfer, etc	..	57.9	98.1	162.1	176.4	..	10.4	10.9	10.2	9.9
5110 General taxes	..	39.8	65.5	119.3	130.8	..	7.2	7.3	7.5	7.4
5111 Value added taxes	..	39.8	65.5	119.3	130.8	..	7.2	7.3	7.5	7.4
5120 Taxes on specific goods and services	..	18.1	32.6	42.8	45.6	..	3.2	3.6	2.7	2.6
5121 Excises	..	16.7	29.9	39.1	42.7	..	3.0	3.3	2.5	2.4
5200 Taxes on use of goods and perform activities	..	4.5	7.7	11.3	12.0	..	0.8	0.9	0.7	0.7
5300 Unallocable between 5100 and 5200	..	0.0	0.0	0.0	0.0	..	0.0	0.0	0.0	0.0
6000 Other taxes	..	0.0	0.0	0.0	0.0	..	0.0	0.0	0.0	0.0
Non-wastable tax credits										
Non-wastable tax credits against 1000	..	..	0.1	0.9	1.9	..	..	0.0	0.1	0.1
Transfer component	..	..	0.1	0.9	1.9	..	..	0.0	0.1	0.1
Tax expenditure component	..	..	0.0	0.0	0.0	..	..	0.0	0.0	0.0

.. Not available

Note: More detailed country data and country notes are available in Chapter 5 "Detailed country tables". Full time series can be accessed at http://data-explorer.oecd.org/s/nb.

Source: Israel Central Bureau of Statistics and Israel Ministry of Finance.

Table 4.36. Israel, tax revenue and % of GDP by level of government and main taxes

	Billion ILS					% of GDP				
	1990	2000	2010	2021	2022	1990	2000	2010	2021	2022
Federal or Central government										
Total tax revenue	..	148.0	199.9	391.6	444.6	..	26.6	22.3	24.6	25.1
1000 Taxes on income, profits and capital gains	..	74.6	78.3	182.9	216.4	..	13.4	8.7	11.5	12.2
2000 Social security contributions	..	0.0	0.0	0.0	0.0	..	0.0	0.0	0.0	0.0
3000 Taxes on payroll and workforce	..	6.8	10.3	16.1	16.3	..	1.2	1.1	1.0	0.9
4000 Taxes on property	..	4.8	6.6	20.8	25.3	..	0.9	0.7	1.3	1.4
5000 Taxes on goods and services	..	61.8	104.7	171.8	186.6	..	11.1	11.7	10.8	10.5
6000 Other taxes	..	0.0	0.0	0.0	0.0	..	0.0	0.0	0.0	0.0
State/Regional										
Total tax revenue	..	..	..	..	..	..	..	..	..	..
1000 Taxes on income, profits and capital gains	..	..	..	..	..	..	..	..	..	..
2000 Social security contributions	..	..	..	..	..	..	..	..	..	..
3000 Taxes on payroll and workforce	..	..	..	..	..	..	..	..	..	..
4000 Taxes on property	..	..	..	..	..	..	..	..	..	..
5000 Taxes on goods and services	..	..	..	..	..	..	..	..	..	..
6000 Other taxes	..	..	..	..	..	..	..	..	..	..
Local government										
Total tax revenue	..	13.7	24.5	42.8	47.8	..	2.5	2.7	2.7	2.7
1000 Taxes on income, profits and capital gains	..	0.0	0.0	0.0	0.0	..	0.0	0.0	0.0	0.0
2000 Social security contributions	..	0.0	0.0	0.0	0.0	..	0.0	0.0	0.0	0.0
3000 Taxes on payroll and workforce	..	0.0	0.0	0.0	0.0	..	0.0	0.0	0.0	0.0
4000 Taxes on property	..	13.2	23.5	41.2	46.0	..	2.4	2.6	2.6	2.6
5000 Taxes on goods and services	..	0.6	1.0	1.6	1.7	..	0.1	0.1	0.1	0.1
6000 Other taxes	..	0.0	0.0	0.0	0.0	..	0.0	0.0	0.0	0.0
Social Security Funds										
Total tax revenue	..	27.6	45.3	79.6	88.8	..	5.0	5.1	5.0	5.0
1000 Taxes on income, profits and capital gains	..	0.0	0.0	0.0	0.0	..	0.0	0.0	0.0	0.0
2000 Social security contributions	..	27.6	45.3	79.6	88.8	..	5.0	5.1	5.0	5.0
3000 Taxes on payroll and workforce	..	0.0	0.0	0.0	0.0	..	0.0	0.0	0.0	0.0
4000 Taxes on property	..	0.0	0.0	0.0	0.0	..	0.0	0.0	0.0	0.0
5000 Taxes on goods and services	..	0.0	0.0	0.0	0.0	..	0.0	0.0	0.0	0.0
6000 Other taxes	..	0.0	0.0	0.0	0.0	..	0.0	0.0	0.0	0.0

.. Not available

Note: More detailed country data and country notes are available in Chapter 6 "Tax revenues by sub-sectors of general government". Full time series can be accessed at http://data-explorer.oecd.org/s/nb.

Source: Israel Central Bureau of Statistics and Israel Ministry of Finance.

Table 4.37. Italy, tax revenue and % of GDP by selected tax category

	Billion EUR					% of GDP				
	1990	2000	2010	2021	2022	1990	2000	2010	2021	2022
Total tax revenue	265.1	503.1	671.9	773.6	840.8	36.3	40.5	41.7	42.5	42.8
1000 Taxes on income, profits and capital gains	96.7	166.9	219.5	246.1	275.7	13.2	13.4	13.6	13.5	14.0
1100 Of individuals	69.7	124.9	180.5	200.0	214.5	9.5	10.1	11.2	11.0	10.9
1200 Corporate	26.6	34.7	36.7	34.4	56.3	3.6	2.8	2.3	1.9	2.9
1300 Unallocable between 1100 and 1200	0.4	7.3	2.3	11.7	4.9	0.1	0.6	0.1	0.6	0.2
2000 Social security contributions	87.3	143.6	209.1	240.7	256.4	11.9	11.6	13.0	13.2	13.1
2100 Employees	16.8	27.3	37.6	45.6	47.0	2.3	2.2	2.3	2.5	2.4
2200 Employers	62.5	99.9	144.3	161.0	171.8	8.6	8.0	9.0	8.8	8.8
2300 Self-employed or non-employed	0.0	0.0	0.0	0.0	0.0	0.0	0.0	0.0	0.0	0.0
2400 Unallocable between 2100, 2200 and 2300	0.0	0.0	0.0	0.0	0.0	0.0	0.0	0.0	0.0	0.0
3000 Taxes on payroll and workforce	0.9	0.0	0.0	0.0	0.0	0.1	0.0	0.0	0.0	0.0
4000 Taxes on property	6.0	23.4	32.4	45.1	48.2	0.8	1.9	2.0	2.5	2.5
4100 Recurrent taxes on immovable property	0.0	9.4	9.7	22.4	22.7	0.0	0.8	0.6	1.2	1.2
4200 Recurrent taxes on net wealth	0.0	0.0	2.1	0.6	0.4	0.0	0.0	0.1	0.0	0.0
4300 Estate, inheritance and gift taxes	0.4	1.0	0.5	0.9	1.1	0.1	0.1	0.0	0.0	0.1
4400 Taxes on financial and capital transactions	5.6	12.3	17.4	19.6	21.2	0.8	1.0	1.1	1.1	1.1
4500 Non-recurrent taxes	0.0	0.0	0.0	0.0	0.0	0.0	0.0	0.0	0.0	0.0
4600 Other recurrent taxes on property	0.0	0.6	1.9	1.5	2.5	0.0	0.0	0.1	0.1	0.1
5000 Taxes on goods and services	74.3	141.9	178.9	219.1	232.5	10.2	11.4	11.1	12.0	11.8
5100 Taxes on production, sale, transfer, etc	67.1	127.3	160.8	189.6	201.8	9.2	10.3	10.0	10.4	10.3
5110 General taxes	38.9	77.5	97.6	121.3	138.9	5.3	6.2	6.1	6.7	7.1
5111 Value added taxes	38.9	77.5	97.6	121.0	138.5	5.3	6.2	6.1	6.6	7.1
5120 Taxes on specific goods and services	28.0	49.8	63.2	68.3	62.9	3.8	4.0	3.9	3.7	3.2
5121 Excises	20.3	31.5	36.4	42.4	32.1	2.8	2.5	2.3	2.3	1.6
5200 Taxes on use of goods and perform activities	4.5	8.5	10.5	15.3	16.0	0.6	0.7	0.7	0.8	0.8
5300 Unallocable between 5100 and 5200	2.7	6.1	7.6	14.2	14.7	0.4	0.5	0.5	0.8	0.7
6000 Other taxes	0.0	27.3	31.9	22.6	28.1	0.0	2.2	2.0	1.2	1.4
Non-wastable tax credits										
Non-wastable tax credits against 1000	..	..	0.0	14.4	6.6	..	..	0.0	0.8	0.3
Transfer component	..	..	0.1	2.1	2.1	..	..	0.0	0.1	0.1
Tax expenditure component	..	..	-0.1	12.3	4.5	..	..	-0.0	0.7	0.2
Revenues collected on behalf of the EU										
Revenues collected on behalf of the EU, total	1.3	1.5	2.2	3.5	5.1	0.2	0.1	0.1	0.2	0.3
Customs duties	0.8	1.5	2.2	2.4	3.7	0.1	0.1	0.1	0.1	0.2
SRF contributions	..	..	..	1.1	1.4	..	..	..	0.1	0.1

.. Not available

Note: More detailed country data and country notes are available in Chapter 5 "Detailed country tables". Full time series can be accessed at http://data-explorer.oecd.org/s/nb.

Source: Ministero dell'economia e delle finanze; Istituto nazionale di statistica.

Table 4.38. Italy, tax revenue and % of GDP by level of government and main taxes

	Billion EUR					% of GDP				
	1990	2000	2010	2021	2022	1990	2000	2010	2021	2022
Federal or Central government										
Total tax revenue	168.9	280.8	357.3	444.5	487.4	23.1	22.6	22.2	24.4	24.8
1000 Taxes on income, profits and capital gains	92.7	154.2	193.9	229.4	257.7	12.7	12.4	12.0	12.6	13.1
2000 Social security contributions	0.0	0.0	0.0	0.0	0.0	0.0	0.0	0.0	0.0	0.0
3000 Taxes on payroll and workforce	0.9	0.0	0.0	0.0	0.0	0.1	0.0	0.0	0.0	0.0
4000 Taxes on property	6.0	12.9	21.0	26.2	29.4	0.8	1.0	1.3	1.4	1.5
5000 Taxes on goods and services	69.3	113.6	142.5	188.8	200.3	9.5	9.2	8.8	10.4	10.2
6000 Other taxes	0.0	0.0	0.0	0.0	0.0	0.0	0.0	0.0	0.0	0.0
State/Regional										
Total tax revenue	..	..	..	..	..	..	..	..	..	..
1000 Taxes on income, profits and capital gains	..	..	..	..	..	..	..	..	..	..
2000 Social security contributions	..	..	..	..	..	..	..	..	..	..
3000 Taxes on payroll and workforce	..	..	..	..	..	..	..	..	..	..
4000 Taxes on property	..	..	..	..	..	..	..	..	..	..
5000 Taxes on goods and services	..	..	..	..	..	..	..	..	..	..
6000 Other taxes	..	..	..	..	..	..	..	..	..	..
Local government										
Total tax revenue	7.7	77.2	103.2	85.0	91.9	1.1	6.2	6.4	4.7	4.7
1000 Taxes on income, profits and capital gains	4.0	12.7	25.6	16.8	17.9	0.6	1.0	1.6	0.9	0.9
2000 Social security contributions	0.0	0.0	0.0	0.0	0.0	0.0	0.0	0.0	0.0	0.0
3000 Taxes on payroll and workforce	0.0	0.0	0.0	0.0	0.0	0.0	0.0	0.0	0.0	0.0
4000 Taxes on property	0.0	10.5	11.5	18.8	18.8	0.0	0.8	0.7	1.0	1.0
5000 Taxes on goods and services	3.7	26.7	34.2	26.7	27.0	0.5	2.1	2.1	1.5	1.4
6000 Other taxes	0.0	27.3	31.9	22.6	28.1	0.0	2.2	2.0	1.2	1.4
Social Security Funds										
Total tax revenue	87.3	143.6	209.1	240.7	256.4	11.9	11.6	13.0	13.2	13.1
1000 Taxes on income, profits and capital gains	0.0	0.0	0.0	0.0	0.0	0.0	0.0	0.0	0.0	0.0
2000 Social security contributions	87.3	143.6	209.1	240.7	256.4	11.9	11.6	13.0	13.2	13.1
3000 Taxes on payroll and workforce	0.0	0.0	0.0	0.0	0.0	0.0	0.0	0.0	0.0	0.0
4000 Taxes on property	0.0	0.0	0.0	0.0	0.0	0.0	0.0	0.0	0.0	0.0
5000 Taxes on goods and services	0.0	0.0	0.0	0.0	0.0	0.0	0.0	0.0	0.0	0.0
6000 Other taxes	0.0	0.0	0.0	0.0	0.0	0.0	0.0	0.0	0.0	0.0

.. Not available

Note: More detailed country data and country notes are available in Chapter 6 "Tax revenues by sub-sectors of general government". Full time series can be accessed at http://data-explorer.oecd.org/s/nb.

Source: Ministero dell'economia e delle finanze; Istituto nazionale di statistica.

Table 4.39. Japan, tax revenue and % of GDP by selected tax category

	Billion JPY					% of GDP				
	1990	2000	2010	2021	2022	1990	2000	2010	2021	2022
Total tax revenue	130 842.7	136 235.8	132 484.2	187 991.9	195 847.8	27.7	25.3	26.2	33.9	34.4
1000 Taxes on income, profits and capital gains	65 681.6	47 398.2	40 034.3	60 005.8	63 669.2	13.9	8.8	7.9	10.8	11.2
1100 Of individuals	36 393.6	28 677.3	24 662.7	35 439.0	36 835.4	7.7	5.3	4.9	6.4	6.5
1200 Corporate	29 288.0	18 720.9	15 371.6	24 566.8	26 833.8	6.2	3.5	3.0	4.4	4.7
1300 Unallocable between 1100 and 1200	0.0	0.0	0.0	0.0	0.0	0.0	0.0	0.0	0.0	0.0
2000 Social security contributions	34 612.6	47 968.3	54 460.5	73 701.9	75 458.0	7.3	8.9	10.8	13.3	13.3
2100 Employees	13 895.0	19 829.9	22 686.7	31 461.1	32 194.0	2.9	3.7	4.5	5.7	5.7
2200 Employers	16 648.8	22 455.5	24 689.1	34 310.8	35 265.4	3.5	4.2	4.9	6.2	6.2
2300 Self-employed or non-employed	0.0	0.0	0.0	0.0	0.0	0.0	0.0	0.0	0.0	0.0
2400 Unallocable between 2100, 2200 and 2300	0.0	0.0	0.0	0.0	0.0	0.0	0.0	0.0	0.0	0.0
3000 Taxes on payroll and workforce	0.0	0.0	0.0	0.0	0.0	0.0	0.0	0.0	0.0	0.0
4000 Taxes on property	12 296.3	14 294.4	12 878.3	14 778.6	15 414.4	2.6	2.7	2.6	2.7	2.7
4100 Recurrent taxes on immovable property	7 098.5	10 413.7	10 225.0	10 655.5	11 044.4	1.5	1.9	2.0	1.9	1.9
4200 Recurrent taxes on net wealth	0.0	0.0	0.0	0.0	0.0	0.0	0.0	0.0	0.0	0.0
4300 Estate, inheritance and gift taxes	1 918.0	1 782.2	1 250.4	2 770.2	2 969.4	0.4	0.3	0.2	0.5	0.5
4400 Taxes on financial and capital transactions	3 279.8	2 098.5	1 402.9	1 352.9	1 400.6	0.7	0.4	0.3	0.2	0.2
4500 Non-recurrent taxes	0.0	0.0	0.0	0.0	0.0	0.0	0.0	0.0	0.0	0.0
4600 Other recurrent taxes on property	0.0	0.0	0.0	0.0	0.0	0.0	0.0	0.0	0.0	0.0
5000 Taxes on goods and services	17 916.8	26 227.2	24 730.2	39 009.7	40 827.0	3.8	4.9	4.9	7.0	7.2
5100 Taxes on production, sale, transfer, etc	15 646.5	23 180.2	22 160.4	36 408.7	38 148.9	3.3	4.3	4.4	6.6	6.7
5110 General taxes	5 778.3	12 350.3	12 675.2	28 058.9	29 494.4	1.2	2.3	2.5	5.1	5.2
5111 Value added taxes	5 778.3	12 350.3	12 675.2	28 058.9	29 494.4	1.2	2.3	2.5	5.1	5.2
5120 Taxes on specific goods and services	9 868.2	10 829.9	9 485.2	8 349.9	8 654.5	2.1	2.0	1.9	1.5	1.5
5121 Excises	8 637.2	9 837.0	8 622.4	7 397.9	7 581.9	1.8	1.8	1.7	1.3	1.3
5200 Taxes on use of goods and perform activities	2 270.3	3 047.0	2 569.8	2 601.0	2 678.1	0.5	0.6	0.5	0.5	0.5
5300 Unallocable between 5100 and 5200	0.0	0.0	0.0	0.0	0.0	0.0	0.0	0.0	0.0	0.0
6000 Other taxes	335.4	347.7	381.1	495.9	479.2	0.1	0.1	0.1	0.1	0.1
Non-wastable tax credits										
Non-wastable tax credits against 1000	..	..	..	..	..	..	..	..	..	..
Transfer component	..	..	..	..	..	..	..	..	..	..
Tax expenditure component	..	..	..	..	..	..	..	..	..	..

.. Not available

Note: More detailed country data and country notes are available in Chapter 5 "Detailed country tables". Full time series can be accessed at http://data-explorer.oecd.org/s/nb.

Source: Tax Bureau, Ministry of Finance.

Table 4.40. Japan, tax revenue and % of GDP by level of government and main taxes

	Billion JPY					% of GDP				
	1990	2000	2010	2021	2022	1990	2000	2010	2021	2022
Federal or Central government										
Total tax revenue	62 779.7	52 720.8	43 707.4	71 881.1	76 337.7	13.3	9.8	8.7	13.0	13.4
1000 Taxes on income, profits and capital gains	44 379.1	30 536.2	23 372.1	39 184.7	41 988.7	9.4	5.7	4.6	7.1	7.4
2000 Social security contributions	0.0	0.0	0.0	0.0	0.0	0.0	0.0	0.0	0.0	0.0
3000 Taxes on payroll and workforce	0.0	0.0	0.0	0.0	0.0	0.0	0.0	0.0	0.0	0.0
4000 Taxes on property	4 601.6	3 314.9	2 274.5	3 731.1	3 951.5	1.0	0.6	0.5	0.7	0.7
5000 Taxes on goods and services	13 799.0	18 869.7	18 060.9	28 930.1	30 389.9	2.9	3.5	3.6	5.2	5.3
6000 Other taxes	0.0	0.0	0.0	35.2	7.6	0.0	0.0	0.0	0.0	0.0
State/Regional										
Total tax revenue	..	..	..	..	..	..	..	..	..	..
1000 Taxes on income, profits and capital gains	..	..	..	..	..	..	..	..	..	..
2000 Social security contributions	..	..	..	..	..	..	..	..	..	..
3000 Taxes on payroll and workforce	..	..	..	..	..	..	..	..	..	..
4000 Taxes on property	..	..	..	..	..	..	..	..	..	..
5000 Taxes on goods and services	..	..	..	..	..	..	..	..	..	..
6000 Other taxes	..	..	..	..	..	..	..	..	..	..
Local government										
Total tax revenue	33 450.4	35 546.7	34 316.3	42 408.9	44 052.2	7.1	6.6	6.8	7.6	7.7
1000 Taxes on income, profits and capital gains	21 302.5	16 862.0	16 662.2	20 821.1	21 680.5	4.5	3.1	3.3	3.8	3.8
2000 Social security contributions	0.0	0.0	0.0	0.0	0.0	0.0	0.0	0.0	0.0	0.0
3000 Taxes on payroll and workforce	0.0	0.0	0.0	0.0	0.0	0.0	0.0	0.0	0.0	0.0
4000 Taxes on property	7 694.7	10 979.5	10 603.8	11 047.5	11 462.9	1.6	2.0	2.1	2.0	2.0
5000 Taxes on goods and services	4 117.8	7 357.5	6 669.3	10 079.7	10 437.1	0.9	1.4	1.3	1.8	1.8
6000 Other taxes	335.4	347.7	381.1	460.7	471.6	0.1	0.1	0.1	0.1	0.1
Social Security Funds										
Total tax revenue	34 612.6	47 968.3	54 460.5	73 701.9	75 458.0	7.3	8.9	10.8	13.3	13.3
1000 Taxes on income, profits and capital gains	0.0	0.0	0.0	0.0	0.0	0.0	0.0	0.0	0.0	0.0
2000 Social security contributions	34 612.6	47 968.3	54 460.5	73 701.9	75 458.0	7.3	8.9	10.8	13.3	13.3
3000 Taxes on payroll and workforce	0.0	0.0	0.0	0.0	0.0	0.0	0.0	0.0	0.0	0.0
4000 Taxes on property	0.0	0.0	0.0	0.0	0.0	0.0	0.0	0.0	0.0	0.0
5000 Taxes on goods and services	0.0	0.0	0.0	0.0	0.0	0.0	0.0	0.0	0.0	0.0
6000 Other taxes	0.0	0.0	0.0	0.0	0.0	0.0	0.0	0.0	0.0	0.0

.. Not available

Note: More detailed country data and country notes are available in Chapter 6 "Tax revenues by sub-sectors of general government". Full time series can be accessed at http://data-explorer.oecd.org/s/nb.

Source: Tax Bureau, Ministry of Finance.

Table 4.41. Korea, tax revenue and % of GDP by selected tax category

	Billion KRW					% of GDP				
	1990	2000	2010	2021	2022	1990	2000	2010	2021	2022
Total tax revenue	37 261.7	136 295.0	295 968.0	619 084.0	691 257.0	18.6	20.9	22.4	29.8	32.0
1000 Taxes on income, profits and capital gains	12 203.5	39 254.0	82 905.0	205 574.0	258 193.0	6.1	6.0	6.3	9.9	11.9
1100 Of individuals	7 440.4	19 950.0	42 098.0	126 210.0	141 926.0	3.7	3.1	3.2	6.1	6.6
1200 Corporate	4 756.6	19 271.0	40 807.0	79 364.0	116 267.0	2.4	3.0	3.1	3.8	5.4
1300 Unallocable between 1100 and 1200	6.5	33.0	0.0	0.0	0.0	0.0	0.0	0.0	0.0	0.0
2000 Social security contributions	3 760.0	22 759.0	69 090.0	162 209.0	176 747.0	1.9	3.5	5.2	7.8	8.2
2100 Employees	1 464.0	8 578.0	28 213.0	70 297.0	77 530.0	0.7	1.3	2.1	3.4	3.6
2200 Employers	1 694.0	9 409.0	30 856.0	72 773.0	80 600.0	0.8	1.4	2.3	3.5	3.7
2300 Self-employed or non-employed	0.0	0.0	0.0	0.0	0.0	0.0	0.0	0.0	0.0	0.0
2400 Unallocable between 2100, 2200 and 2300	0.0	0.0	0.0	0.0	0.0	0.0	0.0	0.0	0.0	0.0
3000 Taxes on payroll and workforce	152.8	258.0	714.0	1 755.0	1 982.0	0.1	0.0	0.1	0.1	0.1
4000 Taxes on property	4 388.9	16 846.0	33 516.0	93 263.0	82 065.0	2.2	2.6	2.5	4.5	3.8
4100 Recurrent taxes on immovable property	980.0	3 385.0	9 270.0	24 486.0	26 510.0	0.5	0.5	0.7	1.2	1.2
4200 Recurrent taxes on net wealth	0.0	0.0	0.0	0.0	0.0	0.0	0.0	0.0	0.0	0.0
4300 Estate, inheritance and gift taxes	353.9	989.0	3 076.0	15 006.0	14 594.0	0.2	0.2	0.2	0.7	0.7
4400 Taxes on financial and capital transactions	2 959.7	11 935.0	21 170.0	53 771.0	40 961.0	1.5	1.8	1.6	2.6	1.9
4500 Non-recurrent taxes	0.0	0.0	0.0	0.0	0.0	0.0	0.0	0.0	0.0	0.0
4600 Other recurrent taxes on property	0.0	0.0	0.0	0.0	0.0	0.0	0.0	0.0	0.0	0.0
5000 Taxes on goods and services	16 497.5	52 271.0	99 769.0	143 100.0	156 778.0	8.2	8.0	7.5	6.9	7.3
5100 Taxes on production, sale, transfer, etc	16 023.5	50 023.0	96 573.0	134 745.0	149 448.0	8.0	7.7	7.3	6.5	6.9
5110 General taxes	6 964.4	23 212.0	51 800.0	89 022.0	105 558.0	3.5	3.6	3.9	4.3	4.9
5111 Value added taxes	6 964.4	23 212.0	51 800.0	89 022.0	105 558.0	3.5	3.6	3.9	4.3	4.9
5120 Taxes on specific goods and services	9 059.1	26 811.0	44 773.0	45 723.0	43 890.0	4.5	4.1	3.4	2.2	2.0
5121 Excises	4 923.7	18 155.0	31 340.0	35 792.0	30 834.0	2.5	2.8	2.4	1.7	1.4
5200 Taxes on use of goods and perform activities	473.9	2 248.0	3 196.0	8 355.0	7 330.0	0.2	0.3	0.2	0.4	0.3
5300 Unallocable between 5100 and 5200	0.0	0.0	0.0	0.0	0.0	0.0	0.0	0.0	0.0	0.0
6000 Other taxes	259.1	4 907.0	9 974.0	13 183.0	15 492.0	0.1	0.8	0.8	0.6	0.7
Non-wastable tax credits										
Non-wastable tax credits against 1000	..	..	..	..	..	..	..	..	..	..
Transfer component	..	..	..	..	..	..	..	..	..	..
Tax expenditure component	..	..	..	..	..	..	..	..	..	..

.. Not available

Note: More detailed country data and country notes are available in Chapter 5 "Detailed country tables". Full time series can be accessed at http://data-explorer.oecd.org/s/nb.

Source: Ministry of Finance and Economy, Ministry of Home Affairs.

Table 4.42. Korea, tax revenue and % of GDP by level of government and main taxes

	Billion KRW					% of GDP				
	1990	2000	2010	2021	2022	1990	2000	2010	2021	2022
Federal or Central government										
Total tax revenue	27 140.8	92 935.0	177 718.0	344 077.0	395 939.0	13.5	14.3	13.4	16.5	18.3
1000 Taxes on income, profits and capital gains	11 655.2	35 824.0	75 352.0	185 459.0	233 535.0	5.8	5.5	5.7	8.9	10.8
2000 Social security contributions	0.0	0.0	0.0	0.0	0.0	0.0	0.0	0.0	0.0	0.0
3000 Taxes on payroll and workforce	29.3	0.0	0.0	0.0	0.0	0.0	0.0	0.0	0.0	0.0
4000 Taxes on property	866.3	5 866.0	11 288.0	40 207.0	34 042.0	0.4	0.9	0.9	1.9	1.6
5000 Taxes on goods and services	14 377.5	46 812.0	86 629.0	113 264.0	121 046.0	7.2	7.2	6.5	5.4	5.6
6000 Other taxes	212.5	4 433.0	4 449.0	5 147.0	7 316.0	0.1	0.7	0.3	0.2	0.3
State/Regional										
Total tax revenue	..	..	..	..	..	..	..	..	..	..
1000 Taxes on income, profits and capital gains	..	..	..	..	..	..	..	..	..	..
2000 Social security contributions	..	..	..	..	..	..	..	..	..	..
3000 Taxes on payroll and workforce	..	..	..	..	..	..	..	..	..	..
4000 Taxes on property	..	..	..	..	..	..	..	..	..	..
5000 Taxes on goods and services	..	..	..	..	..	..	..	..	..	..
6000 Other taxes	..	..	..	..	..	..	..	..	..	..
Local government										
Total tax revenue	6 360.9	20 601.0	49 160.0	112 798.0	118 571.0	3.2	3.2	3.7	5.4	5.5
1000 Taxes on income, profits and capital gains	548.3	3 430.0	7 553.0	20 115.0	24 658.0	0.3	0.5	0.6	1.0	1.1
2000 Social security contributions	0.0	0.0	0.0	0.0	0.0	0.0	0.0	0.0	0.0	0.0
3000 Taxes on payroll and workforce	123.5	258.0	714.0	1 755.0	1 982.0	0.1	0.0	0.1	0.1	0.1
4000 Taxes on property	3 522.6	10 980.0	22 228.0	53 056.0	48 023.0	1.8	1.7	1.7	2.6	2.2
5000 Taxes on goods and services	2 120.0	5 459.0	13 140.0	29 836.0	35 732.0	1.1	0.8	1.0	1.4	1.7
6000 Other taxes	46.6	474.0	5 525.0	8 036.0	8 176.0	0.0	0.1	0.4	0.4	0.4
Social Security Funds										
Total tax revenue	3 760.0	22 759.0	69 090.0	162 209.0	176 747.0	1.9	3.5	5.2	7.8	8.2
1000 Taxes on income, profits and capital gains	0.0	0.0	0.0	0.0	0.0	0.0	0.0	0.0	0.0	0.0
2000 Social security contributions	3 760.0	22 759.0	69 090.0	162 209.0	176 747.0	1.9	3.5	5.2	7.8	8.2
3000 Taxes on payroll and workforce	0.0	0.0	0.0	0.0	0.0	0.0	0.0	0.0	0.0	0.0
4000 Taxes on property	0.0	0.0	0.0	0.0	0.0	0.0	0.0	0.0	0.0	0.0
5000 Taxes on goods and services	0.0	0.0	0.0	0.0	0.0	0.0	0.0	0.0	0.0	0.0
6000 Other taxes	0.0	0.0	0.0	0.0	0.0	0.0	0.0	0.0	0.0	0.0

.. Not available

Note: More detailed country data and country notes are available in Chapter 6 "Tax revenues by sub-sectors of general government". Full time series can be accessed at http://data-explorer.oecd.org/s/nb.

Source: Ministry of Finance and Economy, Ministry of Home Affairs.

Table 4.43. Latvia, tax revenue and % of GDP by selected tax category

	Billion EUR					% of GDP				
	1990	2000	2010	2021	2022	1990	2000	2010	2021	2022
Total tax revenue	..	2.0	5.2	10.3	11.8	..	29.0	28.5	30.7	30.8
1000 Taxes on income, profits and capital gains	..	0.5	1.3	2.3	2.7	..	7.0	7.1	6.9	6.9
1100 Of individuals	..	0.4	1.1	2.0	2.3	..	5.5	6.2	6.0	5.9
1200 Corporate	..	0.1	0.2	0.3	0.4	..	1.5	1.0	0.9	1.0
1300 Unallocable between 1100 and 1200	..	0.0	0.0	0.0	0.0	..	0.0	0.0	0.0	0.0
2000 Social security contributions	..	0.7	1.6	3.2	3.6	..	9.7	8.6	9.6	9.4
2100 Employees	..	0.2	0.4	1.0	1.2	..	2.4	2.2	3.1	3.1
2200 Employers	..	0.5	1.2	2.1	2.4	..	7.3	6.4	6.3	6.2
2300 Self-employed or non-employed	..	0.0	0.0	0.0	0.0	..	0.0	0.0	0.0	0.0
2400 Unallocable between 2100, 2200 and 2300	..	0.0	0.0	0.0	0.0	..	0.0	0.0	0.0	0.0
3000 Taxes on payroll and workforce	..	0.0	0.0	0.0	0.0	..	0.0	0.0	0.0	0.0
4000 Taxes on property	..	0.1	0.2	0.3	0.3	..	1.1	0.9	0.9	0.8
4100 Recurrent taxes on immovable property	..	0.1	0.1	0.2	0.2	..	0.9	0.7	0.7	0.6
4200 Recurrent taxes on net wealth	..	0.0	0.0	0.0	0.0	..	0.0	0.0	0.0	0.0
4300 Estate, inheritance and gift taxes	..	0.0	0.0	0.0	0.0	..	0.0	0.0	0.0	0.0
4400 Taxes on financial and capital transactions	..	0.0	0.0	0.0	0.0	..	0.2	0.1	0.1	0.1
4500 Non-recurrent taxes	..	0.0	0.0	0.0	0.0	..	0.0	0.0	0.0	0.0
4600 Other recurrent taxes on property	..	0.0	0.0	0.0	0.0	..	0.0	0.0	0.0	0.0
5000 Taxes on goods and services	..	0.8	2.2	4.5	5.2	..	11.2	11.9	13.4	13.7
5100 Taxes on production, sale, transfer, etc	..	0.7	2.0	4.2	5.0	..	10.8	11.2	12.7	12.9
5110 General taxes	..	0.5	1.3	3.0	3.7	..	6.9	7.2	9.0	9.5
5111 Value added taxes	..	0.5	1.2	2.9	3.6	..	6.9	6.6	8.6	9.5
5120 Taxes on specific goods and services	..	0.3	0.7	1.2	1.3	..	3.8	4.0	3.7	3.4
5121 Excises	..	0.2	0.7	1.1	1.1	..	3.4	3.6	3.3	3.0
5200 Taxes on use of goods and perform activities	..	0.0	0.1	0.2	0.3	..	0.5	0.7	0.7	0.7
5300 Unallocable between 5100 and 5200	..	0.0	0.0	0.0	0.0	..	0.0	0.0	0.0	0.0
6000 Other taxes	..	0.0	0.0	0.0	0.0	..	0.0	0.0	0.0	0.0
Non-wastable tax credits										
Non-wastable tax credits against 1000	..	..	..	..	..	..	..	..	..	..
Transfer component	..	..	..	..	..	..	..	..	..	..
Tax expenditure component	..	..	..	..	..	..	..	..	..	..
Revenues collected on behalf of the EU										
Revenues collected on behalf of the EU, total	..	..	0.0	0.1	0.1	..	..	0.1	0.2	0.2
Customs duties	..	..	0.0	0.1	0.1	..	..	0.1	0.2	0.2
SRF contributions	..	..	..	0.0	0.0	..	..	..	0.0	0.0

.. Not available

Note: More detailed country data and country notes are available in Chapter 5 "Detailed country tables". Full time series can be accessed at http://data-explorer.oecd.org/s/nb.

Source: Ministry of Finance.

Table 4.44. Latvia, tax revenue and % of GDP by level of government and main taxes

	Billion EUR					% of GDP				
	1990	2000	2010	2021	2022	1990	2000	2010	2021	2022
Federal or Central government										
Total tax revenue	..	1.0	2.5	5.3	6.3	..	14.4	14.1	15.9	16.4
1000 Taxes on income, profits and capital gains	..	0.2	0.4	0.8	1.0	..	3.1	2.2	2.3	2.5
2000 Social security contributions	..	0.0	0.0	0.1	0.1	..	0.0	0.0	0.3	0.3
3000 Taxes on payroll and workforce	..	0.0	0.0	0.0	0.0	..	0.0	0.0	0.0	0.0
4000 Taxes on property	..	0.0	0.0	0.1	0.1	..	0.2	0.2	0.2	0.1
5000 Taxes on goods and services	..	0.8	2.1	4.4	5.1	..	11.1	11.7	13.1	13.4
6000 Other taxes	..	0.0	0.0	0.0	0.0	..	0.0	0.0	0.0	0.0
State/Regional										
Total tax revenue	..	..	..	..	..	..	..	..	..	..
1000 Taxes on income, profits and capital gains	..	..	..	..	..	..	..	..	..	..
2000 Social security contributions	..	..	..	..	..	..	..	..	..	..
3000 Taxes on payroll and workforce	..	..	..	..	..	..	..	..	..	..
4000 Taxes on property	..	..	..	..	..	..	..	..	..	..
5000 Taxes on goods and services	..	..	..	..	..	..	..	..	..	..
6000 Other taxes	..	..	..	..	..	..	..	..	..	..
Local government										
Total tax revenue	..	0.3	1.0	1.8	1.9	..	4.9	5.7	5.3	5.1
1000 Taxes on income, profits and capital gains	..	0.3	0.9	1.5	1.7	..	3.9	4.9	4.6	4.4
2000 Social security contributions	..	0.0	0.0	0.0	0.0	..	0.0	0.0	0.0	0.0
3000 Taxes on payroll and workforce	..	0.0	0.0	0.0	0.0	..	0.0	0.0	0.0	0.0
4000 Taxes on property	..	0.1	0.1	0.2	0.2	..	0.9	0.7	0.7	0.6
5000 Taxes on goods and services	..	0.0	0.0	0.0	0.0	..	0.1	0.1	0.0	0.0
6000 Other taxes	..	0.0	0.0	0.0	0.0	..	0.0	0.0	0.0	0.0
Social Security Funds										
Total tax revenue	..	0.7	1.6	3.1	3.5	..	9.7	8.6	9.3	9.1
1000 Taxes on income, profits and capital gains	..	0.0	0.0	0.0	0.0	..	0.0	0.0	0.0	0.0
2000 Social security contributions	..	0.7	1.6	3.1	3.5	..	9.7	8.6	9.3	9.1
3000 Taxes on payroll and workforce	..	0.0	0.0	0.0	0.0	..	0.0	0.0	0.0	0.0
4000 Taxes on property	..	0.0	0.0	0.0	0.0	..	0.0	0.0	0.0	0.0
5000 Taxes on goods and services	..	0.0	0.0	0.0	0.0	..	0.0	0.0	0.0	0.0
6000 Other taxes	..	0.0	0.0	0.0	0.0	..	0.0	0.0	0.0	0.0

.. Not available

Note: More detailed country data and country notes are available in Chapter 6 "Tax revenues by sub-sectors of general government". Full time series can be accessed at http://data-explorer.oecd.org/s/nb.

Source: Ministry of Finance.

Table 4.45. Lithuania, tax revenue and % of GDP by selected tax category

	Billion EUR					% of GDP				
	1990	2000	2010	2021	2022	1990	2000	2010	2021	2022
Total tax revenue	..	4.1	7.9	18.0	21.3	..	30.8	28.3	31.9	31.6
1000 Taxes on income, profits and capital gains	..	1.1	1.3	5.4	6.7	..	8.3	4.6	9.5	9.9
1100 Of individuals	..	1.0	1.0	4.2	5.1	..	7.6	3.6	7.5	7.6
1200 Corporate	..	0.1	0.3	1.2	1.6	..	0.7	1.0	2.1	2.3
1300 Unallocable between 1100 and 1200	..	0.0	0.0	0.0	0.0	..	0.0	0.0	0.0	0.0
2000 Social security contributions	..	1.3	3.3	5.7	6.6	..	9.9	11.6	10.1	9.8
2100 Employees	..	0.1	0.6	4.3	5.1	..	0.8	2.2	7.7	7.5
2200 Employers	..	1.1	2.1	0.4	0.5	..	8.1	7.4	0.7	0.7
2300 Self-employed or non-employed	..	0.0	0.0	0.0	0.0	..	0.0	0.0	0.0	0.0
2400 Unallocable between 2100, 2200 and 2300	..	0.0	0.0	0.0	0.0	..	0.0	0.0	0.0	0.0
3000 Taxes on payroll and workforce	..	0.0	0.0	0.0	0.0	..	0.0	0.0	0.0	0.0
4000 Taxes on property	..	0.1	0.1	0.2	0.2	..	0.5	0.4	0.3	0.3
4100 Recurrent taxes on immovable property	..	0.1	0.1	0.2	0.2	..	0.5	0.4	0.3	0.3
4200 Recurrent taxes on net wealth	..	0.0	0.0	0.0	0.0	..	0.0	0.0	0.0	0.0
4300 Estate, inheritance and gift taxes	..	0.0	0.0	0.0	0.0	..	0.0	0.0	0.0	0.0
4400 Taxes on financial and capital transactions	..	0.0	0.0	0.0	0.0	..	0.0	0.0	0.0	0.0
4500 Non-recurrent taxes	..	0.0	0.0	0.0	0.0	..	0.0	0.0	0.0	0.0
4600 Other recurrent taxes on property	..	0.0	0.0	0.0	0.0	..	0.0	0.0	0.0	0.0
5000 Taxes on goods and services	..	1.6	3.3	6.8	7.8	..	12.1	11.7	12.0	11.5
5100 Taxes on production, sale, transfer, etc	..	1.6	3.2	6.6	7.6	..	11.7	11.4	11.7	11.3
5110 General taxes	..	1.1	2.2	4.7	5.7	..	8.1	7.8	8.4	8.4
5111 Value added taxes	..	1.0	2.2	4.7	5.6	..	7.5	7.8	8.3	8.4
5120 Taxes on specific goods and services	..	0.5	1.0	1.9	1.9	..	3.5	3.6	3.4	2.9
5121 Excises	..	0.4	0.9	1.7	1.7	..	3.2	3.2	3.0	2.5
5200 Taxes on use of goods and perform activities	..	0.1	0.1	0.1	0.2	..	0.5	0.3	0.2	0.2
5300 Unallocable between 5100 and 5200	..	0.0	0.0	0.0	0.0	..	0.0	0.0	0.0	0.0
6000 Other taxes	..	0.0	0.0	0.0	0.0	..	0.0	0.0	0.0	0.0
Non-wastable tax credits										
Non-wastable tax credits against 1000	..	..	..	..	..	..	..	..	..	..
Transfer component	..	..	..	..	..	..	..	..	..	..
Tax expenditure component	..	..	..	..	..	..	..	..	..	..
Revenues collected on behalf of the EU										
Revenues collected on behalf of the EU, total	..	..	0.1	0.2	0.2	..	..	0.2	0.3	0.3
Customs duties	..	..	0.1	0.2	0.2	..	..	0.2	0.3	0.3
SRF contributions	..	..	..	0.0	0.0	..	..	..	0.0	0.0

.. Not available

Note: More detailed country data and country notes are available in Chapter 5 "Detailed country tables". Full time series can be accessed at http://data-explorer.oecd.org/s/nb.

The total tax revenue has been reduced by the amount of any capital transfer that represents uncollected taxes. The capital transfers were subtracted directly from the specific taxes to which they relate. Therefore, the tax revenue amounts are different to those reported in the detailed country data available in Chapter 5 "Detailed country tables".

Source: Ministry of Finance.

Table 4.46. Lithuania, tax revenue and % of GDP by level of government and main taxes

	Billion EUR					% of GDP				
	1990	2000	2010	2021	2022	1990	2000	2010	2021	2022
Federal or Central government										
Total tax revenue	..	2.7	4.5	11.9	14.2	..	20.3	16.0	21.1	21.1
1000 Taxes on income, profits and capital gains	..	1.1	1.3	5.4	6.7	..	8.3	4.6	9.5	9.9
2000 Social security contributions	..	0.0	0.0	0.0	0.0	..	0.0	0.0	0.0	0.0
3000 Taxes on payroll and workforce	..	0.0	0.0	0.0	0.0	..	0.0	0.0	0.0	0.0
4000 Taxes on property	..	0.0	0.0	0.0	0.0	..	0.0	0.0	0.0	0.0
5000 Taxes on goods and services	..	1.6	3.2	6.5	7.5	..	12.0	11.4	11.6	11.2
6000 Other taxes	..	0.0	0.0	0.0	0.0	..	0.0	0.0	0.0	0.0
State/Regional										
Total tax revenue	..	..	..	..	..	..	..	..	..	..
1000 Taxes on income, profits and capital gains	..	..	..	..	..	..	..	..	..	..
2000 Social security contributions	..	..	..	..	..	..	..	..	..	..
3000 Taxes on payroll and workforce	..	..	..	..	..	..	..	..	..	..
4000 Taxes on property	..	..	..	..	..	..	..	..	..	..
5000 Taxes on goods and services	..	..	..	..	..	..	..	..	..	..
6000 Other taxes	..	..	..	..	..	..	..	..	..	..
Local government										
Total tax revenue	..	0.1	0.1	0.2	0.2	..	0.6	0.5	0.3	0.3
1000 Taxes on income, profits and capital gains	..	0.0	0.0	0.0	0.0	..	0.0	0.0	0.0	0.0
2000 Social security contributions	..	0.0	0.0	0.0	0.0	..	0.0	0.0	0.0	0.0
3000 Taxes on payroll and workforce	..	0.0	0.0	0.0	0.0	..	0.0	0.0	0.0	0.0
4000 Taxes on property	..	0.1	0.1	0.2	0.2	..	0.5	0.4	0.3	0.3
5000 Taxes on goods and services	..	0.0	0.0	0.0	0.0	..	0.1	0.1	0.1	0.1
6000 Other taxes	..	0.0	0.0	0.0	0.0	..	0.0	0.0	0.0	0.0
Social Security Funds										
Total tax revenue	..	1.3	3.3	5.7	6.6	..	9.9	11.6	10.1	9.8
1000 Taxes on income, profits and capital gains	..	0.0	0.0	0.0	0.0	..	0.0	0.0	0.0	0.0
2000 Social security contributions	..	1.3	3.3	5.7	6.6	..	9.9	11.6	10.1	9.8
3000 Taxes on payroll and workforce	..	0.0	0.0	0.0	0.0	..	0.0	0.0	0.0	0.0
4000 Taxes on property	..	0.0	0.0	0.0	0.0	..	0.0	0.0	0.0	0.0
5000 Taxes on goods and services	..	0.0	0.0	0.0	0.0	..	0.0	0.0	0.0	0.0
6000 Other taxes	..	0.0	0.0	0.0	0.0	..	0.0	0.0	0.0	0.0

.. Not available

Note: More detailed country data and country notes are available in Chapter 6 "Tax revenues by sub-sectors of general government". Full time series can be accessed at http://data-explorer.oecd.org/s/nb.

The total tax revenue has been reduced by the amount of any capital transfer that represents uncollected taxes. The capital transfers were subtracted directly from the specific taxes to which they relate. Therefore, the tax revenue amounts are different to those reported in the detailed country data available in Chapter 6 "Tax revenues by sub-sectors of general government".

Source: Ministry of Finance.

Table 4.47. Luxembourg, tax revenue and % of GDP by selected tax category

	Billion EUR					% of GDP				
	1990	2000	2010	2021	2022	1990	2000	2010	2021	2022
Total tax revenue	3.7	8.5	15.1	27.6	29.7	34.7	37.0	35.7	38.2	38.3
1000 Taxes on income, profits and capital gains	1.5	3.1	5.5	10.6	11.4	13.9	13.5	12.9	14.6	14.8
1100 Of individuals	0.9	1.6	3.2	7.3	8.0	8.3	6.8	7.4	10.1	10.4
1200 Corporate	0.6	1.5	2.3	3.3	3.4	5.6	6.7	5.4	4.5	4.4
1300 Unallocable between 1100 and 1200	0.0	0.0	0.0	0.0	0.0	0.0	0.0	0.0	0.0	0.0
2000 Social security contributions	1.0	2.2	4.4	7.7	8.2	9.6	9.7	10.3	10.6	10.6
2100 Employees	0.4	1.0	2.0	3.5	3.8	3.7	4.3	4.8	4.9	5.0
2200 Employers	0.5	1.0	1.9	3.1	3.4	4.7	4.2	4.5	4.4	4.4
2300 Self-employed or non-employed	0.0	0.0	0.0	0.0	0.0	0.0	0.0	0.0	0.0	0.0
2400 Unallocable between 2100, 2200 and 2300	0.0	0.0	0.0	0.0	0.0	0.0	0.0	0.0	0.0	0.0
3000 Taxes on payroll and workforce	0.0	0.0	0.0	0.0	0.0	0.0	0.0	0.0	0.0	0.0
4000 Taxes on property	0.3	0.9	1.1	2.9	2.9	2.9	4.0	2.5	4.0	3.7
4100 Recurrent taxes on immovable property	0.0	0.0	0.0	0.0	0.0	0.1	0.1	0.1	0.1	0.1
4200 Recurrent taxes on net wealth	0.2	0.6	0.8	2.1	2.1	1.6	2.8	2.0	2.9	2.7
4300 Estate, inheritance and gift taxes	0.0	0.0	0.1	0.1	0.1	0.1	0.1	0.1	0.2	0.2
4400 Taxes on financial and capital transactions	0.1	0.2	0.2	0.6	0.6	1.1	1.0	0.4	0.9	0.7
4500 Non-recurrent taxes	0.0	0.0	0.0	0.0	0.0	0.0	0.0	0.0	0.0	0.0
4600 Other recurrent taxes on property	0.0	0.0	0.0	0.0	0.0	0.0	0.0	0.0	0.0	0.0
5000 Taxes on goods and services	0.9	2.3	4.2	6.4	7.1	8.2	9.8	9.9	8.9	9.1
5100 Taxes on production, sale, transfer, etc	0.8	2.2	4.1	6.4	7.0	8.0	9.7	9.7	8.8	9.0
5110 General taxes	0.4	1.1	2.6	4.1	4.7	4.2	4.9	6.2	5.7	6.1
5111 Value added taxes	0.4	1.1	2.6	4.1	4.7	4.2	4.9	6.2	5.7	6.1
5120 Taxes on specific goods and services	0.4	1.1	1.5	2.2	2.3	3.8	4.8	3.5	3.1	3.0
5121 Excises	0.4	1.0	1.4	1.8	1.8	3.4	4.5	3.3	2.5	2.3
5200 Taxes on use of goods and perform activities	0.0	0.0	0.1	0.1	0.1	0.2	0.1	0.2	0.1	0.1
5300 Unallocable between 5100 and 5200	0.0	0.0	0.0	0.0	0.0	0.0	0.0	0.0	0.0	0.0
6000 Other taxes	0.0	0.0	0.0	0.0	0.0	0.1	0.0	0.1	0.0	0.0
Non-wastable tax credits										
Non-wastable tax credits against 1000	..	..	..	0.2	0.4	..	..	..	0.3	0.6
Transfer component	..	..	..	..	..	..	..	..	..	..
Tax expenditure component	..	..	..	..	..	..	..	..	..	..
Revenues collected on behalf of the EU										
Revenues collected on behalf of the EU, total	0.0	0.0	0.0	0.3	0.3	0.2	0.1	0.0	0.4	0.4
Customs duties	0.0	0.0	0.0	0.0	0.0	0.1	0.1	0.0	0.0	0.0
SRF contributions	..	..	..	0.2	0.3	..	..	..	0.3	0.4

.. Not available

Note: The total tax revenue has been reduced by the amount of any capital transfer that represents uncollected taxes. The capital transfers were subtracted directly from the specific taxes to which they relate. Therefore, the tax revenue amounts are different to those reported in the detailed country data available in Chapter 5 "Detailed country tables".

More detailed country data and country notes are available in Chapter 5 "Detailed country tables". Full time series can be accessed at http://data-explorer.oecd.org/s/nb.

Source: General account of the State.

Table 4.48. Luxembourg, tax revenue and % of GDP by level of government and main taxes

	Billion EUR					% of GDP				
	1990	2000	2010	2021	2022	1990	2000	2010	2021	2022
Federal or Central government										
Total tax revenue	2.4	5.8	10.2	18.8	20.2	22.9	25.4	24.0	26.0	26.1
1000 Taxes on income, profits and capital gains	1.3	2.6	4.9	9.6	10.4	12.0	11.5	11.5	13.2	13.5
2000 Social security contributions	0.0	0.1	0.1	0.2	0.2	0.2	0.3	0.3	0.3	0.3
3000 Taxes on payroll and workforce	0.0	0.0	0.0	0.0	0.0	0.0	0.0	0.0	0.0	0.0
4000 Taxes on property	0.3	0.9	1.0	2.8	2.8	2.7	3.8	2.4	3.9	3.6
5000 Taxes on goods and services	0.8	2.2	4.2	6.2	6.7	8.0	9.7	9.8	8.5	8.7
6000 Other taxes	0.0	0.0	0.0	0.0	0.0	0.1	0.0	0.0	0.0	0.0
State/Regional										
Total tax revenue	..	..	..	..	..	..	..	..	..	..
1000 Taxes on income, profits and capital gains	..	..	..	..	..	..	..	..	..	..
2000 Social security contributions	..	..	..	..	..	..	..	..	..	..
3000 Taxes on payroll and workforce	..	..	..	..	..	..	..	..	..	..
4000 Taxes on property	..	..	..	..	..	..	..	..	..	..
5000 Taxes on goods and services	..	..	..	..	..	..	..	..	..	..
6000 Other taxes	..	..	..	..	..	..	..	..	..	..
Local government										
Total tax revenue	0.2	0.5	0.7	1.1	1.1	2.2	2.2	1.5	1.5	1.4
1000 Taxes on income, profits and capital gains	0.2	0.5	0.6	1.0	1.0	2.0	2.0	1.4	1.4	1.3
2000 Social security contributions	0.0	0.0	0.0	0.0	0.0	0.0	0.0	0.0	0.0	0.0
3000 Taxes on payroll and workforce	0.0	0.0	0.0	0.0	0.0	0.0	0.0	0.0	0.0	0.0
4000 Taxes on property	0.0	0.0	0.0	0.1	0.1	0.2	0.1	0.1	0.1	0.1
5000 Taxes on goods and services	0.0	0.0	0.0	0.0	0.0	0.0	0.0	0.0	0.0	0.0
6000 Other taxes	0.0	0.0	0.0	0.0	0.0	0.0	0.0	0.0	0.0	0.0
Social Security Funds										
Total tax revenue	1.0	2.2	4.3	7.4	8.0	9.4	9.4	10.1	10.3	10.3
1000 Taxes on income, profits and capital gains	0.0	0.0	0.0	0.0	0.0	0.0	0.0	0.0	0.0	0.0
2000 Social security contributions	1.0	2.2	4.3	7.4	8.0	9.4	9.4	10.1	10.3	10.3
3000 Taxes on payroll and workforce	0.0	0.0	0.0	0.0	0.0	0.0	0.0	0.0	0.0	0.0
4000 Taxes on property	0.0	0.0	0.0	0.0	0.0	0.0	0.0	0.0	0.0	0.0
5000 Taxes on goods and services	0.0	0.0	0.0	0.0	0.0	0.0	0.0	0.0	0.0	0.0
6000 Other taxes	0.0	0.0	0.0	0.0	0.0	0.0	0.0	0.0	0.0	0.0

.. Not available

Note: The total tax revenue has been reduced by the amount of any capital transfer that represents uncollected taxes. The capital transfers were subtracted directly from the specific taxes to which they relate. Therefore, the tax revenue amounts are different to those reported in the detailed country data available in Chapter 6 "Tax revenues by sub-sectors of general government".

More detailed country data and country notes are available in Chapter 6 "Tax revenues by sub-sectors of general government". Full time series can be accessed at http://data-explorer.oecd.org/s/nb.

Source: General account of the State.

Table 4.49. Mexico, tax revenue and % of GDP by selected tax category

	Billion MXN					% of GDP				
	1990	2000	2010	2021	2022	1990	2000	2010	2021	2022
Total tax revenue	102.0	767.2	1 716.2	4 452.4	4 948.3	11.5	10.9	12.3	16.7	16.8
1000 Taxes on income, profits and capital gains	34.7	276.5	683.6	1 903.0	2 280.8	3.9	3.9	4.9	7.1	7.7
1100 Of individuals	..	..	313.5	938.6	1067.0	..	..	2.2	3.5	3.6
1200 Corporate	..	..	246.7	898.8	1136.6	..	..	1.8	3.4	3.9
1300 Unallocable between 1100 and 1200	34.7	276.5	123.4	65.7	77.2	3.9	3.9	0.9	0.2	0.3
2000 Social security contributions	17.2	138.2	277.5	612.2	681.7	1.9	2.0	2.0	2.3	2.3
2100 Employees	..	..	..	..	..	..	..	..	..	..
2200 Employers	..	..	..	..	..	..	..	..	..	..
2300 Self-employed or non-employed	..	..	..	..	..	..	..	..	..	..
2400 Unallocable between 2100, 2200 and 2300	17.2	138.2	277.5	612.2	681.7	1.9	2.0	2.0	2.3	2.3
3000 Taxes on payroll and workforce	1.8	11.2	36.9	116.9	141.2	0.2	0.2	0.3	0.4	0.5
4000 Taxes on property	1.9	14.0	39.0	90.2	105.2	0.2	0.2	0.3	0.3	0.4
4100 Recurrent taxes on immovable property	1.0	9.9	25.7	56.1	64.9	0.1	0.1	0.2	0.2	0.2
4200 Recurrent taxes on net wealth	0.0	0.0	0.0	0.0	0.0	0.0	0.0	0.0	0.0	0.0
4300 Estate, inheritance and gift taxes	0.0	0.0	0.0	0.0	0.0	0.0	0.0	0.0	0.0	0.0
4400 Taxes on financial and capital transactions	0.9	4.0	13.2	34.1	40.3	0.1	0.1	0.1	0.1	0.1
4500 Non-recurrent taxes	0.0	0.0	0.0	0.0	0.0	0.0	0.0	0.0	0.0	0.0
4600 Other recurrent taxes on property	0.0	0.0	0.0	0.0	0.0	0.0	0.0	0.0	0.0	0.0
5000 Taxes on goods and services	44.8	319.6	651.9	1 647.9	1 623.6	5.1	4.6	4.7	6.2	5.5
5100 Taxes on production, sale, transfer, etc	44.2	310.3	630.1	1 630.6	1 606.1	5.0	4.4	4.5	6.1	5.5
5110 General taxes	26.6	189.6	504.5	1123.7	1 221.8	3.0	2.7	3.6	4.2	4.1
5111 Value added taxes	26.6	189.6	504.5	1123.7	1 221.8	3.0	2.7	3.6	4.2	4.1
5120 Taxes on specific goods and services	17.5	120.7	125.6	506.9	384.3	2.0	1.7	0.9	1.9	1.3
5121 Excises	10.1	86.2	86.1	410.4	259.3	1.1	1.2	0.6	1.5	0.9
5200 Taxes on use of goods and perform activities	0.7	9.3	21.8	17.3	17.5	0.1	0.1	0.2	0.1	0.1
5300 Unallocable between 5100 and 5200	0.0	0.0	0.0	0.0	0.0	0.0	0.0	0.0	0.0	0.0
6000 Other taxes	1.6	7.7	27.4	82.1	115.8	0.2	0.1	0.2	0.3	0.4
Non-wastable tax credits										
Non-wastable tax credits against 1000	..	..	40.3	53.4	43.2	..	..	0.3	0.2	0.1
Transfer component	..	..	9.7	0.5	0.1	..	..	0.1	0.0	0.0
Tax expenditure component	..	..	30.6	52.9	43.1	..	..	0.2	0.2	0.1

.. Not available

Note: More detailed country data and country notes are available in Chapter 5 "Detailed country tables". Full time series can be accessed at http://data-explorer.oecd.org/s/nb.

Source: Ministry of Finance, Economic Department.

Table 4.50. Mexico, tax revenue and % of GDP by level of government and main taxes

	Billion MXN					% of GDP				
	1990	2000	2010	2021	2022	1990	2000	2010	2021	2022
Federal or Central government										
Total tax revenue	81.4	600.5	1 351.5	3 579.5	3 957.6	9.2	8.6	9.7	13.4	13.4
1000 Taxes on income, profits and capital gains	34.7	276.5	683.6	1 903.0	2 280.8	3.9	3.9	4.9	7.1	7.7
2000 Social security contributions	0.0	0.0	0.0	0.0	0.0	0.0	0.0	0.0	0.0	0.0
3000 Taxes on payroll and workforce	0.8	0.0	0.0	0.0	0.0	0.1	0.0	0.0	0.0	0.0
4000 Taxes on property	0.0	0.0	0.0	0.0	0.0	0.0	0.0	0.0	0.0	0.0
5000 Taxes on goods and services	44.6	318.1	645.6	1 621.9	1 592.9	5.0	4.5	4.6	6.1	5.4
6000 Other taxes	1.3	5.9	22.2	54.5	83.9	0.2	0.1	0.2	0.2	0.3
State/Regional										
Total tax revenue	2.2	20.5	58.3	182.6	218.7	0.2	0.3	0.4	0.7	0.7
1000 Taxes on income, profits and capital gains	0.0	0.0	0.0	0.0	0.0	0.0	0.0	0.0	0.0	0.0
2000 Social security contributions	0.0	0.0	0.0	0.0	0.0	0.0	0.0	0.0	0.0	0.0
3000 Taxes on payroll and workforce	1.0	11.2	36.8	116.9	141.2	0.1	0.2	0.3	0.4	0.5
4000 Taxes on property	0.9	7.0	13.1	30.1	33.7	0.1	0.1	0.1	0.1	0.1
5000 Taxes on goods and services	0.1	1.3	5.8	25.4	29.4	0.0	0.0	0.0	0.1	0.1
6000 Other taxes	0.2	0.9	2.5	10.2	14.5	0.0	0.0	0.0	0.0	0.0
Local government										
Total tax revenue	1.3	8.0	29.0	78.1	90.3	0.1	0.1	0.2	0.3	0.3
1000 Taxes on income, profits and capital gains	0.0	0.0	0.0	0.0	0.0	0.0	0.0	0.0	0.0	0.0
2000 Social security contributions	0.0	0.0	0.0	0.0	0.0	0.0	0.0	0.0	0.0	0.0
3000 Taxes on payroll and workforce	0.0	0.0	0.1	0.0	0.0	0.0	0.0	0.0	0.0	0.0
4000 Taxes on property	1.0	6.9	25.8	60.1	71.6	0.1	0.1	0.2	0.2	0.2
5000 Taxes on goods and services	0.1	0.2	0.5	0.6	1.3	0.0	0.0	0.0	0.0	0.0
6000 Other taxes	0.1	0.9	2.6	17.4	17.4	0.0	0.0	0.0	0.1	0.1
Social Security Funds										
Total tax revenue	17.2	138.2	277.5	612.2	681.7	1.9	2.0	2.0	2.3	2.3
1000 Taxes on income, profits and capital gains	0.0	0.0	0.0	0.0	0.0	0.0	0.0	0.0	0.0	0.0
2000 Social security contributions	17.2	138.2	277.5	612.2	681.7	1.9	2.0	2.0	2.3	2.3
3000 Taxes on payroll and workforce	0.0	0.0	0.0	0.0	0.0	0.0	0.0	0.0	0.0	0.0
4000 Taxes on property	0.0	0.0	0.0	0.0	0.0	0.0	0.0	0.0	0.0	0.0
5000 Taxes on goods and services	0.0	0.0	0.0	0.0	0.0	0.0	0.0	0.0	0.0	0.0
6000 Other taxes	0.0	0.0	0.0	0.0	0.0	0.0	0.0	0.0	0.0	0.0

Note: More detailed country data and country notes are available in Chapter 6 "Tax revenues by sub-sectors of general government". Full time series can be accessed at http://data-explorer.oecd.org/s/nb.
Source: Ministry of Finance, Economic Department.

Table 4.51. Netherlands, tax revenue and % of GDP by selected tax category

	Billion EUR					% of GDP				
	1990	2000	2010	2021	2022	1990	2000	2010	2021	2022
Total tax revenue	104.4	166.8	227.9	341.1	378.3	39.6	36.9	35.4	38.3	38.1
1000 Taxes on income, profits and capital gains	33.7	43.3	63.6	107.8	123.8	12.8	9.6	9.9	12.1	12.5
1100 Of individuals	25.8	25.1	49.0	74.4	76.7	9.8	5.6	7.6	8.3	7.7
1200 Corporate	7.9	18.1	14.6	33.4	47.2	3.0	4.0	2.3	3.7	4.7
1300 Unallocable between 1100 and 1200	0.0	0.0	0.0	0.0	0.0	0.0	0.0	0.0	0.0	0.0
2000 Social security contributions	39.1	64.5	82.7	112.7	124.5	14.8	14.3	12.9	12.6	12.5
2100 Employees	24.1	35.3	41.6	42.2	46.9	9.2	7.8	6.5	4.7	4.7
2200 Employers	7.8	18.7	29.4	45.1	49.3	3.0	4.1	4.6	5.1	5.0
2300 Self-employed or non-employed	0.0	0.0	0.0	0.0	0.0	0.0	0.0	0.0	0.0	0.0
2400 Unallocable between 2100, 2200 and 2300	0.0	0.0	0.0	0.0	0.0	0.0	0.0	0.0	0.0	0.0
3000 Taxes on payroll and workforce	0.0	0.0	0.0	0.0	0.0	0.0	0.0	0.0	0.0	0.0
4000 Taxes on property	3.8	8.8	8.8	14.1	14.8	1.4	1.9	1.4	1.6	1.5
4100 Recurrent taxes on immovable property	1.7	3.1	4.2	7.8	7.6	0.6	0.7	0.7	0.9	0.8
4200 Recurrent taxes on net wealth	0.6	0.8	0.0	0.0	0.0	0.2	0.2	0.0	0.0	0.0
4300 Estate, inheritance and gift taxes	0.5	1.5	1.7	2.5	2.6	0.2	0.3	0.3	0.3	0.3
4400 Taxes on financial and capital transactions	1.0	3.4	2.8	3.8	4.6	0.4	0.8	0.4	0.4	0.5
4500 Non-recurrent taxes	0.0	0.0	0.0	0.0	0.0	0.0	0.0	0.0	0.0	0.0
4600 Other recurrent taxes on property	0.0	0.0	0.0	0.0	0.0	0.0	0.0	0.0	0.0	0.0
5000 Taxes on goods and services	27.6	49.5	71.9	105.5	114.0	10.5	10.9	11.2	11.8	11.5
5100 Taxes on production, sale, transfer, etc	25.1	44.9	64.2	95.7	103.6	9.5	9.9	10.0	10.7	10.4
5110 General taxes	17.2	28.9	42.7	65.5	70.5	6.5	6.4	6.6	7.3	7.1
5111 Value added taxes	17.2	28.8	42.7	65.4	70.5	6.5	6.4	6.6	7.3	7.1
5120 Taxes on specific goods and services	7.9	16.0	21.6	30.3	33.1	3.0	3.5	3.4	3.4	3.3
5121 Excises	6.0	13.8	18.4	21.1	22.4	2.3	3.0	2.9	2.4	2.3
5200 Taxes on use of goods and perform activities	2.5	4.6	7.6	9.8	10.5	1.0	1.0	1.2	1.1	1.1
5300 Unallocable between 5100 and 5200	0.0	0.0	0.0	0.0	0.0	0.0	0.0	0.0	0.0	0.0
6000 Other taxes	0.3	0.8	1.0	1.0	1.2	0.1	0.2	0.1	0.1	0.1
Non-wastable tax credits										
Non-wastable tax credits against 1000	..	..	..	..	..	..	..	..	..	..
Transfer component	..	..	..	..	..	..	..	..	..	..
Tax expenditure component	..	..	..	..	..	..	..	..	..	..
Revenues collected on behalf of the EU										
Revenues collected on behalf of the EU, total	1.5	1.6	2.0	4.1	5.1	0.6	0.4	0.3	0.5	0.5
Customs duties	..	1.3	1.7	3.0	3.8	..	0.3	0.3	0.3	0.4
SRF contributions	..	..	..	0.8	1.0	..	..	..	0.1	0.1

.. Not available

Note: More detailed country data and country notes are available in Chapter 5 "Detailed country tables". Full time series can be accessed at http://data-explorer.oecd.org/s/nb.

Source: Social security contributions and local taxes: Central Bureau of Statistics. Other taxes: Ministry of Finance.

Table 4.52. Netherlands, tax revenue and % of GDP by level of government and main taxes

	Billion EUR					% of GDP				
	1990	2000	2010	2021	2022	1990	2000	2010	2021	2022
Federal or Central government										
Total tax revenue	61.4	95.1	135.1	212.8	236.6	23.3	21.0	21.0	23.9	23.8
1000 Taxes on income, profits and capital gains	33.7	43.3	63.6	107.8	123.8	12.8	9.6	9.9	12.1	12.5
2000 Social security contributions	0.0	0.0	0.0	0.0	0.0	0.0	0.0	0.0	0.0	0.0
3000 Taxes on payroll and workforce	0.0	0.0	0.0	0.0	0.0	0.0	0.0	0.0	0.0	0.0
4000 Taxes on property	2.1	5.7	4.6	7.8	8.1	0.8	1.3	0.7	0.9	0.8
5000 Taxes on goods and services	25.3	45.4	66.2	96.2	103.5	9.6	10.0	10.3	10.8	10.4
6000 Other taxes	0.3	0.8	0.8	1.0	1.2	0.1	0.2	0.1	0.1	0.1
State/Regional										
Total tax revenue	..	..	..	..	..	..	..	..	..	..
1000 Taxes on income, profits and capital gains	..	..	..	..	..	..	..	..	..	..
2000 Social security contributions	..	..	..	..	..	..	..	..	..	..
3000 Taxes on payroll and workforce	..	..	..	..	..	..	..	..	..	..
4000 Taxes on property	..	..	..	..	..	..	..	..	..	..
5000 Taxes on goods and services	..	..	..	..	..	..	..	..	..	..
6000 Other taxes	..	..	..	..	..	..	..	..	..	..
Local government										
Total tax revenue	2.5	5.6	8.1	11.6	12.1	0.9	1.2	1.3	1.3	1.2
1000 Taxes on income, profits and capital gains	0.0	0.0	0.0	0.0	0.0	0.0	0.0	0.0	0.0	0.0
2000 Social security contributions	0.0	0.0	0.0	0.0	0.0	0.0	0.0	0.0	0.0	0.0
3000 Taxes on payroll and workforce	0.0	0.0	0.0	0.0	0.0	0.0	0.0	0.0	0.0	0.0
4000 Taxes on property	1.7	3.1	4.2	6.3	6.6	0.6	0.7	0.6	0.7	0.7
5000 Taxes on goods and services	0.8	2.5	3.7	5.3	5.4	0.3	0.6	0.6	0.6	0.5
6000 Other taxes	0.0	0.0	0.2	0.0	0.0	0.0	0.0	0.0	0.0	0.0
Social Security Funds										
Total tax revenue	39.1	64.5	82.7	112.7	124.5	14.8	14.3	12.9	12.6	12.5
1000 Taxes on income, profits and capital gains	0.0	0.0	0.0	0.0	0.0	0.0	0.0	0.0	0.0	0.0
2000 Social security contributions	39.1	64.5	82.7	112.7	124.5	14.8	14.3	12.9	12.6	12.5
3000 Taxes on payroll and workforce	0.0	0.0	0.0	0.0	0.0	0.0	0.0	0.0	0.0	0.0
4000 Taxes on property	0.0	0.0	0.0	0.0	0.0	0.0	0.0	0.0	0.0	0.0
5000 Taxes on goods and services	0.0	0.0	0.0	0.0	0.0	0.0	0.0	0.0	0.0	0.0
6000 Other taxes	0.0	0.0	0.0	0.0	0.0	0.0	0.0	0.0	0.0	0.0

.. Not available

Note: More detailed country data and country notes are available in Chapter 6 "Tax revenues by sub-sectors of general government". Full time series can be accessed at http://data-explorer.oecd.org/s/nb.

Source: Social security contributions and local taxes: Central Bureau of Statistics. Other taxes: Ministry of Finance.

Table 4.53. New Zealand, tax revenue and % of GDP by selected tax category

	Billion NZD					% of GDP				
	1990	2000	2010	2021	2022	1990	2000	2010	2021	2022
Total tax revenue	27.5	39.8	62.3	125.8	130.8	36.2	32.5	30.3	34.5	33.1
1000 Taxes on income, profits and capital gains	16.4	23.9	33.5	73.6	76.1	21.6	19.5	16.3	20.2	19.3
1100 Of individuals	13.2	17.1	23.5	51.4	54.4	17.4	14.0	11.4	14.1	13.8
1200 Corporate	1.8	4.9	7.6	19.8	17.9	2.3	4.0	3.7	5.4	4.5
1300 Unallocable between 1100 and 1200	1.4	1.8	2.4	2.5	3.8	1.9	1.5	1.2	0.7	1.0
2000 Social security contributions	0.0	0.0	0.0	0.0	0.0	0.0	0.0	0.0	0.0	0.0
2100 Employees	0.0	0.0	0.0	0.0	0.0	0.0	0.0	0.0	0.0	0.0
2200 Employers	0.0	0.0	0.0	0.0	0.0	0.0	0.0	0.0	0.0	0.0
2300 Self-employed or non-employed	0.0	0.0	0.0	0.0	0.0	0.0	0.0	0.0	0.0	0.0
2400 Unallocable between 2100, 2200 and 2300	0.0	0.0	0.0	0.0	0.0	0.0	0.0	0.0	0.0	0.0
3000 Taxes on payroll and workforce	0.0	0.0	0.0	0.0	0.0	0.0	0.0	0.0	0.0	0.0
4000 Taxes on property	1.9	2.1	4.1	7.0	7.6	2.5	1.7	2.0	1.9	1.9
4100 Recurrent taxes on immovable property	1.7	2.0	4.0	6.9	7.4	2.3	1.7	2.0	1.9	1.9
4200 Recurrent taxes on net wealth	0.0	0.0	0.0	0.0	0.0	0.0	0.0	0.0	0.0	0.0
4300 Estate, inheritance and gift taxes	0.1	0.0	0.0	0.0	0.0	0.1	0.0	0.0	0.0	0.0
4400 Taxes on financial and capital transactions	0.1	0.1	0.1	0.1	0.2	0.1	0.0	0.0	0.0	0.0
4500 Non-recurrent taxes	0.0	0.0	0.0	0.0	0.0	0.0	0.0	0.0	0.0	0.0
4600 Other recurrent taxes on property	0.0	0.0	0.0	0.0	0.0	0.0	0.0	0.0	0.0	0.0
5000 Taxes on goods and services	9.2	13.8	24.7	45.1	47.1	12.1	11.3	12.0	12.4	11.9
5100 Taxes on production, sale, transfer, etc	8.7	12.9	23.1	42.4	44.7	11.4	10.5	11.2	11.6	11.3
5110 General taxes	6.2	9.9	19.1	36.9	39.7	8.1	8.1	9.3	10.1	10.0
5111 Value added taxes	6.2	9.9	19.1	36.9	39.7	8.1	8.1	9.3	10.1	10.0
5120 Taxes on specific goods and services	2.5	3.0	4.0	5.5	5.0	3.3	2.5	1.9	1.5	1.3
5121 Excises	1.9	2.1	1.8	1.7	1.0	2.5	1.8	0.9	0.5	0.2
5200 Taxes on use of goods and perform activities	0.5	0.9	1.6	2.8	2.4	0.7	0.7	0.8	0.8	0.6
5300 Unallocable between 5100 and 5200	0.0	0.0	0.0	0.0	0.0	0.0	0.0	0.0	0.0	0.0
6000 Other taxes	0.0	0.0	0.0	0.0	0.0	0.0	0.0	0.0	0.0	0.0
Non-wastable tax credits										
Non-wastable tax credits against 1000	..	1.1	2.8	2.8	2.9	..	0.9	1.4	0.8	0.7
Transfer component	..	0.7	1.8	1.3	1.4	..	0.6	0.9	0.4	0.4
Tax expenditure component	..	0.3	1.0	1.5	1.6	..	0.3	0.5	0.4	0.4

.. Not available

Note: More detailed country data and country notes are available in Chapter 5 "Detailed country tables". Full time series can be accessed at http://data-explorer.oecd.org/s/nb.

Source: Statistics New Zealand.

Table 4.54. New Zealand, tax revenue and % of GDP by level of government and main taxes

	Billion NZD					% of GDP				
	1990	2000	2010	2021	2022	1990	2000	2010	2021	2022
Federal or Central government										
Total tax revenue	25.8	37.5	57.9	118.0	122.4	34.0	30.7	28.1	32.4	31.0
1000 Taxes on income, profits and capital gains	16.4	23.9	33.5	73.6	76.1	21.6	19.5	16.3	20.2	19.3
2000 Social security contributions	0.0	0.0	0.0	0.0	0.0	0.0	0.0	0.0	0.0	0.0
3000 Taxes on payroll and workforce	0.0	0.0	0.0	0.0	0.0	0.0	0.0	0.0	0.0	0.0
4000 Taxes on property	0.3	0.1	0.1	0.1	0.2	0.4	0.1	0.0	0.0	0.0
5000 Taxes on goods and services	9.1	13.6	24.3	44.3	46.1	12.0	11.1	11.8	12.2	11.7
6000 Other taxes	0.0	0.0	0.0	0.0	0.0	0.0	0.0	0.0	0.0	0.0
State/Regional										
Total tax revenue	..	..	..	..	..	..	..	..	..	..
1000 Taxes on income, profits and capital gains	..	..	..	..	..	..	..	..	..	..
2000 Social security contributions	..	..	..	..	..	..	..	..	..	..
3000 Taxes on payroll and workforce	..	..	..	..	..	..	..	..	..	..
4000 Taxes on property	..	..	..	..	..	..	..	..	..	..
5000 Taxes on goods and services	..	..	..	..	..	..	..	..	..	..
6000 Other taxes	..	..	..	..	..	..	..	..	..	..
Local government										
Total tax revenue	1.7	2.3	4.5	7.8	8.3	2.2	1.9	2.2	2.1	2.1
1000 Taxes on income, profits and capital gains	0.0	0.0	0.0	0.0	0.0	0.0	0.0	0.0	0.0	0.0
2000 Social security contributions	0.0	0.0	0.0	0.0	0.0	0.0	0.0	0.0	0.0	0.0
3000 Taxes on payroll and workforce	0.0	0.0	0.0	0.0	0.0	0.0	0.0	0.0	0.0	0.0
4000 Taxes on property	1.6	2.0	4.0	6.9	7.4	2.0	1.7	2.0	1.9	1.9
5000 Taxes on goods and services	0.1	0.2	0.4	0.9	0.9	0.2	0.2	0.2	0.2	0.2
6000 Other taxes	0.0	0.0	0.0	0.0	0.0	0.0	0.0	0.0	0.0	0.0
Social Security Funds										
Total tax revenue	0.0	0.0	0.0	0.0	0.0	0.0	0.0	0.0	0.0	0.0
1000 Taxes on income, profits and capital gains	0.0	0.0	0.0	0.0	0.0	0.0	0.0	0.0	0.0	0.0
2000 Social security contributions	0.0	0.0	0.0	0.0	0.0	0.0	0.0	0.0	0.0	0.0
3000 Taxes on payroll and workforce	0.0	0.0	0.0	0.0	0.0	0.0	0.0	0.0	0.0	0.0
4000 Taxes on property	0.0	0.0	0.0	0.0	0.0	0.0	0.0	0.0	0.0	0.0
5000 Taxes on goods and services	0.0	0.0	0.0	0.0	0.0	0.0	0.0	0.0	0.0	0.0
6000 Other taxes	0.0	0.0	0.0	0.0	0.0	0.0	0.0	0.0	0.0	0.0

.. Not available

Note: More detailed country data and country notes are available in Chapter 6 "Tax revenues by sub-sectors of general government". Full time series can be accessed at http://data-explorer.oecd.org/s/nb.

Source: Statistics New Zealand.

Table 4.55. Norway, tax revenue and % of GDP by selected tax category

	Billion NOK					% of GDP				
	1990	2000	2010	2021	2022	1990	2000	2010	2021	2022
Total tax revenue	303.3	630.8	1 087.4	1 787.7	2 479.5	40.4	41.8	41.7	41.3	43.4
1000 Taxes on income, profits and capital gains	106.3	284.9	512.9	881.3	1510.7	14.2	18.9	19.7	20.4	26.5
1100 Of individuals	79.1	152.7	257.2	459.4	463.0	10.5	10.1	9.9	10.6	8.1
1200 Corporate	27.2	132.2	255.7	421.9	1047.7	3.6	8.8	9.8	9.8	18.4
1300 Unallocable between 1100 and 1200	0.0	0.0	0.0	0.0	0.0	0.0	0.0	0.0	0.0	0.0
2000 Social security contributions	79.4	132.2	243.0	402.0	428.5	10.6	8.8	9.3	9.3	7.5
2100 Employees	25.3	45.2	81.0	142.1	148.3	3.4	3.0	3.1	3.3	2.6
2200 Employers	50.1	79.2	148.0	232.6	251.0	6.7	5.3	5.7	5.4	4.4
2300 Self-employed or non-employed	0.0	0.0	0.0	0.0	0.0	0.0	0.0	0.0	0.0	0.0
2400 Unallocable between 2100, 2200 and 2300	0.0	0.0	0.0	0.0	0.0	0.0	0.0	0.0	0.0	0.0
3000 Taxes on payroll and workforce	0.0	0.0	0.0	2.2	2.4	0.0	0.0	0.0	0.1	0.0
4000 Taxes on property	8.9	13.8	27.9	47.6	55.2	1.2	0.9	1.1	1.1	1.0
4100 Recurrent taxes on immovable property	2.2	2.7	7.1	15.6	16.1	0.3	0.2	0.3	0.4	0.3
4200 Recurrent taxes on net wealth	5.1	7.0	12.5	18.9	26.9	0.7	0.5	0.5	0.4	0.5
4300 Estate, inheritance and gift taxes	0.4	1.3	2.4	0.0	0.0	0.1	0.1	0.1	0.0	0.0
4400 Taxes on financial and capital transactions	1.1	2.7	5.9	13.1	12.2	0.1	0.2	0.2	0.3	0.2
4500 Non-recurrent taxes	0.0	0.0	0.0	0.0	0.0	0.0	0.0	0.0	0.0	0.0
4600 Other recurrent taxes on property	0.0	0.0	0.0	0.0	0.0	0.0	0.0	0.0	0.0	0.0
5000 Taxes on goods and services	108.7	200.0	303.6	454.6	482.7	14.5	13.3	11.7	10.5	8.5
5100 Taxes on production, sale, transfer, etc	102.9	185.9	284.6	430.6	458.1	13.7	12.3	10.9	10.0	8.0
5110 General taxes	56.7	125.0	201.8	340.4	373.5	7.6	8.3	7.7	7.9	6.5
5111 Value added taxes	56.7	124.2	201.2	338.9	371.7	7.6	8.2	7.7	7.8	6.5
5120 Taxes on specific goods and services	46.2	60.9	82.8	90.2	84.6	6.2	4.0	3.2	2.1	1.5
5121 Excises	37.5	54.9	76.3	79.6	72.7	5.0	3.6	2.9	1.8	1.3
5200 Taxes on use of goods and perform activities	5.8	14.1	18.9	23.9	24.6	0.8	0.9	0.7	0.6	0.4
5300 Unallocable between 5100 and 5200	0.0	0.0	0.0	0.0	0.0	0.0	0.0	0.0	0.0	0.0
6000 Other taxes	0.0	0.0	0.0	0.0	0.0	0.0	0.0	0.0	0.0	0.0
Non-wastable tax credits										
Non-wastable tax credits against 1000	..	..	1.2	3.7	3.5	..	..	0.0	0.1	0.1
Transfer component	..	..	1.2	3.0	2.7	..	..	0.0	0.1	0.0
Tax expenditure component	..	..	0.1	0.8	0.8	..	..	0.0	0.0	0.0
Revenues collected on behalf of the EU										
Revenues collected on behalf of the EU, total	..	..	..	..	..	..	..	..	..	..
Customs duties	..	..	..	..	..	..	..	..	..	..
SRF contributions	..	..	..	..	..	..	..	..	..	..

.. Not available

Note: More detailed country data and country notes are available in Chapter 5 "Detailed country tables". Full time series can be accessed at http://data-explorer.oecd.org/s/nb.

Source: Statistics Norway; National Accounts.

Table 4.56. Norway, tax revenue and % of GDP by level of government and main taxes

	Billion NOK					% of GDP				
	1990	2000	2010	2021	2022	1990	2000	2010	2021	2022
Federal or Central government										
Total tax revenue	166.9	535.3	939.7	1 504.1	2 224.6	22.3	35.5	36.1	34.8	39.0
1000 Taxes on income, profits and capital gains	50.6	199.1	381.7	630.1	1291.8	6.8	13.2	14.7	14.6	22.6
2000 Social security contributions	4.7	132.2	243.0	402.0	428.5	0.6	8.8	9.3	9.3	7.5
3000 Taxes on payroll and workforce	0.0	0.0	0.0	2.2	2.4	0.0	0.0	0.0	0.1	0.0
4000 Taxes on property	3.4	6.2	13.0	16.9	20.9	0.5	0.4	0.5	0.4	0.4
5000 Taxes on goods and services	108.2	197.9	302.0	452.9	481.0	14.4	13.1	11.6	10.5	8.4
6000 Other taxes	0.0	0.0	0.0	0.0	0.0	0.0	0.0	0.0	0.0	0.0
State/Regional										
Total tax revenue	..	..	..	..	..	..	..	..	..	..
1000 Taxes on income, profits and capital gains	..	..	..	..	..	..	..	..	..	..
2000 Social security contributions	..	..	..	..	..	..	..	..	..	..
3000 Taxes on payroll and workforce	..	..	..	..	..	..	..	..	..	..
4000 Taxes on property	..	..	..	..	..	..	..	..	..	..
5000 Taxes on goods and services	..	..	..	..	..	..	..	..	..	..
6000 Other taxes	..	..	..	..	..	..	..	..	..	..
Local government										
Total tax revenue	61.6	95.5	147.7	283.6	254.9	8.2	6.3	5.7	6.6	4.5
1000 Taxes on income, profits and capital gains	55.7	85.8	131.2	251.2	218.9	7.4	5.7	5.0	5.8	3.8
2000 Social security contributions	0.0	0.0	0.0	0.0	0.0	0.0	0.0	0.0	0.0	0.0
3000 Taxes on payroll and workforce	0.0	0.0	0.0	0.0	0.0	0.0	0.0	0.0	0.0	0.0
4000 Taxes on property	5.5	7.6	14.9	30.8	34.3	0.7	0.5	0.6	0.7	0.6
5000 Taxes on goods and services	0.4	2.1	1.6	1.7	1.7	0.1	0.1	0.1	0.0	0.0
6000 Other taxes	0.0	0.0	0.0	0.0	0.0	0.0	0.0	0.0	0.0	0.0
Social Security Funds										
Total tax revenue	74.8	0.0	0.0	0.0	0.0	10.0	0.0	0.0	0.0	0.0
1000 Taxes on income, profits and capital gains	0.0	0.0	0.0	0.0	0.0	0.0	0.0	0.0	0.0	0.0
2000 Social security contributions	74.6	0.0	0.0	0.0	0.0	10.0	0.0	0.0	0.0	0.0
3000 Taxes on payroll and workforce	0.0	0.0	0.0	0.0	0.0	0.0	0.0	0.0	0.0	0.0
4000 Taxes on property	0.0	0.0	0.0	0.0	0.0	0.0	0.0	0.0	0.0	0.0
5000 Taxes on goods and services	0.2	0.0	0.0	0.0	0.0	0.0	0.0	0.0	0.0	0.0
6000 Other taxes	0.0	0.0	0.0	0.0	0.0	0.0	0.0	0.0	0.0	0.0

.. Not available

Note: More detailed country data and country notes are available in Chapter 6 "Tax revenues by sub-sectors of general government". Full time series can be accessed at http://data-explorer.oecd.org/s/nb.

Source: Statistics Norway; National Accounts.

Table 4.57. Poland, tax revenue and % of GDP by selected tax category

	Billion PLN					% of GDP				
	1990	2000	2010	2021	2022	1990	2000	2010	2021	2022
Total tax revenue	..	246.0	453.3	965.6	1057.1	..	32.9	31.6	36.7	34.4
1000 Taxes on income, profits and capital gains	..	50.3	91.0	209.3	224.0	..	6.7	6.3	8.0	7.3
1100 Of individuals	..	32.4	62.9	140.7	138.3	..	4.3	4.4	5.3	4.5
1200 Corporate	..	17.9	28.1	68.6	85.8	..	2.4	2.0	2.6	2.8
1300 Unallocable between 1100 and 1200	..	0.0	0.0	0.0	0.0	..	0.0	0.0	0.0	0.0
2000 Social security contributions	..	96.4	156.0	341.2	392.5	..	12.9	10.9	13.0	12.8
2100 Employees	..	42.2	59.6	148.3	171.8	..	5.6	4.2	5.6	5.6
2200 Employers	..	41.4	66.3	124.6	142.6	..	5.5	4.6	4.7	4.6
2300 Self-employed or non-employed	..	0.0	0.0	0.0	0.0	..	0.0	0.0	0.0	0.0
2400 Unallocable between 2100, 2200 and 2300	..	0.0	0.0	0.0	0.0	..	0.0	0.0	0.0	0.0
3000 Taxes on payroll and workforce	..	1.6	3.7	14.5	17.2	..	0.2	0.3	0.6	0.6
4000 Taxes on property	..	10.6	19.1	33.6	35.8	..	1.4	1.3	1.3	1.2
4100 Recurrent taxes on immovable property	..	8.4	16.4	28.1	30.1	..	1.1	1.1	1.1	1.0
4200 Recurrent taxes on net wealth	..	0.0	0.0	0.0	0.0	..	0.0	0.0	0.0	0.0
4300 Estate, inheritance and gift taxes	..	0.2	0.3	0.4	0.6	..	0.0	0.0	0.0	0.0
4400 Taxes on financial and capital transactions	..	2.0	2.4	5.1	5.2	..	0.3	0.2	0.2	0.2
4500 Non-recurrent taxes	..	0.0	0.0	0.0	0.0	..	0.0	0.0	0.0	0.0
4600 Other recurrent taxes on property	..	0.0	0.0	0.0	0.0	..	0.0	0.0	0.0	0.0
5000 Taxes on goods and services	..	86.9	182.8	365.7	386.1	..	11.6	12.7	13.9	12.6
5100 Taxes on production, sale, transfer, etc	..	84.9	176.0	344.7	351.5	..	11.3	12.3	13.1	11.4
5110 General taxes	..	51.6	109.7	228.1	226.7	..	6.9	7.6	8.7	7.4
5111 Value added taxes	..	51.6	109.7	225.1	223.4	..	6.9	7.6	8.6	7.3
5120 Taxes on specific goods and services	..	33.3	66.3	116.6	124.8	..	4.4	4.6	4.4	4.1
5121 Excises	..	27.2	62.0	98.4	102.1	..	3.6	4.3	3.7	3.3
5200 Taxes on use of goods and perform activities	..	2.0	6.8	21.1	34.6	..	0.3	0.5	0.8	1.1
5300 Unallocable between 5100 and 5200	..	0.0	0.0	0.0	0.0	..	0.0	0.0	0.0	0.0
6000 Other taxes	..	0.3	0.6	1.3	1.5	..	0.0	0.0	0.0	0.0
Non-wastable tax credits										
Non-wastable tax credits against 1000	..	..	..	..	..	..	..	..	..	..
Transfer component	..	..	..	..	..	..	..	..	..	..
Tax expenditure component	..	..	..	..	..	..	..	..	..	..
Revenues collected on behalf of the EU										
Revenues collected on behalf of the EU, total	..	..	1.7	5.9	8.4	..	..	0.1	0.2	0.3
Customs duties	..	..	1.6	5.9	8.4	..	..	0.1	0.2	0.3
SRF contributions	..	..	..	..	..	..	..	..	..	..

.. Not available

Note: The total tax revenue has been reduced by the amount of any capital transfer that represents uncollected taxes. The capital transfers were subtracted directly from the specific taxes to which they relate. Therefore, the tax revenue amounts are different to those reported in the detailed country data available in Chapter 5 "Detailed country tables".

More detailed country data and country notes are available in Chapter 5 "Detailed country tables". Full time series can be accessed at http://data-explorer.oecd.org/s/nb.

Source: Ministry of Finance, Economic Department.

Table 4.58. Poland, tax revenue and % of GDP by level of government and main taxes

	Billion PLN					% of GDP				
	1990	2000	2010	2021	2022	1990	2000	2010	2021	2022
Federal or Central government										
Total tax revenue	..	126.9	238.4	502.4	529.0	..	17.0	16.6	19.1	17.2
1000 Taxes on income, profits and capital gains	..	40.0	57.7	133.9	140.5	..	5.3	4.0	5.1	4.6
2000 Social security contributions	..	0.0	0.0	0.0	0.0	..	0.0	0.0	0.0	0.0
3000 Taxes on payroll and workforce	..	1.6	3.7	14.5	17.2	..	0.2	0.3	0.6	0.6
4000 Taxes on property	..	0.0	0.0	0.0	0.0	..	0.0	0.0	0.0	0.0
5000 Taxes on goods and services	..	85.3	177.0	354.0	371.3	..	11.4	12.3	13.5	12.1
6000 Other taxes	..	0.0	0.0	0.0	0.0	..	0.0	0.0	0.0	0.0
State/Regional										
Total tax revenue	..	..	..	..	..	..	..	..	..	..
1000 Taxes on income, profits and capital gains	..	..	..	..	..	..	..	..	..	..
2000 Social security contributions	..	..	..	..	..	..	..	..	..	..
3000 Taxes on payroll and workforce	..	..	..	..	..	..	..	..	..	..
4000 Taxes on property	..	..	..	..	..	..	..	..	..	..
5000 Taxes on goods and services	..	..	..	..	..	..	..	..	..	..
6000 Other taxes	..	..	..	..	..	..	..	..	..	..
Local government										
Total tax revenue	..	22.7	57.1	114.6	125.2	..	3.0	4.0	4.4	4.1
1000 Taxes on income, profits and capital gains	..	10.3	33.3	75.4	83.5	..	1.4	2.3	2.9	2.7
2000 Social security contributions	..	0.0	0.0	0.0	0.0	..	0.0	0.0	0.0	0.0
3000 Taxes on payroll and workforce	..	0.0	0.0	0.0	0.0	..	0.0	0.0	0.0	0.0
4000 Taxes on property	..	10.6	19.1	33.6	35.8	..	1.4	1.3	1.3	1.2
5000 Taxes on goods and services	..	1.5	4.1	4.3	4.3	..	0.2	0.3	0.2	0.1
6000 Other taxes	..	0.3	0.6	1.3	1.5	..	0.0	0.0	0.0	0.0
Social Security Funds										
Total tax revenue	..	96.4	156.0	342.8	394.5	..	12.9	10.9	13.0	12.8
1000 Taxes on income, profits and capital gains	..	0.0	0.0	0.0	0.0	..	0.0	0.0	0.0	0.0
2000 Social security contributions	..	96.4	156.0	341.2	392.5	..	12.9	10.9	13.0	12.8
3000 Taxes on payroll and workforce	..	0.0	0.0	0.0	0.0	..	0.0	0.0	0.0	0.0
4000 Taxes on property	..	0.0	0.0	0.0	0.0	..	0.0	0.0	0.0	0.0
5000 Taxes on goods and services	..	0.0	0.0	1.5	2.0	..	0.0	0.0	0.1	0.1
6000 Other taxes	..	0.0	0.0	0.0	0.0	..	0.0	0.0	0.0	0.0

.. Not available

Note: The total tax revenue has been reduced by the amount of any capital transfer that represents uncollected taxes. The capital transfers were subtracted directly from the specific taxes to which they relate. Therefore, the tax revenue amounts are different to those reported in the detailed country data available in Chapter 6 "Tax revenues by sub-sectors of general government".

More detailed country data and country notes are available in Chapter 6 "Tax revenues by sub-sectors of general government". Full time series can be accessed at http://data-explorer.oecd.org/s/nb.

Source: Ministry of Finance, Economic Department.

Table 4.59. Portugal, tax revenue and % of GDP by selected tax category

	Billion EUR					% of GDP				
	1990	2000	2010	2021	2022	1990	2000	2010	2021	2022
Total tax revenue	14.8	39.7	54.5	76.0	87.3	26.5	30.9	30.4	35.2	36.0
1000 Taxes on income, profits and capital gains	3.8	11.7	14.6	20.2	25.0	6.8	9.1	8.1	9.3	10.3
1100 Of individuals	2.4	6.8	9.6	15.0	16.9	4.2	5.3	5.4	6.9	7.0
1200 Corporate	1.2	4.7	4.9	5.2	8.1	2.1	3.7	2.7	2.4	3.3
1300 Unallocable between 1100 and 1200	0.3	0.2	0.0	0.0	0.0	0.5	0.1	0.0	0.0	0.0
2000 Social security contributions	4.0	10.2	15.5	22.5	24.7	7.2	7.9	8.6	10.4	10.2
2100 Employees	1.5	4.3	6.7	9.0	9.7	2.6	3.3	3.7	4.2	4.0
2200 Employers	2.4	5.9	8.8	13.5	15.0	4.3	4.6	4.9	6.2	6.2
2300 Self-employed or non-employed	0.0	0.0	0.0	0.0	0.0	0.0	0.0	0.0	0.0	0.0
2400 Unallocable between 2100, 2200 and 2300	0.0	0.0	0.0	0.0	0.0	0.0	0.0	0.0	0.0	0.0
3000 Taxes on payroll and workforce	0.0	0.0	0.0	0.0	0.0	0.0	0.0	0.0	0.0	0.0
4000 Taxes on property	0.4	1.5	2.0	3.3	3.7	0.7	1.1	1.1	1.5	1.5
4100 Recurrent taxes on immovable property	0.1	0.5	1.1	1.6	1.6	0.2	0.4	0.6	0.7	0.7
4200 Recurrent taxes on net wealth	0.0	0.0	0.0	0.0	0.0	0.0	0.0	0.0	0.0	0.0
4300 Estate, inheritance and gift taxes	0.1	0.1	0.0	0.0	0.0	0.1	0.1	0.0	0.0	0.0
4400 Taxes on financial and capital transactions	0.2	0.9	0.9	1.7	2.1	0.3	0.7	0.5	0.8	0.9
4500 Non-recurrent taxes	0.0	0.0	0.0	0.0	0.0	0.0	0.0	0.0	0.0	0.0
4600 Other recurrent taxes on property	0.0	0.0	0.0	0.0	0.0	0.0	0.0	0.0	0.0	0.0
5000 Taxes on goods and services	6.6	16.3	22.2	29.6	33.4	11.7	12.7	12.4	13.7	13.8
5100 Taxes on production, sale, transfer, etc	6.4	15.9	21.5	28.1	31.4	11.5	12.3	12.0	13.0	13.0
5110 General taxes	2.9	9.7	13.5	19.2	22.7	5.2	7.6	7.5	8.9	9.4
5111 Value added taxes	2.9	9.7	13.5	19.2	22.7	5.2	7.6	7.5	8.9	9.4
5120 Taxes on specific goods and services	3.5	6.1	8.0	8.9	8.7	6.3	4.8	4.4	4.1	3.6
5121 Excises	2.1	4.5	5.7	5.8	5.2	3.7	3.5	3.1	2.7	2.2
5200 Taxes on use of goods and perform activities	0.1	0.4	0.7	1.5	2.0	0.2	0.3	0.4	0.7	0.8
5300 Unallocable between 5100 and 5200	0.0	0.0	0.0	0.0	0.0	0.0	0.0	0.0	0.0	0.0
6000 Other taxes	0.0	0.1	0.2	0.4	0.4	0.1	0.1	0.1	0.2	0.2
Non-wastable tax credits										
Non-wastable tax credits against 1000	..	..	..	..	..	..	..	..	..	..
Transfer component	..	..	..	..	..	..	..	..	..	..
Tax expenditure component	..	..	..	..	..	..	..	..	..	..
Revenues collected on behalf of the EU										
Revenues collected on behalf of the EU, total	0.2	0.2	0.2	0.4	0.5	0.3	0.2	0.1	0.2	0.2
Customs duties	..	0.2	0.2	0.2	0.4	..	0.2	0.1	0.1	0.2
SRF contributions	..	..	..	0.1	0.2	..	..	..	0.1	0.1

.. Not available

Note: More detailed country data and country notes are available in Chapter 5 "Detailed country tables". Full time series can be accessed at http://data-explorer.oecd.org/s/nb.

Source: Instituto Nacional de Estatística.

Table 4.60. Portugal, tax revenue and % of GDP by level of government and main taxes

	Billion EUR					% of GDP				
	1990	2000	2010	2021	2022	1990	2000	2010	2021	2022
Federal or Central government										
Total tax revenue	9.8	26.5	34.7	48.8	56.9	17.6	20.6	19.3	22.6	23.5
1000 Taxes on income, profits and capital gains	3.6	11.1	13.5	18.9	23.5	6.4	8.7	7.5	8.7	9.7
2000 Social security contributions	0.0	0.2	0.3	2.2	2.2	0.0	0.1	0.2	1.0	0.9
3000 Taxes on payroll and workforce	0.0	0.0	0.0	0.0	0.0	0.0	0.0	0.0	0.0	0.0
4000 Taxes on property	0.1	0.3	0.3	0.5	0.6	0.1	0.2	0.2	0.2	0.2
5000 Taxes on goods and services	6.1	14.8	20.4	26.7	30.2	10.9	11.5	11.4	12.4	12.4
6000 Other taxes	0.0	0.1	0.2	0.4	0.4	0.1	0.1	0.1	0.2	0.2
State/Regional										
Total tax revenue	..	..	..	..	..	..	..	..	..	..
1000 Taxes on income, profits and capital gains	..	..	..	..	..	..	..	..	..	..
2000 Social security contributions	..	..	..	..	..	..	..	..	..	..
3000 Taxes on payroll and workforce	..	..	..	..	..	..	..	..	..	..
4000 Taxes on property	..	..	..	..	..	..	..	..	..	..
5000 Taxes on goods and services	..	..	..	..	..	..	..	..	..	..
6000 Other taxes	..	..	..	..	..	..	..	..	..	..
Local government										
Total tax revenue	0.8	3.7	5.3	5.5	6.2	1.5	2.8	2.9	2.5	2.5
1000 Taxes on income, profits and capital gains	0.2	0.6	1.1	1.3	1.5	0.4	0.4	0.6	0.6	0.6
2000 Social security contributions	0.0	1.1	1.7	0.0	0.0	0.0	0.9	0.9	0.0	0.0
3000 Taxes on payroll and workforce	0.0	0.0	0.0	0.0	0.0	0.0	0.0	0.0	0.0	0.0
4000 Taxes on property	0.3	1.2	1.7	2.8	3.2	0.6	0.9	1.0	1.3	1.3
5000 Taxes on goods and services	0.3	0.7	0.8	1.4	1.5	0.5	0.6	0.4	0.6	0.6
6000 Other taxes	0.0	0.0	0.0	0.0	0.0	0.0	0.0	0.0	0.0	0.0
Social Security Funds										
Total tax revenue	4.0	9.4	14.4	21.4	23.7	7.2	7.3	8.0	9.9	9.8
1000 Taxes on income, profits and capital gains	0.0	0.0	0.0	0.0	0.0	0.0	0.0	0.0	0.0	0.0
2000 Social security contributions	4.0	8.8	13.5	20.2	22.5	7.2	6.9	7.5	9.4	9.3
3000 Taxes on payroll and workforce	0.0	0.0	0.0	0.0	0.0	0.0	0.0	0.0	0.0	0.0
4000 Taxes on property	0.0	0.0	0.0	0.0	0.0	0.0	0.0	0.0	0.0	0.0
5000 Taxes on goods and services	0.0	0.5	0.8	1.1	1.2	0.0	0.4	0.5	0.5	0.5
6000 Other taxes	0.0	0.0	0.0	0.0	0.0	0.0	0.0	0.0	0.0	0.0

.. Not available

Note: More detailed country data and country notes are available in Chapter 6 "Tax revenues by sub-sectors of general government". Full time series can be accessed at http://data-explorer.oecd.org/s/nb.

Source: Instituto Nacional de Estatística.

Table 4.61. Slovak Republic, tax revenue and % of GDP by selected tax category

	Billion EUR					% of GDP				
	1990	2000	2010	2021	2022	1990	2000	2010	2021	2022
Total tax revenue	..	10.6	19.2	35.5	38.4	..	33.6	27.9	35.4	35.0
1000 Taxes on income, profits and capital gains	..	2.2	3.6	7.7	8.5	..	6.9	5.2	7.7	7.7
1100 Of individuals	..	1.1	1.8	3.8	4.1	..	3.3	2.6	3.8	3.8
1200 Corporate	..	0.8	1.7	3.6	4.0	..	2.6	2.4	3.6	3.7
1300 Unallocable between 1100 and 1200	..	0.3	0.2	0.3	0.3	..	1.0	0.2	0.3	0.3
2000 Social security contributions	..	4.4	8.2	15.3	16.0	..	13.9	11.9	15.2	14.5
2100 Employees	..	0.9	2.1	3.7	4.0	..	2.8	3.0	3.7	3.7
2200 Employers	..	2.9	4.6	9.1	9.5	..	9.0	6.7	9.1	8.6
2300 Self-employed or non-employed	..	0.0	0.0	0.0	0.0	..	0.0	0.0	0.0	0.0
2400 Unallocable between 2100, 2200 and 2300	..	0.0	0.0	0.0	0.0	..	0.0	0.0	0.0	0.0
3000 Taxes on payroll and workforce	..	0.0	0.0	0.0	0.0	..	0.0	0.0	0.0	0.0
4000 Taxes on property	..	0.2	0.3	0.5	0.5	..	0.6	0.4	0.5	0.4
4100 Recurrent taxes on immovable property	..	0.1	0.3	0.5	0.5	..	0.5	0.4	0.5	0.4
4200 Recurrent taxes on net wealth	..	0.0	0.0	0.0	0.0	..	0.0	0.0	0.0	0.0
4300 Estate, inheritance and gift taxes	..	0.0	0.0	0.0	0.0	..	0.0	0.0	0.0	0.0
4400 Taxes on financial and capital transactions	..	0.0	0.0	0.0	0.0	..	0.1	0.0	0.0	0.0
4500 Non-recurrent taxes	..	0.0	0.0	0.0	0.0	..	0.0	0.0	0.0	0.0
4600 Other recurrent taxes on property	..	0.0	0.0	0.0	0.0	..	0.0	0.0	0.0	0.0
5000 Taxes on goods and services	..	3.9	7.1	12.1	13.5	..	12.2	10.4	12.1	12.3
5100 Taxes on production, sale, transfer, etc	..	3.6	6.6	11.1	12.5	..	11.5	9.6	11.1	11.4
5110 General taxes	..	2.2	4.2	7.5	8.4	..	6.8	6.1	7.5	7.7
5111 Value added taxes	..	2.2	4.2	7.5	8.4	..	6.8	6.1	7.5	7.7
5120 Taxes on specific goods and services	..	1.5	2.4	3.6	4.1	..	4.6	3.5	3.6	3.7
5121 Excises	..	1.0	2.1	3.0	2.8	..	3.1	3.0	3.0	2.5
5200 Taxes on use of goods and perform activities	..	0.2	0.4	0.7	0.8	..	0.7	0.6	0.7	0.7
5300 Unallocable between 5100 and 5200	..	0.0	0.1	0.2	0.2	..	0.0	0.2	0.2	0.2
6000 Other taxes	..	0.0	0.0	0.0	0.0	..	0.0	0.0	0.0	0.0
Non-wastable tax credits										
Non-wastable tax credits against 1000	..	..	0.3	0.4	0.5	..	..	0.4	0.4	0.5
Transfer component	..	..	..	..	..	..	..	..	..	..
Tax expenditure component	..	..	..	..	..	..	..	..	..	..
Revenues collected on behalf of the EU										
Revenues collected on behalf of the EU, total	..	..	0.1	0.2	0.2	..	..	0.2	0.2	0.2
Customs duties	..	..	0.1	0.1	0.2	..	..	0.2	0.1	0.1
SRF contributions	..	..	..	0.0	0.0	..	..	..	0.0	0.0

.. Not available

Note: More detailed country data and country notes are available in Chapter 5 "Detailed country tables". Full time series can be accessed at http://data-explorer.oecd.org/s/nb.

Source: Ministry of Finance.

Table 4.62. Slovak Republic, tax revenue and % of GDP by level of government and main taxes

	Billion EUR					% of GDP				
	1990	2000	2010	2021	2022	1990	2000	2010	2021	2022
Federal or Central government										
Total tax revenue	..	6.2	10.5	19.8	22.0	..	19.5	15.3	19.8	20.0
1000 Taxes on income, profits and capital gains	..	2.2	3.6	7.7	8.5	..	6.9	5.2	7.7	7.7
2000 Social security contributions	..	0.1	0.2	0.4	0.4	..	0.3	0.3	0.4	0.4
3000 Taxes on payroll and workforce	..	0.0	0.0	0.0	0.0	..	0.0	0.0	0.0	0.0
4000 Taxes on property	..	0.1	0.0	0.0	0.0	..	0.2	0.0	0.0	0.0
5000 Taxes on goods and services	..	3.9	6.7	11.7	13.1	..	12.2	9.8	11.7	11.9
6000 Other taxes	..	0.0	0.0	0.0	0.0	..	0.0	0.0	0.0	0.0
State/Regional										
Total tax revenue	..	..	..	..	..	..	..	..	..	..
1000 Taxes on income, profits and capital gains	..	..	..	..	..	..	..	..	..	..
2000 Social security contributions	..	..	..	..	..	..	..	..	..	..
3000 Taxes on payroll and workforce	..	..	..	..	..	..	..	..	..	..
4000 Taxes on property	..	..	..	..	..	..	..	..	..	..
5000 Taxes on goods and services	..	..	..	..	..	..	..	..	..	..
6000 Other taxes	..	..	..	..	..	..	..	..	..	..
Local government										
Total tax revenue	..	0.1	0.5	0.7	0.7	..	0.5	0.8	0.7	0.6
1000 Taxes on income, profits and capital gains	..	0.0	0.0	0.0	0.0	..	0.0	0.0	0.0	0.0
2000 Social security contributions	..	0.0	0.0	0.0	0.0	..	0.0	0.0	0.0	0.0
3000 Taxes on payroll and workforce	..	0.0	0.0	0.0	0.0	..	0.0	0.0	0.0	0.0
4000 Taxes on property	..	0.1	0.3	0.5	0.5	..	0.4	0.4	0.5	0.4
5000 Taxes on goods and services	..	0.0	0.3	0.2	0.2	..	0.0	0.4	0.2	0.2
6000 Other taxes	..	0.0	0.0	0.0	0.0	..	0.0	0.0	0.0	0.0
Social Security Funds										
Total tax revenue	..	4.3	7.9	14.8	15.5	..	13.6	11.5	14.8	14.1
1000 Taxes on income, profits and capital gains	..	0.0	0.0	0.0	0.0	..	0.0	0.0	0.0	0.0
2000 Social security contributions	..	4.3	7.9	14.8	15.5	..	13.6	11.5	14.8	14.1
3000 Taxes on payroll and workforce	..	0.0	0.0	0.0	0.0	..	0.0	0.0	0.0	0.0
4000 Taxes on property	..	0.0	0.0	0.0	0.0	..	0.0	0.0	0.0	0.0
5000 Taxes on goods and services	..	0.0	0.0	0.0	0.0	..	0.0	0.0	0.0	0.0
6000 Other taxes	..	0.0	0.0	0.0	0.0	..	0.0	0.0	0.0	0.0

.. Not available

Note: More detailed country data and country notes are available in Chapter 6 "Tax revenues by sub-sectors of general government". Full time series can be accessed at http://data-explorer.oecd.org/s/nb.

Source: Ministry of Finance.

Table 4.63. Slovenia, tax revenue and % of GDP by selected tax category

	Billion EUR					% of GDP				
	1990	2000	2010	2021	2022	1990	2000	2010	2021	2022
Total tax revenue	..	7.1	13.7	20.0	21.3	..	37.7	37.8	38.3	37.4
1000 Taxes on income, profits and capital gains	..	1.3	2.7	4.1	4.3	..	6.8	7.4	7.9	7.5
1100 Of individuals	..	1.0	2.0	2.8	3.0	..	5.5	5.6	5.4	5.2
1200 Corporate	..	0.2	0.7	1.3	1.3	..	1.1	1.8	2.5	2.3
1300 Unallocable between 1100 and 1200	..	0.0	0.0	0.0	0.0	..	0.1	0.0	0.0	0.0
2000 Social security contributions	..	2.8	5.7	8.6	9.1	..	14.9	15.8	16.4	16.0
2100 Employees	..	1.4	2.8	4.3	4.6	..	7.7	7.7	8.2	8.0
2200 Employers	..	1.0	2.1	3.1	3.3	..	5.3	5.7	6.0	5.9
2300 Self-employed or non-employed	..	0.0	0.0	0.0	0.0	..	0.0	0.0	0.0	0.0
2400 Unallocable between 2100, 2200 and 2300	..	0.0	0.0	0.0	0.0	..	0.0	0.0	0.0	0.0
3000 Taxes on payroll and workforce	..	0.3	0.0	0.0	0.0	..	1.5	0.1	0.0	0.0
4000 Taxes on property	..	0.1	0.2	0.3	0.3	..	0.6	0.6	0.6	0.6
4100 Recurrent taxes on immovable property	..	0.1	0.2	0.3	0.3	..	0.4	0.5	0.5	0.5
4200 Recurrent taxes on net wealth	..	0.0	0.0	0.0	0.0	..	0.0	0.0	0.0	0.0
4300 Estate, inheritance and gift taxes	..	0.0	0.0	0.0	0.0	..	0.0	0.0	0.0	0.0
4400 Taxes on financial and capital transactions	..	0.0	0.0	0.1	0.1	..	0.1	0.1	0.1	0.1
4500 Non-recurrent taxes	..	0.0	0.0	0.0	0.0	..	0.0	0.0	0.0	0.0
4600 Other recurrent taxes on property	..	0.0	0.0	0.0	0.0	..	0.0	0.0	0.0	0.0
5000 Taxes on goods and services	..	2.6	5.1	7.0	7.5	..	13.8	13.9	13.3	13.2
5100 Taxes on production, sale, transfer, etc	..	2.5	4.8	6.5	7.0	..	13.2	13.3	12.5	12.4
5110 General taxes	..	1.6	2.9	4.3	4.7	..	8.7	8.1	8.2	8.2
5111 Value added taxes	..	1.6	2.9	4.3	4.7	..	8.5	8.1	8.2	8.2
5120 Taxes on specific goods and services	..	0.8	1.9	2.2	2.4	..	4.5	5.3	4.2	4.1
5121 Excises	..	0.6	1.6	1.7	1.7	..	3.1	4.3	3.2	3.0
5200 Taxes on use of goods and perform activities	..	0.1	0.2	0.4	0.5	..	0.6	0.6	0.9	0.9
5300 Unallocable between 5100 and 5200	..	0.0	0.0	0.0	0.0	..	0.0	0.0	0.0	0.0
6000 Other taxes	..	0.0	0.0	0.0	0.0	..	0.0	0.0	0.0	0.0
Non-wastable tax credits										
Non-wastable tax credits against 1000	..	..	..	..	..	..	..	..	..	..
Transfer component	..	..	..	..	..	..	..	..	..	..
Tax expenditure component	..	..	..	..	..	..	..	..	..	..
Revenues collected on behalf of the EU										
Revenues collected on behalf of the EU, total	..	..	0.1	0.1	0.1	..	..	0.2	0.2	0.2
Customs duties	..	..	0.1	0.1	0.1	..	..	0.2	0.2	0.2
SRF contributions	..	..	..	0.0	0.0	..	..	..	0.0	0.0

.. Not available

Note: The total tax revenue has been reduced by the amount of any capital transfer that represents uncollected taxes. The capital transfers were subtracted directly from the specific taxes to which they relate. Therefore, the tax revenue amounts are different to those reported in the detailed country data available in Chapter 5 "Detailed country tables".

More detailed country data and country notes are available in Chapter 5 "Detailed country tables". Full time series can be accessed at http://data-explorer.oecd.org/s/nb.

Source: Statistical Office of the Republic of Slovenia.

Table 4.64. Slovenia, tax revenue and % of GDP by level of government and main taxes

	Billion EUR					% of GDP				
	1990	2000	2010	2021	2022	1990	2000	2010	2021	2022
Federal or Central government										
Total tax revenue	..	3.8	6.5	9.7	10.4	..	20.2	18.0	18.6	18.2
1000 Taxes on income, profits and capital gains	..	0.9	1.6	2.8	2.9	..	4.8	4.3	5.3	5.1
2000 Social security contributions	..	0.0	0.1	0.1	0.1	..	0.1	0.2	0.2	0.2
3000 Taxes on payroll and workforce	..	0.3	0.0	0.0	0.0	..	1.5	0.1	0.0	0.0
4000 Taxes on property	..	0.0	0.0	0.0	0.0	..	0.1	0.0	0.0	0.0
5000 Taxes on goods and services	..	2.6	4.9	6.8	7.3	..	13.7	13.5	13.0	12.8
6000 Other taxes	..	0.0	0.0	0.0	0.0	..	0.0	0.0	0.0	0.0
State/Regional										
Total tax revenue	..	..	..	..	..	..	..	..	..	..
1000 Taxes on income, profits and capital gains	..	..	..	..	..	..	..	..	..	..
2000 Social security contributions	..	..	..	..	..	..	..	..	..	..
3000 Taxes on payroll and workforce	..	..	..	..	..	..	..	..	..	..
4000 Taxes on property	..	..	..	..	..	..	..	..	..	..
5000 Taxes on goods and services	..	..	..	..	..	..	..	..	..	..
6000 Other taxes	..	..	..	..	..	..	..	..	..	..
Local government										
Total tax revenue	..	0.5	1.5	1.7	1.8	..	2.7	4.0	3.3	3.2
1000 Taxes on income, profits and capital gains	..	0.4	1.1	1.3	1.4	..	2.0	3.1	2.6	2.4
2000 Social security contributions	..	0.0	0.0	0.0	0.0	..	0.0	0.0	0.0	0.0
3000 Taxes on payroll and workforce	..	0.0	0.0	0.0	0.0	..	0.0	0.0	0.0	0.0
4000 Taxes on property	..	0.1	0.2	0.3	0.3	..	0.6	0.6	0.6	0.6
5000 Taxes on goods and services	..	0.0	0.1	0.1	0.1	..	0.1	0.3	0.1	0.2
6000 Other taxes	..	0.0	0.0	0.0	0.0	..	0.0	0.0	0.0	0.0
Social Security Funds										
Total tax revenue	..	2.8	5.7	8.5	9.0	..	14.8	15.6	16.2	15.9
1000 Taxes on income, profits and capital gains	..	0.0	0.0	0.0	0.0	..	0.0	0.0	0.0	0.0
2000 Social security contributions	..	2.8	5.7	8.5	9.0	..	14.8	15.6	16.2	15.9
3000 Taxes on payroll and workforce	..	0.0	0.0	0.0	0.0	..	0.0	0.0	0.0	0.0
4000 Taxes on property	..	0.0	0.0	0.0	0.0	..	0.0	0.0	0.0	0.0
5000 Taxes on goods and services	..	0.0	0.0	0.0	0.0	..	0.0	0.0	0.0	0.0
6000 Other taxes	..	0.0	0.0	0.0	0.0	..	0.0	0.0	0.0	0.0

.. Not available

Note: The total tax revenue has been reduced by the amount of any capital transfer that represents uncollected taxes. The capital transfers were subtracted directly from the specific taxes to which they relate. Therefore, the tax revenue amounts are different to those reported in the detailed country data available in Chapter 6 "Tax revenues by sub-sectors of general government".

More detailed country data and country notes are available in Chapter 6 "Tax revenues by sub-sectors of general government". Full time series can be accessed at http://data-explorer.oecd.org/s/nb.

Source: Statistical Office of the Republic of Slovenia.

Table 4.65. Spain, tax revenue and % of GDP by selected tax category

	Billion EUR					% of GDP				
	1990	2000	2010	2021	2022	1990	2000	2010	2021	2022
Total tax revenue	103.7	214.1	335.6	462.2	506.1	31.5	33.0	31.3	37.8	37.6
1000 Taxes on income, profits and capital gains	31.8	60.1	93.8	137.7	158.7	9.7	9.3	8.7	11.3	11.8
1100 Of individuals	22.5	41.2	74.1	105.4	122.2	6.9	6.4	6.9	8.6	9.1
1200 Corporate	9.1	18.9	19.7	32.3	36.6	2.8	2.9	1.8	2.6	2.7
1300 Unallocable between 1100 and 1200	0.1	0.0	0.0	0.0	0.0	0.0	0.0	0.0	0.0	0.0
2000 Social security contributions	36.7	74.7	127.2	163.8	172.4	11.2	11.5	11.9	13.4	12.8
2100 Employees	6.0	11.7	19.4	24.1	26.3	1.8	1.8	1.8	2.0	2.0
2200 Employers	26.4	54.2	89.7	118.8	127.6	8.0	8.4	8.4	9.7	9.5
2300 Self-employed or non-employed	0.0	0.0	0.0	0.0	0.0	0.0	0.0	0.0	0.0	0.0
2400 Unallocable between 2100, 2200 and 2300	0.0	0.0	0.0	0.0	0.0	0.0	0.0	0.0	0.0	0.0
3000 Taxes on payroll and workforce	0.0	0.0	0.0	0.0	0.0	0.0	0.0	0.0	0.0	0.0
4000 Taxes on property	5.7	13.8	22.2	33.7	34.9	1.7	2.1	2.1	2.8	2.6
4100 Recurrent taxes on immovable property	1.5	4.0	9.7	14.0	14.1	0.4	0.6	0.9	1.1	1.0
4200 Recurrent taxes on net wealth	0.6	1.4	0.7	2.4	2.6	0.2	0.2	0.1	0.2	0.2
4300 Estate, inheritance and gift taxes	0.4	1.4	2.4	3.5	3.7	0.1	0.2	0.2	0.3	0.3
4400 Taxes on financial and capital transactions	2.5	5.9	7.6	11.1	12.7	0.8	0.9	0.7	0.9	0.9
4500 Non-recurrent taxes	0.0	0.0	0.0	0.0	0.0	0.0	0.0	0.0	0.0	0.0
4600 Other recurrent taxes on property	0.0	0.0	0.0	0.0	0.0	0.0	0.0	0.0	0.0	0.0
5000 Taxes on goods and services	29.4	65.5	92.3	126.8	139.8	9.0	10.1	8.6	10.4	10.4
5100 Taxes on production, sale, transfer, etc	26.7	59.4	85.0	116.3	128.3	8.1	9.2	7.9	9.5	9.5
5110 General taxes	16.6	37.8	55.6	83.9	94.7	5.1	5.8	5.2	6.9	7.0
5111 Value added taxes	16.3	37.8	55.3	83.5	94.2	5.0	5.8	5.2	6.8	7.0
5120 Taxes on specific goods and services	10.1	21.6	29.4	32.4	33.6	3.1	3.3	2.7	2.7	2.5
5121 Excises	6.0	18.0	24.4	24.1	23.8	1.8	2.8	2.3	2.0	1.8
5200 Taxes on use of goods and perform activities	2.6	6.1	7.4	10.5	11.5	0.8	0.9	0.7	0.9	0.9
5300 Unallocable between 5100 and 5200	0.1	0.0	0.0	0.0	0.0	0.0	0.0	0.0	0.0	0.0
6000 Other taxes	0.0	0.0	0.0	0.2	0.2	0.0	0.0	0.0	0.0	0.0
Non-wastable tax credits										
Non-wastable tax credits against 1000	..	..	1.9	4.1	3.2	..	..	0.2	0.3	0.2
Transfer component	..	..	1.2	2.9	1.9	..	..	0.1	0.2	0.1
Tax expenditure component	..	..	0.7	1.2	1.3	..	..	0.1	0.1	0.1
Revenues collected on behalf of the EU										
Revenues collected on behalf of the EU, total	0.5	1.0	1.5	3.0	3.9	0.2	0.2	0.1	0.2	0.3
Customs duties	..	1.0	1.5	2.0	2.8	..	0.1	0.1	0.2	0.2
SRF contributions	..	..	..	1.0	1.1	..	..	..	0.1	0.1

.. Not available

Note: More detailed country data and country notes are available in Chapter 5 "Detailed country tables". Full time series can be accessed at http://data-explorer.oecd.org/s/nb.

Source: Information from the Ministry of Finance for taxes and from Social Security System for social security contributions up to 1994. Since 1995 (accrual basis), national account data (IGAE-Ministry of Finance).

Table 4.66. Spain, tax revenue and % of GDP by level of government and main taxes

	Billion EUR					% of GDP				
	1990	2000	2010	2021	2022	1990	2000	2010	2021	2022
Federal or Central government										
Total tax revenue	53.7	104.7	135.9	186.1	215.3	16.3	16.2	12.7	15.2	16.0
1000 Taxes on income, profits and capital gains	29.5	51.0	60.6	79.0	98.6	9.0	7.9	5.6	6.5	7.3
2000 Social security contributions	0.4	2.3	3.5	3.5	3.6	0.1	0.4	0.3	0.3	0.3
3000 Taxes on payroll and workforce	0.0	0.0	0.0	0.0	0.0	0.0	0.0	0.0	0.0	0.0
4000 Taxes on property	0.4	0.4	0.1	0.7	0.8	0.1	0.1	0.0	0.1	0.1
5000 Taxes on goods and services	23.4	51.1	71.7	102.7	112.0	7.1	7.9	6.7	8.4	8.3
6000 Other taxes	0.0	0.0	0.0	0.1	0.2	0.0	0.0	0.0	0.0	0.0
State/Regional										
Total tax revenue	5.0	16.9	44.1	72.7	76.6	1.5	2.6	4.1	5.9	5.7
1000 Taxes on income, profits and capital gains	0.4	5.6	28.1	51.4	52.1	0.1	0.9	2.6	4.2	3.9
2000 Social security contributions	0.0	0.0	0.0	0.0	0.0	0.0	0.0	0.0	0.0	0.0
3000 Taxes on payroll and workforce	0.0	0.0	0.0	0.0	0.0	0.0	0.0	0.0	0.0	0.0
4000 Taxes on property	3.0	7.7	9.7	15.2	16.9	0.9	1.2	0.9	1.2	1.3
5000 Taxes on goods and services	1.6	3.6	6.3	6.1	7.6	0.5	0.6	0.6	0.5	0.6
6000 Other taxes	0.0	0.0	0.0	0.0	0.0	0.0	0.0	0.0	0.0	0.0
Local government										
Total tax revenue	8.1	19.0	30.3	40.1	41.5	2.5	2.9	2.8	3.3	3.1
1000 Taxes on income, profits and capital gains	1.9	3.5	5.2	7.3	8.0	0.6	0.5	0.5	0.6	0.6
2000 Social security contributions	0.0	0.0	0.0	0.0	0.0	0.0	0.0	0.0	0.0	0.0
3000 Taxes on payroll and workforce	0.0	0.0	0.0	0.0	0.0	0.0	0.0	0.0	0.0	0.0
4000 Taxes on property	2.3	5.8	12.4	17.8	17.2	0.7	0.9	1.2	1.5	1.3
5000 Taxes on goods and services	3.9	9.7	12.8	14.9	16.3	1.2	1.5	1.2	1.2	1.2
6000 Other taxes	0.0	0.0	0.0	0.0	0.0	0.0	0.0	0.0	0.0	0.0
Social Security Funds										
Total tax revenue	36.4	72.4	123.7	160.4	168.8	11.1	11.2	11.5	13.1	12.5
1000 Taxes on income, profits and capital gains	0.0	0.0	0.0	0.0	0.0	0.0	0.0	0.0	0.0	0.0
2000 Social security contributions	36.4	72.4	123.7	160.4	168.8	11.1	11.2	11.5	13.1	12.5
3000 Taxes on payroll and workforce	0.0	0.0	0.0	0.0	0.0	0.0	0.0	0.0	0.0	0.0
4000 Taxes on property	0.0	0.0	0.0	0.0	0.0	0.0	0.0	0.0	0.0	0.0
5000 Taxes on goods and services	0.0	0.0	0.0	0.0	0.0	0.0	0.0	0.0	0.0	0.0
6000 Other taxes	0.0	0.0	0.0	0.0	0.0	0.0	0.0	0.0	0.0	0.0

Note: More detailed country data and country notes are available in Chapter 6 "Tax revenues by sub-sectors of general government". Full time series can be accessed at http://data-explorer.oecd.org/s/nb.

Source: Information from the Ministry of Finance for taxes and from Social Security System for social security contributions up to 1994. Since 1995 (accrual basis), national account data (IGAE-Ministry of Finance).

Table 4.67. Sweden, tax revenue and % of GDP by selected tax category

	Billion SEK					% of GDP				
	1990	2000	2010	2021	2022	1990	2000	2010	2021	2022
Total tax revenue	756.0	1 204.8	1 532.3	2 336.8	2 493.4	48.8	50.0	43.1	42.8	42.5
1000 Taxes on income, profits and capital gains	314.8	514.7	546.7	858.4	897.9	20.3	21.4	15.4	15.7	15.3
1100 Of individuals	291.1	427.0	430.9	676.2	697.2	18.8	17.7	12.1	12.4	11.9
1200 Corporate	23.7	87.8	115.8	182.3	200.7	1.5	3.6	3.3	3.3	3.4
1300 Unallocable between 1100 and 1200	0.0	0.0	0.0	0.0	0.0	0.0	0.0	0.0	0.0	0.0
2000 Social security contributions	205.9	307.0	384.7	489.9	518.4	13.3	12.7	10.8	9.0	8.8
2100 Employees	0.8	63.1	89.2	137.3	145.3	0.1	2.6	2.5	2.5	2.5
2200 Employers	196.9	237.6	288.3	348.6	370.4	12.7	9.9	8.1	6.4	6.3
2300 Self-employed or non-employed	0.0	0.0	0.0	0.0	0.0	0.0	0.0	0.0	0.0	0.0
2400 Unallocable between 2100, 2200 and 2300	0.0	0.8	-0.4	-0.7	-2.0	0.0	0.0	-0.0	-0.0	-0.0
3000 Taxes on payroll and workforce	18.7	50.1	107.5	280.8	301.3	1.2	2.1	3.0	5.1	5.1
4000 Taxes on property	26.6	39.9	36.5	52.2	55.0	1.7	1.7	1.0	1.0	0.9
4100 Recurrent taxes on immovable property	8.9	23.3	26.4	36.1	38.6	0.6	1.0	0.7	0.7	0.7
4200 Recurrent taxes on net wealth	3.2	8.2	0.0	0.0	0.0	0.2	0.3	0.0	0.0	0.0
4300 Estate, inheritance and gift taxes	1.4	2.5	0.0	0.0	0.0	0.1	0.1	0.0	0.0	0.0
4400 Taxes on financial and capital transactions	13.1	5.8	10.1	16.1	16.4	0.8	0.2	0.3	0.3	0.3
4500 Non-recurrent taxes	0.0	0.0	0.0	0.0	0.0	0.0	0.0	0.0	0.0	0.0
4600 Other recurrent taxes on property	0.0	0.0	0.0	0.0	0.0	0.0	0.0	0.0	0.0	0.0
5000 Taxes on goods and services	188.7	291.6	455.4	652.9	717.5	12.2	12.1	12.8	11.9	12.2
5100 Taxes on production, sale, transfer, etc	181.6	284.2	439.1	630.4	695.0	11.7	11.8	12.4	11.5	11.8
5110 General taxes	112.4	199.6	326.7	499.5	552.4	7.3	8.3	9.2	9.1	9.4
5111 Value added taxes	112.4	197.5	322.6	499.4	552.2	7.3	8.2	9.1	9.1	9.4
5120 Taxes on specific goods and services	69.2	84.6	112.4	130.9	142.6	4.5	3.5	3.2	2.4	2.4
5121 Excises	55.3	70.3	91.5	108.7	118.6	3.6	2.9	2.6	2.0	2.0
5200 Taxes on use of goods and perform activities	7.1	7.4	16.4	22.5	22.5	0.5	0.3	0.5	0.4	0.4
5300 Unallocable between 5100 and 5200	0.0	0.0	0.0	0.0	0.0	0.0	0.0	0.0	0.0	0.0
6000 Other taxes	1.3	1.5	1.4	2.6	3.3	0.1	0.1	0.0	0.0	0.1
Non-wastable tax credits										
Non-wastable tax credits against 1000	..	..	..	..	..	..	..	..	..	..
Transfer component	..	..	..	..	..	..	..	..	..	..
Tax expenditure component	..	..	..	..	..	..	..	..	..	..
Revenues collected on behalf of the EU										
Revenues collected on behalf of the EU, total	..	3.8	5.7	7.3	9.3	..	0.2	0.2	0.1	0.2
Customs duties	..	3.4	5.4	7.3	9.3	..	0.1	0.2	0.1	0.2
SRF contributions	..	..	..	..	..	..	..	..	..	..

.. Not available

Note: More detailed country data and country notes are available in Chapter 5 "Detailed country tables". Full time series can be accessed at http://data-explorer.oecd.org/s/nb.

Source: National Financial Management Authority, Stockholm.

Table 4.68. Sweden, tax revenue and % of GDP by level of government and main taxes

	Billion SEK					% of GDP				
	1990	2000	2010	2021	2022	1990	2000	2010	2021	2022
Federal or Central government										
Total tax revenue	383.9	737.9	806.2	1 218.9	1 309.6	24.8	30.6	22.7	22.3	22.3
1000 Taxes on income, profits and capital gains	94.7	178.4	23.8	52.0	45.4	6.1	7.4	0.7	1.0	0.8
2000 Social security contributions	54.8	180.2	201.2	206.4	217.9	3.5	7.5	5.7	3.8	3.7
3000 Taxes on payroll and workforce	18.7	50.1	107.5	280.8	301.3	1.2	2.1	3.0	5.1	5.1
4000 Taxes on property	26.6	39.9	22.5	31.6	33.6	1.7	1.7	0.6	0.6	0.6
5000 Taxes on goods and services	187.8	287.8	449.8	645.6	708.2	12.1	11.9	12.7	11.8	12.1
6000 Other taxes	1.3	1.5	1.4	2.6	3.3	0.1	0.1	0.0	0.0	0.1
State/Regional										
Total tax revenue	..	..	..	..	..	..	..	..	..	..
1000 Taxes on income, profits and capital gains	..	..	..	..	..	..	..	..	..	..
2000 Social security contributions	..	..	..	..	..	..	..	..	..	..
3000 Taxes on payroll and workforce	..	..	..	..	..	..	..	..	..	..
4000 Taxes on property	..	..	..	..	..	..	..	..	..	..
5000 Taxes on goods and services	..	..	..	..	..	..	..	..	..	..
6000 Other taxes	..	..	..	..	..	..	..	..	..	..
Local government										
Total tax revenue	221.0	336.3	536.9	827.1	873.9	14.3	14.0	15.1	15.1	14.9
1000 Taxes on income, profits and capital gains	220.1	336.3	522.9	806.4	852.5	14.2	14.0	14.7	14.8	14.5
2000 Social security contributions	0.0	0.0	0.0	0.0	0.0	0.0	0.0	0.0	0.0	0.0
3000 Taxes on payroll and workforce	0.0	0.0	0.0	0.0	0.0	0.0	0.0	0.0	0.0	0.0
4000 Taxes on property	0.0	0.0	14.0	20.6	21.4	0.0	0.0	0.4	0.4	0.4
5000 Taxes on goods and services	0.9	0.0	0.0	0.0	0.0	0.1	0.0	0.0	0.0	0.0
6000 Other taxes	0.0	0.0	0.0	0.0	0.0	0.0	0.0	0.0	0.0	0.0
Social Security Funds										
Total tax revenue	151.1	126.8	183.5	283.5	300.5	9.8	5.3	5.2	5.2	5.1
1000 Taxes on income, profits and capital gains	0.0	0.0	0.0	0.0	0.0	0.0	0.0	0.0	0.0	0.0
2000 Social security contributions	151.1	126.8	183.5	283.5	300.5	9.8	5.3	5.2	5.2	5.1
3000 Taxes on payroll and workforce	0.0	0.0	0.0	0.0	0.0	0.0	0.0	0.0	0.0	0.0
4000 Taxes on property	0.0	0.0	0.0	0.0	0.0	0.0	0.0	0.0	0.0	0.0
5000 Taxes on goods and services	0.0	0.0	0.0	0.0	0.0	0.0	0.0	0.0	0.0	0.0
6000 Other taxes	0.0	0.0	0.0	0.0	0.0	0.0	0.0	0.0	0.0	0.0

.. Not available

Note: More detailed country data and country notes are available in Chapter 6 "Tax revenues by sub-sectors of general government". Full time series can be accessed at http://data-explorer.oecd.org/s/nb.

Source: National Financial Management Authority, Stockholm.

Table 4.69. Switzerland, tax revenue and % of GDP by selected tax category

	Billion CHF					% of GDP				
	1990	2000	2010	2021	2022	1990	2000	2010	2021	2022
Total tax revenue	85.5	127.5	161.2	208.4	210.3	23.2	27.0	25.8	28.0	26.9
1000 Taxes on income, profits and capital gains	40.0	55.8	73.6	99.4	98.1	10.8	11.8	11.8	13.4	12.5
1100 Of individuals	27.7	37.5	51.2	63.2	65.1	7.5	7.9	8.2	8.5	8.3
1200 Corporate	6.3	11.2	16.2	22.8	25.0	1.7	2.4	2.6	3.1	3.2
1300 Unallocable between 1100 and 1200	6.1	7.1	6.2	13.4	7.9	1.6	1.5	1.0	1.8	1.0
2000 Social security contributions	19.9	30.8	38.3	50.5	52.2	5.4	6.5	6.1	6.8	6.7
2100 Employees	9.3	14.5	17.5	24.0	24.6	2.5	3.1	2.8	3.2	3.1
2200 Employers	9.3	14.5	17.6	23.2	24.5	2.5	3.1	2.8	3.1	3.1
2300 Self-employed or non-employed	0.0	0.0	0.0	0.0	0.0	0.0	0.0	0.0	0.0	0.0
2400 Unallocable between 2100, 2200 and 2300	0.0	0.0	0.0	0.0	0.0	0.0	0.0	0.0	0.0	0.0
3000 Taxes on payroll and workforce	0.0	0.0	0.0	0.0	0.0	0.0	0.0	0.0	0.0	0.0
4000 Taxes on property	7.6	12.3	12.4	16.6	17.0	2.1	2.6	2.0	2.2	2.2
4100 Recurrent taxes on immovable property	0.4	0.7	1.0	1.4	1.5	0.1	0.2	0.2	0.2	0.2
4200 Recurrent taxes on net wealth	3.4	5.3	7.1	10.3	10.6	0.9	1.1	1.1	1.4	1.4
4300 Estate, inheritance and gift taxes	0.9	1.2	1.0	1.4	1.5	0.2	0.3	0.2	0.2	0.2
4400 Taxes on financial and capital transactions	2.2	4.3	2.4	2.2	2.1	0.6	0.9	0.4	0.3	0.3
4500 Non-recurrent taxes	0.0	0.0	0.0	0.0	0.0	0.0	0.0	0.0	0.0	0.0
4600 Other recurrent taxes on property	0.6	0.8	0.9	1.4	1.4	0.2	0.2	0.1	0.2	0.2
5000 Taxes on goods and services	17.9	28.3	36.4	40.8	41.9	4.8	6.0	5.8	5.5	5.4
5100 Taxes on production, sale, transfer, etc	16.0	25.3	32.1	35.4	36.4	4.3	5.4	5.1	4.8	4.7
5110 General taxes	9.9	16.9	20.9	23.8	24.8	2.7	3.6	3.3	3.2	3.2
5111 Value added taxes	9.9	16.6	20.5	23.5	24.5	2.7	3.5	3.3	3.2	3.1
5120 Taxes on specific goods and services	6.1	8.3	11.2	11.6	11.5	1.6	1.8	1.8	1.6	1.5
5121 Excises	4.6	6.8	8.3	8.5	8.2	1.2	1.4	1.3	1.1	1.1
5200 Taxes on use of goods and perform activities	1.9	3.0	4.2	5.4	5.5	0.5	0.6	0.7	0.7	0.7
5300 Unallocable between 5100 and 5200	0.0	0.0	0.0	0.0	0.0	0.0	0.0	0.0	0.0	0.0
6000 Other taxes	0.1	0.2	0.6	1.1	1.2	0.0	0.0	0.1	0.1	0.1
Non-wastable tax credits										
Non-wastable tax credits against 1000	..	..	..	..	..	..	..	..	..	..
Transfer component	..	..	..	..	..	..	..	..	..	..
Tax expenditure component	..	..	..	..	..	..	..	..	..	..

.. Not available

Note: More detailed country data and country notes are available in Chapter 5 "Detailed country tables". Full time series can be accessed at http://data-explorer.oecd.org/s/nb.

The total tax revenue has been reduced by the amount of any capital transfer that represents uncollected taxes. The capital transfers were subtracted directly from the specific taxes to which they relate. Therefore, the tax revenue amounts are different to those reported in the detailed country data available in Chapter 5 "Detailed country tables".

Source: Financial Statistics, Federal Finance Administration.

Table 4.70. Switzerland, tax revenue and % of GDP by level of government and main taxes

	Billion CHF					% of GDP				
	1990	2000	2010	2021	2022	1990	2000	2010	2021	2022
Federal or Central government										
Total tax revenue	29.4	47.3	58.5	75.0	71.1	8.0	10.0	9.4	10.1	9.1
1000 Taxes on income, profits and capital gains	10.9	17.0	22.7	35.6	30.9	2.9	3.6	3.6	4.8	3.9
2000 Social security contributions	0.0	0.0	0.0	0.0	0.0	0.0	0.0	0.0	0.0	0.0
3000 Taxes on payroll and workforce	0.0	0.0	0.0	0.0	0.0	0.0	0.0	0.0	0.0	0.0
4000 Taxes on property	2.1	4.1	2.2	1.9	1.7	0.6	0.9	0.4	0.3	0.2
5000 Taxes on goods and services	16.4	26.1	33.5	37.5	38.5	4.4	5.5	5.4	5.0	4.9
6000 Other taxes	0.0	0.0	0.0	0.1	0.1	0.0	0.0	0.0	0.0	0.0
State/Regional										
Total tax revenue	21.3	28.9	39.9	51.0	53.8	5.8	6.1	6.4	6.9	6.9
1000 Taxes on income, profits and capital gains	16.4	21.7	30.8	38.4	40.7	4.4	4.6	4.9	5.2	5.2
2000 Social security contributions	0.0	0.0	0.0	0.0	0.0	0.0	0.0	0.0	0.0	0.0
3000 Taxes on payroll and workforce	0.0	0.0	0.0	0.0	0.0	0.0	0.0	0.0	0.0	0.0
4000 Taxes on property	3.5	5.1	6.4	9.2	9.5	0.9	1.1	1.0	1.2	1.2
5000 Taxes on goods and services	1.4	2.1	2.7	3.1	3.2	0.4	0.4	0.4	0.4	0.4
6000 Other taxes	0.0	0.0	0.0	0.4	0.4	0.0	0.0	0.0	0.1	0.1
Local government										
Total tax revenue	14.9	20.5	24.6	31.8	33.2	4.0	4.3	3.9	4.3	4.2
1000 Taxes on income, profits and capital gains	12.7	17.1	20.1	25.5	26.5	3.4	3.6	3.2	3.4	3.4
2000 Social security contributions	0.0	0.0	0.0	0.0	0.0	0.0	0.0	0.0	0.0	0.0
3000 Taxes on payroll and workforce	0.0	0.0	0.0	0.0	0.0	0.0	0.0	0.0	0.0	0.0
4000 Taxes on property	2.0	3.1	3.8	5.6	5.8	0.5	0.7	0.6	0.7	0.7
5000 Taxes on goods and services	0.1	0.1	0.1	0.2	0.3	0.0	0.0	0.0	0.0	0.0
6000 Other taxes	0.1	0.2	0.6	0.6	0.6	0.0	0.0	0.1	0.1	0.1
Social Security Funds										
Total tax revenue	19.9	30.8	38.3	50.5	52.2	5.4	6.5	6.1	6.8	6.7
1000 Taxes on income, profits and capital gains	0.0	0.0	0.0	0.0	0.0	0.0	0.0	0.0	0.0	0.0
2000 Social security contributions	19.9	30.8	38.3	50.5	52.2	5.4	6.5	6.1	6.8	6.7
3000 Taxes on payroll and workforce	0.0	0.0	0.0	0.0	0.0	0.0	0.0	0.0	0.0	0.0
4000 Taxes on property	0.0	0.0	0.0	0.0	0.0	0.0	0.0	0.0	0.0	0.0
5000 Taxes on goods and services	0.0	0.0	0.0	0.0	0.0	0.0	0.0	0.0	0.0	0.0
6000 Other taxes	0.0	0.0	0.0	0.0	0.0	0.0	0.0	0.0	0.0	0.0

Note: More detailed country data and country notes are available in Chapter 6 "Tax revenues by sub-sectors of general government". Full time series can be accessed at http://data-explorer.oecd.org/s/nb.

The total tax revenue has been reduced by the amount of any capital transfer that represents uncollected taxes. The capital transfers were subtracted directly from the specific taxes to which they relate. Therefore, the tax revenue amounts are different to those reported in the detailed country data available in Chapter 6 "Tax revenues by sub-sectors of general government".

Source: Financial Statistics, Federal Finance Administration.

Table 4.71. Türkiye, tax revenue and % of GDP by selected tax category

	Billion TRY					% of GDP				
	1990	2000	2010	2021	2022	1990	2000	2010	2021	2022
Total tax revenue	0.1	40.3	287.9	1 662.7	3 144.3	14.5	23.5	24.7	22.9	20.9
1000 Taxes on income, profits and capital gains	0.0	11.9	61.3	397.6	863.9	4.9	6.9	5.3	5.5	5.8
1100 Of individuals	0.0	9.0	40.4	219.7	356.5	3.9	5.2	3.5	3.0	2.4
1200 Corporate	0.0	2.9	20.9	178.0	507.5	1.0	1.7	1.8	2.5	3.4
1300 Unallocable between 1100 and 1200	0.0	0.0	0.0	0.0	0.0	0.0	0.0	0.0	0.0	0.0
2000 Social security contributions	0.0	7.5	71.7	481.2	767.5	2.9	4.4	6.1	6.6	5.1
2100 Employees	0.0	2.7	26.9	182.7	296.0	1.1	1.6	2.3	2.5	2.0
2200 Employers	0.0	3.6	39.4	272.4	440.6	1.6	2.1	3.4	3.8	2.9
2300 Self-employed or non-employed	0.0	0.0	0.0	0.0	0.0	0.0	0.0	0.0	0.0	0.0
2400 Unallocable between 2100, 2200 and 2300	0.0	0.0	0.0	0.0	0.0	0.0	0.0	0.0	0.0	0.0
3000 Taxes on payroll and workforce	0.0	0.0	0.0	0.0	0.0	0.0	0.0	0.0	0.0	0.0
4000 Taxes on property	0.0	1.3	11.7	70.2	109.5	0.3	0.7	1.0	1.0	0.7
4100 Recurrent taxes on immovable property	0.0	0.2	2.7	13.6	18.6	0.0	0.1	0.2	0.2	0.1
4200 Recurrent taxes on net wealth	0.0	0.0	0.0	0.0	0.0	0.0	0.0	0.0	0.0	0.0
4300 Estate, inheritance and gift taxes	0.0	0.0	0.2	2.3	2.9	0.0	0.0	0.0	0.0	0.0
4400 Taxes on financial and capital transactions	0.0	1.1	8.8	54.3	87.9	0.3	0.6	0.8	0.7	0.6
4500 Non-recurrent taxes	0.0	0.0	0.0	0.0	0.0	0.0	0.0	0.0	0.0	0.0
4600 Other recurrent taxes on property	0.0	0.0	0.0	0.0	0.0	0.0	0.0	0.0	0.0	0.0
5000 Taxes on goods and services	0.0	16.9	137.3	696.3	1370.1	4.1	9.9	11.8	9.6	9.1
5100 Taxes on production, sale, transfer, etc	0.0	16.3	131.9	676.0	1344.2	4.0	9.5	11.3	9.3	9.0
5110 General taxes	0.0	9.7	62.5	385.3	754.1	2.9	5.7	5.4	5.3	5.0
5111 Value added taxes	0.0	9.7	62.5	385.3	754.1	2.7	5.7	5.4	5.3	5.0
5120 Taxes on specific goods and services	0.0	6.6	69.3	290.6	590.1	1.1	3.8	5.9	4.0	3.9
5121 Excises	0.0	4.7	57.3	205.4	419.8	0.1	2.8	4.9	2.8	2.8
5200 Taxes on use of goods and perform activities	0.0	0.6	5.4	20.4	25.9	0.1	0.3	0.5	0.3	0.2
5300 Unallocable between 5100 and 5200	0.0	0.0	0.0	0.0	0.0	0.0	0.0	0.0	0.0	0.0
6000 Other taxes	0.0	2.7	5.9	17.4	33.2	2.4	1.6	0.5	0.2	0.2
Non-wastable tax credits										
Non-wastable tax credits against 1000	..	..	..	..	..	..	..	..	..	..
Transfer component	..	..	..	..	..	..	..	..	..	..
Tax expenditure component	..	..	..	..	..	..	..	..	..	..

.. Not available

Note: More detailed country data and country notes are available in Chapter 5 "Detailed country tables". Full time series can be accessed at http://data-explorer.oecd.org/s/nb.

Source: Bulletin of national accounts and the Budget revenue Bulletin.

Table 4.72. Türkiye, tax revenue and % of GDP by level of government and main taxes

	Billion TRY					% of GDP				
	1990	2000	2010	2021	2022	1990	2000	2010	2021	2022
Federal or Central government										
Total tax revenue	0.1	29.1	189.4	1024.0	2 070.5	10.4	17.0	16.2	14.1	13.8
1000 Taxes on income, profits and capital gains	0.0	10.5	54.6	350.2	761.2	4.3	6.1	4.7	4.8	5.1
2000 Social security contributions	0.0	0.0	0.0	0.0	0.0	0.0	0.0	0.0	0.0	0.0
3000 Taxes on payroll and workforce	0.0	0.0	0.0	0.0	0.0	0.0	0.0	0.0	0.0	0.0
4000 Taxes on property	0.0	0.9	8.1	50.0	80.3	0.3	0.5	0.7	0.7	0.5
5000 Taxes on goods and services	0.0	15.2	124.0	616.2	1215.4	3.6	8.9	10.6	8.5	8.1
6000 Other taxes	0.0	2.5	2.7	7.6	13.6	2.2	1.4	0.2	0.1	0.1
State/Regional										
Total tax revenue	..	..	..	..	..	..	..	..	..	..
1000 Taxes on income, profits and capital gains	..	..	..	..	..	..	..	..	..	..
2000 Social security contributions	..	..	..	..	..	..	..	..	..	..
3000 Taxes on payroll and workforce	..	..	..	..	..	..	..	..	..	..
4000 Taxes on property	..	..	..	..	..	..	..	..	..	..
5000 Taxes on goods and services	..	..	..	..	..	..	..	..	..	..
6000 Other taxes	..	..	..	..	..	..	..	..	..	..
Local government										
Total tax revenue	0.0	3.6	26.8	157.5	306.2	1.3	2.1	2.3	2.2	2.0
1000 Taxes on income, profits and capital gains	0.0	1.4	6.7	47.4	102.7	0.6	0.8	0.6	0.7	0.7
2000 Social security contributions	0.0	0.0	0.0	0.0	0.0	0.0	0.0	0.0	0.0	0.0
3000 Taxes on payroll and workforce	0.0	0.0	0.0	0.0	0.0	0.0	0.0	0.0	0.0	0.0
4000 Taxes on property	0.0	0.3	3.6	20.2	29.1	0.0	0.2	0.3	0.3	0.2
5000 Taxes on goods and services	0.0	1.7	13.3	80.1	154.8	0.5	1.0	1.1	1.1	1.0
6000 Other taxes	0.0	0.2	3.2	9.8	19.6	0.2	0.1	0.3	0.1	0.1
Social Security Funds										
Total tax revenue	0.0	7.5	71.7	481.2	767.5	2.9	4.4	6.1	6.6	5.1
1000 Taxes on income, profits and capital gains	0.0	0.0	0.0	0.0	0.0	0.0	0.0	0.0	0.0	0.0
2000 Social security contributions	0.0	7.5	71.7	481.2	767.5	2.9	4.4	6.1	6.6	5.1
3000 Taxes on payroll and workforce	0.0	0.0	0.0	0.0	0.0	0.0	0.0	0.0	0.0	0.0
4000 Taxes on property	0.0	0.0	0.0	0.0	0.0	0.0	0.0	0.0	0.0	0.0
5000 Taxes on goods and services	0.0	0.0	0.0	0.0	0.0	0.0	0.0	0.0	0.0	0.0
6000 Other taxes	0.0	0.0	0.0	0.0	0.0	0.0	0.0	0.0	0.0	0.0

.. Not available

Note: More detailed country data and country notes are available in Chapter 6 "Tax revenues by sub-sectors of general government". Full time series can be accessed at http://data-explorer.oecd.org/s/nb.

Source: Bulletin of national accounts and the Budget revenue Bulletin.

Table 4.73. United Kingdom, tax revenue and % of GDP by selected tax category

	Billion GBP					% of GDP				
	1990	2000	2010	2021	2022	1990	2000	2010	2021	2022
Total tax revenue	202.4	359.5	515.5	781.8	887.6	32.9	32.7	32.0	34.2	35.4
1000 Taxes on income, profits and capital gains	79.6	142.3	192.8	295.1	335.2	12.9	12.9	12.0	12.9	13.4
1100 Of individuals	59.5	104.1	147.0	227.9	253.6	9.7	9.5	9.1	10.0	10.1
1200 Corporate	20.1	38.2	45.8	67.2	81.6	3.3	3.5	2.8	2.9	3.3
1300 Unallocable between 1100 and 1200	0.0	0.0	0.0	0.0	0.0	0.0	0.0	0.0	0.0	0.0
2000 Social security contributions	34.5	60.3	97.3	156.2	177.0	5.6	5.5	6.1	6.8	7.1
2100 Employees	13.3	24.2	38.7	60.0	65.3	2.2	2.2	2.4	2.6	2.6
2200 Employers	20.0	34.0	55.9	91.0	106.0	3.2	3.1	3.5	4.0	4.2
2300 Self-employed or non-employed	0.0	0.0	0.0	0.0	0.0	0.0	0.0	0.0	0.0	0.0
2400 Unallocable between 2100, 2200 and 2300	0.0	0.0	0.0	0.0	0.0	0.0	0.0	0.0	0.0	0.0
3000 Taxes on payroll and workforce	0.0	0.0	0.0	3.1	3.5	0.0	0.0	0.0	0.1	0.1
4000 Taxes on property	16.5	41.1	61.8	89.6	100.6	2.7	3.7	3.8	3.9	4.0
4100 Recurrent taxes on immovable property	13.5	30.5	50.0	64.6	71.7	2.2	2.8	3.1	2.8	2.9
4200 Recurrent taxes on net wealth	0.0	0.0	0.0	0.0	0.0	0.0	0.0	0.0	0.0	0.0
4300 Estate, inheritance and gift taxes	1.3	2.2	2.6	6.0	6.8	0.2	0.2	0.2	0.3	0.3
4400 Taxes on financial and capital transactions	1.8	8.4	9.1	18.7	21.7	0.3	0.8	0.6	0.8	0.9
4500 Non-recurrent taxes	0.0	0.0	0.0	0.0	0.0	0.0	0.0	0.0	0.0	0.0
4600 Other recurrent taxes on property	0.0	0.0	0.0	0.0	0.0	0.0	0.0	0.0	0.0	0.0
5000 Taxes on goods and services	62.8	115.8	163.6	237.8	271.3	10.2	10.5	10.2	10.4	10.8
5100 Taxes on production, sale, transfer, etc	59.4	110.8	156.1	228.9	257.6	9.6	10.1	9.7	10.0	10.3
5110 General taxes	34.1	65.0	97.6	158.6	184.3	5.5	5.9	6.1	6.9	7.4
5111 Value added taxes	34.1	65.0	97.6	158.1	183.6	5.5	5.9	6.1	6.9	7.3
5120 Taxes on specific goods and services	25.2	45.8	58.5	70.3	73.4	4.1	4.2	3.6	3.1	2.9
5121 Excises	19.7	37.3	45.5	48.3	47.8	3.2	3.4	2.8	2.1	1.9
5200 Taxes on use of goods and perform activities	3.4	5.0	7.4	8.8	13.7	0.6	0.5	0.5	0.4	0.5
5300 Unallocable between 5100 and 5200	0.0	0.0	0.0	0.0	0.0	0.0	0.0	0.0	0.0	0.0
6000 Other taxes	9.0	0.0	0.0	0.0	0.0	1.5	0.0	0.0	0.0	0.0
Non-wastable tax credits										
Non-wastable tax credits against 1000	7.5	4.7	30.2	19.0	18.0	1.2	0.4	1.9	0.8	0.7
Transfer component	0.5	3.4	23.7	15.2	14.2	0.1	0.3	1.5	0.7	0.6
Tax expenditure component	7.0	1.2	6.5	3.7	3.8	1.1	0.1	0.4	0.2	0.2
Revenues collected on behalf of the EU										
Revenues collected on behalf of the EU, total	1.8	2.1	2.9	0.0	..	0.3	0.2	0.2	0.0	..
Customs duties	..	1.8	2.9	0.0	..	..	0.2	0.2	0.0	..
SRF contributions	..	..	..	..	..	..	..	..	..	..

.. Not available

Note: Please note that the non-wastable tax credit data for the United Kingdom is on a cash basis and includes estimates in some years. Please see the footnotes in the table for the United Kingdom in Chapter 5 for more information.

Supranational taxes reported by the United Kingdom are reported until 2020 in Revenue Statistics. From 2021, at the end of the Brexit transition period, this came to an end and taxes subsequently introduced by the United Kingdom are reflected in the appropriate tax category at the national or subnational levels of government, as appropriate.

More detailed country data and country notes are available in Chapter 5 "Detailed country tables". Full time series can be accessed at http://data-explorer.oecd.org/s/nb.

Source: National Income and Expenditure; Central Statistical Office; Annual reports of His Majesty's Revenue and Customs.

Table 4.74. United Kingdom, tax revenue and % of GDP by level of government and main taxes

	Billion GBP					% of GDP				
	1990	2000	2010	2021	2022	1990	2000	2010	2021	2022
Federal or Central government										
Total tax revenue	151.9	282.9	388.9	584.6	667.6	24.7	25.7	24.2	25.6	26.6
1000 Taxes on income, profits and capital gains	79.6	142.3	192.8	295.1	335.2	12.9	12.9	12.0	12.9	13.4
2000 Social security contributions	0.0	0.0	0.0	0.0	0.0	0.0	0.0	0.0	0.0	0.0
3000 Taxes on payroll and workforce	0.0	0.0	0.0	3.1	3.5	0.0	0.0	0.0	0.1	0.1
4000 Taxes on property	11.4	26.9	35.5	48.6	57.5	1.9	2.4	2.2	2.1	2.3
5000 Taxes on goods and services	60.9	113.7	160.6	237.8	271.3	9.9	10.3	10.0	10.4	10.8
6000 Other taxes	0.0	0.0	0.0	0.0	0.0	0.0	0.0	0.0	0.0	0.0
State/Regional										
Total tax revenue	..	..	..	..	..	..	..	..	..	..
1000 Taxes on income, profits and capital gains	..	..	..	..	..	..	..	..	..	..
2000 Social security contributions	..	..	..	..	..	..	..	..	..	..
3000 Taxes on payroll and workforce	..	..	..	..	..	..	..	..	..	..
4000 Taxes on property	..	..	..	..	..	..	..	..	..	..
5000 Taxes on goods and services	..	..	..	..	..	..	..	..	..	..
6000 Other taxes	..	..	..	..	..	..	..	..	..	..
Local government										
Total tax revenue	14.1	14.2	26.2	41.0	43.1	2.3	1.3	1.6	1.8	1.7
1000 Taxes on income, profits and capital gains	0.0	0.0	0.0	0.0	0.0	0.0	0.0	0.0	0.0	0.0
2000 Social security contributions	0.0	0.0	0.0	0.0	0.0	0.0	0.0	0.0	0.0	0.0
3000 Taxes on payroll and workforce	0.0	0.0	0.0	0.0	0.0	0.0	0.0	0.0	0.0	0.0
4000 Taxes on property	5.1	14.2	26.2	41.0	43.1	0.8	1.3	1.6	1.8	1.7
5000 Taxes on goods and services	0.0	0.0	0.0	0.0	0.0	0.0	0.0	0.0	0.0	0.0
6000 Other taxes	9.0	0.0	0.0	0.0	0.0	1.5	0.0	0.0	0.0	0.0
Social Security Funds										
Total tax revenue	34.5	60.3	97.3	156.2	177.0	5.6	5.5	6.1	6.8	7.1
1000 Taxes on income, profits and capital gains	0.0	0.0	0.0	0.0	0.0	0.0	0.0	0.0	0.0	0.0
2000 Social security contributions	34.5	60.3	97.3	156.2	177.0	5.6	5.5	6.1	6.8	7.1
3000 Taxes on payroll and workforce	0.0	0.0	0.0	0.0	0.0	0.0	0.0	0.0	0.0	0.0
4000 Taxes on property	0.0	0.0	0.0	0.0	0.0	0.0	0.0	0.0	0.0	0.0
5000 Taxes on goods and services	0.0	0.0	0.0	0.0	0.0	0.0	0.0	0.0	0.0	0.0
6000 Other taxes	0.0	0.0	0.0	0.0	0.0	0.0	0.0	0.0	0.0	0.0

.. Not available

Note: More detailed country data and country notes are available in Chapter 6 "Tax revenues by sub-sectors of general government". Full time series can be accessed at http://data-explorer.oecd.org/s/nb.

Source: National Income and Expenditure; Central Statistical Office; Annual reports of His Majesty's Revenue and Customs.

Table 4.75. United States, tax revenue and % of GDP by selected tax category

	Billion USD					% of GDP				
	1990	2000	2010	2021	2022	1990	2000	2010	2021	2022
Total tax revenue	1 552.4	2 900.5	3 517.1	6 301.7	7 107.1	26.0	28.3	23.4	26.7	27.6
1000 Taxes on income, profits and capital gains	701.7	1 453.9	1 488.7	3 122.1	3 654.9	11.8	14.2	9.9	13.2	14.2
1100 Of individuals	584.7	1 224.5	1 223.2	2 731.2	3 127.3	9.8	11.9	8.1	11.6	12.1
1200 Corporate	117.0	229.3	265.5	390.8	527.5	2.0	2.2	1.8	1.7	2.0
1300 Unallocable between 1100 and 1200	0.0	0.0	0.0	0.0	0.0	0.0	0.0	0.0	0.0	0.0
2000 Social security contributions	397.0	683.1	917.4	1 430.3	1 556.7	6.7	6.7	6.1	6.1	6.0
2100 Employees	173.9	305.6	406.4	658.0	716.4	2.9	3.0	2.7	2.8	2.8
2200 Employers	204.1	343.2	461.7	699.6	757.1	3.4	3.3	3.1	3.0	2.9
2300 Self-employed or non-employed	0.0	0.0	0.0	0.0	0.0	0.0	0.0	0.0	0.0	0.0
2400 Unallocable between 2100, 2200 and 2300	0.0	0.0	0.0	0.0	0.0	0.0	0.0	0.0	0.0	0.0
3000 Taxes on payroll and workforce	0.0	0.0	2.3	3.4	3.6	0.0	0.0	0.0	0.0	0.0
4000 Taxes on property	182.4	299.5	473.4	691.6	736.8	3.1	2.9	3.1	2.9	2.9
4100 Recurrent taxes on immovable property	161.5	254.7	438.6	621.7	660.0	2.7	2.5	2.9	2.6	2.6
4200 Recurrent taxes on net wealth	0.0	0.0	0.0	0.0	0.0	0.0	0.0	0.0	0.0	0.0
4300 Estate, inheritance and gift taxes	15.8	35.6	19.7	34.4	40.6	0.3	0.3	0.1	0.1	0.2
4400 Taxes on financial and capital transactions	2.1	4.4	7.5	24.5	24.6	0.0	0.0	0.0	0.1	0.1
4500 Non-recurrent taxes	0.0	0.0	0.0	0.0	0.0	0.0	0.0	0.0	0.0	0.0
4600 Other recurrent taxes on property	3.0	4.8	7.7	10.9	11.6	0.0	0.0	0.1	0.0	0.0
5000 Taxes on goods and services	271.3	464.0	635.3	1054.5	1 155.1	4.5	4.5	4.2	4.5	4.5
5100 Taxes on production, sale, transfer, etc	235.2	404.1	546.7	919.2	1005.7	3.9	3.9	3.6	3.9	3.9
5110 General taxes	125.6	221.4	295.1	514.5	570.8	2.1	2.2	2.0	2.2	2.2
5111 Value added taxes	0.0	0.0	0.0	0.0	0.0	0.0	0.0	0.0	0.0	0.0
5120 Taxes on specific goods and services	109.7	182.7	251.6	404.7	434.9	1.8	1.8	1.7	1.7	1.7
5121 Excises	65.0	108.6	146.6	174.6	171.6	1.1	1.1	1.0	0.7	0.7
5200 Taxes on use of goods and perform activities	36.1	59.9	88.6	135.3	149.4	0.6	0.6	0.6	0.6	0.6
5300 Unallocable between 5100 and 5200	0.0	0.0	0.0	0.0	0.0	0.0	0.0	0.0	0.0	0.0
6000 Other taxes	0.0	0.0	0.0	0.0	0.0	0.0	0.0	0.0	0.0	0.0
Non-wastable tax credits										
Non-wastable tax credits against 1000	6.2	36.5	171.9	562.5	452.5	0.1	0.4	1.1	2.4	1.8
Transfer component	4.4	26.9	101.8	450.7	324.2	0.1	0.3	0.7	1.9	1.3
Tax expenditure component	1.8	9.6	70.1	111.8	128.3	0.0	0.1	0.5	0.5	0.5

Note: More detailed country data and country notes are available in Chapter 5 "Detailed country tables". Full time series can be accessed at http://data-explorer.oecd.org/s/nb.

Source: Federal estimates are derived from the US Budget, the Final Monthly Treasury Statement and the Annual Report of the US Treasury Department. The State and Local estimates are derived from Government Finances, published by the Bureau of the Census.

Table 4.76. United States, tax revenue and % of GDP by level of government and main taxes

	Billion USD					% of GDP				
	1990	2000	2010	2021	2022	1990	2000	2010	2021	2022
Federal or Central government										
Total tax revenue	632.2	1 316.6	1 288.7	2 666.2	3 135.1	10.6	12.8	8.6	11.3	12.2
1000 Taxes on income, profits and capital gains	569.7	1 201.3	1 176.8	2 460.3	2 908.1	9.6	11.7	7.8	10.4	11.3
2000 Social security contributions	0.0	0.0	0.0	0.0	0.0	0.0	0.0	0.0	0.0	0.0
3000 Taxes on payroll and workforce	0.0	0.0	0.0	0.0	0.0	0.0	0.0	0.0	0.0	0.0
4000 Taxes on property	11.6	28.1	15.1	27.3	32.8	0.2	0.3	0.1	0.1	0.1
5000 Taxes on goods and services	50.9	87.3	96.8	178.6	194.2	0.9	0.9	0.6	0.8	0.8
6000 Other taxes	0.0	0.0	0.0	0.0	0.0	0.0	0.0	0.0	0.0	0.0
State/Regional										
Total tax revenue	309.7	547.6	723.9	1330.1	1 483.2	5.2	5.3	4.8	5.6	5.8
1000 Taxes on income, profits and capital gains	120.2	231.0	279.4	606.5	685.9	2.0	2.3	1.9	2.6	2.7
2000 Social security contributions	0.0	0.0	0.0	0.0	0.0	0.0	0.0	0.0	0.0	0.0
3000 Taxes on payroll and workforce	0.0	0.0	2.3	3.4	3.6	0.0	0.0	0.0	0.0	0.0
4000 Taxes on property	12.2	21.9	23.1	45.6	47.4	0.2	0.2	0.2	0.2	0.2
5000 Taxes on goods and services	177.3	294.7	419.1	674.6	746.2	3.0	2.9	2.8	2.9	2.9
6000 Other taxes	0.0	0.0	0.0	0.0	0.0	0.0	0.0	0.0	0.0	0.0
Local government										
Total tax revenue	213.6	353.2	587.2	875.2	932.2	3.6	3.4	3.9	3.7	3.6
1000 Taxes on income, profits and capital gains	11.9	21.6	32.5	55.3	60.9	0.2	0.2	0.2	0.2	0.2
2000 Social security contributions	0.0	0.0	0.0	0.0	0.0	0.0	0.0	0.0	0.0	0.0
3000 Taxes on payroll and workforce	0.0	0.0	0.0	0.0	0.0	0.0	0.0	0.0	0.0	0.0
4000 Taxes on property	158.6	249.5	435.3	618.6	656.6	2.7	2.4	2.9	2.6	2.6
5000 Taxes on goods and services	43.1	82.0	119.4	201.2	214.7	0.7	0.8	0.8	0.9	0.8
6000 Other taxes	0.0	0.0	0.0	0.0	0.0	0.0	0.0	0.0	0.0	0.0
Social Security Funds										
Total tax revenue	397.0	683.1	917.4	1 430.3	1 556.7	6.7	6.7	6.1	6.1	6.0
1000 Taxes on income, profits and capital gains	0.0	0.0	0.0	0.0	0.0	0.0	0.0	0.0	0.0	0.0
2000 Social security contributions	397.0	683.1	917.4	1 430.3	1 556.7	6.7	6.7	6.1	6.1	6.0
3000 Taxes on payroll and workforce	0.0	0.0	0.0	0.0	0.0	0.0	0.0	0.0	0.0	0.0
4000 Taxes on property	0.0	0.0	0.0	0.0	0.0	0.0	0.0	0.0	0.0	0.0
5000 Taxes on goods and services	0.0	0.0	0.0	0.0	0.0	0.0	0.0	0.0	0.0	0.0
6000 Other taxes	0.0	0.0	0.0	0.0	0.0	0.0	0.0	0.0	0.0	0.0

Note: More detailed country data and country notes are available in Chapter 6 "Tax revenues by sub-sectors of general government". Full time series can be accessed at http://data-explorer.oecd.org/s/nb.

Source: Federal estimates are derived from the US Budget, the Final Monthly Treasury Statement and the Annual Report of the US Treasury Department. The State and Local estimates are derived from Government Finances, published by the Bureau of the Census.

Memorandum tables

Table 4.77 shows different sources for financing social benefits, beyond compulsory social security contributions reported in section 4.1. In addition, this table shows also data on other taxes, on voluntary contributions to government and on compulsory contributions to private sector.

Table 4.78 shows social security contributions and payroll taxes paid by government. During the revision of the Interpretative Guide in 1984, the question arose of how to treat taxes paid by government. The two most prominent examples of such taxes are social security contributions and payroll taxes paid by government in respect of its employees. After a long discussion it was decided that the data shown in this publication should continue to include taxes paid by government (see §7 of the Interpretative Guide in Annex A).

Whilst it was recognised that for certain purposes (e.g. to show the cash flow to the government sector from the private sector) it would be appropriate to eliminate taxes paid by one sector of government to another or tax payments between different units of the same sector of government, the view was taken that to record tax flows in the context of the economy as a whole required that taxes paid by government should be included in the data. This treatment ensures that the different resource flows of an economy, including the calculation of the output of government, are measured consistently in after-tax units. Nevertheless, it was decided that data on identifiable taxes paid by government should be separately identified in a memorandum item and this is the purpose of the country tables which follow.

The data that are reproduced in the following tables refer to actual compulsory payments made by general government in respect of their employees. Fictive, voluntary and imputed contributions are excluded from these data. The definitions of social security contributions, payroll taxes and general government are those set out in §40 to §46, §47 and §3 to §4 of the Interpretative Guide. Information on the other taxes paid by government (namely property taxes and consumption taxes) is not available in most countries, although it is believed that in all countries taxes based upon payroll are the most important taxes paid by government. In many cases, the data are estimates and are not always constructed on a basis consistent with that used in the main tables.

Table 4.77. Financing of social security benefits

As % of GDP

	Total					2022				
	1990	2000	2010	2021	2022	Social security contributions	Other taxes	Voluntary contributions to government	Compulsory contributions to private sector	Total
Australia	0.0	0.0	0.0	0.0	0.0	..	..	..	..	0.0
Austria	13.0	14.4	14.1	15.5	14.8	14.7	0.0	0.1	0.0	14.8
Belgium	14.2	15.6	18.5	17.5	17.0	12.9	4.1	0.0	0.0	17.0
Canada	4.3	4.7	4.6	4.8	4.7	4.7	0.0	0.0	0.0	4.7
Chile	4.6	6.2	6.2	6.9	6.7	1.0	0.0	0.0	5.8	6.7
Colombia	0.9	2.6	7.1	5.8	5.3	1.6	0.0	0.0	3.7	5.3
Costa Rica	6.5	6.4	7.3	8.9	8.8	8.8	..	..	..	8.8
Czechia	..	14.4	14.5	16.1	15.4	15.2	0.0	0.0	0.1	15.4
Denmark	1.1	2.0	1.3	0.8	0.7	0.1	0.0	0.5	0.1	0.7
Estonia	..	10.9	13.0	12.6	12.1	11.3	0.0	0.0	0.8	12.1
Finland	12.2	12.4	12.5	12.4	12.3	11.9	0.0	0.1	0.2	12.3
France	18.6	21.1	22.9	24.9	25.1	14.8	10.3	0.0	0.0	25.1
Germany	14.2	15.6	14.4	15.4	15.3	14.6	0.0	0.2	0.4	15.3
Greece	7.6	10.1	11.0	12.9	12.2	12.2	0.0	0.0	0.0	12.2
Hungary	..	13.2	12.9	10.7	10.1	9.8	0.3	0.0	0.0	10.1
Iceland	10.0	13.4	14.1	17.8	15.3	3.0	6.2	0.0	6.1	15.3
Ireland	4.6	3.7	5.1	3.0	3.1	3.1	0.0	0.0	0.0	3.1
Israel	..	5.0	6.1	7.7	7.8	5.0	0.0	0.0	2.8	7.8
Italy	11.9	11.6	13.0	13.3	13.1	13.1	0.0	0.0	0.0	13.1
Japan	7.3	8.9	10.8	13.3	13.3	13.3	0.0	0.0	0.0	13.3
Korea	1.9	3.5	5.2	7.8	8.2	8.2	0.0	0.0	0.0	8.2
Latvia	..	9.9	8.8	10.0	9.8	9.4	0.4	0.0	0.0	9.8
Lithuania	..	9.9	12.0	10.1	9.8	9.8	0.0	0.0	0.0	9.8
Luxembourg	9.6	9.8	10.4	10.7	10.7	10.6	0.0	0.1	0.0	10.7
Mexico	2.4	2.9	3.0	3.7	3.7	2.3	0.0	0.0	1.4	3.7
Netherlands	17.1	22.5	12.9	12.6	12.2	12.2	0.0	0.0	..	12.2
New Zealand	0.0	0.0	0.0	0.0	0.0	..	..	..	..	0.0
Norway	10.6	8.8	9.3	9.3	7.5	7.5	0.0	0.0	0.0	7.5
Poland	..	12.9	10.9	13.0	12.8	12.8	0.1	0.0	0.0	12.8
Portugal	7.2	8.3	9.0	10.8	10.6	10.2	0.4	0.0	0.0	10.6
Slovak Republic	..	13.9	12.9	16.2	15.6	14.5	0.0	0.0	1.0	15.6
Slovenia	..	14.9	15.8	16.4	16.0	16.0	0.0	0.0	0.0	16.0
Spain	11.2	11.6	12.0	13.5	12.9	12.8	0.0	0.1	0.0	12.9
Sweden	13.3	13.1	11.2	9.5	9.4	8.8	0.0	0.5	0.0	9.4
Switzerland	11.3	13.8	14.6	15.5	15.2	6.7	0.4	0.0	8.1	15.2
Türkiye	2.9	4.4	6.1	6.6	5.1	5.1	0.0	0.0	0.0	5.1
United Kingdom	7.4	7.0	8.0	8.6	8.8	7.1	0.0	1.7	0.0	8.8
United States	6.9	6.9	6.5	6.6	6.6	6.0	0.0	0.5	0.0	6.6

.. Not available

Table 4.78. Social security contributions and payroll taxes paid by government, totals

As % of GDP

	Total					2022				
	1990	2000	2010	2021	2022	Federal or Central government	State/Regional	Local government	Social security Funds	Total
Australia[1]	0.0	0.0	0.0	0.0	0.0	0.0	0.0	0.0	0.0	0.0
Austria	1.0	1.4	1.9	2.1	2.0	0.7	0.6	0.6	0.1	2.0
Belgium	1.0	1.2	1.5	1.8	1.8	0.2	0.6	0.9	0.1	1.8
Canada	..	0.6	0.6	0.6	0.6	0.1	0.3	0.2	0.0	0.6
Chile	..	0.1	0.2	0.1	0.1	0.1	..	0.0	0.0	0.1
Colombia	..	..	..	0.2	0.2	0.0	0.0	0.0	0.2	0.2
Costa Rica	0.7	0.9	1.1	1.0	1.0	0.9	0.0	0.1	0.0	1.0
Czechia	..	1.4	1.4	2.1	1.9	0.8	..	1.1	0.0	1.9
Denmark	0.0	0.0	0.0	0.0	0.0	..	..	..	..	0.0
Estonia	..	2.6	2.9	3.0	2.8	1.7	..	1.1	0.0	2.8
Finland	2.1	2.8	3.0	2.4	2.3	0.5	..	1.7	0.0	2.3
France	2.2	2.5	2.7	2.7	2.7	0.7	..	0.9	1.0	2.7
Germany	1.0	0.8	0.8	0.9	0.9	0.1	0.3	0.4	0.1	0.9
Greece	0.3	0.5	0.8	1.6	1.4	1.2	..	0.2	0.0	1.4
Hungary	..	2.8	2.4	1.2	1.0	0.8	..	0.2	0.0	1.0
Iceland	..	..	..	..	..	..	..	..	..	..
Ireland	0.4	0.4	0.7	0.4	0.4	0.1	..	0.3	0.0	0.4
Israel	..	0.8	0.7	0.8	0.7	0.6	..	0.1	0.0	0.7
Italy	..	3.0	3.1	3.0	2.9	0.0	..	0.0	2.9	2.9
Japan	0.4	0.5	0.6	0.6	0.6	0.2	0.0	0.5	0.0	0.6
Korea	..	..	..	..	..	..	..	..	..	..
Latvia	..	0.6	1.0	1.1	1.1	..	..	..	..	1.1
Lithuania	..	2.7	2.5	0.2	0.2	0.1	..	0.1	0.0	0.2
Luxembourg	2.5	1.3	1.2	1.2	1.2	1.2	..	0.0	0.0	1.2
Mexico	0.3	0.6	0.7	0.7	0.7	0.7	0.0	0.0	0.0	0.7
Netherlands	0.1	0.4	0.0	0.0	0.0	..	..	..	..	0.0
New Zealand	0.0	0.0	0.0	0.0	0.0	..	..	..	..	0.0
Norway	2.4	2.4	2.9	3.0	2.4	1.1	..	1.3	0.0	2.4
Poland	..	1.5	1.3	1.3	1.3	0.5	..	0.7	0.0	1.3
Portugal	0.1	0.2	0.0	0.0	0.0	..	..	..	..	0.0
Slovak Republic	..	2.0	2.0	2.8	2.4	1.4	..	1.0	0.1	2.4
Slovenia	..	1.9	1.7	1.7	1.5	1.0	..	0.5	0.0	1.5
Spain	1.2	1.5	1.7	2.1	2.0	0.2	1.3	0.5	0.0	2.0
Sweden	4.5	4.2	3.9	3.8	3.7	0.9	..	2.8	0.0	3.7
Switzerland	0.4	0.4	0.5	0.5	0.5	0.1	0.3	0.1	0.0	0.5
Türkiye	1.6	2.1	3.4	3.8	2.9	2.9	..	0.0	0.0	2.9
United Kingdom	0.7	0.6	0.7	0.8	0.8	0.6	..	0.3	0.0	0.8
United States	0.5	0.4	0.5	0.4	0.4	0.1	0.2	0.0	0.0	0.4

.. Not available

1. For Australia, the total differs from the sum of the four levels of government. The difference is due to a multi-jurisdictional (University) sector specific to this country. This sector contains units where jurisdiction is shared between two or more governments, or where classification of a unit to a jurisdiction is otherwise unclear. The main type of units currently falling into this category is public universities.

5 Detailed country tables, 1965-2022

Chapter 5 provides detailed country information on tax revenues for each OECD country.

Tax revenues

In all the following tables, the symbol (..) indicates not available or not applicable. The main series in this chapter cover a selection of years between 1965 and 2022. A complete series is available online. Data for 1955 and 1960 (for nineteen OECD countries) are provided in Part V of the 1998 edition of this Report.

Table 5.1. Australia: Details of tax revenue, 1965-2022

Million AUD

	1965	1980	1990	2000	2007	2010	2015	2020	2021	2022
Total tax revenue	5 024	39 878	116 500	214 753	346 772	356 747	460 729	590 140	680 262	753 193
1000 Taxes on income, profits and capital gains	2 547	22 383	66 542	124 427	206 134	202 184	261 345	347 854	418 320	468 871
1100 Of individuals	1 729	17 532	50 062	80 991	127 587	138 163	191 720	236 868	265 367	304 566
1110 On income and profits	1 729	17 532	49 888	80 991	127 587	138 163	191 720	236 868	265 367	304 566
1120 On capital gains	0	0	174	0	0	0	0	0	0	0
1200 Corporate	818	4 851	16 480	43 436	78 547	64 021	69 625	110 985	152 952	164 305
1210 On profits	818	4 851	16 315	43 436	78 547	64 021	69 625	110 985	152 952	164 305
Income tax on companies	791	4 574	15 220	42 221	76 655	62 549	67 794	109 456	151 315	161 846
Dividend and interest taxes	17	161	899	846	1 892	1 472	1 831	1 529	1 637	2 459
Other withholding taxes	0	116	196	369	..	..	..	..	..	..
1220 On capital gains	0	0	165	0	0	0	0	0	0	0
1300 Unallocable between 1100 and 1200	0	0	0	0	0	0	0	0	0	0
2000 Social security contributions	0	0	0	0	0	0	0	0	0	0
2100 Employees	0	0	0	0	0	0	0	0	0	0
2110 On a payroll basis	..	..	..	..	..	..	..	..	..	..
2120 On an income tax basis	..	..	..	..	..	..	..	..	..	..
2200 Employers	0	0	0	0	0	0	0	0	0	0
2210 On a payroll basis of employers SSC	..	..	..	..	..	..	..	..	..	..
2220 On an income tax basis of employers SSC	..	..	..	..	..	..	..	..	..	..
2300 Selfemployed or nonemployed	0	0	0	0	0	0	0	0	0	0
2310 On a payroll basis of self/nonemployed SSC	..	..	..	..	..	..	..	..	..	..
2320 On an income tax basis of self/nonemployed SSC	..	..	..	..	..	..	..	..	..	..
2400 Unallocable between 2100, 2200 and 2300	0	0	0	0	0	0	0	0	0	0
2410 On a payroll basis unallocable between 2100, 2200 and 2300 SSC	..	..	..	..	..	..	..	..	..	..
2420 On an income tax basis unallocable between 2100, 2200 and 2300 SSC	..	..	..	..	..	..	..	..	..	..
3000 Taxes on payroll and workforce	157	1 988	7 115	9 624	16 407	18 492	23 354	26 383	29 399	35 309
4000 Taxes on property	576	3 105	10 427	18 825	31 130	33 498	49 168	59 509	74 152	69 904
4100 Recurrent taxes on immovable property	341	1 886	6 148	9 067	15 615	19 907	26 649	34 471	36 521	40 188
4110 Households	..	..	..	..	..	..	..	..	..	..
4120 Others	..	..	..	..	..	..	..	..	..	..
4200 Recurrent taxes on net wealth	0	0	0	0	0	0	0	0	0	0
4210 Individual	..	..	..	..	..	..	..	..	..	..
4220 Corporate	..	..	..	..	..	..	..	..	..	..
4300 Estate, inheritance and gift taxes	137	175	0	0	0	0	0	0	0	0
4310 Estate and inheritance taxes	131	174	..	..	..	..	..	..	..	..
Estate duty central government	36	17	..	..	..	..	..	..	..	..
St. and loc. estate probate and succession	95	157	..	..	..	..	..	..	..	..
4320 Gift taxes	7	1	..	..	..	..	..	..	..	..
4400 Taxes on financial and capital transactions	98	1 044	4 279	9 758	15 515	13 591	22 519	25 038	37 631	29 716
4500 Nonrecurrent taxes	0	0	0	0	0	0	0	0	0	0
4510 On net wealth	..	..	..	..	..	..	..	..	..	..
4520 Other nonrecurrent taxes	..	..	..	..	..	..	..	..	..	..
4600 Other recurrent taxes on property	0	0	0	0	0	0	0	0	0	0
5000 Taxes on goods and services	1 744	12 402	32 416	61 877	93 101	102 573	126 862	156 394	158 391	179 109
5100 Taxes on production, sale, transfer, etc	1 508	11 097	27 213	56 179	84 104	90 824	109 050	134 792	134 780	152 421
5110 General taxes	370	2 102	9 365	25 830	44 739	48 146	60 680	75 298	77 661	88 602
5111 Value added taxes	0	0	0	23 854	43 634	46 910	59 177	73 297	75 565	86 274
5112 Sales tax	370	2 102	9 365	1 976	1 105	1 236	1 503	2 001	2 096	2 328
5113 Other	0	0	0	0	0	0	0	0	0	0
5120 Taxes on specific goods and services	1 138	8 995	17 848	30 349	39 365	42 678	48 370	59 494	57 119	63 819
5121 Excises	781	6 183	11 975	19 768	24 357	26 689	22 541	25 548	23 721	27 626
Excises central government	752	5 834	10 359	19 019	23 526	25 803	21 625	24 503	22 562	26 281
Excise on beer			0	1 697	1 862	1 957	1 998	2 185	2 136	2 284
Excise on spirits			0	238	205	253	477	786	809	883
Excise on other alcoholic beverages			0	0	744	900	896	1 282	1 391	1 591
Excise on tobacco			0	4 637	5 631	6 387	290	0	0	0
Other excise			0	12 447	15 085	16 305	17 964	20 250	18 226	21 523
Statutory corporate payments	0	83	378	295	231	452	405	511	513	668
Primary production charges	29	266	1 238	454	600	434	511	534	646	677
5122 Profits of fiscal monopolies	0	0	0	0	0	0	0	0	0	0
5123 Customs and import duties	271	1 799	3 319	4 606	6 070	5 828	14 046	18 123	16 945	17 079

	1965	1980	1990	2000	2007	2010	2015	2020	2021	2022
Customs duties central government	271	1 799	3 319	4 606	6 070	5 828	14 046	18 123	16 945	17 079
Excise equivalent customs duty on beer			0	37	164	221	388	363	328	283
Excise equivalent customs duty on spirits			0	975	1 265	1 544	1 594	2 375	2 706	2 474
Excise equivalent customs duty on other alcoholic beverages			0	0	0	0	22	21	66	35
Excise equivalent customs duty on tobacco			0	386	621	1 215	9 639	14 264	12 659	12 667
Other customs duty			0	3 208	4 021	2 849	2 404	1 100	1 186	1 619
5124 Taxes on exports	1	117	57	0	10	11	11	0	0	0
Customs duties on coal exports	0	85	54	..	0	0	0	..	..	..
Other	1	32	3	..	10	11	11	..	..	..
5125 Taxes on investment goods	0	0	0	0	0	0	0	0	0	0
5126 Taxes on specific services	85	896	2 497	5 975	8 928	10 150	11 772	15 823	16 453	19 114
Taxes race meetings	31	240	651	301	359	373	265	795	931	1 155
Poker machines	16	140	295	2 074	3 009	3 125	3 684	3 935	3 856	5 313
Lotteries	7	122	325	890	1 118	1 141	1 362	1 813	2 005	1 951
Levies on fire insurance companies	16	157	363	574	937	1 232	786	1 115	942	1 213
Other	15	237	863	2 136	3 505	4 279	5 675	8 165	8 719	9 482
5127 Other taxes on internat. trade and transactions	0	0	0	0	0	0	0	0	0	0
5128 Other taxes	0	0	0	0	0	0	0	0	0	0
5130 Unallocable between 5110 and 5120	0	0	0	0	0	0	0	0	0	0
5200 Taxes on use of goods and perform activities	236	1 305	5 203	5 698	8 997	11 749	17 812	21 602	23 611	26 688
5210 Recurrent taxes	197	1 260	5 109	5 698	8 997	11 749	15 898	19 969	21 629	23 532
5211 Paid by households: motor vehicles	65	448	1 373	2 748	4 381	5 064	7 253	8 723	9 194	9 927
5212 Paid by others: motor vehicles	65	351	937	1 285	2 005	2 397	2 649	3 409	3 661	3 996
Fees on motor vehicle registry	46	312	794	778	1 165	1 499	1 530	1 957	2 126	2 248
Drivers licences	12	30	111	0	0	0	0	0	0	0
Stamp duty on vehicle registry	6	9	32	506	839	898	1 119	1 452	1 535	1 748
5213 Paid in respect of other goods	67	461	2 799	1 665	2 611	4 288	5 996	7 837	8 774	9 609
Broadcasting tv licences	37	21	125	210	288	150	128	14	46	44
Business franchise lic. tobac. fuel	0	221	2 016	227	0	0	1	0	0	0
Other taxes	2	12	33	1 129	2 321	4 136	5 846	7 813	8 697	9 544
Liquor taxes	28	206	603	97	2	1	22	10	31	21
Dog licenses	0	1	22	0	0	0	0	0	0	0
5220 Nonrecurrent taxes	39	45	94	0	0	0	1 914	1 633	1 982	3 156
5300 Unallocable between 5100 and 5200	0	0	0	0	0	0	0	0	0	0
6000 Other taxes	0	0	0	0	0	0	0	0	0	0
6100 Paid solely by business	..	..	..	..	..	..	..	..	..	..
6200 Other	..	..	..	..	..	..	..	..	..	..
Non-wastable tax credits against 1110	..	..	..	195	2 585	991	460	446	414	346
Tax expenditure component	..	..	..	175	178	110	334	310	288	245
Transfer component	..	..	..	20	2 407	881	126	136	126	101
Non-wastable tax credits against 1210	..	..	..	0	4 564	5 726	8 951	10 582	10 599	11 542
Tax expenditure component	..	..	..	..	1 922	2 253	3 438	3 621	3 325	3 388
Transfer component	..	..	..	..	2 642	3 473	5 513	6 961	7 275	8 154
Total tax revenue on cash basis	5 024	39 878	116 500	..	..	..	..	..	..	..
Total tax revenue on accrual basis	..	..	..	214 753	346 772	356 747	460 729	590 140	680 262	753 193
Additional taxes included in National Accounts	..	..	..	0	0	0	0	0	0	0
Taxes excluded from National Accounts	..	..	..	0	0	0	0	0	0	0
Difference in treatment of tax credits	..	..	..	175	2 100	2 363	3 772	3 930	3 612	3 633
Capital transfer for uncollected revenue	..	..	..	0	0	0	0	0	0	0
Voluntary social security contributions	..	..	..	0	0	0	0	0	0	0
Miscellaneous differences	..	..	..	0	0	0	0	0	0	0
National Accounts: Taxes and actual social contributions	..	..	..	214 928	348 872	359 110	464 501	594 070	683 874	756 826
Imputed social contributions	..	..	..	0	0	0	0	0	0	0
National Accounts: Taxes and all social contributions	..	..	..	214 928	348 872	359 110	464 501	594 070	683 874	756 826

.. Not available

Note: Data are on a fiscal year basis beginning 1st July.

From 1998 taxes are recorded on an accrual basis; prior to that they were on a cash basis.

Direct taxes paid by public trading enterprises are excluded from receipts.

The figures for total tax revenue do not match the published totals in Taxation Revenue Australia. The latter is based on an accrual IMF GFS methodology and there are some differences between that and the OECD equivalent.

Heading 5213 includes radio and television licenses fees, though these are usually not regarded as a tax revenue in the OECD list.

Headings for non-wastable tax credits 1110 and 1210 include the private health insurance tax offset, family benefit, baby bonus tax offsets (paid during the 2003-04 budget year), film tax offset, and research and development tax offsets. The estimation of non-wastable credits into the expenditure and transfer components is in accordance with the OECD guidelines on the treatment and the data for this memorandum item has been provided by the Australian Taxation Office.

Source: Australian Bureau of Statistics.

Table 5.2. Austria: Details of tax revenue, 1965-2022

Million EUR

	1965	1980	1990	2000	2007	2010	2015	2020	2021	2022
Total tax revenue	6 210	29 759	54 040	90 324	115 146	121 192	148 469	160 713	176 120	193 204
Total tax revenue exclusive of taxes collected for the EU	..	..	54 040	89 897	114 728	120 843	147 841	159 995	175 343	192 164
1000 Taxes on income, profits and capital gains	1 584	7 959	13 797	25 553	34 319	34 021	44 796	44 597	51 922	59 732
1100 Of individuals	1 240	6 899	11 326	19 890	25 741	27 098	35 841	35 595	39 442	43 039
1110 On income and profits	1 240	6 899	11 326	19 890	25 741	27 098	35 841	35 595	39 442	43 039
Income tax	415	1 576	2 501	3 202	3 253	3 358	4 274	4 210	4 690	6 619
Special income tax	0	0	0	0	0	0	0	0	0	0
Wage tax	417	4 626	7 823	15 630	20 607	21 783	28 429	28 686	31 096	32 595
Tax on industry and trade	196	402	454	7	0	0	0	0	0	0
Tax on capital yields	2	14	46	354	970	938	1 979	1 342	2 205	2 274
Contribution to chambers	60	279	501	697	910	1 018	1 159	1 358	1 451	1 552
Water supply fund	151	0	0	0	0	0	0	0	0	0
Contribution emergency fund	0	0	0	0	0	0	0	0	0	0
1120 On capital gains	0	0	0	0	0	0	0	0	0	0
1200 Corporate	334	1 049	1 930	4 157	6 622	5 519	7 659	8 182	11 168	15 325
1210 On profits	334	1 049	1 930	4 157	6 622	5 519	7 659	8 182	11 168	15 325
Corporation tax	195	698	998	3 865	6 094	4 978	6 752	7 526	10 180	14 216
Tax on industry and trade	83	254	624	10	0	1	0	0	0	0
Special tax on income	0	0	0	0	0	0	0	0	0	0
Tax on capital yields	5	33	108	118	346	347	684	447	735	758
Water supply fund	35	0	0	0	0	0	0	0	0	0
Contribution emergency fund	0	0	0	0	0	0	0	0	0	0
Contribution to chambers	14	58	200	164	182	193	224	210	253	272
Directors tax	2	6	0	0	0	0	0	0	0	0
Energy surtaxes			0	0	0	0	0	0	0	79
1220 On capital gains	0	0	0	0	0	0	0	0	0	0
1300 Unallocable between 1100 and 1200	10	12	540	1 506	1 956	1 405	1 295	819	1 312	1 367
Fines related to tax offences	10	12	18	33	77	99	70	28	34	62
Tax on interest	0	0	522	1 473	1 879	1 305	1 225	791	1 278	1 305
2000 Social security contributions	1 548	9 200	17 763	30 510	38 453	41 423	49 867	59 094	62 312	65 893
2100 Employees	686	3 792	7 512	12 477	15 612	16 846	20 115	23 857	25 030	26 601
2110 On a payroll basis	..	..	..	12 477	15 612	16 846	20 115	23 857	25 030	26 601
Health insurance contributions	..	..	..	2 606	3 326	3 675	4 347	5 249	5 487	5 853
Pension insurance contributions	..	..	..	6 410	8 274	8 986	10 896	13 350	14 042	15 043
Pension contributions, civil servants	..	..	..	1 489	1 579	1 625	1 629	1 504	1 451	1 400
Unemployment insurance contributions	..	..	..	1 854	2 284	2 385	3 040	3 504	3 786	4 025
Health insurance contributions, local government employees	..	..	..	100	130	156	181	222	232	246
Special unemployment insurance contributions	..	..	..	17	19	20	23	29	33	34
2120 On an income tax basis	..	..	..	0	0	0	0	0	0	0
2200 Employers	721	4 563	8 768	14 651	18 091	19 421	23 281	27 733	29 189	31 080
2210 On a payroll basis of employers SSC	..	..	..	14 651	18 091	19 421	23 281	27 733	29 189	31 080
Health insurance contributions	..	..	..	2 667	3 395	3 669	4 339	5 240	5 477	5 842
Pension insurance contributions	..	..	..	7 888	10 214	11 145	13 549	16 648	17 517	18 777
Pension contributions, civil servants	..	..	..	438	376	361	298	244	230	217
Accident insurance contributions	..	..	..	952	1 157	1 254	1 394	1 459	1 519	1 625
Unemployment insurance contributions	..	..	..	1 854	2 284	2 385	3 040	3 504	3 786	4 025
Health insurance contributions, local government employees	..	..	..	101	141	157	181	222	232	246
Contributions to sickness benefit fund	..	..	..	341	0	0	0	0	0	0
Special pension contributions, nightshift workers	..	..	..	11	18	15	38	46	48	57
Contributions to insolvency fund	..	..	..	381	488	416	419	234	226	130
Special unemployment insurance contributions construction workers	..	..	..	17	19	20	23	136	154	160
2220 On an income tax basis of employers SSC	..	..	..	0	0	0	0	0	0	0
2300 Selfemployed or nonemployed	141	845	1 482	3 382	4 750	5 155	6 470	7 504	8 093	8 212
2310 On a payroll basis of self/non-employed SSC	..	..	..	3 382	4 750	5 155	6 470	7 504	8 093	8 212
Health insurance contributions	..	..	..	1 971	2 724	3 090	3 664	4 219	4 422	4 426

	1965	1980	1990	2000	2007	2010	2015	2020	2021	2022
Pension insurance contributions	..	..	..	1 117	1 527	1 524	2 210	2 574	2 945	3 049
Pension contributions, civil servants (retired)	..	..	..	116	274	297	317	311	307	305
Accident insurance contributions	..	..	..	77	85	88	98	178	187	187
Health insurance contributions, local government employees	..	..	..	101	140	156	181	222	232	246
2320 On an income tax basis of self/non-employed SSC	..	..	..	0	0	0	0	0	0	0
2400 Unallocable between 2100, 2200 and 2300	0	0	0	0	0	0	0	0	0	0
2410 On a payroll basis unallocable between 2100, 2200 and 2300 SSC	..	..	..	..	..	..	..	..	..	..
2420 On an income tax basis unallocable between 2100, 2200 and 2300 SSC	..	..	..	..	..	..	..	..	..	..
3000 Taxes on payroll and workforce	472	2 097	3 259	5 788	7 266	8 359	10 040	10 447	11 348	12 111
Emplr. contr. equaliz. of family.burdens	318	1 397	2 147	3 140	3 915	4 762	5 623	5 389	5 989	6 316
Tax on sum of wages	82	375	669	1 735	2 238	2 402	2 911	3 326	3 531	3 867
Promotion residential buildings	44	217	389	595	754	811	965	1 149	1 229	1 301
Tax on employment (Vienna undergr.)	0	20	21	21	22	22	65	69	65	70
Special levy for households allowances	26	80	0	0	0	0	0	0	0	0
Disabled persons equalization levy	2	8	34	54	83	91	148	163	159	167
Contributions to chambers	0	0	0	242	253	271	327	352	374	390
4000 Taxes on property	246	858	1 473	1 206	1 572	1 555	1 965	2 195	2 558	2 634
4100 Recurrent taxes on immovable property	92	231	355	526	626	682	761	861	889	897
4110 Households	47	66	84	87	92	93	107	142	145	134
Duty on farms	9	15	20	20	20	20	30	32	36	26
Farm contr. equaliz. of family burdens	5	6	6	6	6	6	6	7	7	6
Farm contribution to chambers	14	23	32	32	39	40	44	49	47	49
Contr. residential buildings reconstruction	4	0	0	0	0	0	0	0	0	0
Land tax A	16	22	25	28	26	26	26	31	31	30
Tax on secondary residences			0	0	0	0	0	23	23	23
4120 Others	45	165	271	440	534	589	654	719	744	764
Tax on vacant plots	1	4	5	5	5	6	6	5	5	9
Land tax B	44	161	266	435	529	583	649	714	738	754
4200 Recurrent taxes on net wealth	103	401	642	1	0	0	0	0	0	0
4210 Individual	37	140	189	1	..	..	..	..	..	..
Capital tax	25	109	189	1	..	..	..	..	..	..
Contribution emergency fund	0	0	0	0	..	..	..	..	..	..
Tax on industry and trade	10	26	0	0	..	..	..	..	..	..
Contribution to chambers	2	6	0	0	..	..	..	..	..	..
4220 Corporate	66	260	453	0	..	..	..	..	..	..
Capital tax	24	139	322	0	..	..	..	..	..	..
Capital death duty	20	53	131	0	..	..	..	..	..	..
Contribution emergency fund	0	0	0	0	..	..	..	..	..	..
Tax on industry and trade	19	56	0	0	..	..	..	..	..	..
Contribution to chambers	3	13	0	0	..	..	..	..	..	..
4300 Estate, inheritance and gift taxes	16	50	77	111	155	35	12	0	0	0
4310 Estate and inheritance taxes	..	..	..	..	..	..	..	..	..	..
4320 Gift taxes	..	..	..	..	..	..	..	..	..	..
4400 Taxes on financial and capital transactions	35	176	399	568	791	828	1 116	1 320	1 657	1 694
Land transfer tax	30	150	251	452	644	727	1 014	1 319	1 658	1 693
Capital transfer tax	5	27	148	115	147	102	102	1	- 1	0
4500 Nonrecurrent taxes	0	0	0	0	0	10	76	14	13	43
4510 On net wealth	..	..	..	..	..	0	4	0	0	0
Withholding Tax	..	..	..	..	..	..	4	0	0	..
4520 Other nonrecurrent taxes	..	..	..	..	..	10	72	14	13	43
Foundation tax	..	..	..	..	..	10	72	14	13	43
4600 Other recurrent taxes on property	0	0	0	0	0	0	0	0	0	0
5000 Taxes on goods and services	2 321	9 379	17 034	26 497	32 609	34 740	41 064	43 691	47 238	52 055
5100 Taxes on production, sale, transfer, etc	2 275	9 006	16 169	24 616	30 180	32 114	37 633	39 626	43 107	47 646
5110 General taxes	1 160	5 984	11 229	16 857	20 941	22 711	26 282	28 480	31 060	35 802
5111 Value added taxes	0	5 984	11 229	16 857	20 941	22 711	26 282	28 437	30 980	35 706
5112 Sales tax	0	0	0	0	0	0	0	0	0	0
5113 Other	1 160	0	0	0	0	0	0	43	80	96
Turnover tax	664	..	..	..	..	..	..	0	0	0
Additional federal levy-turnover	332	..	..	..	..	..	..	0	0	0
Additional lieu invoice stp.	164	..	..	..	..	..	..	0	0	0
Tax on online advertisement			..	..	..	..	..	43	80	96
5120 Taxes on specific goods and services	1 115	2 996	4 873	7 721	9 236	9 400	11 348	11 144	12 043	11 838
5121 Excises	610	2 219	3 290	5 484	6 760	6 921	7 749	7 246	8 001	7 506
Tax on beer	39	44	56	161	200	198	189	194	178	206
Tax on wine	7	0	0	0	0	0	0	0	0	0
Tax on sparkling wine	1	7	25	25	1	1	19	13	3	2
Tax on tobacco	188	519	820	1 197	1 446	1 502	1 782	1 983	2 073	2 075
Tax on mineral oils	50	136	1 426	2 726	3 689	3 854	4 218	3 579	4 201	3 994

	1965	1980	1990	2000	2007	2010	2015	2020	2021	2022
Additional federal levy mineral oils	202	876	0	0	0	0	0	0	0	0
Special duty alcoholic drinks	0	142	193	0	0	0	0	0	0	0
Special duty vehicles	0	0	0	0	0	0	0	0	0	0
Duty on starch products	0	4	12	0	0	0	0	0	0	0
Beverage tax	46	216	364	178	3	- 1	0	0	0	0
Other receipts-Market Organisation Act	26	35	9	0	1	0	0	0	0	0
Transport equality levy	0	5	1	0	0	0	0	0	0	0
Market Organisation Act - milk	35	177	192	0	0	0	0	0	0	0
Market Organisation Act - livestock	0	0	0	0	0	0	0	0	0	0
Market Organisation Act - grain	16	23	142	0	0	0	0	0	0	0
Duty promotion milk distrib.	0	34	13	0	0	0	0	0	0	0
Special tax on mineral oils	0	0	37	0	0	0	0	0	0	0
Duty on vehicles (fuel consumption)	0	0	0	433	457	453	395	440	406	423
Agricultural fund	0	0	0	23	16	18	17	17	17	18
Tax on energy	0	0	0	562	764	726	931	836	925	300
Social contributions to the artists' fund	0	0	0	0	11	6	13	8	9	13
Duty on exceeding milk-quota	0	0	0	36	24	6	11	0	0	0
Car registration taxes	0	0	0	143	148	158	174	175	189	161
Tax on Non-ETS emissions (carbon tax)			0	0	0	0	0	0	0	313
5122 Profits of fiscal monopolies	37	57	52	130	122	129	328	380	459	428
Duty on spirits	5	14	17	130	122	129	120	138	161	174
Federal monopolies salt	1	0	0	0	0	0	0	0	0	0
Federal monopolies spirits	30	43	35	0	0	0	0	0	0	0
Federal monopolies gambling	0	0	0	0	0	0	208	242	298	254
5123 Customs and import duties	332	354	677	351	390	340	415	476	497	665
Customs duties	310	237	418	352	390	339	415	476	497	665
Other import duties	0	21	61	0	0	0	0	0	0	0
Contribution promote foreign trade	10	63	171	0	0	0	0	0	0	0
Import equalization duties	12	33	27	0	0	0	0	0	0	0
5124 Taxes on exports	8	36	1	0	0	0	0	0	0	0
Contribution to promote foreign trade	8	36	1	..	..	..	..	..	..	..
5125 Taxes on investment goods	0	33	0	0	0	0	0	0	0	0
5126 Taxes on specific services	129	297	854	1 720	1 967	2 005	2 852	3 043	3 085	3 239
Insurance tax	25	135	384	745	993	1 017	1 122	1 240	1 287	1 366
Transport tax	63	0	0	0	0	0	0	0	0	0
Duty on casinos	2	28	64	105	71	55	70	80	45	96
Fire protection tax	5	24	50	45	54	56	61	67	70	75
Advertisement tax	7	31	65	62	0	0	0	0	0	0
Entertainment tax	2	2	2	5	8	9	18	0	0	0
Tax on tourism	8	43	71	103	142	171	186	235	251	258
Amusement tax	13	17	51	73	94	107	30	9	8	14
Announcement tax	3	18	40	81	0	1	0	0	0	0
Tax on interest yields	0	0	0	0	0	0	0	0	0	0
Tax on gambling stakes - licenses	0	0	116	197	202	221	254	276	318	307
Tax on advertisement	0	0	0	33	108	110	107	88	101	98
Levy on dangerous waste	0	0	10	71	72	51	56	57	66	66
Duty for airways security	0	0	0	28	56	30	0	0	0	0
Tax on gambling stakes - gains	0	0	0	171	166	176	0	0	0	0
Flight Charge	0	0	0	0	0	0	109	23	46	117
Financial Institutions Stability Fee	0	0	0	0	0	0	640	724	613	466
SRF Contributions			0	0	0	0	198	242	280	374
5127 Other taxes on internat. trade and transactions	0	0	0	0	0	0	0	0	0	0
5128 Other taxes	0	0	0	34	- 3	4	4	0	0	0
Levy on sugar	..	..	..	34	- 3	4	4	..	..	..
5130 Unallocable between 5110 and 5120	0	26	66	38	3	4	4	2	4	6
Fines related to tax offenses	..	26	66	38	3	4	4	2	4	6
5200 Taxes on use of goods and perform activities	46	373	865	1 881	2 429	2 626	3 431	4 065	4 131	4 409
5210 Recurrent taxes	38	335	757	1 733	2 253	2 416	3 124	3 631	3 711	3 803
5211 Paid by households: motor vehicles	22	156	366	811	1 173	1 293	1 814	2 172	2 230	2 271
5212 Paid by others: motor vehicles	13	41	97	298	370	334	421	496	514	524
5213 Paid in respect of other goods	3	138	294	624	710	789	890	963	967	1 008
Hunting and fishing duties	1	4	7	10	10	10	22	15	14	16
Dog tax	1	4	6	8	10	11	18	21	22	22
Contribution to promotion of arts	1	3	8	71	120	132	143	162	166	173
Tax on radio and tv - licenses	0	15	46	450	571	636	708	765	765	784
Road transport duty	0	112	226	84	0	0	0	0	0	0
Mandatory cap on market revenues for electricity			0	0	0	0	0	0	0	13
5220 Nonrecurrent taxes	8	38	108	147	175	210	307	434	420	605
Certain user fees	8	38	108	147	175	210	307	434	420	605
5300 Unallocable between 5100 and 5200	0	0	0	0	0	0	0	0	0	0
6000 Other taxes	38	266	714	770	928	1 095	737	688	741	780

	1965	1980	1990	2000	2007	2010	2015	2020	2021	2022
Tax on financial institutions	0	0	123	- 3	0	0	0	0	0	0
Administration duties	4	17	32	278	366	521	302	352	365	370
Stamp fees	7	46	76	135	92	84	32	25	24	32
Contributions of interested persons	0	0	130	0	0	0	0	0	0	0
Parking duty	0	0	6	0	0	0	0	0	0	0
Contrbutions to students' associations	0	0	0	4	8	11	11	14	15	17
Duty on contribution to political parties	0	0	0	0	- 1	1	0	0	0	0
Other fees, taxes on production n.e.c.	0	0	0	272	346	353	252	223	262	278
Embossing fee	0	0	0	0	1	1	1	0	0	0
Other taxes	28	202	347	82	115	124	137	70	71	79
Compensation levy according to the Vienna Tree Protection Act			0	1	1	2	2	3	5	6
6100 Paid solely by business	..	..	..	..	..	..	..	..	..	..
6200 Other	..	..	..	..	..	..	..	..	..	..
Custom duties collected for the EU	..	..	..	352	390	339	415	476	497	665
SRF Contributions collected for the EU			..	..	..	..	198	242	280	374
Non-wastable tax credits against 1110	..	..	..	650	650	650	540	330	325	350
Tax expenditure component	..	..	..	590	450	422	295	210	190	185
Transfer component	..	..	..	60	200	228	245	120	135	165
Non-wastable tax credits against 1210	..	..	..	..	..	..	..	..	..	..
Tax expenditure component	..	..	..	..	..	..	..	..	..	..
Transfer component	..	..	..	..	..	..	..	..	..	..
Total tax revenue on cash basis	6 210	29 759	54 040	90 299	115 045	120 735	148 036	158 727	176 063	193 158
Total tax revenue on accrual basis	..	..	..	90 324	115 146	121 192	148 469	160 713	176 120	193 204
Additional taxes included in National Accounts	..	..	..	..	..	..	..	..	..	..
Taxes excluded from National Accounts	..	..	..	..	..	..	..	..	..	..
Difference in treatment of tax credits	..	..	..	590	450	422	295	210	190	185
Capital transfer for uncollected revenue	..	..	..	..	..	..	..	- 349	- 314	- 92
Voluntary social security contributions	..	..	..	206	256	339	321	344	358	373
Miscellaneous differences	..	..	..	0	0	0	0	0	0	0
National Accounts: Taxes and actual social contributions	..	..	..	91 120	115 853	121 953	149 085	160 917	176 354	193 670
Imputed social contributions	..	..	..	2 485	2 177	2 106	1 925	1 640	1 567	1 526
National Accounts: Taxes and all social contributions	..	..	..	93 605	118 030	124 060	151 010	162 557	177 920	195 196

.. Not available

Note: Year ending 31st December.

From 1995 data are on accrual basis.

The pre-1995 figures are not in all cases comparable with those from the following years (due to the switch to the new System of National Accounts implemented only from 1995 onwards).

Source: Statistics Austria.

Table 5.3. Belgium: Details of tax revenue, 1965-2022

Million EUR

	1965	1980	1990	2000	2007	2010	2015	2020	2021	2022
Total tax revenue	6 421	37 443	70 408	112 710	147 861	156 317	184 374	195 050	214 264	235 398
Total tax revenue exclusive of taxes collected for the EU	..	..	..	111 675	146 411	155 042	182 758	193 204	212 313	232 671
1000 Taxes on income, profits and capital gains	1 774	15 379	25 983	43 461	52 854	53 313	65 572	69 204	76 329	87 956
1100 Taxes on income, profits and capital gains of individuals	1 317	13 626	22 538	35 318	41 020	44 027	51 877	54 136	57 234	66 196
1110 On income and profits of individuals	1 317	13 626	22 538	35 318	41 020	44 027	51 877	54 136	57 234	66 196
Immovable income withholding tax	148	532	1 053	1 857	0	0	0	0	0	0
Movable income withholding tax	119	1 062	3 014	1 755	2 351	2 426	4 104	3 066	3 694	4 376
Earned income withholding tax	740	9 119	15 422	27 778	36 022	39 829	45 658	48 417	50 846	57 353
Advance payments PIT	125	1 776	2 144	1 959	1 747	1 611	1 547	1 474	1 503	1 482
Non residents tax	0	- 3	4	585	792	810	926	1 229	1 256	1 246
Assessments PIT	183	1 128	878	774	- 915	- 1 697	- 1 512	- 1 327	- 1 414	359
Special social contributions	0	0	19	602	957	1 032	1 106	1 223	1 327	1 347
Other income taxes	0	12	2	8	65	17	48	54	21	33
1120 On capital gains of individuals	0	0	0	0	0	0	0	0	0	0
1200 Taxes on income, profits and capital gains of corporates	397	1 744	3 405	8 065	11 749	9 249	13 644	15 001	19 020	21 679
1210 On profits of corporates	397	1 744	3 405	8 065	11 749	9 249	13 644	15 001	19 020	21 679
Immovable income withholding tax (corporate)	33	0	0	0	0	0	0	0	0	0
Movable income withholding tax (corporate)	41	367	1 206	527	686	315	466	254	356	466
Advance payments (corporate)	262	1 273	2 735	7 112	9 733	7 691	8 539	12 426	15 539	18 011
Assessments (corporate)	60	79	- 553	404	1 270	1 196	4 466	2 246	2 964	3 160
Non residents tax (corporate)	0	- 6	18	17	41	43	154	52	149	31
Other income taxes (corporate)	0	32	- 2	5	19	4	19	24	12	11
1220 On capital gains of corporates	0	0	0	0	0	0	0	0	0	0
1300 Unallocable between 1100 and 1200	61	9	40	77	85	38	51	67	75	81
Former income taxes	51	0	0	0	0	0	0	0	0	0
Penalties	3	0	0	0	0	0	0	0	0	0
Other	7	9	40	77	85	38	51	67	75	81
2000 Social security contributions (SSC)	2 018	10 798	23 386	34 865	45 929	50 674	58 812	62 293	65 580	71 520
2100 Employees SSC	569	3 130	7 152	10 932	13 847	14 996	17 036	18 837	19 841	21 645
2110 On a payroll basis of employees SSC	..	3 130	7 152	10 932	13 847	14 996	17 036	18 837	19 841	21 645
On gross wages	..	3 130	7 062	10 932	13 847	14 996	17 036	18 837	19 841	21 645
On social benefits	..	0	89	0	0	0	0	0	0	0
2120 On an income tax basis of employees SSC	..	0	0	0	0	0	0	0	0	0
2200 Employers SSC	1 320	6 791	14 689	21 027	28 216	31 041	36 240	37 352	39 412	43 137
2210 On a payroll basis of employers SSC	..	6 791	14 689	21 027	28 216	31 041	36 240	37 352	39 412	43 137
Contributions by government	..	1 059	1 769	3 105	4 493	5 381	7 686	8 824	9 158	9 741
Contributions by other sectors	..	5 732	12 920	17 922	23 723	25 661	28 554	28 528	30 254	33 396
2220 On an income tax basis of employers SSC	..	0	0	0	0	0	0	0	0	0
2300 Self-employed or non-employed SSC	129	877	1 546	2 906	3 866	4 637	5 537	6 104	6 328	6 738
Self-employed	..	803	1 230	2 053	2 678	3 342	3 975	4 088	4 433	4 596
Unemployed	..	0	0	0	0	0	0	0	0	0
Retired	..	29	198	709	1 012	1 134	1 449	1 890	1 762	1 996
Other	..	45	118	144	176	161	113	127	133	146
2310 On a payroll basis of self/non-employed SSC	..	877	1 546	2 906	3 866	4 637	5 537	6 104	6 328	6 738
2320 On an income tax basis of self/non-employed SSC	..	0	0	0	0	0	0	0	0	0
2400 Unallocable between 2100, 2200 and 2300 SSC	0	0	0	0	0	0	0	0	0	0
2410 On a payroll basis unallocable between 2100, 2200 and 2300 SSC	..	..	..	..	..	..	..	..	..	..
2420 On an income tax basis unallocable between 2100, 2200 and 2300 SSC	..	..	..	..	..	..	..	..	..	..
3000 Taxes on payroll and workforce	0	0	0	0	6	7	8	5	5	5
Levy on public mandates	..	..	..	..	6	7	8	5	5	5
4000 Taxes on property	240	1 161	2 679	5 282	10 550	11 252	14 408	15 616	18 002	18 031
4100 Recurrent taxes on immovable property	2	210	599	1 164	4 146	4 632	5 433	6 059	6 249	6 663
4110 Households recurrent taxes on immovable property	0	26	63	102	2 779	3 115	3 651	4 129	4 263	4 554
4120 Other than households recurrent taxes on immovable property	2	184	536	1 063	1 367	1 517	1 782	1 930	1 986	2 110
Tax on non profit institutions	2	7	17	41	32	33	41	50	51	54
Immovable income withholding tax (corporate)	0	177	519	929	1 269	1 416	1 651	1 794	1 841	1 965
Regional tax (Brussels)	0	0	0	94	66	68	90	86	94	90
4200 Recurrent taxes on net wealth	0	0	0	92	253	237	661	984	1 031	1 096
4210 Individual recurrent taxes on net wealth	..	..	..	0	0	0	0	0	0	0
4220 Corporate recurrent taxes on net wealth	..	..	..	92	253	237	661	984	1 031	1 096
4300 Estate, inheritance and gift taxes	75	309	504	1 101	2 053	2 269	2 996	2 967	3 663	3 578

	1965	1980	1990	2000	2007	2010	2015	2020	2021	2022
4310 Estate and inheritance taxes	69	281	475	1 042	1 702	1 939	2 504	2 411	2 948	2 801
4320 Gift taxes	6	29	29	59	351	330	492	556	716	777
4400 Taxes on financial and capital transactions	163	633	1 478	2 669	3 704	3 493	4 358	4 961	5 943	5 617
Registration duties	153	527	1 213	1 967	3 325	3 210	3 899	4 403	5 337	5 098
Mortgage duties	2	10	29	37	76	75	93	84	93	92
Court duties	2	8	29	38	31	34	41	19	30	39
Economic expansion fund	0	0	0	0	0	0	0	0	0	0
Tax on stock exchange transactions	4	31	92	386	234	134	287	413	435	335
Tax on stock exchange listings	2	4	21	0	0	0	0	0	0	0
Tax on bearer securities	0	0	0	79	3	0	0	0	0	0
Stamp duties	0	53	94	161	35	40	38	42	48	54
4500 Non-recurrent taxes on property	0	0	0	74	163	327	643	321	416	325
4510 Non-recurrent taxes on net wealth	..	..	..	0	0	0	0	0	0	0
4520 Non-recurrent taxes on property other than net wealth	..	..	..	74	163	327	643	321	416	325
Tax on long term savings	..	..	..	74	163	194	413	203	207	212
Voluntary disclosure tax	..	..	..	0	0	0	0	0	0	0
Voluntary disclosure tax (Diamond)	..	..	..	0	0	0	0	0	0	0
Voluntary disclosure tax (bis)	..	..	..	0	0	133	152	26	37	10
Voluntary disclosure tax (ter)	..	..	..	0	0	0	78	92	172	103
Special contribution on credit associations	..	..	..	0	0	0	0	0	0	0
4600 Other recurrent taxes on property except 4100 and 4200	0	8	99	182	232	294	318	325	700	752
Levy for fighting the non-use of an electric power production site by a producer	..	..	..	0	- 17	0	0	0	0	0
Transfer to the Fund for Industrial Accidents of recognized private insurance corporations	..	..	..	182	249	294	318	297	321	343
Tax on securities accounts	..	..	..	0	0	0	0	27	379	410
Custom duties collected for the EU	..	..	..	960	1 388	1 234	1 373	1 545	1 604	2 280
Non-wastable tax credits against 1110: Total value	..	..	..	..	348	1 037	830	1 449	1 099	1 229
Non-wastable tax credits against 1110: Tax expenditure component	..	..	..	..	78	588	537	1 073	799	895
Non-wastable tax credits against 1110: Transfer component	..	..	..	..	270	449	293	376	300	333
Non-wastable tax credits against 1210: Total value	..	..	..	..	..	..	..	..	..	..
Non-wastable tax credits against 1210: Tax expenditure component	..	..	..	..	..	..	..	..	..	..
Non-wastable tax credits against 1210: Transfer component	..	..	..	..	..	..	..	..	..	..
5000 Taxes on goods and services	2 386	10 105	18 360	29 103	38 462	41 035	45 535	47 932	54 348	57 886
5100 Taxes on production, sale, transfer, etc	2 187	9 606	17 387	27 000	36 091	38 646	43 043	45 182	51 524	54 727
5110 General taxes on goods and services	1 355	6 321	11 570	18 258	24 411	25 882	28 170	29 785	35 076	36 714
5111 Value added taxes	0	6 321	11 547	18 132	24 140	25 628	27 952	29 538	34 713	36 442
VAT	..	6 293	11 491	18 132	24 140	25 628	27 952	29 538	34 713	36 442
Vehicle immatriculation tax	..	28	56	0	0	0	0	0	0	0
5112 Sales tax	0	0	23	126	271	253	219	247	363	272
5113 Other (than value added and sales tax)	1 355	0	0	0	0	0	0	0	0	0
Taxes assimilated to stamp duties	1 355	..	..	..	..	..	..	..	..	..
5120 Taxes on specific goods and services	832	3 285	5 818	8 742	11 680	12 764	14 873	15 397	16 448	18 013
5121 Excises	531	1 997	3 478	5 690	7 367	7 783	8 649	9 031	9 858	9 970
Mineral oil	278	1 109	2 017	3 392	3 891	4 148	4 556	4 401	5 202	5 147
Liquified gases and benzol	0	4	0	0	0	0	0	0	0	0
Tobacco	132	501	868	1 342	1 821	1 885	2 262	2 451	2 580	2 767
Spirits	23	123	191	206	225	235	318	344	322	334
Consumption tax on alcohol and spirits	26	54	0	0	0	0	0	0	0	0
Fermented sparkling beverages	1	7	11	24	39	57	92	90	106	105
Fermented fruit beverages	18	57	88	101	115	116	148	186	169	170

	1965	1980	1990	2000	2007	2010	2015	2020	2021	2022
Beer	38	93	170	208	191	188	194	180	167	191
Non-alcoholic beverages	10	44	113	148	49	54	56	186	164	189
Coffee, sugar and syrup	5	5	22	13	12	13	14	15	14	14
Levy on energy	0	0	0	193	341	383	343	321	340	431
Intermediate alcoholic products	0	0	0	32	28	26	26	26	24	22
Inspection fee on domestic fuel oil	0	0	0	29	43	51	36	32	30	25
Ecotax	0	0	0	2	1	0	0	0	0	0
Levy on packaging	0	0	0	0	296	320	336	372	321	349
Federal contribution on electricity and natural gas	0	0	0	0	311	292	269	430	418	226
Environmental charge	0	0	0	0	5	15	1	0	0	0
5122 Profits of fiscal monopolies	0	0	0	0	0	0	0	0	0	0
5123 Customs and import duties	272	627	809	960	1 388	1 234	1 373	1 545	1 604	2 280
Import duties	206	0	0	0	0	0	0	0	0	0
Levies on agricultural products	63	0	0	0	0	0	0	0	0	0
ECSC levies	2	0	0	0	0	0	0	0	0	0
EU levies, import duties	0	383	716	932	1 365	1 210	1 368	1 545	1 604	2 280
EU levies on agricultural products	0	244	93	28	23	23	5	0	0	0
5124 Taxes on exports	0	1	0	0	0	0	0	0	0	0
5125 Taxes on investment goods	0	0	0	0	0	0	0	0	0	0
5126 Taxes on specific services	29	452	937	1 365	2 044	2 454	3 210	3 398	3 551	3 793
Gambling and betting tax	9	47	51	45	64	77	80	93	104	136
Insurance levy	19	404	885	1 282	1 930	2 123	2 307	2 566	2 653	2 728
Bill-posting tax	0	0	1	1	3	3	3	3	2	4
Deposit insurance	0	0	0	36	48	252	441	435	446	457
Resolution fund	..	..	..	0	0	0	380	302	347	448
5127 Other taxes on internat. trade and transactions not included within 5121 to 5126 inclusive	0	0	0	0	0	0	0	0	0	0
5128 Other taxes not included within 5121 to 5127 inclusive	0	208	593	726	881	1 294	1 640	1 424	1 435	1 971
5130 Unallocable between 5110 and 5120	0	0	0	0	0	0	0	0	0	0
5200 Taxes on use of goods and perform activities	199	496	966	2 096	2 363	2 384	2 482	2 738	2 812	3 145
5210 Recurrent taxes on use of goods and perform activities	199	496	966	1 887	2 032	2 005	2 032	1 934	1 946	2 034
Traffic tax	100	368	712	1 413	1 693	1 702	1 851	1 880	1 909	1 956
5211 Recurrent taxes paid by households: motor vehicles	0	204	458	889	1 051	1 054	1 163	1 260	1 279	1 310
5212 Recurrent taxes paid by others: motor vehicles	0	164	254	525	642	648	689	620	630	646
5213 Recurrent taxes paid on use of goods and perform activities other than on motor vehicles	99	127	254	474	338	303	181	54	37	78
Tax on entertainment devices	6	20	20	71	56	58	56	30	13	53
Tax on pubs	1	5	24	18	0	0	0	0	0	0
Hunting tax	2	0	0	0	0	0	0	0	0	0
Local taxes	90	15	19	38	99	112	22	24	24	25
Radio and television licence fees	0	87	191	347	184	133	103	0	0	0
5220 Non-recurrent taxes on use of goods and perform activities	0	0	0	209	332	379	451	804	866	1 112
Vehicle registration tax	..	..	..	209	332	379	349	455	479	406
Vehicle registration tax (households)	..	..	..	139	221	252	233	303	320	271
Vehicle registration tax (others)	..	..	..	70	111	126	116	152	160	135
Emission permits	..	..	..	0	0	0	101	349	387	705
5300 Unallocable between 5100 and 5200	0	3	7	7	7	6	9	12	13	13
6000 Taxes other than 1000, 2000, 3000, 4000 and 5000	2	0	0	0	61	36	40	0	0	0
6100 Paid solely by business	0	..	..	..	0	0	0	..	0	..
6200 Other taxes not solely paid by business	2	..	..	..	61	36	40	..	0	..
Fines and interest	2	..	..	..	0	0	0	..	0	..
Other taxes collected on behalf of the EU				75	62	42	9	..	..	..
SRF Contributions collected for the EU				..	..	..	380	302	347	448
Taxes and compulsory social security contributions paid by EU civil servants				310	521	685	731	951	939	957
Taxes paid by EU civil servants: income taxes				174	270	345	370	482	475	485
Taxes paid by EU civil servants: compulsory social security contributions				136	250	340	360	469	464	472
Total tax revenue on cash basis	6 421	37 438	70 268	..	..	..	..	..	..	..
Total tax revenue on accrual basis	..	37 443	70 408	112 710	147 861	156 317	184 374	195 050	214 264	235 398
Additional taxes included in National Accounts	..	107	447	1 300	1 740	2 458	3 670	5 248	5 490	5 241
National lottery profits	..	107	262	279	225	243	206	185	185	200

	1965	1980	1990	2000	2007	2010	2015	2020	2021	2022
Water levies	..	0	66	378	119	137	104	135	144	136
Sanitel levy	..	0	0	14	13	15	6	12	12	12
Levy on industrial waste	..	0	27	74	68	54	55	76	77	93
Levy on manure	..	0	0	11	11	5	1	4	6	5
Levy on household waste	..	0	0	20	..	..	..	..	..	..
Earned income withholding tax (EU)	..	0	93	174	270	345	370	482	475	485
Social contributions (EU)	..	0	0	136	250	340	360	469	464	472
Imputed social contributions (EU)	..	0	0	213	431	508	554	721	723	735
Green certificates				..	354	812	1 959	2 433	2 528	1 847
Contracts art. 81 (Managed entry agreements)				..	..	..	55	733	876	1 257
Taxes excluded from National Accounts	..	0	0	0	0	0	0	0	0	0
Deposit insurance	..	..	..	..	..	..	..	..	..	..
Difference in treatment of tax credits	..	0	..	..	78	588	537	1 073	799	895
Capital transfer for uncollected revenue	..	0	0	- 291	- 381	- 597	- 547	- 617	- 547	- 540
VAT on products assessed but unlikely to be collected				- 18	- 276	- 367	- 357	- 477	- 430	- 411
Earned income withholding tax assessed but unlikely to be collected				- 40	- 53	- 71	- 49	- 44	- 44	- 39
Employers' actual social contributions assessed but unlikely to be collected				- 233	- 52	- 159	- 141	- 97	- 73	- 90
Voluntary social security contributions	..	41	52	58	57	59	70	82	83	72
Miscellaneous differences	..	0	0	0	0	0	0	0	0	0
Reallocation national levels of government	..	..	..	..	..	..	..	..	..	..
Reallocation EU	..	..	..	..	..	..	..	..	..	..
National Accounts: Taxes and actual social contributions	..	37 590	70 907	113 564	148 924	158 318	187 550	200 116	219 366	240 332
Imputed social contributions	..	1 497	2 886	5 377	7 568	8 713	9 812	11 446	11 722	12 733
National Accounts: Taxes and all social contributions	..	39 087	73 793	118 940	156 492	167 031	197 362	211 562	231 088	253 065

.. Not available

Note: Year ending 31st December. From 1970, data are on accrual basis.

Source: Institute for National Accounts; Federal Ministry of Finance.

Table 5.4. Canada: Details of tax revenue, 1965-2022

Million CAD

	1965	1980	1990	2000	2007	2010	2015	2020	2021	2022
Total tax revenue	15 318	101 015	244 152	390 234	512 663	516 591	653 269	765 375	875 924	951 779
1000 Taxes on income, profits and capital gains	5 910	47 064	118 566	195 320	251 198	240 961	314 841	386 815	451 841	490 947
1100 Of individuals	3 464	34 451	99 722	143 652	190 025	180 894	240 304	287 205	318 034	346 169
1110 On income and profits	3 464	34 451	99 722	143 652	190 025	180 894	240 304	287 205	318 034	346 169
Taxes federal government	2 635	21 231	60 252	90 694	116 395	109 341	143 315	173 110	191 964	207 161
Taxes on individuals - province	829	13 220	39 470	52 958	73 630	71 553	96 989	114 095	126 070	139 008
1120 On capital gains	0	0	0	0	0	0	0	0	0	0
1200 Corporate	2 276	11 741	17 190	47 643	54 272	54 101	67 894	92 132	123 325	132 032
1210 On profits	2 276	11 741	17 190	47 643	54 272	54 101	67 894	92 132	123 325	132 032
Taxes federal government (1)	1 752	8 110	11 726	31 570	37 093	33 419	41 726	57 424	77 697	83 597
Taxes on corporations - province	524	3 631	5 464	16 073	17 179	20 682	26 168	34 708	45 628	48 435
1220 On capital gains	0	0	0	0	0	0	0	0	0	0
1300 Unallocable between 1100 and 1200	170	872	1 654	4 025	6 901	5 966	6 643	7 479	10 483	12 747
Non-resident withhold taxes - federal	170	872	1 654	4 025	6 901	5 966	6 643	7 479	10 483	12 747
2000 Social security contributions	854	10 649	29 653	53 109	73 722	76 787	96 371	107 496	120 919	133 578
2100 Employees	318	3 756	10 634	21 361	29 361	30 626	38 685	44 348	50 463	55 762
Canada pension plan	47	1 265	3 745	9 401	16 194	16 852	21 491	25 606	29 667	32 259
Quebec pension plan	15	431	1 108	2 897	4 124	5 449	6 293	8 026	9 257	10 832
Employment insurance	164	1 393	5 284	7 782	7 084	7 388	9 772	9 331	9 900	10 922
Hospital insurance premiums	92	667	496	1 281	1 959	937	1 128	1 385	1 639	1 749
2110 On a payroll basis	..	..	10 634	20 976	28 654	29 689	37 557	42 963	48 824	54 013
2120 On an income tax basis	..	..	0	385	707	937	1 128	1 385	1 639	1 749
2200 Employers	536	6 697	18 449	30 307	41 922	43 525	54 380	59 165	65 843	72 737
Canada pension plan	48	1 266	3 745	9 401	16 194	16 852	21 491	25 606	29 667	32 259
Quebec pension plan	15	432	1 108	2 897	4 124	5 449	6 293	8 026	9 257	10 832
Employment insurance	164	2 006	7 398	10 894	9 917	10 343	13 681	13 064	13 861	15 290
Hospital insurance premiums	92	1 270	496	897	1 252	0	0	0	0	0
Social insurance levies	217	1 723	5 702	6 218	10 434	10 881	12 914	12 469	13 059	14 356
2210 On a payroll basis of employers SSC	..	..	18 449	30 307	41 922	43 525	54 380	59 165	65 843	72 737
2220 On an income tax basis of employers SSC	..	..	0	0	0	0	0	0	0	0
2300 Selfemployed or nonemployed	0	196	570	1 442	2 440	2 636	3 307	3 984	4 612	5 079
Canada pension plan	..	153	478	1 200	2 096	2 181	2 781	3 313	3 839	4 174
Quebec pension plan	..	43	92	242	344	455	525	670	773	904
2310 On a payroll basis of self/non-employed SSC	..	196	570	1 442	2 440	2 636	3 307	3 984	4 612	5 079
2320 On an income tax basis of self/non-employed SSC	..	0	0	0	0	0	0	0	0	0
2400 Unallocable between 2100, 2200 and 2300	0	0	0	0	0	0	0	0	0	0
2410 On a payroll basis unallocable between 2100, 2200 and 2300 SSC	..	..	..	..	..	..	..	..	..	..
2420 On an income tax basis unallocable between 2100, 2200 and 2300 SSC	..	..	..	..	..	..	..	..	..	..
3000 Taxes on payroll and workforce	0	0	5 499	8 013	10 038	10 760	13 256	17 198	18 890	20 697
4000 Taxes on property	2 186	9 195	24 467	37 157	54 507	63 735	77 778	89 816	97 959	98 540
4100 Recurrent taxes on immovable property	1 830	8 315	20 189	30 242	44 567	51 702	62 651	71 797	73 455	74 700
On property provincial government	11	133	1 645	3 078	3 164	4 476	5 410	6 707	7 220	7 791
Personal property local government	17	0	18 544	27 165	41 403	47 226	57 241	65 090	66 235	66 909
Real property local government	1 802	8 182	0	0	0	0	0	0	0	0
4110 Households	..	..	..	..	..	..	..	..	..	..
4120 Others	..	..	..	..	..	..	..	..	..	..
4200 Recurrent taxes on net wealth	25	512	1 911	4 171	2 970	1 523	372	464	490	561
4210 Individual	0	0	0	0	0	0	0	0	0	0
4220 Corporate	25	512	1 911	4 171	2 970	1 523	372	464	490	561
4300 Estate, inheritance and gift taxes	223	75	3	2	0	178	268	339	443	489
4310 Estate and inheritance taxes	216	75	3	2	..	178	268	339	443	489
On inheritances federal government	108	0	0	0	..	0	0	0	0	0
Succession duties provincial government	108	75	3	2	..	178	268	339	443	489
4320 Gift taxes	7	0	0	0	..	0	0	0	0	0
On gifts federal government	7	..	..	..	..	..	..	..	..	..
4400 Taxes on financial and capital transactions	0	0	0	0	2 868	3 077	4 975	8 121	12 296	10 818
4500 Nonrecurrent taxes	108	293	2 365	2 742	4 102	7 254	9 512	9 095	11 275	11 972
4510 On net wealth	0	0	0	0	0	0	0	0	0	0
4520 Other nonrecurrent taxes	108	293	2 365	2 742	4 102	7 254	9 512	9 095	11 275	11 972
Special assessments and charges local govt.	108	293	2 365	2 742	4 102	7 254	9 512	9 095	11 275	11 972
4600 Other recurrent taxes on property	0	0	0	0	0	0	0	0	0	0
5000 Taxes on goods and services	6 202	32 909	63 092	94 468	122 855	123 752	150 275	163 156	185 298	206 964
5100 Taxes on production, sale, transfer, etc	5 310	24 808	59 627	88 879	114 701	116 160	140 750	152 702	172 000	192 866
5110 General taxes	2 730	11 658	34 475	55 313	71 242	72 130	90 598	102 805	117 021	129 139
5111 Value added taxes	0	0	0	35 884	46 072	70 712	86 694	100 493	115 366	127 188
5112 Sales tax	2 730	11 658	34 475	19 429	25 170	1 418	3 904	2 311	1 655	1 951

	1965	1980	1990	2000	2007	2010	2015	2020	2021	2022
Sales taxes federal government	813	5 429	16 866	0	0	0	0	0	0	0
Sales taxes provincial, local govt.	1 917	6 229	17 609	19 429	25 170	1 418	3 904	2 311	1 655	1 951
5113 Other	0	0	0	0	0	0	0	0	0	0
5120 Taxes on specific goods and services	2 580	13 150	25 153	33 565	43 459	44 030	50 152	49 897	54 979	63 727
5121 Excises	1 499	6 805	14 473	18 417	22 759	23 281	25 284	28 384	29 922	31 703
Excises federal government	740	3 850	6 405	8 377	9 249	10 244	10 372	14 705	16 272	19 105
Liquor	..	..	926	1 103	1 224	1 554	1 521	2 023	1 991	2 045
Tobacco	..	..	2 247	2 176	2 466	3 025	2 875	3 024	3 223	2 936
Gasoline and motive fuel	..	..	2 472	4 807	5 272	5 306	5 678	4 917	5 091	5 511
Remitted gaming profits	..	..	45	0	0	0	0	0	0	0
Miscellaneous consumption taxes	..	..	715	291	287	358	297	4 741	5 967	8 613
Excises provincial government	759	2 955	8 067	10 039	13 510	13 037	14 912	13 679	13 650	12 598
Motor fuel	680	1 863	4 674	7 031	8 065	8 198	9 727	8 611	8 771	8 018
Tobacco	53	772	2 776	2 279	4 181	4 620	5 108	4 556	4 128	3 589
Other	26	320	617	730	1 264	219	77	512	751	991
5122 Profits of fiscal monopolies	294	1 406	3 758	8 756	11 565	11 565	13 016	10 450	12 072	15 707
Own enterprises contributions	294	1 406	3 758	8 756	11 565	11 565	13 016	10 450	12 072	15 707
5123 Customs and import duties	686	3 199	4 021	2 824	3 829	3 441	5 181	4 025	5 188	6 100
Customs and import duties federal govt.	686	3 199	4 021	2 824	3 829	3 441	5 181	4 025	5 188	6 100
5124 Taxes on exports	0	842	0	0	0	0	0	0	0	0
5125 Taxes on investment goods	0	0	0	0	0	0	0	0	0	0
5126 Taxes on specific services	84	575	2 385	2 524	4 088	4 489	5 213	5 799	6 363	8 253
Tax on insurance premiums, provincial govt.	45	261	1 141	1 740	2 796	3 305	3 962	5 401	5 729	6 849
Tax on insurance premiums, federal govt.	0	1	1	1	11	28	10	13	18	21
Amusement and admission taxes	4	25	126	538	537	322	291	74	81	179
Air transportation taxes	0	166	488	0	403	600	722	146	256	691
Racetrack betting	35	122	155	55	36	36	33	19	21	21
Tax on meals and hotels	0	0	473	191	305	198	195	146	258	492
5127 Other taxes on internat. trade and transactions	0	0	0	0	0	0	0	0	0	0
5128 Other taxes	17	323	517	1 045	1 217	1 255	1 458	1 238	1 434	1 964
Other taxes federal government	0	98	272	758	762	557	544	349	318	325
Other taxes provincial government	17	225	245	287	455	698	914	889	1 116	1 639
5130 Unallocable between 5110 and 5120	0	0	0	0	0	0	0	0	0	0
5200 Taxes on use of goods and perform activities	892	8 101	3 465	5 589	8 154	7 592	9 525	10 454	13 298	14 098
5210 Recurrent taxes	306	1 500	2 393	3 644	4 368	4 452	5 589	6 272	6 323	5 354
5211 Paid by households: motor vehicles	103	666	1 056	1 696	2 241	1 986	2 478	2 992	2 988	2 017
5212 Paid by others: motor vehicles	141	509	697	1 039	1 242	1 153	1 552	1 710	1 743	1 740
5213 Paid in respect of other goods	62	325	640	909	885	1 313	1 559	1 570	1 592	1 597
5220 Nonrecurrent taxes	586	6 601	1 072	1 945	3 786	3 140	3 936	4 182	6 975	8 744
Licences and permits local govt.	36	132	317	499	889	807	1 023	1 057	1 189	1 186
Licences and permits provincial govt.	550	6 469	755	1 446	2 897	2 333	2 913	3 125	5 786	7 558
5300 Unallocable between 5100 and 5200	0	0	0	0	0	0	0	0	0	0
6000 Other taxes	166	1 198	2 875	2 167	342	596	748	894	1 017	1 053
6100 Paid solely by business	139	943	2 386	1 280	0	0	0	0	0	0
6200 Other	27	255	489	887	342	596	748	894	1 017	1 053
Poll tax local government	5	0	0	0	0	0	0	0	0	0
Miscellaneous local government	11	358	489	887	342	596	748	894	1 017	1 053
Other federal government	11	- 103	0	0	0	0	0	0	0	0
Non-wastable tax credits against 1110	..	..	..	1 633	5 550	6 415	7 510	8 364	14 096	16 875
Tax expenditure component	..	..	..	276	824	875	968	1 246	2 307	2 735
Transfer component	..	..	..	1 357	4 726	5 540	6 542	7 118	11 789	14 140
Non-wastable tax credits against 1210	..	..	..	1 758	3 445	4 726	3 768	4 775	4 727	5 069
Tax expenditure component	..	..	..	20	12	19	15	25	31	27
Transfer component	..	..	..	1 738	3 433	4 707	3 753	4 750	4 696	5 042
Total tax revenue on cash basis	15 318	101 015	244 152	388 833	527 734	..	0	0	0	0
Total tax revenue on accrual basis	..	..	..	390 234	512 663	516 591	653 269	765 375	875 924	951 779
Additional taxes included in National Accounts	..	..	..	0	0	0	0	0	0	0
Taxes excluded from National Accounts	..	..	..	0	0	0	0	0	0	0
Difference in treatment of tax credits	..	..	..	296	836	894	983	1 272	2 338	2 762
Capital transfer for uncollected revenue	..	..	..	0	0	0	0	0	0	0
Voluntary social security contributions	..	..	..	0	0	0	0	0	0	0
Miscellaneous differences	..	..	..	0	0	0	0	0	0	0
National Accounts: Taxes and actual social contributions	..	..	..	390 234	513 499	517 485	654 252	766 647	878 262	954 541
Imputed social contributions	..	..	..	0	0	0	0	0	0	0
National Accounts: Taxes and all social contributions	..	..	..	390 234	513 499	517 485	654 252	766 647	878 262	954 541

.. Not available

Note: From 2001, all data are for the year ending 31st December. For 2000 and earlier years, data for the Federal, Provincial and Territorial governments and Social security funds are on a fiscal year basis commencing 1st April. Data for local government are on a fiscal year basis commencing 1st January. From 1999 data are on accrual basis.

There are some minor differences between the data for the years 1965 to 1978 and those for subsequent years. These mostly relate to the inclusion of fines and penalities or late payment of taxes and deductions for the child tax credits in the data for the years 1979 to 1983.

Heading 1210 - Taxes federal government: Federal corporate taxes include capital taxes.

Heading 2000: Includes receipts from the Canadian Pension Plan, Quebec Pension Plan, Unemployment Insurance Fund and Provincial Health Insurance. Premiums, Medicare Premiums and Social Insurance levies but excludes that part of the taxes on income and sales taxes earmarked for old age security. The practice of earmarking these taxes was discontinued in June 1975.

Heading 4400: From 2002 onward includes land transfer taxes of the provincial, territorial and local governments. Prior to 2002 land transfer taxes of the local government were included in line 6000 and those provincial and territorial governments were included in line 4520.

Heading 5121: The large increase in this heading between 1980 and 1981 is due to the introduction of a 'special petroleum compensation charge', a 'Canadian ownership special charge' and to an increase in the natural gas tax of C$ 2399 millions.

Heading 5122: From 1988, profits on fiscal monopolies include lottery profits.

Heading 5128: From 1988, other taxes of Federal Government does not include the annual fees for managing the spectrum (airwaves) allocation to the cellular industry.

Heading 5211: Some Québec motor vehicle licence administrative fees are included in sales of goods and services for the period 1988-89 to 1997-98. From 1998-99 onward, these fees are included under other taxes - motor vehicle licences.

Source: Statistics Canada.

Table 5.5. Chile: Details of tax revenue, 1965-2022

Million CLP

	1965	1980	1990	2000	2007	2010	2015	2020	2021	2022
Total tax revenue	..	..	1 777 218	7 901 998	20 598 963	21 815 391	32 533 542	38 823 397	53 463 334	62 901 438
1000 Taxes on income, profits and capital gains	..	..	412 974	1 841 630	9 412 056	8 329 058	11 840 521	12 540 342	20 456 920	27 491 879
1100 Of individuals	..	..	99 154	604 100	989 348	1 492 837	3 199 876	3 976 009	5 780 432	6 626 617
Second category tax	..	..	65 552	490 980	993 129	1 449 099	2 350 120	3 051 177	3 442 651	3 914 343
Global complementary tax	..	..	33 603	113 120	- 3 781	43 738	- 36 757	132 551	620 904	1 087 034
Others	..	..	0	0	0	0	886 513	792 281	1 716 877	1 625 240
1110 On income and profits	..	..	..	..	..	..	..	..	..	..
1120 On capital gains	..	..	..	..	..	..	..	..	..	..
1200 Corporate	..	..	219 586	882 896	6 054 487	4 448 745	6 839 133	9 429 787	9 145 873	14 900 568
First category tax	..	..	200 891	815 747	5 084 996	3 913 870	6 183 830	8 745 612	8 360 928	13 034 540
Surtax on state owned enterprises	..	..	16 074	47 634	113 334	194 203	132 352	203 416	249 073	475 034
Mining tax	..	..	0	0	835 452	298 558	323 507	267 544	393 548	1 223 807
Other	..	..	2 621	19 516	20 705	42 114	199 444	213 216	142 323	167 188
1210 On profits	..	..	..	..	..	..	..	..	..	..
1220 On capital gains	..	..	..	..	..	..	..	..	..	..
1300 Unallocable between 1100 and 1200	..	..	94 233	354 634	2 368 221	2 387 477	1 801 512	- 865 454	5 530 616	5 964 694
Adicionel tax	..	..	59 082	350 301	1 462 715	1 414 057	1 429 758	2 063 149	2 534 906	2 731 170
Other	..	..	35 151	4 332	905 507	973 420	371 755	-2 928 603	2 995 710	3 233 524
2000 Social security contributions	..	..	159 559	576 758	1 148 647	1 493 987	2 252 489	3 104 866	2 815 090	2 585 421
2100 Employees	..	..	154 021	553 937	1 098 620	1 433 159	2 188 575	2 994 036	2 686 021	2 435 398
2110 On a payroll basis	..	..	154 021	553 937	1 098 620	1 433 159	2 188 575	2 994 036	2 686 021	2 435 398
2120 On an income tax basis	..	..	0	0	0	0	0	0	0	0
2200 Employers	..	..	5 538	22 821	50 027	60 828	63 914	110 830	129 068	150 023
2210 On a payroll basis of employers SSC	..	..	5 538	22 821	50 027	60 828	63 914	110 830	129 068	150 023
2220 On an income tax basis of employers SSC	..	..	0	0	0	0	0	0	0	0
2300 Selfemployed or nonemployed	..	..	0	0	0	0	0	0	0	0
2310 On a payroll basis of self/non-employed SSC	..	..	..	..	..	..	..	..	..	..
2320 On an income tax basis of self/non-employed SSC	..	..	..	..	..	..	..	..	..	..
2400 Unallocable between 2100, 2200 and 2300	..	..	0	0	0	0	0	0	0	0
2410 On a payroll basis unallocable between 2100, 2200 and 2300 SSC	..	..	..	..	..	..	..	..	..	..
2420 On an income tax basis unallocable between 2100, 2200 and 2300 SSC	..	..	..	..	..	..	..	..	..	..
3000 Taxes on payroll and workforce	..	..	0	0	0	0	0	0	0	0
4000 Taxes on property	..	..	109 319	554 037	1 013 571	867 908	1 419 338	2 262 822	2 885 059	3 466 181
4100 Recurrent taxes on immovable property	..	..	59 968	302 244	496 311	631 669	1 054 984	1 753 218	2 002 413	2 284 253
4110 Households	..	..	..	..	..	..	..	..	..	..
4120 Others	..	..	..	..	..	..	..	..	..	..
4200 Recurrent taxes on net wealth	..	..	0	0	0	0	0	0	0	0
4210 Individual	..	..	..	..	..	..	..	..	..	..
4220 Corporate	..	..	..	..	..	..	..	..	..	..
4300 Estate, inheritance and gift taxes	..	..	3 444	10 906	28 501	39 338	92 236	155 433	291 830	416 219
4310 Estate and inheritance taxes	..	..	..	..	..	..	..	..	..	..
4320 Gift taxes	..	..	..	..	..	..	..	..	..	..
4400 Taxes on financial and capital transactions	..	..	45 907	240 886	488 759	196 901	272 118	354 171	590 816	765 709
4500 Nonrecurrent taxes	..	..	0	0	0	0	0	0	0	0
4510 On net wealth	..	..	..	..	..	..	..	..	..	..
4520 Other nonrecurrent taxes	..	..	..	..	..	..	..	..	..	..
4600 Other recurrent taxes on property	..	..	0	0	0	0	0	0	0	0
5000 Taxes on goods and services	..	..	1 118 722	5 041 769	9 023 666	11 185 157	17 598 086	21 275 452	28 368 617	30 080 511
5100 Taxes on production, sale, transfer, etc	..	..	1 074 009	4 789 827	8 578 636	10 532 905	16 516 194	19 613 567	26 628 027	28 078 680
5110 General taxes	..	..	664 421	3 306 350	6 781 501	8 399 927	13 273 958	15 963 032	22 785 935	24 515 246
5111 Value added taxes	..	..	664 421	3 306 350	6 781 501	8 399 927	13 273 958	15 963 032	22 785 935	24 515 246
5112 Sales tax	..	..	0	0	0	0	0	0	0	0
5113 Other	..	..	0	0	0	0	0	0	0	0
5120 Taxes on specific goods and services	..	..	409 588	1 483 477	1 797 135	2 132 978	3 242 236	3 650 535	3 842 092	3 563 434
5121 Excises	..	..	166 050	816 160	1 299 844	1 561 205	2 413 482	2 899 252	2 799 017	2 331 072
Cigarettes and tobacco	..	..	60 604	283 275	455 595	647 637	982 609	1 021 917	1 201 968	1 171 382
Gasolene and diesel	..	..	105 445	532 885	844 249	913 568	1 388 218	1 799 846	1 507 872	1 028 982
Oil stabilisation fund	..	..	0	0	0	0	0	0	0	1 547
Fisheries Law Extraction Rights	..	..	0	0	0	0	8 558	33 104	8 967	21 566
Additional tax on new motor vehicles	..	..	0	0	0	0	34 097	44 385	80 210	107 596
5122 Profits of fiscal monopolies	..	..	0	0	0	0	0	0	0	0
5123 Customs and import duties	..	..	222 486	548 571	300 416	267 331	343 491	294 204	468 128	555 863
5124 Taxes on exports	..	..	0	0	0	0	0	0	0	0

	1965	1980	1990	2000	2007	2010	2015	2020	2021	2022
5125 Taxes on investment goods	..	..	0	0	0	0	0	0	0	0
5126 Taxes on specific services	..	..	21 052	118 746	196 875	304 442	485 263	457 079	574 947	676 499
5127 Other taxes on internat. trade and transactions	..	..	0	0	0	0	0	0	0	0
5128 Other taxes	..	..	0	0	0	0	0	0	0	0
5130 Unallocable between 5110 and 5120	..	..	0	0	0	0	0	0	0	0
5200 Taxes on use of goods and perform activities	..	..	44 714	251 942	445 030	652 252	1 081 893	1 661 885	1 740 590	2 001 831
5210 Recurrent taxes	..	..	44 714	251 942	445 030	652 252	1 081 893	1 504 291	1 617 710	1 855 378
Motor vehicles	..	..	24 469	93 880	155 158	218 219	397 608	585 651	671 258	821 559
5211 Paid by households: motor vehicles	..	..	0	0	0	0	0	0	0	0
5212 Paid by others: motor vehicles	..	..	0	0	0	0	0	0	0	0
5213 Paid in respect of other goods	..	..	20 245	158 062	289 872	434 033	684 285	918 640	946 452	1 033 819
Municipal permits	..	..	18 401	136 138	263 996	396 944	630 943	862 685	885 324	967 043
Mining patents	..	..	3 374	34 730	25 184	36 213	51 767	54 932	59 801	65 122
Other	..	..	- 1 530	- 12 806	692	876	1 575	1 023	1 327	1 653
5220 Nonrecurrent taxes	..	..	0	0	0	0	0	157 594	122 880	146 453
Tax on polluting fixed sources			..	..	..	..	..	157 594	122 880	146 453
5300 Unallocable between 5100 and 5200	..	..	0	0	0	0	0	0	0	0
6000 Other taxes	..	..	- 23 356	- 112 195	1 023	- 60 720	- 576 893	- 360 084	-1 062 352	- 722 555
6100 Paid solely by business	..	..	0	0	0	0	0	0	0	0
6200 Other	..	..	- 23 356	- 112 195	1 023	- 60 720	- 576 893	- 360 084	-1 062 352	- 722 555
Non-wastable tax credits against 1110	..	..	0	0	0	0	0	0	0	0
Tax expenditure component	..	..	..	..	..	..	..	..	..	..
Transfer component	..	..	..	..	..	..	..	..	..	..
Non-wastable tax credits against 1210	..	..	0	0	0	0	175 468	297 981	279 353	352 801
Tax expenditure component	..	..	..	..	..	..	45 774	74 949	63 520	102 393
Transfer component	..	..	..	..	..	..	129 694	223 032	215 833	250 407
Total tax revenue on cash basis	..	..	1 777 218	7 901 998	20 598 963	21 815 391	32 533 542	38 823 397	53 463 334	62 901 438
Total tax revenue on accrual basis	..	..	..	..	..	..	..	..	..	..
Additional taxes included in National Accounts	..	..	..	..	..	..	..	..	..	..
Taxes excluded from National Accounts	..	..	..	..	..	..	..	..	..	..
Difference in treatment of tax credits	..	..	..	..	..	..	..	..	..	..
Capital transfer for uncollected revenue	..	..	..	..	..	..	..	..	..	..
Voluntary social security contributions	..	..	..	..	..	..	..	..	..	..
Miscellaneous differences	..	..	..	..	..	..	..	..	..	..
National Accounts: Taxes and actual social contributions	..	..	..	..	..	..	..	..	..	..
Imputed social contributions	..	..	..	..	..	..	..	..	..	..
National Accounts: Taxes and all social contributions	..	..	..	..	..	..	..	..	..	..

.. Not available

Note: Year ending 31st December.

The data are on a cash basis.

Source: Servicio de Impuestos internos (Chile's Tax Service).

Table 5.6. Colombia: Details of tax revenue, 1965-2022

Million COP

	1965	1980	1990	2000	2007	2010	2015	2020	2021	2022
Total tax revenue	..	..	2 579 426	30 598 630	82 697 457	98 455 335	160 157 693	187 438 661	228 906 840	288 842 327
1000 Taxes on income, profits and capital gains	..	..	771 694	7 103 525	24 010 404	26 218 852	52 656 876	61 812 525	73 222 876	95 911 106
1100 Taxes on income, profits and capital gains of individuals	..	..	47 210	1 499 345	4 751 580	5 192 384	9 218 735	14 340 067	15 825 275	20 356 452
1110 On income and profits of individuals	..	..	47 210	1 499 345	4 751 580	5 192 384	9 218 735	14 340 067	15 825 275	20 356 452
Income tax			47 210	1 499 345	4 751 580	5 192 384	9 218 735	14 304 469	15 754 931	20 224 214
Simple tax regime			0	0	0	0	0	35 598	70 344	132 238
1120 On capital gains of individuals	..	..	..	..	..	..	..	..	..	..
1200 Taxes on income, profits and capital gains of corporates	..	..	359 758	5 119 828	18 427 899	20 405 209	41 406 848	43 257 502	54 442 473	73 300 918
1210 On profits of corporates	..	..	359 758	5 119 828	18 427 899	20 405 209	41 406 848	43 257 502	54 442 473	73 300 918
Income Tax	..	..	359 758	5 119 828	18 427 899	20 405 209	27 480 679	43 131 163	54 248 966	72 907 780
Pro Equity Income Tax - CREE	..	..	0	0	0	0	13 926 169	39 871	28 428	56 854
Simple tax regime			0	0	0	0	0	86 469	165 079	336 285
1220 On capital gains of corporates	..	..	..	..	..	..	..	..	..	..
1300 Unallocable between 1100 and 1200	..	..	364 726	484 352	830 925	621 258	2 031 293	4 214 956	2 955 127	2 253 735
Income tax	..	..	364 726	484 352	830 925	621 258	2 031 293	4 214 956	2 955 127	2 253 735
Pro equity income tax -CREE	..	..	0	0	0	0	0	0	0	0
2000 Social security contributions (SSC)	..	..	203 596	4 989 000	9 694 000	11 478 085	13 585 138	18 389 481	21 673 981	23 908 538
2100 Employees SSC	..	..	..	..	..	..	..	..	..	..
2110 On a payroll basis of employees SSC	..	..	..	..	..	..	..	..	..	..
2120 On an income tax basis of employees SSC	..	..	..	..	..	..	..	..	..	..
2200 Employers SSC	..	..	..	..	..	..	..	..	..	..
2210 On a payroll basis of employers SSC	..	..	..	..	..	..	..	..	..	..
2220 On an income tax basis of employers SSC	..	..	..	..	..	..	..	..	..	..
2300 Self-employed or non-employed SSC	..	..	..	..	..	..	..	..	..	..
2310 On a payroll basis of self/non-employed SSC	..	..	..	..	..	..	..	..	..	..
2320 On an income tax basis of self/non-employed SSC	..	..	..	..	..	..	..	..	..	..
2400 Unallocable between 2100, 2200 and 2300 SSC	..	..	203 596	4 989 000	9 694 000	11 478 085	13 585 138	18 389 481	21 673 981	23 908 538
2410 On a payroll basis unallocable between 2100, 2200 and 2300 SSC	..	..	203 596	4 989 000	9 694 000	11 478 085	13 585 138	18 389 481	21 673 981	23 908 538
2420 On an income tax basis unallocable between 2100, 2200 and 2300 SSC	..	..	0	0	0	0	0	0	0	0
3000 Taxes on payroll and workforce	..	..	0	1 286 803	2 798 906	4 022 503	2 797 308	3 670 490	3 927 070	4 421 997
4000 Taxes on property	..	..	56 160	2 027 654	6 459 259	8 535 238	18 156 105	18 167 358	20 652 565	22 525 146
4100 Recurrent taxes on immovable property	..	..	56 160	991 070	2 298 829	3 338 935	6 061 965	9 109 598	9 643 729	9 937 041
4110 Households recurrent taxes on immovable property	..	..	0	0	0	0	0	0	0	0
4120 Other than households recurrent taxes on immovable property	..	..	56 160	991 070	2 298 829	3 338 935	6 061 965	9 109 598	9 643 729	9 937 041
4200 Recurrent taxes on net wealth	..	..	0	0	1 170 908	1 970 530	5 352 940	957 137	1 032 058	73 113
4210 Individual recurrent taxes on net wealth	..	..	..	..	..	..	..	..	..	..
4220 Corporate recurrent taxes on net wealth	..	..	..	..	..	..	..	..	..	..
4300 Estate, inheritance and gift taxes	..	..	0	0	0	0	0	0	0	0
4310 Estate and inheritance taxes	..	..	..	..	..	..	..	..	..	..
4320 Gift taxes	..	..	..	..	..	..	..	..	..	..
4400 Taxes on financial and capital transactions	..	..	0	1 036 584	2 989 522	3 225 773	6 741 200	7 476 295	9 831 204	12 281 751
4500 Non-recurrent taxes on property	..	..	0	0	0	0	0	624 327	145 573	233 241
4510 Non-recurrent taxes on net wealth	..	..	..	..	..	..	..	0	0	0
4520 Non-recurrent taxes on property other than net wealth	..	..	..	..	..	..	..	624 327	145 573	233 241
4600 Other recurrent taxes on property except 4100 and 4200	..	..	0	0	0	0	0	0	0	0
5000 Taxes on goods and services	..	..	1 388 653	14 180 450	36 766 741	44 411 642	65 716 566	77 752 543	99 258 009	129 331 933
5100 Taxes on production, sale, transfer, etc	..	..	1 388 653	14 048 655	36 447 297	44 038 074	64 688 081	75 960 351	97 214 920	127 046 376
5110 General taxes on goods and services	..	..	672 368	9 585 866	26 910 512	33 333 802	48 684 900	62 866 653	80 093 904	105 084 119
5111 Value added taxes	..	..	583 078	8 445 776	23 377 821	28 811 682	41 659 696	53 912 648	69 883 378	91 723 278
5112 Sales tax	..	..	89 290	1 140 090	3 532 691	4 522 121	7 025 204	8 954 004	10 210 526	13 360 841
Industry and commerce tax (State)	..	..	89 290	1 140 090	3 532 691	4 522 121	7 025 204	8 954 004	10 210 526	13 360 841
5113 Other (than value added and sales tax)	..	..	0	0	0	0	0	0	0	0
5120 Taxes on specific goods and services	..	..	716 285	4 462 789	9 536 785	10 704 271	16 003 181	13 093 698	17 121 016	21 962 257
5121 Excises	..	..	404 699	2 718 692	5 276 999	6 052 273	11 412 250	10 159 930	12 906 426	15 703 712
Diesel surcharge			0	85 716	388 091	500 405	598 993	505 000	570 600	655 000
Sugar-sweetened ultra-processed beverages			0	0	0	0	0	0	0	0
Ultra-processed foods and/or with high content of added sugars, sodium or saturated fats			0	0	0	0	0	0	0	0
Petrol surcharge			0	595 031	1 309 154	1 380 848	1 747 969	1 737 050	2 265 855	2 690 737
Petrol	..	..	141 270	833 004	1 211 511	1 418 766	3 297 392	1 205 806	1 732 540	1 650 801

	1965	1980	1990	2000	2007	2010	2015	2020	2021	2022
Restaurant service, vehicle sale and mobile telephone service	..	..	0	0	0	0	1 684 179	1 226 863	1 279 312	2 531 110
Tobacco (State)	..	..	52 898	213 412	330 016	390 472	524 357	1 239 269	1 451 431	1 638 694
Beer (State)	..	..	85 722	471 135	1 203 838	1 432 453	2 305 895	2 243 811	2 723 800	3 049 682
Liquors (State)	..	..	124 808	520 394	834 390	929 328	1 253 466	1 675 472	2 503 248	3 075 170
Carbon			0	0	0	0	0	281 911	330 567	361 899
Plastic bags			0	0	0	0	0	43 777	48 079	49 697
Medicinal cannabis			0	0	0	0	0	972	993	921
National Accounts: Taxes and all social contributions	..	..	..	..	..	..	..	..	..	..
5122 Profits of fiscal monopolies	..	..	0	0	0	0	0	0	0	0
5123 Customs and import duties	..	..	311 586	1 744 097	4 259 786	4 651 999	4 590 931	2 933 768	4 214 590	6 258 546
Custom duties	..	..	180 989	1 744 097	4 259 786	4 651 999	4 590 931	2 933 768	4 214 590	6 258 546
Imports surcharge	..	..	130 597	0	0	0	0	0	0	0
5124 Taxes on exports	..	..	0	0	0	0	0	0	0	0
5125 Taxes on investment goods	..	..	0	0	0	0	0	0	0	0
5126 Taxes on specific services	..	..	0	0	0	0	0	0	0	0
5127 Other taxes on internat. trade and transactions not included within 5121 to 5126 inclusive	..	..	0	0	0	0	0	0	0	0
5128 Other taxes not included within 5121 to 5127 inclusive	..	..	0	0	0	0	0	0	0	0
5130 Unallocable between 5110 and 5120	..	..	0	0	0	0	0	0	0	0
5200 Taxes on use of goods and perform activities	..	..	0	131 795	319 444	373 568	1 028 485	1 792 192	2 043 090	2 285 557
5210 Recurrent taxes on use of goods and perform activities	..	..	..	131 795	319 444	373 568	1 028 485	1 792 192	2 043 090	2 285 557
5211 Recurrent taxes paid by households: motor vehicles	..	..	..	131 795	319 444	373 568	1 028 485	1 792 192	2 043 090	2 285 557
Tax on motor vehicle ownership			..	131 795	319 444	373 568	1 028 485	1 792 192	2 043 090	2 285 557
5212 Recurrent taxes paid by others: motor vehicles	..	..	..	..	..	..	..	..	..	..
5213 Recurrent taxes paid on use of goods and perform activities other than on motor vehicles	..	..	..	..	..	..	..	..	..	..
5220 Non-recurrent taxes on use of goods and perform activities	..	..	..	..	..	..	..	..	..	..
5300 Unallocable between 5100 and 5200	..	..	0	0	0	0	0	0	0	0
6000 Taxes other than 1000, 2000, 3000, 4000 and 5000	..	..	159 323	1 011 197	2 968 147	3 789 014	7 245 701	7 646 264	10 172 339	12 743 607
6100 Paid solely by business	..	..	0	0	0	0	0	0	0	0
6200 Other taxes not solely paid by business	..	..	159 323	1 011 197	2 968 147	3 789 014	7 245 701	7 646 264	10 172 339	12 743 607
Stamp tax	..	..	0	401 497	759 787	357 160	101 668	41 373	83 115	134 457
Other	..	..	78 306	79 287	86 297	126 602	318 271	245 541	423 822	788 653
Other (sub-national)	..	..	81 017	530 413	2 122 062	3 305 252	6 825 762	7 359 350	9 665 402	11 820 497
Total tax revenue on cash basis	..	..	2 579 426	30 598 630	82 697 457	98 455 335	160 157 693	187 438 661	228 906 840	288 842 327
Total tax revenue on accrual basis	..	..	..	..	..	..	..	..	..	..
Additional taxes included in National Accounts	..	..	..	..	..	..	..	..	..	..
Taxes excluded from National Accounts	..	..	..	..	..	..	..	..	..	..
Difference in treatment of tax credits	..	..	..	..	..	..	..	..	..	..
Capital transfer for uncollected revenue	..	..	..	..	..	..	..	..	..	..
Voluntary social security contributions	..	..	..	..	..	..	..	..	..	..
Miscellaneous differences	..	..	..	..	..	..	..	..	..	..
National Accounts: Taxes and actual social contributions	..	..	..	..	..	..	..	..	..	..
Imputed social contributions	..	..	..	..	..	..	..	..	..	..

.. Not available

Note: Year ending 31st December.

Data on an cash basis.

Includes the reported consolidated revenues of the territorial entities (departments and municipalities).

Heading 2000: Before 2013, social security contributions did not include all the contributions entering FOSYGA (Solidarity and Guarantee Fund). Only the portion of the contributions used to finance the subsidised regime (up to 1.5 pp of the 12.5% of the monthly wage paid by employers and employees as an obligatory health contribution) was included. The part of the contributions entering FOSYGA to finance the contributory regime was classified in the social security sector as "other incomes".

From 2013 onwards, all of the health contributions entering FOSYGA are classified as social security contributions. The portion of the contributions not entering FOSYGA that is both collected and spent by the health insurers – EPS - is not part of the fiscal accounts.

Headings 1100 and 1200: The data for the preliminary year are estimates.

Source: Dirección de Impuestos y Aduanas Nacionales de Colombia, Ministerio de Hacienda y Crédito Público y Banco Central de Colombia.

(National Tax and Customs Administration, Ministry of Finance and Public Credit and Central Bank of Colombia).

Table 5.7. Costa Rica: Details of tax revenue, 1965-2022

Million CRC

	1965	1980	1990	2000	2007	2010	2015	2020	2021	2022
Total tax revenue	..	..	117 711	978 114	3 213 401	4 382 367	6 923 575	8 235 528	10 019 264	11 285 967
National Accounts: Taxes and all social contributions	..	..	..	..	..	..	..	..	..	..
1000 Taxes on income, profits and capital gains	..	..	11 820	128 805	531 552	748 093	1 247 308	1 651 249	2 063 810	2 430 200
1100 Of individuals	..	..	..	..	123 194	202 849	386 241	556 084	622 772	691 305
1110 On income and profits	..	..	..	..	123 194	202 849	386 241	554 486	618 550	682 875
1120 On capital gains	..	..	..	..	0	0	0	1 598	4 222	8 430
1200 Corporate	..	..	..	..	348 826	450 312	659 951	692 551	970 546	1 188 835
1210 On profits	..	..	..	..	348 826	450 312	659 951	685 470	952 951	1 162 697
1220 On capital gains	..	..	..	..	0	0	0	7 081	17 595	26 138
1300 Unallocable between 1100 and 1200	..	..	11 820	128 805	59 531	94 932	201 116	402 613	470 492	550 059
2000 Social security contributions	..	..	33 990	297 069	885 053	1 450 531	2 305 133	2 971 589	3 605 731	3 925 692
2100 Employees	..	..	..	..	..	..	..	..	..	..
2110 On a payroll basis	..	..	..	..	..	..	..	..	..	..
2120 On an income tax basis	..	..	..	..	..	..	..	..	..	..
2200 Employers	..	..	3 447	37 313	107 398	207 206	318 652	387 840	389 183	412 852
Government contributions	..	..	3 447	37 313	107 398	207 206	318 652	387 840	389 183	412 852
2210 On a payroll basis of employers SSC	..	..	..	..	..	..	..	..	..	..
2220 On an income tax basis of employers SSC	..	..	..	..	..	..	..	..	..	..
2300 Selfemployed or nonemployed	..	..	..	..	..	..	..	..	..	..
2310 On a payroll basis of self/non-employed SSC	..	..	..	..	..	..	..	..	..	..
2320 On an income tax basis of self/non-employed SSC	..	..	..	..	..	..	..	..	..	..
2400 Unallocable between 2100, 2200 and 2300	..	..	30 543	259 756	777 654	1 243 325	1 986 481	2 583 749	3 216 548	3 512 840
Contributions by employees and non-government employers	..	..	30 543	249 182	727 844	1 139 265	1 785 522	2 212 249	2 447 640	2 697 026
Contributions for the special regimes	..	..	0	10 574	49 811	104 060	200 959	292 072	299 713	300 083
2410 On a payroll basis unallocable between 2100, 2200 and 2300 SSC	..	..	..	..	..	..	..	..	..	..
2420 On an income tax basis unallocable between 2100, 2200 and 2300 SSC	..	..	..	..	..	..	..	..	..	..
3000 Taxes on payroll and workforce	..	..	7 575	61 796	170 996	260 664	423 616	537 654	569 339	639 737
Contributions by non-government employers	..	..	7 484	59 129	165 677	248 259	406 296	515 624	546 262	616 504
Contributions by government employers	..	..	91	2 666	5 320	12 405	17 321	22 030	23 077	23 233
4000 Taxes on property	..	..	1 566	8 396	42 658	63 706	123 261	162 950	208 531	220 741
4100 Recurrent taxes on immovable property	..	..	1 200	5 390	23 293	48 963	90 003	127 625	150 279	154 930
Land tax	..	..	0	0	0	0	0	0	0	0
Additional land tax	..	..	0	0	0	0	0	0	0	0
Tax on sumptuary constructions	..	..	0	0	0	0	0	0	0	0
Immovable property tax	..	..	0	0	0	3 527	4 076	4 655	5 108	5 206
Municipal immovable property tax	..	..	1 200	5 390	23 293	45 436	85 927	122 970	145 171	149 724
4110 Households	..	..	..	..	..	..	..	..	..	..
4120 Others	..	..	..	..	..	..	..	..	..	..
4200 Recurrent taxes on net wealth	..	..	0	0	0	0	0	0	0	0
4210 Individual	..	..	..	..	..	..	..	..	..	..
4220 Corporate	..	..	..	..	..	..	..	..	..	..
4300 Estate, inheritance and gift taxes	..	..	0	0	0	0	0	0	0	0
4310 Estate and inheritance taxes	..	..	..	..	..	..	..	..	..	..
4320 Gift taxes	..	..	..	..	..	..	..	..	..	..
4400 Taxes on financial and capital transactions	..	..	366	3 007	19 366	14 743	33 258	35 300	58 206	65 802
4500 Nonrecurrent taxes	..	..	0	0	0	0	0	24	46	8
4510 On net wealth	..	..	..	..	..	..	..	0	0	0
4520 Other nonrecurrent taxes	..	..	..	..	..	..	..	24	46	8
4600 Other recurrent taxes on property	..	..	0	0	0	0	0	0	0	0
5000 Taxes on goods and services	..	..	53 509	456 851	1 505 510	1 766 914	2 661 902	2 745 118	3 488 535	3 674 723
5100 Taxes on production, sale, transfer, etc	..	..	49 867	425 713	1 406 100	1 600 302	2 388 900	2 500 510	3 150 398	3 330 772
5110 General taxes	..	..	21 326	222 775	797 850	920 298	1 368 601	1 649 531	2 065 623	2 217 743
5111 Value added taxes	..	..	21 326	222 775	797 850	920 298	1 336 075	1 623 695	2 039 997	2 193 160
5112 Sales tax	..	..	0	0	0	0	0	0	0	0
5113 Other	..	..	0	0	0	0	32 526	25 836	25 626	24 583
5120 Taxes on specific goods and services	..	..	28 541	202 939	608 250	680 004	1 020 299	850 979	1 084 775	1 113 029
5121 Excises	..	..	11 096	157 204	447 168	523 617	798 412	688 784	863 133	883 105
Fuels and energy	..	..	0	0	250 577	320 638	457 827	436 384	522 063	530 195
Alcoholic beverages	..	..	0	8 229	23 802	28 035	43 095	44 373	53 118	55 539
Non alcoholic beverages	..	..	0	0	18 263	26 566	36 353	38 510	43 234	49 556
Soaps	..	..	0	0	883	1 317	2 562	3 052	3 200	2 810
Cement	..	..	0	0	0	227	304	123	0	5 358
Tobaco	..	..	0	0	0	0	33 681	23 896	27 019	22 336
Abolished specific taxes on production and consumption	..	..	0	0	0	0	0	0	0	0

	1965	1980	1990	2000	2007	2010	2015	2020	2021	2022
Other specific taxes on consumption	..	..	11 096	148 975	153 643	146 834	224 590	142 447	214 499	217 311
5122 Profits of fiscal monopolies	..	..	0	0	0	0	0	0	0	0
5123 Customs and import duties	..	..	15 052	40 485	134 576	126 134	174 568	133 733	177 948	164 137
Import duties	..	..	13 977	32 336	107 565	103 851	148 666	114 777	152 133	137 668
Custom duties	..	..	1 075	8 149	27 011	22 284	25 902	18 956	25 815	26 469
Import duties on animals	..	..	0	0	0	0	0	0	0	0
5124 Taxes on exports	..	..	2 113	2 238	2 432	3 973	4 468	5 471	6 274	4 842
Export duties	..	..	2 113	2 088	2 260	3 816	2 701	3 777	4 064	3 100
Export duties Law 133	..	..	0	0	0	0	0	0	0	0
Export duties Law 5519	..	..	0	0	0	0	0	0	0	0
Tax on banana exports	..	..	0	150	172	157	156	199	203	150
Export tax on ground transportation	..	..	0	0	0	0	1 611	1 494	2 007	1 593
5125 Taxes on investment goods	..	..	0	0	0	0	0	0	0	0
5126 Taxes on specific services	..	..	280	2 929	23 242	24 767	38 687	18 463	31 742	55 167
Casinos and gambling	..	..	0	225	442	445	1 455	378	431	455
Port cargo movements	..	..	0	6	0	0	0	0	0	0
Overseas departure tax	..	..	0	0	22 799	24 322	37 232	18 085	31 311	54 711
10% on public shows	..	..	0	0	0	0	0	0	0	0
Pro-national airports stamp tax	..	..	0	0	0	0	0	0	0	0
Stamp tax on the use of borders and ports	..	..	280	2 697	0	0	0	0	0	0
5127 Other taxes on internat. trade and transactions	..	..	0	83	832	1 513	3 093	3 304	3 916	3 919
5128 Other taxes	..	..	0	0	0	0	1 071	1 225	1 761	1 860
5130 Unallocable between 5110 and 5120	..	..	0	0	0	0	0	0	0	0
5200 Taxes on use of goods and perform activities	..	..	3 642	31 138	99 410	166 612	273 003	244 608	338 138	343 951
5210 Recurrent taxes	..	..	3 642	31 138	99 410	166 612	273 003	244 608	338 138	343 951
5211 Paid by households: motor vehicles	..	..	0	0	0	0	0	0	0	0
5212 Paid by others: motor vehicles	..	..	1 425	15 374	52 511	94 102	145 894	108 198	183 368	186 226
Property tax on vehicles, aircraft and boats	..	..	1 425	15 374	52 511	94 102	145 894	108 198	183 368	186 226
5213 Paid in respect of other goods	..	..	2 217	15 763	46 899	72 510	127 109	136 410	154 769	157 725
Local taxes	..	..	1 262	11 898	43 874	68 808	122 248	130 332	147 349	151 320
Hunting and fishing licences	..	..	0	0	0	0	0	0	0	0
Spirits license	..	..	0	0	0	0	0	0	0	0
Revenue stamps	..	..	955	3 866	3 025	3 702	4 861	6 078	7 421	6 405
Sport stamp tax	..	..	0	0	0	0	0	0	0	0
5220 Nonrecurrent taxes	..	..	0	0	0	0	0	0	0	0
5300 Unallocable between 5100 and 5200	..	..	0	0	0	0	0	0	0	0
6000 Other taxes	..	..	9 251	25 198	77 632	92 460	162 355	166 969	83 319	394 874
6100 Paid solely by business	..	..	0	0	0	0	0	0	0	0
6200 Other	..	..	9 251	25 198	77 632	92 460	162 355	166 969	83 319	394 874
Transfers of vehicles, aircraft and boats	..	..	497	2 530	9 937	12 311	20 999	22 593	28 064	27 597
Tax revenue from decentralised units	..	..	2 764	15 048	22 257	29 969	49 334	60 054	0	0
Other taxes	..	..	5 990	7 620	45 438	50 180	92 022	84 266	55 122	367 079
Total tax revenue on cash basis	..	..	..	..	..	..	..	..	..	..
Total tax revenue on accrual basis	..	..	..	..	..	..	..	..	..	..
Additional taxes included in National Accounts	..	..	..	..	..	..	..	..	..	..
Taxes excluded from National Accounts	..	..	..	..	..	..	..	..	..	..
Difference in treatment of tax credits	..	..	..	..	..	..	..	..	..	..
Capital transfer for uncollected revenue	..	..	..	..	..	..	..	..	..	..
Voluntary social security contributions	..	..	..	..	..	..	..	..	..	..
Miscellaneous differences	..	..	..	..	..	..	..	..	..	..
National Accounts: Taxes and actual social contributions	..	..	..	..	..	..	..	..	..	..
Imputed social contributions	..	..	..	..	..	..	..	..	..	..

.. Not available

Note: Note: Year ending 31st December.

Data on a cash basis.

Heading 2000: The data include social security contributions paid by the governments for their employees as well as the contributions for special regimes (teachers and magistrates). In ECLAC data, social security contributions also include INA (National Institute of Apprenticeship), IMAS (Joint Social Aid Institute) and FODESAF (Social Development and Family Allowances Fund).

Heading 3000: In Costa Rica and for ECLAC, payments from decentralised institutions are classified under heading 2000.

Heading 5212: In ECLAC data, tax on ownership of vehicles, aircraft and boats is classified in category 4000.

In ECLAC data, the tax on the transfer of used vehicles Law No. 7088 of 30/11/87 is classified as a property tax.

Source: Secretaría Técnica de la Autoridad Presupuestaria, Ministerio de Finanzas y Contraloría General de la República.
(Technical Secretary of the Budgeting Authority, Ministry of Finance and National General Comptroller).

Table 5.8. Czechia: Details of tax revenue, 1965-2022

Million CZK

	1965	1980	1990	2000	2007	2010	2015	2020	2021	2022
Total tax revenue	..	..	..	771 596	1 316 197	1 286 861	1 532 565	1 984 321	2 122 826	2 339 641
Total tax revenue exclusive of taxes collected for the EU	..	..	..	771 596	1 309 754	1 280 288	1 524 653	1 976 244	2 112 170	2 326 909
1000 Taxes on income, profits and capital gains	..	..	..	175 846	327 771	259 934	329 768	454 979	441 143	515 371
1100 Of individuals	..	..	..	99 668	155 817	131 706	164 678	268 362	198 761	214 131
1110 On income and profits	..	..	..	99 668	155 817	131 706	164 678	268 362	198 761	214 131
Wages and salaries withholding	..	..	..	73 474	127 524	115 755	139 888	233 421	155 614	161 419
Of unincorporated individuals	..	..	..	17 254	19 568	5 747	9 100	13 929	18 183	19 751
Withheld on interest and dividends paid to individuals	..	..	..	8 940	8 725	10 204	15 691	21 012	24 964	32 962
1120 On capital gains	..	..	..	0	0	0	0	0	0	0
1200 Corporate	..	..	..	76 178	171 954	128 228	165 090	186 617	242 381	301 240
1210 On profits	..	..	..	76 178	171 954	128 228	165 090	186 617	242 381	301 240
Profit tax	..	..	..	68 945	164 016	118 248	147 157	172 720	224 588	276 947
Withheld on interest and dividends paid to corporations	..	..	..	7 233	7 162	9 156	9 415	4 187	4 775	6 996
Levy on lottery revenue	..	..	..	0	776	824	8 518	9 709	13 019	17 298
Temporary windfall tax				0	0	0	0	0	0	0
1220 On capital gains	..	..	..	0	0	0	0	0	0	0
1300 Unallocable between 1100 and 1200	..	..	..	0	0	0	0	0	0	0
2000 Social security contributions	..	..	..	341 544	573 417	576 029	659 743	901 670	1 004 804	1 074 201
2100 Employees	..	..	..	77 272	127 662	116 818	133 878	187 733	200 968	215 214
2110 On a payroll basis	..	..	..	77 272	127 662	116 818	133 878	187 733	200 968	215 214
Retirement	..	..	..	40 489	66 644	69 272	78 120	107 988	117 893	126 039
State employment policy	..	..	..	2 492	4 101	0	0	0	0	0
Sick leave	..	..	..	6 852	11 279	0	0	0	0	0
Health insurance	..	..	..	27 439	45 638	47 546	55 758	79 745	83 075	89 175
2120 On an income tax basis	..	..	..	0	0	0	0	0	0	0
2200 Employers	..	..	..	220 207	359 493	363 074	417 778	573 753	618 255	661 335
2210 On a payroll basis of employers SSC	..	..	..	220 207	359 493	363 074	417 778	573 753	618 255	661 335
Retirement	..	..	..	121 547	220 591	229 450	261 786	357 887	390 597	417 557
State employment policy	..	..	..	19 933	12 303	12 756	14 604	19 961	21 789	23 293
Sick leave	..	..	..	20 555	33 834	24 332	27 851	34 687	37 870	40 474
Health insurance	..	..	..	54 879	91 275	95 095	111 517	159 493	166 150	178 342
Penalties	..	..	..	3 293	1 490	1 441	2 020	1 725	1 849	1 669
2220 On an income tax basis of employers SSC	..	..	..	0	0	0	0	0	0	0
2300 Selfemployed or nonemployed	..	..	..	44 065	86 262	96 137	108 088	140 184	185 581	197 653
2310 On a payroll basis of self/non-employed SSC	..	..	..	44 065	86 262	96 137	108 088	140 184	185 581	197 653
Retirement	..	..	..	7 819	19 508	20 510	22 472	20 882	28 297	32 935
State employment policy	..	..	..	1 082	1 114	1 173	962	896	1 213	1 412
Sick leave	..	..	..	0	0	0	0	0	0	0
Health insurance	..	..	..	34 992	65 483	74 299	84 460	118 288	155 924	163 153
Self-employed	..	..	..	7 328	15 921	17 603	20 748	17 846	26 326	30 076
Non-employed	..	..	..	200	2 103	3 996	2 768	3 180	3 275	3 681
Government	..	..	..	27 464	47 459	52 700	60 944	97 262	126 323	129 396
Penalties	..	..	..	172	157	155	193	118	147	153
2320 On an income tax basis of self/non-employed SSC	..	..	..	0	0	0	0	0	0	0
2400 Unallocable between 2100, 2200 and 2300	..	..	..	0	0	0	0	0	0	0
2410 On a payroll basis unallocable between 2100, 2200 and 2300 SSC	..	..	..	..	..	..	..	..	..	..
2420 On an income tax basis unallocable between 2100, 2200 and 2300 SSC	..	..	..	..	..	..	..	..	..	..
3000 Taxes on payroll and workforce	..	..	..	0	0	0	0	0	0	0
4000 Taxes on property	..	..	..	10 890	15 495	16 364	21 920	11 615	11 939	12 501
4100 Recurrent taxes on immovable property	..	..	..	4 469	5 126	8 752	10 333	11 606	11 864	12 446
4110 Households	..	..	..	1 452	2 228	4 302	5 433	6 079	6 253	6 460
Real property tax	..	..	..	1 452	2 228	4 302	5 433	6 079	6 253	6 460
4120 Others	..	..	..	3 017	2 898	4 450	4 900	5 526	5 611	5 986
Levy collected by Winery Fund	..	..	..	0	2	5	20	26	28	27
Real property tax	..	..	..	3 017	2 895	4 445	4 880	5 501	5 583	5 959
4200 Recurrent taxes on net wealth	..	..	..	0	0	0	0	0	0	0
4210 Individual	..	..	..	..	..	..	..	..	..	..
4220 Corporate	..	..	..	..	..	..	..	..	..	..
4300 Estate, inheritance and gift taxes	..	..	..	587	460	218	20	7	1	0
4310 Estate and inheritance taxes	..	..	..	112	115	78	10	8	0	..
Inheritance tax	..	..	..	112	115	78	10	8	0	..
4320 Gift taxes	..	..	..	475	345	140	10	- 2	0	..
Gift tax	..	..	..	475	345	140	10	- 2	0	..
4400 Taxes on financial and capital transactions	..	..	..	5 834	9 909	7 394	11 566	3	74	55

	1965	1980	1990	2000	2007	2010	2015	2020	2021	2022
Real property transfer tax	..	..	..	5 834	9 909	7 394	11 566	3	74	55
4500 Nonrecurrent taxes	..	..	..	0	0	0	0	0	0	0
4510 On net wealth	..	..	..	..	..	..	..	..	..	..
4520 Other nonrecurrent taxes	..	..	..	..	..	..	..	..	..	..
4600 Other recurrent taxes on property	..	..	..	0	0	0	0	0	0	0
5000 Taxes on goods and services	..	..	..	242 960	399 484	434 386	520 747	615 888	664 721	737 336
5100 Taxes on production, sale, transfer, etc	..	..	..	226 354	372 441	408 645	495 291	588 343	635 978	708 671
5110 General taxes	..	..	..	141 235	232 288	263 457	333 274	422 479	463 521	536 896
5111 Value added taxes	..	..	..	141 235	232 288	263 457	333 274	422 479	463 521	536 896
5112 Sales tax	..	..	..	0	0	0	0	0	0	0
5113 Other	..	..	..	0	0	0	0	0	0	0
Previous turnover tax	..	..	..	..	..	..	..	..	..	..
5120 Taxes on specific goods and services	..	..	..	85 119	140 153	145 188	162 017	165 864	172 457	171 775
5121 Excises	..	..	..	71 404	133 492	138 401	153 785	157 444	161 597	158 695
On mineral oils	..	..	..	46 998	81 661	80 508	83 460	83 308	83 147	78 114
On alcohol and liquor	..	..	..	5 629	7 201	5 820	7 203	6 787	8 789	8 810
On beer	..	..	..	3 410	3 564	4 396	4 648	4 344	4 308	4 551
On wine	..	..	..	350	342	317	332	439	530	532
On tobacco products	..	..	..	14 984	40 713	44 062	53 380	57 148	59 168	58 297
Duty on CFC	..	..	..	33	0	0	0	0	0	0
Levy collected by Winery Fund	..	..	..	0	11	24	0	5	5	5
On electricity	..	..	..	0	0	1 433	1 229	1 497	1 600	1 537
On natural gas	..	..	..	0	0	1 347	1 146	1 434	1 601	1 410
On solid fuels	..	..	..	0	0	495	415	323	350	349
Fee on electricity from solar radiation	..	..	..	0	0	0	1 972	2 159	2 100	5 090
5122 Profits of fiscal monopolies	..	..	..	0	0	0	0	0	0	0
5123 Customs and import duties	..	..	..	13 572	6 443	6 573	7 912	8 077	10 656	12 733
Customs duties	..	..	..	13 572	6 443	6 573	7 912	8 077	10 656	12 733
Previous import surcharge	..	..	..	0	0	0	0	0	0	0
5124 Taxes on exports	..	..	..	0	0	0	0	0	0	0
5125 Taxes on investment goods	..	..	..	0	0	0	0	0	0	0
5126 Taxes on specific services	..	..	..	143	218	214	320	343	204	348
Fees on entry tickets	..	..	..	65	61	53	53	19	15	65
Fees on recreational units (based on capacity)	..	..	..	69	144	147	240	132	6	72
Fees on advertising facilities	..	..	..	0	0	0	0	0	0	0
Restaurant sale alcoh. beverages and tobac. products	..	..	..	0	0	0	0	0	0	0
Fees collected by the cinematography EBF	..	..	..	9	13	14	27	0	0	0
Fees on advertisement				0	0	0	191	191	183	210
Revenue from abolished local fees				0	0	0	0	0	0	0
5127 Other taxes on internat. trade and transactions	..	..	..	0	0	0	0	0	0	0
5128 Other taxes	..	..	..	0	0	0	0	0	0	0
5130 Unallocable between 5110 and 5120	..	..	..	0	0	0	0	0	0	0
5200 Taxes on use of goods and perform activities	..	..	..	16 606	27 043	25 740	25 456	27 545	28 743	28 665
5210 Recurrent taxes	..	..	..	10 788	18 100	18 461	19 023	20 999	21 343	21 313
Highway fee	..	..	..	1 753	2 429	3 061	4 397	4 930	5 356	5 839
5211 Paid by households: motor vehicles	..	..	..	0	0	0	0	0	0	0
5212 Paid by others: motor vehicles	..	..	..	5 456	5 882	5 138	5 868	5 933	5 430	1 071
Road tax (commercial)	..	..	..	5 456	5 882	5 138	5 868	5 933	5 430	1 071
5213 Paid in respect of other goods	..	..	..	3 579	9 790	10 262	8 758	10 137	10 557	14 403
Resort and recreation fees on visitors	..	..	..	232	312	284	327	322	397	1 092
Dog fees	..	..	..	191	277	281	277	287	300	297
Motor vehicle entry fees	..	..	..	32	25	23	13	14	11	13
Water pollution fee	..	..	..	520	404	202	173	228	236	191
Air pollution fee	..	..	..	685	525	399	283	451	339	338
Waste deposit fee	..	..	..	454	5 728	5 948	6 218	7 065	7 453	9 369
Levy on temp. withdrawal of land from agriculture	..	..	..	94	40	34	39	68	79	85
Radioactive waste fee	..	..	..	642	1 310	1 430	1 393	1 668	1 708	1 703
Fees on operated gambling machines	..	..	..	722	1 145	927	0	0	0	0
Fees on registration and recording of packaging	..	..	..	0	17	17	18	17	17	17
Levy on temp. withdrawal of land from forestry	..	..	..	7	6	6	7	11	7	8
Other environmental fees	..	..	..	0	0	710	11	5	10	10

	1965	1980	1990	2000	2007	2010	2015	2020	2021	2022
Temporary mandatory cap on market revenues				0	0	0	0	0	0	1 279
Other levies on selected activities and services				0	0	0	0	0	0	0
5220 Nonrecurrent taxes	..	..	..	5 818	8 943	7 280	6 433	6 546	7 400	7 352
Levy on withdrawal of land from agriculture	..	..	..	532	361	306	348	609	707	767
Levy on withdrawal of land from forestry	..	..	..	40	57	57	59	103	63	72
Tax on use of public space	..	..	..	645	639	626	632	506	579	716
Misc. licence and permit fees	..	..	..	4 601	7 881	6 279	5 382	5 293	6 031	5 772
Land betterment fee	..	..	..	0	4	11	11	35	21	25
Licence for lorry transport	..	..	..	0	1	1	1	0	0	0
Levy on substances that deplete or threaten the Earth's ozone layer				0	0	0	0	0	0	0
Fee for the use of natural mineral water				0	0	0	0	0	0	0
Other levies on selected activities and services				0	0	0	0	0	0	0
5300 Unallocable between 5100 and 5200	..	..	..	0	0	0	0	0	0	0
6000 Other taxes	..	..	..	356	29	149	387	170	219	232
Unallocated previous taxes and levies	..	..	..	0	0	0	0	0	0	0
6100 Paid solely by business	..	..	..	0	0	0	0	0	0	0
6200 Other	..	..	..	356	29	149	387	170	219	232
Other taxes, fees and related payments	..	..	..	356	29	149	387	170	219	232
Customs duties collected for the EU	..	..	..	..	6 443	6 573	7 912	8 077	10 656	12 733
Non-wastable tax credits against 1110	..	..	..	0	13 093	25 727	31 415	38 913	41 145	42 099
Tax expenditure component	..	..	..	..	10 487	17 922	22 532	29 323	29 192	29 194
Transfer component	..	..	..	..	2 606	7 805	8 883	9 590	11 952	12 905
Total tax revenue on cash basis	..	..	..	772 272	1 310 618	1 273 676	1 478 758	1 937 606	2 055 661	2 264 745
Total tax revenue on accrual basis	..	..	..	771 596	1 316 197	1 286 861	1 532 565	1 984 321	2 122 826	2 339 641
Additional taxes included in National Accounts	..	..	..	2 837	5 757	6 094	0	0	0	0
Compulsory injury insurance	..	..	..	2 837	5 757	6 094	0	0	0	0
Driving licence fees	..	..	..	0	0	0	0	0	0	0
Taxes excluded from National Accounts	..	..	..	- 9 488	- 17 797	- 20 096	- 20 314	- 21 838	- 23 382	- 26 015
Tax on use of public space	..	..	..	- 645	- 639	- 632	- 632	- 506	- 579	- 716
Waste deposit fee	..	..	..	- 454	- 5 728	- 5 948	- 6 218	- 7 065	- 7 453	- 9 369
Misc. licence and permit fees	..	..	..	- 2 301	- 3 940	- 3 139	- 2 691	- 2 646	- 3 015	- 2 886
Radioactive waste fee	..	..	..	- 642	- 1 310	- 1 430	- 1 393	- 1 668	- 1 708	- 1 703
Health insurance: non-employed	..	..	..	- 200	- 2 103	- 3 996	- 2 768	- 3 180	- 3 275	- 3 681
Health insurance: government	..	..	..	0	0	0	0	0	0	0
Soc. Security contr. employers: Penalties	..	..	..	- 3 293	- 1 490	- 1 441	- 2 020	- 1 725	- 1 849	- 1 669
Soc. Security contr. Self-employed or non-employed: Penalties	..	..	..	- 200	- 157	- 155	- 193	- 118	- 147	- 153
Licence for lorry transport	..	..	..	0	- 1	- 1	- 1	0	0	0
Highway fee	..	..	..	- 1 753	- 2 429	- 3 061	- 4 397	- 4 930	- 5 356	- 5 839
Other environmental fees	..	..	..	0	0	- 105	0	0	0	0
Levy on loterry revenue	..	..	..	0	0	- 187	0	0	0	0
Value added taxes	..	..	..	0	0	0	0	0	0	0
Difference in treatment of tax credits	..	..	..	0	- 127	451	118	1 734	- 198	- 643
Capital transfer for uncollected revenue	..	..	..	0	0	0	0	0	0	0
Voluntary social security contributions	..	..	..	1 099	974	661	386	537	573	618
Miscellaneous differences	..	..	..	2 162	0	0	0	0	0	0
National Accounts: Taxes and actual social contributions	..	..	..	768 206	1 305 004	1 273 971	1 512 755	1 964 755	2 099 819	2 313 601
Imputed social contributions	..	..	..	423	299	600	1 027	3 179	3 557	4 803
National Accounts: Taxes and all social contributions	..	..	..	768 629	1 305 303	1 274 571	1 513 782	1 967 934	2 103 376	2 318 404

.. Not available

Note: Year ending 31st December.

From 1995 data are on accrual basis.

Source: Ministry of Finance, Tax Analyses Department.

Table 5.9. Denmark: Details of tax revenue, 1965-2022

Million DKK

	1965	1980	1990	2000	2007	2010	2015	2020	2021	2022
Total tax revenue	20 821	165 753	381 079	623 197	813 613	816 787	964 234	1 109 759	1 222 051	1 202 275
Total tax revenue exclusive of taxes collected for the EU	..	164 363	378 393	620 561	809 961	813 512	960 915	1 106 670	1 218 338	1 197 692
1000 Taxes on income, profits and capital gains	9 712	92 098	232 729	382 555	489 765	503 083	609 743	716 667	806 312	776 225
1100 Of individuals	8 758	86 958	206 531	327 864	427 372	423 958	525 168	600 682	640 823	670 771
1110 On income and profits	8 758	86 909	206 387	327 637	427 030	423 637	524 880	600 415	640 507	670 370
Central government income tax	5 020	33 351	91 638	77 473	155 441	125 790	169 557	208 075	227 519	248 241
County income tax	0	10 742	31 361	56 131	0	0	0	0	0	0
Municipality income tax	2 948	33 555	77 571	121 967	173 110	193 097	221 084	263 055	278 619	282 574
Seaman's income tax	66	457	0	0	0	0	0	0	0	0
Old-age pension fund contributions	592	2 163	0	0	0	0	0	0	0	0
Social pension fund contributions	0	3 340	0	0	0	0	0	0	0	0
Sickness benefit fund contributions	0	1 804	0	0	0	0	0	0	0	0
Pension schemes and annuity insurance	22	355	2 687	6 242	9 017	9 571	22 160	6 342	6 296	7 223
Special income tax	101	1 054	2 802	0	0	0	0	0	0	0
Duty on canceled pension schemes	9	82	0	0	0	0	0	0	0	0
Duty on feed rent increases	0	8	5	0	0	0	0	0	0	0
Duty on employees' remuneration compens. fund releases	0	0	325	632	1 183	963	11 091	1 608	1 419	775
Duty on interest on consumer loans	0	0	0	0	0	0	0	0	0	0
Labour market contributions	0	0	0	56 794	76 564	81 604	87 392	106 260	112 454	117 116
Imputed income from owner-occupied dwelling	0	0	0	8 399	11 714	12 613	13 596	15 074	14 199	14 442
1120 On capital gains	0	49	144	226	343	321	289	267	316	402
Tax on winnings from lotteries, pools, etc.	..	49	144	226	343	321	289	267	316	402
1200 Corporate	954	5 139	13 597	42 258	57 928	42 590	61 854	67 720	102 130	94 281
1210 On profits	954	5 139	13 597	42 258	57 928	42 590	61 854	67 720	102 130	94 281
1220 On capital gains	0	0	0	0	0	0	0	0	0	0
1300 Unallocable between 1100 and 1200	0	0	12 601	12 434	4 465	36 535	22 721	48 265	63 359	11 173
2000 Social security contributions	690	710	101	8 453	2 030	2 280	1 874	2 156	2 493	2 340
2100 Employees	567	1	98	8 209	1 057	900	826	751	736	697
Sickness benefit fund contributions	30	0	0	0	0	0	0	0	0	0
Sickday benefit contributions, ordinary	534	0	0	0	0	0	0	0	0	0
Sickday benefit contributions, special	3	0	0	0	0	0	0	0	0	0
Contribution to merchant marine's welf. board	0	1	1	0	0	0	0	0	0	0
Special pension scheme savings	0	0	0	6 846	0	0	0	0	0	0
Contr. to pension funds from officials in companies	0	0	0	879	555	450	438	402	428	409
Contr. to pension funds from officials in non-profit institutions	0	0	96	485	502	450	388	349	308	288
2110 On a payroll basis	..	..	..	..	..	..	..	..	..	..
2120 On an income tax basis	..	..	..	..	..	..	..	..	..	..
2200 Employers	123	709	3	244	973	1 379	1 048	1 406	1 758	1 643
Unemployment insurance contributions	41	598	0	0	0	0	0	0	0	0
Disablement insurance contributions	21	58	0	0	0	0	0	0	0	0
Sickness benefit fund contributions	61	0	0	0	0	0	0	0	0	0
Contribution to employee's wage guarantee fund	0	50	0	241	227	908	542	601	802	544
Contribution to merchant marine's welf. board	0	1	1	0	0	0	0	0	0	0
Shipping owners contr. sickness assist. seamen	0	1	2	3	2	6	10	8	4	5
Contribution to maternity/paternity compensation scheme	0	..	0	0	744	465	496	797	952	1 095
2210 On a payroll basis of employers SSC	..	..	..	..	..	..	..	..	..	..
2220 On an income tax basis of employers SSC	..	..	..	..	..	..	..	..	..	..
2300 Selfemployed or nonemployed	0	0	0	0	0	0	0	0	0	0
2310 On a payroll basis of self/non-employed SSC	..	..	..	..	..	..	..	..	..	..
2320 On an income tax basis of self/non-employed SSC	..	..	..	..	..	..	..	..	..	..
2400 Unallocable between 2100, 2200 and 2300	0	0	0	0	0	0	0	0	0	0
2410 On a payroll basis unallocable between 2100, 2200 and 2300 SSC	..	..	..	..	..	..	..	..	..	..
2420 On an income tax basis unallocable between 2100, 2200 and 2300 SSC	..	..	..	..	..	..	..	..	..	..
3000 Taxes on payroll and workforce	0	0	2 494	2 258	3 975	4 160	5 894	4 230	6 656	7 150
4000 Taxes on property	1 691	9 490	16 242	20 737	31 556	33 533	39 361	45 629	47 605	48 475
4100 Recurrent taxes on immovable property	1 029	5 412	8 891	13 565	18 996	24 161	28 085	31 581	32 432	33 080
Central government land tax	130	0	0	0	0	0	0	0	0	0
County land tax	169	2 315	2 915	4 070	0	0	0	0	0	0
Municipal land tax	408	2 257	4 123	7 049	15 601	19 645	24 707	28 440	29 270	29 964
Centr. Govt. fixed tax on real property	32	11	0	0	0	0	0	0	0	0
County fixed tax on real property	45	0	0	0	0	0	0	0	0	0
Municipal fixed tax on real property	190	91	0	0	0	0	0	0	0	0
County duty on land (public property)	4	22	22	25	0	0	0	0	0	0

	1965	1980	1990	2000	2007	2010	2015	2020	2021	2022
County duty on buildings (public property)	0	53	88	97	0	0	0	0	0	0
Municipal duty on land (public property)	26	103	244	383	393	434	364	332	332	885
Municipal duty on buildings (residential)	0	195	335	381	757	814	599	567	575	1
Municipal duty on buildings (business)	25	366	1 165	1 560	2 244	3 269	2 416	2 242	2 255	2 230
4110 Households	..	..	..	..	..	..	..	..	..	..
4120 Others	..	..	..	..	..	..	..	..	..	..
4200 Recurrent taxes on net wealth	306	965	922	0	0	0	0	0	0	0
4210 Individual	306	965	922	..	..	..	..	..	..	..
4220 Corporate	0	0	0	..	..	..	..	..	..	..
4300 Estate, inheritance and gift taxes	137	738	2 197	2 863	3 896	3 646	5 177	6 676	6 616	7 444
4310 Estate and inheritance taxes	..	..	..	..	..	..	..	..	..	..
4320 Gift taxes	..	..	..	..	..	..	..	..	..	..
4400 Taxes on financial and capital transactions	219	2 259	4 151	4 170	8 659	5 726	6 099	7 372	8 557	7 951
Stamp duties	214	2 189	2 838	4 125	8 574	5 695	6 071	7 313	8 500	7 897
Duty on share capital creation	0	32	477	0	0	0	0	0	0	0
Duty to land registry office	5	38	27	45	85	30	28	59	57	54
Duty on transfers of shares	0	0	809	0	0	0	0	0	0	0
4500 Nonrecurrent taxes	0	116	81	140	6	0	0	0	0	0
4510 On net wealth	..	0	0	0	0	0	..	..	..	..
4520 Other nonrecurrent taxes	..	116	81	140	6	0	..	..	..	..
4600 Other recurrent taxes on property	0	0	0	0	0	0	0	0	0	0
5000 Taxes on goods and services	8 727	63 456	129 514	208 803	286 096	273 526	304 582	339 877	357 646	366 703
5100 Taxes on production, sale, transfer, etc	8 239	60 563	123 529	197 967	266 797	253 848	280 875	315 199	333 805	342 575
5110 General taxes	2 139	37 727	80 508	121 955	174 639	171 583	191 328	231 650	251 278	266 040
5111 Value added taxes	2 139	37 727	71 978	121 955	174 639	171 583	191 328	231 650	251 278	266 040
5112 Sales tax	0	0	0	0	0	0	0	0	0	0
5113 Other	0	0	8 530	0	0	0	0	0	0	0
Labour market contrib. concerning imports	..	..	4 903	..	..	..	..	..	..	..
Labour market contrib. concerning value added	..	..	3 627	..	..	..	..	..	..	..
5120 Taxes on specific goods and services	6 100	22 836	43 021	76 012	92 159	82 265	89 546	83 549	82 527	76 535
5121 Excises	5 466	20 487	38 364	68 775	82 835	73 597	81 784	76 027	73 789	66 743
Duty on petrol	1 016	3 713	5 637	10 005	9 155	8 029	7 348	7 055	7 367	7 317
Motor vehicle registration duty	818	2 989	7 917	13 858	24 289	13 587	17 988	18 683	16 381	11 541
Cigarettes and tobacco duties	1 469	4 483	6 470	7 595	7 169	7 896	7 561	9 371	8 554	7 303
Duties on cigars, cheroots and cigarillos	234	220	128	75	43	32	113	51	52	45
Sale of revenue labels	0	3	12	7	4	7	0	0	0	0
Sales duties on chocolate and sugar	254	331	801	1 201	1 282	1 455	2 156	2 285	2 410	2 366
Raw material duty on chocolate and sugar	11	14	54	59	92	143	187	0	0	0
Special tax on chocolate and sugar	0	2	13	76	46	50	103	121	109	119
Duty on ice-cream	33	58	135	168	180	201	297	408	393	380
Duty on coffee	5	249	224	263	250	253	280	274	284	283
Duty on mineral water	68	195	466	506	418	383	0	0	0	0
Duty on beer	622	1 983	3 100	1 510	1 080	895	916	781	846	843
Duty on wine	122	611	1 448	1 166	1 032	1 071	1 764	1 803	1 822	1 670
Duty on spirits	412	1 432	1 982	1 756	1 213	1 028	1 201	1 179	1 330	1 375
Duty on restaurant sales of alcoholic bev.	150	0	0	0	0	0	0	0	0	0
Duty on wireless sets	55	67	0	0	0	0	0	0	0	0
Duty on television sets	0	93	0	0	0	0	0	0	0	0
Duty on video recorders	0	17	0	0	0	0	0	0	0	0
Duty on major household appliances	0	199	0	0	0	0	0	0	0	0
Duty on grammophone records	10	46	86	0	0	0	0	0	0	0
Duty on playing cards	1	2	0	0	0	0	0	0	0	0
Duty on matches	5	3	0	0	0	0	0	0	0	0
Duty on lighters	1	8	0	0	0	0	0	0	0	0
Duty on electric bulbs	36	67	152	177	211	117	86	38	33	27
Duty on perfumery and toilet articles	91	214	506	0	0	0	0	0	0	0
Duty on almanacs	3	0	0	0	0	0	0	0	0	0
Duty on salmon	0	0	0	0	0	0	0	0	0	0
Duty on paper and cardboard	45	0	0	0	0	0	0	0	0	0
Duty on sugar	0	174	0	0	0	0	0	0	0	0
Duty on tea	0	12	10	9	8	8	8	0	0	0
Duty on electricity	0	1 222	4 317	7 533	8 665	10 195	11 501	11 203	11 693	9 760
Duty on certain oil products	0	1 719	2 938	6 451	8 549	8 623	9 347	9 467	10 171	9 927
Duty on certain retail containers	0	100	397	611	725	705	316	132	146	134
Duty on gas	0	56	47	0	0	0	0	0	0	0
Duty on extraction and import of raw materials	0	16	108	172	220	119	148	183	200	188
Duty on disposable tableware	0	0	72	65	126	120	138	267	303	334
Duty on insecticides, herbicides, etc.	0	0	13	368	499	466	598	563	614	670
Duty on videotapes	0	0	0	0	0	0	0	0	0	0
Duty on coal, etc.	0	0	849	1 225	1 450	2 587	2 255	1 600	1 797	1 801
Other duties on goods and services	5	191	- 36	10	117	146	179	119	139	158
Duty on waste	0	0	492	1 025	1 225	51	130	158	193	155

	1965	1980	1990	2000	2007	2010	2015	2020	2021	2022
Duty on CFC	0	0	28	0	53	56	65	41	52	55
Duty on CO2	0	0	0	4 698	5 108	5 822	3 652	3 306	3 502	3 388
Duty on cigarette paper	0	0	0	68	32	28	38	30	28	30
Duty on nicotine products	0	..	0	0	0	0	0	0	0	146
Energy producers payback in relation to extraordinary high energy prices	0	..	0	0	0	0	0	0	0	2 000
Duty on rechargeable Ni-Cd batteries	0	0	0	24	17	4	2	1	1	0
Duty on piped water	0	0	0	1 392	1 371	1 334	1 688	1 687	1 704	1 696
Duty on carrier bags made of paper, plastic, etc.	0	0	0	160	210	201	208	324	307	254
Duty on tires	0	0	0	29	45	61	57	56	54	52
Duty on sulpher	0	0	0	165	110	48	42	35	38	33
Duty on chlorinated solvents	0	0	0	2	0	0	0	0	0	0
Duty on natural gas	0	0	0	2 625	3 375	4 524	3 160	2 784	2 934	2 476
Duty on nitrogen	0	0	0	30	27	26	17	15	22	17
Duty on specific growth stimulants	0	0	0	0	0	0	0	0	0	0
Duty on PVC-film	0	0	0	7	12	11	11	0	17	21
Duty on PVC and phathalates	0	0	0	31	42	23	19	0	17	20
Duty on lead accumulators	0	0	0	14	0	0	0	0	0	0
Duty on mineral phosphorus	0	0	0	0	51	51	52	0	0	0
Surcharge on alcoholic soft drinks	0	0	0	0	17	26	33	0	0	0
Duty on nitrogen oxides	0	0	0	0	0	212	820	155	165	157
Duty on saturated fat	0	0	0	0	0	0	0	0	0	0
Duty on PSO (Public Service Obligations)	0	0	0	3 641	4 319	3 004	7 302	1 853	114	0
5122 Profits of fiscal monopolies	16	183	404	1 402	1 565	1 445	1 247	1 334	1 507	1 479
5123 Customs and import duties	556	1 113	1 849	2 325	3 282	3 242	3 285	3 089	3 713	4 583
Customs duties	0	1 032	1 779	2 325	3 282	3 242	3 285	3 089	3 713	4 583
Temporary import surcharge	556	0	0	0	0	0	0	0	0	0
Import duties on agricultural produce	0	81	70	0	0	0	0	0	0	0
5124 Taxes on exports	0	0	0	0	0	0	0	0	0	0
5125 Taxes on investment goods	0	0	0	0	0	0	0	0	0	0
5126 Taxes on specific services	62	775	1 568	3 198	4 503	3 949	3 196	3 098	3 518	3 730
Sales tax on gambling stakes races	17	28	20	11	19	16	13	0	0	0
Tax on football pools	31	156	285	954	1 127	1 088	0	0	0	0
Tax on cinema tickets	14	0	0	0	0	0	0	0	0	0
Duty on motor vehicle compl. insurance	0	470	923	1 494	2 104	1 854	1 529	1 444	1 420	1 413
Duty on insurance on pleasure boats	0	13	57	66	100	122	126	104	105	117
Duty on charter flight	0	109	283	0	0	0	0	0	0	0
Turnover tax on 6-win horse race betting	0	0	0	0	0	0	0	0	0	0
Duty on casinos	0	0	0	180	261	173	200	132	117	195
Passenger duty	0	0	0	477	0	0	0	0	0	0
Duty on the Danish State Lottery	0	0	0	16	35	41	44	45	45	45
Duty on slot machines	0	0	0	0	858	656	618	414	328	484
Duty on gambling	0	0	0	0	0	0	402	460	690	669
Duty on online casinos	0	0	0	0	0	0	263	501	813	807
5127 Other taxes on internat. trade and transactions	0	0	0	0	0	0	0	0	0	0
5128 Other taxes	0	277	837	312	- 26	33	33	0	0	0
Duty paid to ECSC	..	4	5	0	0	0	0	..	..	..
Sugar storing duty	..	83	113	62	0	0	0	..	..	..
Duty on the production of sugar	..	81	145	249	- 26	33	33	..	..	..
Duty on milk co-reponsibility levy	..	109	255	0	0	0	0	..	..	..
Grain co-reponsibility levy	..	0	319	0	0	0	0	..	..	..
Restructuring scheme for EU sugar system	..	0	0	0	397	0	0	..	..	..
5130 Unallocable between 5110 and 5120	0	0	0	0	0	0	0	0	0	0
5200 Taxes on use of goods and perform activities	488	2 893	4 410	7 468	14 575	14 730	16 530	15 073	13 864	13 546
5210 Recurrent taxes	488	2 893	4 410	7 468	14 484	14 730	16 171	13 833	12 624	11 368
5211 Paid by households: motor vehicles	199	1 874	2 922	5 485	7 105	7 613	8 136	7 135	7 113	7 093
Weight duty automobiles	199	1 874	2 922	5 318	6 954	7 467	7 859	6 879	6 852	6 829
Recycling fee on cars	0	0	0	167	151	147	277	256	261	263
5212 Paid by others: motor vehicles	287	1 014	1 441	1 919	3 125	2 980	3 483	3 946	4 188	4 173
Weight duty automobiles	287	1 014	1 441	1 612	2 652	2 611	3 088	3 391	3 617	3 605
Road charges	0	0	0	307	473	370	395	555	571	569
5213 Paid in respect of other goods	2	5	47	64	4 255	4 137	4 552	2 752	1 323	102
5220 Nonrecurrent taxes	0	0	0	0	91	0	359	1 240	1 241	2 178
5300 Unallocable between 5100 and 5200	0	0	1 575	3 368	4 724	4 948	7 177	9 606	9 976	10 582
6000 Other taxes	0	0	0	391	190	206	2 781	1 199	1 339	1 382
6100 Paid solely by business	..	..	..	391	190	206	2 781	1 199	1 339	1 382
6200 Other	..	..	..	0	0	0	0	0	0	0
Custom duties collected for the EU	..	..	0	2 325	3 282	3 242	3 285	3 089	3 713	4 583
Non-wastable tax credits against 1110	..	..	..	..	..	4 959	4 230	3 026	3 020	2 260

	1965	1980	1990	2000	2007	2010	2015	2020	2021	2022
Tax expenditure component	..	..	..	..	..	4 711	4 018	2 874	2 869	2 147
Transfer component	..	..	..	..	..	248	211	151	151	113
Non-wastable tax credits against 1210	..	..	..	..	..	0	0	0	0	0
Tax expenditure component	..	..	..	..	..	..	..	..	..	..
Transfer component	..	..	..	..	..	..	..	..	..	..
Total tax revenue on cash basis	..	..	..	..	..	..	..	..	..	..
Total tax revenue on accrual basis	20 821	165 753	381 079	623 197	813 613	816 787	964 234	1 109 759	1 222 051	1 202 275
Additional taxes included in National Accounts	0	0	..	..	..	..	..	..	..	..
Taxes excluded from National Accounts	0	0	..	..	..	..	..	..	..	..
Difference in treatment of tax credits	0	0	0	0	0	4 711	4 018	2 874	2 869	2 147
Capital transfer for uncollected revenue	0	- 1 363	- 3 091	- 2 744	- 3 251	- 4 712	- 20 451	- 10 754	- 8 927	- 9 576
Voluntary social security contributions	0	1 673	8 177	16 633	17 061	17 192	14 721	14 873	15 277	14 844
Miscellaneous differences	0	0	..	..	..	..	..	..	..	..
National Accounts: Taxes and actual social contributions	20 821	166 063	386 165	637 086	827 423	833 978	962 522	1 116 752	1 231 270	1 209 691
Imputed social contributions	0	5 958	4 351	6 223	5 693	5 356	4 063	3 094	2 999	2 955
National Accounts: Taxes and all social contributions	20 821	172 021	390 515	643 309	833 116	839 335	966 585	1 119 846	1 234 269	1 212 646

.. Not available

Note: Year ending 31st December.

The figures are on an accrual basis.

Heading 2300 includes a small amount of voluntary contributions which cannot be isolated.

Source: Statistics Denmark.

Table 5.10. Estonia: Details of tax revenue, 1965-2022

Million EUR

	1965	1980	1990	2000	2007	2010	2015	2020	2021	2022
Total tax revenue	..	..	..	1 919	5 082	4 894	6 874	9 134	10 536	11 862
Total tax revenue exclusive of taxes collected for the EU	..	..	..	1 919	5 047	4 870	6 840	9 084	10 462	11 761
1000 Taxes on income, profits and capital gains	..	..	..	476	1 197	970	1 607	2 102	2 627	2 876
1100 Of individuals	..	..	..	421	936	776	1 182	1 652	2 146	2 279
1110 On income and profits	..	..	..	421	936	776	1 182	1 652	2 146	2 279
1120 On capital gains	..	..	..	0	0	0	0	0	0	0
1200 Corporate	..	..	..	55	261	194	424	450	481	596
1210 On profits	..	..	..	55	65	35	38	82	96	110
1220 On capital gains	..	..	..	0	196	159	386	368	386	486
1300 Unallocable between 1100 and 1200	..	..	..	0	0	0	0	0	0	0
2000 Social security contributions	..	..	..	674	1 683	1 879	2 300	3 331	3 652	4 122
2100 Employees	..	..	..	0	28	116	99	139	150	171
2110 On a payroll basis	..	..	..	..	28	116	99	139	150	171
2120 On an income tax basis	..	..	..	..	0	0	0	0	0	0
2200 Employers	..	..	..	662	1 635	1 742	2 181	2 974	3 280	3 771
2210 On a payroll basis of employers SSC	..	..	..	662	1 635	1 742	2 181	2 974	3 280	3 771
2220 On an income tax basis of employers SSC	..	..	..	0	0	0	0	0	0	0
2300 Selfemployed or nonemployed	..	..	..	12	21	21	20	217	221	180
2310 On a payroll basis of self/non-employed SSC	..	..	..	12	21	21	20	217	221	180
2320 On an income tax basis of self/non-employed SSC	..	..	..	0	0	0	0	0	0	0
2400 Unallocable between 2100, 2200 and 2300	..	..	..	0	0	0	0	0	0	0
2410 On a payroll basis unallocable between 2100, 2200 and 2300 SSC	..	..	..	..	..	..	..	..	..	..
2420 On an income tax basis unallocable between 2100, 2200 and 2300 SSC	..	..	..	..	..	..	..	..	..	..
3000 Taxes on payroll and workforce	..	..	..	0	0	0	0	0	0	0
4000 Taxes on property	..	..	..	24	35	51	58	58	59	59
4100 Recurrent taxes on immovable property	..	..	..	24	35	51	58	58	59	59
Land tax	..	..	..	24	35	51	58	58	59	59
4110 Households	..	..	..	..	..	..	..	..	..	..
4120 Others	..	..	..	..	..	..	..	..	..	..
4200 Recurrent taxes on net wealth	..	..	..	0	0	0	0	0	0	0
4210 Individual	..	..	..	..	..	..	..	..	..	..
4220 Corporate	..	..	..	..	..	..	..	..	..	..
4300 Estate, inheritance and gift taxes	..	..	..	0	0	0	0	0	0	0
4310 Estate and inheritance taxes	..	..	..	..	..	..	..	..	..	..
4320 Gift taxes	..	..	..	..	..	..	..	..	..	..
4400 Taxes on financial and capital transactions	..	..	..	0	0	0	0	0	0	0
4500 Nonrecurrent taxes	..	..	..	0	0	0	0	0	0	0
4510 On net wealth	..	..	..	..	..	..	..	..	..	..
4520 Other nonrecurrent taxes	..	..	..	..	..	..	..	..	..	..
4600 Other recurrent taxes on property	..	..	..	0	0	0	0	0	0	0
5000 Taxes on goods and services	..	..	..	745	2 166	1 993	2 909	3 643	4 198	4 805
5100 Taxes on production, sale, transfer, etc	..	..	..	723	2 099	1 938	2 829	3 438	3 994	4 482
5110 General taxes	..	..	..	521	1 423	1 263	1 873	2 439	2 877	3 309
5111 Value added taxes	..	..	..	520	1 423	1 257	1 873	2 439	2 877	3 309
5112 Sales tax	..	..	..	0	0	6	0	0	0	0
5113 Other	..	..	..	0	0	0	0	0	0	0
5120 Taxes on specific goods and services	..	..	..	202	675	675	956	999	1 117	1 173
5121 Excises	..	..	..	183	577	619	869	897	981	996
Alcohol	..	..	..	62	153	154	207	211	223	241
Tobacco	..	..	..	36	134	91	183	231	242	246
Fuel	..	..	..	76	290	343	444	437	507	500
Motor vehicle	..	..	..	9	0	0	0	0	0	0
Package	..	..	..	0	0	0	1	0	0	0
Fur	..	..	..	0	0	0	0	0	0	0
Electricity	..	..	..	0	0	31	34	18	8	8
5122 Profits of fiscal monopolies	..	..	..	0	0	0	0	0	0	0
5123 Customs and import duties	..	..	..	2	35	24	34	42	62	85
5124 Taxes on exports	..	..	..	0	0	0	0	0	0	0
5125 Taxes on investment goods	..	..	..	0	0	0	0	0	0	0
5126 Taxes on specific services	..	..	..	17	64	33	53	60	73	93
Gambling tax	..	..	..	7	30	21	23	28	33	47
Advertising tax	..	..	..	1	3	2	4	0	0	0
Postal service payment	..	..	..	0	0	0	0	5	7	7
Liquid fuel stockpiling fee	..	..	..	0	2	5	5	4	5	6
Contributions to the Guarantee Fund	..	..	..	9	29	5	20	23	28	33

	1965	1980	1990	2000	2007	2010	2015	2020	2021	2022
5127 Other taxes on internat. trade and transactions	..	..	..	0	0	0	0	0	0	0
5128 Other taxes	..	..	..	0	0	0	0	0	0	0
5130 Unallocable between 5110 and 5120	..	..	..	0	0	0	0	0	0	0
5200 Taxes on use of goods and perform activities	..	..	..	22	68	55	80	204	204	323
5210 Recurrent taxes	..	..	..	22	68	55	73	61	62	79
Car registration fee	..	..	..	2	5	4	7	6	8	8
Heavy vehicle tax	..	..	..	0	4	4	5	5	5	5
5211 Paid by households: motor vehicles	..	..	..	..	..	..	..	..	..	..
5212 Paid by others: motor vehicles	..	..	..	..	..	..	..	..	..	..
5213 Paid in respect of other goods	..	..	..	20	58	47	61	50	49	66
Business and professional licenses	..	..	..	3	2	1	1	4	5	5
Pollution fee	..	..	..	10	44	31	44	29	25	43
Specific use of water	..	..	..	4	9	13	13	14	14	15
Fees for closure of roads, streets and squares	..	..	..	0	1	1	2	2	2	2
Fishing fees	..	..	..	1	1	1	2	2	2	2
Tax on motor vehicle	..	..	..	2	0	0	0	0	0	0
Boat tax	..	..	..	0	0	0	0	0	0	0
Animal tax	..	..	..	0	0	0	0	0	0	0
5220 Nonrecurrent taxes	..	..	..	0	0	0	7	143	142	244
Revenue from the sale of emission permits	..	..	..	..	..	..	7	143	142	244
5300 Unallocable between 5100 and 5200	..	..	..	0	0	0	0	0	0	0
6000 Other taxes	..	..	..	0	0	0	0	0	0	0
6100 Paid solely by business	..	..	..	..	..	..	..	..	..	..
6200 Other	..	..	..	..	..	..	..	..	..	..
Other taxes	..	..	..	..	..	..	..	..	..	..
Customs duties collected for the EU	..	..	..	..	35	24	34	42	62	85
SRF Contributions collected for the EU				..	..	..	..	8	12	16
Total tax revenue on cash basis	..	..	..	1 907	5 003	4 921	6 848	9 204	10 426	11 807
Total tax revenue on accrual basis	..	..	..	1 919	5 082	4 894	6 874	9 134	10 536	11 862
Additional taxes included in National Accounts	..	..	..	0	0	0	0	0	0	0
Taxes excluded from National Accounts	..	..	..	0	0	0	0	0	0	0
Difference in treatment of tax credits	..	..	..	0	0	0	0	0	0	0
Capital transfer for uncollected revenue	..	..	..	0	0	0	0	0	0	0
Voluntary social security contributions	..	..	..	0	0	0	0	0	0	0
Miscellaneous differences	..	..	..	0	0	0	0	0	0	0
National Accounts: Taxes and actual social contributions	..	..	..	1 919	5 082	4 894	6 874	9 134	10 536	11 862
Imputed social contributions	..	..	..	4	20	30	49	86	95	108
National Accounts: Taxes and all social contributions	..	..	..	1 922	5 102	4 924	6 923	9 220	10 631	11 970

.. Not available

Note: Year ending 31st December.

Data on an accrual basis.

Source: Statistics Estonia.

Table 5.11. Finland: Details of tax revenue, 1965-2022

Million EUR

	1965	1980	1990	2000	2007	2010	2015	2020	2021	2022
Total tax revenue	1 362	11 895	39 052	62 435	77 447	76 315	92 003	99 610	108 314	115 575
Total tax revenue exclusive of taxes collected for the EU	..	..	39 052	62 296	77 247	76 163	91 760	99 201	107 839	114 958
1000 Taxes on income, profits and capital gains	564	4 654	15 323	26 910	30 358	27 104	32 371	34 962	39 115	42 660
1100 Of individuals	453	4 248	13 562	19 118	23 396	22 545	27 824	29 873	32 270	34 604
1110 On income and profits	453	4 234	13 520	19 118	23 396	22 545	27 824	29 873	32 270	34 604
Tax on income	125	1 827	5 917	9 036	9 086	6 465	9 138	9 360	11 417	12 828
The final withdrawal tax on interest income	0	0	0	92	254	205	110	36	26	15
Communal tax	279	2 376	7 603	9 990	14 056	15 875	18 576	20 477	20 827	21 761
Seaman's tax	3	31	0	0	0	0	0	0	0	0
National pension contributions	32	0	0	0	0	0	0	0	0	0
National health insurance contributions	15	0	0	0	0	0	0	0	0	0
1120 On capital gains	0	14	42	0	0	0	0	0	0	0
Tax on lottery prizes	..	14	42	..	..	..	..	..	..	..
1200 Corporate	111	405	1 761	7 792	6 962	4 559	4 547	5 089	6 845	8 056
1210 On profits	111	405	1 761	7 792	6 962	4 559	4 547	5 089	6 845	8 056
Tax on income	72	202	1 001	4 758	5 298	2 972	2 761	2 933	3 797	5 279
Communal tax	36	187	699	2 900	1 541	1 471	1 668	2 156	3 048	2 777
Church tax	3	16	61	134	123	116	118	0	0	0
1220 On capital gains	0	0	0	0	0	0	0	0	0	0
1300 Unallocable between 1100 and 1200	0	0	0	0	0	0	0	0	0	0
2000 Social security contributions	93	2 776	10 012	15 756	21 384	22 648	26 639	27 326	30 186	31 954
2100 Employees	1	394	1 152	2 926	4 050	4 710	6 364	8 553	9 133	9 580
For employment pension schemes	1	10	23	2 120	2 950	3 386	4 714	6 239	6 546	6 972
For unemployment schemes	0	0	0	435	369	267	489	1 072	1 239	1 421
2110 On a payroll basis	..	10	23	2 565	3 319	3 653	5 203	7 311	7 785	8 393
2120 On an income tax basis	..	384	1 129	361	731	1 057	1 161	1 242	1 348	1 187
National pension contributions	..	251	502	2	0	0	0	0	0	0
National health insurance contributions	..	133	627	359	731	1 057	1 161	1 242	1 348	1 187
2200 Employers	93	2 230	8 127	11 571	15 715	16 041	18 232	16 704	18 890	20 283
For national pension schemes	29	685	1 502	1 566	1 331	0	0	0	0	0
For national health insurance	10	244	792	839	1 142	1 590	1 662	1 197	1 445	1 347
For unemployment schemes	3	106	206	1 143	1 346	1 377	1 676	1 006	1 172	1 344
For employment pension schemes	50	1 195	5 627	8 023	11 896	13 074	14 894	14 501	16 273	17 592
For accident and group life insurance premiums	0	0	0	0	0	0	0	0	0	0
2210 On a payroll basis of employers SSC	..	2 230	8 127	11 571	15 715	16 041	18 232	16 704	18 890	20 283
2220 On an income tax basis of employers SSC	..	0	0	0	0	0	0	0	0	0
2300 Selfemployed or nonemployed	0	152	733	1 259	1 619	1 897	2 043	2 069	2 163	2 091
For employment pension schemes	..	84	394	576	817	932	1 269	1 241	1 246	1 280
2310 On a payroll basis of self/non-employed SSC	..	84	394	576	817	932	1 269	1 241	1 246	1 280
2320 On an income tax basis of self/non-employed SSC	..	68	339	683	802	965	774	828	917	811
National pension contributions	..	43	151	5	0	0	0	0	0	0
National health insurance contributions	..	25	188	678	802	965	774	828	917	811
2400 Unallocable between 2100, 2200 and 2300	0	0	0	0	0	0	0	0	0	0
2410 On a payroll basis unallocable between 2100, 2200 and 2300 SSC	..	..	..	..	..	..	..	..	..	..
2420 On an income tax basis unallocable between 2100, 2200 and 2300 SSC	..	..	..	..	..	..	..	..	..	..
3000 Taxes on payroll and workforce	70	22	0	0	0	0	0	0	0	0
Soc. Sec. contr. for children allowance	70	22	..	..	..	..	..	..	..	..
4000 Taxes on property	54	221	956	1 518	2 012	2 087	3 017	3 569	3 788	3 864
4100 Recurrent taxes on immovable property	0	0	76	570	855	1 169	1 603	1 950	1 960	2 046
4110 Households	..	..	46	273	405	576	733	899	904	940
4120 Others	..	..	30	297	450	593	870	1 051	1 056	1 106
4200 Recurrent taxes on net wealth	24	24	27	179	0	0	0	0	0	0
4210 Individual	11	23	25	175	..	..	..	..	..	..
4220 Corporate	13	2	2	4	..	..	..	..	..	..
4300 Estate, inheritance and gift taxes	3	26	146	368	459	387	631	797	826	901
4310 Estate and inheritance taxes	3	21	121	307	384	324	528	650	662	705
4320 Gift taxes	1	5	25	61	75	63	103	147	164	196
4400 Taxes on financial and capital transactions	27	170	707	401	698	531	783	822	1 002	917
Stamp duty excluded entertainment	27	170	688	- 20	0	0	0	0	0	0
Credit tax	0	0	19	0	0	0	0	0	0	0
Transfer tax	0	0	0	421	698	531	783	822	1 002	917
4500 Nonrecurrent taxes	0	0	0	0	0	0	0	0	0	0
4510 On net wealth	..	..	..	..	..	..	..	..	..	..
4520 Other nonrecurrent taxes	..	..	..	..	..	..	..	..	..	..
4600 Other recurrent taxes on property	0	0	0	0	0	0	0	0	0	0
5000 Taxes on goods and services	578	4 202	12 711	18 221	23 624	24 407	29 895	33 680	35 117	37 010

	1965	1980	1990	2000	2007	2010	2015	2020	2021	2022
5100 Taxes on production, sale, transfer, etc	570	4 158	12 555	17 781	22 953	23 642	28 836	32 224	33 680	35 333
5110 General taxes	251	2 062	7 519	10 869	15 207	15 533	18 974	22 005	23 551	25 061
5111 Value added taxes	251	2 062	7 519	10 869	15 207	15 533	18 974	22 005	23 551	25 061
Value added taxes	251	2 062	7 519	9 616	13 657	13 691	16 680	18 802	20 226	21 409
VAT repayments of local government	0	0	0	849	1 550	1 842	2 294	3 203	3 325	3 652
Social Insur. Institutions' part of VAT revenue	0	0	0	404	0	0	0	0	0	0
5112 Sales tax	0	0	0	0	0	0	0	0	0	0
5113 Other	0	0	0	0	0	0	0	0	0	0
Suppl. sales tax on consumer durables	..	..	..	..	..	..	..	..	..	..
5120 Taxes on specific goods and services	319	2 096	5 036	6 912	7 746	8 109	9 862	10 219	10 129	10 272
5121 Excises	183	1 615	3 813	5 613	6 013	6 286	7 678	8 006	7 834	7 893
Excise on tobacco products	52	206	473	561	622	655	885	1 054	1 019	1 140
Excise on sweetments	6	23	26	0	0	0	0	0	0	0
Excise on medium, strong beer	3	109	419	0	0	0	0	0	0	0
Excise on non-alcoholic beverages	2	17	22	32	35	37	250	209	221	219
Excise on certain foodstuffs	3	218	36	0	0	0	0	0	0	0
Excise on liquid fuels	58	504	986	2 583	2 907	3 167	4 054	4 253	4 272	4 316
Excise on motor cars	28	238	697	1 059	1 217	941	882	713	515	477
Tax on alcoholic beverages	29	353	813	1 239	1 016	1 279	1 356	1 521	1 543	1 478
Levies on pharmacy	2	16	46	85	113	122	165	198	202	208
Levies for price reduction on butter	0	3	0	0	0	0	0	0	0	0
Levies for marketing of milk	0	12	58	0	0	0	0	0	0	0
Excise on margarines	0	18	55	0	0	0	0	0	0	0
Stock-building levies on liquid fuels	0	15	44	46	50	48	43	40	44	40
Excise on sugar products	0	18	34	0	0	0	0	0	0	0
Excise on feeding stuffs	0	0	0	0	0	0	0	0	0	0
Excise on fertilizers	0	21	21	0	0	0	0	0	0	0
Excise on oil-based concentrated feed	0	1	0	0	0	0	0	0	0	0
Excise on protein feed	0	0	0	0	0	0	0	0	0	0
Equalization fee agricultural products	0	8	29	0	0	0	0	0	0	0
Excise on albumen	0	0	30	0	0	0	0	0	0	0
Tax on electricity	0	65	0	0	0	0	0	0	0	0
Oil damage levy	0	0	7	5	8	20	24	2	0	0
Oil waste levy	0	0	4	3	4	4	4	0	0	0
Price difference compensations	0	- 231	0	0	0	0	0	0	0	0
The milk quota charge	0	0	6	0	0	0	0	0	0	0
Levies for marketing of special agric. prod.	0	0	0	0	0	0	0	0	0	0
Excise on phosphorous fertilizers	0	0	7	0	0	0	0	0	0	0
Excise on certain beverage packages	0	0	0	0	41	13	15	16	18	15
5122 Profits of fiscal monopolies	38	86	202	0	0	0	0	0	0	0
Excess profits on alcohol	38	86	202	..	..	..	..	..	..	..
5123 Customs and import duties	88	235	423	130	199	151	166	174	205	297
Import duties	62	126	232	0	0	0	0	0	0	0
Import levies on agricultural products	26	6	12	0	0	0	0	0	0	0
Local import duties (Town dues)	1	0	0	0	0	0	0	0	0	0
Import levies price stabilisation fund	0	3	0	0	0	0	0	0	0	0
Agricultural levies	0	0	0	0	0	0	0	0	0	0
Equalization tax	0	100	179	0	0	0	0	0	0	0
Custom duties			0	130	199	151	166	174	205	297
5124 Taxes on exports	0	0	0	0	0	0	0	0	0	0
Export duties	..	..	..	..	..	..	..	..	..	..
Levies on export	..	..	..	..	..	..	..	..	..	..
Counter-cyclical tax exports	..	..	..	..	..	..	..	..	..	..
5125 Taxes on investment goods	0	0	0	0	0	0	0	0	0	0
Investment tax on buildings	..	..	..	..	..	..	..	..	..	..
5126 Taxes on specific services	9	161	598	1 160	1 533	1 671	2 017	2 039	2 090	2 082
Net revenue of betting	8	94	328	704	807	874	967	746	819	748
Tax on motion pictures	0	0	0	0	0	0	0	0	0	0
Stamp duties on entertainment	2	5	0	0	0	0	0	0	0	0
Fire protection levy	0	3	7	6	8	9	11	11	12	12
Tax on waste	0	0	0	33	56	42	32	7	3	4
Rail tax	0	0	0	0	18	18	6	0	0	0
Tax on insurance premiums	0	58	263	337	509	584	777	820	848	875
Tax on lottery prizes	0	0	0	80	135	144	222	163	67	42
Tax on telecommunications	0	0	0	0	0	0	0	0	0	0
Bank tax	0	0	0	0	0	0	- 74	- 2	- 1	- 1
Contributions to the Resolution Fund	..	..	0	0	0	0	76	235	270	320
Contributions to the Deposit Guarantee Fund			0	0	0	0	0	59	72	82
5127 Other taxes on internat. trade and transactions	0	0	0	0	0	0	0	0	0	0

	1965	1980	1990	2000	2007	2010	2015	2020	2021	2022
Tax on charter flights	..	..	..	..	..	..	..	..	..	..
5128 Other taxes	0	0	0	9	1	1	1	0	0	0
Sugar levy	..	..	..	9	1	1	1	..	..	..
Steel and coal levy	..	..	..	0	0	0	0	..	..	..
5130 Unallocable between 5110 and 5120	0	0	0	0	0	0	0	0	0	0
5200 Taxes on use of goods and perform activities	8	44	156	440	671	765	1 059	1 456	1 437	1 677
5210 Recurrent taxes	8	44	156	423	637	725	960	1 208	1 170	1 144
5211 Paid by households: motor vehicles	0	2	5	165	486	541	748	965	938	916
5212 Paid by others: motor vehicles	7	32	135	235	126	150	182	203	196	193
5213 Paid in respect of other goods	1	10	16	23	25	34	30	40	36	35
Dog licenses	1	2	4	5	3	2	1	0	0	0
Hunting and fishing licenses	1	7	12	17	17	24	22	28	27	26
Seamens welfare and rescue levy	0	0	0	1	1	1	0	0	0	0
Nuclear energy research levy	0	0	0	0	4	7	7	12	9	9
5220 Nonrecurrent taxes	0	0	0	17	34	40	99	248	267	533
Vehicle registration tax	..	..	..	17	34	40	36	27	29	30
Income from auction of emission allowances	..	..	..	0	0	0	63	221	238	503
5300 Unallocable between 5100 and 5200	0	0	0	0	0	0	0	0	0	0
6000 Other taxes	2	21	50	30	69	69	81	73	108	87
6100 Paid solely by business	0	0	0	0	0	0	0	0	0	0
6200 Other	2	21	50	30	69	69	81	73	108	87
Custom duties collected for the EU	..	..	..	130	199	151	166	174	205	297
SRF Contributions collected for the EU			..	..	..	..	76	235	270	320
Total tax revenue on cash basis	1 362	11 895	39 396	61 638	77 110	76 176	91 846	98 048	107 070	116 092
Total tax revenue on accrual basis	..	..	39 052	62 435	77 447	76 315	92 003	99 610	108 314	115 575
Additional taxes included in National Accounts	..	0	0	0	0	0	0	0	0	0
Taxes excluded from National Accounts	..	0	0	0	0	0	0	0	0	0
Difference in treatment of tax credits	..	0	0	0	0	0	0	0	0	0
Capital transfer for uncollected revenue	..	0	0	0	0	0	0	0	0	0
Voluntary social security contributions	..	262	632	236	228	254	303	235	261	246
Miscellaneous differences	..	0	0	0	0	0	0	0	0	0
National Accounts: Taxes and actual social contributions	..	12 157	39 684	62 671	77 675	76 569	92 306	99 845	108 575	115 821
Imputed social contributions	..	513	688	30	0	0	0	..	..	..
National Accounts: Taxes and all social contributions	..	12 670	40 372	62 701	77 675	76 569	92 306	99 845	108 575	115 821

.. Not available

Note: Year ending 31st December.

From 1988 data are on accrual basis.

The comparability of the time series to earlier years is slightly lower.

Headings 2120 and 2320: The breakdown of contributions paid by employees and self-employed or non-employed is estimated, except for the healthcare fee of students in higher education included also into 2320 (in effect from 2021).

Headings 4110 and 4120: The breakdown of contributions paid by households and others is estimated.

Heading 4400: Negative values in Stamp duties are due to repayments during transition time from Stamp duties to Transfer tax.

Heading 5121: Negative items in Price difference compensations were due to subsidies under the price compensation scheme, which could be offset against any positive tax liability.

Heading 5126: Negative values are due to repayments temporary bank tax.

Heading 5212: Prior to 1990, a part of the tax was paid by households.

Source: Statistics Finland, basing on data from State Treasury, Tax Administration, Finnish Customs, Finnish Transport and Communication Agency, Financial Stability Authority and Financial Supervisory Authority. Supplementary information from unpublished sources.

Table 5.12. France: Details of tax revenue, 1965-2022

Million EUR

	1965	1980	1990	2000	2007	2010	2015	2020	2021	2022
Total tax revenue	25 776	178 576	433 771	646 630	836 425	847 878	1 004 517	1 058 550	1 136 864	1 219 771
Total tax revenue exclusive of taxes collected for the EU	..	..	..	644 757	834 610	845 906	1 001 450	1 053 496	1 131 396	1 212 830
1000 Taxes on income, profits and capital gains	4 095	30 019	69 649	160 298	202 472	192 477	235 080	274 251	296 111	334 170
1100 Taxes on income, profits and capital gains of individuals	2 736	20 734	46 272	116 989	148 328	151 762	192 051	221 534	235 813	258 542
1110 On income and profits of individuals	2 723	20 674	46 252	116 988	148 328	151 762	192 051	221 534	235 813	258 542
Tax on individual income	..	18 207	39 237	49 548	53 295	52 511	74 712	75 901	80 915	90 730
Tax on non business profits	..	51	189	293	559	446	927	603	833	784
Tax on financial assets	..	2 333	3 971	1 460	3 492	5 952	3 933	3 207	4 695	3 498
CSG, FSV, CRDS	..	0	0	65 597	90 937	92 763	112 379	131 251	137 461	150 175
Flat-rate tax on precious metals	..	70	58	47	37	52	71	79	95	108
Tax on multiple wages	..	7	20	38	0	0	0	0	0	0
Solidarity levy	..	0	2 207	5	0	0	0	10 219	11 480	12 771
Others	..	6	571	0	8	38	29	274	334	476
1120 On capital gains of individuals	14	59	20	1	0	0	0	0	0	0
On capital gains	..	0	0	0	..	..	..	..	..	..
Levies on construction profits	..	59	20	1	..	..	..	..	..	..
1200 Taxes on income, profits and capital gains of corporates	1 358	9 158	23 117	43 309	54 144	40 715	43 029	52 717	60 298	75 628
1210 On profits of corporates	1 358	9 158	23 117	43 309	54 144	40 715	43 029	52 717	60 298	75 628
Corporations' tax (excluding tax credits to reduce or remove the taxation)	..	8 524	20 804	40 046	52 165	38 842	39 758	50 425	58 652	73 556
3% tax on dividends	..	0	0	0	0	0	2 165	0	0	0
Tax on financial assets	..	487	1 333	0	0	0	0	0	0	0
Precount on distributed profits (exceptional levy of 25% since 2005)	..	36	247	1 135	88	28	4	0	20	0
Exceptional levies on temporary work corporations	..	0	0	0	0	0	0	0	0	0
Social contribution on corporation profits	..	0	0	589	158	842	971	1 171	1 042	1 589
Annual flat-rate tax	..	111	658	1 484	1 656	599	4	0	0	0
Exceptionnal levies on insurances	..	0	61	55	64	94	127	1 121	584	105
Inframarginal rent caps on electricity production				0	0	0	0	0	0	378
Other taxes	..	0	14	0	13	310	0	0	0	0
1220 On capital gains of corporates	0	0	0	0	0	0	0	0	0	0
1300 Unallocable between 1100 and 1200	0	127	260	0	0	0	0	0	0	0
2000 Social security contributions (SSC)	8 804	76 235	191 141	231 766	305 929	322 078	368 660	346 095	372 809	395 489
2100 Employees SSC	1 701	19 851	57 347	57 686	76 012	77 407	92 853	83 369	89 938	95 535
Actual cotisations	0	19 851	57 347	57 686	76 012	77 407	92 853	83 369	89 938	95 535
2110 On a payroll basis of employees SSC	0	0	0	57 686	76 012	77 407	92 853	83 369	89 938	95 535
2120 On an income tax basis of employees SSC	0	0	0	0	0	0	0	0	0	0
2200 Employers SSC	6 525	50 742	118 079	159 367	207 757	218 810	247 372	235 532	254 127	268 049
Actual cotisations	0	50 742	118 079	159 367	207 757	218 810	247 372	235 532	254 127	268 049
2210 On a payroll basis of employers SSC	0	0	0	159 367	207 757	218 810	247 372	235 532	254 127	268 049
2220 On an income tax basis of employers SSC	0	0	0	0	0	0	0	0	0	0
2300 Self-employed or non-employed SSC	578	5 642	15 714	14 713	22 160	25 861	28 435	27 194	28 744	31 905
Actual cotisations	..	5 642	15 714	14 713	22 160	25 861	28 435	27 194	28 744	31 905
2310 On a payroll basis of self/non-employed SSC	0	0	0	14 713	22 160	25 861	28 435	27 194	28 744	31 905
2320 On an income tax basis of self/non-employed SSC	0	0	0	0	0	0	0	0	0	0
2400 Unallocable between 2100, 2200 and 2300 SSC	0	0	0	0	0	0	0	0	0	0
2410 On a payroll basis unallocable between 2100, 2200 and 2300 SSC	0	0	0	..	..	..	..	..	..	..
2420 On an income tax basis unallocable between 2100, 2200 and 2300 SSC	0	0	0	..	..	..	..	..	..	..
3000 Taxes on payroll and workforce	1 189	3 935	8 254	16 118	24 243	28 531	36 354	45 242	47 381	52 035
Tax on wages	0	2 413	5 208	7 583	10 272	11 440	13 165	14 537	15 206	15 971
Corporate social contributions	0	0	0	0	0	657	5 019	5 428	5 137	6 193
Apprenticeship tax	0	172	101	102	964	1 130	1 436	0	0	0
Tax benefitting the wage garantee scheme (AGS)	0	263	379	551	736	1 759	1 479	798	865	936
Tax on vocational training	0	236	30	97	19	13	17	8 441	9 093	10 695
Taxes benefitting the national housing fund (FNAL)	0	120	754	1 506	2 412	2 465	2 629	2 478	2 648	2 687
Employers' contribution to building effort				1 032	1 171	1 211	1 450	1 368	1 310	1 392
Others	0	0	159	1 021	298	290	227	230	258	278
Payment benefitting the UNEDIC	0	0	23	24	0	0	0	0	0	0
Tax on re-employed pensioners income	0	0	0	0	0	0	0	0	0	0
Contributions on redundancy and early retirements compensations and on top-hat pension plans	0	0	0	415	773	1 120	415	282	309	290
Contribution for mobility	0	731	1 600	3 786	5 738	6 344	7 842	9 042	9 642	10 505
Additional solidarity contribution for autonomy	0	0	0	0	1 860	1 917	1 891	1 993	2 115	2 262

	1965	1980	1990	2000	2007	2010	2015	2020	2021	2022
Employers' contribution to the early retirement of asbestos workers regime (FCAATA)	0	0	0	0	0	0	0	0	0	0
Employer's contributions on stock options				0	0	185	430	644	795	826
Exceptional levy on high wages	0	0	0	0	0	0	354	1	3	0
4000 Taxes on property	1 105	8 591	27 434	44 115	65 453	70 864	89 883	92 798	97 530	98 333
4100 Recurrent taxes on immovable property	506	5 358	14 808	27 375	39 925	47 674	57 527	55 384	51 971	51 806
4110 Households recurrent taxes on immovable property	198	4 454	11 493	20 221	30 633	36 565	43 957	40 353	38 409	37 543
Council tax	0	2 306	5 100	8 366	12 433	15 254	18 424	10 456	7 889	5 416
Tax on real-estate properties	0	1 034	4 040	8 460	11 983	14 403	17 557	20 879	21 396	22 530
Waste collection tax	0	534	1 219	3 103	5 117	5 699	6 567	7 490	7 763	8 269
Tax on non-developped land	0	506	979	172	851	919	980	1 001	1 011	1 048
Chamber of Agriculture tax	0	0	0	53	59	61	61	69	69	69
Street-cleaning tax	0	0	0	68	74	75	109	112	115	116
Other taxes	0	74	156	- 1	116	154	259	346	166	95
4120 Other than households recurrent taxes on immovable property	308	904	3 315	7 154	9 291	11 109	13 570	15 031	13 562	14 263
Tax on real-estate properties	0	759	3 032	6 256	9 054	10 865	13 246	14 751	13 285	13 986
Tax on non-developped land	0	127	245	688	0	0	0	0	0	0
Chamber of Agriculture tax	0	18	39	210	237	244	242	204	205	203
Other taxes	0	0	0	0	0	0	82	76	72	74
4200 Recurrent taxes on net wealth	0	0	2 615	2 440	4 390	4 461	5 224	1 997	2 025	2 283
4210 Individual recurrent taxes on net wealth	..	..	938	2 440	4 390	4 461	5 224	1 997	2 025	2 283
4220 Corporate recurrent taxes on net wealth	..	..	1 677	0	0	0	0	0	0	0
4300 Estate, inheritance and gift taxes	145	1 010	4 124	6 907	8 910	7 738	12 477	15 365	19 054	18 981
4310 Estate and inheritance taxes	140	875	3 490	5 508	7 853	6 862	10 850	12 904	15 189	15 651
Inheritance taxes	0	861	3 453	5 428	7 794	6 806	10 540	12 527	14 719	15 182
Levy on insurance proceeds in the event of death				0	0	0	160	336	346	364
Various receipts and tax fines	0	14	37	80	59	56	150	41	124	105
4320 Gift taxes	5	135	634	1 399	1 057	876	1 627	2 461	3 865	3 330
Donations	0	113	568	1 399	1 057	876	1 627	2 461	3 865	3 330
Various receipts and tax fines	0	0	0	0	0	0	0	0	0	0
Other taxes	0	22	66	0	0	0	0	0	0	0
4400 Taxes on financial and capital transactions	447	2 224	5 886	7 393	12 228	10 991	14 655	20 052	24 480	25 263
Debts, annuities, offices	0	30	209	279	443	279	335	322	452	507
Business assets	0	253	518	199	268	154	132	159	153	189
Tangible movable assets	0	14	18	0	0	1	1	0	0	0
Properties and real property rights	0	63	4	2	2	3	1	0	0	1
Conventions and civil transactions between corporations	0	95	218	4	5	8	7	0	0	0
Various receipts and tax fines	0	35	60	367	179	253	6	1	1	1
Judicial and extra-judicial documents	0	6	10	0	0	0	0	0	0	0
Land registration tax	0	781	38	68	130	140	770	991	1 175	1 188
Various stamps and fees	0	94	242	0	0	0	0	0	0	0
Taxes on stock exchange transactions	0	168	525	407	271	0	0	0	0	0
Tax on financial transactions	0	0	0	0	0	0	917	1 290	1 204	1 314
Additional registration taxes	0	679	4 002	5 349	10 481	9 733	11 934	16 931	21 033	21 628
Other taxes and receipts	0	5	44	718	449	420	552	358	462	435
4500 Non-recurrent taxes on property	8	0	0	0	0	0	0	0	0	0
4510 Non-recurrent taxes on net wealth	8	..	..	..	..	..	..	..	..	..
4520 Non-recurrent taxes on property other than net wealth	0	..	..	..	..	..	..	..	..	..
4600 Other recurrent taxes on property except 4100 and 4200	0	0	0	0	0	0	0	0	0	0
5000 Taxes on goods and services	9 902	54 317	123 235	169 922	210 532	224 158	262 430	284 575	306 924	317 902
5100 Taxes on production, sale, transfer, etc	9 676	52 719	119 201	163 725	203 138	216 239	253 138	274 277	296 490	309 989
5110 General taxes on goods and services	5 994	37 760	81 341	110 118	141 779	151 269	169 530	181 560	197 017	213 259
5111 Value added taxes	5 173	37 282	79 972	107 334	136 883	135 833	152 167	162 090	185 350	199 362
VAT (general budget)	0	36 895	78 902	103 223	137 059	135 833	152 167	162 090	185 350	199 362
VAT (BAPSA)	0	62	101	4 111	0	0	0	0	0	0
Other VAT	0	325	969	0	0	0	0	0	0	0
Sub-compensations of agricultural VAT	0	0	0	0	- 248	0	0	0	0	0
Value added taxes on subsidies	0	0	0	0	72	0	0	0	0	0
5112 Sales tax	822	0	0	0	0	0	0	0	0	0
5113 Other (than value added and sales tax)	0	477	1 369	2 784	4 896	15 436	17 363	19 470	11 667	13 897
Social solidarity contribution	..	477	1 369	2 784	4 896	5 090	4 390	4 109	3 664	4 274
Contributions on the value added of the corporations				0	0	10 346	12 973	14 986	7 529	9 002
Taxe sur les services numériques				0	0	0	0	375	474	621
5120 Taxes on specific goods and services	3 682	14 960	37 860	53 606	61 360	64 970	83 608	92 717	99 473	96 730

	1965	1980	1990	2000	2007	2010	2015	2020	2021	2022
5121 Excises	2 775	11 013	26 834	39 881	44 512	46 102	57 487	61 323	65 931	59 507
Domestic duty on energy products	0	7 136	17 476	23 493	24 232	23 330	26 029	26 187	30 001	30 370
Exceptional levies on oil product corporations	0	0	0	0	0	0	0	0	0	0
Taxes on wines, ciders and meads	0	97	174	0	121	121	123	100	109	109
Taxes on alcohol	0	1 238	1 593	3 025	2 649	2 578	3 033	2 969	3 113	3 102
Taxes on beer and mineral water	0	58	91	20	409	538	931	1 048	1 096	1 186
Other taxes and receipts	0	136	38	19	4	4	33	0	0	0
Taxes on tobaccos and matches	0	1 188	2 989	7 965	9 473	10 912	12 130	15 417	15 326	14 361
Contribution on sugar-sweetened beverages and bottled water				0	0	0	378	433	456	497
Fines and confiscations	0	2	1	0	0	0	0	0	0	0
Local tax	0	5	8	241	247	325	126	95	76	102
Exceptional contribution on pharmacies and laboratories	0	16	0	0	0	0	0	0	0	0
Sugar market fund tax	0	0	0	0	0	0	0	0	0	0
Tax on pollution, distribution, collection and extraction of water	0	217	609	1 624	1 821	1 763	2 268	2 169	2 325	2 276
Other taxes	0	30	772	78	102	55	199	558	559	565
Tax on meat	0	25	36	0	19	1	0	0	0	0
Tax on water consumption	0	34	51	74	5	11	2	0	0	5
National Literature Fund tax	0	23	0	0	0	0	0	0	0	0
Tax on food fats	0	32	89	99	114	112	126	0	0	0
Solidarity tax on oil seeds	0	8	41	0	0	0	0	0	0	0
Tax on beet, sugar and alcohol	0	22	400	0	0	0	0	0	0	0
Taxes on sales of pharmaceutical products and medical devices	0	4	559	553	585	515	755	757	696	813
Surtax on appetizers	0	12	17	0	0	0	0	0	0	0
Tax on electricity and heating	0	426	1 340	1 061	2 990	3 717	8 703	9 047	9 356	3 108
Mining fees	0	16	59	43	23	25	16	18	17	17
Tax on logging products	0	11	0	0	0	0	0	0	0	0
National Book Fund tax	0	7	17	0	0	0	0	0	0	0
Fees included in fuel price	0	36	32	453	485	495	493	499	547	551
Tax on flour	0	0	0	38	72	59	62	0	0	0
Fees on potash salt	0	0	0	0	0	0	0	0	0	0
Fees on tobacco stores	0	0	0	0	0	0	0	0	0	0
Tax on cereals	0	147	275	19	19	24	14	0	0	0
Tax on health protection and meats market organisation	0	0	0	48	46	43	43	41	42	40
ANDA taxes	0	84	147	89	0	0	0	0	0	0
Gold and silver warranty	0	6	19	29	2	0	0	0	0	0
French petrol institute (IFP) tax	0	0	0	193	0	0	0	0	0	0
Contribution of low voltage electric energy suppliers	0	0	0	183	322	324	375	376	377	378
ADEME tax	0	0	0	80	212	489	449	0	0	0
Dock dues	0	0	0	449	544	645	703	833	881	880
General tax on polluting activities	0	0	0	6	16	16	117	392	594	775
Tax on oil products	0	0	0	0	0	0	379	384	360	372
5122 Profits of fiscal monopolies	0	0	0	0	0	0	0	0	0	0
5123 Customs and import duties	471	966	1 669	1 810	2 188	2 281	2 549	2 507	2 657	2 929
Import duties (State)	0	0	0	0	0	0	0	0	0	0
Import duties (UE)	0	873	1 623	0	0	0	0	0	0	0
Dock dues	0	0	0	267	327	297	397	402	488	601
Other taxes	0	94	46	30	204	232	220	39	46	48
Custom duties collected for the EU				1 513	1 657	1 752	1 932	2 066	2 123	2 280
5124 Taxes on exports	0	75	15	0	0	0	0	0	0	0
Agricultural levies (State part)	..	0	0	..	..	..	..	..	..	..
Agricultural levies (EU part)	..	75	15	..	..	..	..	..	..	..
5125 Taxes on investment goods	0	0	0	0	0	0	0	0	0	0
5126 Taxes on specific services	431	2 690	8 373	11 556	14 647	16 532	23 518	28 887	30 885	34 294
Levies on horse-race bets	0	446	545	502	719	626	446	362	395	417
Levies on gambling casinos	0	0	0	727	1 022	748	691	476	388	861
Levies on the French national lottery	0	200	702	1 305	1 982	1 968	2 305	2 113	2 706	2 869
Exceptionnal levies on banks and lending institutions	0	0	0	0	0	0	0	0	0	0
Tax on insurance policies	0	1 292	4 782	5 097	6 571	7 099	7 923	8 956	9 434	9 950
Tax on leases	0	264	633	573	29	- 5	0	0	1	0
Taxes on funerals	0	11	32	14	11	12	12	15	7	7
Stamp taxes for transportation contracts	0	9	77	10	0	0	0	0	0	0
Tax on expertise and technical checks	0	0	0	0	0	0	0	0	0	0
ANAEM tax	0	0	0	33	58	129	146	0	0	0
Tax on the use of inland waterways	0	0	0	73	20	8	- 6	0	0	0
Other various taxes	0	98	272	249	449	288	794	2 280	2 295	2 086
Taxes on entertainment	0	75	195	664	1 004	997	1 359	1 712	2 142	2 480
Insurances contributions to the guarantee funds	0	32	135	223	274	323	450	783	823	808

	1965	1980	1990	2000	2007	2010	2015	2020	2021	2022
Tax on automobile insurance	0	0	0	55	0	0	0	0	0	0
Additional contribution on insurance contracts to the FNGCA	0	0	0	261	96	101	125	70	71	75
Tax on retail surfaces	0	114	258	678	604	604	932	999	991	1 057
Movie-making corporations contributions to the CNC	0	52	207	299	26	594	547	476	515	620
Agricultural insurances fund tax on food	0	0	0	0	0	0	0	0	0	0
National Sports Fund tax	0	3	0	0	0	0	0	0	0	0
Annuities and pensions upgrading fund tax	0	15	0	0	0	0	0	0	0	0
Annual tax on outstanding loans	0	0	0	0	0	0	0	0	0	0
Tax on advertisement	0	0	26	52	38	156	232	173	194	209
Levies on mortgage recording officers wages	0	67	188	0	0	0	0	0	0	0
Tax on safety and security	0	0	0	220	353	459	574	261	362	647
Tax on systemic risk	0	0	0	0	0	0	591	28	28	28
Additional solidarity tax	0	0	0	262	680	1 802	4 422	5 770	5 773	5 781
Major natural disasters prevention fund (FPRNM) tax	0	0	0	0	0	0	205	223	135	194
SRF Contributions collected for the EU				0	0	0	916	2 988	3 345	4 661
Tax on electronic communications supply				0	0	239	201	230	236	247
Contribution on rents				100	143	166	246	531	540	539
Other taxes	0	10	320	159	568	218	407	441	504	758
5127 Other taxes on internat. trade and transactions not included within 5121 to 5126 inclusive	0	0	0	0	0	0	0	0	0	0
5128 Other taxes not included within 5121 to 5127 inclusive	5	215	970	360	13	55	54	0	0	0
Co-responsibility tax on milk	0	48	119	0	0	0	0	..	..	..
Co-responsibility tax on cereals	0	0	520	0	0	0	0	..	..	..
European Coal and Steel Community levy	0	14	0	0	0	0	0	..	..	..
Collector of customs	0	9	24	0	0	0	0	..	..	..
Various taxes (local government)	0	0	0	0	0	0	0	..	..	..
Contributions on sugar	0	68	185	270	0	42	41	..	..	..
Sugar market fund tax	0	76	120	76	0	0	0	..	..	..
Other taxes	0	0	2	14	13	13	13	..	..	..
5130 Unallocable between 5110 and 5120	0	0	0	0	0	0	0	0	0	0
5200 Taxes on use of goods and perform activities	226	1 598	4 034	6 198	7 394	7 919	9 292	10 298	10 434	7 913
5210 Recurrent taxes on use of goods and perform activities	178	1 226	3 024	4 562	4 785	4 776	5 294	5 266	5 259	2 341
5211 Recurrent taxes paid by households: motor vehicles	27	545	1 236	126	0	0	0	0	0	0
Tax differential (central and local government)	0	545	1 236	126	..	..	..	..	..	..
5212 Recurrent taxes paid by others: motor vehicles	79	545	1 086	1 280	1 559	1 269	1 028	997	945	900
Tax on corporation vehicles	0	197	345	644	891	992	753	801	756	693
Tax on vehicles (central and local government)	0	348	741	636	668	277	275	196	189	207
5213 Recurrent taxes paid on use of goods and perform activities other than on motor vehicles	72	136	702	3 156	3 226	3 507	4 266	4 269	4 314	1 441
Special tax on use of roads	0	0	0	420	526	539	574	535	611	843
Weighing tax	0	17	14	0	0	0	0	0	0	0
Various taxes (local government)	0	7	33	0	0	0	0	0	0	0
Tax on video recorders	0	0	0	0	0	0	0	0	0	0
Fee on nuclear power plants monitoring	0	8	41	0	0	0	0	0	0	0
Tax on use of slaughterhouses	0	19	13	0	0	0	0	0	0	0
Corporation contributions on medicines preparation	0	0	20	0	0	0	34	0	10	8
Tax on electric pylons	0	1	66	128	183	213	231	283	290	299
Beverage licences	0	8	22	23	0	0	0	0	0	0
Gallicisation and navigation annual right (DAFN)	0	0	0	0	0	39	37	43	43	44
Fees on radio frequencies use	0	0	0	0	0	0	0	0	0	0
Contribution to public broadcasting				2 181	2 350	2 574	3 122	3 157	3 109	0
Other taxes	0	75	493	404	167	142	268	251	251	247
5220 Non-recurrent taxes on use of goods and perform activities	47	372	1 010	1 636	2 609	3 143	3 998	5 032	5 175	5 572
Entry into service receipt	0	75	0	0	0	0	0	0	0	0
Carbon emission allowances				0	0	0	215	727	728	1 469
Tax on exceeding the density legal ceiling	0	38	270	38	45	82	52	0	0	0
Other taxes	0	35	423	0	0	0	0	0	0	0
Beverage taxes and licences	0	0	0	3	0	0	0	0	0	0
Fee for the right to build	0	79	53	72	0	18	0	0	0	0
Building permit tax	0	146	263	150	625	940	1 343	1 606	1 801	1 726

	1965	1980	1990	2000	2007	2010	2015	2020	2021	2022
Car registration tax	0	0	0	1 373	1 939	1 917	2 086	2 130	2 167	1 891
Additional tax on car registration	0	0	0	0	0	186	302	569	479	486
5300 Unallocable between 5100 and 5200	0	0	0	0	0	0	0	0	0	0
6000 Taxes other than 1000, 2000, 3000, 4000 and 5000	681	5 480	14 060	24 412	27 796	9 770	12 110	15 589	16 109	21 842
6100 Paid solely by business	678	5 480	14 060	22 726	27 787	9 764	12 104	15 567	16 089	21 823
National Institute of intellectual property (INPI) tax on services	0	43	67	115	156	165	193	234	129	102
Tax on general charges	0	0	0	0	0	0	0	0	0	0
Tax on the use of fixed assets	0	5 152	13 381	19 641	22 035	0	0	0	0	0
Tax on union benefits (local government)	0	36	197	293	0	0	0	0	0	0
Various taxes (central government)	0	0	0	61	236	255	649	848	919	876
Annual tax on outstanding loans	0	110	0	0	0	0	0	0	0	0
Exceptionnal levies on insurance corporations	0	0	0	0	0	0	0	0	0	0
Fees of the chambers of commerce and industry	0	36	125	155	203	275	253	201	190	213
Industrial corporation tax to the FNE	0	4	240	204	33	10	0	0	0	0
(ANDA) and (ADAR) tax	0	0	0	32	0	0	0	0	0	0
Property contributions of the corporations	0	0	0	0	0	4 941	6 356	7 142	5 951	6 540
Flat-rate tax on network corporations	0	0	0	0	0	1 223	1 297	1 444	1 395	1 588
Exit tax on insurance	0	0	0	0	0	0	0	0	0	0
Fees of the chambers of commerce and industry	0	0	0	770	835	1 103	458	644	531	511
Tax on railway companies profit	0	0	0	0	0	0	400	227	0	0
Tax on pharmaceutical companies' advertising expenses				122	217	232	197	172	179	99
Discounts from pharmaceutical companies				85	178	255	632	3 281	5 275	6 597
Contractual prices on renewable energy				0	0	0	0	0	0	3 554
Other taxes	0	98	50	1 248	3 894	1 305	1 669	1 374	1 520	1 743
6200 Other taxes not solely paid by business	3	0	0	1 686	8	6	6	22	20	19
Other taxes	0	..	..	1 686	8	6	6	22	20	19
Sectors accounts differential	0	..	..	0	0	0	0	0	0	0
Custom duties collected for the EU	..	..	..	1 513	1 657	1 752	1 932	2 066	2 123	2 280
SRF Contributions collected for the EU				..	..	..	916	2 988	3 345	4 661
Non-wastable tax credits against 1110: Total value	..	..	..	0	7 663	10 761	8 041	7 848	6 644	7 490
Non-wastable tax credits against 1110: Transfer component	..	..	..	..	4 698	5 463	4 334	1 483	1 715	1 995
Non-wastable tax credits against 1110: Tax expenditure component	..	..	..	..	2 965	5 298	3 707	6 365	4 929	5 495
Non-wastable tax credits against 1210: Total value	..	..	..	457	1 860	6 655	19 007	18 564	15 972	16 009
Non-wastable tax credits against 1210: Tax expenditure component	..	..	..	88	357	1 277	10 949	5 704	3 884	4 850
Non-wastable tax credits against 1210: Transfer component	..	..	..	369	1 503	5 378	8 058	12 860	12 088	11 159
Non-wastable tax credits against 3000	..	..	..	0	0	0	0	0	0	0
Non-wastable tax credits against 3000: Transfer component	..	..	..	..	..	..	..	..	..	..
Non-wastable tax credits against 3000: Tax expenditure component	..	..	..	..	..	..	..	..	..	..
Total tax revenue on cash basis	25 776	178 576	433 771	643 427	831 750	843 102	998 620	1 048 775	1 130 134	1 215 509
Total tax revenue on accrual basis	..	..	..	646 630	836 425	847 878	1 004 517	1 058 550	1 136 864	1 219 771
Additional taxes included in National Accounts	..	..	..	0	0	0	0	0	0	0
Taxes excluded from National Accounts	..	..	..	- 3 171	- 5 191	- 5 774	- 6 676	- 7 602	- 7 878	- 8 385
Waste collection tax	..	..	..	- 3 103	- 5 117	- 5 699	- 6 567	- 7 490	- 7 763	- 8 269
Tax on electric pylons	..	..	..	0	0	0	0	0	0	0
Street-cleaning tax	..	..	..	- 68	- 74	- 75	- 109	- 112	- 115	- 116
Difference in treatment of tax credits	..	..	..	88	3 322	6 575	14 656	12 069	8 813	10 345
Capital transfer for uncollected revenue	..	..	..	- 3 204	- 4 675	- 4 776	- 5 897	- 9 775	- 6 730	- 4 262
Voluntary social security contributions	..	..	..	0	0	0	0	0	0	0
Miscellaneous differences	..	..	..	0	0	0	0	0	0	0
National Accounts: Taxes and actual social contributions	..	..	..	640 344	829 881	843 903	1 006 600	1 053 242	1 131 069	1 217 469
Imputed social contributions	..	..	..	25 981	33 639	38 171	42 655	44 617	44 866	46 775
National Accounts: Taxes and all social contributions	..	..	..	666 325	863 519	882 074	1 049 255	1 097 859	1 175 935	1 264 244

.. Not available

Note: Calendar year ending on December 31st.

From 1992, the data are on an accrual basis.

From 1970, figures were calculated according to the new System of National Accounts and are not, therefore, comparable to those of the previous years.

The section 2000 includes certain voluntary contributions.

Source: National accounts for France, Insee.

Table 5.13. Germany: Details of tax revenue, 1965-2022

Million EUR

	1965	1980	1990	2000	2007	2010	2015	2020	2021	2022
Total tax revenue	74 359	287 373	454 764	767 045	892 257	919 827	1 151 532	1 315 613	1 439 067	1 537 045
Total tax revenue exclusive of taxes collected for the EU	..	..	450 620	763 300	888 512	915 585	1 144 736	1 308 649	1 431 276	1 526 962
1000 Taxes on income, profits and capital gains	25 059	100 821	147 257	231 249	273 596	257 817	351 386	403 713	463 278	506 014
1100 Of individuals	19 254	85 134	125 296	194 173	218 848	219 387	299 362	348 846	379 110	413 386
1110 On income and profits	19 254	85 134	125 296	194 173	218 848	219 387	299 362	348 846	379 110	413 386
Taxes on wages and salaries	8 558	57 039	90 801	135 733	146 365	145 202	194 116	227 507	239 528	256 556
Assessed income tax	7 567	18 813	18 672	12 225	25 341	31 346	48 902	59 447	72 289	81 576
Withholding tax on dividends	691	2 135	5 538	13 515	13 572	12 982	17 944	21 498	27 394	32 628
Supplementary tax	0	0	0	10 347	10 907	10 706	14 555	17 105	7 886	9 142
Enterprise tax	2 438	7 147	10 285	16 486	14 630	13 709	18 553	18 884	25 535	29 300
Stabilisation tax	0	0	0	0	0	0	0	0	0	0
Withholding tax on interest	0	0	0	5 867	8 033	5 442	5 292	4 405	6 478	4 184
1120 On capital gains	0	0	0	0	0	0	0	0	0	0
1200 Corporate	5 806	15 686	21 961	37 076	54 748	38 430	52 024	54 867	84 168	92 628
1210 On profits	5 806	15 686	21 961	37 076	54 748	38 430	52 024	54 867	84 168	92 628
Corporation tax	4 177	10 902	15 385	23 575	23 386	12 516	20 178	24 514	42 304	46 564
Supplementary tax	0	20	1	1 494	1 550	982	1 409	1 460	2 513	2 663
Sacrifice for Berlin	3	0	0	0	0	0	0	0	0	0
Enterprise tax	1 625	4 765	6 576	10 540	25 486	22 002	27 589	26 521	35 863	41 149
Stabilisation tax	0	0	0	0	0	0	0	0	0	0
Withholding tax on interest	0	0	0	1 467	4 326	2 930	2 848	2 372	3 488	2 252
Absorption of windfall profits in the energy market (Emergency Regulation (EU) 2022/1854)			0	0	0	0	0	0	0	0
1220 On capital gains	0	0	0	0	0	0	0	0	0	0
1300 Unallocable between 1100 and 1200	0	0	0	0	0	0	0	0	0	0
2000 Social security contributions	19 876	98 659	170 449	299 440	320 750	354 320	424 842	512 279	534 374	567 083
2100 Employees	8 723	43 833	73 580	131 610	139 927	152 843	186 307	217 264	229 146	246 434
Payments by employees total	8 723	43 833	73 580	131 610	139 927	152 843	186 307	217 264	229 146	246 434
2110 On a payroll basis	..	..	..	131 610	139 927	152 843	186 307	217 264	229 146	246 434
2120 On an income tax basis	..	..	..	0	0	0	0	0	0	0
2200 Employers	10 693	52 985	86 659	147 410	151 094	165 469	196 665	244 759	253 465	266 727
Payments by employers total	10 693	52 985	86 659	147 410	151 094	165 469	196 665	244 759	253 465	266 727
2210 On a payroll basis of employers SSC	..	..	..	147 410	151 094	165 469	196 665	244 759	253 465	266 727
2220 On an income tax basis of employers SSC	..	..	..	0	0	0	0	0	0	0
2300 Selfemployed or nonemployed	460	1 841	10 210	20 420	29 729	36 008	41 870	50 256	51 763	53 922
Payments total	460	1 841	10 210	20 420	29 729	36 008	41 870	50 256	51 763	53 922
2310 On a payroll basis of self/non-employed SSC	..	..	..	20 420	29 729	36 008	41 870	50 256	51 763	53 922
2320 On an income tax basis of self/non-employed SSC	..	..	..	0	0	0	0	0	0	0
2400 Unallocable between 2100, 2200 and 2300	0	0	0	0	0	0	0	0	0	0
2410 On a payroll basis unallocable between 2100, 2200 and 2300 SSC	..	..	..	..	..	..	..	..	..	..
2420 On an income tax basis unallocable between 2100, 2200 and 2300 SSC	..	..	..	..	..	..	..	..	..	..
3000 Taxes on payroll and workforce	477	445	0	0	0	0	0	0	0	0
Payroll tax	477	445	..	..	..	..	..	..	..	..
4000 Taxes on property	4 313	9 414	15 321	17 505	21 874	21 011	32 439	42 427	44 831	43 244
4100 Recurrent taxes on immovable property	1 079	2 968	4 461	8 849	10 714	11 314	13 214	14 675	14 985	15 282
4110 Households	644	1 187	1 784	3 540	4 286	4 526	5 286	5 870	5 994	6 113
4120 Others	435	1 780	2 676	5 309	6 428	6 788	7 928	8 805	8 991	9 169
4200 Recurrent taxes on net wealth	2 530	4 362	6 213	433	5	2	1 686	1 517	1 758	1 614
4210 Individual	973	977	1 425	191	2	1	- 1	0	0	0
General wealth tax	471	954	1 425	191	2	1	- 1	..	..	..
Equalization of war burden	502	23	0	0	0	0	0	..	..	..
4220 Corporate	1 557	3 385	4 788	242	3	1	1 687	1 517	1 758	1 614
General wealth tax	490	1 431	1 813	242	3	1	- 1	0	0	0
Equalization of war burden	350	15	0	0	0	0	0	0	0	0
Enterprise tax	717	1 939	2 975	0	0	0	0	0	0	0
Bank levy	0	0	0	0	0	0	0	21	30	30
Contribution to Deposit Protection Fund	0	0	0	0	0	0	1 688	1 496	1 728	1 584
4300 Estate, inheritance and gift taxes	162	520	1 545	2 982	4 203	4 405	6 290	8 657	9 775	9 226
4310 Estate and inheritance taxes	134	416	1 359	2 624	3 699	3 876	5 535	7 618	8 602	8 119
4320 Gift taxes	28	104	186	358	504	529	755	1 039	1 173	1 107
4400 Taxes on financial and capital transactions	542	1 564	3 103	5 241	6 952	5 290	11 249	17 578	18 313	17 122
Real property transfer tax	150	521	1 999	5 081	6 952	5 290	11 249	17 578	18 313	17 122
Additional real property transfer	198	680	148	160	0	0	0	0	0	0
Capital transfer tax	111	200	807	0	0	0	0	0	0	0
Bill of exchange tax	83	163	149	0	0	0	0	0	0	0
4500 Nonrecurrent taxes	0	0	0	0	0	0	0	0	0	0

	1965	1980	1990	2000	2007	2010	2015	2020	2021	2022
4510 On net wealth	..	..	..	..	..	..	..	..	..	..
4520 Other nonrecurrent taxes	..	..	..	..	..	..	..	..	..	..
4600 Other recurrent taxes on property	0	0	0	0	0	0	0	0	0	0
5000 Taxes on goods and services	24 462	77 863	121 577	218 686	275 941	286 579	342 649	356 986	396 328	420 346
5100 Taxes on production, sale, transfer, etc	23 079	74 406	117 209	211 444	259 598	269 863	323 865	336 002	375 524	389 159
5110 General taxes	12 235	47 779	75 459	140 871	170 387	180 533	211 936	221 882	260 654	289 962
5111 Value added taxes	0	47 779	75 459	140 871	170 387	180 533	211 936	221 882	260 654	289 962
5112 Sales tax	0	0	0	0	0	0	0	0	0	0
5113 Other	12 235	0	0	0	0	0	0	0	0	0
Turnover tax old	11 028	..	..	..	..	..	..	..	..	..
Old turnover tax on import	1 208	..	..	..	..	..	..	..	..	..
5120 Taxes on specific goods and services	10 844	26 627	41 750	70 573	88 859	88 990	111 637	113 884	114 618	98 937
5121 Excises	8 213	20 566	31 158	57 224	72 018	72 163	88 111	88 504	87 868	67 575
Duty on mineral oils	3 798	10 917	17 701	37 826	38 877	39 601	39 605	37 703	37 191	33 340
Duty on power	0	0	0	3 356	6 439	6 167	6 560	6 569	6 730	6 813
Duty on tobacco	2 402	5 771	8 898	11 443	14 108	13 453	14 963	14 789	14 673	14 152
Duty on alcohol	771	1 986	2 162	2 151	2 172	2 052	2 075	2 098	2 208	2 176
Duty on beer	501	645	693	843	750	708	679	572	582	597
Duty on coffee	488	756	986	1 087	985	998	1 034	1 070	1 058	1 057
Duty on sugar	59	72	79	0	0	0	0	0	0	0
Duty on tea	16	32	31	0	0	0	0	0	0	0
Duty on salt	20	20	23	0	0	0	0	0	0	0
Duty on electric lamps	34	63	83	0	0	0	0	0	0	0
Duty on playing cards	2	4	0	0	0	0	0	0	0	0
Duty on beverages	46	22	8	6	1	0	0	0	0	0
Duty on acetic acid	3	2	0	0	0	0	0	0	0	0
Duty on champagne	69	274	494	512	451	462	416	391	381	390
Duty on matches	5	2	0	0	0	0	0	0	0	0
Duty on ice cream	1	0	0	0	0	0	0	0	0	0
EEG surcharge			0	0	7 594	8 326	22 025	23 044	22 624	6 595
KWKG surcharge			0	0	641	396	571	853	933	986
Offshore-network surcharge			0	0	0	0	183	1 415	1 488	1 469
5122 Profits of fiscal monopolies	8	2	0	0	0	0	0	0	0	0
5123 Customs and import duties	1 658	3 125	3 847	3 394	3 774	4 212	5 180	4 734	5 300	6 708
Monetary compensation accounts	0	368	1	0	0	0	0	0	0	0
Customs (mainly UE)	1 294	2 353	3 662	3 394	3 774	4 212	5 180	4 734	5 300	6 708
Agricultural levies UE	364	404	184	0	0	0	0	0	0	0
5124 Taxes on exports	0	0	0	0	0	0	0	0	0	0
5125 Taxes on investment goods	0	0	0	0	0	0	0	0	0	0
5126 Taxes on specific services	942	2 689	6 443	9 599	13 095	12 583	18 306	20 645	21 447	24 653
Duty transport goods on residents	0	0	0	0	0	0	0	0	0	0
Transport tax	452	0	0	0	0	0	0	0	0	0
Insurance tax	198	910	2 266	7 243	10 410	10 261	12 445	14 551	14 955	15 684
Fire insurance tax	33	124	200	288	319	326	413	510	537	580
Entertainment tax	55	44	140	267	210	376	881	746	433	872
Taxes on betting and gambling	204	655	1 046	1 801	1 702	1 412	1 711	2 043	2 332	2 569
Tax on electricity bills	0	956	2 792	0	0	0	0	0	0	0
Aviation tax	0	0	0	0	0	0	1 027	349	539	1 168
Gaming casinos levy	0	0	0	0	454	208	251	216	161	404
SRF Contributions			0	0	0	0	1 578	2 230	2 490	3 376
5127 Other taxes on internat. trade and transactions	0	0	4	5	1	2	2	1	2	2
5128 Other taxes	24	244	298	351	- 29	30	38	0	1	- 1
Levies CECA	24	56	36	0	0	0	0	..	0	0
Cotisation sugar UE	0	112	224	351	- 29	30	38	..	1	- 1
Levy on milk	0	75	38	0	0	0	0	..	0	0
5130 Unallocable between 5110 and 5120	0	0	0	0	352	340	292	236	252	260
Contributions to the German National Petroleum Stockpiling Agency	..	..	..	..	352	340	292	236	252	260
5200 Taxes on use of goods and perform activities	1 383	3 457	4 368	7 242	16 343	16 716	18 784	20 984	20 804	31 187
5210 Recurrent taxes	1 369	3 454	4 368	7 239	16 343	16 189	18 034	17 821	18 142	18 224
5211 Paid by households: motor vehicles	614	1 892	2 950	5 177	6 823	6 447	6 992	7 439	7 389	7 307
5212 Paid by others: motor vehicles	728	1 475	1 300	1 838	2 075	2 041	1 812	2 089	2 158	2 192
5213 Paid in respect of other goods	27	87	118	224	7 445	7 701	9 230	8 293	8 595	8 725
Dog taxes	24	75	101	198	240	258	322	380	401	414
Hunting and fishing taxes	4	13	17	26	23	19	10	8	7	7
Nuclear fuel tax	0	0	0	0	0	0	1 018	0	0	0

	1965	1980	1990	2000	2007	2010	2015	2020	2021	2022
Licence fee (private households)	0	0	0	0	6 464	6 681	7 155	7 178	7 433	7 540
Licence fee (companies)	0	0	0	0	718	743	725	727	754	764
5220 Nonrecurrent taxes	14	3	1	3	0	527	750	3 163	2 662	12 963
Non-recurrent taxes	..	..	0	0	..	0	0	0	0	0
CO2 emission certificates	..	..	0	0	..	527	750	3 163	2 662	12 963
5300 Unallocable between 5100 and 5200	0	0	0	0	0	0	0	0	0	0
6000 Other taxes	172	172	160	165	96	100	216	208	256	358
6100 Paid solely by business	0	0	0	0	0	0	0	0	0	0
6200 Other	172	172	160	165	96	100	216	208	256	358
Custom duties collected for the EU	..	..	3 662	3 394	3 774	4 212	5 180	4 734	5 300	6 708
SRF Contributions collected for the EU			..	..	..	..	1 578	2 230	2 490	3 376
Taxes and compulsory social security contributions paid by EU civil servants			..	..	..	..	43	56	64	66
Taxes paid by EU civil servants: income taxes			..	..	..	..	22	29	33	34
Taxes paid by EU civil servants: compulsory social security contributions			..	..	..	..	21	27	31	32
Non-wastable tax credits against 1110	..	..	..	38 356	43 602	45 475	41 951	51 861	52 038	51 685
Tax expenditure component	..	..	..	..	29 499	28 268	26 817	32 398	32 866	33 115
Transfer component	..	..	..	..	14 104	17 207	15 134	19 463	19 172	18 569
Non-wastable tax credits against 1210	..	..	..	962	804	802	200	- 2	16	136
Tax expenditure component	..	..	..	..	348	326	120	0	16	130
Transfer component	..	..	..	..	456	474	80	- 2	0	6
Total tax revenue on cash basis	74 359	287 373	454 764	767 045	889 756	919 842	1 149 760	1 314 335	1 427 656	1 521 716
Total tax revenue on accrual basis	..	..	..	..	892 257	919 827	1 151 532	1 315 613	1 439 067	1 537 045
Additional taxes included in National Accounts	..	..	..	..	2 179	1 799	2 624	2 421	2 641	2 687
Several duties, administrative fees and other revenues	..	..	..	..	2 179	1 799	2 624	2 421	2 641	2 687
Taxes excluded from National Accounts	..	..	..	..	0	0	0	..	..	..
Difference in treatment of tax credits	..	..	..	..	12 623	9 230	5 619	7 532	6 696	6 008
Capital transfer for uncollected revenue	..	..	..	..	0	0	0	..	..	..
Voluntary social security contributions	..	..	..	..	21 409	5 102	6 068	7 399	7 937	8 295
Miscellaneous differences	..	..	..	..	33 339	34 336	35 647	49 615	48 625	49 196
National Accounts: Taxes and actual social contributions	..	..	..	..	961 807	970 294	1 201 490	1 382 580	1 504 966	1 603 231
Imputed social contributions	..	..	..	..	29 511	32 705	34 533	41 380	42 401	43 969
National Accounts: Taxes and all social contributions	..	..	..	..	991 318	1 002 999	1 236 023	1 423 960	1 547 367	1 647 200

.. Not available

Note: Year ending 31st December.

From 2002 data are on accrual basis.

The tax revenues for Germany refer to the old Länder until 1990 and to all Germany beginning in 1991.

Heading 1000: In the years up to 2000, the revenues shown take into account the whole amount of non-wastable tax credits including that part paid out by the tax authorities which should, under the OECD criteria, be treated as expenditure. From 2001, the data necessary to make the adjustment have become available and the revenue figures comply with the OECD criteria from that year.

Heading for non-wastable tax credits against 1110 comprise child tax credits (paid out of wage tax revenue), tax credits for owner occupied housing (paid out of assessed income tax revenue), retirement allowance ("Riester allowance", paid out of wage tax revenue), investment tax credits for unincorporated businesses (for investment in former East Germany; paid out of assessed income tax revenue), research allowance for unincorporated businesses (paid out of assessed income tax revenue) and employee savings allowance.

Heading for non-wastable tax credits against 1210 are investment tax credits for incorporated businesses (for investment in former East Germany; paid out of corporate income tax revenue) and research allowance for incorporated businesses (paid out of corporate income tax revenue).

Source: Finanzbericht, Bonn; Tax Statistics. Unpublished estimates by the Ministry of Finance.

Table 5.14. Greece: Details of tax revenue, 1965-2022

Million EUR

	1965	1980	1990	2000	2007	2010	2015	2020	2021	2022
Total tax revenue	116	1 475	11 472	47 211	73 990	72 414	65 162	65 196	72 674	85 153
Total tax revenue exclusive of taxes collected for the EU	..	..	11 361	46 990	73 683	72 134	64 887	64 854	72 299	84 603
1000 Taxes on income, profits and capital gains	11	286	2 283	12 662	17 176	15 953	14 586	13 462	15 170	17 461
1100 Of individuals	8	220	1 619	6 127	10 554	9 015	10 155	10 447	10 833	11 549
1110 On income and profits	8	220	1 619	6 102	10 500	8 948	10 047	10 359	10 705	11 432
Personal income tax	..	..	1 414	..	..	..	..	..	..	..
Receipts from previous years	..	..	62	..	..	..	..	..	..	..
Agricultural social security fund	..	..	143	..	..	..	..	..	..	..
1120 On capital gains	0	0	0	25	54	67	108	88	128	117
1200 Corporate	2	56	631	5 625	5 304	5 717	3 800	2 350	3 634	5 127
1210 On profits	2	56	631	5 625	5 304	5 717	3 800	2 350	3 634	5 127
Corporation income tax	2	39	553	..	..	..	..	..	..	..
Receipts from previous years	0	8	33	..	..	..	..	..	..	..
Agricultural social security fund	0	9	46	..	..	..	..	..	..	..
1220 On capital gains	0	0	0	0	0	0	0	0	0	0
1300 Unallocable between 1100 and 1200	1	10	32	910	1 318	1 221	631	665	703	785
Extraordinary taxes	0	10	32	..	..	..	..	..	..	..
Other taxes on income and profits	1	0	0	..	..	..	..	..	..	..
2000 Social security contributions	37	485	3 466	14 284	24 940	24 748	18 807	21 352	23 417	25 186
2100 Employees	15	214	1 735	7 629	13 417	13 292	11 095	11 622	12 215	13 619
2110 On a payroll basis	..	..	..	..	..	..	..	..	..	..
2120 On an income tax basis	..	..	..	..	..	..	..	..	..	..
2200 Employers	14	213	1 728	6 655	11 523	11 456	7 712	9 730	11 202	11 567
2210 On a payroll basis of employers SSC	..	..	..	..	..	..	..	..	..	..
2220 On an income tax basis of employers SSC	..	..	..	..	..	..	..	..	..	..
2300 Selfemployed or nonemployed	0	0	3	0	0	0	0	0	0	0
2310 On a payroll basis of self/non-employed SSC	..	..	..	..	..	..	..	..	..	..
2320 On an income tax basis of self/non-employed SSC	..	..	..	..	..	..	..	..	..	..
2400 Unallocable between 2100, 2200 and 2300	7	58	0	0	0	0	0	0	0	0
2410 On a payroll basis unallocable between 2100, 2200 and 2300 SSC	..	..	..	..	..	..	..	..	..	..
2420 On an income tax basis unallocable between 2100, 2200 and 2300 SSC	..	..	..	..	..	..	..	..	..	..
3000 Taxes on payroll and workforce	1	27	79	0	0	0	0	0	0	0
4000 Taxes on property	11	68	532	3 631	4 908	3 741	5 418	5 042	5 290	5 659
4100 Recurrent taxes on immovable property	0	4	22	372	709	553	3 592	3 068	3 200	3 173
4110 Households	0	3	22	..	..	..	..	..	..	..
4120 Others	0	1	0	..	..	..	..	..	..	..
Taxes on immovable property	0	0	..	..	..	..	..	..	..	..
4200 Recurrent taxes on net wealth	0	0	0	714	1 208	1 272	1 083	1 161	1 157	1 294
4210 Individual	..	..	..	..	..	..	..	..	..	..
4220 Corporate	..	..	..	..	..	..	..	..	..	..
4300 Estate, inheritance and gift taxes	1	18	141	372	208	165	134	169	198	232
4310 Estate and inheritance taxes	1	13	85	..	..	..	..	..	..	..
4320 Gift taxes	0	4	55	..	..	..	..	..	..	..
4400 Taxes on financial and capital transactions	10	44	368	2 035	2 556	1 146	547	630	722	945
Stamp and transaction taxes	10	41	368	2 035	2 556	1 146	547	630	722	945
Receipts from previous years	0	3	0	0	0	0	0	0	0	0
4500 Nonrecurrent taxes	0	2	1	27	0	1	0	0	0	0
4510 On net wealth	0	0	0	..	..	..	..	..	..	..
4520 Other nonrecurrent taxes	0	2	1	..	..	..	..	..	..	..
4600 Other recurrent taxes on property	0	0	0	111	227	604	62	14	13	15
5000 Taxes on goods and services	57	608	5 109	16 634	26 966	27 972	26 351	25 340	28 797	36 847
5100 Taxes on production, sale, transfer, etc	51	564	4 881	14 797	24 541	25 505	22 131	21 736	24 561	32 194
5110 General taxes	12	194	3 040	9 234	17 020	16 504	13 077	13 008	15 291	18 854
5111 Value added taxes	0	0	2 821	8 927	16 511	15 958	12 885	12 925	15 160	18 621
5112 Sales tax	9	185	123	0	0	0	0	0	0	0
5113 Other	2	9	96	307	509	546	192	83	131	233
Other taxes on goods and services	1	9	34	307	509	546	192	83	131	233
Receipts from previous years	1	0	62	0	0	0	0	0	0	0
5120 Taxes on specific goods and services	39	370	1 789	5 526	7 407	8 922	8 953	8 693	9 226	13 296
5121 Excises	20	165	1 372	4 069	5 876	7 567	7 580	6 944	7 490	7 797
Duty on tobacco products	8	45	357	1 769	2 657	2 712	2 365	2 081	2 148	2 190
Duty on alcohol and spirits	1	7	50	262	334	501	393	375	467	547
Duty on beer			0	61	60	120	105	151	175	188
Duty on other alcoholic drinks			0	201	274	381	288	224	292	359
Duty on mineral oil	7	75	637	2 016	2 878	4 242	3 971	3 607	3 852	4 021
Duty on sugar	3	6	0	0	0	0	0	0	0	0

	1965	1980	1990	2000	2007	2010	2015	2020	2021	2022
Duty on coton and other products	0	30	328	22	7	112	851	881	1 023	1 039
5122 Profits of fiscal monopolies	2	6	0	0	0	0	0	0	0	0
5123 Customs and import duties	12	94	112	220	314	279	181	255	305	432
Import duties	11	90	111	220	314	279	181	255	305	432
Agricultural social security fund	1	5	1	0	0	0	0	0	0	0
5124 Taxes on exports	0	1	1	0	0	0	0	0	27	0
5125 Taxes on investment goods	0	0	0	0	0	0	0	0	0	0
5126 Taxes on specific services	2	47	293	1 237	1 217	1 076	1 192	1 494	1 404	5 067
5127 Other taxes on internat. trade and transactions	0	0	0	0	0	0	0	0	0	0
5128 Other taxes	4	58	10	0	0	0	0	0	0	0
Agricultural social security fund	2	..	0	..	..	..	..	..	..	..
Other taxes	2	..	0	..	..	..	..	..	..	..
5130 Unallocable between 5110 and 5120	0	0	52	37	114	79	101	35	44	44
5200 Taxes on use of goods and perform activities	6	44	228	1 320	2 169	1 682	3 218	2 941	3 578	3 950
5210 Recurrent taxes	5	24	219	1 320	2 169	1 682	3 218	2 941	3 578	3 950
Motor vehicle tax	5	0	0	0	0	0	0	0	0	0
5211 Paid by households: motor vehicles	..	23	210	281	598	825	780	789	801	800
5212 Paid by others: motor vehicles	..	0	8	735	1 182	272	207	240	296	384
5213 Paid in respect of other goods	0	1	1	304	389	585	2 231	1 912	2 481	2 766
Taxes on boats/ships	0	0	1	0	0	0	0	0	0	0
5220 Nonrecurrent taxes	1	20	9	0	0	0	0	0	0	0
Exceptional tax on construction of buildings	0	..	9	..	..	..	..	..	..	..
Building permits	0	..	0	..	..	..	..	..	..	..
5300 Unallocable between 5100 and 5200	0	0	0	517	256	785	1 002	663	658	703
6000 Other taxes	0	1	3	0	0	0	0	0	0	0
6100 Paid solely by business	..	0	0	..	..	..	..	..	..	..
6200 Other	..	1	3	..	..	..	..	..	..	..
Custom duties collected for the EU	..	..	100	210	307	278	181	255	284	429
SRF Contributions collected for the EU			..	..	..	..	92	87	91	121
Total tax revenue on cash basis	116	1 475	11 472	45 979	72 429	73 083	63 210	62 172	69 344	77 582
Total tax revenue on accrual basis	..	..	..	47 211	73 990	72 414	65 162	65 196	72 674	85 153
Additional taxes included in National Accounts	..	..	..	0	0	0	0	0	0	0
Taxes excluded from National Accounts	..	..	..	0	0	0	0	0	0	0
Difference in treatment of tax credits	..	..	..	0	0	0	0	0	0	0
Capital transfer for uncollected revenue	..	..	..	0	0	0	0	0	0	0
Tax (Employer's actual social contributions)	..	..	..	..	..	..	..	..	0	0
Tax (Employee's actual social contributions)	..	..	..	..	..	..	..	..	0	0
Voluntary social security contributions	..	..	..	0	0	0	0	0	0	0
Miscellaneous differences	..	..	..	0	0	0	0	0	0	0
National Accounts: Taxes and actual social contributions	..	..	..	47 211	73 990	72 414	65 162	65 196	72 674	85 153
Imputed social contributions	..	..	..	2 055	3 952	4 952	5 615	4 086	3 856	3 855
National Accounts: Taxes and all social contributions	..	..	..	49 266	77 942	77 366	70 777	69 282	76 530	89 008

.. Not available

Note: Year ending 31st December.

From 1998 data are on accrual basis.

Source: Ministry of Finance, General accounting Office, Directorate of General Government Budget in collaboration with the National Statistical Authority (ELSTAT).

Table 5.15. Hungary: Details of tax revenue, 1965-2022

Million HUF

	1965	1980	1990	2000	2007	2010	2015	2020	2021	2022
Total tax revenue	..	..	..	5 132 570	10 098 955	10 121 687	13 519 622	17 425 190	18 646 419	23 181 302
Total tax revenue exclusive of custom duties	..	..	..	5 132 570	10 055 315	10 096 033	13 479 897	17 361 695	18 573 604	23 076 449
1000 Taxes on income, profits and capital gains	..	..	..	1 247 420	2 539 389	2 093 830	2 425 958	3 165 880	3 011 836	4 618 426
1100 Of individuals	..	..	..	954 698	1 838 563	1 764 082	1 824 671	2 543 593	2 254 978	3 524 479
1110 On income and profits	..	..	..	954 698	1 838 563	1 764 082	1 824 671	2 543 593	2 254 978	3 524 479
1120 On capital gains	..	..	..	0	0	0	0	0	0	0
1200 Corporate	..	..	..	292 722	700 826	329 748	601 287	622 287	756 858	1 093 947
Corporate income tax	..	..	..	292 722	510 781	323 370	539 777	549 822	674 002	866 241
Research and development fund levy	..	..	..	0	0	0	0	0	0	0
Credit institutions' special tax	..	..	..	0	10 890	21 618	19 902	8 842	5 580	8 729
Separate tax for companies	..	..	..	0	178 598	- 32 390	0	0	0	0
Medicine tax	..	..	..	0	558	163	0	0	0	0
Energy corporations' special tax	..	..	..	0	0	16 987	41 608	63 623	77 276	218 977
1210 On profits	..	..	..	..	..	..	..	..	..	..
1220 On capital gains	..	..	..	..	..	..	..	..	..	..
1300 Unallocable between 1100 and 1200	..	..	..	0	0	0	0	0	0	0
Interest withholding	..	..	..	..	..	..	..	..	..	..
2000 Social security contributions	..	..	..	1 506 755	3 402 194	3 179 509	4 433 464	5 364 400	5 781 454	6 481 845
2100 Employees	..	..	..	275 323	941 682	1 112 583	1 770 923	2 813 766	3 165 758	3 829 813
Pensions	..	..	..	150 585	336 855	537 556	969 908	1 539 523	1 731 635	2 093 935
Health	..	..	..	81 874	513 633	467 208	656 147	1 046 999	1 181 988	1 430 647
Unemployment	..	..	..	42 864	91 194	107 819	144 868	227 244	252 135	305 231
2110 On a payroll basis	..	..	..	..	..	..	..	..	..	..
2120 On an income tax basis	..	..	..	..	..	..	..	..	..	..
2200 Employers	..	..	..	1 213 190	2 402 941	2 043 771	2 637 330	2 521 328	2 585 742	2 619 374
Pensions	..	..	..	734 456	1 508 490	1 800 864	2 235 536	1 781 571	1 824 993	1 846 964
Health	..	..	..	385 019	693 705	169 202	398 618	738 365	759 253	770 186
Unemployment	..	..	..	93 715	200 746	73 705	3 176	1 392	1 496	2 224
2210 On a payroll basis of employers SSC	..	..	..	..	..	..	..	..	..	..
2220 On an income tax basis of employers SSC	..	..	..	..	..	..	..	..	..	..
2300 Selfemployed or nonemployed	..	..	..	873	2 534	0	0	0	0	0
Pensions: of which	..	..	..	0	0	..	..	..	..	..
Self-employed	..	..	..	0	0	..	..	..	..	..
Unemployed	..	..	..	0	0	..	..	..	..	..
Retired	..	..	..	0	0	..	..	..	..	..
Other	..	..	..	0	0	..	..	..	..	..
Health: of which	..	..	..	873	2 534	..	..	..	..	..
Self-employed	..	..	..	873	2 534	..	..	..	..	..
Unemployed	..	..	..	0	0	..	..	..	..	..
Retired	..	..	..	0	0	..	..	..	..	..
Other	..	..	..	0	0	..	..	..	..	..
2310 On a payroll basis of self/non-employed SSC	..	..	..	..	..	..	..	..	..	..
2320 On an income tax basis of self/non-employed SSC	..	..	..	..	..	..	..	..	..	..
2400 Unallocable between 2100, 2200 and 2300	..	..	..	17 368	55 037	23 155	25 211	29 306	29 954	32 658
2410 On a payroll basis unallocable between 2100, 2200 and 2300 SSC	..	..	..	..	..	..	..	..	..	..
2420 On an income tax basis unallocable between 2100, 2200 and 2300 SSC	..	..	..	..	..	..	..	..	..	..
3000 Taxes on payroll and workforce	..	..	..	183 430	82 068	113 689	241 750	501 292	598 811	472 433
Rehabilitation contribution	..	..	..	2 184	13 559	56 004	67 460	107 943	113 893	138 103
Training levy	..	..	..	13 186	36 612	47 083	96 427	140 481	162 573	106
Wage guarantee contribution	..	..	..	0	0	0	0	0	0	0
Communal tax on enterprises	..	..	..	1 192	1 261	1 170	0	0	0	0
Health contribution	..	..	..	166 869	20 427	0	0	0	0	0
Medicine tax	..	..	..	0	10 209	9 431	10 283	9 543	8 574	8 886
Tax on home-workers	..	..	..	0	0	1	29	20	19	17
Lump sum tax for small taxpayers	..	..	..	0	0	0	55 409	158 736	197 020	175 899
Small business tax				0	0	0	12 142	84 569	116 732	149 422
4000 Taxes on property				89 024	202 711	312 059	437 329	507 379	482 670	531 943
4100 Recurrent taxes on immovable property	..	..	..	30 810	72 071	92 525	200 906	224 590	235 959	238 114
Land tax	..	..	..	0	0	0	0	0	0	0
Building tax	..	..	..	22 262	54 556	71 025	111 963	130 529	137 766	140 310
Development land tax	..	..	..	3 099	6 900	9 861	19 102	26 168	28 324	28 189
Communal tax on recreational howes	..	..	..	893	1 412	1 515	26	0	0	0
Communal tax on households	..	..	..	4 557	9 069	10 124	13 451	14 770	15 047	15 291

	1965	1980	1990	2000	2007	2010	2015	2020	2021	2022
Luxury tax	..	..	..	0	134	0	0	0	0	0
Public utility tax	..	..	..	0	0	0	55 906	52 502	54 127	53 495
Community tax	..	..	..	0	0	0	458	621	695	829
4110 Households	..	..	..	..	..	..	..	..	..	..
4120 Others	..	..	..	..	..	..	..	..	..	..
4200 Recurrent taxes on net wealth	..	..	..	0	0	135 652	135 661	108 104	52 308	66 657
Surtax payable by financial institutions	..	..	..	..	..	135 652	135 661	108 104	52 308	66 657
4210 Individual	..	..	..	..	..	..	..	..	..	..
4220 Corporate	..	..	..	..	..	..	..	..	..	..
4300 Estate, inheritance and gift taxes	..	..	..	5 460	13 175	6 264	7 373	9 493	9 132	11 399
4310 Estate and inheritance taxes	..	..	..	4 020	10 775	4 243	6 230	8 026	7 255	9 289
Inheritance tax-local	..	..	..	2 010	4 658	1 858	0	0	0	0
Inheritance tax-central	..	..	..	2 010	6 117	2 385	6 230	8 026	7 255	9 289
4320 Gift taxes	..	..	..	1 440	2 400	2 021	1 143	1 467	1 877	2 110
Gift tax-local	..	..	..	720	1 038	885	0	0	0	0
Gift tax-central	..	..	..	720	1 363	1 136	1 143	1 467	1 877	2 110
4400 Taxes on financial and capital transactions	..	..	..	52 754	117 465	77 618	93 389	165 192	185 271	215 773
Property transfer tax-local	..	..	..	26 349	50 783	33 990	0	0	0	0
Property transfer tax-central	..	..	..	26 405	66 682	43 628	93 389	165 192	185 271	215 773
4500 Nonrecurrent taxes	..	..	..	0	0	0	0	0	0	0
4510 On net wealth	..	..	..	..	..	..	..	..	..	..
4520 Other nonrecurrent taxes	..	..	..	..	..	..	..	..	..	..
4600 Other recurrent taxes on property	..	..	..	0	0	0	0	0	0	0
5000 Taxes on goods and services	..	..	..	2 081 439	3 832 361	4 383 865	5 936 435	7 863 946	8 790 416	11 002 045
5100 Taxes on production, sale, transfer, etc	..	..	..	2 052 712	3 751 218	4 272 312	5 798 298	7 645 017	8 550 634	10 716 185
5110 General taxes	..	..	..	1 340 572	2 622 027	3 010 781	4 099 741	5 632 941	6 420 284	7 796 722
5111 Value added taxes	..	..	..	1 153 750	2 013 271	2 325 608	3 309 540	4 717 048	5 460 243	6 691 200
5112 Sales tax	..	..	..	0	0	37 795	50 635	96 406	110 311	104 266
Public health product tax	..	..	..	..	..	0	29 882	57 685	66 346	77 272
Hydrocarbons stockholding fee	..	..	..	..	..	37 795	20 753	38 721	43 965	26 994
5113 Other	..	..	..	186 823	608 756	647 378	739 566	819 487	849 730	1 001 256
Local tax on company sales	..	..	..	186 823	427 134	443 093	584 380	729 000	754 982	890 118
Simplified business tax	..	..	..	0	152 812	181 880	89 406	1 690	0	0
Research and development contribution	..	..	..	0	28 810	22 405	65 780	88 797	94 748	111 138
5120 Taxes on specific goods and services	..	..	..	712 140	1 129 192	1 261 531	1 698 557	2 012 076	2 130 350	2 919 463
5121 Excises	..	..	..	533 502	969 730	929 881	1 119 189	1 318 427	1 352 067	1 389 645
Road fund petrol tax	..	..	..	0	0	0	0	0	0	0
Alcohol production duty	..	..	..	3 848	5 621	3 021	8 007	6 535	3 043	79
Water fund tax	..	..	..	6 017	13 171	14 444	12 305	12 632	12 425	12 652
Forestry fund tax	..	..	..	2 858	3 353	284	0	0	0	0
Environment petrol tax	..	..	..	14 837	19 447	17 274	65 534	74 825	83 568	87 649
Budget excises (central budget)	..	..	..	505 942	916 869	877 778	1 015 555	1 207 253	1 232 865	1 270 278
Coffee	..	..	..	3 200	0	0	0	0	0	0
Alcohol	..	..	..	53 500	88 600	83 078	87 369	90 640	97 549	119 759
Tobacco	..	..	..	107 000	252 400	251 778	321 922	409 123	399 787	504 137
Petrol	..	..	..	156 000	218 200	216 728	206 220	227 025	239 539	214 283
Diesel	..	..	..	157 000	256 600	293 588	375 026	459 231	477 138	414 577
Other oil	..	..	..	6 000	2 200	2 567	3 608	1 711	1 882	1 796
Other budget excises	..	..	..	30 343	93 442	30 039	21 410	19 523	16 970	15 726
Energy tax	..	..	..	0	11 269	17 080	17 788	17 182	20 166	18 987
5122 Profits of fiscal monopolies	..	..	..	0	0	0	0	0	0	0
5123 Customs and import duties	..	..	..	137 730	37 174	33 446	52 395	79 357	96 177	141 761
Customs duties	..	..	..	137 730	37 174	33 446	52 395	79 357	96 177	141 761
5124 Taxes on exports	..	..	..	0	0	0	0	0	0	0
5125 Taxes on investment goods	..	..	..	0	0	0	0	0	0	0
5126 Taxes on specific services	..	..	..	40 908	106 629	297 554	465 479	590 136	649 330	1 344 563
Gambling tax	..	..	..	27 935	71 804	62 718	44 972	48 956	39 237	57 073
Tourism tax	..	..	..	4 379	0	0	0	0	0	0
Communal tourism tax	..	..	..	2 943	4 935	5 798	10 475	3 953	6 815	16 599
Cultural contribution	..	..	..	4 387	8 432	1 096	127	0	0	0
Pork slaughterhouse tax	..	..	..	32	0	0	0	0	0	0
Breeding contribution	..	..	..	899	919	0	0	0	0	0
Medicine tax	..	..	..	0	19 789	28 104	45 529	53 064	53 447	70 979
Surtax payable by financial institutions	..	..	..	0	0	39 611	4 155	3 513	3 833	251 660
Specific sectors' surtax	..	..	..	0	0	151 693	285	0	0	0
Telecommunication services tax	..	..	..	0	0	0	54 516	58 709	57 793	95 903
Accident tax	..	..	..	0	0	0	27 694	- 10	0	0
Insurance tax	..	..	..	0	0	4 018	30 108	97 220	105 121	171 235
Financial transaction levy	..	..	..	0	0	0	205 616	213 979	235 246	300 035
Waste dumping contribution	..	..	..	0	0	0	11 123	15 473	16 078	15 752
Advertising tax	..	..	..	0	0	0	5 675	0	0	0
Protection Fund levies (KA)				0	0	0	0	4 744	4 814	4 752

	1965	1980	1990	2000	2007	2010	2015	2020	2021	2022
Departure tax				0	0	0	0	0	0	17 899
Tourism development contribution				0	0	0	0	7 445	339	38 330
Protection Fund levies (BEVA)	..	..	..	0	0	1 036	2 600	7 624	7 714	8 933
Protection Fund levies (OBA)	..	..	..	0	0	2 435	14 391	10 027	13 536	99 943
Protection Fund levies (Resolution Fund)	..	..	..	0	0	0	7 290	16 576	23 634	17 376
Protection Fund Levies (PGA)				332	750	1 045	0	0	0	0
Retail tax				0	0	0	0	47 637	78 594	176 748
Protection Fund levies (SZHTKA)	..	..	..	0	0	0	923	1 226	3 129	1 346
5127 Other taxes on internat. trade and transactions	..	..	..	0	0	0	0	0	0	0
Previous differential producer's turnover tax	..	..	..	..	..	..	..	..	..	..
5128 Other taxes	..	..	..	0	15 659	650	61 494	24 156	32 776	43 494
Sugar duty	..	..	..	..	15 659	650	765	0	0	0
Payments by companies in the energy sector (MAVIR)				..	0	0	60 729	24 156	32 776	43 494
5130 Unallocable between 5110 and 5120	..	..	..	0	0	0	0	0	0	0
5200 Taxes on use of goods and perform activities	..	..	..	28 727	81 143	111 553	138 137	218 929	239 782	285 860
5210 Recurrent taxes	..	..	..	25 454	74 268	106 903	130 238	206 069	223 463	269 487
Tax on domestically registered vehicles-local	..	..	..	12 622	62 432	71 112	73 248	85 563	95 038	95 944
Tax on domestically registered vehicles-extra budget	..	..	..	0	0	0	0	0	0	0
Tax on domestically registered vehicles-central	..	..	..	8 250	0	79	0	0	0	0
Tax on foreign registered vehicles extra budget fund	..	..	..	0	0	0	0	0	0	0
Tax on foreign registered vehicles-central	..	..	..	3 078	1 655	1 397	0	0	0	0
Company car tax	..	..	..	0	0	25 867	31 570	37 511	39 689	58 544
5211 Paid by households: motor vehicles	..	..	..	0	0	0	0	0	0	0
5212 Paid by others: motor vehicles	..	..	..	0	0	0	0	0	0	0
5213 Paid in respect of other goods	..	..	..	1 504	10 181	8 448	25 420	82 995	88 736	114 999
Environmental protection fee	..	..	..	5	13	27	0	0	0	0
Fishing development contribution	..	..	..	40	104	0	0	0	0	0
Environmental protection charge	..	..	..	0	8 785	7 653	6 680	6 357	6 181	6 152
Air pollution levy	..	..	..	751	610	53	0	0	0	0
Water pollution levy	..	..	..	225	186	0	0	0	0	0
Toxic waste levy	..	..	..	65	42	130	0	0	0	0
Noise abatement levy	..	..	..	13	8	19	0	0	0	0
Unidentified environmental protection levies paid to local governments	..	..	..	404	433	566	265	155	155	139
Sale of emission allowances	..	..	..	0	0	0	17 479	74 177	79 585	102 919
Carbon dioxide quota tax				0	0	0	0	0	0	0
Concession fees (tobacco shops)				0	0	0	996	2 306	2 815	5 789
5220 Nonrecurrent taxes	..	..	..	3 273	6 875	4 650	7 899	12 860	16 319	16 373
Land protection levy	..	..	..	1 640	3 777	2 488	3 610	5 776	7 368	8 327
Vehicle weight fee	..	..	..	805	1 288	820	0	2 059	3 305	2 554
Game protection contribution	..	..	..	178	176	1	0	0	0	0
Casino license fee	..	..	..	650	1 635	1 341	4 289	5 025	5 646	5 492
5300 Unallocable between 5100 and 5200	..	..	..	0	0	0	0	0	0	0
6000 Other taxes	..	..	..	24 503	40 232	38 735	44 686	22 293	- 18 768	74 610
Unallocable tax penalties	..	..	..	23 546	33 321	36 250	35 530	22 293	- 18 768	35 910
6100 Paid solely by business	..	..	..	957	6 911	2 485	9 156	0	0	38 700
Nuclear contribution	..	..	..	957	6 711	2 485	9 156	..	..	0
Medicine tax	..	..	..	0	200	0	0	..	..	38 700
6200 Other	..	..	..	0	0	0	0	0	0	0
Custom duties collected for the EU	..	..	..	..	27 981	25 004	38 960	63 495	72 815	104 853
Total tax revenue on cash basis	..	..	..	5 132 570	10 020 734	10 137 257	13 218 609	16 994 769	18 789 624	22 044 857
Total tax revenue on accrual basis	..	..	..	..	10 098 955	10 121 687	13 519 622	17 425 190	18 646 419	23 181 302
Additional taxes included in National Accounts	..	..	..	..	45 120	49 057	76 364	32 597	29 688	34 689
Social security contributions	..	..	..	..	0	11 675	40 688	84	43	11
Duty for state procedures	..	..	..	..	45 084	37 331	35 653	32 498	29 633	34 666
Other taxes	..	..	..	..	36	51	23	15	12	12
Taxes excluded from National Accounts	..	..	..	..	- 49 439	- 53 707	- 48 414	- 35 100	6 169	- 48 718
Water fund tax	..	..	..	..	- 13 171	- 14 444	- 12 305	- 12 632	- 12 425	- 12 652
Tax on foreign registered vehicles	..	..	..	..	- 1 655	- 1 397	0	0	0	0
Environmental protection fee	..	..	..	..	- 446	- 593	- 265	- 155	- 155	- 139
Air pollution levy	..	..	..	..	- 610	- 53	0	0	0	0
Water pollution levy	..	..	..	..	- 186	0	0	0	0	0
Toxic waste levy	..	..	..	..	- 42	- 130	0	0	0	0
Noise abatement levy	..	..	..	..	- 8	- 19	0	0	0	0
Vehicle weight fee	..	..	..	..	0	- 820	0	0	0	0
Unallocable tax penalties	..	..	..	..	- 33 321	- 36 250	- 35 530	- 22 293	18 768	- 35 910
Tax on home-workers	..	..	..	..	0	- 1	- 29	- 20	- 19	- 17
Specific sectors' surtax correction	..	..	..	..	0	0	- 285	0	0	0
Difference in treatment of tax credits	..	..	..	..	0	0	0	0	0	0

	1965	1980	1990	2000	2007	2010	2015	2020	2021	2022
Capital transfer for uncollected revenue	..	..	..	..	0	0	0	0	0	0
Voluntary social security contributions	..	..	..	..	1 762	1 693	1 229	953	963	1 045
Miscellaneous differences	..	..	..	..	- 2 687	- 28	- 43	1 433	2 737	6 129
Inheritance tax	..	..	..	..	0	0	0	0	0	0
Gift tax	..	..	..	..	0	0	0	0	0	0
Property transfer tax	..	..	..	..	0	0	0	0	0	0
Rounding	..	..	..	..	4	- 2	0	- 1	- 1	- 1
Taxes on income and profits	..	..	..	..	- 2 087	0	0	0	0	0
Corporate income tax	..	..	..	..	0	0	0	0	0	0
Customs duties	..	..	..	..	- 604	- 26	- 43	1 434	2 738	6 130
Vehicle weight fee	..	..	..	..	0	0	0	0	0	0
Environment petrol tax	..	..	..	..	0	0	0	0	0	0
Social security contributions	..	..	..	..	0	0	0	0	0	0
Credit institutions' special tax	..	..	..	..	0	0	0	0	0	0
National Accounts: Taxes and actual social contributions	..	..	..	..	10 093 712	10 118 702	13 548 758	17 425 073	18 685 976	23 174 447
Imputed social contributions	..	..	..	..	21 113	24 841	28 783	29 221	31 020	40 573
National Accounts: Taxes and all social contributions	..	..	..	..	10 114 825	10 143 543	13 577 541	17 454 294	18 716 996	23 215 020

.. Not available

Note: Year ending 31st December.

From 2002 onwards, data are on accrual basis, except for the preliminary year, which is on a cash basis.

Heading 5121: the aggregate figure for excise tax revenues is on a cash basis. Revenue from specific excises is in several cases reported on an accrual basis.

Tax base for "Environment petrol tax" is broader than petrol only.

Source: Ministry of Finance, Economic Department.

Table 5.16. Iceland: Details of tax revenue, 1965-2022

Million ISK

	1965	1980	1990	2000	2007	2010	2015	2020	2021	2022
Total tax revenue	60	4 731	114 932	254 570	532 769	541 578	812 002	1 061 089	1 139 978	1 365 413
1000 Taxes on income, profits and capital gains	13	1 211	34 106	101 488	241 378	239 664	380 979	542 035	569 645	702 954
1100 Of individuals	12	1 092	30 908	88 492	180 070	197 318	297 979	457 255	471 865	545 134
1110 On income and profits	..	..	30 908	88 492	180 070	197 318	297 979	457 255	471 865	545 134
1120 On capital gains	..	..	..	0	0	0	0	0	0	0
1200 Corporate	1	119	3 198	8 371	32 555	14 609	52 544	64 447	65 454	100 909
1210 On profits	..	..	3 198	8 371	32 555	14 609	52 544	64 447	65 454	100 909
1220 On capital gains	..	..	..	0	0	0	0	0	0	0
1300 Unallocable between 1100 and 1200	0	0	0	4 625	28 754	27 737	30 457	20 333	32 327	56 911
2000 Social security contributions	5	102	3 607	19 680	39 594	63 599	79 707	88 364	97 414	115 564
2100 Employees	0	0	315	..	..	..	..	..	..	..
2110 On a payroll basis	..	..	..	..	..	..	..	..	..	..
2120 On an income tax basis	..	..	..	..	..	..	..	..	..	..
2200 Employers	5	102	3 292	..	..	..	..	..	..	..
2210 On a payroll basis of employers SSC	..	..	..	..	..	..	..	..	..	..
2220 On an income tax basis of employers SSC	..	..	..	..	..	..	..	..	..	..
2300 Selfemployed or nonemployed	0	0	0	..	..	..	..	..	..	..
2310 On a payroll basis of self/non-employed SSC	..	..	..	..	..	..	..	..	..	..
2320 On an income tax basis of self/non-employed SSC	..	..	..	..	..	..	..	..	..	..
2400 Unallocable between 2100, 2200 and 2300	0	0	0	19 680	39 594	63 599	79 707	88 364	97 414	115 564
2410 On a payroll basis unallocable between 2100, 2200 and 2300 SSC	..	..	..	19 680	39 594	63 599	79 707	88 364	97 414	115 564
2420 On an income tax basis unallocable between 2100, 2200 and 2300 SSC	..	..	..	0	0	0	0	0	0	0
3000 Taxes on payroll and workforce	1	180	4 071	184	1 519	2 827	6 638	9 233	9 160	10 003
4000 Taxes on property	2	297	9 689	16 839	23 039	35 412	39 160	66 312	67 752	76 161
4100 Recurrent taxes on immovable property	1	138	4 131	10 107	20 567	28 542	34 879	56 040	58 209	62 439
4110 Households	0	50	1 862	..	..	..	..	..	..	..
4120 Others	1	88	2 269	..	..	..	..	..	..	..
4200 Recurrent taxes on net wealth	0	69	2 402	5 173	- 8	3 849	657	34	13	0
4210 Individual	..	29	1 476	..	..	..	..	..	..	..
4220 Corporate	..	40	926	..	..	..	..	..	..	..
4300 Estate, inheritance and gift taxes	0	6	235	765	1 663	2 613	2 919	9 059	8 393	12 154
4310 Estate and inheritance taxes	0	6	235	765	1 663	2 613	2 919	9 059	8 393	12 154
4320 Gift taxes	0	0	0	0	0	0	0	0	0	0
4400 Taxes on financial and capital transactions	1	84	2 921	0	0	0	0	0	0	0
4500 Nonrecurrent taxes	0	0	0	113	460	146	362	612	524	802
4510 On net wealth	..	..	..	0	0	0	0	0	0	0
4520 Other nonrecurrent taxes	..	..	..	113	460	146	362	612	524	802
4600 Other recurrent taxes on property	0	0	0	681	356	263	343	567	613	767
5000 Taxes on goods and services	37	2 834	58 943	115 389	225 480	194 088	267 155	335 971	382 756	446 508
5100 Taxes on production, sale, transfer, etc	37	2 778	56 564	103 813	202 449	182 953	254 422	312 821	361 377	419 446
5110 General taxes	10	1 368	37 084	75 811	148 085	126 351	188 001	239 773	284 536	329 554
5111 Value added taxes	0	0	32 698	72 668	138 601	123 695	183 674	233 732	277 808	323 469
5112 Sales tax	10	1 368	4 386	0	0	0	0	0	0	0
5113 Other	0	0	0	3 143	9 484	2 656	4 327	6 040	6 728	6 085
5120 Taxes on specific goods and services	27	1 410	19 480	28 002	54 364	56 603	66 421	73 049	76 841	89 892
5121 Excises	1	311	2 346	23 585	45 891	46 711	56 909	64 251	66 591	77 118
Excises on alcohol			0	5 772	8 057	10 214	13 302	20 511	22 724	23 800
Excises on tobacco			0	0	3 903	4 573	5 874	5 923	5 662	5 007
5122 Profits of fiscal monopolies	5	263	5 986	0	0	0	0	0	0	0
5123 Customs and import duties	20	715	9 181	2 702	5 446	5 952	4 989	2 575	4 122	5 991
5124 Taxes on exports	1	2	0	0	0	0	0	0	0	0
5125 Taxes on investment goods	0	0	0	0	0	0	0	0	0	0
5126 Taxes on specific services	1	69	1 404	1 715	3 026	3 940	4 523	6 223	6 127	6 782
5127 Other taxes on internat. trade and transactions	0	50	563	0	0	0	0	0	0	0
5128 Other taxes	0	0	0	0	0	0	0	0	0	0
5130 Unallocable between 5110 and 5120	0	0	0	0	0	0	0	0	0	0
5200 Taxes on use of goods and perform activities	1	56	2 379	11 576	23 032	11 135	12 733	23 150	21 379	27 062
5210 Recurrent taxes	1	56	2 379	..	..	..	..	..	..	..
5211 Paid by households: motor vehicles	0	10	970	..	..	..	..	..	..	..
5212 Paid by others: motor vehicles	0	41	1 331	..	..	..	..	..	..	..
5213 Paid in respect of other goods	0	5	78	..	..	..	..	..	..	..
5220 Nonrecurrent taxes	0	0	0	..	..	..	..	..	..	..
5300 Unallocable between 5100 and 5200	0	0	0	0	0	0	0	0	0	0
6000 Other taxes	2	107	4 516	991	1 758	5 988	38 364	19 174	13 251	14 223
6100 Paid solely by business	2	107	4 145	418	628	763	32 477	12 046	5 927	6 228
6200 Other	0	0	371	573	1 130	5 225	5 887	7 127	7 324	7 995

	1965	1980	1990	2000	2007	2010	2015	2020	2021	2022
Non-wastable tax credits against 1110	..	..	..	..	..	..	0	0	0	0
Tax expenditure component	..	..	..	..	..	..	..	..	..	..
Transfer component	..	..	..	..	..	..	..	..	..	..
Non-wastable tax credits against 1210	..	..	..	..	..	..	1 190	5 186	10 431	11 603
Tax expenditure component	..	..	..	..	..	..	173	824	716	715
Transfer component	..	..	..	..	..	..	1 017	4 362	9 715	10 888
Total tax revenue on cash basis	60	4 731	114 932	..	..	..	..	..	..	..
Total tax revenue on accrual basis	..	..	..	254 570	532 769	541 578	812 002	1 061 089	1 139 978	1 365 413
Additional taxes included in National Accounts	..	..	..	0	0	0	0	0	0	0
Taxes excluded from National Accounts	..	..	..	- 765	- 1 663	- 2 613	- 2 919	- 9 059	- 8 393	- 12 154
Estate and inheritance taxes (4310)	..	..	..	- 765	- 1 663	- 2 613	- 2 919	- 9 059	- 8 393	- 12 154
Difference in treatment of tax credits	..	..	..	0	0	0	0	0	0	0
Capital transfer for uncollected revenue	..	..	..	0	0	0	0	0	0	0
Voluntary social security contributions	..	..	..	0	0	0	0	0	0	0
Miscellaneous differences	..	..	..	0	0	0	0	0	0	0
National Accounts: Taxes and actual social contributions	..	..	..	253 806	531 105	538 964	809 084	1 052 029	1 131 584	1 353 259
Imputed social contributions	..	..	..	0	0	0	0	0	0	0
National Accounts: Taxes and all social contributions	..	..	..	253 806	531 105	538 964	809 084	1 052 029	1 131 584	1 353 259

.. Not available

Note: Year ending 31st December.

From 1998 data are on accrual basis.

Source: Statistics Iceland.

Table 5.17. Ireland: Details of tax revenue, 1965-2022

Million EUR

	1965	1980	1990	2000	2007	2010	2015	2020	2021	2022
Total tax revenue	317	4 046	12 260	33 363	60 790	46 399	60 898	74 033	90 028	105 515
Total tax revenue exclusive of taxes collected for the EU	..	..	12 075	33 155	60 517	46 170	60 572	73 623	89 294	104 640
1000 Taxes on income, profits and capital gains	82	1 478	4 662	14 551	25 364	18 617	26 599	36 333	44 737	55 679
1100 Of individuals	53	1 294	4 059	10 650	18 970	14 665	19 722	24 380	29 413	33 033
1110 On income and profits	53	1 286	4 023	9 876	15 872	14 320	19 053	23 428	27 768	31 286
Income tax	66	1 286	4 023	9 876	15 872	14 320	19 053	23 428	27 768	31 286
Surtax	3	0	0	0	0	0	0	0	0	0
Income tax paid by corporations	- 17	0	0	0	0	0	0	0	0	0
1120 On capital gains	0	8	36	774	3 097	345	669	952	1 645	1 747
1200 Corporate	29	184	603	3 900	6 395	3 945	6 873	11 954	15 324	22 646
1210 On profits	29	184	603	3 900	6 395	3 945	6 873	11 954	15 324	22 646
Corporation profits tax	12	2	0	0	0	0	0	0	0	0
Corporation tax	0	176	603	3 885	6 393	3 944	6 872	11 953	15 323	22 645
Income tax paid by corporation	17	0	0	0	0	0	0	0	0	0
Agricultural produce duty	0	6	0	14	1	1	1	1	1	1
1220 On capital gains	0	0	0	0	0	0	0	0	0	0
1300 Unallocable between 1100 and 1200	0	0	0	2	0	7	4	0	0	0
2000 Social security contributions	21	578	1 729	3 966	8 143	8 458	9 999	12 266	13 792	15 967
2100 Employees	10	190	570	962	1 926	3 195	3 327	3 766	4 217	5 419
2110 On a payroll basis	..	..	570	962	1 926	3 195	3 327	3 766	4 217	5 419
2120 On an income tax basis	..	..	0	0	0	0	0	0	0	0
2200 Employers	10	380	1 092	2 814	5 796	4 932	6 211	7 868	8 885	9 917
2210 On a payroll basis of employers SSC	..	..	1 092	2 814	5 796	4 932	6 211	7 868	8 885	9 917
2220 On an income tax basis of employers SSC	..	..	0	0	0	0	0	0	0	0
2300 Selfemployed or nonemployed	0	8	67	190	421	331	460	632	690	631
2310 On a payroll basis of self/non-employed SSC	..	..	67	190	421	331	460	632	690	631
2320 On an income tax basis of self/non-employed SSC	..	..	0	0	0	0	0	0	0	0
2400 Unallocable between 2100, 2200 and 2300	0	0	0	0	0	0	0	0	0	0
2410 On a payroll basis unallocable between 2100, 2200 and 2300 SSC	..	..	..	..	..	..	..	..	..	..
2420 On an income tax basis unallocable between 2100, 2200 and 2300 SSC	..	..	..	..	..	..	..	..	..	..
3000 Taxes on payroll and workforce	0	9	159	15	411	310	357	717	797	951
4000 Taxes on property	48	213	569	1 902	4 789	2 389	3 918	3 687	4 843	5 009
4100 Recurrent taxes on immovable property	39	139	312	587	1 233	1 322	1 864	1 215	1 668	2 051
4110 Households	..	..	..	..	..	..	..	..	..	..
4120 Others	..	..	..	..	..	..	..	..	..	..
4200 Recurrent taxes on net wealth	0	1	0	0	0	0	169	0	0	0
4210 Individual	..	..	..	..	..	..	0	0	0	0
4220 Corporate	..	..	..	..	..	..	169	0	0	0
4300 Estate, inheritance and gift taxes	6	14	48	225	405	235	401	505	582	615
4310 Estate and inheritance taxes	6	14	45	210	337	192	365	499	576	609
Estate duty	5	..	0	0	0	0	0	0	0	0
Legacy duty	1	..	0	0	0	0	0	0	0	0
Succession duty	0	..	0	0	0	0	0	0	0	0
4320 Gift taxes	0	0	3	15	68	43	36	6	6	5
4400 Taxes on financial and capital transactions	3	59	209	1 090	3 151	832	1 484	1 968	2 592	2 344
Stamp duty	3	59	209	1 090	3 151	832	1 484	1 968	2 592	2 344
4500 Nonrecurrent taxes	0	0	0	0	0	0	0	0	0	0
4510 On net wealth	..	..	..	..	..	..	..	..	..	..
4520 Other nonrecurrent taxes	..	..	..	..	..	..	..	..	..	..
4600 Other recurrent taxes on property	0	0	0	0	0	0	0	0	0	0
5000 Taxes on goods and services	167	1 769	5 140	12 929	22 082	16 619	20 013	21 021	25 850	27 896
5100 Taxes on production, sale, transfer, etc	155	1 741	4 939	12 374	20 982	15 319	18 036	19 183	23 842	26 194
5110 General taxes	18	597	2 500	7 643	14 355	10 067	11 831	12 753	16 642	19 176
5111 Value added taxes	0	597	2 500	7 643	14 355	10 067	11 831	12 753	16 642	19 176
Value added tax	..	597	2 500	7 643	14 355	10 067	11 831	12 753	16 642	19 176
5112 Sales tax	18	0	0	0	0	0	0	0	0	0
Turnover tax	18	..	..	..	..	..	..	..	..	..
Wholesale tax	0	..	..	..	..	..	..	..	..	..
5113 Other	0	0	0	0	0	0	0	0	0	0
5120 Taxes on specific goods and services	137	1 143	2 439	4 731	6 627	5 252	6 205	6 430	7 200	7 018
5121 Excises	124	1 045	2 084	4 402	6 125	4 859	5 474	5 470	5 867	5 559
Beer	19	192	356	475	459	316	418	348	346	407
Oils	31	330	745	1 491	2 204	2 099	2 120	1 805	1 927	1 504
Spirits	16	148	153	241	363	244	313	379	383	414
Table waters	0	11	23	0	0	0	0	0	0	0
Tobacco	50	187	419	1 035	1 192	1 160	1 055	1 202	1 317	1 160

	1965	1980	1990	2000	2007	2010	2015	2020	2021	2022
Wine, cider, perry	1	18	46	154	297	266	414	478	428	428
Motor vehicle (incl. tyres)	7	148	331	985	1 554	395	702	717	763	782
Others	1	11	11	20	57	379	451	515	672	831
Sugar-sweetened drinks			0	0	0	0	0	26	31	32
5122 Profits of fiscal monopolies	0	0	0	0	0	0	0	0	0	0
5123 Customs and import duties	10	62	147	208	273	229	327	272	519	618
5124 Taxes on exports	0	0	0	0	0	0	0	0	0	0
UE agriculture levies	..	..	0	..	..	..	..	..	..	..
5125 Taxes on investment goods	0	0	0	0	0	0	0	0	0	0
5126 Taxes on specific services	3	21	171	122	229	164	404	688	814	841
Duty on betting	2	19	37	59	36	30	37	83	92	104
Sweepstakes duty	1	1	0	0	0	0	0	0	0	0
Bank levy	0	0	46	61	66	- 70	190	427	528	520
Other	0	1	88	2	127	204	178	178	194	217
5127 Other taxes on internat. trade and transactions	0	0	0	0	0	0	0	0	0	0
5128 Other taxes	0	14	37	0	0	0	0	0	0	0
5130 Unallocable between 5110 and 5120	0	0	0	0	0	0	0	0	0	0
5200 Taxes on use of goods and perform activities	11	28	201	555	1 100	1 300	1 977	1 838	2 008	1 702
5210 Recurrent taxes	11	28	201	555	1 100	1 300	1 977	1 838	2 008	1 702
5211 Paid by households: motor vehicles	6	14	100	373	723	768	904	756	747	754
5212 Paid by others: motor vehicles	5	11	82	124	239	256	281	235	227	226
5213 Paid in respect of other goods	0	3	20	58	138	276	792	846	1 034	723
5220 Nonrecurrent taxes	0	0	0	0	0	0	0	0	0	0
5300 Unallocable between 5100 and 5200	0	0	0	0	0	0	0	0	0	0
6000 Other taxes	0	0	0	0	0	6	12	9	10	13
6100 Paid solely by business	..	..	..	..	..	0	0	0	0	0
6200 Other	..	..	..	..	..	6	12	9	10	13
Custom duties collected for the EU	..	..	148	208	273	229	327	272	519	618
SRF Contributions collected for the EU			..	..	..	..	..	138	216	258
Non-wastable tax credits against 1110	..	..	..	..	843	1 073	555	400	400	380
Tax expenditure component	..	..	..	..	843	1 073	555	400	400	380
Transfer component	..	..	..	..	0	0	0	0	0	0
Total tax revenue on cash basis	317	4 046	12 260	32 997	60 836	46 609	60 867	73 732	88 574	105 361
Total tax revenue on accrual basis	..	..	..	33 363	60 790	46 399	60 898	74 033	90 028	105 515
Additional taxes included in National Accounts	..	..	..	0	0	178	177	185	184	164
Taxes excluded from National Accounts	..	..	..	0	0	0	0	0	0	0
Difference in treatment of tax credits	..	..	..	0	0	0	0	0	0	0
Capital transfer for uncollected revenue	..	..	..	0	0	0	0	0	0	0
Voluntary social security contributions	..	..	..	0	0	0	0	0	0	0
Miscellaneous differences	..	..	..	0	0	0	0	0	0	0
National Accounts: Taxes and actual social contributions	..	..	..	33 363	60 790	46 577	61 075	74 218	90 212	105 679
Imputed social contributions	..	..	..	1 366	2 579	1 053	2 223	3 144	3 697	4 053
National Accounts: Taxes and all social contributions	..	..	..	34 729	63 369	47 630	63 298	77 362	93 909	109 733

.. Not available

Note: The personal income tax data shown for the country table for Ireland is different to the ESA2010 presentation as the expenditure component of the payable tax credits are excluded in accordance with the OECD Interpretative Guide.

The data for years 1965 to 1973 are on fiscal year basis (commencing on 1st April) and are therefore not strictly comparable with the data for later years, which are on a calendar year basis.

From 1998, data are on accrual basis.

Heading 1200: Capital gains taxes paid by corporations are included in heading 1210.

Heading 2100: Includes contributions by self-employed and certain voluntary contributions.

Heading 2200: Since 1976 income tax paid by corporations and corporation profits tax have been replaced by corporation tax.

Heading 5111: Includes arrears of the wholesale and turnover taxes.

Tax receipts in 1988 were inflated by the success of the new arrangements for assessment and collection of tax. These arrangements included an amnesty for tax arrears paid by 30th September. This amnesty waived penalties and interest charge tax. It resulted in payments of 631 million euros spread across the main tax headings.

Source: Annual Report of the Revenue Commissioners, Financial Accounts and National Income and Expenditure Accounts.

Table 5.18. Israel: Details of tax revenue, 1965-2022

Million ILS

	1965	1980	1990	2000	2007	2010	2015	2020	2021	2022
Total tax revenue	..	..	..	189 301	252 037	269 674	366 064	420 750	514 035	581 132
1000 Taxes on income, profits and capital gains	..	..	..	74 551	91 530	78 265	113 976	138 952	182 913	216 384
1100 Of individuals	..	..	..	54 753	56 434	48 214	70 895	91 204	113 200	127 900
1110 On income and profits	..	..	..	53 698	55 213	47 550	69 215	89 354	108 160	124 310
On wages – deduction at source	..	..	..	45 278	45 515	40 159	54 097	70 318	83 836	96 831
On self employement income – deduction at source	..	..	..	0	0	2 063	2 805	0	0	471
On self employement income – other	..	..	..	8 420	9 698	5 328	12 313	19 036	24 324	27 008
1120 On capital gains	..	..	..	1 055	1 221	664	1 680	1 850	5 040	3 590
1200 Corporate	..	..	..	18 001	30 210	23 113	34 676	39 006	56 466	76 187
1210 On profits	..	..	..	16 109	27 582	22 291	32 936	36 416	53 536	72 147
Deduction at source	..	..	..	0	0	1 097	1 411	0	0	165
In lieu of VAT on the profits of Financial Institutions	..	..	..	1 290	2 200	1 920	1 910	3 070	4 000	4 400
Other	..	..	..	14 819	25 382	19 274	29 615	33 346	49 536	67 582
1220 On capital gains	..	..	..	1 892	2 628	822	1 740	2 590	2 930	4 040
1300 Unallocable between 1100 and 1200	..	..	..	1 797	4 886	6 938	8 405	8 742	13 247	12 297
Tax deducted at the source on the capital market	..	..	..	1 797	4 886	6 938	8 405	8 742	13 247	12 297
2000 Social security contributions	..	..	..	27 565	37 909	45 343	59 561	73 031	79 602	88 775
2100 Employees	..	..	..	15 771	23 093	27 788	34 692	40 797	44 414	49 880
2110 On a payroll basis	..	..	..	15 771	23 093	27 788	34 692	40 797	44 414	49 880
2120 On an income tax basis	..	..	..	0	0	0	0	0	0	0
2200 Employers	..	..	..	8 182	9 960	11 427	17 247	22 564	24 675	27 845
2210 On a payroll basis of employers SSC	..	..	..	8 182	9 960	11 427	17 247	22 564	24 675	27 845
2220 On an income tax basis of employers SSC	..	..	..	0	0	0	0	0	0	0
2300 Selfemployed or nonemployed	..	..	..	3 612	4 856	6 128	7 622	9 670	10 513	11 050
2310 On a payroll basis of self/non-employed SSC	..	..	..	3 612	4 856	6 128	7 622	9 670	10 513	11 050
2320 On an income tax basis of self/non-employed SSC	..	..	..	0	0	0	0	0	0	0
2400 Unallocable between 2100, 2200 and 2300	..	..	..	0	0	0	0	0	0	0
2410 On a payroll basis unallocable between 2100, 2200 and 2300 SSC	..	..	..	..	..	..	..	..	..	..
2420 On an income tax basis unallocable between 2100, 2200 and 2300 SSC	..	..	..	..	..	..	..	..	..	..
3000 Taxes on payroll and workforce	..	..	..	6 850	9 920	10 280	13 760	16 570	16 147	16 253
Employers tax on the the non-profit sector other than govt	..	..	..	1 250	1 500	320	420	500	532	64
In lieu of VAT on the wage-bill in the non-profit sector	..	..	..	4 260	6 580	7 650	10 320	12 700	13 233	13 587
In lieu VAT on the wage-bill in Financial Institutions	..	..	..	1 340	1 840	2 310	3 020	3 370	2 382	2 602
4000 Taxes on property	..	..	..	17 987	25 049	30 028	40 609	43 542	62 019	71 378
4100 Recurrent taxes on immovable property	..	..	..	11 311	16 156	18 768	23 702	24 778	29 015	31 516
Land tax	..	..	..	442	52	48	44	10	23	22
4110 Households	..	..	..	0	0	0	0	0	0	0
4120 Others	..	..	..	10 869	16 104	18 720	23 658	24 768	28 992	31 494
4200 Recurrent taxes on net wealth	..	..	..	0	0	0	0	0	0	0
4210 Individual	..	..	..	..	..	..	..	..	..	..
4220 Corporate	..	..	..	..	..	..	..	..	..	..
4300 Estate, inheritance and gift taxes	..	..	..	0	0	0	0	0	0	0
4310 Estate and inheritance taxes	..	..	..	..	..	..	..	..	..	..
4320 Gift taxes	..	..	..	..	..	..	..	..	..	..
4400 Taxes on financial and capital transactions	..	..	..	3 181	3 555	4 071	6 732	6 915	12 645	14 438
Transaction tax on the buyer of real estate	..	..	..	1 972	3 084	4 024	6 731	6 914	12 642	14 438
Transaction tax on the seller of real estate	..	..	..	206	404	27	1	1	3	0
Stamp tax	..	..	..	1 003	67	20	0	0	0	0
4500 Nonrecurrent taxes	..	..	..	3 495	5 338	7 190	10 175	11 849	20 359	25 424
4510 On net wealth	..	..	..	0	0	0	0	0	0	0
4520 Other nonrecurrent taxes	..	..	..	3 495	5 338	7 190	10 175	11 849	20 359	25 424
Capital gains tax on real estate	..	..	..	3 495	5 338	7 190	10 175	11 849	20 359	25 424
4600 Other recurrent taxes on property	..	..	..	0	0	0	0	0	0	0
5000 Taxes on goods and services	..	..	..	62 348	87 629	105 758	138 157	148 655	173 354	188 342
5100 Taxes on production, sale, transfer, etc	..	..	..	57 888	81 108	98 094	128 277	138 750	162 099	176 388
5110 General taxes	..	..	..	39 805	53 983	65 510	90 824	100 373	119 346	130 757
5111 Value added taxes	..	..	..	39 805	53 983	65 510	90 824	100 373	119 346	130 757
5112 Sales tax	..	..	..	0	0	0	0	0	0	0
5113 Other	..	..	..	0	0	0	0	0	0	0
5120 Taxes on specific goods and services	..	..	..	18 083	27 125	32 584	37 453	38 377	42 753	45 631
5121 Excises	..	..	..	16 666	24 910	29 895	34 583	35 502	39 076	42 659
Fuel	..	..	..	5 891	11 814	15 493	18 058	17 243	19 059	18 947
Tobacco products	..	..	..	2 346	3 490	4 681	6 239	7 288	7 492	7 485

	1965	1980	1990	2000	2007	2010	2015	2020	2021	2022
Alcoholic beverages				330	500	630	1 062	951	1 121	1 165
Sugar-sweetened beverages				0	0	0	0	0	0	880
Disposable plastic products				0	0	0	0	0	70	330
Vehicles and other products				8 099	9 106	9 091	9 225	10 020	11 333	13 852
5122 Profits of fiscal monopolies	..	..	..	0	0	0	0	0	0	0
5123 Customs and import duties	..	..	..	1 417	2 215	2 689	2 870	2 875	3 677	2 972
5124 Taxes on exports	..	..	..	0	0	0	0	0	0	0
5125 Taxes on investment goods	..	..	..	0	0	0	0	0	0	0
5126 Taxes on specific services	..	..	..	0	0	0	0	0	0	0
5127 Other taxes on internat. trade and transactions	..	..	..	0	0	0	0	0	0	0
5128 Other taxes	..	..	..	0	0	0	0	0	0	0
5130 Unallocable between 5110 and 5120	..	..	..	0	0	0	0	0	0	0
5200 Taxes on use of goods and perform activities	..	..	..	4 460	6 521	7 664	9 880	9 905	11 255	11 954
5210 Recurrent taxes	..	..	..	4 460	6 521	7 664	9 880	9 905	11 255	11 954
5211 Paid by households: motor vehicles	..	..	..	1 436	1 895	2 274	2 515	2 868	3 088	3 170
5212 Paid by others: motor vehicles	..	..	..	479	632	758	1 723	1 898	2 029	2 066
5213 Paid in respect of other goods	..	..	..	2 546	3 995	4 632	5 642	5 139	6 138	6 718
Licences collected by the Ministry of Transportation	..	..	..	257	535	350	196	30	51	102
Licences collected by the Ministry of Communication	..	..	..	151	0	274	338	356	423	351
Licences collected by other ministries	..	..	..	1 587	2 605	2 990	3 800	3 366	4 064	4 541
Business and professional licences paid locally	..	..	..	500	769	917	1 181	1 238	1 449	1 574
Other local authority fees	..	..	..	51	86	101	128	150	150	150
5220 Nonrecurrent taxes	..	..	..	0	0	0	0	0	0	0
5300 Unallocable between 5100 and 5200	..	..	..	0	0	0	0	0	0	0
6000 Other taxes	..	..	..	0	0	0	0	0	0	0
6100 Paid solely by business	..	..	..	..	..	..	..	..	..	..
6200 Other	..	..	..	..	..	..	..	..	..	..
Non-wastable tax credits against 1110	..	..	..	..	..	87	1 415	1 932	894	1 911
Tax expenditure component	..	..	..	..	..	3	67	0	0	0
Transfer component	..	..	..	..	..	84	1 348	1 932	894	1 911
Non-wastable tax credits against 1210	..	..	..	..	..	0	0	0	0	0
Tax expenditure component	..	..	..	..	..	..	..	..	..	..
Transfer component	..	..	..	..	..	..	..	..	..	..
Total tax revenue on cash basis	..	..	..	189 301	252 037	269 674	366 064	420 750	514 035	581 132
Total tax revenue on accrual basis	..	..	..	..	..	..	..	..	..	..
Additional taxes included in National Accounts	..	..	..	0	0	0	0	0	0	0
Taxes excluded from National Accounts	..	..	..	..	..	..	..	..	..	..
Difference in treatment of tax credits	..	..	..	..	..	..	..	..	..	..
Capital transfer for uncollected revenue	..	..	..	..	..	..	..	..	..	..
Voluntary social security contributions	..	..	..	..	..	..	..	..	..	..
Miscellaneous differences	..	..	..	..	..	..	..	..	..	..
National Accounts: Taxes and actual social contributions	..	..	..	189 301	252 037	269 674	366 064	420 750	514 035	581 132
Imputed social contributions	..	..	..	6 172	7 131	8 203	9 186	8 804	8 594	8 345
National Accounts: Taxes and all social contributions	..	..	..	195 473	259 168	277 877	375 250	429 554	522 629	589 476

.. Not available

Note: Year ending 31st December.

Data are on a cash basis.

Source: Israel Central Bureau of Statistics and Israel Ministry of Finance.

Table 5.19. Italy: Details of tax revenue, 1965-2022

Million EUR

	1965	1980	1990	2000	2007	2010	2015	2020	2021	2022
Total tax revenue	5 505	60 422	265 116	503 096	671 189	671 912	711 114	707 382	773 609	840 824
Total tax revenue exclusive of taxes collected for the EU	..	..	263 829	501 560	668 928	669 687	706 522	704 430	770 104	835 734
1000 Taxes on income, profits and capital gains	982	18 821	96 707	166 912	226 498	219 547	225 934	231 910	246 146	275 661
1100 Taxes on income, profits and capital gains of individuals	603	13 940	69 654	124 918	172 136	180 512	184 622	189 241	200 039	214 461
1110 On income and profits of individuals	603	13 796	68 786	124 233	172 122	180 505	184 619	189 241	200 039	214 461
Personal income tax	0	11 538	57 318	121 211	162 644	173 991	173 007	178 974	186 671	202 309
Local income tax paid by households	0	829	4 492	67	0	0	0	0	0	0
Tax on income from investiments (60%)	319	55	15	0	0	0	80	53	61	67
10% Surcharge on income	94	37	5	0	0	0	0	0	0	0
10% proportional surcharge	1	0	0	0	0	0	0	0	0	0
Withholding tax on company dividends paid by households	23	51	496	110	542	393	875	1 742	2 601	3 569
Law 1177 proportional surcharge (60%)	39	0	1	0	0	0	0	0	0	0
Direct taxes 5% proportional surcharge (60%)	0	8	72	0	0	0	0	0	0	0
Additional Treasury increase (60%)	23	6	1	0	0	0	0	0	0	0
Decree 1132 revenues (60%)	0	0	0	0	0	0	0	0	0	0
Tax on households	65	7	0	0	0	0	0	0	0	0
Rental value tax	2	0	0	0	0	0	0	0	0	0
Driving licence tax	1	0	0	0	0	0	0	0	0	0
Municipal surcharge on buildings (40%)	37	5	0	22	0	0	0	0	0	0
Withholding tax on income from deposits paid by households	0	1 206	6 223	2 823	8 402	5 440	10 076	7 583	9 511	7 312
Direct taxes refund (60%)	0	0	41	0	0	0	0	0	0	0
Other	0	53	123	0	534	681	581	890	1 196	1 204
1120 On capital gains of individuals	0	144	867	685	14	7	3	0	0	0
Tax on capitail gains on land	..	0	0	0	0	0	0	..	..	..
Municipal capital gains tax on buildings paid by households (60%)	..	144	867	685	14	7	3	..	..	..
1200 Taxes on income, profits and capital gains of corporates	379	4 710	26 605	34 699	50 529	36 740	33 530	34 165	34 362	56 319
1210 On profits of corporates	379	4 494	26 027	34 242	50 520	36 736	33 528	34 163	34 361	56 317
Corporation tax	0	1 245	9 042	28 877	47 192	34 841	31 927	31 939	28 695	48 614
Municipal surcharge on buildings (60%)	37	8	0	32	0	0	0	0	0	0
Tax on income from investiments (40%)	213	37	10	0	0	0	54	36	41	45
Company franchise and liabilities tax	88	12	2	0	0	0	0	0	0	0
Law 1177 proportional surcharge (40%)	26	0	0	0	0	0	0	0	0	0
Direct taxes 5% proportional surcharge (40%)	0	20	48	0	0	0	0	0	0	0
Decree 1132 revenues (40%)	0	0	0	0	0	0	0	0	0	0
Additional Treasury increase (40 %)	15	4	0	0	0	0	0	0	0	0
Withholding tax on company dividends paid by firms	0	77	745	166	0	0	0	0	0	0
Withholding tax on income from deposits paid by firms	0	1 810	9 334	4 235	2 370	605	759	592	502	431
Local income tax paid by firms	0	1 245	6 738	100	15	13	12	4	4	4
Direct taxes refund (40%)	0	0	27	0	0	0	0	0	0	0
Other	0	36	82	832	943	1 277	776	1 592	5 119	4 463
1220 On capital gains of corporates	0	216	578	457	9	4	2	2	1	2
Municipal capital gains tax on buildings paid by firms (40%)	..	216	578	457	9	4	2	2	1	2
1300 Unallocable between 1100 and 1200	0	171	448	7 295	3 833	2 295	7 782	8 503	11 744	4 881
Refunds tax on income	..	- 240	- 1 768	- 5 175	0	0	0	0	0	0
Other	..	412	2 216	12 470	3 833	2 295	7 782	8 503	11 744	4 881
2000 Social security contributions (SSC)	1 881	22 976	87 256	143 629	200 772	209 122	214 376	224 741	240 690	256 430
2100 Employees SSC	..	4 171	16 753	27 333	35 715	37 598	39 805	41 312	45 570	46 967
2110 On a payroll basis of employees SSC	..	..	..	27 333	35 715	37 598	39 805	41 312	45 570	46 967
2120 On an income tax basis of employees SSC	..	..	..	0	0	0	0	0	0	0
2200 Employers SSC	..	17 152	62 540	99 904	137 924	144 281	143 273	149 791	161 044	171 799
2210 On a payroll basis of employers SSC	..	..	..	99 904	137 924	144 281	143 273	149 791	161 044	171 799
2220 On an income tax basis of employers SSC	..	..	..	0	0	0	0	0	0	0
2300 Self-employed or non-employed SSC	..	1 654	7 962	16 392	27 133	27 243	31 298	33 638	34 076	37 664
2310 On a payroll basis of self/non-employed SSC	..	..	..	16 392	27 133	27 243	31 298	33 638	34 076	37 664
2320 On an income tax basis of self/non-employed SSC	..	..	..	0	0	0	0	0	0	0
2400 Unallocable between 2100, 2200 and 2300 SSC	1 881	0	0	0	0	0	0	0	0	0
2410 On a payroll basis unallocable between 2100, 2200 and 2300 SSC	..	..	..	..	..	..	..	..	..	..
2420 On an income tax basis unallocable between 2100, 2200 and 2300 SSC	..	..	..	..	..	..	..	..	..	..
3000 Taxes on payroll and workforce	0	387	890	0	0	0	0	0	0	0

	1965	1980	1990	2000	2007	2010	2015	2020	2021	2022
Contributions to GESCAL	..	387	890	..	..	..	..	..	..	..
4000 Taxes on property	397	2 248	5 983	23 360	32 646	32 441	46 259	40 432	45 062	48 157
4100 Recurrent taxes on immovable property	96	7	1	9 354	12 778	9 663	25 558	21 270	22 389	22 676
Income tax on landowners	2	0	0	0	0	0	0	0	0	0
Income tax on buildings	12	2	1	0	0	0	0	0	0	0
Income tax on luxury buildings	1	0	0	0	0	0	0	0	0	0
Surcharge on land (provincial)	16	0	0	0	0	0	0	0	0	0
Surcharge on land (municipal)	18	0	0	0	0	0	0	0	0	0
Surcharge on buildings (provincial)	26	2	0	0	0	0	0	0	0	0
Surcharge on buildings (municipal)	21	3	0	0	0	0	0	0	0	0
Municipal real estate tax	0	0	0	9 354	12 778	9 663	20 798	21 137	22 292	22 611
Tax on indivisible services (TASI)	0	0	0	0	0	0	4 760	133	97	65
4110 Households recurrent taxes on immovable property	..	..	..	..	..	..	..	..	..	..
4120 Other than households recurrent taxes on immovable property	..	..	..	..	..	..	..	..	..	..
4200 Recurrent taxes on net wealth	0	0	0	14	1	2 118	231	427	579	447
4210 Individual recurrent taxes on net wealth	..	..	..	5	0	0	0	0	0	0
4220 Corporate recurrent taxes on net wealth	..	..	..	9	1	2 118	231	427	579	447
4300 Estate, inheritance and gift taxes	47	128	376	1 005	149	483	674	396	855	1 067
Inheritance and gift duty	33	119	376	1 005	149	483	674	396	855	1 067
Estate duty	11	9	0	0	0	0	0	0	0	0
Proportional surcharge and premium	3	0	0	0	0	0	0	0	0	0
4310 Estate and inheritance taxes	..	..	..	..	..	..	..	..	..	..
4320 Gift taxes	..	..	..	..	..	..	..	..	..	..
4400 Taxes on financial and capital transactions	255	2 113	5 606	12 320	18 256	17 365	17 245	17 262	19 599	21 230
Registration tax	120	1 048	2 421	6 794	9 410	9 019	7 625	8 118	9 734	10 390
Mortgage taxes and land registry duties	22	190	469	1 067	2 525	2 071	1 529	1 464	1 825	1 853
5% proportional surcharge	6	0	0	0	0	0	0	0	0	0
Additional surcharge	4	0	0	0	0	0	0	0	0	0
Stamp duties and surcharges accruing on cadastral acts	104	751	2 185	4 459	6 321	6 275	7 600	7 261	7 574	8 462
Other	0	123	530	0	0	0	491	419	466	525
4500 Non-recurrent taxes on property	0	0	0	98	151	916	309	121	164	193
4510 Non-recurrent taxes on net wealth	..	..	..	0	0	0	0	0	0	0
4520 Non-recurrent taxes on property other than net wealth	..	..	..	98	151	916	309	121	164	193
4600 Other recurrent taxes on property except 4100 and 4200	0	0	0	569	1 311	1 896	2 242	956	1 476	2 544
5000 Taxes on goods and services	2 173	15 990	74 280	141 852	171 869	178 863	196 473	190 896	219 073	232 465
5100 Taxes on production, sale, transfer, etc	2 037	15 251	67 083	127 281	155 191	160 775	174 443	164 855	189 580	201 832
Direct taxes refund	0	- 73	- 86	0	0	0	0	0	0	0
5110 General taxes on goods and services	710	9 438	38 940	77 473	95 623	97 586	100 692	99 916	121 283	138 925
5111 Value added taxes	0	9 438	38 940	77 473	95 623	97 586	100 692	99 683	120 980	138 533
VAT	..	9 438	38 940	77 473	95 623	97 586	100 692	99 683	120 980	138 533
5112 Sales tax	0	0	0	0	0	0	0	0	0	0
5113 Other (than value added and sales tax)	710	0	0	0	0	0	0	233	303	392
General tax on receipts	662	..	..	..	..	..	..	0	0	0
Compensation tax on imported products	48	..	..	..	..	..	..	0	0	0
Digital Services Tax			..	..	..	..	..	233	303	392
5120 Taxes on specific goods and services	1 327	5 886	28 048	49 808	59 568	63 189	73 751	64 939	68 297	62 907
5121 Excises	816	4 088	20 304	31 479	32 904	36 414	46 238	40 181	42 421	32 055
Duty on mineral oils	465	3 462	15 928	22 172	23 252	22 884	25 759	21 454	24 421	18 218
Duty on spirits	27	87	206	486	595	570	600	593	701	759
Duty on beer	12	54	172	242	489	476	633	624	698	718
Duty on sugars	22	25	68	120	0	5	5	0	0	0

	1965	1980	1990	2000	2007	2010	2015	2020	2021	2022
Duty on electricity	20	51	2 018	3 079	3 034	7 152	15 246	13 569	12 527	7 777
Duty on bananas	9	53	97	0	0	0	0	0	0	0
Duty on coffee	31	60	74	0	0	0	0	0	0	0
Duty on cocoa	3	4	7	0	0	0	0	0	0	0
Duty on olive oil	0	0	0	0	0	0	0	0	0	0
Other duty	44	190	1 037	5 201	5 385	5 268	3 898	3 922	4 048	4 556
Alcohol, spirits, liquor	5	0	0	0	0	0	0	0	0	0
On matches and flints	13	22	47	0	0	0	0	0	0	0
Meat	26	0	0	0	0	0	0	0	0	0
In-bond surcharge	0	81	650	174	143	54	90	12	19	22
Combustible materials	39	0	0	0	0	0	0	0	0	0
Construction materials	30	0	0	0	0	0	0	0	0	0
Excise duty on sound and video	3	0	0	0	0	0	0	0	0	0
Tax on phonograph records	1	0	0	0	0	0	0	0	0	0
Stamp duty on playing cards	1	0	0	0	0	0	0	0	0	0
Other	66	0	0	5	6	5	7	7	7	5
5122 Profits of fiscal monopolies	303	1 033	3 248	7 718	10 440	10 983	10 711	10 539	10 945	10 959
Duty on tobacco	292	1 033	3 248	7 712	10 436	10 978	10 710	10 538	10 943	10 958
On salt	10	0	0	0	0	0	0	0	0	0
Duty on products of Monopoli di Stato	1	0	0	6	4	5	1	1	2	1
5123 Customs and import duties	142	261	1 164	1 536	2 261	2 225	2 246	1 971	2 431	3 734
Common Customs tariff (CEE)	0	0	836	1 536	2 261	2 225	2 246	1 971	2 431	3 734
Customs and shipping duties	115	14	0	0	0	0	0	0	0	0
Administrative services duties	11	0	0	0	0	0	0	0	0	0
Tax on agriculture	15	228	207	0	0	0	0	0	0	0
Other duties	0	9	68	0	0	0	0	0	0	0
Compensatory amounts	0	9	53	0	0	0	0	0	0	0
5124 Taxes on exports	0	0	0	0	0	0	0	0	0	0
5125 Taxes on investment goods	0	0	0	0	0	0	0	0	0	0
5126 Taxes on specific services	67	483	3 141	9 029	13 932	13 567	14 556	12 248	12 500	16 159
Entertainment tax	20	59	167	118	68	58	40	15	15	25
Stamp duty	6	0	0	0	0	0	0	0	0	0
Tax on advertisements	6	56	168	389	392	384	405	382	382	422
Tax on lotto, lotteries, betting and Totocalcio game	3	123	617	4 164	7 144	7 983	7 488	6 930	6 603	9 899
Casino takings, special duties, etc.	0	0	0	158	152	192	112	45	61	119
Single tax on games of skill and betting-levied inderectly	9	74	476	487	405	242	116	214	274	309
Aerotaxi passengers tax	0	0	0	0	0	0	8	5	12	16
Local tax (including insurance)	23	171	1 714	3 713	5 771	4 708	3 835	3 676	4 079	4 013
Bank levy for the National Resolution Fund	..	..	0	0	0	0	2 552	981	1 074	1 356
5127 Other taxes on internat. trade and transactions not included within 5121 to 5126 inclusive	0	0	0	0	0	0	0	0	0	0
Special Duty on foreign payments and currency selling	..	..	..	..	..	..	..	..	..	..
5128 Other taxes not included within 5121 to 5127 inclusive	0	21	192	46	31	0	0	0	0	0
ECSC taxes and contributions on sugar and other levies	..	21	121	0	0	..	..	..	..	..
Other	..	0	70	46	31	..	..	..	..	..
Bank contribution to the unique European Resolution Fund	..	0	0	0	0	..	..	..	..	..
5130 Unallocable between 5110 and 5120	0	0	180	0	0	0	0	0	0	0
5200 Taxes on use of goods and perform activities	136	456	4 474	8 479	10 550	10 531	11 130	13 069	15 324	15 977
5210 Recurrent taxes on use of goods and perform activities	136	456	4 474	8 479	10 550	1 155	1 653	1 571	1 769	1 587
Public motor vehicle register tax	64	152	967	1 034	1 326	1 155	1 653	1 571	1 769	1 587
Tax on vehicles 5% proportional surcharge	3	13	450	0	0	0	0	0	0	0
Surcharge on diesel cars	0	66	683	0	0	0	0	0	0	0
Surcharge on gas cars	0	0	171	0	0	0	0	0	0	0
5211 Recurrent taxes paid by households: motor vehicles	..	..	..	3 433	4 652	4 628	4 710	4 974	5 467	5 424
5212 Recurrent taxes paid by others: motor vehicles	..	..	..	1 006	1 332	1 300	1 446	1 235	1 458	1 473
Motor vehicle duty paid by firms	..	..	..	1 006	1 332	1 300	1 446	1 235	1 458	1 473
5213 Recurrent taxes paid on use of goods and perform activities other than on motor vehicles	67	225	2 203	3 006	3 240	3 448	3 321	5 289	6 630	7 493
Law 1177 proportional surcharge	22	0	0	0	0	0	0	0	0	0
Taxes on signs	2	4	0	0	0	0	0	0	0	0
Tax on dog tags	0	7	12	0	0	0	0	0	0	0
Tax on hunting and fishing	0	0	0	0	0	0	0	0	0	0

	1965	1980	1990	2000	2007	2010	2015	2020	2021	2022
Duty on official franchises	43	215	2 191	3 006	3 240	3 448	3 321	3 389	4 713	5 544
Television tax (households)	0	0	0	0	0	0	0	1 900	1 917	1 949
5220 Non-recurrent taxes on use of goods and perform activities	0	0	0	0	0	0	0	0	0	0
Motor vehicles, airplanes	..	..	..	..	..	..	..	..	..	..
Pro-Friuli tax on vehicles	..	..	..	..	..	..	..	..	..	..
5300 Unallocable between 5100 and 5200	0	283	2 724	6 092	6 128	7 557	10 900	12 972	14 169	14 656
Indirect taxes refund	..	0	160	288	616	693	715	525	598	882
Other	..	283	2 564	5 804	5 512	6 864	10 185	12 447	13 571	13 774
6000 Other	72	0	0	27 343	39 404	31 939	28 072	19 403	22 638	28 111
6100 Paid solely by business	0	..	..	27 343	39 404	31 939	28 072	19 403	22 638	28 111
6200 Other taxes not solely paid by business	72	..	..	0	0	0	0	0	0	0
Capital levies	2	..	..	..	..	..	..	..	..	..
Other taxes	71	..	..	..	..	..	..	..	..	..
Custom duties collected for the EU	..	..	836	1 536	2 261	2 225	2 246	1 971	2 431	3 734
SRF Contributions collected for the EU			..	..	..	..	2 346	981	1 074	1 356
Taxes paid by EU civil servants			..	..	..	..	61	77	70	71
Taxes paid by EU civil servants: income taxes			..	..	..	..	31	39	35	36
Taxes paid by EU civil servants: compulsory social security contributions			..	..	..	..	30	38	34	35
Non-wastable tax credits against 1110	..	..	..	..	0	0	9 793	11 667	13 915	6 100
Tax expenditure component	..	..	..	..	..	- 109	8 615	10 246	12 250	4 472
Transfer component	..	..	..	..	..	109	1 178	1 420	1 665	1 628
Non-wastable tax credits against 1210	..	..	..	..	0	0	4 866	469	469	469
Tax expenditure component	..	..	..	..	..	..	0	0	0	0
Transfer component	..	..	..	..	..	..	4 866	469	469	469
Total tax revenue on cash basis	5 505	60 422	265 116	488 738	653 836	659 704	711 837	452 854	497 995	533 789
Total tax revenue on accrual basis	..	..	..	503 096	671 189	671 912	711 114	707 382	773 609	840 824
Additional taxes included in National Accounts	..	..	..	0	0	0	0	0	0	0
Taxes excluded from National Accounts	..	..	..	- 5 416	- 5 470	- 6 538	- 9 801	- 10 911	- 11 646	- 11 563
The tax for the urban solid waste disposal (TARSU)	..	..	..	- 4 387	- 4 443	- 5 519	- 8 519	- 9 667	- 9 677	- 9 680
Other	..	..	..	- 1 029	- 1 027	- 1 019	- 1 282	- 1 244	- 1 969	- 1 883
Difference in treatment of tax credits	..	..	..	0	0	- 109	8 615	10 246	12 250	4 472
Capital transfer for uncollected revenue	..	..	..	0	0	0	0	0	0	0
Voluntary social security contributions	..	..	..	464	567	561	750	763	804	924
Miscellaneous differences	..	..	..	0	0	0	0	0	0	0
National Accounts: Taxes and actual social contributions	..	..	..	498 144	666 286	665 826	710 678	707 480	775 017	834 657
Imputed social contributions	..	..	..	3 884	3 980	3 984	3 938	4 148	4 546	4 047
National Accounts: Taxes and all social contributions	..	..	..	502 028	670 266	669 810	714 616	711 628	779 563	838 704

.. Not available

Note: The tax year ends in December 31th.

As from 2000, revenues data are computed on accrual basis.

As from 1997, revenues data are based on data provided to the European Union as for the Treaty of Maastricht excessive deficit procedure.

Section 6000: Regional Tax on Productive Activities (IRAP); it is a tax on the value of production therefore its taxable base is different from other groups tax bases.

Regarding the section “Taxes excluded National Accounts” the item “Others” includes: tax on the public areas utilization and tax on the collection and disposal of waste water.

Source: Ministero dell'economia e delle finanze; Istituto nazionale di statistica.

Table 5.20. Japan: Details of tax revenue, 1965-2022

Billion JPY

	1965	1980	1990	2000	2007	2010	2015	2020	2021	2022
Total tax revenue	6 172	62 443	130 843	136 236	146 248	132 484	163 532	177 321	187 992	195 848
1000 Taxes on income, profits and capital gains	2 708	28 800	65 682	47 398	53 174	40 034	50 969	53 934	60 006	63 669
1100 Of individuals	1 338	15 180	36 394	28 677	28 600	24 663	30 847	33 189	35 439	36 835
1110 On income and profits	1 338	15 180	36 394	28 677	28 600	24 663	30 847	33 189	35 439	36 835
Income tax	970	10 800	25 996	18 789	16 080	12 984	18 178	19 591	21 829	22 992
Prefectural inhabitants tax	123	1 415	3 675	3 621	5 008	4 699	5 252	4 955	5 054	5 039
Municipal inhabitants tax	220	2 890	6 475	6 044	7 294	6 795	7 224	8 427	8 332	8 544
Enterprise tax	25	75	249	223	218	184	194	216	225	260
1120 On capital gains	0	0	0	0	0	0	0	0	0	0
1200 Corporate	1 370	13 620	29 288	18 721	24 573	15 372	20 122	20 745	24 567	26 834
1210 On profits	1 370	13 620	29 288	18 721	24 573	15 372	20 122	20 745	24 567	26 834
Corporation tax	927	8 923	18 384	11 747	14 744	8 968	10 832	11 235	13 643	14 940
Prefectural inhabitants tax	53	557	1 414	879	1 206	777	859	548	512	525
Municipal inhabitants tax	85	1 297	3 198	2 176	3 015	1 954	2 324	1 813	1 956	2 072
Enterprise tax	305	2 843	6 293	3 918	5 608	2 253	3 510	4 082	4 743	5 240
Local special corporate tax	0	0	0	0	0	1 420	2 081	978	0	0
Local corporate tax	0	0	0	0	0	0	516	1 418	1 881	1 888
Special corporate enterprise tax			0	0	0	0	0	672	1 832	2 169
1220 On capital gains	0	0	0	0	0	0	0	0	0	0
1300 Unallocable between 1100 and 1200	0	0	0	0	0	0	0	0	0	0
2000 Social security contributions	1 344	18 178	34 613	47 968	53 325	54 461	64 464	71 563	73 702	75 458
2100 Employees	446	6 393	13 895	19 830	21 975	22 687	27 139	30 463	31 461	32 194
2110 On a payroll basis	..	..	13 895	19 830	21 975	22 687	27 139	30 463	31 461	32 194
2120 On an income tax basis	..	..	0	0	0	0	0	0	0	0
2200 Employers	588	9 267	16 649	22 456	24 243	24 689	29 494	33 245	34 311	35 265
2210 On a payroll basis of employers SSC	..	..	16 649	22 456	24 243	24 689	29 494	33 245	34 311	35 265
2220 On an income tax basis of employers SSC	..	..	0	0	0	0	0	0	0	0
2300 Selfemployed or nonemployed	107	2 518	4 069	5 683	7 108	7 085	7 832	7 855	7 930	7 999
2310 On a payroll basis of self/non-employed SSC	..	..	4 069	5 683	7 108	7 085	7 832	7 855	7 930	7 999
2320 On an income tax basis of self/non-employed SSC	..	..	0	0	0	0	0	0	0	0
2400 Unallocable between 2100, 2200 and 2300	203	0	0	0	0	0	0	0	0	0
2410 On a payroll basis unallocable between 2100, 2200 and 2300 SSC	..	..	..	..	..	..	..	..	..	..
2420 On an income tax basis unallocable between 2100, 2200 and 2300 SSC	..	..	..	..	..	..	..	..	..	..
3000 Taxes on payroll and workforce	0	0	0	0	0	0	0	0	0	0
4000 Taxes on property	498	5 114	12 296	14 294	13 138	12 878	13 400	14 328	14 779	15 414
4100 Recurrent taxes on immovable property	319	3 326	7 099	10 414	9 949	10 225	10 005	10 719	10 655	11 044
Prefectural property tax	4	8	15	11	14	5	2	9	8	4
Municipal property tax	296	2 784	6 023	9 041	8 729	8 961	8 755	9 380	9 322	9 666
City planning tax	19	469	942	1 318	1 202	1 256	1 244	1 330	1 326	1 374
Special landholding tax	0	65	118	43	4	3	3	0	0	0
Water and land utilization tax	0	0	0	0	0	0	0	0	0	0
Land value tax	0	0	0	1	0	0	0	0	0	0
4110 Households	..	..	..	..	..	..	..	..	..	..
4120 Others	..	..	..	..	..	..	..	..	..	..
4200 Recurrent taxes on net wealth	0	0	0	0	0	0	0	0	0	0
4210 Individual	..	..	..	..	..	..	..	..	..	..
4220 Corporate	..	..	..	..	..	..	..	..	..	..
4300 Estate, inheritance and gift taxes	44	441	1 918	1 782	1 503	1 250	1 968	2 315	2 770	2 969
4310 Estate and inheritance taxes	34	375	..	..	..	..	..	..	..	..
Inheritance tax	34	375	..	..	..	..	..	..	..	..
4320 Gift taxes	10	65	..	..	..	..	..	..	..	..
Tax on gifts	10	65	..	..	..	..	..	..	..	..
4400 Taxes on financial and capital transactions	135	1 347	3 280	2 099	1 686	1 403	1 426	1 294	1 353	1 401
Bourse tax	3	15	41	0	0	0	0	0	0	0
Securities transaction	8	209	748	0	0	0	0	0	0	0
Bank of Japan note issue tax	0	0	0	0	0	0	0	0	0	0
Stamp revenues	83	841	1 894	1 532	1 202	1 024	1 050	920	961	982
Real property acquisition tax	41	282	596	567	485	379	377	374	392	418
4500 Nonrecurrent taxes	0	0	0	0	0	0	0	0	0	0
4510 On net wealth	..	..	..	..	..	..	..	..	..	..
4520 Other nonrecurrent taxes	..	..	..	..	..	..	..	..	..	..
4600 Other recurrent taxes on property	0	0	0	0	0	0	0	0	0	0
5000 Taxes on goods and services	1 620	10 200	17 917	26 227	26 256	24 730	34 286	37 053	39 010	40 827
5100 Taxes on production, sale, transfer, etc	1 544	8 822	15 647	23 180	23 241	22 160	31 871	34 433	36 409	38 149
5110 General taxes	0	0	5 778	12 350	12 841	12 675	22 400	26 395	28 059	29 494
5111 Value added taxes	..	..	5 778	12 350	12 841	12 675	22 400	26 395	28 059	29 494

	1965	1980	1990	2000	2007	2010	2015	2020	2021	2022
5112 Sales tax	..	..	0	0	0	0	0	0	0	0
5113 Other	..	..	0	0	0	0	0	0	0	0
5120 Taxes on specific goods and services	1 544	8 822	9 868	10 830	10 400	9 485	9 470	8 038	8 350	8 654
5121 Excises	1 062	6 674	8 637	9 837	9 374	8 622	8 351	7 167	7 398	7 582
Liquor tax	353	1 424	1 935	1 816	1 524	1 389	1 338	1 134	1 132	1 188
Sugar excises	29	43	0	0	0	0	0	0	0	0
Local gasoline tax	46	278	361	296	302	294	264	220	222	221
Gasoline tax	254	1 547	2 007	2 769	2 820	2 750	2 465	2 058	2 076	2 065
Liquefied petroleum gas tax	0	30	31	28	27	24	18	9	10	9
Aviation fuel tax	0	58	76	104	104	89	66	11	45	45
Commodity tax	138	1 038	5	0	0	0	0	0	0	0
Playing-card tax	1	1	0	0	0	0	0	0	0	0
Prefectural tobacco tax	44	229	361	282	278	256	153	134	142	150
Municipal tobacco tax	73	402	636	865	853	788	936	817	871	921
Timber delivery tax	3	3	0	0	0	0	0	0	0	0
Mineral product tax	2	5	3	2	2	2	2	2	2	2
Electricity and gas tax	54	386	0	0	0	0	0	0	0	0
Diesel oil tax	65	447	834	1 208	1 034	918	925	910	927	920
Vehicle acquisition tax	0	270	613	464	425	192	137	0	0	0
Promotion of power resources development tax	0	109	295	375	352	349	316	311	316	312
Petroleum and coal tax	0	404	487	489	513	502	630	608	636	663
Tobacco tax	0	0	996	876	925	908	954	840	906	957
Special tobacco tax	0	0	0	264	214	163	148	112	112	116
International tourist tax			0	0	0	0	0	1	2	13
5122 Profits of fiscal monopolies	179	808	0	0	0	0	0	0	0	0
Monopoly profits	179	808	..	..	..	..	..	..	..	..
5123 Customs and import duties	222	786	928	877	941	786	1 049	820	893	1 008
Customs duty	222	786	928	877	941	786	1 049	820	893	1 008
5124 Taxes on exports	0	0	0	0	0	0	0	0	0	0
5125 Taxes on investment goods	0	0	0	0	0	0	0	0	0	0
5126 Taxes on specific services	81	554	303	116	85	77	70	52	59	64
Travel tax	4	64	0	0	0	0	0	0	0	0
Admission tax	10	5	0	0	0	0	0	0	0	0
Local entertainment tax	10	74	0	0	0	0	0	0	0	0
Golf course utilization tax	0	0	90	81	60	55	48	39	44	45
Meal and lodging tax	56	398	0	0	0	0	0	0	0	0
Special local consumption tax	0	0	195	12	0	0	0	0	0	0
Bathing tax	1	13	18	23	25	22	23	12	14	19
5127 Other taxes on internat. trade and transactions	0	0	0	0	0	0	0	0	0	0
5128 Other taxes	0	0	0	0	0	0	0	0	0	0
5130 Unallocable between 5110 and 5120	0	0	0	0	0	0	0	0	0	0
5200 Taxes on use of goods and perform activities	76	1 378	2 270	3 047	3 015	2 570	2 416	2 620	2 601	2 678
5210 Recurrent taxes	69	1 358	2 250	3 027	2 993	2 548	2 393	2 599	2 580	2 657
Automobile tax	55	781	1 276	1 765	1 717	1 616	1 543	1 623	1 614	1 654
Light vehicle tax	13	43	88	125	164	178	200	285	294	310
Motor vehicle tonnage tax	0	527	881	1 134	1 110	753	649	690	671	692
Hunter licence tax	0	3	2	2	0	0	0	0	0	0
Hunting tax	0	3	2	1	2	2	1	1	1	1
Mine lot tax	1	1	1	1	0	0	0	0	0	0
5211 Paid by households: motor vehicles	..	..	..	..	..	..	..	..	..	..
5212 Paid by others: motor vehicles	..	..	..	..	..	..	..	..	..	..
5213 Paid in respect of other goods	..	..	..	..	..	..	..	..	..	..
5220 Nonrecurrent taxes	7	20	20	20	22	21	22	21	21	22
5300 Unallocable between 5100 and 5200	0	0	0	0	0	0	0	0	0	0
6000 Other taxes	2	151	335	348	356	381	413	444	496	479
6100 Paid solely by business	0	139	288	324	313	330	361	385	397	398
Business office tax	..	139	288	324	313	330	361	385	397	398
6200 Other	2	12	47	24	43	52	52	60	99	82
Taxes not in local tax law	2	12	47	24	43	52	52	60	63	74
Other	0	0	0	0	0	0	0	0	35	8
Total tax revenue on cash basis	6 172	62 443	..	..	..	..	..	..	..	..
Total tax revenue on accrual basis	..	..	130 843	136 236	146 248	132 484	163 532	177 321	187 992	195 848
Additional taxes included in National Accounts	..	..	..	..	..	..	..	..	..	..
Taxes excluded from National Accounts	..	..	..	..	..	..	..	..	..	..
Difference in treatment of tax credits	..	..	..	..	..	..	..	..	..	..
Capital transfer for uncollected revenue	..	..	..	..	..	..	..	..	..	..
Voluntary social security contributions	..	..	..	..	..	..	..	..	..	..
Miscellaneous differences	..	..	..	..	..	..	..	..	..	..
National Accounts: Taxes and actual social contributions	..	..	..	..	..	..	..	..	..	..
Imputed social contributions	..	..	..	..	..	..	..	..	..	..

	1965	1980	1990	2000	2007	2010	2015	2020	2021	2022
National Accounts: Taxes and all social contributions	..	..	..	..	..	..	..	..	..	..

.. Not available

Note: Data are on a fiscal year basis beginning 1st April.

From 1990, data are on accrual basis.

The figures for different groups of taxes are reported on different reporting bases, namely: Social security contributions (heading 2000) : in principle accrual basis, Central government taxes : accrual basis (revenues accrued during the fiscal year plus cash receipts collected before the end of May (the end of April until 1977), Local government taxes : accrual basis (due to be paid during the fiscal year and cash receipts collected before the end of May).

The Japanese authorities take the view that the Enterprise tax (classified in 1100 and 1200) and the Mineral product tax (classified in 5121) should be classified in heading 6000 since under articles 72 and 519 of the Local Tax Law these taxes are regarded as levies on the business or mining activity itself.

Heading 2000 includes some unidentifiable voluntary contributions.

Heading 2300: Includes contributions to the National pension, National Health Insurance and the Farmer's pension fund. Contributions to the Farmer's pension fund are not available for the years before 1999.

Heading 4100: Municipal property tax, includes Prefectural property tax from 1990 to 1994 because data is not available to provide a breakdown.

Heading 5121: Municipal tobacco tax, includes Prefectural tobacco tax from 1990 to 1994 because data is not available to provide a breakdown.

Heading 5121: In sub-item Petroleum and coal tax, the data before 2003 refer to petroleum tax.

Source: Tax Bureau, Ministry of Finance.

Table 5.21. Korea: Details of tax revenue, 1965-2022

Billion KRW

	1965	1980	1990	2000	2007	2010	2015	2020	2021	2022
Total tax revenue	..	6 687	37 262	136 295	258 571	295 968	393 559	538 450	619 084	691 257
1000 Taxes on income, profits and capital gains	..	1 704	12 203	39 254	82 239	82 905	119 151	166 564	205 574	258 193
1100 Of individuals	..	766	7 440	19 950	43 276	42 098	67 600	101 286	126 210	141 926
1110 On income and profits	..	766	6 327	18 569	31 984	33 935	55 744	77 630	89 503	109 693
Income tax	..	0	0	0	0	0	0	0	0	0
Dividends and interest income tax	..	0	0	0	4 682	4 425	4 561	5 830	6 863	6 785
Wages and salaries income tax	..	0	0	0	14 124	15 517	27 055	40 905	47 231	57 442
Other income tax	..	0	0	0	2 607	2 986	4 467	6 645	7 321	8 350
Global income tax	..	661	4 723	16 128	6 151	6 369	12 784	16 073	15 990	23 939
Defence tax on income tax	..	105	938	0	0	0	0	0	0	0
Education tax on income tax	..	0	325	0	0	0	0	0	0	0
Rural development tax on interest, bus. Inc. & cap.gains relief	..	0	0	156	160	179	105	225	326	347
Inhabitant tax on income tax (local)	..	0	341	2 285	4 260	4 459	6 772	7 952	11 772	12 830
1120 On capital gains	..	0	1 113	1 381	11 292	8 163	11 856	23 656	36 707	32 233
Capital gains tax	..	..	1 113	1 381	11 292	8 163	11 856	23 656	36 707	32 233
1200 Corporate	..	738	4 757	19 271	38 963	40 807	51 551	65 278	79 364	116 267
1210 On profits	..	738	4 757	19 271	38 963	40 807	51 551	65 278	79 364	116 267
Corporation tax - withholding	..	..	677	8 577	8 360	9 095	12 317	13 179	14 928	16 586
Corporation tax - final returns	..	..	2 549	9 302	27 057	28 173	32 713	42 335	55 468	86 984
Defence tax on corporation tax	..	..	1 323	0	0	0	0	0	0	0
Inhabitant tax on corporation tax (local)	..	..	207	1 142	3 152	3 094	6 217	9 293	8 343	11 828
Rural development tax corporate income	..	..	0	251	394	445	304	471	625	869
Excess profit tax	..	0	0	0	0	0	0	0	0	0
1220 On capital gains	..	0	0	0	0	0	0	0	0	0
Capital gains tax	..	..	..	..	..	..	..	..	..	..
1300 Unallocable between 1100 and 1200	..	199	6	33	0	0	0	0	0	0
Business income tax	..	0	0	0	..	..	..	..	..	..
Real estate income tax	..	0	0	0	..	..	..	..	..	..
Defence tax on real estate & business income	..	0	0	0	..	..	..	..	..	..
Rural dev. tax on bus. inc. & cap. gains relief	..	0	0	30	..	..	..	..	..	..
Inhabitant tax before 1990 (local)	..	117	0	0	..	..	..	..	..	..
Farm land tax (local)	..	83	6	3	..	..	..	..	..	..
Inhabitant tax on farm land tax (local)	..	0	0	0	..	..	..	..	..	..
2000 Social security contributions	..	73	3 760	22 759	53 588	69 090	104 693	150 854	162 209	176 747
2100 Employees	..	0	1 464	8 578	21 773	28 213	44 281	65 384	70 297	77 530
Veterans' relief fund	..	0	0	0	0	0	0	0	0	0
Soldiers' annuity fund	..	0	0	0	0	0	0	0	0	0
Unemployment assurance	..	0	0	598	1 164	1 358	3 076	4 895	5 159	6 061
National welfare pension fund	..	0	429	4 325	9 338	11 004	15 821	21 722	22 879	24 310
Social benefit fund	..	0	0	0	0	0	0	0	0	0
Health Insurance	..	0	483	2 066	8 180	11 783	19 868	30 184	33 453	38 209
Teachers' pensions	..	0	86	279	581	868	1 125	1 780	1 818	1 837
Government employees pensions	..	0	406	1 144	2 202	2 878	3 876	6 134	6 302	6 409
Military personal pensions	..	0	60	166	308	322	515	669	686	704
2110 On a payroll basis	..	..	..	8 578	21 773	28 213	44 281	65 384	70 297	77 530
2120 On an income tax basis	..	..	..	0	0	0	0	0	0	0
2200 Employers	..	73	1 694	9 409	23 557	30 856	47 846	67 676	72 773	80 600
Ind. works' insurance fund	..	73	550	1 876	4 431	4 632	6 062	7 088	7 498	8 195
Soldiers' annuity fund	..	0	0	0	0	0	0	0	0	0
Pneumoconiosis fund	..	0	0	0	0	0	0	0	0	0
Unemployment insurance	..	0	0	1 449	2 474	2 860	5 499	8 024	8 398	9 658
Veterans' relief fund	..	0	0	0	0	0	0	0	0	0
National welfare pension fund	..	0	430	4 340	9 383	11 052	15 895	21 722	22 879	24 310
Social benefit fund	..	0	0	0	0	0	0	0	0	0
Health Insurance	..	0	658	1 547	6 844	11 718	19 493	29 288	32 373	36 759
Teachers' pensions	..	0	56	197	425	594	897	1 554	1 625	1 678
Government employees pensions	..	0	0	0	0	0	0	0	0	0
2210 On a payroll basis of employers SSC	..	..	..	9 409	23 557	30 856	47 846	67 676	72 773	80 600
2220 On an income tax basis of employers SSC	..	..	..	0	0	0	0	0	0	0
2300 Selfemployed or nonemployed	..	0	602	4 772	8 258	10 021	12 566	17 794	19 139	18 617
2310 On a payroll basis of self/non-employed SSC	..	..	0	0	0	0	0	0	0	0
2320 On an income tax basis of self/non-employed SSC	..	..	602	4 772	8 258	10 021	12 566	17 794	19 139	18 617
2400 Unallocable between 2100, 2200 and 2300	..	0	0	0	0	0	0	0	0	0
2410 On a payroll basis unallocable between 2100, 2200 and 2300 SSC	..	..	..	..	..	..	..	..	..	..
2420 On an income tax basis unallocable between 2100, 2200 and 2300 SSC	..	..	..	..	..	..	..	..	..	..

	1965	1980	1990	2000	2007	2010	2015	2020	2021	2022
3000 Taxes on payroll and workforce	..	34	153	258	619	714	1 122	1 607	1 755	1 982
Workshop tax on workforce (local)	..	31	124	258	619	714	1 122	1 607	1 755	1 982
Vocational training promotion fund	..	3	29	0	0	0	0	0	0	0
4000 Taxes on property	..	537	4 389	16 846	33 109	33 516	48 625	76 512	93 263	82 065
4100 Recurrent taxes on immovable property	..	183	980	3 385	9 196	9 270	12 486	20 044	24 486	26 510
Property tax (local)	..	119	227	728	3 755	4 817	9 294	13 773	14 974	16 277
City planning tax on urban real estate (local)	..	51	244	815	1 883	2 465	0	0	0	0
Community facilities tax (local)	..	13	86	341	543	650	1 351	1 777	1 841	1 915
Tax on excessive land holdings (local)	..	0	1	0	0	0	0	0	0	0
Tax on aggregate land holdings (local)	..	0	400	1 282	5	0	0	0	0	0
Rural dev. tax on local agg. land holdings tax	..	0	0	81	1	0	0	0	0	0
Tax on excessively increased land value	..	0	0	0	0	0	0	0	0	0
Comprehensive real estate tax	..	0	0	0	2 414	1 029	1 399	3 601	6 130	6 799
Rural dev. tax on comprehensive real estate tax	..	0	0	0	483	208	267	680	1 172	1 300
4110 Households	..	..	0	0	0	0	0	0	0	0
4120 Others	..	..	22	138	112	101	175	213	369	219
Workshop tax on property (local)	..	..	22	138	112	101	175	213	369	219
4200 Recurrent taxes on net wealth	..	0	0	0	0	0	0	0	0	0
4210 Individual	..	..	..	..	..	..	..	..	..	..
4220 Corporate	..	..	..	..	..	..	..	..	..	..
4300 Estate, inheritance and gift taxes	..	12	354	989	2 842	3 076	5 044	10 375	15 006	14 594
4310 Estate and inheritance taxes	..	5	85	449	1 059	1 203	1 944	3 904	6 945	7 611
Inheritance tax	..	3	71	449	1 059	1 203	1 944	3 904	6 945	7 611
Defence tax on inheritance tax	..	2	14	0	0	0	0	0	0	0
4320 Gift taxes	..	7	269	540	1 783	1 873	3 100	6 471	8 061	6 983
Gift tax	..	7	225	540	1 783	1 873	3 100	6 471	8 061	6 983
Defence tax on gift tax	..	0	44	0	0	0	0	0	0	0
4400 Taxes on financial and capital transactions	..	319	2 960	11 935	21 071	21 170	31 095	46 093	53 771	40 961
Registration tax (local)	..	122	1 378	4 528	7 254	7 370	1 831	2 053	2 155	1 896
Registration tax	..	0	0	0	0	0	0	0	0	0
Defence tax on registration tax	..	0	0	0	0	0	0	0	0	0
Rural dev. tax on local acquisition tax	..	0	0	246	627	632	969	1 164	1 343	1 179
Rural dev. tax on local registration tax	..	0	0	66	143	144	1	0	0	0
Securities transactions tax	..	0	224	2 736	3 469	3 667	4 670	8 759	10 256	6 303
Rural dev. tax on securities transaction tax	..	0	0	823	1 729	2 010	1 861	3 616	5 340	3 068
Acquisition tax (local)	..	163	1 165	3 148	7 261	6 825	20 810	29 536	33 717	27 716
Stamp tax	..	34	193	388	588	522	953	965	960	799
4500 Nonrecurrent taxes	..	22	95	537	0	0	0	0	0	0
Asset revaluation tax	..	22	95	537	..	..	..	..	..	..
4510 On net wealth	..	..	0	0	..	..	..	..	..	..
4520 Other nonrecurrent taxes	..	..	0	0	..	..	..	..	..	..
4600 Other recurrent taxes on property	..	0	0	0	0	0	0	0	0	0
5000 Taxes on goods and services	..	4 190	16 497	52 271	80 861	99 769	110 326	131 353	143 100	156 778
5100 Taxes on production, sale, transfer, etc	..	4 114	16 024	50 023	78 414	96 573	103 254	123 219	134 745	149 448
5110 General taxes	..	1 471	6 964	23 212	40 942	51 800	60 162	81 452	89 022	105 558
5111 Value added taxes	..	1 471	6 964	23 212	40 942	51 800	60 162	81 452	89 022	105 558
Value added tax	..	1 471	6 964	23 212	40 942	51 800	60 162	81 452	89 022	105 558
5112 Sales tax	..	0	0	0	0	0	0	0	0	0
Business tax	..	..	..	..	..	..	..	..	..	..
5113 Other	..	0	0	0	0	0	0	0	0	0
5120 Taxes on specific goods and services	..	2 643	9 059	26 811	37 472	44 773	43 092	41 767	45 723	43 890
5121 Excises	..	1 029	4 924	18 155	27 880	31 340	31 857	33 013	35 792	30 834
Commodity tax	..	0	0	0	0	0	0	0	0	0
Defence tax on commodity tax	..	0	0	0	0	0	0	0	0	0
Liquor tax	..	298	1 022	1 963	2 268	2 878	3 228	3 008	2 673	3 767
Defence tax on liquor tax	..	78	0	0	0	0	0	0	0	0
Education tax on liquor tax	..	0	81	516	580	724	808	733	608	865
Textile tax	..	0	0	0	0	0	0	0	0	0
Petroleum tax	..	0	0	0	0	0	0	0	0	0
Transport tax on petrol products	..	0	0	8 404	11 464	13 970	14 055	13 938	16 598	11 116
Education tax on transport tax	..	0	0	1 247	1 715	2 133	2 154	2 041	2 497	1 670
Electricity and gas tax	..	0	0	0	0	0	0	0	0	0
Special excise tax	..	583	1 912	2 985	5 161	5 066	8 001	9 218	9 364	9 318
Defence tax on special excise tax	..	70	337	0	0	0	0	0	0	0
Education tax on special excise tax	..	0	0	498	607	501	515	440	435	404
Rural development on special excise tax	..	0	0	37	54	24	61	57	59	64
Tobacco sales tax (local)	..	0	0	0	0	0	0	0	0	0
Tobacco consumption tax (local)	..	0	1 572	2 251	2 761	2 875	3 035	3 578	3 558	3 630
Motor fuel tax (local)	..	0	0	254	3 270	3 169	0	0	0	0
5122 Profits of fiscal monopolies	..	510	0	0	0	0	0	0	0	0
Monopoly profit	..	510	..	..	..	..	..	..	..	..

	1965	1980	1990	2000	2007	2010	2015	2020	2021	2022
5123 Customs and import duties	..	1 014	3 692	5 936	7 690	11 046	8 907	7 413	8 629	10 794
Customs duties	..	762	2 765	5 800	7 411	10 666	8 495	7 059	8 227	10 324
Defence tax on customs duties	..	248	919	0	0	0	0	0	0	0
Special customs duties	..	0	0	0	0	0	0	0	0	0
Tonnage tax	..	0	0	0	0	0	0	0	0	0
Education tax on imports	..	0	7	99	234	336	390	341	388	452
Rural dev. tax on customs exemptions	..	0	0	37	45	44	22	13	14	18
Previous year receipts	..	4	0	0	0	0	0	0	0	0
5124 Taxes on exports	..	0	0	0	0	0	0	0	0	0
5125 Taxes on investment goods	..	0	0	0	0	0	0	0	0	0
5126 Taxes on specific services	..	90	444	2 720	1 902	2 387	2 328	1 341	1 302	2 262
Telephone tax	..	50	262	1 457	0	0	0	0	0	0
Defence tax on telephone tax	..	33	0	0	0	0	0	0	0	0
Entertainment tax	..	0	0	0	0	0	0	0	0	0
Defence tax on entertainment tax	..	0	0	0	0	0	0	0	0	0
Entertainment tax (local)	..	0	0	0	0	0	0	0	0	0
Travel tax	..	0	0	0	0	0	0	0	0	0
Admission tax	..	0	0	0	0	0	0	0	0	0
Defence tax on admission tax	..	0	0	0	0	0	0	0	0	0
Education tax on banking & insurance	..	0	108	473	721	951	1 004	1 138	1 175	1 253
Horse race tax (local)	..	3	56	566	864	1 068	1 089	169	106	841
Rural dev. tax on horse race tax	..	0	0	84	165	215	235	34	21	168
Butchery tax (local)	..	5	18	51	52	58	0	0	0	0
Regional development tax (local)	..	0	0	89	100	95	0	0	0	0
5127 Other taxes on internat. trade and transactions	..	0	0	0	0	0	0	0	0	0
5128 Other taxes	..	0	0	0	0	0	0	0	0	0
5130 Unallocable between 5110 and 5120	..	0	0	0	0	0	0	0	0	0
5200 Taxes on use of goods and perform activities	..	75	474	2 248	2 447	3 196	7 072	8 134	8 355	7 330
5210 Recurrent taxes	..	75	474	2 248	2 447	3 196	7 072	8 134	8 355	7 330
License tax (local)	..	18	48	241	77	76	0	0	0	0
Automobile tax (local)	..	57	426	2 007	2 370	3 120	7 072	8 134	8 355	7 330
5211 Paid by households: motor vehicles	..	..	..	..	..	..	..	..	..	..
5212 Paid by others: motor vehicles	..	..	..	..	..	..	..	..	..	..
5213 Paid in respect of other goods	..	..	..	..	..	..	..	..	..	..
5220 Nonrecurrent taxes	..	0	0	0	0	0	0	0	0	0
5300 Unallocable between 5100 and 5200	..	0	0	0	0	0	0	0	0	0
6000 Other taxes	..	150	259	4 907	8 155	9 974	9 642	11 560	13 183	15 492
6100 Paid solely by business	..	0	0	0	0	0	0	0	0	0
6200 Other	..	150	259	4 907	8 155	9 974	9 642	11 560	13 183	15 492
Unallocable tax revenue	..	143	0	0	0	0	0	0	0	0
Previous year tax	..	0	213	1 474	2 965	4 449	3 435	4 165	5 147	7 316
Previous year tax (local)	..	6	47	474	672	654	392	259	437	656
Unallocable defence tax	..	0	0	- 3	0	0	0	0	0	0
Education tax on local taxes	..	0	0	2 962	4 518	4 871	5 815	7 136	7 599	7 520
Total tax revenue on cash basis	..	6 687	37 262	136 295	258 571	295 968	393 559	538 450	619 084	691 257
Total tax revenue on accrual basis	..	..	..	..	..	..	..	..	..	..
Additional taxes included in National Accounts	..	..	..	..	..	..	..	..	..	..
Taxes excluded from National Accounts	..	..	..	..	..	..	..	..	..	..
Difference in treatment of tax credits	..	..	..	..	..	..	..	..	..	..
Capital transfer for uncollected revenue	..	..	..	..	..	..	..	..	..	..
Voluntary social security contributions	..	..	..	..	..	..	..	..	..	..
Miscellaneous differences	..	..	..	..	..	..	..	..	..	..
National Accounts: Taxes and actual social contributions	..	..	..	..	..	..	..	..	..	..
Imputed social contributions	..	..	..	..	..	..	..	..	..	..
National Accounts: Taxes and all social contributions	..	..	..	..	..	..	..	..	..	..

.. Not available

Note: Year ending 31st December.

Data are on cash basis.

Heading 2000: From 1997 the contributions to the three funds (civil servant pension fund, private school teachers pension fund and medical insurance fund) are classified as security social contributions. The reasons for the change are that the contributions either became mandatory or the fund started to be managed by public authorities in that year, thereby meeting the OECD definition of social security contributions.

Heading 2200: From 2007, this includes long-term care insurance.

Source: Ministry of Finance and Economy, Ministry of Home Affairs.

Table 5.22. Latvia: Details of tax revenue, 1965-2022

Million EUR

	1965	1980	1990	2000	2007	2010	2015	2020	2021	2022
Total tax revenue	..	..	..	1 995	6 401	5 162	7 320	9 374	10 253	11 808
Total tax revenue exclusive of taxes collected for the EU	..	..	..	1 995	6 362	5 137	7 272	9 322	10 177	11 716
1000 Taxes on income, profits and capital gains	..	..	..	480	1 857	1 292	1 833	2 019	2 296	2 653
1100 Taxes on income, profits and capital gains of individuals	..	..	..	376	1 287	1 116	1 445	1 803	2 009	2 264
1110 On income and profits of individuals	..	..	..	376	1 287	1 116	1 445	1 803	2 009	2 264
Personal income tax	..	..	..	376	1 287	1 116	1 445	1 803	2 009	2 264
Solidarity tax	..	..	..	0	0	0	0	0	0	0
1120 On capital gains of individuals	..	..	..	0	0	0	0	0	0	0
1200 Taxes on income, profits and capital gains of corporates	..	..	..	105	570	175	389	217	288	388
1210 On profits of corporates	..	..	..	105	570	175	389	217	288	388
1220 On capital gains of corporates	..	..	..	0	0	0	0	0	0	0
1300 Unallocable between 1100 and 1200	..	..	..	0	0	0	0	0	0	0
2000 Social security contributions (SSC)	..	..	..	669	1 774	1 554	2 030	2 985	3 191	3 610
2100 Employees SSC	..	..	..	167	479	389	585	978	1 042	1 183
2110 On a payroll basis of employees SSC	..	..	..	167	479	389	585	978	1 042	1 183
2120 On an income tax basis of employees SSC	..	..	..	0	0	0	0	0	0	0
2200 Employers SSC	..	..	..	501	1 283	1 155	1 432	1 979	2 107	2 374
2210 On a payroll basis of employers SSC	..	..	..	501	1 283	1 155	1 432	1 979	2 107	2 374
2220 On an income tax basis of employers SSC	..	..	..	0	0	0	0	0	0	0
2300 Self-employed or non-employed SSC	..	..	..	1	12	9	12	29	43	53
2310 On a payroll basis of self/non-employed SSC	..	..	..	1	12	9	12	29	43	53
2320 On an income tax basis of self/non-employed SSC	..	..	..	0	0	0	0	0	0	0
2400 Unallocable between 2100, 2200 and 2300 SSC	..	..	..	0	0	0	0	0	0	0
2410 On a payroll basis unallocable between 2100, 2200 and 2300 SSC	..	..	..	..	..	..	..	..	..	..
2420 On an income tax basis unallocable between 2100, 2200 and 2300 SSC	..	..	..	..	..	..	..	..	..	..
3000 Taxes on payroll and workforce	..	..	..	0	4	3	3	3	3	3
Risk duty of business	..	..	..	..	4	3	3	3	3	3
4000 Taxes on property	..	..	..	76	195	157	249	281	296	294
4100 Recurrent taxes on immovable property	..	..	..	63	106	128	197	222	226	231
4110 Households recurrent taxes on immovable property	..	..	..	0	0	0	24	39	39	40
4120 Other than households recurrent taxes on immovable property	..	..	..	63	106	128	173	183	187	190
Tax on property	..	..	..	63	106	128	173	183	187	190
Tax on land	..	..	..	0	0	0	0	0	0	0
4200 Recurrent taxes on net wealth	..	..	..	0	0	0	0	0	0	0
4210 Individual recurrent taxes on net wealth	..	..	..	..	..	..	..	..	..	..
4220 Corporate recurrent taxes on net wealth	..	..	..	..	..	..	..	..	..	..
4300 Estate, inheritance and gift taxes	..	..	..	0	3	3	7	12	15	13
4310 Estate and inheritance taxes	..	..	..	..	3	3	7	12	15	13
Duty for legacies and donations	..	..	..	..	0	2	4	9	12	9
Stamp duty for transactions made in Land Register in relation to legacies and donations	..	..	..	..	1	0	1	1	1	1
Duty for consolidation of ownership and legal cliens in Land Register anent legacies and donations	..	..	..	..	2	2	2	2	3	3
4320 Gift taxes	..	..	..	..	0	0	0	0	0	0
4400 Taxes on financial and capital transactions	..	..	..	13	86	26	42	44	50	47
Duties on transactions with privatization vouchers	..	..	..	0	0	0	0	0	0	0
Stamp duty for transactions made in Land Register, which have been collected from juridical persons, except legacies and donations	..	..	..	0	1	1	1	1	1	1
Duty for consolidation of ownership and legal liens in Land Register, which have been collected from juridical persons, except legacies and donations	..	..	..	4	27	13	18	18	21	21
Stamp duty for transactions made in Land Register, which have been collected from physical persons, except legacies and donations	..	..	..	1	8	1	2	2	2	2
Duty for consolidation of ownership and legal liens in Land Register, which have been collected from physical persons, except legacies and donations	..	..	..	7	51	11	20	23	26	23
4500 Non-recurrent taxes on property	..	..	..	0	0	0	3	3	5	4
4510 Non-recurrent taxes on net wealth	..	..	..	..	..	..	0	0	0	0
4520 Non-recurrent taxes on property other than net wealth	..	..	..	..	..	..	3	3	5	4
4520 The payment made by a foreigner before receiving temporary residence permit				..	..	..	3	3	5	4

	1965	1980	1990	2000	2007	2010	2015	2020	2021	2022
4600 Other recurrent taxes on property except 4100 and 4200	..	..	..	0	0	0	0	0	0	0
5000 Taxes on goods and services	..	..	..	770	2 572	2 157	3 205	4 086	4 467	5 248
5100 Taxes on production, sale, transfer, etc	..	..	..	739	2 515	2 031	3 052	3 867	4 234	4 962
5110 General taxes on goods and services	..	..	..	476	1 753	1 301	2 130	2 690	2 997	3 657
5111 Value added taxes	..	..	..	476	1 727	1 202	1 876	2 541	2 880	3 639
5112 Sales tax	..	..	..	0	0	0	31	0	0	0
Subsidised electricity tax	..	..	..	..	..	..	31	..	..	..
5113 Other (than value added and sales tax)	..	..	..	0	27	99	223	149	118	18
Mandatory procurement public service obligation fee				..	27	99	223	149	118	18
5120 Taxes on specific goods and services	..	..	..	262	761	730	922	1 177	1 237	1 305
5121 Excises	..	..	..	232	654	659	810	1 067	1 113	1 142
Excise duty on alcoholic beverages	..	..	..	63	127	111	128	190	195	208
Excise duty on wine				5	7	9	11	20	21	22
Excise duty on fermented beverages				0	4	3	3	8	9	9
Excise duty on intermediate products (the absolute alcohol content up to 15 per cent by volume)				1	1	1	2	4	5	6
Excise duty on intermediate products (the absolute alcohol content from 15 to 22 per cent by volume)				1	1	1	2	4	4	4
Excise duty on other alcoholic drinks (ethyl alcohol)				55	114	96	110	153	155	167
Excise duty on beer	..	..	..	4	15	25	27	52	52	52
Excise duty on oil products	..	..	..	124	359	360	428	560	579	566
Excise duty on tobacco	..	..	..	27	92	130	178	223	241	262
Excise duty on cigarettes				26	91	127	172	208	219	238
Excise duty on cigars and cigarillos				0	0	2	2	3	3	3
Excise duty on smoking tobacco				0	0	1	3	7	9	9
Excise duty on heated tobacco				0	0	0	0	5	10	12
Excise duty on coffee, non alcoholic beverages, refill liquids for electronic cigarettes and tobacco substitute products	..	..	..	6	8	13	14	19	22	33
Excise duty on non alcoholic beverages	..	..	..	2	4	5	7	9	9	14
Excise duty on liquids used in e-cigarettes	..	..	..	0	0	0	0	1	3	8
Excise duty on tobacco substitutes				0	0	0	0	0	1	2
Excise duty on coffee				4	4	7	7	9	9	9
Excise duty on natural gas	..	..	..	0	0	1	20	17	19	13
Excise duty on cars and motorcycles / Tax on cars and motocycles				8	24	5	11	0	0	0
Tax on electricity	..	..	..	0	1	1	2	5	5	5
Excise duty of imported goods for omission for free turnover				0	28	14	3	0	1	4
5122 Profits of fiscal monopolies	..	..	..	0	0	0	0	0	0	0
5123 Customs and import duties	..	..	..	21	42	25	40	48	71	88
Customs duties	..	..	..	21	40	25	40	48	71	88
Levies on imported agricultural products	..	..	..	0	2	0	0	0	0	0
5124 Taxes on exports	..	..	..	0	0	0	0	0	0	0
5125 Taxes on investment goods	..	..	..	0	0	0	0	0	0	0
5126 Taxes on specific services	..	..	..	10	66	47	72	63	53	75
Taxes on lotteries and gambling	..	..	..	7	42	22	32	34	20	40
Financial stability fee	..	..	..	0	0	0	4	6	8	8
Passenger departure duty	..	..	..	3	0	0	0	0	0	0
Other special target State duties				0	0	0	0	1	1	1
Contributions to the EU Single Resolution Fund	..	..	..	0	0	0	8	4	5	5
Contributions to the fund for the protection of the insured	..	..	..	0	1	1	1	0	0	0
Contributions to the deposit guarantee fund	..	..	..	0	22	24	28	18	20	22
5127 Other taxes on internat. trade and transactions not included within 5121 to 5126 inclusive	..	..	..	0	0	0	0	0	0	0
5128 Other taxes not included within 5121 to 5127 inclusive	..	..	..	0	0	0	0	0	0	0
5130 Unallocable between 5110 and 5120	..	..	..	0	0	0	0	0	0	0
5200 Taxes on use of goods and perform activities	..	..	..	32	57	126	153	219	233	286
5210 Recurrent taxes on use of goods and perform activities	..	..	..	32	57	73	142	178	189	209
5211 Recurrent taxes paid by households: motor vehicles	..	..	..	12	16	34	54	66	68	70
Vehicle tax for vehicles which have been registered on physical persons	..	..	..	0	0	0	54	66	68	70
Annual vehicle duty for vehicles which have been registered on physical persons	..	..	..	12	16	34	0	0	0	0
5212 Recurrent taxes paid by others: motor vehicles	..	..	..	0	20	22	46	53	54	54

	1965	1980	1990	2000	2007	2010	2015	2020	2021	2022
Tax on cars belonging to enterprises	..	..	..	..	0	0	20	22	23	22
Vehicle tax for vehicles which have been registered on judical persons	..	..	..	..	0	0	26	31	32	31
Annual vehicle duty for vehicles which have been registered on judical persons	..	..	..	..	20	22	0	0	0	0
5213 Recurrent taxes paid on use of goods and perform activities other than on motor vehicles	..	..	..	20	21	17	42	59	66	85
Duty for keeping animals	..	..	..	0	0	0	0	0	0	0
Income from lease of reservoirs and fishing rights and non-production use of fishing rights (fishing cards)	..	..	..	0	0	0	1	1	1	1
State fee from weapon				0	0	0	0	0	0	0
Business and professional licences	..	..	..	5	6	4	20	23	21	30
State duties and payments for issue of special permits (licences) and registration of documents that commensurate correspondence of professional qualification	..	..	..	1	0	0	0	0	0	0
Lottery and gambling state duty	..	..	..	1	4	2	2	4	4	4
Gambling equipment marking duty	..	..	..	0	1	1	0	0	0	0
Payment for rental of commercial fishing rights	..	..	..	0	0	0	1	0	0	0
Lottery of goods and services organization duty	..	..	..	2	0	0	0	0	0	0
State duty for using numerative rights	..	..	..	0	0	0	0	0	0	0
State duty for keeping oil products` security reserves	..	..	..	0	0	0	16	18	16	24
Tax on natural resources	..	..	..	15	15	12	22	35	44	54
5220 Non-recurrent taxes on use of goods and perform activities	..	..	..	0	0	53	11	42	44	77
Revenue from state-owned greenhouse gas emission unit trade	..	..	..	..	..	53	0	0	0	0
Payment for emission quota trading	..	..	..	..	..	0	11	42	44	77
The fee for the appeal of procurement	..	..	..	..	..	0	0	0	0	0
5300 Unallocable between 5100 and 5200	..	..	..	0	0	0	0	0	0	0
6000 Other	..	..	..	0	0	0	0	0	0	0
6100 Paid solely by business	..	..	..	..	..	..	..	..	..	..
6200 Other taxes not solely paid by business	..	..	..	..	..	..	..	..	..	..
Customs duties collected for the EU	..	..	..	..	37	25	40	48	72	87
SRF Contributions collected for the EU				..	..	..	8	4	5	5
Total tax revenue on cash basis	..	..	..	..	..	..	..	..	..	..
Total tax revenue on accrual basis	..	..	..	1 995	6 401	5 162	7 320	9 374	10 253	11 808
Additional taxes included in National Accounts	..	..	..	14	1	1	0	0	0	0
Taxes excluded from National Accounts	..	..	..	0	0	0	0	0	0	0
Difference in treatment of tax credits	..	..	..	0	0	0	0	0	0	0
Capital transfer for uncollected revenue	..	..	..	0	0	0	0	0	0	0
Voluntary social security contributions	..	..	..	0	0	0	0	0	0	0
Miscellaneous differences	..	..	..	0	0	0	0	0	0	0
National Accounts: Taxes and actual social contributions	..	..	..	2 009	6 402	5 163	7 320	9 374	10 254	11 809
Imputed social contributions	..	..	..	12	51	36	80	128	138	165
National Accounts: Taxes and all social contributions	..	..	..	2 022	6 453	5 199	7 401	9 502	10 391	11 974

.. Not available

Note: Year ending 31st December.
Data on accrual basis.

Source: Ministry of Finance.

Table 5.23. Lithuania: Details of tax revenue, 1965-2022

Million EUR

	1965	1980	1990	2000	2007	2010	2015	2020	2021	2022
Total tax revenue	..	..	..	4 154	8 730	7 961	10 826	15 623	18 044	21 314
Total tax revenue exclusive of taxes collected for the EU	..	..	..	4 154	8 656	7 908	10 716	15 490	17 870	21 108
1000 Taxes on income, profits and capital gains	..	..	..	1 111	2 625	1 281	2 013	4 453	5 375	6 678
1100 Taxes on income, profits and capital gains of individuals	..	..	..	1 020	1 891	1 005	1 439	3 628	4 215	5 105
1110 On income and profits of individuals	..	..	..	1 020	1 810	972	1 390	3 628	4 215	5 105
Tax on payroll and workforce	..	..	..	950	1 628	793	1 148	3 628	4 215	5 105
Tax on income from individual activities	..	..	..	40	81	36	55	0	0	0
Tax on capital income	..	..	..	31	102	143	187	0	0	0
1120 On capital gains of individuals	..	..	..	0	81	33	50	0	0	0
1200 Taxes on income, profits and capital gains of corporates	..	..	..	90	734	276	574	825	1 161	1 573
1210 On profits of corporates	..	..	..	90	734	276	574	825	1 161	1 573
1220 On capital gains of corporates	..	..	..	0	0	0	0	0	0	0
1300 Unallocable between 1100 and 1200	..	..	..	0	0	0	0	0	0	0
2000 Social security contributions (SSC)	..	..	..	1 362	2 643	3 293	4 338	5 127	5 750	6 656
2100 Employees SSC	..	..	..	107	233	641	873	3 872	4 367	5 091
2110 On a payroll basis of employees SSC	..	..	..	107	233	641	873	3 872	4 367	5 091
2120 On an income tax basis of employees SSC	..	..	..	0	0	0	0	0	0	0
2200 Employers SSC	..	..	..	1 119	2 180	2 109	2 916	378	421	503
2210 On a payroll basis of employers SSC	..	..	..	1 119	2 180	2 109	2 916	378	421	503
2220 On an income tax basis of employers SSC	..	..	..	0	0	0	0	0	0	0
2300 Self-employed or non-employed SSC	..	..	..	135	230	544	549	877	962	1 062
2310 On a payroll basis of self/non-employed SSC	..	..	..	135	230	544	549	877	962	1 062
2320 On an income tax basis of self/non-employed SSC	..	..	..	0	0	0	0	0	0	0
2400 Unallocable between 2100, 2200 and 2300 SSC	..	..	..	0	0	0	0	0	0	0
2410 On a payroll basis unallocable between 2100, 2200 and 2300 SSC	..	..	..	..	..	..	..	..	..	..
2420 On an income tax basis unallocable between 2100, 2200 and 2300 SSC	..	..	..	..	..	..	..	..	..	..
3000 Taxes on payroll and workforce	..	..	..	0	0	0	0	0	0	0
4000 Taxes on property	..	..	..	62	83	103	126	150	166	194
4100 Recurrent taxes on immovable property	..	..	..	61	82	102	125	148	164	191
4110 Households recurrent taxes on immovable property	..	..	..	3	6	7	17	40	45	49
4120 Other than households recurrent taxes on immovable property	..	..	..	58	76	95	108	108	119	142
Tax on land from corporations	..	..	..	3	8	9	10	6	7	6
Tax on immovable property	..	..	..	55	69	86	98	102	112	136
4200 Recurrent taxes on net wealth	..	..	..	0	0	0	0	0	0	0
4210 Individual recurrent taxes on net wealth	..	..	..	..	..	..	..	..	..	..
4220 Corporate recurrent taxes on net wealth	..	..	..	..	..	..	..	..	..	..
4300 Estate, inheritance and gift taxes	..	..	..	1	2	1	1	2	3	3
4310 Estate and inheritance taxes	..	..	..	1	2	1	1	2	3	3
4320 Gift taxes	..	..	..	0	0	0	0	0	0	0
4400 Taxes on financial and capital transactions	..	..	..	0	0	0	0	0	0	0
4500 Non-recurrent taxes on property	..	..	..	0	0	0	0	0	0	0
4510 Non-recurrent taxes on net wealth	..	..	..	..	..	..	..	..	..	..
4520 Non-recurrent taxes on property other than net wealth	..	..	..	..	..	..	..	..	..	..
4600 Other recurrent taxes on property except 4100 and 4200	..	..	..	0	0	0	0	0	0	0
5000 Taxes on goods and services	..	..	..	1 619	3 378	3 284	4 348	5 893	6 752	7 786
5100 Taxes on production, sale, transfer, etc	..	..	..	1 556	3 298	3 202	4 275	5 771	6 612	7 626
5110 General taxes on goods and services	..	..	..	1 086	2 339	2 183	2 913	4 033	4 719	5 693
5111 Value added taxes	..	..	..	1 005	2 330	2 180	2 889	4 008	4 688	5 644
5112 Sales tax	..	..	..	0	0	0	0	0	0	0

	1965	1980	1990	2000	2007	2010	2015	2020	2021	2022
5113 Other (than value added and sales tax)	..	..	..	81	8	3	24	24	31	49
Deductions from revenue according to the RoL on the financing of road maintence and development	..	..	..	81	0	0	0	0	0	0
Deductions from revenue according to the RoL Forestry Law	..	..	..	0	0	0	24	24	31	49
Turnover tax on goods	..	..	..	0	0	0	0	0	0	0
Deductions from Ignalina nuclear power plant income generated by sales of electricity	..	..	..	0	8	3	0	0	0	0
Turnover tax on publications of erotic and violent nature	..	..	..	0	0	0	0	0	0	0
Turnover tax on motor cars	..	..	..	0	0	0	0	0	0	0
Turnover tax on goods containing ethyl	..	..	..	0	0	0	0	0	0	0
5120 Taxes on specific goods and services	..	..	..	470	960	1 019	1 362	1 738	1 894	1 933
5121 Excises	..	..	..	428	835	903	1 165	1 569	1 675	1 657
Alcoholic beverages	..	..	..	10	2	10	6	21	16	8
Manufactured tabacco	..	..	..	41	121	170	270	309	329	348
Oil and other oil products	..	..	..	230	451	487	619	861	915	872
Electricity	..	..	..	2	0	3	4	5	2	2
Luxury cars	..	..	..	1	0	0	0	0	0	0
Sugar	..	..	..	25	13	1	1	0	0	0
Other former minor excises	..	..	..	5	0	0	0	0	0	0
Wine and sparkling wine	..	..	..	6	23	30	36	53	56	59
Beer	..	..	..	24	38	44	50	87	85	96
Other alcoholic beverages	..	..	..	84	186	158	179	234	271	272
5122 Profits of fiscal monopolies	..	..	..	0	0	0	0	0	0	0
5123 Customs and import duties	..	..	..	41	61	53	99	128	167	199
Taxes on international trades and transactions	..	..	..	41	0	0	0	0	0	0
Imported sugar tax	..	..	..	0	0	0	0	0	0	0
Custom duties collected for the EU				0	61	53	99	128	167	199
5124 Taxes on exports	..	..	..	0	0	0	0	0	0	0
5125 Taxes on investment goods	..	..	..	0	0	0	0	0	0	0
5126 Taxes on specific services	..	..	..	0	64	63	98	41	52	76
Tax on lotteries and gambling	..	..	..	..	9	8	15	17	24	41
Contributions to the Guarantee Fund	..	..	..	..	11	5	16	0	0	0
Deposit and investment insurance tax	..	..	..	..	43	48	56	17	20	26
Resolution Fund	..	..	..	..	0	0	10	6	6	7
Other taxes on specific services	..	..	..	..	0	1	1	2	1	2
5127 Other taxes on internat. trade and transactions not included within 5121 to 5126 inclusive	..	..	..	0	0	0	0	0	0	0
5128 Other taxes not included within 5121 to 5127 inclusive	..	..	..	0	0	0	0	0	0	0
5130 Unallocable between 5110 and 5120	..	..	..	0	0	0	0	0	0	0
5200 Taxes on use of goods and perform activities	..	..	..	64	80	83	74	122	140	160
5210 Recurrent taxes on use of goods and perform activities	..	..	..	64	80	83	74	122	140	160
5211 Recurrent taxes paid by households: motor vehicles	..	..	..	0	0	0	0	0	0	0
5212 Recurrent taxes paid by others: motor vehicles	..	..	..	7	30	13	32	52	68	68
Car registration taxes	..	..	..	0	0	0	15	30	47	48
Conveyance taxes	..	..	..	7	30	13	17	22	21	20
5213 Recurrent taxes paid on use of goods and perform activities other than on motor vehicles	..	..	..	57	50	70	42	70	72	92
Pollution taxes	..	..	..	6	18	7	13	25	20	33
Payments by households for licences (not for business purposes)	..	..	..	5	3	6	2	2	2	3
Tax on market place	..	..	..	2	0	0	0	0	0	0
State - imposed fees and charges	..	..	..	34	22	44	5	6	7	9
Other taxes on production	..	..	..	10	6	13	22	38	42	48
5220 Non-recurrent taxes on use of goods and perform activities	..	..	..	0	0	0	0	0	0	0
5300 Unallocable between 5100 and 5200	..	..	..	0	0	0	0	0	0	0
6000 Taxes other than 1000, 2000, 3000, 4000 and 5000	..	..	..	0	0	0	0	0	0	0
6100 Paid solely by business	..	..	..	..	..	..	..	..	..	..
6200 Other taxes not solely paid by business	..	..	..	..	..	..	..	..	..	..
Customs duties collected for the EU	..	..	..	..	61	53	99	128	167	199
SRF Contributions collected for the EU				..	..	..	10	6	6	7
Total tax revenue on cash basis	..	..	..	..	..	..	..	..	..	..
Total tax revenue on accrual basis	..	..	..	4 154	8 730	7 961	10 826	15 623	18 044	21 314
Additional taxes included in National Accounts	..	..	..	0	0	0	0	0	0	0

	1965	1980	1990	2000	2007	2010	2015	2020	2021	2022
Taxes excluded from National Accounts	..	..	..	0	0	0	0	0	0	0
Difference in treatment of tax credits	..	..	..	0	0	0	0	0	0	0
Capital transfer for uncollected revenue	..	..	..	- 39	- 9	- 32	- 18	- 41	- 30	- 35
Voluntary social security contributions	..	..	..	0	2	2	2	0	0	0
Miscellaneous differences	..	..	..	0	0	0	0	0	0	0
National Accounts: Taxes and actual social contributions	..	..	..	4 115	8 723	7 932	10 811	15 582	18 014	21 279
Imputed social contributions	..	..	..	3	91	103	116	171	183	215
National Accounts: Taxes and all social contributions	..	..	..	4 118	8 814	8 035	10 927	15 753	18 197	21 494

.. Not available

Note: Year ending 31st December.

Data on an accrual basis.

Source: Ministry of Finance.

Table 5.24. Luxembourg: Details of tax revenue, 1965-2022

Million EUR

	1965	1980	1990	2000	2007	2010	2015	2020	2021	2022
Total tax revenue	266	1 543	3 671	8 510	13 456	15 117	18 830	24 711	27 632	29 700
Total tax revenue exclusive of taxes collected for the EU	..	..	3 654	8 482	13 432	15 099	18 777	24 502	27 366	29 355
1000 Taxes on income, profits and capital gains	95	667	1 476	3 106	4 654	5 467	7 011	9 370	10 592	11 436
1100 Taxes on income, profits and capital gains of individuals	66	417	884	1 573	2 677	3 156	4 716	6 290	7 318	8 028
1110 On income and profits of individuals	66	417	884	1 573	2 677	3 156	4 716	6 290	7 318	8 028
Personal income tax - fixed by assessment	27	106	184	258	389	540	721	874	1 023	1 171
Tax on wages and salaries	36	287	601	1 177	1 909	2 136	3 227	4 468	4 932	5 568
Withholding tax on income from capital	2	11	52	88	188	315	313	456	817	694
Special tax on company directors fees	1	2	5	11	20	26	44	53	59	64
Tax on certain income of non-residents	0	1	1	2	1	1	1	1	1	1
Supplementary solidarity income tax	0	10	41	37	59	74	305	410	462	503
Tax withheld on savings income (non-residents)	0	0	0	0	51	33	0	0	0	0
Withholding tax on interest	0	0	0	0	60	31	20	21	18	21
Crisis Tax	0	0	0	0	0	0	0	0	0	0
Temporary budgetary balance tax	0	0	0	0	0	0	85	1	1	0
Tax withheld on contributions to a registered supplementary pension plan for self-employed persons			0	0	0	0	0	6	6	6
1120 On capital gains of individuals	0	0	0	0	0	0	0	0	0	0
Tax on betting gains	..	..	..	..	..	..	..	..	..	..
1200 Taxes on income, profits and capital gains of corporates	29	250	592	1 533	1 977	2 311	2 295	3 080	3 273	3 407
1210 On profits of corporates	29	250	592	1 533	1 977	2 311	2 295	3 080	3 273	3 407
Corporation tax	18	168	376	1 031	1 381	1 646	1 569	1 965	2 096	2 244
Real estate levy			0	0	0	0	0	0	0	0
Supplementary solidarity corporation tax	0	2	8	43	58	61	120	146	161	163
Trade tax	0	80	209	460	538	603	606	969	1 016	1 001
1220 On capital gains of corporates	0	0	0	0	0	0	0	0	0	0
1300 Unallocable between 1100 and 1200	0	0	0	0	0	0	0	0	0	0
2000 Social security contributions (SSC)	86	443	1 011	2 224	3 710	4 387	5 548	7 208	7 651	8 286
2100 Employees SSC	32	175	388	993	1 691	2 017	2 498	3 340	3 531	3 841
2110 On a payroll basis of employees SSC	..	175	388	993	1 691	2 017	2 498	3 340	3 531	3 841
2120 On an income tax basis of employees SSC	..	0	0	0	0	0	0	0	0	0
2200 Employers SSC	49	243	494	964	1 580	1 888	2 335	2 955	3 149	3 417
2210 On a payroll basis of employers SSC	..	243	494	964	1 580	1 888	2 335	2 955	3 149	3 417
2220 On an income tax basis of employers SSC	..	0	0	0	0	0	0	0	0	0
2300 Self-employed or non-employed SSC	5	25	129	266	438	482	715	913	971	1 028
2310 On a payroll basis of self/non-employed SSC	..	25	129	266	438	482	715	913	971	1 028
2320 On an income tax basis of self/non-employed SSC	..	0	0	0	0	0	0	0	0	0
2400 Unallocable between 2100, 2200 and 2300 SSC	0	0	0	0	0	0	0	0	0	0
2410 On a payroll basis unallocable between 2100, 2200 and 2300 SSC	..	..	..	..	..	..	..	..	..	..
2420 On an income tax basis unallocable between 2100, 2200 and 2300 SSC	..	..	..	..	..	..	..	..	..	..
3000 Taxes on payroll and workforce	2	10	0	0	0	0	0	0	0	0
Payroll tax	2	10	..	..	..	..	..	..	..	..
4000 Taxes on property	16	87	309	910	1 294	1 062	1 715	2 463	2 912	2 863
4100 Recurrent taxes on immovable property	4	9	14	21	27	29	36	39	41	44
Taxes on ownership of lands and buildings	4	9	14	21	27	29	36	39	41	44

	1965	1980	1990	2000	2007	2010	2015	2020	2021	2022
4110 Households recurrent taxes on immovable property	..	..	..	..	..	..	..	..	..	..
4120 Other than households recurrent taxes on immovable property	..	..	..	..	..	..	..	..	..	..
4200 Recurrent taxes on net wealth	7	44	172	633	878	831	1 318	1 852	2 129	2 101
4210 Individual recurrent taxes on net wealth	0	0	0	0	0	0	0	0	0	0
Wealth tax	..	..	..	..	..	..	..	..	..	..
4220 Corporate recurrent taxes on net wealth	7	44	172	633	878	831	1 318	1 852	2 129	2 101
Wealth tax	2	15	58	152	172	208	385	780	796	876
Holding tax	3	29	114	481	706	622	933	1 072	1 333	1 225
4300 Estate, inheritance and gift taxes	1	5	11	23	47	50	74	84	118	145
4310 Estate and inheritance taxes	1	5	11	23	47	50	74	84	118	145
4320 Gift taxes	0	0	0	0	0	0	0	0	0	0
4400 Taxes on financial and capital transactions	4	30	112	232	343	152	287	487	623	573
Registration taxes	4	26	94	208	288	116	221	381	497	457
Mortgage taxes	1	3	9	12	29	21	39	72	79	83
Stamp duties	0	2	2	5	7	5	8	9	9	9
Tax on contruction in dense sectors	0	0	0	0	1	1	2	3	4	2
Tax on sale of real estate	0	0	6	7	17	8	16	22	33	20
Mortgage tax on salaries	0	0	1	1	1	1	1	1	1	1
Tax on secondary residence	0	0	0	0	0	1	0	0	0	0
Building permits	0	0	0	0	0	0	0	0	0	0
Infrastructure tax	0	0	0	0	0	0	0	0	0	0
Authorization taxes on oil tanks	0	0	0	0	0	0	0	0	0	0
4500 Non-recurrent taxes on property	0	0	0	0	0	0	0	0	0	0
4510 Non-recurrent taxes on net wealth	..	..	..	..	..	..	..	..	..	..
4520 Non-recurrent taxes on property other than net wealth	..	..	..	..	..	..	..	..	..	..
4600 Other recurrent taxes on property except 4100 and 4200	0	0	0	0	0	0	0	0	0	0
5000 Taxes on goods and services	66	336	868	2 260	3 784	4 180	4 528	5 648	6 449	7 085
5100 Taxes on production, sale, transfer, etc	62	327	848	2 229	3 709	4 105	4 442	5 555	6 351	6 991
5110 General taxes on goods and services	33	179	443	1 127	2 231	2 616	2 946	3 699	4 121	4 692
5111 Value added taxes	0	179	443	1 127	2 231	2 616	2 946	3 699	4 121	4 692
VAT Own resources	..	18	75	92	50	41	45	56	63	87
5112 Sales tax	0	0	0	0	0	0	0	0	0	0
5113 Other (than value added and sales tax)	33	0	0	0	0	0	0	0	0	0
Turnover tax	33	..	..	..	..	..	..	..	..	..
5120 Taxes on specific goods and services	30	148	404	1 103	1 478	1 489	1 496	1 855	2 230	2 299
5121 Excises	26	134	365	1 036	1 394	1 401	1 374	1 516	1 787	1 811
Excice duties on mineral oils	1	1	10	100	135	145	184	180	183	114
Tax on the consumption of national alcoholic beverages and spirits	1	5	19	20	21	20	28	47	50	53
Excice duties on tobacco (part on national production)	..	0	8	24	66	70	81	176	207	245
Autonomous excise duties on mineral oils	..	76	173	414	559	536	495	436	449	405
Excice duties on tobacco	..	40	141	407	418	422	394	481	562	647
Supplementary tax on fuels	..	0	0	59	145	132	117	106	114	109
Tax on control of domestic fuel	..	0	0	2	3	3	2	2	2	2
Excice duty on liquefied petroleum	..	0	0	0	0	0	0	0	0	0
Excice duty on benzol	..	0	0	1	1	1	1	1	1	1
Excice duties on imported alcoholic beverages	..	3	5	5	6	5	8	13	14	14
Excice duties on beers (part on national production)	..	4	2	3	4	4	5	3	4	4
Excice duty on fermented fruit beverages	..	2	3	0	0	0	0	0	0	0
Excice duties on fermented sparkling beverages	..	0	1	0	0	0	0	0	0	0
Excice duty on sugar	..	0	1	0	0	0	0	0	0	0
U.E.B.L. excises adjustment			0	0	0	0	0	0	0	0
Excice duties on nationally produced alcoholic beverages	..	1	1	0	0	0	0	0	0	0
Excice duty on Kyoto	..	0	0	0	37	62	58	70	1	0
Excice duty on alcopops	..	0	0	0	0	0	0	0	0	0
CO2 tax	..	0	0	0	0	0	0	0	201	217
5122 Profits of fiscal monopolies	0	0	0	0	0	0	0	0	0	0
5123 Customs and import duties	1	5	11	27	24	18	23	24	21	21
Levies on imported agricultural products	1	0	0	0	1	0	0	0	0	0
Customs duty	0	0	0	0	0	0	0	0	0	0
Customs duty + mobiles + C.E.C.A. + anti-dumping	0	4	11	27	23	18	23	24	20	21
Agricultural compensatory amounts	0	0	0	0	0	0	0	0	0	0
5124 Taxes on exports	0	0	0	0	0	0	0	0	0	0
5125 Taxes on investment goods	0	0	0	0	0	0	0	0	0	0
5126 Taxes on specific services	2	6	22	39	60	69	98	316	422	467
Tax on betting stakes	0	0	0	0	0	0	0	0	0	0

	1965	1980	1990	2000	2007	2010	2015	2020	2021	2022
Tax on insurance	1	5	15	23	32	40	46	61	72	62
Tax on transport	1	0	0	0	0	0	0	0	0	0
Tourist tax	0	0	1	1	2	2	3	1	1	3
Tax on national lottery	0	0	3	4	3	3	0	0	0	0
Tax on casino gambling	0	0	3	9	21	23	19	12	21	20
Entertainment tax	0	1	1	2	2	1	2	0	0	1
Tax on bank notes	0	0	0	0	0	0	0	0	0	0
Contributions to FGDL	0	0	0	0	0	0	0	50	75	52
Contributions to FRL	..	..	0	0	0	0	29	185	246	323
Special tax for insurers in the interest of the rescue service	0	0	0	0	0	0	0	6	6	5
5127 Other taxes on internat. trade and transactions not included within 5121 to 5126 inclusive	0	0	0	0	0	0	0	0	0	0
5128 Other taxes not included within 5121 to 5127 inclusive	0	4	6	1	0	1	1	0	0	0
C.E.C.A.	..	3	4	0	0	0	0	..	..	..
Co-responsibility tax on milk	..	1	2	1	0	1	1	..	..	..
Co-responsibility tax on cereals	..	0	0	0	0	0	0	..	..	..
5130 Unallocable between 5110 and 5120	0	0	0	0	0	0	0	0	0	0
5200 Taxes on use of goods and perform activities	3	9	20	30	75	75	86	94	98	94
5210 Recurrent taxes on use of goods and perform activities	3	8	18	28	68	68	71	71	71	71
5211 Recurrent taxes paid by households: motor vehicles	2	4	9	16	39	39	41	41	41	41
5212 Recurrent taxes paid by others: motor vehicles	1	4	7	11	26	26	28	28	28	28
5213 Recurrent taxes paid on use of goods and perform activities other than on motor vehicles	0	0	1	2	2	3	3	3	3	3
Tax on licenced premises	0	0	0	0	1	1	1	0	1	1
Ship registration tax	0	0	0	1	1	1	1	1	1	1
Dog tax	0	0	1	1	1	1	1	1	1	1
Tax on ships	0	0	0	0	0	0	0	0	0	0
Tax on peddeling	0	0	0	0	0	0	0	0	0	0
5220 Non-recurrent taxes on use of goods and perform activities	0	0	2	2	7	7	15	23	27	23
Emission permits	..	..	0	0	0	0	7	14	17	14
Car registration taxes	..	..	2	2	7	7	8	9	9	9
5300 Unallocable between 5100 and 5200	0	0	0	0	0	0	0	0	0	0
6000 Taxes other than 1000, 2000, 3000, 4000 and 5000	0	0	7	11	14	22	28	23	29	29
6100 Paid solely by business	..	0	6	11	13	16	28	23	29	29
Supplementary tax on electricity	..	0	0	2	2	2	2	2	2	2
Tax on distribution of electricity	..	0	3	4	1	1	1	1	1	1
Tax on production of electricity	..	0	2	2	1	1	0	0	4	2
Tax on natural gas consumption	..	0	0	0	3	4	4	4	4	5
Tax on enterprise register	..	0	1	1	0	0	0	0	0	0
Tax concerning foreign affair departments	..	0	0	0	2	5	4	6	6	6
Chancellery stamps	..	0	1	2	4	3	1	1	1	1
VAT reclassified as tax on production	..	0	0	1	1	1	1	2	2	2
Under-compensation of VAT (flat rate system)	..	0	2	0	0	0	0	0	0	0
Tax on water	..	0	0	0	0	5	15	6	8	10
6200 Other taxes not solely paid by business	..	0	0	0	0	0	0	0	0	0
Custom duties collected for the EU	..	..	11	27	23	18	23	24	20	21
SRF Contributions collected for the EU			..	..	..	..	29	185	246	323
Taxes and compulsory social security contributions paid by EU civil servants			56	82	243	207	228	317	318	333
Taxes paid by EU civil servants: income taxes			37	55	103	112	125	175	177	186
Taxes paid by EU civil servants: compulsory social security contributions			20	27	140	95	103	142	142	148
Non-wastable tax credits against 1110	..	..	..	..	..	..	198	189	184	445
Tax expenditure component	..	..	..	..	..	..	..	..	..	..
Transfer component	..	..	..	..	..	..	..	..	..	..
Total tax revenue on cash basis	266	1 543	3 722	8 612	13 385	14 746	19 087	24 707	27 886	30 297
Total tax revenue on accrual basis	..	..	3 671	8 510	13 456	15 117	18 830	24 711	27 632	29 700
Additional taxes included in National Accounts	..	..	0	0	0	0	0	0	0	0
Taxes excluded from National Accounts	..	..	0	0	0	0	0	0	0	0
Difference in treatment of tax credits	..	..	0	0	0	0	0	0	0	0
Capital transfer for uncollected revenue	..	..	0	0	0	0	- 1	- 17	0	- 39

	1965	1980	1990	2000	2007	2010	2015	2020	2021	2022
Voluntary social security contributions	..	..	4	18	18	28	38	53	57	66
Miscellaneous differences	..	..	0	0	0	0	0	0	0	0
National Accounts: Taxes and actual social contributions	..	..	3 675	8 528	13 474	15 146	18 867	24 747	27 689	29 727
Imputed social contributions	..	..	267	288	429	505	669	855	891	947
National Accounts: Taxes and all social contributions	..	..	3 941	8 816	13 903	15 651	19 536	25 602	28 581	30 673

.. Not available

Note: The civil year ends December 31st.

Data are on an accrual basis.

Under the heading 2000, the difference between the total social security contributions and those collected by the social security parastatals corresponds to the levy for realignment of pensions operated on the remuneration and pensions of employees and former agents of P&T and BCEE; one of these establishments belonging to the "non-corporate and quasi-corporate sector" and the other to the "credit institutions sector".

Compulsory social security contributions paid by EU civil servants include imputed social security contributions.

Source: General account of the State.

Table 5.25. Mexico: Details of tax revenue, 1965-2022

Million MXN

	1965	1980	1990	2000	2007	2010	2015	2020	2021	2022
Total tax revenue	..	771	102 005	767 216	1 382 103	1 716 243	2 953 480	4 148 699	4 452 360	4 948 318
1000 Taxes on income, profits and capital gains	..	230	34 673	276 548	554 099	683 604	1 230 555	1 768 161	1 903 047	2 280 791
1100 Of individuals	..	..	..	..	238 938	313 473	609 384	872 598	938 623	1 066 965
Tax on income of individuals	..	..	..	..	238 938	313 473	609 384	872 598	938 623	1 066 965
1110 On income and profits	..	..	..	..	..	..	..	..	..	..
1120 On capital gains	..	..	..	..	..	..	..	..	..	..
1200 Corporate	..	..	..	..	217 790	246 745	592 443	832 120	898 767	1 136 636
Tax on income of corporations	..	..	..	..	217 790	246 745	592 443	832 120	898 767	1 136 636
1210 On profits	..	..	..	..	..	..	..	..	..	..
1220 On capital gains	..	..	..	..	..	..	..	..	..	..
1300 Unallocable between 1100 and 1200	..	230	34 673	276 548	97 370	123 386	28 728	63 443	65 657	77 190
Tax on income of other individuals and corporations	..	..	..	244 841	54 785	66 937	36 268	58 196	58 306	70 239
Tax on asset	..	..	..	13 913	15 670	- 625	- 502	- 1 245	- 380	31
Credit on salary	..	..	..	17 794	23 177	9 708	993	479	512	107
Oil yields tax	..	..	..	0	3 738	2 296	0	0	0	0
IETU	..	..	..	0	0	45 069	- 11 777	- 888	200	- 346
Imposed by Activity Exploration and extraction of hydrocarbon	..	..	..	0	0	0	3 746	6 902	7 019	7 160
2000 Social security contributions	..	109	17 165	138 223	236 727	277 459	409 249	576 019	612 175	681 672
2100 Employees	..	..	..	..	..	..	..	..	..	..
2110 On a payroll basis	..	..	..	..	..	..	..	..	..	..
2120 On an income tax basis	..	..	..	..	..	..	..	..	..	..
2200 Employers	..	..	..	..	..	..	..	..	..	..
2210 On a payroll basis of employers SSC	..	..	..	..	..	..	..	..	..	..
2220 On an income tax basis of employers SSC	..	..	..	..	..	..	..	..	..	..
2300 Selfemployed or nonemployed	..	..	..	..	..	..	..	..	..	..
2310 On a payroll basis of self/non-employed SSC	..	..	..	..	..	..	..	..	..	..
2320 On an income tax basis of self/non-employed SSC	..	..	..	..	..	..	..	..	..	..
2400 Unallocable between 2100, 2200 and 2300	..	109	17 165	138 223	236 727	277 459	409 249	576 019	612 175	681 672
2410 On a payroll basis unallocable between 2100, 2200 and 2300 SSC	..	..	..	138 223	236 727	277 459	409 249	576 019	612 175	681 672
2420 On an income tax basis unallocable between 2100, 2200 and 2300 SSC	..	..	..	0	0	0	0	0	0	0
3000 Taxes on payroll and workforce	..	8	1 797	11 217	28 071	36 911	70 221	105 456	116 910	141 161
Substitute tax on salary	..	..	..	0	0	0	0	0	0	0
Payroll tax	..	..	..	11 101	20 277	27 813	69 866	104 825	115 974	139 977
Tax on remuneration to the personal work	..	..	..	65	7 578	8 841	152	407	579	837
Tax on professions and fees	..	..	..	36	68	71	106	177	235	263
Tax on operations by contract	..	..	..	15	148	186	96	47	121	84
4000 Taxes on property	..	15	1 914	13 964	33 161	38 955	57 673	79 237	90 206	105 244
4100 Recurrent taxes on immovable property	..	10	1 036	9 948	19 425	25 724	37 961	52 728	56 148	64 903
4110 Households	..	0	0	0	0	0	0	0	0	0
4120 Others	..	10	1 036	9 948	19 425	25 724	37 961	52 728	56 148	64 903
Property tax	..	..	..	9 948	19 425	25 724	37 961	52 728	56 148	64 903
4200 Recurrent taxes on net wealth	..	0	0	0	0	0	0	0	0	0
4210 Individual	..	..	..	..	..	..	..	..	..	..
4220 Corporate	..	..	..	..	..	..	..	..	..	..
4300 Estate, inheritance and gift taxes	..	0	8	0	0	0	0	0	0	0
4310 Estate and inheritance taxes	..	..	8	..	..	..	..	..	..	..
4320 Gift taxes	..	..	0	..	..	..	..	..	..	..
4400 Taxes on financial and capital transactions	..	5	870	4 017	13 736	13 231	19 712	26 509	34 058	40 341
Alienation of immovable property	..	..	..	1 763	1 076	1 122	1 595	1 982	2 486	2 837
Transfer of ownership of real estate	..	..	..	2 236	8 147	5 027	6 671	12 072	11 394	16 705
Purchasing property	..	..	..	18	4 513	7 082	11 447	12 456	20 177	20 799
4500 Nonrecurrent taxes	..	0	0	0	0	0	0	0	0	0
4510 On net wealth	..	..	..	..	..	..	..	..	..	..
4520 Other nonrecurrent taxes	..	..	..	..	..	..	..	..	..	..
4600 Other recurrent taxes on property	..	0	0	0	0	0	0	0	0	0
5000 Taxes on goods and services	..	395	44 837	319 613	513 140	651 915	1 141 170	1 544 156	1 647 927	1 623 605
5100 Taxes on production, sale, transfer, etc	..	388	44 171	310 326	491 928	630 123	1 120 610	1 527 674	1 630 616	1 606 144
5110 General taxes	..	121	26 635	189 606	409 013	504 509	707 213	987 525	1 123 699	1 221 803
5111 Value added taxes	..	120	26 635	189 606	409 013	504 509	707 213	987 525	1 123 699	1 221 803
5112 Sales tax	..	0	0	0	0	0	0	0	0	0
5113 Other	..	1	0	0	0	0	0	0	0	0
5120 Taxes on specific goods and services	..	265	17 519	120 720	82 915	125 614	413 397	540 149	506 917	384 341
5121 Excises	..	45	10 072	86 163	47 008	86 098	361 538	469 040	410 450	259 306
Special tax on production and services on tobacco	..	..	..	8 083	20 069	26 925	36 891	43 848	45 657	47 948
Special tax on production and services on alcohol and beer	..	..	..	7 250	21 463	25 152	43 014	52 312	57 395	68 050

	1965	1980	1990	2000	2007	2010	2015	2020	2021	2022
Special tax on production and services on sugar-sweetened beverages	..	..	..	0	0	0	21 402	29 124	30 478	34 247
Special tax on production and services on no staple foods with high caloric density			0	0	0	0	15 926	21 049	25 590	30 333
Other special tax on production and services			0	66 211	0	29 349	237 061	314 340	240 034	63 668
Tax on new automobiles			0	4 619	5 476	4 671	7 244	8 366	11 296	15 060
Tax on luxury goods and services			0	0	0	0	0	0	0	0
5122 Profits of fiscal monopolies	..	0	0	0	0	0	0	0	0	0
5123 Customs and import duties	..	45	6 998	33 285	33 344	26 602	45 366	59 247	77 236	95 901
Step customs officer	..	..	..	423	1 156	2 071	1 270	1 309	1 697	2 229
Import taxes	..	..	..	32 861	32 188	24 531	44 096	57 938	75 539	93 672
5124 Taxes on exports	..	2	75	4	3	0	1	0	0	0
Tax on exports	..	..	..	4	3	0	1	0	0	0
5125 Taxes on investment goods	..	0	0	0	0	0	0	0	0	0
5126 Taxes on specific services	..	8	132	1 042	2 146	10 958	1 763	5 625	9 265	13 863
IDE	..	8	..	0	0	8 022	- 3 323	- 252	- 135	- 152
Tax on lodging	..	0	..	504	1 059	1 384	2 561	2 500	4 119	6 411
Public entertainment tax	..	0	..	240	365	462	689	467	393	1 225
Tax on lotteries, raffles and gambling	..	0	..	267	705	923	1 416	2 114	3 799	5 055
Tax on commercials	..	0	..	4	17	166	210	0	0	0
Various indirect taxes	..	0	..	28	0	1	209	795	1 089	1 324
5127 Other taxes on internat. trade and transactions	..	0	0	0	0	0	0	0	0	0
5128 Other taxes	..	165	242	226	414	1 956	4 730	6 238	9 966	15 271
Mining fees	..	..	..	226	414	1 956	4 730	6 238	9 966	15 271
5130 Unallocable between 5110 and 5120	..	2	17	0	0	0	0	0	0	0
5200 Taxes on use of goods and perform activities	..	7	666	9 287	21 212	21 793	20 560	16 482	17 311	17 461
5210 Recurrent taxes	..	7	666	9 287	21 212	21 793	20 560	16 482	17 311	17 461
5211 Paid by households: motor vehicles	..	3	567	8 878	20 692	21 319	19 880	15 699	16 422	16 311
Tax on motor vehicules	..	..	..	8 878	20 692	21 319	19 880	15 699	16 422	16 311
5212 Paid by others: motor vehicles	..	0	0	301	275	281	439	437	605	705
Tax on federal auto transport	..	..	..	301	275	281	439	437	605	705
5213 Paid in respect of other goods	..	4	99	108	246	193	240	347	285	445
Sport fishing	..	..	..	40	98	59	62	55	69	87
Sport hunting	..	..	..	3	0	0	0	0	0	0
Tax on commercial activities	..	..	..	63	147	50	64	159	39	112
Trade in books and magazines	..	..	..	0	0	0	1	0	0	1
Tax on industrial activities	..	..	..	2	0	82	93	113	113	51
Mining	..	..	..	0	0	1	21	19	64	196
5220 Nonrecurrent taxes	..	0	0	0	0	0	0	0	0	0
5300 Unallocable between 5100 and 5200	..	0	0	0	0	0	0	0	0	0
6000 Other taxes	..	14	1 619	7 651	16 905	27 398	44 612	75 671	82 094	115 845
6100 Paid solely by business	..	0	0	0	0	0	0	0	0	0
6200 Other	..	14	1 619	7 651	16 905	27 398	44 612	75 671	82 094	115 845
Accessories	..	..	..	5 504	12 403	22 206	23 211	56 793	54 231	83 591
Unallocable between 1000 and 5000 caused in exercices fiscal previous liquidation slopes or of payment	..	..	..	374	222	30	4 168	218	304	328
Additional state and local taxes	..	..	..	1 773	4 280	5 162	17 232	18 660	27 560	31 926
Adjustment	..	0	0	0	0	0	0	843 545	917 268	1 062 434
Non-wastable tax credits against 1000	..	..	..	..	59 065	40 344	43 806	50 476	53 399	43 238
Tax expenditure component	..	..	..	..	35 888	30 635	42 813	49 997	52 887	43 131
Transfer component	..	..	..	..	23 177	9 708	993	479	512	107
Total tax revenue on cash basis	..	771	102 005	767 216	1 382 103	1 716 243	2 953 480	4 148 699	4 452 360	4 948 318
Total tax revenue on accrual basis	..	..	..	..	..	..	..	..	..	..
Additional taxes included in National Accounts	..	..	..	..	..	..	..	..	..	..
Taxes excluded from National Accounts	..	..	..	..	..	..	..	..	..	..
Difference in treatment of tax credits	..	..	..	..	..	..	..	..	..	..
Capital transfer for uncollected revenue	..	..	..	..	..	..	..	..	..	..
Voluntary social security contributions	..	..	..	..	..	..	..	..	..	..
Miscellaneous differences	..	..	..	..	..	..	..	..	..	..
National Accounts: Taxes and actual social contributions	..	..	..	..	..	..	..	..	..	..
Imputed social contributions	..	..	..	..	..	..	..	..	..	..
National Accounts: Taxes and all social contributions	..	..	..	..	..	..	..	..	..	..

.. Not available

Note: Year ending 31st December.

Data are on cash basis.

Source: Ministry of Finance, Economic Department.

Table 5.26. Netherlands: Details of tax revenue, 1965-2022

Million EUR

	1965	1980	1990	2000	2007	2010	2015	2020	2021	2022
Total tax revenue	10 860	69 982	104 419	166 824	220 950	227 911	255 348	318 601	341 143	378 305
Total tax revenue exclusive of taxes collected for the EU	..	..	102 926	165 227	218 926	225 943	252 272	315 077	337 080	373 220
1000 Taxes on income, profits and capital gains	3 884	22 998	33 689	43 256	62 463	63 581	70 849	97 810	107 846	123 828
1100 Of individuals	3 008	18 383	25 806	25 116	41 414	48 992	52 405	73 116	74 429	76 656
1110 On income and profits	3 007	18 364	25 757	25 057	41 276	48 771	52 167	72 937	74 253	76 448
Income tax	1 359	2 895	2 455	- 880	2 294	2 076	- 2 566	8 109	6 893	5 611
Wage tax	1 466	14 984	22 258	24 433	37 729	46 102	53 953	62 077	65 314	69 284
Dividend tax	123	486	1 044	1 504	1 253	593	780	2 751	2 046	1 553
Directors tax	14	0	0	0	0	0	0	0	0	0
Inhabited house tax	45	0	0	0	0	0	0	0	0	0
1120 On capital gains	1	18	50	59	138	221	238	179	176	208
Tax on games of chance	1	18	50	59	138	221	238	179	176	208
1200 Corporate	876	4 615	7 882	18 140	21 049	14 589	18 444	24 694	33 417	47 172
1210 On profits	876	4 615	7 882	18 140	21 049	14 589	18 444	24 694	33 417	47 172
Corporate income and dividend taxes	876	4 615	7 882	18 140	21 049	14 589	18 444	24 694	33 417	47 172
1220 On capital gains	0	0	0	0	0	0	0	0	0	0
1300 Unallocable between 1100 and 1200	0	0	0	0	0	0	0	0	0	0
2000 Social security contributions	3 342	26 641	39 075	64 522	77 072	82 732	96 426	108 685	112 666	124 463
2100 Employees	1 659	11 018	24 109	35 305	40 918	41 637	48 213	40 295	42 179	46 899
2110 On a payroll basis	..	..	..	35 305	40 918	41 637	48 213	40 295	42 179	46 899
2120 On an income tax basis	..	..	..	0	0	0	0	0	0	0
2200 Employers	1 371	12 465	7 837	18 671	25 925	29 351	34 614	44 135	45 071	49 303
2210 On a payroll basis of employers SSC	..	..	..	18 671	25 925	29 351	34 614	44 135	45 071	49 303
2220 On an income tax basis of employers SSC	..	..	..	0	0	0	0	0	0	0
2300 Selfemployed or nonemployed	311	3 158	7 129	10 546	10 229	11 744	13 599	24 255	25 416	28 261
2310 On a payroll basis of self/non-employed SSC	..	..	..	0	0	0	0	0	0	0
2320 On an income tax basis of self/non-employed SSC	..	..	..	10 546	10 229	11 744	13 599	24 255	25 416	28 261
2400 Unallocable between 2100, 2200 and 2300	0	0	0	0	0	0	0	0	0	0
2410 On a payroll basis unallocable between 2100, 2200 and 2300 SSC	..	..	..	..	..	..	..	..	..	..
2420 On an income tax basis unallocable between 2100, 2200 and 2300 SSC	..	..	..	..	..	..	..	..	..	..
3000 Taxes on payroll and workforce	0	0	0	0	0	0	0	0	0	0
4000 Taxes on property	476	2 509	3 816	8 797	10 363	8 770	9 768	13 544	14 110	14 778
4100 Recurrent taxes on immovable property	111	1 021	1 711	3 094	3 488	4 241	6 382	7 910	7 795	7 562
Municipal immovable property tax	- 59	821	1 398	..	..	..	..	..	..	..
Other municipal taxes	66	5	18	..	..	..	..	..	..	..
Contributions polder boards	44	195	295	..	..	..	..	..	..	..
Tax on land	59	0	0	..	..	..	..	..	..	..
4110 Households	..	..	..	1 806	1 642	2 058	3 741	4 769	4 501	4 093
Municipal immovable property tax	..	..	..	1 651	1 368	1 553	1 882	2 243	2 375	2 490
Contributions polder boards	..	..	..	155	274	429	514	638	667	685
Levies on social housing corporations	..	..	..	0	0	76	1 345	1 888	1 459	918
4120 Others	..	..	..	1 288	1 846	2 183	2 641	3 141	3 294	3 469
Municipal immovable property tax	..	..	..	893	1 319	1 488	1 809	2 156	2 282	2 392
Contributions polder boards	..	..	..	395	527	695	832	985	1 012	1 077
4200 Recurrent taxes on net wealth	86	517	554	824	30	23	0	0	0	0
4210 Individual	86	517	554	824	30	23	..	..	..	..
Property tax of individuals	86	517	554	824	30	23	..	..	..	..
4220 Corporate	0	0	0	0	0	0	..	..	..	..
4300 Estate, inheritance and gift taxes	117	336	522	1 483	1 877	1 721	1 614	2 081	2 496	2 614
4310 Estate and inheritance taxes	..	304	472	1 303	1 877	1 721	1 614	2 081	2 496	2 614
Estate tax	..	0	0	0	0	0	0	0	0	0
Inheritance tax	..	304	472	1 303	1 877	1 721	1 614	2 081	2 496	2 614
4320 Gift taxes	..	32	50	180	0	0	0	0	0	0
4400 Taxes on financial and capital transactions	162	635	1 030	3 396	4 968	2 785	1 772	3 553	3 819	4 602
Stamp duties	44	0	0	0	0	0	0	0	0	0
Registration duties	118	0	0	0	0	0	0	0	0	0
Tax on legal transactions	0	635	1 030	0	0	0	0	0	0	0
Real estate transfer tax	0	0	0	2 804	4 925	2 785	1 772	3 553	3 819	4 602
Tax on capital formation	0	0	0	592	43	0	0	0	0	0
4500 Nonrecurrent taxes	0	0	0	0	0	0	0	0	0	0
4510 On net wealth	..	..	..	..	..	..	..	..	..	..
4520 Other nonrecurrent taxes	..	..	..	..	..	..	..	..	..	..
4600 Other recurrent taxes on property	0	0	0	0	0	0	0	0	0	0
5000 Taxes on goods and services	3 110	17 675	27 585	49 472	70 084	71 866	77 889	97 033	105 511	114 037
5100 Taxes on production, sale, transfer, etc	2 943	16 204	25 067	44 871	63 673	64 247	69 315	87 507	95 730	103 572
5110 General taxes	1 344	11 081	17 216	28 857	42 884	42 674	44 922	59 038	65 472	70 458

	1965	1980	1990	2000	2007	2010	2015	2020	2021	2022
5111 Value added taxes	0	11 081	17 216	28 849	42 873	42 654	44 879	58 971	65 400	70 458
5112 Sales tax	0	0	0	0	0	0	0	0	0	0
5113 Other	1 344	0	0	8	11	20	43	67	72	0
Turnover tax	1 344	..	..	0	0	0	0	0	0	..
5120 Taxes on specific goods and services	1 600	5 123	7 850	16 014	20 789	21 573	24 393	28 469	30 258	33 114
5121 Excises	880	3 789	5 985	13 755	17 724	18 392	18 020	20 410	21 058	22 399
Excise on spirits	129	463	422	397	335	331	314	321	372	376
Excise on beer	34	123	259	263	310	389	451	384	392	476
Excise on sugar	45	9	27	0	0	0	0	0	0	0
Excise on tobacco	307	839	948	1 590	2 136	2 437	2 222	3 178	2 909	2 901
Excise on wine	14	82	91	173	257	304	354	329	351	354
Registration tax on motor vehicles	0	613	1 189	2 875	3 647	2 096	1 462	1 501	1 489	1 477
Excise on soft drinks	0	59	186	216	155	156	207	269	268	291
Levies for nuclear reactor	0	0	0	0	0	0	0	0	0	0
Excise on petrol	310	1 280	1 684	3 151	4 010	4 086	4 109	3 888	4 044	3 617
Excise on other mineral oils	41	295	808	2 139	2 965	3 573	3 757	3 483	3 604	3 146
Levies on air pollution	0	27	304	0	0	0	0	0	0	0
Taxes on pollution/resources	0	0	68	462	456	655	345	532	561	549
Levies on energy	0	0	0	2 387	3 333	4 250	4 679	6 409	6 963	9 099
Other excise duties and consumption taxes	0	0	0	0	0	0	0	0	0	0
Other environmental taxes	0	0	0	34	35	15	14	21	16	17
Strategic stockpile tax on mineral oils	0	0	0	68	85	100	106	95	89	96
5122 Profits of fiscal monopolies	0	0	0	0	0	0	0	0	0	0
5123 Customs and import duties	702	971	1 375	1 310	1 679	1 732	2 266	2 533	3 005	3 759
Agriculture levy	338	295	168	0	0	0	0	0	0	0
MCA levy	0	9	0	0	0	0	0	0	0	0
Remaining import duties	364	667	1 207	0	0	0	0	0	0	0
Custom duties collected for the EU			0	1 310	1 679	1 732	2 266	2 533	3 005	3 759
5124 Taxes on exports	0	0	0	0	0	0	0	0	0	0
5125 Taxes on investment goods	0	77	0	0	0	0	0	0	0	0
Selective investment regulation levy	..	77	..	..	..	..	..	..	..	..
5126 Taxes on specific services	16	222	372	662	1 041	1 213	3 751	5 283	5 964	6 646
Tax on fire insurance	2	0	0	0	0	0	0	0	0	0
Entertainment tax	14	0	0	0	0	0	0	0	0	0
Tax on insurances	0	209	340	512	807	861	2 375	3 048	3 204	3 401
Tourist tax	0	14	32	83	125	131	206	211	240	396
Tax on games of chance	0	0	0	67	109	221	238	181	167	643
Flight tax	0	0	0	0	0	0	0	0	69	164
Bank levies	0	0	0	0	0	0	478	1 095	1 457	1 026
Contribution to EU Single Resolution Fund	..	..	0	0	0	0	454	748	827	1 016
5127 Other taxes on internat. trade and transactions	0	0	0	0	0	0	0	0	0	0
5128 Other taxes	1	64	118	287	345	236	356	243	231	310
ESCC levy	1	5	0	0	0	0	0	0	0	0
Sugar contribution	0	23	36	0	0	0	0	0	0	0
Milk levy	0	36	82	0	0	0	0	0	0	0
EU levies on food products	0	0	0	273	345	236	356	243	231	310
Sugar storage duty	0	0	0	14	0	0	0	0	0	0
5130 Unallocable between 5110 and 5120	0	0	0	0	0	0	0	0	0	0
5200 Taxes on use of goods and perform activities	167	1 470	2 518	4 601	6 411	7 619	8 574	9 526	9 781	10 465
5210 Recurrent taxes	165	1 470	2 518	4 601	6 411	7 619	8 410	9 083	9 293	9 425
5211 Paid by households: motor vehicles	27	463	799	2 288	3 211	4 084	4 470	4 784	4 889	4 951
Motor vehicle tax	27	427	744	2 288	3 211	4 084	4 470	4 784	4 889	4 951
Motor vehicle licence	0	36	54	0	0	0	0	0	0	0
5212 Paid by others: motor vehicles	132	604	1 044	554	760	976	1 069	1 144	1 169	1 184
Motor vehicle tax	132	590	1 026	554	760	976	1 069	1 144	1 169	1 184
Motor vehicle licence	0	14	18	0	0	0	0	0	0	0
Heavy motor vehicle tax	0	0	0	0	0	0	0	0	0	0
5213 Paid in respect of other goods	6	404	676	1 759	2 440	2 559	2 871	3 155	3 235	3 290
Dog licences	3	23	27	40	54	59	65	50	50	44
Commuter tax	0	5	5	12	21	25	29	39	41	46
Levies on water pollution	1	372	644	1 003	1 220	1 127	1 212	1 351	1 399	1 437
Permission to sell spirits	2	5	0	0	0	0	0	0	0	0
Sewerage charges	0	0	0	650	1 094	1 304	1 531	1 702	1 737	1 761
Levies on manure surplus	0	0	0	18	- 4	2	3	12	7	1
Noise nuisance tax civil aviation	0	0	0	36	55	42	31	1	1	1
5220 Nonrecurrent taxes	2	0	0	0	0	0	164	443	488	1 040
Emission permits	..	..	..	..	..	..	164	443	488	1 040
5300 Unallocable between 5100 and 5200	0	0	0	0	0	0	0	0	0	0
6000 Other taxes	48	159	254	777	968	962	416	1 529	1 010	1 199
6100 Paid solely by business	48	159	254	410	322	326	0	0	0	58
Administrative levies	48	159	254	410	322	326	..	..	..	58

	1965	1980	1990	2000	2007	2010	2015	2020	2021	2022
6200 Other	0	0	0	367	646	636	416	1 529	1 010	1 141
Wage Tax reductions	..	..	..	331	497	609	208	1 226	864	770
Other taxes	..	..	..	36	149	14	80	155	- 15	161
Tax revenue from Carribean Netherlands	..	..	..	0	0	13	128	148	161	210
Custom duties collected for the EU	..	..	..	1 310	1 679	1 732	2 266	2 533	3 005	3 759
SRF Contributions collected for the EU			..	..	..	..	454	748	827	1 016
Total tax revenue on cash basis	10 860	69 982	104 419	165 503	..	..	..	..	..	..
Total tax revenue on accrual basis	..	..	..	166 824	220 950	227 911	255 348	318 601	341 143	378 305
Additional taxes included in National Accounts	..	..	..	1 400	0	0	0	0	0	0
Wage Tax reductions	..	..	..	1 400	..	..	..	..	..	..
Taxes excluded from National Accounts	..	..	..	0	0	0	0	0	0	0
Difference in treatment of tax credits	..	..	..	0	0	0	0	0	0	0
Capital transfer for uncollected revenue	..	..	..	0	0	0	0	0	0	0
Voluntary social security contributions	..	..	..	0	0	0	0	0	0	0
Miscellaneous differences	..	..	..	- 70	0	0	0	0	0	0
National Accounts: Taxes and actual social contributions	..	..	..	168 154	220 950	227 911	255 348	318 601	341 143	378 305
Imputed social contributions	..	..	..	3 808	3 509	3 545	3 160	3 801	4 073	5 220
National Accounts: Taxes and all social contributions	..	..	..	171 962	224 459	231 456	258 508	322 402	345 216	383 525

.. Not available

Note: Year ending 31st December.

From 1999 data are on accrual basis.

Heading 2000: From 1998 the figures include some violuntary contributions and the breakdown between premiums paid by employees (2100) and by self-employed / non-employed has been estimated. This is also the case for the breakdown between premiums paid on a payroll or on an income tax basis for those years where both apply.

Heading 4100: From 1992, there was a structural break in the data for the 'municipal immovable property tax'. The tax ceased to be collected by the central government at that time and the figures are presented on a different type of statistical registration (no longer cash basis).

Heading 5110: Includes 358 millions of euros (1969) and 186 millions of euros (1970) in respect of deduction of turnover tax on stocks existing at 1st January 1969.

Heading 5213: Small amounts (less than 2.3 millions euros) of hunting and fishing licence receipts which should be classified here have been omitted.

Source: Social security contributions and local taxes: Central Bureau of Statistics.

Other taxes: Ministry of Finance.

Table 5.27. New Zealand: Details of tax revenue, 1965-2022

Million NZD

	1965	1980	1990	2000	2007	2010	2015	2020	2021	2022
Total tax revenue	1 001	7 594	27 471	39 765	64 046	62 310	81 499	115 596	125 753	130 786
1000 Taxes on income, profits and capital gains	606	5 299	16 370	23 861	40 308	33 494	44 723	65 298	73 629	76 139
1100 Of individuals	394	4 679	13 177	17 126	26 965	23 519	30 297	44 494	51 398	54 402
1110 On income and profits	394	4 679	13 177	17 126	26 965	23 519	30 297	44 494	51 398	54 402
1120 On capital gains	0	0	0	0	0	0	0	0	0	0
1200 Corporate	207	589	1 780	4 914	9 069	7 609	11 407	17 819	19 771	17 905
1210 On profits	207	589	1 780	4 914	9 069	7 609	11 407	17 819	19 771	17 905
1220 On capital gains	0	0	0	0	0	0	0	0	0	0
1300 Unallocable between 1100 and 1200	5	31	1 413	1 821	4 274	2 366	3 019	2 985	2 460	3 832
NRWT	5	24	277	760	1 506	467	733	470	514	618
Property speculation	0	0	0	0	0	0	0	0	0	0
Absentee income tax	0	7	0	0	0	0	0	0	0	0
Interest	0	0	1 028	990	2 699	1 704	1 660	999	841	2 091
Dividends	0	0	83	71	69	195	626	1 516	1 105	1 123
Other	0	0	25	0	0	0	0	0	0	0
2000 Social security contributions	0	0	0	0	0	0	0	0	0	0
2100 Employees	0	0	0	0	0	0	0	0	0	0
2110 On a payroll basis	..	..	..	..	..	..	..	..	..	..
2120 On an income tax basis	..	..	..	..	..	..	..	..	..	..
2200 Employers	0	0	0	0	0	0	0	0	0	0
2210 On a payroll basis of employers SSC	..	..	..	..	..	..	..	..	..	..
2220 On an income tax basis of employers SSC	..	..	..	..	..	..	..	..	..	..
2300 Selfemployed or nonemployed	0	0	0	0	0	0	0	0	0	0
2310 On a payroll basis of self/non-employed SSC	..	..	..	..	..	..	..	..	..	..
2320 On an income tax basis of self/non-employed SSC	..	..	..	..	..	..	..	..	..	..
2400 Unallocable between 2100, 2200 and 2300	0	0	0	0	0	0	0	0	0	0
2410 On a payroll basis unallocable between 2100, 2200 and 2300 SSC	..	..	..	..	..	..	..	..	..	..
2420 On an income tax basis unallocable between 2100, 2200 and 2300 SSC	..	..	..	..	..	..	..	..	..	..
3000 Taxes on payroll and workforce	0	0	0	0	0	0	0	0	0	0
4000 Taxes on property	116	602	1 880	2 112	3 417	4 119	5 046	6 359	6 982	7 573
4100 Recurrent taxes on immovable property	84	515	1 722	2 049	3 322	4 031	4 962	6 271	6 885	7 420
Local govt rates and services	81	503	1 550	2 049	3 322	4 031	4 962	6 271	6 885	7 420
Land tax	3	12	172	0	0	0	0	0	0	0
4200 Recurrent taxes on net wealth	0	0	0	0	0	0	0	0	0	0
4300 Estate, inheritance and gift taxes	23	39	80	2	3	2	0	0	0	0
4400 Taxes on financial and capital transactions	9	48	78	61	92	86	84	88	97	153
Instrument duty	7	40	62	51	85	82	84	88	97	153
Cheque duty	2	8	16	10	7	4	0	0	0	0
4500 Nonrecurrent taxes	0	0	0	0	0	0	0	0	0	0
4510 On net wealth	..	..	..	..	..	..	..	..	..	..
4520 Other nonrecurrent taxes	..	..	..	..	..	..	..	..	..	..
4600 Other recurrent taxes on property	0	0	0	0	0	0	0	0	0	0
4110 Households	..	..	0	..	..	..	..	..	..	..
4120 Others	..	..	172	..	..	..	..	..	..	..
4210 Individual	..	..	..	..	..	..	..	..	..	..
4220 Corporate	..	..	..	..	..	..	..	..	..	..
4310 Estate and inheritance taxes	21	37	74	0	0	0	..	..	..	..
4320 Gift taxes	2	2	6	2	3	2	..	..	..	..
5000 Taxes on goods and services	280	1 693	9 220	13 792	20 290	24 692	31 728	43 938	45 141	47 074
5100 Taxes on production, sale, transfer, etc	262	1 624	8 680	12 887	18 832	23 107	29 584	41 122	42 352	44 671
5110 General taxes	77	776	6 163	9 885	15 046	19 143	24 587	35 397	36 858	39 661
5111 Value added taxes	0	0	6 163	9 885	15 046	19 143	24 587	35 397	36 858	39 661
5112 Sales tax	77	776	0	0	0	0	0	0	0	0
Motor vehicles	..	231	..	..	..	..	..	..	..	..
Other sales tax	..	544	..	..	..	..	..	..	..	..
5113 Other	0	0	0	0	0	0	0	0	0	0
5120 Taxes on specific goods and services	186	849	2 517	3 002	3 786	3 964	4 997	5 725	5 494	5 010
5121 Excises	124	548	1 929	2 148	1 627	1 782	2 280	2 111	1 729	951
On alcoholic beverages	37	84	411	436	573	622	672	780	738	785
Beer	33	64	0	201	290	207	262	308	374	393
Wine	0	0	0	100	163	181	216	229	186	197
Spirits	4	20	0	135	120	234	194	243	178	195
Tobacco	33	99	568	764	159	220	362	45	2	0
Motor vehicles	0	0	7	0	0	0	0	0	0	0
Refined sugar	2	0	0	0	0	0	0	0	0	0

	1965	1980	1990	2000	2007	2010	2015	2020	2021	2022
CA petroleum fuels	0	140	835	810	819	872	1 185	1 084	802	- 33
NRF fuel excise	49	121	0	0	0	0	0	0	0	0
Local petroleum fuels	0	18	21	27	30	32	33	179	161	176
CA mileage tax	0	0	0	0	0	0	0	0	0	0
NRF mileage tax	3	0	0	0	0	0	0	0	0	0
Road user charges	0	68	0	0	0	0	0	0	0	0
Energy resources levy	0	20	87	111	46	36	28	23	26	23
5122 Profits of fiscal monopolies	0	0	0	0	0	0	0	0	0	0
5123 Customs and import duties	49	231	505	648	1 857	1 916	2 442	3 292	3 493	3 717
On alcoholic beverages			0	106	221	229	276	469	504	505
Beer			0	..	..	..	55	69	76	76
Wine			0	..	..	..	59	85	101	90
Spirits & other alcoholic beverages			0	..	..	..	162	315	327	339
Tobacco			0	76	804	924	1 348	1 593	1 864	1 666
Refined fuels			0	191	528	575	691	1 061	947	1 359
Other tariffs			0	275	304	188	127	169	178	187
5124 Taxes on exports	0	0	0	0	0	0	0	0	0	0
5125 Taxes on investment goods	0	0	0	0	0	0	0	0	0	0
5126 Taxes on specific services	13	57	83	206	302	266	275	322	272	342
Lottery (national)	1	6	26	167	290	253	260	314	269	342
Lottery (overseas)	0	0	0	0	0	0	0	0	0	0
Racing	12	46	57	39	12	13	15	8	3	0
Film hire tax	0	1	0	0	0	0	0	0	0	0
Domestic air travel tax	0	3	0	0	0	0	0	0	0	0
5127 Other taxes on internat. trade and transactions	0	12	0	0	0	0	0	0	0	0
Foreign fishing vessels tax	..	0	..	..	..	..	..	..	..	..
Foreign travel tax	..	0	..	..	..	..	..	..	..	..
International departure tax	..	12	..	..	..	..	..	..	..	..
5128 Other taxes	0	0	0	0	0	0	0	0	0	0
5130 Unallocable between 5110 and 5120	0	0	0	0	0	0	0	0	0	0
5200 Taxes on use of goods and perform activities	18	69	539	905	1 458	1 585	2 144	2 816	2 789	2 403
5210 Recurrent taxes	18	69	539	905	1 458	1 585	2 144	2 816	2 789	2 403
Motor vehicle registration	7	47	154	181	226	172	214	231	234	236
Heavy traffic fees	8	0	285	532	851	1 016	1 381	1 930	1 840	1 414
Accident compensation levies	0	0	0	0	0	0	0	0	0	0
5220 Nonrecurrent taxes	0	0	0	0	0	0	0	0	0	0
5300 Unallocable between 5100 and 5200	0	0	0	0	0	0	0	0	0	0
5211 Paid by households: motor vehicles	0	0	0	0	0	0	0	0	0	0
5212 Paid by others: motor vehicles	0	0	0	0	0	0	0	0	0	0
5213 Paid in respect of other goods	3	23	100	192	381	397	549	655	715	753
Local authority fees and charges	3	23	100	192	381	397	549	655	715	753
6000 Other taxes	0	0	1	0	31	5	2	1	1	0
6100 Paid solely by business	..	..	0	..	0	0	0	0	0	..
6200 Other	..	..	1	..	31	5	2	1	1	..
Non-wastable tax credits against 1110	..	..	..	1 057	2 568	2 794	2 352	2 958	2 844	2 949
Tax expenditure component	..	..	..	311	873	950	1 254	1 520	1 502	1 558
Transfer component	..	..	..	746	1 695	1 844	1 098	1 438	1 342	1 391
Non-wastable tax credits against 1210	..	..	..	0	0	0	0	0	0	0
Tax expenditure component	..	..	..	..	..	..	..	..	..	..
Transfer component	..	..	..	..	..	..	..	..	..	..
Total tax revenue on cash basis	1 001	7 594	27 471	39 276	64 273	62 053	82 481	114 305	124 905	131 772
Total tax revenue on accrual basis	..	..	..	39 765	64 046	62 310	81 499	115 596	125 753	130 786
Additional taxes included in National Accounts	..	..	..	..	0	0	2 807	3 838	4 691	5 677
Taxes excluded from National Accounts	..	..	..	..	0	0	- 5 852	- 9 327	- 10 687	- 10 887
Difference in treatment of tax credits	..	..	..	..	873	950	1 254	1 520	1 502	1 558
Capital transfer for uncollected revenue	..	..	..	..	0	0	0	0	0	0
Voluntary social security contributions	..	..	..	..	0	0	0	0	0	0
Miscellaneous differences	..	..	..	..	0	0	- 1 602	- 8 389	- 823	1 550
National Accounts: Taxes and actual social contributions	..	..	..	..	64 919	63 260	78 106	103 238	120 436	128 684
Imputed social contributions	..	..	..	..	0	0	2 063	2 221	2 417	2 728
National Accounts: Taxes and all social contributions	..	..	..	..	64 919	63 260	80 169	105 459	122 853	131 412

.. Not available

Note: For the years before 1989 data are on a fiscal year basis ending 31st March. The figures provided for 1989 and onwards relate to the financial year ending 30th June of the following year.

From 1993, data are on accrual basis.

Heading 1000: Tax credits to exporters under the export incentives schemes are non-wastable, but that part of the excess of taxliability paid out to taxpayers is not identifiable.

Heading 1100: The figures up to 1969 include revenues collected by a social security income tax. The base of this tax was the same as the ordinary income tax base and the two have now been incorporated into a single income tax.

Heading 5121: From October 1986 incorporates that portion of the selective impost on wine, spirits, tobacco and motor vehicles which was formerly collected and reported as sales tax. The revenue collected on those imported goods which are subject to the equivalent of the domestic excise has been classified as excise duty. In this respect, there is a discontinuity between the excises recorded before and after October 1986.

Heading 5210: The other local authority licence fees include some small items which could be regarded as non-tax revenues.

Heading for non-wastable tax credits 1110 comprises four Family assistance tax credits. The total in item 1100 is net of the tax expenditure component but not net of the transfer component.

Source: Statistics New Zealand.

Table 5.28. Norway: Details of tax revenue, 1965-2022

Million NOK

	1965	1980	1990	2000	2007	2010	2015	2020	2021	2022
Total tax revenue	16 842	133 499	303 297	630 762	990 567	1 087 360	1 200 028	1 340 119	1 787 681	2 479 483
1000 Taxes on income, profits and capital gains	7 316	55 837	106 290	284 853	476 298	512 916	476 301	488 781	881 281	1 510 667
1100 Of individuals	6 671	38 018	79 068	152 677	221 564	257 216	336 126	392 270	459 419	462 977
1110 On income and profits	6 671	38 018	79 068	152 677	221 564	257 216	336 126	392 270	459 419	462 977
Employee social security contributions	1 305	0	0	0	0	0	0	0	0	0
Income taxes	5 366	38 018	79 068	152 677	221 564	257 216	336 126	392 270	459 419	462 977
1120 On capital gains	0	0	0	0	0	0	0	0	0	0
1200 Corporate	645	17 819	27 222	132 176	254 734	255 700	140 175	96 511	421 862	1 047 690
1210 On profits	..	..	..	132 176	254 734	255 700	140 175	96 511	421 862	1 047 690
1220 On capital gains	..	..	..	0	0	0	0	0	0	0
1300 Unallocable between 1100 and 1200	0	0	0	0	0	0	0	0	0	0
2000 Social security contributions	2 009	28 205	79 362	132 170	204 473	243 002	325 130	381 231	401 990	428 463
2100 Employees	0	6 639	25 345	45 162	68 518	81 032	112 662	134 761	142 137	148 315
2110 On a payroll basis	..	..	..	45 162	68 518	81 032	112 662	134 761	142 137	148 315
2120 On an income tax basis	..	..	..	0	0	0	0	0	0	0
2200 Employers	1 716	20 454	50 116	79 242	124 178	148 047	190 923	221 257	232 603	251 048
2210 On a payroll basis of employers SSC	..	..	..	79 242	124 178	148 047	190 923	221 257	232 603	251 048
2220 On an income tax basis of employers SSC	..	..	..	0	0	0	0	0	0	0
2300 Selfemployed or nonemployed	293	1 112	3 901	7 766	11 777	13 923	21 545	25 213	27 250	29 100
2310 On a payroll basis of self/non-employed SSC	..	..	..	7 766	11 777	13 923	21 545	25 213	27 250	29 100
2320 On an income tax basis of self/non-employed SSC	..	..	..	0	0	0	0	0	0	0
2400 Unallocable between 2100, 2200 and 2300	0	0	0	0	0	0	0	0	0	0
2410 On a payroll basis unallocable between 2100, 2200 and 2300 SSC	..	..	..	..	..	..	..	..	..	..
2420 On an income tax basis unallocable between 2100, 2200 and 2300 SSC	..	..	..	..	..	..	..	..	..	..
3000 Taxes on payroll and workforce	0	0	0	0	0	0	0	2 065	2 217	2 415
4000 Taxes on property	523	2 295	8 887	13 758	24 763	27 875	33 094	43 954	47 637	55 228
4100 Recurrent taxes on immovable property	100	431	2 216	2 724	5 571	7 109	11 177	14 818	15 566	16 091
4110 Households	..	431	2 216	2 724	2 149	3 024	5 437	7 224	7 639	8 083
4120 Others	..	0	0	0	3 422	4 085	5 740	7 594	7 927	8 008
4200 Recurrent taxes on net wealth	341	1 450	5 118	7 039	11 062	12 521	13 196	17 720	18 905	26 924
4210 Individual	235	907	3 692	6 869	10 746	12 169	12 902	17 259	18 454	26 100
4220 Corporate	106	543	1 426	170	316	352	294	461	451	824
4300 Estate, inheritance and gift taxes	45	122	446	1 273	2 576	2 377	295	64	48	32
4310 Estate and inheritance taxes	..	122	446	1 273	2 576	2 377	295	64	48	32
4320 Gift taxes	..	0	0	0	0	0	0	0	0	0
4400 Taxes on financial and capital transactions	37	292	1 107	2 722	5 554	5 868	8 426	11 352	13 118	12 181
4500 Nonrecurrent taxes	0	0	0	0	0	0	0	0	0	0
4510 On net wealth	..	..	..	..	..	..	..	..	..	..
4520 Other nonrecurrent taxes	..	..	..	..	..	..	..	..	..	..
4600 Other recurrent taxes on property	0	0	0	0	0	0	0	0	0	0
5000 Taxes on goods and services	6 928	47 154	108 747	199 981	285 033	303 567	365 503	424 088	454 556	482 710
5100 Taxes on production, sale, transfer, etc	6 720	45 882	102 901	185 921	266 456	284 646	342 410	403 931	430 625	458 093
5110 General taxes	3 622	24 350	56 656	124 985	189 424	201 802	256 029	312 936	340 400	373 515
5111 Value added taxes	0	24 350	56 656	124 166	188 705	201 184	255 182	311 600	338 900	371 700
Value added tax	..	24 350	56 656	124 166	188 705	201 184	255 182	311 600	338 900	371 700
5112 Sales tax	0	0	0	0	719	618	0	1 336	1 500	1 815
5113 Other	3 622	0	0	819	0	0	847	0	0	0
5120 Taxes on specific goods and services	3 098	21 532	46 245	60 936	77 032	82 844	86 381	90 995	90 225	84 578
5121 Excises	2 338	14 914	37 453	54 871	71 047	76 328	78 845	81 662	79 584	72 681

	1965	1980	1990	2000	2007	2010	2015	2020	2021	2022
Stamp duty on tobacco	392	1 076	3 750	6 806	6 815	7 768	7 219	9 127	9 308	7 103
Taxes on spirits and wines	449	2 013	3 454	5 217	0	0	0	0	0	0
Excise on beer	162	605	2 195	3 650	0	0	0	0	0	0
Excise on petrol	480	2 310	7 057	9 756	8 132	7 373	5 711	4 409	4 503	4 275
Vehicles transfer tax	395	2 761	4 554	10 956	22 898	21 835	19 355	10 793	9 456	8 133
Chocolate and sweets	123	247	551	789	1 078	1 173	1 324	1 516	0	0
Sugar	0	0	217	230	192	196	206	205	220	174
Non-alcoholic beverages	38	120	487	1 113	1 024	1 739	1 972	3 057	705	0
Electric energy	89	1 515	3 414	5 091	7 079	8 110	9 233	11 322	12 182	9 178
Oil and gas products	0	3 703	8 729	88	92	98	103	111	116	110
Sales of radio and tv sets	0	163	220	920	0	0	0	0	0	0
Mineral oil	0	113	1 098	490	685	1 419	1 986	1 770	1 796	1 760
Cosmetics	0	0	0	159	0	0	0	0	0	0
Recording equipment	0	0	92	35	0	0	0	0	0	0
Others	210	288	1 635	1 249	1 821	1 965	2 535	3 346	3 683	3 669
Taxes on alcoholic beverages	0	0	0	0	10 338	11 317	12 969	17 976	17 847	16 301
Excise on diesel	0	0	0	4 802	6 424	8 653	10 267	9 588	10 289	9 755
Tax on Co2 emissions, petroleum sector excepted	0	0	0	3 520	4 469	4 682	5 965	8 442	9 479	12 223
5122 Profits of fiscal monopolies	31	395	751	2 534	2 902	3 433	3 869	5 311	5 883	6 137
Profits state wine monopoly	31	30	67	41	32	44	0	0	0	0
Norsk tipping	0	365	684	2 493	2 870	3 389	3 869	5 311	5 883	6 137
5123 Customs and import duties	634	697	1 360	1 944	2 132	2 505	3 305	3 625	4 334	4 123
Customs revenue	615	689	1 305	1 944	2 132	2 505	3 305	3 625	4 334	4 123
Loading and lighthouse dues	11	0	0	0	0	0	0	0	0	0
Other import duties	8	8	55	0	0	0	0	0	0	0
5124 Taxes on exports	7	105	227	0	112	151	178	316	363	456
5125 Taxes on investment goods	0	4 274	4 454	0	0	0	0	0	0	0
5126 Taxes on specific services	88	195	1 233	1 386	131	114	138	21	0	962
Excise on race tracks	9	25	15	88	119	114	138	21	..	0
Taxes on specific services	34	49	150	1 298	0	0	0	0	..	962
Pengelotteriet (national lotteries)	45	121	462	0	0	0	0	0	..	0
Excise on lotto games	0	0	606	0	12	0	0	0	..	0
5127 Other taxes on internat. trade and transactions	0	0	0	0	0	0	0	0	0	0
5128 Other taxes	0	952	767	201	708	313	46	60	61	219
5130 Unallocable between 5110 and 5120	0	0	0	0	0	0	0	0	0	0
5200 Taxes on use of goods and perform activities	208	1 272	5 846	14 060	18 577	18 921	23 093	20 157	23 931	24 617
5210 Recurrent taxes	208	1 272	5 846	14 060	18 577	17 446	22 309	17 751	17 626	20 565
5211 Paid by households: motor vehicles	88	458	1 789	4 435	6 699	7 157	8 400	7 640	7 994	8 631
5212 Paid by others: motor vehicles	108	696	2 072	1 346	712	539	352	330	329	273
5213 Paid in respect of other goods	12	118	1 985	8 279	11 166	9 750	13 557	9 781	9 303	11 661
CO2 tax	0	0	0	3 047	3 385	2 166	4 906	5 713	5 035	7 165
Excise on pharmacies	6	32	59	105	153	80	99	64	69	82
Others	6	86	441	2 354	3 132	3 394	3 809	3 949	4 149	4 363
Tax on emissions of NOX	0	0	0	0	1 207	87	69	55	50	51
TV licence paid by households			1 485	2 773	3 289	4 023	4 674	0	0	0
5220 Nonrecurrent taxes	0	0	0	0	0	1 475	784	2 406	6 305	4 052
5300 Unallocable between 5100 and 5200	0	0	0	0	0	0	0	0	0	0
6000 Other taxes	66	8	11	0	0	0	0	0	0	0
6100 Paid solely by business	0	3	2	..	..	..	..	..	..	..
6200 Other	66	5	9	..	..	..	..	..	..	..
Non-wastable tax credits against 1210	..	..	..	..	994	1 229	2 959	3 654	3 713	3 537
Tax expenditure component	..	..	..	..	350	75	484	821	754	800
Transfer component	..	..	..	..	644	1 154	2 475	2 833	2 959	2 737
Total tax revenue on cash basis	16 842	133 499	303 297	575 989	0	0	0	1 362 295	1 489 963	2 288 674
Total tax revenue on accrual basis	..	..	..	630 762	990 567	1 087 360	1 200 028	1 340 119	1 787 681	2 479 483
Additional taxes included in National Accounts	..	..	0	0	0	0	0	0	0	0
Taxes excluded from National Accounts	..	..	..	0	0	0	0	0	0	0
Difference in treatment of tax credits	..	..	..	0	350	75	484	821	754	800
Capital transfer for uncollected revenue	..	..	..	0	0	0	0	0	0	0
Voluntary social security contributions	..	..	..	0	0	0	0	0	0	0
Miscellaneous differences	..	..	..	0	0	0	0	0	0	0
National Accounts: Taxes and actual social contributions	..	..	..	630 762	990 917	1 087 435	1 200 512	1 340 940	1 788 435	2 480 283
Imputed social contributions	..	..	..	2 076	2 931	3 164	3 870	5 530	6 453	6 195
National Accounts: Taxes and all social contributions	..	..	..	632 838	993 848	1 090 599	1 204 382	1 346 470	1 794 888	2 486 478

.. Not available

Note: Year ending 31st December.
From 2000, data are on accrual basis.
Heading 5211: Up to 1971 this item contains motor vehicle licences paid by both households and enterprises.
Heading 5121: From 2005, taxes on alcoholic beverages include both 'taxes on spirits and wines' and 'excise on beer'.
Heading 5125: From 1998, revenue from taxes on investments goods is included in item 5121 "Others".
Source: Statistics Norway; National Accounts.

Table 5.29. Poland: Details of tax revenue, 1965-2022

Million PLN

	1965	1980	1990	2000	2007	2010	2015	2020	2021	2022
Total tax revenue	..	..	..	247 064	412 656	454 660	586 263	834 473	969 137	1 061 095
Total tax revenue exclusive of taxes collected for the EU	..	..	..	247 064	410 945	452 961	583 369	830 079	963 226	1 052 655
1000 Taxes on income, profits and capital gains	..	..	..	50 268	93 795	91 026	117 078	175 845	209 268	224 023
1100 Of individuals	..	..	..	32 415	61 471	62 901	83 974	122 973	140 681	138 258
Individual income tax	..	..	..	32 415	61 403	62 818	83 861	122 817	140 465	138 019
Tax on winnings from lottery or gambling	..	..	..	0	68	83	113	156	216	239
1110 On income and profits	..	..	..	..	..	..	..	..	..	..
1120 On capital gains	..	..	..	..	..	..	..	..	..	..
1200 Corporate	..	..	..	17 853	32 324	28 125	33 104	52 872	68 587	85 765
1210 On profits	..	..	..	..	..	..	..	..	..	..
1220 On capital gains	..	..	..	..	..	..	..	..	..	..
1300 Unallocable between 1100 and 1200	..	..	..	0	0	0	0	0	0	0
2000 Social security contributions	..	..	..	97 411	141 457	157 432	225 711	318 636	344 720	396 507
2100 Employees	..	..	..	42 606	51 745	60 158	92 607	133 065	149 781	173 427
2110 On a payroll basis	..	..	..	..	..	..	..	..	..	..
2120 On an income tax basis	..	..	..	..	..	..	..	..	..	..
2200 Employers	..	..	..	41 834	56 016	66 893	88 749	120 856	125 870	144 069
2210 On a payroll basis of employers SSC	..	..	..	..	..	..	..	..	..	..
2220 On an income tax basis of employers SSC	..	..	..	..	..	..	..	..	..	..
2300 Selfemployed or nonemployed	..	..	..	12 971	33 696	30 381	44 355	64 715	69 069	79 011
2310 On a payroll basis of self/non-employed SSC	..	..	..	..	..	..	..	..	..	..
2320 On an income tax basis of self/non-employed SSC	..	..	..	..	..	..	..	..	..	..
2400 Unallocable between 2100, 2200 and 2300	..	..	..	0	0	0	0	0	0	0
2410 On a payroll basis unallocable between 2100, 2200 and 2300 SSC	..	..	..	..	..	..	..	..	..	..
2420 On an income tax basis unallocable between 2100, 2200 and 2300 SSC	..	..	..	..	..	..	..	..	..	..
3000 Taxes on payroll and workforce	..	..	..	1 628	3 081	3 720	4 028	7 683	14 531	17 154
Rehabilitation fund contribution	..	..	..	1 508	2 860	3 370	3 621	4 937	5 331	5 923
Wage guarantee fund contribution	..	..	..	120	221	350	407	416	488	561
Receipts from employers' obligatory payments to the Fundusz Solidarno?ciowy				0	0	0	0	2 330	8 712	10 670
4000 Taxes on property	..	..	..	10 584	17 116	19 068	24 637	30 293	33 611	35 795
4100 Recurrent taxes on immovable property	..	..	..	8 404	13 515	16 399	22 206	26 454	28 064	30 084
Agricultural tax-local	..	..	..	720	906	969	1 579	1 628	1 635	1 685
Forest tax-local	..	..	..	96	157	165	230	301	306	330
Real estate tax-local	..	..	..	7 588	12 452	15 265	20 397	24 525	26 123	28 069
4110 Households	..	..	..	2 348	3 613	4 555	6 549	7 796	8 339	8 976
4120 Others	..	..	..	6 056	9 902	11 844	15 657	18 658	19 725	21 108
4200 Recurrent taxes on net wealth	..	..	..	0	0	0	0	0	0	0
4210 Individual	..	..	..	..	..	..	..	..	..	..
4220 Corporate	..	..	..	..	..	..	..	..	..	..
4300 Estate, inheritance and gift taxes	..	..	..	172	328	290	246	313	425	555
Inheritance and gift tax-local	..	..	..	172	328	290	246	313	425	555
4310 Estate and inheritance taxes	..	..	..	..	..	..	..	..	..	..
4320 Gift taxes	..	..	..	..	..	..	..	..	..	..
4400 Taxes on financial and capital transactions	..	..	..	2 008	3 273	2 379	2 185	3 526	5 122	5 156
Tax on civil law transactions and stamp tax	..	..	..	2 008	3 273	2 379	2 185	3 526	5 122	5 156
4500 Nonrecurrent taxes	..	..	..	0	0	0	0	0	0	0
4510 On net wealth	..	..	..	..	..	..	..	..	..	..
4520 Other nonrecurrent taxes	..	..	..	..	..	..	..	..	..	..
4600 Other recurrent taxes on property	..	..	..	0	0	0	0	0	0	0
5000 Taxes on goods and services	..	..	..	86 880	156 683	182 820	214 162	301 030	365 723	386 097
5100 Taxes on production, sale, transfer, etc	..	..	..	84 885	151 804	176 044	206 197	283 817	344 650	351 536
5110 General taxes	..	..	..	51 615	97 848	109 717	125 895	185 964	228 088	226 721
5111 Value added taxes	..	..	..	51 615	97 848	109 717	125 895	185 964	225 140	223 395
5112 Sales tax	..	..	..	0	0	0	0	0	2 948	3 326
5113 Other	..	..	..	0	0	0	0	0	0	0
Turnover tax, of which	..	..	..	..	..	..	..	..	..	..
On spirits	..	..	..	..	..	..	..	..	..	..
On fuels	..	..	..	..	..	..	..	..	..	..
On tobacco	..	..	..	..	..	..	..	..	..	..
5120 Taxes on specific goods and services	..	..	..	33 270	53 956	66 327	80 302	97 853	116 562	124 815
5121 Excises	..	..	..	27 170	49 376	62 016	70 632	81 754	98 366	102 139

	1965	1980	1990	2000	2007	2010	2015	2020	2021	2022
On domestic excise products, of which	..	..	..	24 213	45 752	58 935	62 442	77 649	92 044	95 029
On spirits	..	..	..	4 309	5 000	6 154	6 655	8 743	8 953	10 115
On fuels	..	..	..	11 056	22 128	26 545	29 874	39 975	45 156	43 411
On other products				488	3 298	5 270	4 332	3 806	10 629	10 654
On tobacco	..	..	..	6 143	11 973	17 348	17 788	21 455	23 342	25 900
On beer	..	..	..	1 758	2 975	3 303	3 547	3 425	3 245	3 646
On wine	..	..	..	459	378	315	246	229	247	260
On electronic cigarette liquid and novelty products	..	..	..	0	0	0	0	16	472	1 043
On imported excise products, of which	..	..	..	2 957	3 624	3 081	8 190	4 105	4 901	5 511
On spirits	..	..	..	90	253	311	267	500	690	692
On fuels	..	..	..	2 031	2 045	1 051	5 650	928	1 100	1 391
On tobacco	..	..	..	18	214	114	86	52	48	51
On beer	..	..	..	26	12	14	53	70	76	81
On wine	..	..	..	71	106	133	139	194	231	247
On electronic cigarette liquid and novelty products	..	..	..	0	0	0	0	9	53	91
On other products				721	994	1 458	1 995	2 352	2 703	2 958
Levy on foodstuffs				0	0	0	0	0	1 421	1 599
5122 Profits of fiscal monopolies	..	..	..	0	0	0	0	0	0	0
5123 Customs and import duties	..	..	..	5 038	1 711	1 627	2 823	4 394	5 911	8 440
5124 Taxes on exports	..	..	..	0	0	0	0	0	0	0
5125 Taxes on investment goods	..	..	..	0	0	0	0	0	0	0
5126 Taxes on specific services	..	..	..	1 062	1 297	1 974	5 795	10 582	10 907	12 472
Taxes and payments of financial institutions	..	..	..	443	189	375	4 472	3 485	2 525	2 495
Gambling tax	..	..	..	619	1 108	1 599	1 323	2 366	3 030	3 855
Tax from some financial institutions	..	..	..	0	0	0	0	4 731	5 352	6 122
5127 Other taxes on internat. trade and transactions	..	..	..	0	0	0	0	0	0	0
5128 Other taxes	..	..	..	0	1 572	710	1 052	1 123	1 378	1 764
5130 Unallocable between 5110 and 5120	..	..	..	0	0	0	0	0	0	0
5200 Taxes on use of goods and perform activities	..	..	..	1 995	4 879	6 776	7 965	17 213	21 073	34 561
5210 Recurrent taxes	..	..	..	433	2 383	3 667	4 317	3 596	4 048	6 280
5211 Paid by households: motor vehicles	..	..	..	0	0	0	0	0	0	0
5212 Paid by others: motor vehicles	..	..	..	0	0	0	0	0	0	0
5213 Paid in respect of other goods	..	..	..	433	2 383	3 667	4 317	3 596	4 048	6 280
5220 Nonrecurrent taxes	..	..	..	1 562	2 496	3 109	3 648	13 617	17 025	28 281
5300 Unallocable between 5100 and 5200	..	..	..	0	0	0	0	0	0	0
6000 Other taxes	..	..	..	293	524	594	647	986	1 284	1 519
Abolished taxes	..	..	..	0	0	0	0	0	0	0
6100 Paid solely by business	..	..	..	0	0	0	0	0	0	0
6200 Other	..	..	..	293	524	594	647	986	1 284	1 519
Custom duties collected for the EU	..	..	..	..	1 711	1 627	2 823	4 394	5 911	8 440
Total tax revenue on cash basis	..	..	..	..	..	..	..	..	..	..
Total tax revenue on accrual basis	..	..	..	247 064	412 656	454 660	586 263	834 473	969 137	1 061 095
Additional taxes included in National Accounts	..	..	..	..	..	..	..	..	..	..
Taxes excluded from National Accounts	..	..	..	..	..	..	..	..	..	..
Difference in treatment of tax credits	..	..	..	..	..	..	..	..	..	..
Capital transfer for uncollected revenue	..	..	..	1 025	1 371	1 406	2 229	3 201	3 495	3 982
Voluntary social security contributions	..	..	..	..	..	..	49	48	48	50
Miscellaneous differences	..	..	..	..	..	..	..	..	..	1 057 163
National Accounts: Taxes and actual social contributions	..	..	..	246 039	411 285	453 254	584 083	831 323	965 690	25 147
Imputed social contributions	..	..	..	777	10 848	13 841	17 423	20 429	22 548	1 082 310
National Accounts: Taxes and all social contributions	..	..	..	252 943	422 133	467 095	601 506	851 752	988 238	0

.. Not available

Note: Year ending 31st December.

From 2002, data are on accrual basis.

Source: Ministry of Finance, Economic Department.

Table 5.30. Portugal: Details of tax revenue, 1965-2022

Million EUR

	1965	1980	1990	2000	2007	2010	2015	2020	2021	2022
Total tax revenue	99	1 798	14 825	39 705	55 885	54 541	61 788	70 510	76 015	87 277
Total tax revenue exclusive of taxes collected for the EU	..	..	14 675	39 501	55 695	54 363	61 630	70 179	75 644	86 754
1000 Taxes on income, profits and capital gains	24	355	3 805	11 691	15 546	14 585	18 762	19 534	20 179	24 993
1100 Of individuals	..	..	2 350	6 768	9 328	9 637	13 149	13 994	14 973	16 911
Individual income tax	..	..	2 350	6 768	9 328	9 637	13 149	13 994	14 973	16 911
1110 On income and profits	..	..	..	..	..	..	..	..	..	..
1120 On capital gains	..	..	..	..	..	..	..	..	..	..
1200 Corporate	..	..	1 182	4 744	6 128	4 936	5 614	5 540	5 206	8 082
Corporate income tax	..	..	1 088	4 457	5 815	4 670	5 405	5 193	4 908	7 706
Local corporate income tax ("Derrama")	..	..	84	287	313	266	208	347	297	375
Other	..	..	11	0	0	0	0	0	0	0
1210 On profits	..	..	..	..	..	..	..	..	..	..
1220 On capital gains	..	..	..	..	..	..	..	..	..	..
1300 Unallocable between 1100 and 1200	24	355	273	178	90	12	0	0	0	0
Tax on wages and professional income	2	93	9	0	0	0	0	..	..	..
Industrial tax	7	108	129	0	0	0	0	..	..	..
Tax on income from movable capital	2	71	1	0	0	0	0	..	..	..
Property income tax	3	23	17	0	0	0	0	..	..	..
Agricultural income tax	0	0	1	0	0	0	0	..	..	..
Complementary income tax	4	43	58	0	0	0	0	..	..	..
Tax on capital gains	0	3	1	0	0	0	0	..	..	..
Taxes abolished by DL 442-A/88 and DL 442-B/88	0	0	0	0	0	0	0	..	..	..
Other	6	15	58	178	90	12	0	..	..	..
2000 Social security contributions	22	531	4 026	10 168	14 305	15 462	16 182	20 943	22 471	24 734
2100 Employees	8	203	1 470	4 286	6 344	6 670	6 992	8 290	8 986	9 689
2110 On a payroll basis	8	203	1 470	4 286	6 344	6 670	6 992	8 290	8 986	9 689
Compulsory employee's social contributions	8	203	1 470	4 286	6 344	6 670	6 992	8 290	8 986	9 689
2120 On an income tax basis	0	0	0	0	0	0	0	0	0	0
2200 Employers	13	318	2 413	5 882	7 961	8 792	9 191	12 653	13 485	15 045
2210 On a payroll basis of employers SSC	13	318	2 413	5 882	7 961	8 792	9 191	12 653	13 485	15 045
Employers' social contributions	13	318	2 413	5 882	7 961	8 792	9 191	12 653	13 485	15 045
2220 On an income tax basis of employers SSC	0	0	0	0	0	0	0	0	0	0
2300 Selfemployed or nonemployed	0	10	143	0	0	0	0	0	0	0
Compulsory social contributions by self-employed	0	10	143	..	..	..	..	..	..	..
2310 On a payroll basis of self/non-employed SSC	..	..	0	..	..	..	..	..	..	..
2320 On an income tax basis of self/non-employed SSC	..	..	0	..	..	..	..	..	..	..
2400 Unallocable between 2100, 2200 and 2300	0	0	0	0	0	0	0	0	0	0
2410 On a payroll basis unallocable between 2100, 2200 and 2300 SSC	..	..	..	..	..	..	..	..	..	..
2420 On an income tax basis unallocable between 2100, 2200 and 2300 SSC	..	..	..	..	..	..	..	..	..	..
3000 Taxes on payroll and workforce	1	47	0	0	0	0	0	0	0	0
Contributions for Unemployment Fund	1	47	..	..	..	..	..	..	..	..
Stamp duty on wages and salaries	0	0	..	..	..	..	..	..	..	..
4000 Taxes on property	5	26	402	1 468	2 330	2 028	2 307	2 888	3 329	3 731
4100 Recurrent taxes on immovable property	0	0	133	508	1 008	1 112	1 535	1 632	1 612	1 639
Real estate tax	..	..	133	508	1 008	1 112	1 535	1 632	1 612	1 639
4110 Households	..	..	..	..	..	..	..	..	..	..
4120 Others	..	..	..	..	..	..	..	..	..	..
4200 Recurrent taxes on net wealth	0	0	0	0	0	0	0	0	0	0
4210 Individual	..	..	..	..	..	..	..	..	..	..
4220 Corporate	..	..	..	..	..	..	..	..	..	..
4300 Estate, inheritance and gift taxes	2	4	74	103	10	2	0	0	0	0
Inheritance and gift taxes	2	4	74	0	0	0	..	0	..	0
4310 Estate and inheritance taxes	..	..	0	103	10	2	..	0	..	0
4320 Gift taxes	..	..	0	0	0	0	..	0	..	0
4400 Taxes on financial and capital transactions	2	21	195	857	1 312	914	772	1 256	1 717	2 093
Real estate transfer tax	2	21	195	674	973	595	569	949	1 313	1 659
Stamp duty on registrations and mortgages	0	0	0	34	45	35	49	7	9	10
Stamp duty on the raising of capital	0	0	0	0	9	1	0	0	0	0
Stamp duty on real estate transactions	0	0	0	150	285	201	154	300	394	423
Special Tax on capital transfers			0	0	0	83	0	0	0	0
4500 Nonrecurrent taxes	0	0	0	0	0	0	0	0	0	0
4510 On net wealth	..	..	..	..	..	..	..	..	..	..
4520 Other nonrecurrent taxes	..	..	..	..	..	..	..	..	..	..
4600 Other recurrent taxes on property	0	0	0	0	0	0	0	0	0	0
5000 Taxes on goods and services	47	837	6 555	16 283	23 494	22 238	24 194	26 702	29 610	33 401
5100 Taxes on production, sale, transfer, etc	44	810	6 440	15 858	22 841	21 485	23 112	25 209	28 057	31 435

	1965	1980	1990	2000	2007	2010	2015	2020	2021	2022
5110 General taxes	0	290	2 906	9 733	14 333	13 527	15 368	16 803	19 186	22 711
5111 Value added taxes	0	0	2 899	9 733	14 333	13 527	15 368	16 803	19 186	22 711
VAT	..	..	2 899	9 733	14 333	13 527	15 368	16 803	19 186	22 711
5112 Sales tax	0	290	7	0	0	0	0	0	0	0
General sales tax	..	290	7	..	..	..	..	..	..	..
5113 Other	0	0	0	0	0	0	0	0	0	0
5120 Taxes on specific goods and services	44	519	3 534	6 125	8 508	7 958	7 744	8 406	8 872	8 723
5121 Excises	15	295	2 052	4 496	5 937	5 653	5 211	5 490	5 772	5 222
Excise duties on tobacco	3	62	362	1 077	1 165	1 496	1 357	1 474	1 473	1 596
Excise duties on beer	1	0	55	87	97	80	75	82	89	110
Tax on motor vehicle sales	1	59	304	1 239	1 221	832	585	447	432	455
Tax on oil products	6	166	1 251	1 969	3 320	3 126	3 069	3 298	3 551	2 793
Excise duties on alcoholic beverages	0	0	23	123	126	112	115	105	137	168
Excise duties on alcohol	0	0	0	1	1	1	0	1	0	0
Tax on sugary soft drinks	0	0	0	0	0	0	0	52	51	59
Other	4	7	59	0	6	6	11	30	39	40
5122 Profits of fiscal monopolies	0	0	0	261	521	425	582	628	652	685
5123 Customs and import duties	21	96	511	204	190	177	158	203	238	365
Import levies	14	36	392	0	0	0	0	0	0	0
Import surtax	0	26	1	0	0	0	0	0	0	0
Agricultural Levies			0	0	0	0	0	0	0	0
Levy on sugar and isoglucse			0	0	0	0	0	0	0	0
Other	6	34	119	0	0	0	0	0	0	0
Custom duties collected for the EU			0	204	190	177	158	203	238	365
5124 Taxes on exports	0	0	0	0	0	0	0	0	0	0
Taxes on Oporto wine exports	0	0	..	..	..	..	..	..	..	..
Other	0	0	..	..	..	..	..	..	..	..
5125 Taxes on investment goods	0	0	0	0	0	0	0	0	0	0
5126 Taxes on specific services	1	38	547	1 116	1 679	1 539	1 523	1 879	2 004	2 239
Tax on insurance premiums	0	6	47	131	170	215	218	277	302	320
Stamp duty on bank transactions	1	24	405	330	694	619	464	595	627	671
Stamp duty on debt related operations, interest and leasing of buildings	0	0	22	258	386	293	144	136	141	150
Stamp duty on insurance premiums	0	0	0	248	335	325	313	419	446	477
Bank levies	0	0	0	100	48	46	353	412	433	487
Other	2	8	73	47	46	40	30	40	55	133
5127 Other taxes on internat. trade and transactions	0	0	0	0	0	0	0	0	0	0
5128 Other taxes	6	91	424	48	182	163	269	207	205	212
Stamp taxes (miscellaneous)	6	91	424	36	48	111	251	201	194	207
Other	0	0	0	0	0	0	0	0	0	0
5130 Unallocable between 5110 and 5120	0	0	0	12	134	52	18	6	11	5
5200 Taxes on use of goods and perform activities	4	27	115	384	622	736	1 069	1 478	1 539	1 957
5210 Recurrent taxes	4	27	115	384	621	736	990	1 255	1 282	1 441
5211 Paid by households: motor vehicles	0	4	15	55	94	139	209	230	236	254
Local tax on vehicles	..	4	15	55	94	139	209	230	236	254
5212 Paid by others: motor vehicles	2	10	20	67	132	180	330	453	460	505
Local tax on vehicles	0	2	6	0	0	0	0	0	0	0
Road taxes	2	8	14	67	132	180	330	453	460	505
5213 Paid in respect of other goods	2	13	80	261	396	417	451	571	587	682
Gambling tax	0	3	72	110	140	143	108	223	217	261
Tax on the use, carrying and possession of weapons	0	0	1	3	6	4	5	4	4	5
Tax on motor vehicles - compensation	2	8	0	0	0	0	0	0	0	0
Hunting and fishery licenses	0	1	4	1	7	12	13	12	16	16
Fee for the use of water resources	0	0	0	0	2	19	19	19	21	23
Other	0	1	2	148	241	239	307	313	329	378
5220 Nonrecurrent taxes	0	0	0	0	0	0	80	223	257	516
Special tax on motor vehicles	..	..	0	..	0	0	0	0	0	0
Emissions permits			0	..	0	0	80	223	256	514
Tax on noise			0	..	0	0	0	1	1	2
5300 Unallocable between 5100 and 5200	0	0	0	41	31	17	13	15	14	9
Miscellaneous taxes on production	..	..	..	41	31	17	13	15	14	9
6000 Other taxes	0	3	37	95	211	227	342	444	426	418
6100 Paid solely by business	0	2	17	90	200	210	341	443	425	414
General services and licenses granted to corporations	0	2	17	90	200	210	341	443	425	414
6200 Other	0	0	20	5	11	16	1	1	1	4
Fees collected by courts of justice	0	0	0	0	0	0	0	0	0	0
Miscellaneous taxes	0	0	20	5	11	16	1	1	1	4
Customs duties collected for the EU	..	..	..	204	190	177	158	203	238	365
SRF Contributions collected for the EU			..	..	..	..	..	128	133	158
Total tax revenue on cash basis	99	1 798	14 825	..	..	..	..	..	..	..

	1965	1980	1990	2000	2007	2010	2015	2020	2021	2022
Total tax revenue on accrual basis	..	..	..	39 705	55 885	54 541	61 788	70 510	76 015	87 277
Additional taxes included in National Accounts	..	..	..	5	7	14	18	21	24	25
Taxes excluded from National Accounts	..	..	0	0	0	0	0	0	0	0
Difference in treatment of tax credits	..	..	0	0	0	0	0	0	0	0
Capital transfer for uncollected revenue	..	..	0	0	0	0	0	0	0	0
Voluntary social security contributions	..	..	0	0	0	0	0	0	0	0
Miscellaneous differences	..	..	0	0	0	0	0	0	0	0
National Accounts: Taxes and actual social contributions	..	..	..	39 710	55 892	54 555	61 806	70 532	76 039	87 302
Imputed social contributions	..	..	..	3 292	5 592	5 906	4 602	4 656	4 863	4 907
National Accounts: Taxes and all social contributions	..	..	..	43 002	61 484	60 461	66 408	75 188	80 902	92 209

.. Not available

Note: Fiscal year ending 31 December.

From 1995, data are on accrual basis.

Source: Instituto Nacional de Estatística.

Table 5.31. Slovak Republic: Details of tax revenue, 1965-2022

Million EUR

	1965	1980	1990	2000	2007	2010	2015	2020	2021	2022
Total tax revenue	..	..	..	10 648	18 456	19 159	26 049	32 500	35 496	38 429
Total tax revenue exclusive of taxes collected for the EU	..	..	..	10 648	18 321	19 016	25 930	32 362	35 335	38 240
1000 Taxes on income, profits and capital gains	..	..	..	2 181	3 844	3 601	5 542	6 535	7 682	8 453
1100 Of individuals	..	..	..	1 055	1 820	1 790	2 464	3 500	3 760	4 126
1110 On income and profits	..	..	..	1 055	1 820	1 790	2 464	3 500	3 760	4 126
Wages and salaries withholding	..	..	..	0	0	0	0	0	0	0
Of unicorporated individuals	..	..	..	0	0	0	0	0	0	0
1120 On capital gains	..	..	..	0	0	0	0	0	0	0
1200 Corporate	..	..	..	813	1 835	1 659	2 917	2 800	3 633	4 012
1210 On profits	..	..	..	0	0	0	0	0	0	0
1220 On capital gains	..	..	..	0	0	0	0	0	0	0
1300 Unallocable between 1100 and 1200	..	..	..	314	189	152	162	235	290	315
2000 Social security contributions	..	..	..	4 409	7 244	8 154	10 897	14 229	15 261	15 968
2100 Employees	..	..	..	901	1 700	2 077	2 410	3 477	3 724	4 010
Retirement	..	..	..	0	0	0	0	0	0	0
State employment policy	..	..	..	0	0	0	0	0	0	0
Health insurance	..	..	..	0	0	0	0	0	0	0
Sick leave	..	..	..	0	0	0	0	0	0	0
2110 On a payroll basis	..	..	..	901	1 700	2 077	2 410	3 477	3 724	4 010
2120 On an income tax basis	..	..	..	0	0	0	0	0	0	0
2200 Employers	..	..	..	2 850	3 914	4 579	6 319	8 650	9 142	9 465
Retirement	..	..	..	0	0	0	0	0	0	0
State employment policy	..	..	..	0	0	0	0	0	0	0
Health insurance	..	..	..	0	0	0	0	0	0	0
Sick leave	..	..	..	0	0	0	0	0	0	0
2210 On a payroll basis of employers SSC	..	..	..	2 850	3 914	4 579	6 319	8 650	9 142	9 465
2220 On an income tax basis of employers SSC	..	..	..	0	0	0	0	0	0	0
2300 Selfemployed or nonemployed	..	..	..	658	1 631	1 498	2 168	2 103	2 395	2 493
Retirement	..	..	..	0	0	0	0	0	0	0
State employment policy	..	..	..	0	0	0	0	0	0	0
Health insurance	..	..	..	0	0	0	0	0	0	0
Sick leave	..	..	..	0	0	0	0	0	0	0
2310 On a payroll basis of self/non-employed SSC	..	..	..	658	1 631	1 498	2 168	2 103	2 395	2 493
2320 On an income tax basis of self/non-employed SSC	..	..	..	0	0	0	0	0	0	0
2400 Unallocable between 2100, 2200 and 2300	..	..	..	0	0	0	0	0	0	0
2410 On a payroll basis unallocable between 2100, 2200 and 2300 SSC	..	..	..	..	..	..	..	..	..	..
2420 On an income tax basis unallocable between 2100, 2200 and 2300 SSC	..	..	..	..	..	..	..	..	..	..
3000 Taxes on payroll and workforce	..	..	..	0	0	0	0	0	0	0
4000 Taxes on property	..	..	..	194	245	277	335	438	466	469
4100 Recurrent taxes on immovable property	..	..	..	143	243	277	335	438	466	469
4110 Households	..	..	..	28	22	25	29	36	37	37
4120 Others	..	..	..	114	222	252	306	402	428	432
4200 Recurrent taxes on net wealth	..	..	..	0	0	0	0	0	0	0
4210 Individual	..	..	..	..	..	..	..	..	..	..
4220 Corporate	..	..	..	..	..	..	..	..	..	..
4300 Estate, inheritance and gift taxes	..	..	..	8	0	0	0	0	0	0
4310 Estate and inheritance taxes	..	..	..	3	0	0	0	..	..	..
4320 Gift taxes	..	..	..	5	0	0	0	..	..	..
4400 Taxes on financial and capital transactions	..	..	..	43	1	0	0	0	0	0
Real property transfer tax	..	..	..	30	1	0	0	0	0	0
4500 Nonrecurrent taxes	..	..	..	0	0	0	0	0	0	0
4510 On net wealth	..	..	..	..	..	..	..	..	..	..
4520 Other nonrecurrent taxes	..	..	..	..	..	..	..	..	..	..
4600 Other recurrent taxes on property	..	..	..	0	0	0	0	0	0	0
5000 Taxes on goods and services	..	..	..	3 864	7 123	7 127	9 275	11 298	12 087	13 540
5100 Taxes on production, sale, transfer, etc	..	..	..	3 631	6 580	6 573	8 573	10 371	11 142	12 524
5110 General taxes	..	..	..	2 168	4 147	4 182	5 423	6 820	7 494	8 441
5111 Value added taxes	..	..	..	2 168	4 147	4 182	5 423	6 820	7 494	8 441
5112 Sales tax	..	..	..	0	0	0	0	0	0	0
5113 Other	..	..	..	0	0	0	0	0	0	0
5120 Taxes on specific goods and services	..	..	..	1 464	2 433	2 391	3 151	3 551	3 648	4 083
5121 Excises	..	..	..	971	2 171	2 081	2 567	2 752	2 958	2 797
On hydrocarbon fuels and lubricants	..	..	..	617	1 118	1 032	1 139	1 196	1 237	1 294

	1965	1980	1990	2000	2007	2010	2015	2020	2021	2022
On alcohol and liquers	..	..	..	143	201	197	205	208	216	238
On beer	..	..	..	43	66	56	57	57	55	56
On wine	..	..	..	12	4	4	4	5	5	5
On tobacco products	..	..	..	156	783	602	665	732	852	901
On electricity	..	..	..	0	0	16	13	12	10	12
On coal	..	..	..	0	0	1	0	0	0	0
On natural gas	..	..	..	0	0	24	23	24	25	24
Green energy				0	0	150	459	519	559	266
5122 Profits of fiscal monopolies	..	..	..	0	0	0	0	0	0	0
5123 Customs and import duties	..	..	..	437	136	143	119	121	138	163
Customs duties	..	..	..	122	136	143	119	121	138	163
Import surcharges	..	..	..	315	0	0	0	0	0	0
Other customs revenues	..	..	..	0	0	0	0	0	0	0
5124 Taxes on exports	..	..	..	0	0	0	0	0	0	0
5125 Taxes on investment goods	..	..	..	0	0	0	2	3	3	3
5126 Taxes on specific services	..	..	..	55	125	167	462	675	548	1 120
5127 Other taxes on internat. trade and transactions	..	..	..	0	0	0	0	0	0	0
5128 Other taxes	..	..	..	0	0	0	0	0	0	0
5130 Unallocable between 5110 and 5120	..	..	..	0	0	0	0	0	0	0
5200 Taxes on use of goods and perform activities	..	..	..	231	438	421	549	723	723	792
5210 Recurrent taxes	..	..	..	219	372	384	470	453	455	489
5211 Paid by households: motor vehicles	..	..	..	0	0	0	0	0	0	0
5212 Paid by others: motor vehicles	..	..	..	93	153	153	204	200	203	202
5213 Paid in respect of other goods	..	..	..	127	219	231	266	253	252	287
5220 Nonrecurrent taxes	..	..	..	12	66	37	79	270	267	303
5300 Unallocable between 5100 and 5200	..	..	..	2	105	134	153	204	222	225
6000 Other taxes	..	..	..	0	0	0	0	0	0	0
6100 Paid solely by business	..	..	..	..	..	..	..	..	..	..
6200 Other	..	..	..	..	..	..	..	..	..	..
Custom duties collected for the EU	..	..	..	..	136	143	119	121	138	162
SRF Contributions collected for the EU				..	..	..	..	17	24	27
Non-wastable tax credits against 1110	..	..	..	..	252	276	261	368	359	509
Tax expenditure component	..	..	..	..	..	..	..	..	..	..
Transfer component	..	..	..	..	..	..	..	..	..	..
"Non-wastable tax credits against 1210	"	..	..	..	..	0	0	0	0	0
Tax expenditure component	..	..	..	..	..	..	..	..	..	..
Transfer component	..	..	..	..	..	..	..	..	..	..
Total tax revenue on cash basis	..	..	..	10 843	18 033	18 358	25 757	31 087	33 799	37 011
Total tax revenue on accrual basis	..	..	..	10 648	18 456	19 159	26 049	32 500	35 496	38 429
Additional taxes included in National Accounts	..	..	..	53	33	47	43	4	30	32
Taxes excluded from National Accounts	..	..	..	0	- 103	- 131	- 149	- 201	- 219	- 221
Difference in treatment of tax credits	..	..	..	0	0	0	0	0	0	0
Capital transfer for uncollected revenue	..	..	..	0	0	0	0	0	0	0
Voluntary social security contributions	..	..	..	0	22	31	11	12	29	28
Miscellaneous differences	..	..	..	0	0	0	0	0	0	0
National Accounts: Taxes and actual social contributions	..	..	..	10 702	18 409	19 106	25 953	32 315	35 337	38 268
Imputed social contributions	..	..	..	19	80	143	171	258	344	343
National Accounts: Taxes and all social contributions	..	..	..	10 721	18 488	19 250	26 124	32 572	35 681	38 611

.. Not available

Note: Year ending 31st December.

Data are on accrual basis.

Source: Ministry of Finance.

Table 5.32. Slovenia: Details of tax revenue, 1965-2022

Million EUR

	1965	1980	1990	2000	2007	2010	2015	2020	2021	2022
Total tax revenue	..	..	..	7 114	13 377	13 758	14 498	17 692	20 003	21 335
Total tax revenue exclusive of taxes collected for the EU	..	..	..	7 114	13 292	13 698	14 430	17 621	19 913	21 219
1000 Taxes on income, profits and capital gains	..	..	..	1 280	3 041	2 692	2 547	3 403	4 123	4 288
1100 Of individuals	..	..	..	1 041	1 919	2 020	1 977	2 466	2 829	2 954
1110 On income and profits	..	..	..	1 039	1 916	2 017	1 974	2 463	2 826	2 948
Personal income tax	..	..	..	1 039	1 916	2 017	1 974	2 463	2 826	2 948
Special contribution for the reconstruction of the Posocje region	..	..	..	0	0	0	0	0	0	0
1120 On capital gains	..	..	..	2	3	3	3	2	3	6
Taxes on winnings from lottery and gambling	..	..	..	2	3	3	3	2	3	6
1200 Corporate	..	..	..	216	1 116	668	568	935	1 291	1 332
1210 On profits	..	..	..	216	1 116	668	568	935	1 291	1 332
1220 On capital gains	..	..	..	0	0	0	0	0	0	0
1300 Unallocable between 1100 and 1200	..	..	..	24	5	4	2	2	3	3
Tax on income - copy rights, patents and trademarks	..	..	..	24	5	4	2	2	3	3
Tax on profits due to changes in land use	..	..	..	0	0	0	0	0	0	0
2000 Social security contributions	..	..	..	2 820	5 046	5 761	5 983	7 908	8 561	9 134
2100 Employees	..	..	..	1 447	2 490	2 785	2 910	3 895	4 263	4 560
2110 On a payroll basis	..	..	..	1 447	2 490	2 785	2 910	3 895	4 263	4 560
2120 On an income tax basis	..	..	..	0	0	0	0	0	0	0
2200 Employers	..	..	..	1 012	1 852	2 070	2 135	2 865	3 139	3 348
2210 On a payroll basis of employers SSC	..	..	..	1 012	1 852	2 070	2 135	2 865	3 139	3 348
2220 On an income tax basis of employers SSC	..	..	..	0	0	0	0	0	0	0
2300 Selfemployed or nonemployed	..	..	..	361	705	906	938	1 148	1 159	1 226
2310 On a payroll basis of self/non-employed SSC	..	..	..	361	705	906	938	1 148	1 159	1 226
2320 On an income tax basis of self/non-employed SSC	..	..	..	0	0	0	0	0	0	0
2400 Unallocable between 2100, 2200 and 2300	..	..	..	0	0	0	0	0	0	0
2410 On a payroll basis unallocable between 2100, 2200 and 2300 SSC	..	..	..	..	..	..	..	..	..	..
2420 On an income tax basis unallocable between 2100, 2200 and 2300 SSC	..	..	..	..	..	..	..	..	..	..
3000 Taxes on payroll and workforce	..	..	..	289	418	28	20	22	24	27
Payroll tax	..	..	..	272	391	0	0	0	0	0
Tax on work contracts	..	..	..	18	27	28	20	22	24	27
4000 Taxes on property	..	..	..	120	206	222	241	295	322	347
4100 Recurrent taxes on immovable property	..	..	..	81	140	173	199	237	251	261
4110 Households	..	..	..	17	38	46	56	72	74	77
Property tax on weekend cottages	..	..	..	1	1	1	1	1	1	1
Compensation on the use of building ground - paid by individuals	..	..	..	16	37	45	56	71	73	76
Tax on immovable property of higher value	..	..	..	0	0	0	0	0	0	0
4120 Others	..	..	..	65	102	127	142	164	176	183
Property tax on buildings	..	..	..	2	3	3	4	7	7	8
Compensation on the use of building ground - paid by legal entities	..	..	..	63	100	124	139	157	169	175
4200 Recurrent taxes on net wealth	..	..	..	4	0	0	0	0	0	0
4210 Individual	..	..	..	0	..	..	..	..	..	..
4220 Corporate	..	..	..	4	..	..	..	..	..	..
Tax on balance wealth paid by banks	..	..	..	4	..	..	..	..	..	..
4300 Estate, inheritance and gift taxes	..	..	..	2	9	14	8	10	11	17
4310 Estate and inheritance taxes	..	..	..	..	..	..	..	..	..	..
4320 Gift taxes	..	..	..	..	..	..	..	..	..	..
4400 Taxes on financial and capital transactions	..	..	..	23	57	32	29	40	54	55
Taxes on the sale of immovable property - from legal entities	..	..	..	11	19	7	7	7	9	7
Taxes on the sale of immovable property - from individuals	..	..	..	12	38	25	23	33	44	48
4500 Nonrecurrent taxes	..	..	..	10	0	2	4	8	6	14
4510 On net wealth	..	..	..	0	..	0	0	0	0	0
4520 Other nonrecurrent taxes	..	..	..	10	..	2	4	8	6	14
Payments for the change of use of agricultural and forest land	..	..	..	10	..	0	2	2	4	3
Granting of easements and the creation of building rights	..	..	..	0	..	2	3	6	2	10
4600 Other recurrent taxes on property	..	..	..	0	0	0	0	0	0	0
Property tax on boats	..	..	..	0	0	0	0	0	0	0
5000 Taxes on goods and services	..	..	..	2 604	4 666	5 055	5 707	6 065	6 973	7 538
5100 Taxes on production, sale, transfer, etc	..	..	..	2 483	4 451	4 840	5 331	5 625	6 524	7 047

	1965	1980	1990	2000	2007	2010	2015	2020	2021	2022
5110 General taxes	..	..	..	1 642	2 941	2 929	3 224	3 554	4 305	4 681
5111 Value added taxes	..	..	..	1 611	2 941	2 929	3 224	3 554	4 305	4 681
Value added tax	..	..	..	1 599	2 923	2 926	3 220	3 553	4 299	4 674
Negative compensation of farmers in a VAT flat rate system	..	..	..	12	18	3	4	1	6	7
5112 Sales tax	..	..	..	8	0	0	0	0	0	0
Customs duties paid by individuals	..	..	..	1	..	..	..	..	..	..
Special import duties and customs charges	..	..	..	7	..	..	..	..	..	..
5113 Other	..	..	..	23	0	0	0	0	0	0
Turnover tax on goods	..	..	..	11	..	..	..	..	..	..
Turnover tax on services	..	..	..	12	..	..	..	..	..	..
Special turnover tax on alcohol	..	..	..	0	..	..	..	..	..	..
5120 Taxes on specific goods and services	..	..	..	841	1 510	1 911	2 107	2 071	2 220	2 366
5121 Excises	..	..	..	581	1 196	1 555	1 626	1 588	1 695	1 705
Alcohol and alcoholic drinks	..	..	..	39	71	89	108	112	118	125
Mineral oil and gas	..	..	..	405	758	1 016	1 033	852	929	930
Tobacco	..	..	..	97	301	391	419	404	422	471
Duty free shops - alcohol and alcoholic drinks	..	..	..	3	0	0	0	0	0	0
Duty free shops - tobacco	..	..	..	17	0	0	0	0	0	0
Electric power and coal	..	..	..	0	4	19	34	31	32	17
Tax on the sales of new motor vehicles	..	..	..	18	60	40	26	26	14	18
Tax on the sales of used motor vehicles	..	..	..	2	2	0	0	0	0	0
Additional tax on motor vehicles	..	..	..	0	0	0	6	7	0	0
Support for produced electricity from RES and CHP				0	0	0	0	156	180	143
5122 Profits of fiscal monopolies	..	..	..	0	0	0	0	0	0	0
5123 Customs and import duties	..	..	..	158	85	60	53	62	82	104
Import duties	..	..	..	151	0	0	0	0	0	0
Levies on imported agricultural products	..	..	..	7	0	0	0	0	0	0
Custom duties collected for the EU			..	0	85	60	53	62	82	104
5124 Taxes on exports	..	..	..	0	0	0	0	0	0	0
5125 Taxes on investment goods	..	..	..	0	0	0	0	0	0	0
5126 Taxes on specific services	..	..	..	102	230	296	428	421	443	557
Tax on special gambling (gambling in casinos)	..	..	..	25	64	53	48	26	22	46
Tax on classical gambling (lottery...)	..	..	..	1	3	3	3	3	3	4
Special tax on slot machines	..	..	..	4	0	0	0	0	0	0
Tax on insurance services	..	..	..	37	65	69	82	102	108	116
Sojourn tax	..	..	..	3	7	7	11	15	16	24
Concessions	..	..	..	1	29	40	79	64	66	90
Concessions duties on special gambling (gambling in casinos)	..	..	..	26	55	47	37	23	18	40
Fire protection tax	..	..	..	4	6	7	8	10	10	11
Tax on lottery tickets	..	..	..	0	0	0	17	18	19	22
Tax on financial services	..	..	..	0	0	0	57	67	76	78
FIHO, FSO	..	..	..	0	0	25	27	24	24	30
SOS	..	..	..	0	0	23	11	9	11	14
Tax on balance wealth paid by banks	..	..	..	0	0	0	2	0	0	0
Commodity reserve fund	..	..	..	0	0	21	32	26	29	34
Deposit Guarantee Fund	..	..	..	0	0	0	16	31	35	43
Promotional tax of STO				0	0	0	0	3	4	5
5127 Other taxes on internat. trade and transactions	..	..	..	0	0	0	0	0	0	0
5128 Other taxes	..	..	..	0	0	0	0	0	0	0
Sugar levy	..	..	..	..	0	..	..	..	..	..
5130 Unallocable between 5110 and 5120	..	..	..	0	0	0	0	0	0	0
5200 Taxes on use of goods and perform activities	..	..	..	121	215	215	377	440	449	491
5210 Recurrent taxes	..	..	..	121	215	215	353	375	384	361
5211 Paid by households: motor vehicles	..	..	..	49	87	86	118	128	130	132
Registration fees on motor vehicles, boats and airplanes paid by individuals	..	..	..	49	87	86	118	128	130	132
5212 Paid by others: motor vehicles	..	..	..	12	21	20	27	32	33	34
Registration fees on motor vehicles, boats and airplanes paid by legal entities	..	..	..	12	21	20	27	32	33	34
Registration fees on tractors	..	..	..	0	0	0	0	0	0	0
5213 Paid in respect of other goods	..	..	..	59	107	110	208	215	221	195
Charges on the use of water	..	..	..	4	22	23	32	32	31	31

	1965	1980	1990	2000	2007	2010	2015	2020	2021	2022
Taxes on waste pollution	..	..	..	7	10	3	2	1	1	2
Taxes on air pollution - caused by gas and hard fuels	..	..	..	3	8	10	13	16	16	13
Contribution of Nuclear power plant to finance its de-composition	..	..	..	16	8	8	8	6	6	6
Indemnity for the restricted use of area on the territory of Nuclear power plant	..	..	..	0	7	10	12	6	6	6
Taxes on air pollution	..	..	..	29	21	23	114	112	118	93
Special water tax	..	..	..	0	30	33	27	24	23	23
Markup on toll				0	0	0	0	12	13	13
Transhipment fee in the port of Koper				0	0	0	0	6	6	8
5220 Nonrecurrent taxes	..	..	..	0	0	0	24	65	65	130
Emission permits	..	..	..	..	..	..	24	65	65	130
Contribution from excess market revenues in the field of energy				..	..	..	0	0	0	0
5300 Unallocable between 5100 and 5200	..	..	..	0	0	0	0	0	0	0
6000 Other taxes	..	..	..	0	0	0	0	0	0	0
6100 Paid solely by business	..	..	..	..	..	..	..	..	..	..
6200 Other	..	..	..	..	..	..	..	..	..	..
Customs duties collected for the EU	..	..	..	..	85	60	53	62	82	104
SRF Contributions collected for the EU			..	..	..	..	16	9	9	11
Total tax revenue on cash basis	..	..	..	7 135	13 140	13 605	14 560	0	0	0
Total tax revenue on accrual basis	..	..	..	7 114	13 377	13 758	14 498	17 692	20 003	21 335
Additional taxes included in National Accounts	..	..	..	..	..	87	94	96	97	99
Radio and television licence fee	..	..	..	..	..	87	94	96	97	99
Taxes excluded from National Accounts	..	..	..	..	..	..	..	0	0	0
Difference in treatment of tax credits	..	..	..	0	0	0	0	0	0	0
Capital transfer for uncollected revenue	..	..	..	- 7	- 35	- 17	- 2	- 25	- 5	- 2
Voluntary social security contributions	..	..	..	0	0	0	0	0	0	0
Miscellaneous differences	..	..	..	0	0	0	0	0	0	0
National Accounts: Taxes and actual social contributions	..	..	..	7 107	13 342	13 828	14 590	17 764	20 095	21 432
Imputed social contributions	..	..	..	39	81	100	118	165	180	173
National Accounts: Taxes and all social contributions	..	..	..	7 146	13 423	13 928	14 708	17 929	20 275	21 605

.. Not available

Note: Year ending 31st December.
Data are on accrual basis.

Source: Statistical Office of the Republic of Slovenia.

Table 5.33. Spain: Details of tax revenue, 1965-2022

Million EUR

	1965	1980	1990	2000	2007	2010	2015	2020	2021	2022
Total tax revenue	1 238	22 002	103 662	214 114	391 648	335 563	364 683	412 288	462 189	506 104
Total tax revenue exclusive of taxes collected for the EU	..	..	..	213 067	389 927	334 019	362 175	409 786	459 182	502 183
1000 Taxes on income, profits and capital gains	304	5 714	31 763	60 145	130 081	93 798	102 645	119 782	137 742	158 705
1100 Of individuals	177	4 481	22 527	41 248	80 719	74 118	78 896	97 764	105 449	122 151
Personal income tax	..	..	22 527	40 366	79 973	73 534	78 586	97 470	105 073	121 568
Income tax of non-residents	..	..	0	882	746	584	310	294	376	583
1110 On income and profits	..	..	..	..	..	..	..	..	..	..
1120 On capital gains	..	..	..	..	..	..	..	..	..	..
1200 Corporate	114	1 119	9 146	18 897	49 362	19 680	23 749	22 018	32 293	36 554
Corporate income tax	..	..	9 146	18 597	47 499	17 567	22 471	20 752	30 686	34 029
Income tax of non-residents (legal persons)	..	..	0	300	1 863	2 113	1 278	1 266	1 607	2 525
1210 On profits	..	..	..	..	..	..	..	..	..	..
Tax on commercial activity	..	..	..	..	..	..	..	..	..	..
Special tax 4 percent	..	..	..	..	..	..	..	..	..	..
Taxes on profits	..	..	..	..	..	..	..	..	..	..
Temporary levy on credit institutions and specialised credit institutions				..	..	..	..	..	..	..
1220 On capital gains	..	..	..	..	..	..	..	..	..	..
1300 Unallocable between 1100 and 1200	13	114	91	0	0	0	0	0	0	0
Local taxes	13	114	0	..	..	..	..	..	..	..
Other taxes	0	0	91	..	..	..	..	..	..	..
2000 Social security contributions	350	10 682	36 722	74 683	127 088	127 235	122 835	154 315	163 824	172 438
2100 Employees	81	2 376	5 976	11 711	19 625	19 423	18 783	22 229	24 091	26 263
2110 On a payroll basis	..	..	5 976	11 711	19 625	19 423	18 783	22 229	24 091	26 263
2120 On an income tax basis	..	..	0	..	..	..	..	..	..	..
2200 Employers	269	8 306	26 385	54 226	93 234	89 666	87 988	112 444	118 756	127 643
2210 On a payroll basis of employers SSC	..	..	26 385	54 226	93 234	89 666	87 988	112 444	118 756	127 643
2220 On an income tax basis of employers SSC	..	..	0	..	..	..	..	..	..	..
2300 Selfemployed or nonemployed	0	0	4 361	8 746	14 229	18 146	16 064	19 642	20 977	18 532
Self-employment	..	..	2 492	6 788	10 120	10 119	10 872	11 588	11 802	12 083
Unemployment	..	..	1 869	1 958	4 109	8 027	5 192	8 054	9 175	6 449
2310 On a payroll basis of self/non-employed SSC	..	..	..	..	..	..	..	..	..	..
2320 On an income tax basis of self/non-employed SSC	..	..	..	..	..	..	..	..	..	..
2400 Unallocable between 2100, 2200 and 2300	0	0	0	0	0	0	0	0	0	0
2410 On a payroll basis unallocable between 2100, 2200 and 2300 SSC	..	..	..	..	..	..	..	..	..	..
2420 On an income tax basis unallocable between 2100, 2200 and 2300 SSC	..	..	..	..	..	..	..	..	..	..
3000 Taxes on payroll and workforce	0	0	0	0	0	0	0	0	0	0
4000 Taxes on property	79	1 004	5 718	13 827	32 133	22 178	27 855	27 770	33 669	34 939
4100 Recurrent taxes on immovable property	6	41	1 478	3 988	7 281	9 666	12 623	13 267	13 998	14 082
Real State tax (IBI)/Real State tax Surcharge	..	41	1 478	3 982	7 267	9 657	12 581	13 186	13 924	14 052
Special Real State tax for Non-residents	..	0	0	6	6	8	4	3	3	5
Other taxes on property, land or building use	..	0	0	0	3	0	1	0	0	0
4110 Households	..	..	..	..	..	..	..	..	..	..
4120 Others	..	..	..	0	5	1	37	78	71	25
Tax on large Commercial Establishments	..	..	..	..	5	1	37	78	71	25
4200 Recurrent taxes on net wealth	0	107	637	1 413	2 479	688	1 904	2 304	2 370	2 613
4210 Individual	..	107	637	1 413	2 479	688	1 904	2 304	2 370	2 613
Wealth tax	..	..	637	1 199	2 054	104	1 144	1 496	1 518	1 753
Temporary Solidarity Tax on Large Fortunes				0	0	0	0	0	0	0
Real State tax (unoccupied dwellings) and others	..	..	0	214	425	584	760	808	852	860
4220 Corporate	..	0	0	0	0	0	0	0	0	0
4300 Estate, inheritance and gift taxes	13	90	440	1 379	2 901	2 412	2 790	2 493	3 536	3 662
Inheritance and gift tax	..	..	440	1 379	2 901	2 412	2 790	2 493	3 536	3 662
4310 Estate and inheritance taxes	..	..	..	..	..	..	..	..	..	..
4320 Gift taxes	..	..	..	..	..	..	..	..	..	..
4400 Taxes on financial and capital transactions	60	767	2 478	5 939	17 025	7 603	6 984	7 535	11 108	12 661
Taxes on property transactions	60	767	2 478	5 939	17 025	7 603	6 984	7 535	10 812	12 356
Tax on financial transactions				0	0	0	0	0	296	305
4500 Nonrecurrent taxes	0	0	646	1 108	2 447	1 809	3 554	2 171	2 657	1 921
4510 On net wealth	..	..	467	0	495	192	1 006	316	348	330
Tax on land holding gains	..	..	467	..	..	..	0			
Urban use tax	..	..	..	..	495	192	73	82	114	96
Extraordinary resource of FGD	..	..	..	..	0	0	933	234	234	234
4520 Other nonrecurrent taxes	..	..	179	1 108	1 952	1 617	2 548	1 855	2 309	1 591
Special duties	..	..	179	180	168	129	70	59	84	88

	1965	1980	1990	2000	2007	2010	2015	2020	2021	2022
Land development contributions	..	..	0	223	368	225	61	47	71	68
Levy on "Revaluation of Reserve Account"	..	..	..	0	0	0	0	0	0	0
Tax on the increase in value of urban terrains	..	..	0	705	1 416	1 263	2 417	1 749	2 154	1 435
Others	..	..	0	0	0	0	0	0	0	0
4600 Other recurrent taxes on property	0	0	38	0	0	0	0	0	0	0
5000 Taxes on goods and services	506	4 553	29 437	65 456	102 334	92 344	111 159	110 303	126 779	139 807
5100 Taxes on production, sale, transfer, etc	503	4 552	26 732	59 383	93 814	84 985	102 912	100 986	116 314	128 277
5110 General taxes	275	2 234	16 611	37 800	62 778	55 629	69 478	70 846	83 881	94 690
5111 Value added taxes	0	0	16 304	37 785	62 743	55 318	69 294	70 669	83 547	94 234
Value added tax (VAT)	..	..	16 304	37 045	61 472	54 509	67 913	69 435	82 249	92 344
Canary Islands general indirect tax	..	..	0	740	1 271	809	1 381	1 234	1 298	1 890
5112 Sales tax	0	0	0	15	35	311	184	177	168	160
Fees for RTVE (since 2010)	..	..	..	0	0	278	184	177	168	160
Fees from the National Commission of Telecommunications Market	..	..	..	15	35	33	0	0	0	0
5113 Other	275	2 234	307	0	0	0	0	0	166	296
Cascade tax	118	1 483	197	..	..	..	..	..	0	0
Excises on luxury expenditure	96	939	15	..	..	..	..	..	0	0
Other import duties	94	832	128	..	..	..	..	..	0	0
Refund of internal taxes	- 33	- 1 020	- 33	..	..	..	..	..	0	0
Tax on certain digital services				..	..	..	..	..	166	296
5120 Taxes on specific goods and services	228	2 317	10 120	21 583	31 036	29 356	33 434	30 140	32 433	33 587
5121 Excises	69	1 239	6 048	17 952	25 581	24 384	25 908	23 181	24 093	23 757
Special excises	69	1 239	10	0	0	0	0	0	0	0
On beer	0	0	87	202	307	302	316	330	340	375
On wine	0	0	0	0	0	0	0	0	0	0
On alcohol	0	0	481	785	1 008	876	843	673	735	959
On hydrocarbon	0	0	4 222	9 977	11 787	10 907	12 465	11 471	12 718	13 259
On tobacco	0	0	1 123	4 507	7 258	7 976	7 213	6 828	6 601	7 216
On electricity bills	0	0	0	703	1 153	1 483	1 458	1 309	1 142	245
Tax on retail sales of specific hydrocarbons	0	0	0	0	1 356	1 238	7	0	0	1
Tax on oil derived fuels	0	0	120	237	253	220	314	254	289	301
Petrol tax	0	0	0	6	5	5	22	19	23	20
Other taxes	0	0	5	17	21	18	22	20	22	25
On carbon	0	0	0	0	0	0	308	41	29	58
Production and storage of electricity	0	0	0	0	0	0	1 576	1 146	1 108	16
Tax Greenhouse Effect Flourinated	0	0	0	0	0	0	99	67	68	100
Canary Islands taxes on national products	0	0	0	51	86	71	85	86	115	144
Taxes on national products in Ceuta and Melilla	0	0	0	108	110	105	115	81	90	79
Fees from the National Energy Commission	0	0	0	13	27	35	0	0	0	0
Contribution to the National Energy Efficiency Fund	0	0	0	0	0	366	207	206	207	192
Duty on specific means of transport	0	0	0	1 317	2 158	735	358	446	544	717
Fee for the use of continental waters for the production of the electrical power	0	0	0	0	0	0	453	154	0	0
Special duties and other taxes on importes products	0	0	0	29	52	47	47	21	32	19
Excise tax on non-reusable plastic containers				0	0	0	0	0	0	0
Other taxes on products	0	0	0	0	0	0	0	29	30	31
5122 Profits of fiscal monopolies	66	132	546	0	0	0	0	0	0	0
Tobacco	21	77	0	..	..	..	..	..	..	..
Petroleum	45	55	546	..	..	..	..	..	..	..
5123 Customs and import duties	87	561	2 078	1 044	1 816	1 593	1 899	1 742	2 132	2 909
Import duties	87	561	1 394	0	0	0	0	0	0	0
Canary Islands taxes on imported products	0	0	137	33	51	44	53	55	73	90
Taxes on imported products in Ceuta and Melilla	0	0	36	41	42	40	43	31	34	30
Customs duties collected for the EU	..	..	511	970	1 723	1 509	1 803	1 656	2 025	2 789
5124 Taxes on exports	0	0	0	..	..	..	..	..	..	..
5125 Taxes on investment goods	0	0	0	0	0	0	0	0	0	0
5126 Taxes on specific services	7	385	1 427	2 497	3 633	3 166	5 408	4 999	5 967	6 681
Taxes on betting and gambling	0	232	1 307	1 649	2 051	1 635	1 164	816	997	1 203
Taxes on other specific services	6	153	120	0	0	0	0	0	0	0
Taxes on insurance premiums	0	0	0	848	1 581	1 531	1 446	1 704	2 247	2 455
Tax on deposits of credit institution	0	0	0	0	1	0	421	406	439	461
Ordinary resource DGF	0	0	0	0	0	0	1 644	1 161	1 257	1 203
EU SRF contribution	..	..	..	0	0	0	690	846	982	1 132
Tourist tax	0	0	0	0	0	0	43	66	45	227
5127 Other taxes on internat. trade and transactions	0	0	0	0	0	0	0	0	0	0
5128 Other taxes	0	0	22	90	6	213	219	218	241	240
EU levies	..	..	22	77	- 2	35	15	0	0	0
Others	..	..	0	13	8	9	37	66	94	95
Resource CORES	..	..	0	0	0	169	167	152	147	145
5130 Unallocable between 5110 and 5120	0	0	0	0	0	0	0	0	0	0

	1965	1980	1990	2000	2007	2010	2015	2020	2021	2022
5200 Taxes on use of goods and perform activities	3	1	2 633	6 073	8 520	7 359	8 247	9 317	10 465	11 530
5210 Recurrent taxes	3	1	1 616	4 306	5 311	5 782	6 420	6 503	6 881	7 091
Other taxes on luxury expenses	..	..	..	2	7	4	3	3	3	3
5211 Paid by households: motor vehicles	..	0	461	1 117	1 626	1 770	1 725	1 712	1 784	1 798
Car registration tax	..	..	461	1 117	1 626	1 770	1 725	1 712	1 784	1 798
5212 Paid by others: motor vehicles	..	0	117	298	502	498	470	473	493	497
Car registration tax	..	..	117	298	502	498	470	473	493	497
5213 Paid in respect of other goods	..	1	1 038	2 889	3 176	3 510	4 222	4 315	4 601	4 793
Hunting and fishing taxes	..	..	0	28	28	34	30	27	30	26
Economic activity tax	..	..	925	1 934	1 633	1 785	1 794	1 855	2 006	2 032
Advertising	..	..	27	0	0	0	0	0	0	0
Taxes on environment and pollution	..	..	0	42	91	141	563	663	778	615
Tax on effluent, use of hydrocarbon and mines	..	..	0	51	83	67	184	193	184	218
Other fees paid by households for licences	..	..	0	179	264	228	245	280	322	314
Compensation for local taxes	..	..	86	140	176	165	118	126	121	110
Vehicle Inspection duty	..	..	0	6	18	17	19	14	17	17
Municipal fees for private use of public space	..	..	0	509	883	1 073	1 269	1 157	1 143	1 461
Temporary energy levy				0	0	0	0	0	0	0
5220 Nonrecurrent taxes	0	0	1 017	1 767	3 209	1 577	1 827	2 814	3 584	4 439
Tax and building permits	..	..	327	1 117	2 227	859	575	892	1 162	1 295
Urban licenses	..	..	0	451	490	260	200	274	331	391
Greenhouse gas emission trading	..	..	0	0	0	0	412	1 264	1 656	2 318
Parafiscal taxes	..	..	690	199	492	458	640	384	435	435
Tax on waste disposal in landfills, incineration and co-incineration of waste				0	0	0	0	0	0	0
5300 Unallocable between 5100 and 5200	0	0	72	0	0	0	0	0	0	0
6000 Other taxes	0	49	22	3	12	8	189	118	175	215
6100 Paid solely by business	..	49	0	0	0	0	0	0	0	0
6200 Other	..	0	22	3	12	8	189	118	175	215
Other taxes on production	..	..	..	3	12	8	189	118	175	215
Custom duties collected for the EU	..	..	..	970	1 723	1 509	1 803	1 656	2 025	2 789
SRF Contributions collected for the EU				..	..	..	690	846	982	1 132
Non-wastable tax credits against 1110	..	..	..	..	1 323	1 897	1 093	2 822	2 704	2 816
Tax expenditure component	..	..	..	..	522	729	546	1 196	1 199	1 248
Transfer component	..	..	..	..	801	1 168	547	1 626	1 505	1 568
Non-wastable tax credits against 1210	..	..	..	..	0	0	46	296	1 417	387
Tax expenditure component	..	..	..	..	..	..	12	47	38	54
Transfer component	..	..	..	..	..	..	34	249	1 379	333
Total tax revenue on cash basis	1 238	22 002	103 662	212 669	388 829	333 697	360 947	398 682	451 125	501 052
Total tax revenue on accrual basis	..	..	..	214 114	391 648	335 563	364 683	412 288	462 189	506 104
Additional taxes included in National Accounts	..	..	..	0	0	0	0	0	0	0
Taxes excluded from National Accounts	..	..	..	0	0	0	0	0	0	0
Difference in treatment of tax credits	..	..	..	0	522	729	558	1 243	1 237	1 302
Capital transfer for uncollected revenue	..	..	..	0	0	0	0	0	0	0
Voluntary social security contributions	..	..	..	447	937	1 155	1 170	891	931	930
Miscellaneous differences	..	..	..	0	0	0	0	0	0	0
National Accounts: Taxes and actual social contributions	..	..	..	214 561	393 107	337 447	366 411	414 422	464 357	508 336
Imputed social contributions	..	..	..	5 379	7 618	8 585	7 503	6 985	6 932	6 854
National Accounts: Taxes and all social contributions	..	..	..	219 940	400 725	346 032	373 914	421 407	471 289	515 190

.. Not available

Note: Year ending 31st December.

From 1995, data are on accrual basis.

Since 1995, the data are consistent with those transmitted to Eurostat in the framework of Government Finance Statistics (ESA).

From 1981 the figures take into account the classification procedures set out in the OECD Interpretative Guide. Consequently, they are not completely comparable with the figures for earlier years though the amounts involved are quite small.

Heading 2300: Contributions paid by self-employed were shown under heading 2100 until 1982.

Source: Information from the Ministry of Finance for taxes and from Social Security System for social security contributions up to 1994. Since 1995 (accrual basis), national account data (IGAE-Ministry of Finance)

Table 5.34. Sweden: Details of tax revenue, 1965-2022

Million SEK

	1965	1980	1990	2000	2007	2010	2015	2020	2021	2022
Total tax revenue	40 003	259 216	755 953	1 204 794	1 491 190	1 532 259	1 816 166	2 137 949	2 336 817	2 493 410
Total tax revenue exclusive of taxes collected for the EU	..	..	755 953	1 200 999	1 485 306	1 526 585	1 809 891	2 131 737	2 329 478	2 484 082
1000 Taxes on income, profits and capital gains	21 956	112 730	314 797	514 729	580 372	546 696	657 539	768 423	858 446	897 879
1100 Of individuals	19 500	106 376	291 146	426 956	464 435	430 896	533 660	619 939	676 176	697 186
1110 On income and profits	19 390	105 866	289 598	392 532	414 728	396 353	464 596	553 964	571 572	604 294
Coupon tax	9	44	233	2 040	6 306	3 047	4 615	3 545	9 355	12 324
Duties on foreign artists	4	3	3	50	86	89	2	0	0	0
National income tax individual	8 676	31 682	70 755	66 850	44 326	42 595	52 480	52 716	51 534	63 716
Local income tax individual	9 294	78 134	220 072	336 304	479 068	522 850	635 719	766 082	806 447	852 510
Tax reduction individual	0	- 3 997	- 1 465	- 18 872	- 122 029	- 179 890	- 236 613	- 278 728	- 305 764	- 334 469
Public service tax			0	5 061	6 674	6 981	7 759	9 369	9 149	9 352
Other	1 407	0	0	1 098	296	681	635	981	852	860
1120 On capital gains	110	510	1 548	34 425	49 707	34 543	69 064	65 975	104 604	92 892
Lottery prize tax	110	510	1 548	60	0	0	0	0	0	0
1200 Corporate	2 456	6 354	23 651	87 772	115 937	115 800	123 878	148 484	182 270	200 693
1210 On profits	2 456	6 354	23 651	87 772	115 937	115 800	123 878	148 484	182 270	200 693
Tax on profits not distributed	1	10	3	0	0	0	0	0	0	0
National income tax b.c. list	1 425	2 078	19 774	74 501	103 150	103 944	115 507	142 841	175 545	192 400
Local income tax b.c. list	1 030	4 266	0	0	0	0	0	0	0	0
Special tax on profits	0	0	3 874	0	0	0	0	0	0	0
Taxes on pension insurance savings	0	0	0	13 271	12 787	11 856	8 371	5 644	6 724	8 294
1220 On capital gains	0	0	0	0	0	0	0	0	0	0
1300 Unallocable between 1100 and 1200	0	0	0	0	0	0	0	0	0	0
2000 Social security contributions	4 851	74 647	205 867	306 974	388 505	384 668	404 851	455 396	489 876	518 438
2100 Employees	743	254	823	63 074	81 088	89 175	108 356	131 044	137 337	145 337
Health insurance fees	743	9	5	0	0	0	0	0	0	0
Unemployment insurance fees	0	245	818	0	0	0	0	0	0	0
Pension fees	0	0	0	63 074	81 088	89 175	108 356	131 044	137 337	145 337
2110 On a payroll basis	..	..	..	63 074	81 088	89 175	108 356	131 044	137 337	145 337
2120 On an income tax basis	..	..	..	0	0	0	0	0	0	0
2200 Employers	3 568	71 602	196 905	237 576	300 010	288 310	291 646	321 621	348 647	370 375
Survivors pension fees	0	20 343	44 181	14 847	19 611	20 362	17 305	10 493	11 636	12 359
Health insurance fees	717	26 005	58 334	74 097	100 979	71 292	64 332	62 066	68 834	73 103
Unemployment insurance fees	0	0	0	0	0	0	0	0	0	0
Labour market fees	0	982	12 516	45 975	48 471	55 443	37 926	44 078	48 300	51 320
Industrial injury insurance fees	132	1 201	4 663	12 030	7 844	8 146	4 431	3 496	3 878	4 118
Seamen's pension fees	0	10	26	30	0	0	0	0	0	0
Part pension fees	0	1 119	2 897	0	0	0	0	0	0	0
Supplementary pension fees	2 719	21 458	73 129	71 384	97 748	106 712	129 204	156 039	165 587	175 938
Parent insurance fees	0	484	1 159	19 215	25 356	26 355	38 448	45 449	50 411	53 537
2210 On a payroll basis of employers SSC	..	..	..	237 576	300 010	288 310	291 646	321 621	348 647	370 375
2220 On an income tax basis of employers SSC	..	..	..	0	0	0	0	0	0	0
2300 Selfemployed or nonemployed	540	2 791	8 139	5 569	8 391	7 584	5 058	4 100	4 560	4 714
Survivors pension fees	0	943	1 580	451	662	687	443	91	167	175
Health insurance fees	260	992	1 702	1 988	3 297	2 082	256	59	184	206
Industrial injury insurance fees	0	64	191	365	264	275	84	29	54	57
Parent insurance fees	0	58	106	573	856	888	603	279	568	605
Supplementary pension fees	280	734	4 560	2 192	3 312	3 652	3 672	3 641	3 587	3 671
Reduction	0	0	0	0	0	0	0	0	0	0
2310 On a payroll basis of self/non-employed SSC	..	..	..	5 569	8 391	7 584	5 058	4 100	4 560	4 714
2320 On an income tax basis of self/non-employed SSC	..	..	..	0	0	0	0	0	0	0
2400 Unallocable between 2100, 2200 and 2300	0	0	0	756	- 984	- 401	- 209	- 1 368	- 670	- 1 988
2410 On a payroll basis unallocable between 2100, 2200 and 2300 SSC	..	..	..	756	- 984	- 401	- 209	- 1 368	- 670	- 1 988
2420 On an income tax basis unallocable between 2100, 2200 and 2300 SSC	..	..	..	0	0	0	0	0	0	0
3000 Taxes on payroll and workforce	13	6 759	18 686	50 106	83 279	107 515	194 121	255 891	280 766	301 306
Special wage tax	0	61	0	22 391	30 225	33 090	40 283	50 836	51 865	58 320
Child care fees	0	4 740	13 080	0	0	0	0	0	0	0
Adult education fees	0	614	1 555	0	0	0	0	0	0	0
Building research fees	13	105	0	0	0	0	0	0	0	0
Labour welfare fees	0	257	2 033	0	0	0	0	0	0	0
Labour education fees	0	982	0	0	0	0	0	0	0	0
Labour market fees	0	0	0	112	156	219	- 1	0	1	1
General wage fees	0	0	2 018	27 603	52 898	74 207	153 839	205 054	228 899	242 985
4000 Taxes on property	712	2 424	26 630	39 890	36 228	36 509	43 852	47 892	52 203	55 007
4100 Recurrent taxes on immovable property	10	16	8 946	23 286	25 899	26 402	32 444	34 569	36 098	38 615
4110 Households	0	0	3 877	13 321	13 474	11 666	13 320	15 893	17 008	17 560

	1965	1980	1990	2000	2007	2010	2015	2020	2021	2022
Special tax on real estate	..	..	3 877	13 321	13 474	11 666	13 320	15 893	17 008	17 560
4120 Others	10	16	5 069	9 965	12 424	14 736	19 124	18 676	19 090	21 056
Forestry levy	10	16	423	22	34	18	19	11	14	16
Special tax on real estate	0	0	4 646	9 943	12 390	14 718	19 105	18 665	19 076	21 040
4200 Recurrent taxes on net wealth	366	717	3 200	8 223	0	0	0	0	0	0
4210 Individual	361	702	3 135	8 043	..	..	..	..	..	..
4220 Corporate	5	15	65	180	..	..	..	..	..	..
4300 Estate, inheritance and gift taxes	155	545	1 433	2 549	23	9	0	0	0	0
4310 Estate and inheritance taxes	143	495	1 118	2 088	15	9	0	..	..	..
4320 Gift taxes	12	50	315	460	8	0	0	..	..	..
4400 Taxes on financial and capital transactions	181	1 146	13 051	5 833	10 305	10 097	11 408	13 323	16 106	16 391
Taxes on financial and capital transactions	181	1 146	6 946	4 878	9 414	8 968	10 895	12 721	15 525	15 759
Turnover tax on securities	0	0	6 105	0	0	0	0	0	0	0
Tax on life group insurances	0	0	0	955	891	1 129	513	602	581	632
4500 Nonrecurrent taxes	0	0	0	0	0	0	0	0	0	0
4510 On net wealth	..	..	..	..	..	..	..	..	..	..
4520 Other nonrecurrent taxes	..	..	..	..	..	..	..	..	..	..
4600 Other recurrent taxes on property	0	0	0	0	0	0	0	0	0	0
5000 Taxes on goods and services	12 471	62 234	188 709	291 615	401 038	455 450	514 448	607 973	652 909	717 486
5100 Taxes on production, sale, transfer, etc	11 808	58 474	181 587	284 182	387 956	439 050	495 695	586 392	630 360	694 959
5110 General taxes	4 147	34 643	112 399	199 606	286 211	326 685	383 002	461 267	499 497	552 379
5111 Value added taxes	0	34 643	112 399	197 483	282 586	322 603	379 120	461 138	499 360	552 245
5112 Sales tax	4 147	0	0	0	0	0	0	0	0	0
5113 Other	0	0	0	2 123	3 625	4 082	3 882	129	137	135
5120 Taxes on specific goods and services	7 661	23 831	69 188	84 576	101 745	112 365	112 693	125 124	130 863	142 579
5121 Excises	5 953	19 941	55 332	70 313	84 873	91 470	91 534	104 931	108 745	118 626
Taxes on petrol and fuel	1 420	4 229	17 171	39 011	44 501	47 426	44 906	45 847	48 533	40 918
Special sales tax	390	585	1 098	0	0	0	0	0	0	0
Sales tax on motor vehicles	325	553	1 983	195	3	0	0	0	0	0
Tobacco tax	1 150	3 087	5 636	7 747	9 742	10 588	11 825	11 912	11 907	13 158
Tax on spirits	1 548	4 431	6 205	4 902	4 250	4 324	4 208	5 250	5 609	5 514
Tax on wine	149	930	2 922	3 567	4 001	4 589	5 654	6 552	6 635	6 495
Tax on beer and soft drinks	242	964	2 532	2 355	2 773	3 219	3 895	4 477	4 546	4 583
Tax on energy consumption	729	5 162	16 352	11 451	18 994	21 035	20 749	28 583	28 597	44 915
Taxes on electricity from certain sources	0	0	1 018	0	0	0	0	0	0	0
Tax on wastes	0	0	0	1 085	609	289	297	681	1 165	1 428
Tax on cassette tapes	0	0	194	0	0	0	0	0	0	0
Tax on videorecorders	0	0	221	0	0	0	0	0	0	0
Tax on chemicals	0	0	0	0	0	0	0	1 629	1 753	1 614
5122 Profits of fiscal monopolies	72	204	332	3 641	3 952	5 068	5 001	2 094	3 276	2 159
Alcohol monopoly wholesale	23	116	98	0	0	0	0	0	0	0
Alcohol monopoly retailing	49	88	234	80	296	302	198	471	376	159
Gaming monopoly retailing	0	0	0	3 561	3 657	4 766	4 803	1 623	2 900	2 000
5123 Customs and import duties	1 419	2 433	8 308	3 450	5 099	5 412	6 243	6 212	7 339	9 329
Customs	1 080	1 300	3 115	3 450	5 099	5 412	6 243	6 212	7 339	9 329
Agricultural levies	339	1 133	5 193	0	0	0	0	0	0	0
5124 Taxes on exports	0	0	0	0	0	0	0	0	0	0
5125 Taxes on investment goods	0	0	40	0	0	0	0	0	0	0
Investment tax	..	..	40	..	..	..	..	..	..	..
5126 Taxes on specific services	217	1 253	5 176	5 834	3 361	4 712	7 120	10 215	10 579	12 032
Betting tax	79	223	616	0	0	0	0	0	0	0
Advertisement tax	0	202	1 073	1 116	657	335	200	114	103	28
Tax on gambling	0	69	88	1 245	1 315	1 378	1 353	3 777	4 028	4 271
Other specific services	138	656	2 938	3 473	1 388	2 999	5 567	5 829	5 984	6 612
Tax on charter travelling	0	103	461	0	0	0	0	0	0	0
Tax on air travel	..	..	0	0	0	0	0	495	465	1 120
5127 Other taxes on internat. trade and transactions	0	0	0	0	0	0	0	0	0	0
5128 Other taxes	0	0	0	1 339	4 460	5 702	2 795	1 672	925	434
5130 Unallocable between 5110 and 5120	0	0	0	0	0	0	0	0	0	0
5200 Taxes on use of goods and perform activities	663	3 760	7 122	7 433	13 083	16 400	18 752	21 581	22 549	22 527
5210 Recurrent taxes	663	3 760	7 122	7 433	13 083	16 400	18 752	21 581	22 549	22 527
5211 Paid by households: motor vehicles	336	1 241	2 003	4 969	7 414	8 550	10 897	10 342	10 815	10 655
5212 Paid by others: motor vehicles	313	2 476	5 055	2 464	5 669	7 850	7 855	11 239	11 735	11 872
5213 Paid in respect of other goods	14	43	64	0	0	0	0	0	0	0
5220 Nonrecurrent taxes	0	0	0	0	0	0	0	0	0	0
5300 Unallocable between 5100 and 5200	0	0	0	0	0	0	0	0	0	0
6000 Other taxes	0	422	1 264	1 479	1 768	1 421	1 356	2 374	2 617	3 294
6100 Paid solely by business	..	0	0	0	0	0	0	0	0	0
6200 Other	..	422	1 264	1 479	1 768	1 421	1 356	2 374	2 617	3 294
Custom duties collected for the EU	..	..	..	3 450	5 099	5 412	6 243	6 212	7 339	9 329
Total tax revenue on cash basis	40 003	259 216	755 953	1 144 233	1 465 382	1 496 374	1 762 187	0	0	0

	1965	1980	1990	2000	2007	2010	2015	2020	2021	2022
Total tax revenue on accrual basis	..	..	..	1 204 794	1 491 190	1 532 259	1 816 166	2 137 949	2 336 817	2 493 410
Additional taxes included in National Accounts	..	..	..	0	0	0	0	0	0	0
Taxes excluded from National Accounts	..	..	..	0	0	0	0	0	0	0
Difference in treatment of tax credits	..	..	..	0	0	0	0	0	0	0
Capital transfer for uncollected revenue	..	..	..	0	0	0	0	0	0	0
Voluntary social security contributions	..	..	..	7 951	12 376	13 167	16 726	24 731	30 070	26 919
Miscellaneous differences	..	..	..	0	0	0	0	0	0	0
National Accounts: Taxes and actual social contributions	..	..	..	1 212 745	1 503 566	1 545 426	1 832 892	2 162 680	2 366 887	2 520 329
Imputed social contributions	..	..	..	0	0	0	0	0	0	0
National Accounts: Taxes and all social contributions	..	..	..	1 212 745	1 503 566	1 545 426	1 832 892	2 162 680	2 366 887	2 520 329

.. Not available

Note: Year ending 31st December.

From 2000 data are on accrual basis.

Figures prior to 1970 are not strictly comparable with those of later years, though the amounts involved are insignificant.

Heading 1000: Receipts are on accrual and not on a cash basis for all years.

Source: National Financial Management Authority, Stockholm.

Table 5.35. Switzerland: Details of tax revenue, 1965-2022

Million CHF

	1965	1980	1990	2000	2007	2010	2015	2020	2021	2022
Total tax revenue	11 237	46 385	85 774	128 205	151 404	162 356	181 128	195 260	209 311	211 254
1000 Taxes on income, profits and capital gains	4 616	21 022	40 203	56 411	69 790	74 439	84 362	90 452	100 037	98 772
1100 Taxes on income, profits and capital gains of individuals	3 748	18 056	27 824	37 948	47 994	51 835	56 375	62 876	63 762	65 677
1110 On income and profits of individuals	3 547	17 622	27 824	37 948	47 994	51 835	56 375	62 876	63 762	65 677
Direct federal tax	245	2 525	4 432	5 713	8 589	9 880	10 394	12 054	12 693	12 730
Military service exemption tax	35	103	135	163	138	155	173	185	182	167
Cantonal tax individuals	1 473	7 510	12 856	17 592	23 094	24 957	27 156	30 284	30 251	31 756
Municipal tax individuals	1 322	6 235	10 402	14 481	16 174	16 844	18 651	20 353	20 636	21 024
Withholding tax	358	1 249	0	0	0	0	0	0	0	0
Coupons	114	0	0	0	0	0	0	0	0	0
1120 On capital gains of individuals	201	434	0	0	0	0	0	0	0	0
Cantonal tax individuals	84	229	..	..	..	..	..	..	..	..
Municipal tax individuals	112	190	..	..	..	..	..	..	..	..
Direct federal tax	5	15	..	..	..	..	..	..	..	..
1200 Taxes on income, profits and capital gains of corporates	868	2 966	6 300	11 323	16 161	16 378	19 432	21 485	22 876	25 107
1210 On profits of corporates	801	2 818	6 300	11 323	16 161	16 378	19 432	21 485	22 876	25 107
Direct federal tax	153	781	2 214	4 928	6 800	8 006	9 731	12 092	12 701	13 601
Corporate cantonal tax	363	1 230	2 576	3 989	6 098	5 445	6 294	6 127	6 585	7 329
Corporate municipal tax	285	807	1 510	2 406	3 263	2 927	3 407	3 267	3 590	4 178
Withholding tax	0	0	0	0	0	0	0	0	0	0
1220 On capital gains of corporates	67	148	..	..	..	..	..	..	..	..
Corporate tax on gains	2	7	..	..	..	..	..	..	..	..
Corporate cantonal tax	28	77	..	..	..	..	..	..	..	..
Corporate municipal tax	37	64	..	..	..	..	..	..	..	..
1300 Unallocable between 1100 and 1200	0	0	6 079	7 140	5 635	6 226	8 556	6 091	13 399	7 988
Withholding tax	..	..	4 044	6 202	4 211	4 723	6 543	3 316	10 000	4 388
Property gains tax	..	..	2 035	938	1 424	1 502	2 013	2 775	3 399	3 600
Other	..	..	0	0	0	0	0	0	0	0
2000 Social security contributions (SSC)	1 670	10 844	19 952	30 961	34 974	38 385	44 285	49 056	50 655	52 285
2100 Employees SSC	716	4 833	9 341	14 491	16 369	17 581	20 542	23 753	24 103	24 623
2110 On a payroll basis of employees SSC	716	4 833	9 341	14 491	16 369	17 581	20 542	23 753	24 103	24 623
2120 On an income tax basis of employees SSC	0	0	..	..	..	..	..	..	..	..
2200 Employers SSC	747	4 897	9 350	14 504	16 383	17 608	20 574	22 044	23 253	24 512
2210 On a payroll basis of employers SSC	747	4 897	9 350	14 504	16 383	17 608	20 574	22 044	23 253	24 512
2220 On an income tax basis of employers SSC	0	0	..	..	..	..	..	..	..	..
2300 Self-employed or non-employed SSC	208	1 046	1 261	1 967	2 222	3 197	3 169	3 260	3 299	3 149
2310 On a payroll basis of self/non-employed SSC	209	1 046	1 261	1 967	2 222	3 197	3 169	3 260	3 299	3 149
2320 On an income tax basis of self/non-employed SSC	0	0	..	..	..	..	..	..	..	..
2400 Unallocable between 2100, 2200 and 2300 SSC	0	68	0	0	0	0	0	0	0	0
2410 On a payroll basis unallocable between 2100, 2200 and 2300 SSC	..	68	..	..	..	..	..	..	..	..
2420 On an income tax basis unallocable between 2100, 2200 and 2300 SSC	..	0	..	..	..	..	..	..	..	..
3000 Taxes on payroll and workforce	0	0	0	0	0	0	0	0	0	0
4000 Taxes on property	1 108	3 830	7 586	12 333	12 223	12 402	13 140	15 744	16 664	16 991
4100 Recurrent taxes on immovable property	78	304	447	735	895	968	1 138	1 341	1 414	1 499
4110 Households recurrent taxes on immovable property	78	304	447	735	895	968	1 138	1 341	1 414	1 499
Cantonal tax on buildings	20	71	125	187	265	286	349	392	435	440
Municipal tax on buildings	58	233	322	548	630	682	789	949	979	1 059
4120 Other than households recurrent taxes on immovable property	0	0	..	..	..	..	..	..	..	..
4200 Recurrent taxes on net wealth	692	2 201	3 382	5 254	7 002	7 105	8 096	9 950	10 299	10 581
4210 Individual recurrent taxes on net wealth	420	1 383	2 194	3 972	5 309	5 576	6 606	8 246	8 703	8 994
Cantonal wealth tax	206	739	1 232	2 241	3 145	3 324	4 044	5 081	5 292	5 536
Municipal wealth tax	214	644	962	1 731	2 164	2 252	2 562	3 165	3 411	3 458
4220 Corporate recurrent taxes on net wealth	272	818	1 188	1 282	1 693	1 529	1 490	1 704	1 596	1 588
Direct federal tax on capital	21	92	0	0	0	0	0	0	0	0
Cantonal tax on capital	142	436	760	821	1 107	969	947	1 090	985	960
Municipal tax on capital	109	290	428	461	586	561	542	614	611	628
4300 Estate, inheritance and gift taxes	142	393	896	1 215	869	974	1 088	1 272	1 366	1 479
4310 Estate and inheritance taxes	142	393	896	1 215	869	974	1 088	1 272	1 366	1 479
Cantonal inheritance tax	128	361	820	1 118	774	886	964	1 128	1 195	1 292
Municipal inheritance tax	14	32	76	97	96	88	124	144	171	187
4320 Gift taxes	0	0	..	..	..	..	..	..	..	..
4400 Taxes on financial and capital transactions	196	932	2 245	4 342	2 562	2 428	1 902	1 992	2 209	2 057

	1965	1980	1990	2000	2007	2010	2015	2020	2021	2022
Cantonal transfer tax	48	245	115	144	182	182	177	233	265	259
Municipal transfer tax	21	103	39	52	42	50	52	64	79	85
Securities issuance	99	175	0	0	405	779	360	179	272	262
Securities trading	19	409	0	0	1 933	1 417	1 314	1 516	1 594	1 451
Currency effects	9	0	0	0	0	0	0	0	0	0
Securities issuance and trading	0	0	2 091	4 146	0	0	0	0	0	0
4500 Non-recurrent taxes on property	0	0	0	0	0	0	0	0	0	0
4510 Non-recurrent taxes on net wealth	..	..	..	..	..	..	..	..	..	..
4520 Non-recurrent taxes on property other than net wealth	..	..	..	..	..	..	..	..	..	..
4600 Other recurrent taxes on property except 4100 and 4200	0	0	616	786	895	927	915	1 189	1 375	1 375
5000 Taxes on goods and services	3 843	10 689	17 894	28 285	34 168	36 539	38 542	38 958	40 897	42 047
5100 Taxes on production, sale, transfer, etc	3 582	9 863	15 975	25 302	30 669	32 264	33 771	33 544	35 527	36 535
5110 General taxes on goods and services	1 191	4 772	9 871	16 917	19 962	21 035	22 791	22 435	23 869	24 920
5111 Value added taxes	0	0	9 871	16 594	19 604	20 662	22 397	22 104	23 553	24 588
5112 Sales tax	1 191	4 772	0	323	358	373	393	331	316	331
Automobile duty	..	..	..	323	358	373	393	331	316	331
Other sales taxes	..	..	..	0	0	0	0	0	0	0
5113 Other (than value added and sales tax)	0	0	..	..	..	..	..	..	..	..
5120 Taxes on specific goods and services	2 391	5 091	6 058	8 337	10 663	11 191	10 912	11 016	11 559	11 482
5121 Excises	1 016	3 427	4 604	6 810	7 805	8 295	8 056	8 049	8 462	8 209
Beer tax	26	33	0	0	107	112	114	110	107	115
Excises on tobacco	190	634	15	32	2 247	2 417	2 255	2 158	2 204	2 082
Other price supplements	104	542	1 503	1 783	3	0	3	3	3	3
Fuel tax	467	955	1 334	2 975	3 076	3 110	2 864	2 543	2 727	2 664
Additional fuel tax	229	1 263	1 753	2 020	2 071	2 082	1 905	1 683	1 811	1 755
Road tax	0	0	0	0	0	0	0	0	0	0
Mineral oil tax on combustibles	0	0	0	0	20	20	19	17	16	14
Automobile duty	0	0	0	0	0	0	0	0	0	0
Tax on distilled spirits	0	0	0	1	281	296	279	290	305	302
Electricity consumption tax	0	0	0	0	0	259	617	1 245	1 288	1 274
5122 Profits of fiscal monopolies	158	472	..	..	..	..	..	..	..	..
Alcohol monopoly	111	354	..	..	..	..	..	..	..	..
Salt monopoly	16	25	..	..	..	..	..	..	..	..
Water monopoly	30	90	..	..	..	..	..	..	..	..
Other	1	3	..	..	..	..	..	..	..	..
5123 Customs and import duties	1 104	953	1 201	1 096	1 040	1 079	1 056	1 187	1 277	1 221
Import duties	972	923	1 201	1 096	1 040	1 079	1 056	1 187	1 277	1 221
Tobacco duty	114	6	0	0	0	0	0	0	0	0
Additional duties	18	24	0	0	0	0	0	0	0	0
5124 Taxes on exports	0	0	..	..	..	..	..	..	..	..
5125 Taxes on investment goods	0	0	..	..	..	..	..	..	..	..
5126 Taxes on specific services	113	239	253	431	1 818	1 816	1 800	1 780	1 820	2 051
Games in B casinos Confederation	2	2	2	37	449	381	272	250	248	353
Cantonal entertainment tax	17	37	23	27	39	101	67	53	46	66
Municipal entertainment tax	11	19	46	26	18	17	15	5	8	9
Other cantonal expenditure taxes	24	63	0	0	0	0	0	0	0	0
Other municipal expenditure taxes	19	6	0	0	0	0	0	0	0	0
Premium stamp duty	40	112	0	0	645	659	715	726	742	770
Lottery taxes	0	0	181	320	474	459	527	526	544	620
Other	0	0	0	20	193	199	204	220	232	233
5127 Other taxes on internat. trade and transactions not included within 5121 to 5126 inclusive	0	0	..	..	..	..	..	..	..	..
5128 Other taxes not included within 5121 to 5127 inclusive	0	0	..	..	..	..	..	..	..	..
5130 Unallocable between 5110 and 5120	0	0	46	47	44	38	68	92	99	133
5200 Taxes on use of goods and perform activities	261	826	1 918	2 983	3 499	4 276	4 771	5 415	5 370	5 513
5210 Recurrent taxes on use of goods and perform activities	261	826	1 918	2 983	3 499	4 276	4 767	5 406	5 353	5 465
5211 Recurrent taxes paid by households: motor vehicles	152	501	921	1 336	1 580	1 667	1 768	1 875	1 907	1 920
Paid by households in respect of motor vehicles	..	..	921	1 336	1 580	1 667	1 768	1 875	1 907	1 920
Paid by households in respect of motorway tax sticker	..	..	0	0	0	0	0	0	0	0
5212 Recurrent taxes paid by others: motor vehicles	76	251	230	334	395	417	442	469	477	480
Paid by others in respect of motor vehicles	..	..	230	334	395	417	442	469	477	480
Paid by others in respect of motorway tax sticker	..	..	0	0	0	0	0	0	0	0
Paid by others in respect of heavy vehicle charge	..	..	0	0	- 3	- 8	- 5	- 3	- 3	- 2
5213 Recurrent taxes paid on use of goods and perform activities other than on motor vehicles	33	74	768	1 314	1 524	2 192	2 556	3 062	2 969	3 065

	1965	1980	1990	2000	2007	2010	2015	2020	2021	2022
Hunting and fishing	9	20	0	0	0	0	0	0	0	0
Cantonal dog license	3	9	6	9	8	8	9	12	11	11
Municipal dog license	2	8	14	21	25	30	35	44	52	63
Cantonal inns	12	24	0	0	0	0	0	0	0	0
Cantonal royalties	5	12	0	0	0	0	0	0	0	0
Other	2	1	703	1 157	1 261	1 315	1 375	1 387	1 409	1 396
Environmental incentive fees	0	0	3	73	166	755	1 036	1 497	1 365	1 450
Royalties and concessions	0	0	42	53	64	84	101	121	131	145
Radio and television licences			703	1 124	1 228	1 285	1 351	1 377	1 400	1 337
5220 Non-recurrent taxes on use of goods and perform activities	0	0	0	0	0	0	5	8	17	48
5300 Unallocable between 5100 and 5200	0	0	0	0	0	0	0	0	0	0
6000 Taxes other than 1000, 2000, 3000, 4000 and 5000	0	0	140	215	249	590	799	1 050	1 057	1 159
6100 Paid solely by business	..	..	42	65	75	274	342	388	372	424
6200 Other taxes not solely paid by business	..	..	98	151	174	316	457	662	685	735
Exemption tax	..	..	98	151	174	187	190	201	203	208
Other	..	..	0	0	0	130	267	461	482	526
Total tax revenue on cash basis	11 237	46 385	..	..	..	..	..	..	..	..
Total tax revenue on accrual basis	..	..	85 774	128 205	151 404	162 356	181 128	195 260	209 311	211 254
Additional taxes included in National Accounts	..	..	0	0	0	0	0	0	0	0
Taxes excluded from National Accounts	..	..	0	0	0	0	0	0	0	0
Difference in treatment of tax credits	..	..	0	0	0	0	0	0	0	0
Capital transfer for uncollected revenue	..	..	- 242	- 733	- 936	- 1 121	- 1 058	- 818	- 921	- 963
Voluntary social security contributions	..	..	0	0	0	0	0	0	0	0
Miscellaneous differences	..	..	0	0	0	0	0	0	0	0
National Accounts: Taxes and actual social contributions	..	..	85 533	127 472	150 468	161 235	180 070	194 442	208 390	210 291
Imputed social contributions	..	..	362	502	467	454	337	806	565	624
National Accounts: Taxes and all social contributions	..	..	85 895	127 974	150 935	161 689	180 407	195 248	208 954	210 915

.. Not available

Note: Calendar year ending on 31 December.

The data is on an accrual basis.

The pre-1970 figures are not strictly comparable with those from the following years which were revised.

"Parish taxes" are not reported in these statistics from 1985 onward.

In section 1100: payments made in consideration for exemption from military service could be classed under nontax receipts.

Section 2000 (Social security contributions) has been revised from 1985 onward to take account of the sectoring of government units adopted when switching to the ESA 95 system of accounts (currently ESA 2010). Consequently, health insurance contributions and those to the Swiss National Accident Insurance Fund are now excluded from section 2000.

Source: Financial Statistics, Federal Finance Administration.

Table 5.36. Türkiye: Details of tax revenue, 1965-2022

Million TRY

	1965	1980	1990	2000	2007	2010	2015	2020	2021	2022
Total tax revenue	0	1	79	40 263	203 053	287 873	586 722	1 204 629	1 662 669	3 144 266
1000 Taxes on income, profits and capital gains	0	0	26	11 890	48 197	61 317	119 144	263 898	397 629	863 918
1100 Of individuals	0	0	21	8 954	34 447	40 392	85 756	158 842	219 656	356 464
1110 On income and profits	0	0	21	8 954	34 447	40 392	85 756	158 842	219 656	356 464
Income tax	0	0	21	8 954	34 447	40 392	85 756	158 842	219 656	356 464
1120 On capital gains	0	0	0	0	0	0	0	0	0	0
1200 Corporate	0	0	5	2 935	13 751	20 925	33 388	105 057	177 973	507 454
1210 On profits	0	0	5	2 935	13 751	20 925	33 388	105 057	177 973	507 454
Corporation tax	0	0	5	2 935	13 751	20 925	33 388	105 057	177 973	507 454
1220 On capital gains	0	0	0	0	0	0	0	0	0	0
1300 Unallocable between 1100 and 1200	0	0	0	0	0	0	0	0	0	0
Fiscal balance tax	..	0	..	..	..	..	..	..	..	..
Capital gains tax on real estate sales	..	0	..	..	..	..	..	..	..	..
2000 Social security contributions	0	0	15	7 543	44 052	71 696	170 282	357 677	481 163	767 544
2100 Employees	0	0	6	2 712	17 867	26 934	64 214	137 742	182 733	296 029
2110 On a payroll basis	..	..	..	2 712	17 867	26 934	64 214	137 742	182 733	296 029
2120 On an income tax basis	..	..	..	0	0	0	0	0	0	0
2200 Employers	0	0	9	3 619	20 442	39 363	95 067	204 045	272 370	440 551
2210 On a payroll basis of employers SSC	..	..	..	3 619	20 442	39 363	95 067	204 045	272 370	440 551
2220 On an income tax basis of employers SSC	..	..	..	0	0	0	0	0	0	0
2300 Selfemployed or nonemployed	0	0	1	1 211	5 743	5 399	11 001	15 890	26 060	30 965
2310 On a payroll basis of self/non-employed SSC	..	..	..	1 211	5 743	5 399	11 001	15 890	26 060	30 965
2320 On an income tax basis of self/non-employed SSC	..	..	..	0	0	0	0	0	0	0
2400 Unallocable between 2100, 2200 and 2300	0	0	0	0	0	0	0	0	0	0
2410 On a payroll basis unallocable between 2100, 2200 and 2300 SSC	..	..	..	..	..	..	..	..	..	..
2420 On an income tax basis unallocable between 2100, 2200 and 2300 SSC	..	..	..	..	..	..	..	..	..	..
3000 Taxes on payroll and workforce	0	0	0	0	0	0	0	0	0	0
4000 Taxes on property	0	0	2	1 272	7 621	11 684	28 582	53 548	70 179	109 473
4100 Recurrent taxes on immovable property	0	0	0	191	1 464	2 669	5 882	11 204	13 647	18 633
Real estate tax	0	0	..	191	1 464	2 669	5 882	11 204	13 647	18 633
4110 Households	..	..	..	..	..	..	..	..	..	..
4120 Others	..	..	..	..	..	..	..	..	..	..
4200 Recurrent taxes on net wealth	0	0	0	0	0	0	0	0	23	40
4210 Individual	..	..	..	..	..	..	..	..	23	40
4220 Corporate	..	..	..	..	..	..	..	..	0	0
4300 Estate, inheritance and gift taxes	0	0	0	15	125	215	435	1 298	2 255	2 886
Gift and inheritance tax	0	0	0	15	125	215	435	1 298	2 255	2 886
4310 Estate and inheritance taxes	..	..	..	..	..	..	..	..	..	..
4320 Gift taxes	..	..	..	..	..	..	..	..	..	..
4400 Taxes on financial and capital transactions	0	0	2	1 065	6 032	8 800	22 265	41 045	54 254	87 913
Stamp tax	0	0	2	818	3 642	5 083	12 045	20 964	28 203	41 945
Real estate purchase tax	0	0	0	0	0	0	0	0	0	0
Title deed fees	0	0	0	207	2 000	3 329	9 530	19 001	24 739	44 018
Notary fees	0	0	0	40	389	388	690	1 081	1 312	1 950
4500 Nonrecurrent taxes	0	0	0	0	0	0	0	0	0	0
4510 On net wealth	..	..	..	..	..	..	..	..	..	..
4520 Other nonrecurrent taxes	..	..	..	..	..	..	..	..	..	..
4600 Other recurrent taxes on property	0	0	0	0	0	0	0	0	0	0
5000 Taxes on goods and services	0	0	22	16 901	96 766	137 252	259 964	517 288	696 341	1 370 130
5100 Taxes on production, sale, transfer, etc	0	0	22	16 328	92 605	131 878	250 261	500 367	675 957	1 344 247
5110 General taxes	0	0	16	9 735	43 285	62 533	121 070	230 761	385 343	754 109
5111 Value added taxes	..	..	14	9 735	43 285	62 533	121 070	230 761	385 343	754 109
5112 Sales tax	..	..	0	0	0	0	0	0	0	0
5113 Other	..	..	1	0	0	0	0	0	0	0
5120 Taxes on specific goods and services	0	0	6	6 593	49 320	69 345	129 191	269 606	290 614	590 139
5121 Excises	0	0	1	4 718	39 111	57 285	105 922	207 273	205 351	419 791
Sales taxes	0	0	0	0	0	0	0	0	0	0
Domestic production tax	0	0	0	0	0	0	0	0	0	0
Domestic production tax on petrol	0	0	0	0	0	0	0	0	0	0
Production tax on monopoly goods	0	0	0	0	0	0	0	0	0	0
Sugar consumption taxes	0	0	0	0	0	0	0	0	0	0
Motor vehicles purchase tax (Total)	0	0	1	916	4 293	6 193	17 027	46 596	66 372	167 142

	1965	1980	1990	2000	2007	2010	2015	2020	2021	2022
Motor vehicles purchase tax	0	0	0	498	4 293	6 193	17 027	46 596	66 372	167 142
Additional motor vehicle purchase tax	0	0	0	418	0	0	0	0	0	0
Revenue from other excises	0	0	0	533	12 765	19 395	38 066	12 060	15 309	26 736
Petroleum consumption tax	0	0	0	3 269	22 052	31 697	50 830	69 009	31 292	76 765
Alcohol								16 464	22 785	43 702
Tobacco								61 801	67 620	101 275
Sugar-sweetened beverages								1 341	1 973	4 171
5122 Profits of fiscal monopolies	0	0	0	0	0	0	0	0	0	0
5123 Customs and import duties	0	0	4	462	2 478	3 319	8 521	26 246	35 592	79 076
Customs duty	0	0	1	449	2 441	3 240	8 280	25 637	34 444	76 517
Customs duty on petrol	0	0	0	0	0	0	0	0	0	0
Production tax on imports	0	0	0	0	0	0	0	0	0	0
Production tax on petrol imports	0	0	0	0	0	0	0	0	0	0
Stamp duty on imports	0	0	2	0	0	0	0	0	0	0
Wharf duty	0	0	1	0	0	0	0	0	0	0
Other	0	0	0	13	37	80	240	609	1 148	2 560
5124 Taxes on exports	0	0	0	0	0	0	0	0	0	0
5125 Taxes on investment goods	0	0	0	0	0	0	0	0	0	0
5126 Taxes on specific services	0	0	1	997	7 686	4 005	10 014	30 533	39 120	68 939
Bank, insurance transaction tax	0	0	1	997	3 149	3 571	9 172	27 069	33 029	58 639
Transportation tax	0	0	0	0	0	0	0	0	0	0
PTT service tax	0	0	0	0	4 211	0	0	0	0	0
Tax on football pool	0	0	0	0	0	0	0	0	0	0
Lottery tax	0	0	0	0	327	434	842	3 464	6 092	10 300
5127 Other taxes on internat. trade and transactions	0	0	0	0	0	0	0	0	0	0
Foreign travel expenditures tax	0	0	..	..	..	..	..	..	..	..
5128 Other taxes	0	0	0	416	46	4 736	4 734	5 553	10 550	22 332
5130 Unallocable between 5110 and 5120	0	0	0	0	0	0	0	0	0	0
5200 Taxes on use of goods and perform activities	0	0	0	572	4 161	5 374	9 703	16 921	20 384	25 883
5210 Recurrent taxes	0	0	0	359	4 161	5 374	9 703	16 921	20 384	25 883
Motor vehicles tax	0	0	0	359	0	5 374	9 703	16 921	20 384	25 883
5211 Paid by households: motor vehicles	..	..	..	0	0	0	0	0	0	0
5212 Paid by others: motor vehicles	..	..	..	359	4 161	5 374	9 703	16 921	20 384	25 883
Motor vehicles tax	..	..	..	302	3 521	5 033	8 949	15 983	18 836	23 627
Traffic fees	..	..	..	58	640	341	754	938	1 548	2 256
5213 Paid in respect of other goods	..	..	..	0	0	0	0	0	0	0
5220 Nonrecurrent taxes	0	0	0	213	0	0	0	0	0	0
Building construction tax	..	0	..	0	..	..	..	..	..	..
5300 Unallocable between 5100 and 5200	0	0	0	0	0	0	0	0	0	0
6000 Other taxes	0	0	13	2 658	6 417	5 924	8 750	12 218	17 357	33 201
6100 Paid solely by business	..	0	0	0	0	0	0	0	0	0
6200 Other	..	0	13	2 658	6 417	5 924	8 750	12 218	17 357	33 201
Funds	..	..	..	1 938	0	0	0	0	0	0
Vocatial Train Pro.F.	..	..	..	67	0	0	0	0	0	0
Tax penalties and fines	..	..	..	548	4 191	2 689	3 779	5 123	7 580	13 559
Municipalities revenue	..	..	..	106	2 227	3 235	4 971	7 095	9 777	19 642
Total tax revenue on cash basis	0	1	79	40 263	203 053	287 873	586 722	1 204 629	1 654 956	3 144 266
Total tax revenue on accrual basis	..	..	..	..	..	..	..	..	..	..
Additional taxes included in National Accounts	..	..	..	..	..	..	..	..	..	..
Taxes excluded from National Accounts	..	..	..	..	..	..	..	..	..	..
Difference in treatment of tax credits	..	..	..	..	..	..	..	..	..	..
Capital transfer for uncollected revenue	..	..	..	..	..	..	..	..	..	..
Voluntary social security contributions	..	..	..	..	..	..	..	..	..	..
Miscellaneous differences	..	..	..	..	..	..	..	..	..	..
National Accounts: Taxes and actual social contributions	..	..	..	..	..	..	..	..	..	..
Imputed social contributions	..	..	..	..	..	..	..	..	..	..
National Accounts: Taxes and all social contributions	..	..	..	..	..	..	..	..	..	..

.. Not available

Note: From 1982 the data are based on the fiscal year ending 31st December. Before that the data are on a fiscal year basis beginning 1st March.

Revenue is reported on a cash basis except for social security contributions which are reported on an assessment basis.

The figures under the local tax collections include taxes under 'Municipalities Revenues Law' and Property tax. They also include transfers to the local authorities from central budget tax revenues under the revenue sharing system.

Heading 2000: Before 2003, contributions to some private social security schemes are included in this heading.

Source: Bulletin of national accounts and the Budget revenue Bulletin.

Table 5.37. United Kingdom: Details of tax revenue, 1965-2022

Million GBP

	1965	1980	1990	2000	2007	2010	2015	2020	2021	2022
Total tax revenue	10 945	81 153	202 368	359 483	509 222	515 462	611 491	690 452	781 763	887 623
Total tax revenue exclusive of custom duties	..	..	200 520	357 353	506 807	512 517	608 404	687 556	..	..
1000 Taxes on income, profits and capital gains	4 050	30 651	79 576	142 335	201 316	192 771	212 726	248 455	295 065	335 214
1100 Of individuals	3 618	23 868	59 506	104 136	151 157	147 019	168 901	198 165	227 872	253 612
Swiss bank tax				0	0	0	28	0	51	0
1110 On income and profits	3 615	23 376	57 614	101 925	147 309	144 502	163 291	187 913	215 705	238 187
Income tax	..	23 370	57 614	101 925	147 309	144 502	163 291	187 913	215 705	238 187
Surtax	..	6	0	0	0	0	0	0	0	0
1120 On capital gains	3	492	1 892	2 211	3 848	2 517	5 582	10 252	12 116	15 425
1200 Corporate	484	6 783	20 070	38 199	50 159	45 752	43 825	50 289	67 194	81 601
1210 On profits	484	6 510	18 994	35 868	46 841	44 857	42 408	49 259	65 999	80 361
Petroleum revenue tax	..	1 799	941	1 540	1 387	1 349	- 552	- 431	- 360	- 391
Supplementary petroleum duty	..	0	0	0	0	0	0	0	0	0
Corporation tax	..	4 712	18 053	34 328	44 740	42 865	42 340	48 955	65 609	79 968
Corporation tax overspill relief	..	- 1	0	0	0	0	0	0	0	0
Profits tax	..	0	0	0	0	0	0	0	0	0
Windfall tax	..	0	0	0	0	0	0	0	0	0
Betting tax	..	0	0	0	590	568	595	735	750	784
Non fossil fuel obligation levy	..	0	0	0	124	75	25	0	0	0
1220 On capital gains	0	273	1 076	2 331	3 318	895	1 417	1 030	1 195	1 240
1300 Unallocable between 1100 and 1200	- 52	0	0	0	0	0	0	0	0	0
2000 Social security contributions	1 685	13 531	34 457	60 252	93 210	97 346	114 173	143 608	156 208	176 951
2100 Employees	770	5 228	13 296	24 175	36 585	38 703	44 488	56 159	60 015	65 337
2110 On a payroll basis	..	..	13 296	24 175	36 585	38 703	44 488	56 159	60 015	65 337
2120 On an income tax basis	..	..	0	0	0	0	0	0	0	0
2200 Employers	831	8 210	19 984	34 028	53 765	55 887	66 491	82 976	91 049	105 980
2210 On a payroll basis of employers SSC	..	..	19 984	34 028	53 765	55 887	66 491	82 976	91 049	105 980
2220 On an income tax basis of employers SSC	..	..	0	0	0	0	0	0	0	0
2300 Selfemployed or nonemployed	75	317	1 177	2 049	2 860	2 756	3 194	4 473	5 144	5 634
2310 On a payroll basis of self/non-employed SSC	..	..	1 177	2 049	2 860	2 756	3 194	4 473	5 144	5 634
2320 On an income tax basis of self/non-employed SSC	..	..	0	0	0	0	0	0	0	0
2400 Unallocable between 2100, 2200 and 2300	9	- 224	0	0	0	0	0	0	0	0
2410 On a payroll basis unallocable between 2100, 2200 and 2300 SSC	..	..	..	..	..	..	..	..	..	..
2420 On an income tax basis unallocable between 2100, 2200 and 2300 SSC	..	..	..	..	..	..	..	..	..	..
3000 Taxes on payroll and workforce	0	3 498	0	0	0	0	0	2 898	3 148	3 520
Selective employment tax	..	0	..	..	..	..	..	0	0	0
National insurance surcharge	..	3 498	..	..	..	..	..	0	0	0
Apprenticeship Levy	..	0	..	..	..	..	..	2 898	3 148	3 520
4000 Taxes on property	1 591	9 774	16 538	41 109	63 392	61 768	76 399	79 937	89 589	100 591
4100 Recurrent taxes on immovable property	1 228	8 665	13 462	30 527	44 891	50 028	58 019	61 265	64 599	71 683
4110 Households	539	3 687	2 373	14 205	23 609	25 919	29 373	38 055	40 173	42 292
Northern Ireland rates paid to CG	..	37	113	141	265	335	323	432	436	444
Council tax	..	0	0	13 991	23 217	25 438	28 777	37 269	39 373	41 469
Rates paid to LA	..	3 650	2 260	73	127	146	273	354	364	379
4120 Others	689	4 978	11 089	16 322	21 282	24 109	28 646	23 210	24 426	29 391
National non-domestic rates	..	0	7 542	14 912	19 358	21 602	25 834	20 255	21 289	26 367
Rates paid to LA	..	4 925	2 869	149	267	497	480	509	607	552
Northern Ireland rates paid to CG	..	53	115	207	353	361	335	359	346	349
London Regional Transport levy	..	0	47	0	0	0	0	0	0	0
LA payments of NNDR	..	0	469	889	1 111	1 236	1 389	1 389	1 389	1 389
NPISH payments of NNDR	..	0	47	165	193	245	384	501	508	510
Crossrail Business rates supplement	..	0	0	0	0	168	224	197	287	224
4200 Recurrent taxes on net wealth	0	0	0	0	0	0	0	0	0	0
4210 Individual	..	..	..	..	..	..	..	..	..	..
4220 Corporate	..	..	..	..	..	..	..	..	..	..
4300 Estate, inheritance and gift taxes	287	479	1 321	2 215	3 867	2 642	4 442	5 252	5 972	6 808
4310 Estate and inheritance taxes	287	479	1 321	2 215	3 867	2 642	4 442	5 252	5 972	6 808
Death duties	..	423	1 278	2 156	3 764	2 592	4 359	5 202	5 922	6 748

	1965	1980	1990	2000	2007	2010	2015	2020	2021	2022
Development land tax	..	42	6	0	0	0	0	0	0	0
Taxes on other capital transfers	..	14	37	59	50	50	50	50	50	50
Special tax on bank deposits	..	0	0	0	0	0	0	0	0	0
Betterment duty	..	0	0	0	0	0	0	0	0	0
Special charges	..	0	0	0	0	0	0	0	0	0
Special contribution	..	0	0	0	0	0	0	0	0	0
Equal pay on capital transfers	..	0	0	0	53	0	33	0	0	10
4320 Gift taxes	0	0	0	0	0	0	0	0	0	0
4400 Taxes on financial and capital transactions	76	630	1 755	8 367	14 634	9 098	13 791	13 187	18 654	21 670
Stamp duties	..	630	1 755	8 367	14 634	9 098	13 791	13 187	18 654	21 670
4500 Nonrecurrent taxes	0	0	0	0	0	0	147	233	364	430
4510 On net wealth	..	..	..	..	..	..	0	0	0	0
4520 Other nonrecurrent taxes	..	..	..	..	..	..	147	233	364	430
4600 Other recurrent taxes on property	0	0	0	0	0	0	0	0	0	0
5000 Taxes on goods and services	3 619	23 699	62 780	115 787	151 304	163 577	208 193	215 554	237 753	271 347
5100 Taxes on production, sale, transfer, etc	3 406	22 677	59 379	110 804	145 250	156 136	200 750	206 945	228 945	257 624
5110 General taxes	647	11 897	34 136	65 018	93 374	97 646	132 906	140 205	158 610	184 258
5111 Value added taxes	0	11 897	34 136	65 018	93 374	97 646	132 906	139 949	158 121	183 614
Value added tax	..	11 893	33 620	64 918	93 348	97 565	132 790	139 872	158 121	183 614
Adj. to VAT contribution	..	4	516	100	26	81	116	77	0	0
Purchase tax	..	0	0	0	0	0	0	0	0	0
5112 Sales tax	647	0	0	0	0	0	0	0	0	0
5113 Other	0	0	0	0	0	0	0	256	489	644
Digital services tax				..	..	..	..	256	489	644
5120 Taxes on specific goods and services	2 759	10 780	25 243	45 786	51 876	58 490	67 844	66 740	70 335	73 366
5121 Excises	2 383	8 616	19 707	37 315	40 427	45 454	47 294	44 880	48 304	47 831
Beer	..	1 029	2 220	2 813	3 042	3 278	3 294	3 062	3 552	3 680
Wines, spirits, cider and perry	..	1 513	2 627	3 751	5 008	6 075	7 385	9 084	9 334	8 866
Tobacco	..	2 735	5 541	7 666	7 862	9 076	9 190	9 790	10 254	10 079
Hydrocarbon oil	..	3 327	9 302	23 041	24 512	27 013	27 415	22 647	24 828	24 849
Other excise duty	..	12	17	0	0	0	0	0	0	0
Soft Drinks Levy			0	0	0	0	0	297	336	357
Sugar levy	..	12	0	44	3	12	10	0	0	0
5122 Profits of fiscal monopolies	0	0	0	0	0	0	0	0	0	0
5123 Customs and import duties	343	1 109	1 837	2 086	2 522	3 058	3 219	3 041	4 678	5 635
Custom duties	..	..	..	1 800	2 074	2 933	3 077	2 896	0	0
Import duties	..	855	1 722	0	0	0	0	0	0	0
Agricultural levies	..	254	115	286	338	0	0	0	0	0
Temporary charges of import	..	0	0	0	0	0	0	0	0	0
British Transport Police	..	0	0	0	110	125	142	145	145	145
Customs Duties - UK Receipts				0	0	0	0	0	4 533	5 490
5124 Taxes on exports	0	- 1	36	0	0	0	0	0	0	0
Levies on exports	..	- 1	36	..	..	..	..	..	..	..
5125 Taxes on investment goods	0	0	0	0	0	0	0	0	0	0
5126 Taxes on specific services	33	456	1 022	5 826	7 021	7 957	14 188	13 937	13 424	16 461
Betting and gaming	..	456	1 022	1 522	959	1 092	2 053	2 088	2 427	2 631
National Lottery contributions to fund	..	0	0	1 590	1 310	1 625	1 713	1 713	1 713	1 713
Air passenger duty	..	0	0	940	1 883	2 094	3 119	927	790	2 951
Insurance premium tax	..	0	0	1 707	2 306	2 401	3 294	6 306	6 627	7 341
Bank Levy - Stability Fee Scheme	..	0	0	0	0	0	3 369	2 214	1 266	1 308
Pensions Protection Fund Levy				0	498	665	562	619	529	436
Light Dues	..	0	0	67	65	80	78	70	72	81
5127 Other taxes on internat. trade and transactions	0	0	0	0	0	0	0	0	0	0
5128 Other taxes	0	600	2 641	559	1 906	2 021	3 143	4 882	3 929	3 439
Fossil fuel levy	..	0	875	56	0	0	0	0	0	0
European coal and steel levy	..	21	11	0	0	0	0	0	0	0
Gas levy	..	12	291	0	0	0	0	0	0	0
Car tax	..	83	1 464	0	0	0	0	0	0	0
Landfill tax	..	484	0	461	877	1 065	1 028	701	845	782
Climate change levy	..	0	0	0	690	666	1 761	1 779	1 929	2 094
Aggregates levy	..	0	0	0	339	290	354	360	411	375
Hydro benefit	..	0	0	42	0	0	0	0	0	0
Renewable energy obligations	..	0	0	0	0	0	0	0	0	0
Channel 4 advertising formula	..	0	0	0	0	0	0	0	0	0
Milk super levy	..	0	0	0	0	0	0	0	0	0
Contracts for Difference	..	0	0	0	0	0	0	2 042	744	- 10
Pension Protection Fund Levy				0	0	0	0	0	0	198
Plastic Packaging Tax				0	0	0	0	0	0	207
5130 Unallocable between 5110 and 5120	0	0	0	0	0	0	0	0	0	0
5200 Taxes on use of goods and perform activities	212	1 378	3 401	4 983	6 054	7 441	7 443	8 609	8 808	13 723
5210 Recurrent taxes	212	1 378	3 401	4 983	6 054	7 441	7 443	8 455	8 516	8 847

	1965	1980	1990	2000	2007	2010	2015	2020	2021	2022
5211 Paid by households: motor vehicles	118	729	1 841	2 996	4 096	4 561	3 970	4 755	4 922	5 202
Motor vehicle duty	..	726	1 837	2 992	4 096	4 561	3 970	4 755	4 922	5 202
Boat licences	..	3	4	4	0	0	0	0	0	0
Visa and Citizenship Fees				0	372	774	812	914	1 211	1 805
5212 Paid by others: motor vehicles	74	588	1 134	1 614	1 288	1 279	1 929	2 206	2 124	2 127
Motor vehicle levy	..	588	1 134	1 614	1 288	1 279	1 929	2 206	2 124	2 127
5213 Paid in respect of other goods	20	61	426	373	670	1 601	1 544	1 494	1 470	1 518
IBA levy	..	..	134	0	0	0	0	0	0	0
Telecommunications regulator fees	..	..	7	12	17	12	0	0	0	0
Gas regulator fees	..	..	2	0	0	0	0	0	0	0
Electricity regulator fees	..	..	5	0	0	0	0	0	0	0
Water regulator fees	..	..	6	11	11	12	27	27	24	24
Rail regulator fees	..	..	0	14	12	12	12	12	12	12
Company registration surplus fees	..	..	12	0	0	0	0	0	0	0
Consumer and credit act fees	..	..	163	119	281	480	480	480	480	480
Levy funded bodies	..	..	97	217	349	1 040	970	947	925	879
1936 Tithe Act payments	..	..	0	0	0	0	0	0	0	0
Air travel organiser license fees	..	..	0	0	0	45	55	28	29	60
Economic Crime Levy				0	0	0	0	0	0	63
Registers of Scotland				8	16	8	15	16	17	0
UK Emisions Trading Scheme (ETS)				0	0	0	0	0	0	4 347
5220 Nonrecurrent taxes	0	0	0	0	0	0	0	154	292	4 876
UK Emissions Trading Scheme (ETS)				0	0	0	0	0	0	4 347
Immigration Skills Charge	..	..	..	..	..	..	..	154	292	529
5300 Unallocable between 5100 and 5200	1	- 356	0	0	0	0	0	0	0	0
6000 Other taxes	0	0	9 017	0	0	0	0	0	0	0
6100 Paid solely by business	..	..	0	..	..	..	..	..	..	..
6200 Other	..	..	9 017	1 800	2 074	2 933	3 077	2 896	..	..
Community charge	..	..	9 017	..	..	..	..	..	..	..
Custom duties collected for the EU	..	..	..	1 800	2 074	2 933	3 077	2 896	..	..
Non-wastable tax credits against 1110	..	..	7 454	4 651	20 030	28 879	28 539	15 296	10 929	8 910
Tax expenditure component	..	..	6 973	1 233	4 414	5 542	2 571	1 378	984	803
Transfer component	..	..	481	3 418	15 617	23 338	25 968	13 918	9 945	8 107
Non-wastable tax credits against 1210	..	..	0	0	918	1 313	3 273	8 091	8 025	9 137
Tax expenditure component	..	..	0	..	654	915	1 136	2 423	2 761	3 027
Transfer component	..	..	0	..	264	398	2 137	5 668	5 263	6 110
Total tax revenue on cash basis	10 945	81 153	202 400	356 336	509 032	509 501	601 185	639 219	779 924	860 440
Total tax revenue on accrual basis	..	..	202 368	359 483	509 222	515 462	611 491	690 452	781 763	887 623
Additional taxes included in National Accounts	..	..	1 323	2 062	4 072	4 731	7 261	10 147	10 476	11 004
Taxes excluded from National Accounts	..	..	0	0	0	0	0	0	0	0
Difference in treatment of tax credits	..	..	6 973	1 233	5 068	6 457	3 707	3 802	3 746	3 829
Capital transfer for uncollected revenue	..	..	0	0	0	0	0	0	0	0
Voluntary social security contributions	..	..	3 288	8 103	18 629	21 217	25 025	38 013	40 449	42 616
Miscellaneous differences	..	..	0	0	0	0	0	0	0	0
National Accounts: Taxes and actual social contributions	..	..	213 952	370 881	536 991	547 867	647 484	742 414	836 434	945 072
Imputed social contributions	..	..	3 966	3 464	2 125	2 580	1 863	1 205	1 249	1 185
National Accounts: Taxes and all social contributions	..	..	217 918	374 345	539 116	550 447	649 347	743 619	837 683	946 257

.. Not available

Note: Year ending 31st December.

From 1990 data are on accrual basis.

Supranational taxes reported by the United Kingdom continue to be reported for 2020 in Revenue Statistics as in previous years. From 2021, at the end of the Brexit transition period, this will come to an end and taxes subsequently introduced by the United Kingdom will be reflected in the appropriate tax category at the national or subnational levels of government, as appropriate.

Heading 1210: The corporate tax figures include company income tax from 1990 onwards.

Heading 2000: Includes some voluntary contributions which cannot be separately identified.

Heading 5113: Following the SNA 2008 classification, the digital services tax is classified by the ONS as a Tax on imports excluding VAT and import duties (D.2122). However, it is classified in Revenue Statistics in the category Taxes on turnover and other general taxes on goods and services (5113) for consistency across OECD countries reporting the same type of tax.

Heading 6200: The community charge replaced domestic rates in Scotland in April 1989 and was extended to England and Wales in April 1990. This tax has been classified in heading 6200 as it is a lump-sum tax levied on each adult in a household (domestic rates are classified in heading 4100). Headings for non-wastable tax credits 1110 and 1210 are consistent with the guidelines, and the figures in the data are treated accordingly. The following method is adopted separately for Working Families 'Tax Credit and Disabled Persons Tax Credit' paid from 1999 to 2003. For each calendar year, a random sample of awards over-lapping the quarter is taken. Each recipient family's income tax liability for the fiscal year within which the quarter falls is calculated, based on the earned income reported for the award (uprated to the middle of the overlap period). And the result multiplied by the number of days in the overlap period divided by 365. The tax expenditure component is defined as the minimum of this amount and the total amount of award paid in the overlap period. The total amount of award paid and the tax expenditure component are each summed over the sample cases, and the ratio is taken as the tax expenditure ration for the quarter. From 2003, the equivalent breakdown for Child and Working tax credits is based on household survey data. Survey data is used to estimate the breakdown into the tax expenditure and the transfer components for the other smaller tax credits.

The United Kingdom Personal Tax Credit information presented in Revenue Statistics is on a cash basis (rather than an accrual basis as for the rest of the data). PTC information on a financial year basis has been used as a proxy for calendar year. Please note that since 2015-16 tax credits is no longer split into tax expenditure and transfer component. The split for years after 2014-15 is estimated by applying the 2014-15 split to total personal tax credits expenditure. The sum of tax expenditure and transfer components may not match the total due to rounding. Total values are consistent with published figures available here: https://www.gov.uk/government/statistics/hmrc-tax-and-nics-receipts-for-the-uk.

Please note that the sum of the corporate tax credit (CTC) components in the United Kingdom may not match total CTC's due to rounding. The CTC information presented in Revenue Statistics is on a cash basis (rather than an accrual basis as for the rest of the data). CTC information on a financial year basis has been used as a proxy for calendar year. Please note that the breakdown of total CTCs from 2002/03 to 2010/11 have been estimated using historic proportional splits applied to total published CTC information. Total values are consistent with published figures available here: https://www.gov.uk/government/statistics/hmrc-tax-and-nics-receipts-for-the-uk.

Source: National Income and Expenditure; Central Statistical Office; Annual reports of His Majesty's Revenue and Customs.

Table 5.38. United States: Details of tax revenue, 1965-2022

Million USD

	1965	1980	1990	2000	2007	2010	2015	2020	2021	2022
Total tax revenue	167 022	730 672	1 552 413	2 900 519	3 868 612	3 517 144	4 772 710	5 452 240	6 301 741	7 107 112
1000 Taxes on income, profits and capital gains	80 284	364 137	701 731	1 453 865	1 865 205	1 488 699	2 315 228	2 539 776	3 122 063	3 654 869
1100 Of individuals	52 894	285 513	584 733	1 224 538	1 479 085	1 223 218	1 930 079	2 245 147	2 731 244	3 127 332
1110 On income and profits	50 401	272 879	552 859	1 088 967	1 326 736	1 163 737	1 754 568	2 016 852	2 284 907	2 788 194
Individual income tax federal	46 492	233 269	449 239	895 677	1 062 755	910 874	1 413 376	1 600 026	1 824 045	2 263 775
Individual income tax state and local govt.	3 909	39 610	103 620	193 290	263 981	252 863	341 192	416 826	460 862	524 419
1120 On capital gains	2 493	12 634	31 874	135 571	152 349	59 481	175 511	228 295	446 337	339 138
Capital gains federal	2 300	10 800	25 900	111 507	122 036	46 557	141 381	181 113	356 312	275 351
Capital gains tax state and local govt.	193	1 834	5 974	24 064	30 313	12 924	34 130	47 182	90 025	63 787
1200 Corporate	27 390	78 624	116 998	229 327	386 119	265 481	385 150	294 629	390 818	527 536
1210 On profits	26 745	73 586	106 134	170 835	330 597	240 445	337 631	253 909	324 712	472 339
Corporate income tax federal	24 861	60 525	85 736	144 590	281 040	198 698	288 486	191 110	232 553	330 340
Corporate income tax state and local govt.	1 884	13 061	20 398	26 245	49 556	41 747	49 145	62 799	92 159	142 000
1220 On capital gains	645	5 038	10 864	58 492	55 523	25 036	47 519	40 720	66 106	55 197
Capital gains tax corp. federal	600	4 143	8 776	49 506	47 200	20 689	40 602	30 649	47 344	38 603
Capital gains tax corp. state and local govt.	45	895	2 088	8 986	8 323	4 347	6 917	10 071	18 762	16 594
1300 Unallocable between 1100 and 1200	0	0	0	0	0	0	0	0	0	0
2000 Social security contributions	22 192	159 763	396 972	683 104	907 357	917 409	1 125 493	1 327 683	1 430 254	1 556 656
2100 Employees	8 459	67 022	173 860	305 555	400 941	406 404	502 103	605 379	657 954	716 437
Federal insurance contribution Act tax	8 084	66 221	..	..	..	..	..	..	..	..
Less refund federal	- 192	- 507	..	..	..	..	..	..	..	..
Railroad retirement taxes federal	322	590	..	..	..	..	..	..	..	..
Fed. hosp. insur. recpts from railroad retir.	0	111	..	..	..	..	..	..	..	..
Unemployment state tax federal	20	127	..	..	..	..	..	..	..	..
Temp. disability insurance state and local	225	480	..	..	..	..	..	..	..	..
2110 On a payroll basis	..	..	..	..	..	..	..	..	..	..
2120 On an income tax basis	..	..	..	..	..	..	..	..	..	..
2200 Employers	12 703	87 019	204 102	343 184	456 602	461 702	561 936	651 974	699 646	757 071
Federal insurance contributions act tax	7 802	64 768	..	..	..	..	..	..	..	..
Railroad retirement taxes federal	314	1 722	..	..	..	..	..	..	..	..
Fed. hosp. insur. recpts from railroad retir.	0	111	..	..	..	..	..	..	..	..
Military service credit federal	14	652	..	..	..	..	..	..	..	..
Old-age dis. hosp. insur. fed. employer contr.	282	1 453	..	..	..	..	..	..	..	..
Unemployment state tax federal	3 032	11 788	..	..	..	..	..	..	..	..
Federal unemployment tax Act	615	3 246	..	..	..	..	..	..	..	..
Railroad unempl. insurance Act tax federal	152	175	..	..	..	..	..	..	..	..
Workmen's compensation state and local	484	3 039	..	..	..	..	..	..	..	..
Temp. disability insurance state and local	8	65	..	..	..	..	..	..	..	..
2210 On a payroll basis of employers SSC	..	..	..	..	..	..	..	..	..	..
2220 On an income tax basis of employers SSC	..	..	..	..	..	..	..	..	..	..
2300 Selfemployed or nonemployed	1 030	5 722	19 010	34 365	49 814	49 303	61 454	70 330	72 654	83 148
Federal old-age survivors trust	0	4 250	..	..	..	..	..	..	..	..
Federal disability insurance trust	1 030	733	..	..	..	..	..	..	..	..
Federal hospital insurance trust	0	739	..	..	..	..	..	..	..	..
2310 On a payroll basis of self/non-employed SSC	..	..	..	..	..	..	..	..	..	..
2320 On an income tax basis of self/non-employed SSC	..	..	..	..	..	..	..	..	..	..
2400 Unallocable between 2100, 2200 and 2300	0	0	0	0	0	0	0	0	0	0
2410 On a payroll basis unallocable between 2100, 2200 and 2300 SSC	..	..	..	..	..	..	..	..	..	..
2420 On an income tax basis unallocable between 2100, 2200 and 2300 SSC	..	..	..	..	..	..	..	..	..	..
3000 Taxes on payroll and workforce	0	0	0	0	285	2 285	1 774	3 377	3 354	3 634
4000 Taxes on property	26 529	77 913	182 408	299 546	463 052	473 422	537 963	660 674	691 567	736 848
4100 Recurrent taxes on immovable property	22 918	68 499	161 533	254 669	403 688	438 588	489 332	607 621	621 672	660 026
4110 Households	8 548	28 975	..	..	..	..	..	..	..	..
Property tax state and local	8 548	28 975	..	..	..	..	..	..	..	..
Other	0	0	..	..	..	..	..	..	..	..
4120 Others	14 370	39 524	..	..	..	..	..	..	..	..
Property tax state and local	14 370	39 524	..	..	..	..	..	..	..	..
Other	0	0	..	..	..	..	..	..	..	..
4200 Recurrent taxes on net wealth	0	0	0	0	0	0	0	0	0	0
4210 Individual	..	..	..	..	..	..	..	..	..	..
4220 Corporate	..	..	..	..	..	..	..	..	..	..
4300 Estate, inheritance and gift taxes	3 447	8 425	15 755	35 640	31 927	19 699	25 548	25 281	34 410	40 634
4310 Estate and inheritance taxes	3 080	8 149	..	..	..	..	..	..	..	..
Estate tax less refund federal	2 427	6 181	..	..	..	..	..	..	..	..

	1965	1980	1990	2000	2007	2010	2015	2020	2021	2022
Estate tax state and local govt.	653	1 968	..	..	..	..	..	..	..	..
4320 Gift taxes	367	276	..	..	..	..	..	..	..	..
Gift tax less refund federal	289	209	..	..	..	..	..	..	..	..
Gift tax calculate state and local govt.	78	67	..	..	..	..	..	..	..	..
4400 Taxes on financial and capital transactions	164	989	2 148	4 389	20 503	7 460	14 614	17 248	24 547	24 594
Interest equalisation tax federal	15	0	..	..	..	..	..	..	..	..
Document and stock transfer state and local	149	989	2 148	4 389	20 503	7 460	14 614	17 248	24 547	24 594
4500 Nonrecurrent taxes	0	0	0	0	0	0	0	0	0	0
4510 On net wealth	..	..	..	..	..	..	..	0	0	0
4520 Other nonrecurrent taxes	..	..	..	..	..	..	..	..	..	..
4600 Other recurrent taxes on property	0	0	2 972	4 848	6 934	7 675	8 468	10 523	10 938	11 594
5000 Taxes on goods and services	38 017	128 844	271 301	464 004	632 713	635 329	792 251	920 730	1 054 503	1 155 106
5100 Taxes on production, sale, transfer, etc	33 300	111 810	235 233	404 093	540 291	546 710	694 964	803 229	919 215	1 005 659
5110 General taxes	8 016	51 328	125 575	221 358	301 403	295 123	373 249	443 672	514 506	570 794
5111 Value added taxes	0	0	0	0	0	0	0	0	0	0
5112 Sales tax	8 016	51 328	125 575	221 358	301 403	295 123	373 249	443 672	514 506	570 794
General sales - general receipts state and local	7 981	51 328	125 575	221 358	301 403	295 123	373 249	443 672	514 506	570 794
Other state and local	35	0	0	0	0	0	0	0	0	0
5113 Other	0	0	0	0	0	0	0	0	0	0
5120 Taxes on specific goods and services	25 284	60 482	109 658	182 735	238 888	251 587	321 715	359 557	404 709	434 864
5121 Excises	21 209	45 471	64 953	108 600	137 373	146 582	156 995	157 642	174 619	171 574
Alcohol taxes federal govt.	3 689	5 601	5 228	8 120	9 348	9 496	10 367	10 790	11 595	11 550
Tobacco taxes federal govt.	2 142	2 443	4 217	7 216	7 531	16 614	14 450	12 354	12 136	11 259
Airport, airway, highway federal	3 559	6 411	0	0	0	0	0	0	0	0
Manufacturer's excise taxes federal govt.	2 867	6 122	0	0	0	0	0	0	0	0
Sugar tax federal govt.	97	0	0	0	0	0	0	0	0	0
Other taxes excise federal govt.	889	2	0	0	0	0	0	0	0	0
Undistributed tax deposits federal government	- 11	152	0	0	0	0	0	0	0	0
Other taxes excise and undist. fed.govt. -	0	0	13 316	32 005	31 747	26 913	35 287	31 499	40 815	35 634
Less special tax liquor occupations federal	- 22	- 21	0	0	0	0	0	0	0	0
Other federal (refunds)	- 7	- 32	0	0	0	0	0	0	0	0
Alcohol taxes state and local govt.	949	2 642	3 577	4 485	5 684	6 197	7 170	7 567	8 784	9 341
Tobacco taxes state and local govt.	1 386	3 874	6 009	8 726	16 433	18 611	17 973	19 047	19 049	17 839
Public utilities state and local govt.	871	5 888	11 814	17 989	27 879	28 892	28 043	27 793	28 383	31 495
Motor fuel taxes state and local govt.	4 331	9 822	20 792	31 373	38 682	39 634	44 743	51 034	55 640	56 611
Other state and local taxes	469	2 295	0	0	0	0	0	0	0	0
Coal tonnage tax federal govt.	0	272	0	0	0	0	0	0	0	0
Hazardous substances tax federal	0	0	0	0	0	0	0	0	0	0
Transportation fuels tax federal	0	0	0	0	0	0	0	0	0	0
Boat fuels and equipment tax federal	0	0	0	0	0	0	0	0	0	0
Waste site deposits tax federal	0	0	0	0	0	0	0	0	0	0
Leaking underground storage federal	0	0	0	0	0	0	0	0	0	0
Vaccine injury compens. federal	0	0	0	0	0	0	0	0	0	0
Ozone depletion tax federal	0	0	0	0	0	0	0	0	0	0
Oil spill liability federal	0	0	0	0	0	0	0	0	0	0
Luxury tax federal govt.	0	0	0	0	0	0	0	0	0	0
5122 Profits of fiscal monopolies	275	608	..	..	..	..	..	..	..	..
Liquor store revenue state and local govt.	1 447	3 200	..	..	..	..	..	..	..	..
Liquor store expend. state and local govt.	- 1 172	- 2 592	..	..	..	..	..	..	..	..
5123 Customs and import duties	1 442	7 436	17 490	21 123	28 793	28 603	38 123	68 627	89 101	102 333
Custom duties federal	1 442	7 436	17 490	21 123	28 793	28 603	38 123	68 627	89 101	102 333
Petroleum import fees federal govt.	0	0	0	0	0	0	0	0	0	0
5124 Taxes on exports	0	0	0	0	0	0	0	0	0	0
5125 Taxes on investment goods	0	0	0	0	0	0	0	0	0	0
5126 Taxes on specific services	2 358	6 967	8 895	13 857	23 639	23 642	28 608	33 753	39 302	44 420
Amusements state and local govt.	23	234	671	3 668	7 105	7 082	8 230	7 119	11 259	12 829
Parimutuels state and local govt.	386	731	659	326	328	206	184	204	236	236
Transportation of persons federal	126	1 601	0	0	0	0	0	0	0	0
Transport of property	0	92	0	0	0	0	0	0	0	0
General and toll telephone federal	1 079	1 118	0	0	0	0	0	0	0	0
Foreign insurance policies federal	0	75	0	0	0	0	0	0	0	0
Insurance state and local govt.	744	3 113	7 565	9 863	16 206	16 354	20 194	26 430	27 807	31 355
Employee pension plans federal	0	3	0	0	0	0	0	0	0	0
Inland waterway tax federal	0	0	0	0	0	0	0	0	0	0
Ship departure tax federal	0	0	0	0	0	0	0	0	0	0
5127 Other taxes on internat. trade and transactions	0	0	0	0	0	0	0	0	0	0
5128 Other taxes	0	0	18 320	39 155	49 083	52 760	97 989	99 536	101 687	116 538
5130 Unallocable between 5110 and 5120	0	0	0	0	0	0	0	0	0	0
5200 Taxes on use of goods and perform activities	4 717	17 034	36 068	59 910	92 422	88 619	97 287	117 501	135 289	149 448
5210 Recurrent taxes	3 490	9 501	21 262	37 114	68 547	66 440	74 957	90 766	98 048	101 006
5211 Paid by households: motor vehicles	1 211	3 370	8 104	11 409	14 996	16 294	18 820	21 354	22 577	22 911

	1965	1980	1990	2000	2007	2010	2015	2020	2021	2022
Motor vehicle regis. license st. and loc.	1 056	2 981	..	..	..	..	..	..	..	..
Motor vehicle oper. license st. and loc.	152	389	..	..	..	..	..	..	..	..
Other motor vehicle	3	0	..	..	..	..	..	..	..	..
5212 Paid by others: motor vehicles	937	2 343	3 564	6 688	8 484	9 108	10 697	12 210	12 819	13 053
Motor vehicle regis. license st. and loc.	937	2 343	..	..	..	..	..	..	..	..
Motor vehicle oper. license st. and loc.	0	0	..	..	..	..	..	..	..	..
5213 Paid in respect of other goods	1 342	3 788	9 594	19 017	45 067	41 038	45 441	57 202	62 652	65 043
Misc. fees permit license federal	19	0	0	0	0	0	0	0	0	0
Special tax liquor occupations federal	22	21	0	0	0	0	0	0	0	0
Use tax of certain vehicles federal	99	277	0	0	0	0	0	0	0	0
Use of internat. travel facilities federal	0	92	0	0	0	0	0	0	0	0
Use tax of aircraft federal	0	21	0	0	0	0	0	0	0	0
Corporation in general license st. and loc.	528	1 388	3 147	6 736	10 658	9 473	6 605	9 202	10 965	11 441
Alcoholic beverage license tax st. and loc.	133	179	264	308	608	596	822	984	1 044	1 110
Public utilities license tax st. and loc.	30	130	270	395	1 903	1 468	1 689	1 768	1 776	1 852
Amusements license taxes st. and loc.	7	69	202	196	966	638	714	552	622	699
Occupation and business license st. and loc.	349	1 113	3 512	7 651	16 484	17 812	20 543	24 715	25 330	26 025
Wagering occupation tax federal	7	12	0	0	0	0	0	0	0	0
Other license taxes st. and loc.	10	69	2 118	3 619	14 302	10 900	14 906	19 789	22 720	23 729
Hunting and fishing license taxes st. and loc.	138	417	82	112	146	151	161	192	196	187
Other	0	0	0	0	0	0	0	0	0	0
5220 Nonrecurrent taxes	1 227	7 533	14 806	22 796	23 875	22 179	22 330	26 735	37 241	48 441
Severance state and local govt.	503	4 167	5 224	5 285	12 895	11 751	9 833	9 326	18 622	29 778
Poll taxes state and local govt.	9	0	0	0	0	0	0	0	0	0
Other taxes state and local govt.	715	3 366	9 582	17 511	10 980	10 428	12 497	17 410	18 619	18 663
5300 Unallocable between 5100 and 5200	0	0	0	0	0	0	0	0	0	0
6000 Other taxes	0	15	0	0	0	0	0	0	0	0
6100 Paid solely by business	..	0	..	..	..	..	..	..	..	..
6200 Other	..	15	..	..	..	..	..	..	..	..
Non-wastable tax credits against 1110	..	..	6 155	36 511	90 439	171 630	156 656	525 970	562 230	452 130
Tax expenditure component	..	..	1 800	9 602	35 910	69 870	42 826	92 340	111 520	127 960
Transfer component	..	..	4 355	26 909	54 529	101 760	113 830	433 630	450 710	324 170
Non-wastable tax credits against 1210	..	..	..	..	..	250	577	660	300	340
Tax expenditure component	..	..	..	..	..	240	527	630	300	300
Transfer component	..	..	..	..	..	10	50	30	0	40
Unallocable transfer component	..	..	..	..	..	2 420	4 890	2 600	3 980	3 250
Total tax revenue on cash basis	167 022	730 672	..	..	..	..	..	..	..	..
Total tax revenue on accrual basis	..	..	..	..	..	..	..	..	..	..
Additional taxes included in National Accounts	..	..	..	..	..	..	..	..	..	..
Taxes excluded from National Accounts	..	..	..	..	..	..	..	..	..	..
Difference in treatment of tax credits	..	..	..	..	..	..	..	..	..	..
Capital transfer for uncollected revenue	..	..	..	..	..	..	..	..	..	..
Voluntary social security contributions	..	..	11 719	22 562	51 635	61 833	74 886	118 059	124 053	141 377
Miscellaneous differences	..	..	..	..	..	..	..	..	..	..
National Accounts: Taxes and actual social contributions	..	..	1 564 132	2 923 081	3 920 247	3 578 977	4 847 596	5 570 299	6 425 794	7 248 489
Imputed social contributions	..	..	3 384	3 727	7 134	9 428	9 636	8 838	9 029	9 407
National Accounts: Taxes and all social contributions	..	..	1 567 516	2 926 808	3 927 381	3 588 405	4 857 232	5 579 137	6 434 822	7 257 896

.. Not available

Note: From 1990, data are on a year ending 31st December basis. For years up to and including 1976 the dated covered fiscal years ending 30th June. Between 1977 and 1989, Federal government data covered fiscal years ending 30th September and State & Local government data covered fiscal years ending 30th June.

From 1990, data are on accrual basis. There are no separate estimates for the State and Local capital gains tax revenues.

Heading 5121: In 1994 through 1996, some Federal excise taxes formerly shown separately were included in 'Other taxes,excises and undistributed, Federal government'.

Source: Federal estimates are derived from the US Budget, the Final Monthly Treasury Statement and the Annual Report of the US Treasury Department. The State and Local estimates are derived from Government Finances, published by the Bureau of the Census.

Memorandum tables

Table 5.39 shows different sources for financing social benefits, beyond compulsory social security contributions reported in section 5.1. In addition, this table shows also data on other taxes, on voluntary contributions to government and on compulsory contributions to private sector.

Table 5.40 shows social security contributions and payroll taxes paid by government. During the revision of the Interpretative Guide in 1984, the question arose of how to treat taxes paid by government. The two most prominent examples of such taxes are social security contributions and payroll taxes paid by government in respect of its employees. After a long discussion, it was decided that the data shown in this publication should continue to include taxes paid by government (see §7 of the Interpretative Guide in Annex A).

Whilst it was recognised that for certain purposes (e.g. to show the cash flow to the government sector from the private sector) it would be appropriate to eliminate taxes paid by one sector of government to another or tax payments between different units of the same sector of government, the view was taken that to record tax flows in the context of the economy as a whole required that taxes paid by government should be included in the data. This treatment ensures that the different resource flows of an economy, including the calculation of the output of government, are measured consistently in after-tax units. Nevertheless, it was decided that data on identifiable taxes paid by government should be separately identified in a memorandum item. This is the purpose of the country tables that follow.

The data that are reproduced in the following tables refer to actual compulsory payments made by general government in respect of their employees. Fictive, voluntary, and imputed contributions are excluded from these data. The definitions of social security contributions, payroll taxes and general government are those set out in §40 to §46, §47 and §3 to §4 of the Interpretative Guide. Information on the other taxes paid by government (namely property taxes and consumption taxes) is not available for most countries, although it is believed that in all countries taxes based upon payroll are the most important taxes paid by government. In many cases, the data are estimates and are not always constructed on a basis consistent with that used in the main tables.

Table 5.39. Financing social benefits, national currency

	1965	1980	1990	2000	2007	2010	2015	2020	2021	2022
Australia, million AUD										
Contribution under 2000 heading	..	..	..	..	..	..	..	..	..	..
Other taxes	..	..	..	..	..	..	..	..	..	..
Voluntary contributions to government	..	..	..	..	..	..	..	..	..	..
Compulsory contributions to private sector	..	..	..	..	..	..	..	..	..	..
Total	0	0	0	0	0	0	0	0	0	0
Austria, million EUR										
Contribution under 2000 heading	1 548	9 200	17 763	30 510	38 453	41 423	49 867	59 094	62 312	65 893
Other taxes	0	0	0	0	0	0	0	0	0	0
Voluntary contributions to government	32	135	141	206	256	339	321	344	358	373
Compulsory contributions to private sector	0	0	0	0	0	0	0	0	0	0
Total	1 580	9 335	17 904	30 716	38 709	41 762	50 188	59 438	62 670	66 266
Belgium, million EUR										
Contribution under 2000 heading	2 018	10 798	23 386	34 865	45 929	50 674	58 812	62 293	65 580	71 520
Other taxes	0	171	644	5 375	13 659	16 772	12 292	20 009	23 415	22 914
Voluntary contributions to government	0	41	52	58	57	59	70	82	83	72
Compulsory contributions to private sector	0	0	0	0	0	0	0	0	0	0
Total	2 018	11 009	24 082	40 298	59 644	67 505	71 174	82 384	89 078	94 506
Canada, million CAD										
Contribution under 2000 heading	854	10 649	29 653	53 109	73 722	76 787	96 371	107 496	120 919	133 578
Other taxes	1 199	0	0	0	0	0	0	0	0	0
Voluntary contributions to government	0	0	0	0	0	0	0	0	0	0
Compulsory contributions to private sector	0	0	0	0	0	0	0	0	0	0
Total	2 053	10 649	29 653	53 109	73 722	76 787	96 371	107 496	120 919	133 578
Chile, million CLP										
Contribution under 2000 heading	..	..	159 559	576 758	1 148 647	1 493 987	2 252 490	3 104 866	2 815 090	2 585 421
Other taxes	..	..	0	0	0	0	0	0	0	0
Voluntary contributions to government	..	..	0	0	0	0	0	0	0	0
Compulsory contributions to private sector	..	..	328 102	2 021 631	3 808 658	5 408 703	8 914 415	12 194 451	13 597 362	15 217 010
Total	..	..	487 661	2 598 389	4 957 305	6 902 690	11 166 905	15 299 318	16 412 451	17 802 431
Colombia, million COP										
Contribution under 2000 heading	..	..	203 596	4 989 000	9 694 000	11 478 085	13 585 138	18 389 481	21 673 981	23 908 538
Other taxes	..	..	0	0	0	0	0	0	0	0
Voluntary contributions to government	..	..	0	0	0	0	0	0	0	0
Compulsory contributions to private sector	..	..	0	0	18 667 073	27 354 493	31 112 566	40 888 910	46 914 226	53 874 632
Total	..	..	203 596	4 989 000	28 361 073	38 832 579	44 697 703	59 278 391	68 588 208	77 783 170
Costa Rica, million CRC										
Contribution under 2000 heading	..	..	33 990	297 069	885 053	1 450 531	2 305 133	2 971 589	3 605 731	3 925 692
Other taxes	..	..	..	..	..	..	..	..	..	..
Voluntary contributions to government	..	..	..	..	..	..	..	..	..	..
Compulsory contributions to private sector	..	..	..	..	..	..	..	..	..	..
Total	..	..	33 990	297 069	885 053	1 450 531	2 305 133	2 971 589	3 605 731	3 925 692
Czechia, million CZK										
Contribution under 2000 heading	..	..	..	341 544	573 417	576 029	659 743	901 670	1004 804	1 074 201
Other taxes	..	..	..	0	0	0	0	0	0	0
Voluntary contributions to government	..	..	..	1 099	974	661	386	537	573	618
Compulsory contributions to private sector	..	..	..	2 837	5 757	6 094	6 741	9 048	9 539	10 150
Total	..	..	..	345 480	580 148	582 784	666 871	911 255	1014 916	1 084 969
Denmark, million DKK										
Contribution under 2000 heading	690	710	101	8 453	2 030	2 280	1 874	2156	2 493	2 340
Other taxes	0	0	0	0	0	0	0	0	0	0
Voluntary contributions to government	0	1 673	8 087	16 633	17 061	17 192	14 721	14 873	15 277	14 844
Compulsory contributions to private sector	145	554	1 278	1 445	4 526	3 847	2 946	3 024	3 308	3 492
Total	835	2 937	9 466	26 531	23 618	23 319	19 541	20 053	21 078	20 676

	1965	1980	1990	2000	2007	2010	2015	2020	2021	2022
Estonia, million EUR										
Contribution under 2000 heading	..	..	..	674	1 683	1 879	2 300	3 331	3 652	4 122
Other taxes	..	..	..	0	0	0	0	0	0	0
Voluntary contributions to government	..	..	..	0	0	0	0	0	0	0
Compulsory contributions to private sector	..	..	..	1	341	38	389	342	311	288
Total	..	..	..	674	2 024	1 918	2 689	3 673	3 962	4 410
Finland, million EUR										
Contribution under 2000 heading	93	2 776	10 012	15 756	21 384	22 648	26 639	27 326	30 186	31 954
Other taxes	47	22	0	404	0	0	0	0	0	0
Voluntary contributions to government	0	262	632	236	228	254	303	235	261	246
Compulsory contributions to private sector	0	123	431	532	653	619	673	619	637	610
Total	140	3 183	11 075	16 928	22 265	23 521	27 615	28 180	31 084	32 810
France, million EUR										
Contribution under 2000 heading	8 408	77 462	190 784	231 768	305 924	322 078	368 660	346 095	372 809	395 489
Other taxes	0	262	3 387	81 170	127 714	137 592	170 410	234 449	254 310	272 657
Voluntary contributions to government	0	0	0	0	0	0	0	0	0	0
Compulsory contributions to private sector	0	0	0	0	0	0	0	0	0	0
Total	8 408	77 724	194 091	312 938	433 638	459 670	539 070	580 544	627 119	668 146
Germany, million EUR										
Contribution under 2000 heading	19 876	98 659	170 449	299 440	320 750	354 320	424 842	512 279	534 374	567 083
Other taxes	0	0	0	0	0	0	0	0	0	0
Voluntary contributions to government	1 946	8 441	13 002	23 329	21 409	5 102	6 068	7 399	7 937	8 295
Compulsory contributions to private sector	107	690	1 462	6 120	8 243	9 386	11 202	15 465	16 224	17 368
Total	21 929	107 791	184 914	328 889	350 402	368 808	442 112	535 143	558 535	592 746
Greece, million EUR										
Contribution under 2000 heading	37	485	3 466	14 284	24 940	24 748	18 807	21 352	23 417	25 186
Other taxes	8	0	0	0	0	0	0	0	0	0
Voluntary contributions to government	0	0	0	0	0	0	0	0	0	0
Compulsory contributions to private sector	0	0	0	0	0	0	0	0	0	0
Total	44	485	3 466	14 284	24 940	24 748	18 807	21 352	23 417	25 186
Hungary, million HUF										
Contribution under 2000 heading	..	..	..	1 506 755	3 402 194	3 179 509	4 433 464	5 364 400	5 781 454	6 481 845
Other taxes	..	..	..	188 413	85 058	78 629	294 313	128 079	134 966	167 774
Voluntary contributions to government	..	..	..	1 273	1 762	1 693	1 229	953	963	1045
Compulsory contributions to private sector	..	..	..	62 836	190 331	279 814	0	0	0	0
Total	..	..	..	1 759 277	3 679 344	3 539 645	4 729 006	5 493 432	5 917 383	6 650 664
Iceland, million ISK										
Contribution under 2000 heading	5	102	3 607	19 680	39 594	63 599	79 707	88 364	97 414	115 564
Other taxes	0	1 047	20 571	26 732	52 444	77 472	97 987	259 588	277 008	239 643
Voluntary contributions to government	0	0	0	0	0	0	0	0	0	0
Compulsory contributions to private sector	0	459	13 454	48 847	118 117	95 438	139 792	191 784	207 998	238 749
Total	5	1 608	37 632	95 260	210 155	236 509	317 486	539 736	582 420	593 956
Ireland, million EUR										
Contribution under 2000 heading	21	578	1 729	3 966	8 143	8 458	9 999	12 285	13 618	15 967
Other taxes	0	0	0	0	0	0	0	0	0	0
Voluntary contributions to government	0	0	0	0	0	0	0	0	0	0
Compulsory contributions to private sector	0	0	0	0	0	0	0	0	0	0
Total	21	578	1 729	3 966	8 143	8 458	9 999	12 285	13 618	15 967
Israel, million ILS										
Contribution under 2000 heading	..	..	..	27 565	37 909	45 343	59 561	73 031	79 602	88 775
Other taxes	..	..	..	0	0	0	0	0	0	0
Voluntary contributions to government	..	..	..	0	0	0	0	0	0	0
Compulsory contributions to private sector	..	..	..	0	0	9 100	28 700	39 200	43 500	49 100
Total	..	..	..	27 565	37 909	54 443	88 261	112 231	123 102	137 875
Italy, million EUR										
Contribution under 2000 heading	1 881	22 976	87 256	143 629	200 772	209 122	214 376	224 741	240 690	256 430
Other taxes	0	0	0	0	0	0	0	0	0	0
Voluntary contributions to government	0	0	0	464	567	561	750	763	804	924
Compulsory contributions to private sector	0	0	0	0	0	0	0	0	0	0
Total	1 881	22 976	87 256	144 093	201 339	209 683	215 126	225 504	241 494	257 354

	1965	1980	1990	2000	2007	2010	2015	2020	2021	2022
Japan, billion JPY										
Contribution under 2000 heading	1 344	18 178	34 613	47 968	53 325	54 461	64 464	71 562	73 702	75 458
Other taxes	0	0	0	0	0	0	0	0	0	0
Voluntary contributions to government	0	0	0	0	0	0	0	0	0	0
Compulsory contributions to private sector	0	0	0	0	0	0	0	0	0	0
Total	1 344	18 178	34 613	47 968	53 325	54 461	64 464	71 562	73 702	75 458
Korea, billion KRW										
Contribution under 2000 heading	..	73	3 760	22 759	53 588	69 090	104 693	150 854	162 209	176 747
Other taxes	..	0	0	0	0	0	0	0	0	0
Voluntary contributions to government	..	0	0	0	0	0	0	0	0	0
Compulsory contributions to private sector	..	0	0	0	0	0	0	0	0	0
Total	..	73	3 760	22 759	53 588	69 090	104 693	150 854	162 209	176 747
Latvia, million EUR										
Contribution under 2000 heading	..	..	..	669	1 774	1 554	2 030	2 985	3 191	3 610
Other taxes	..	..	..	12	51	36	80	128	138	165
Voluntary contributions to government	..	..	..	0	0	0	0	0	0	0
Compulsory contributions to private sector	..	..	..	0	0	0	0	0	0	0
Total	..	..	..	682	1 825	1 590	2 111	3 113	3 329	3 776
Lithuania, million EUR										
Contribution under 2000 heading	..	..	..	1 362	2 643	3 293	4 338	5 127	5 750	6 656
Other taxes	..	..	..	0	0	0	0	0	0	0
Voluntary contributions to government	..	..	..	0	2	2	2	0	0	0
Compulsory contributions to private sector	..	..	..	0	247	95	140	0	0	0
Total	..	..	..	1 362	2 892	3 391	4 480	5 127	5 750	6 656
Luxembourg, million EUR										
Contribution under 2000 heading	86	443	1 011	2 224	3 710	4 387	5 548	7 208	7 651	8 286
Other taxes	0	0	0	0	0	0	0	0	0	0
Voluntary contributions to government	0	0	4	18	18	28	38	53	57	66
Compulsory contributions to private sector	0	0	0	0	0	0	0	0	0	0
Total	86	443	1 015	2 241	3 728	4 415	5 587	7 261	7 708	8 352
Mexico, million MXN										
Contribution under 2000 heading	..	109	17 165	138 223	236 727	277 459	409 249	576 019	612 175	681 672
Other taxes	..	0	0	0	0	0	0	0	0	0
Voluntary contributions to government	..	0	0	0	0	0	0	0	0	0
Compulsory contributions to private sector	..	25	3 840	67 352	144 331	146 110	206 824	332 725	363 552	417 476
Total	..	134	21 005	205 575	381 057	423 569	616 073	908 743	975 727	1099 148
Netherlands, million EUR										
Contribution under 2000 heading	3 342	26 641	39 075	64 522	77 072	82 732	96 426	108 685	112 666	120 769
Other taxes	0	0	0	0	0	0	0	0	0	0
Voluntary contributions to government	168	1 139	163	0	0	0	0	0	0	0
Compulsory contributions to private sector	1 266	7 642	5 727	37 088	..	..	..	..	..	..
Total	4 776	35 422	44 965	101 610	77 072	82 732	96 426	108 685	112 666	120 769
New Zealand, million NZD										
Contribution under 2000 heading	..	..	..	..	..	..	..	..	..	..
Other taxes	..	..	..	..	..	..	..	..	..	..
Voluntary contributions to government	..	..	..	..	..	..	..	..	..	..
Compulsory contributions to private sector	..	..	..	..	..	..	..	..	..	..
Total	0	0	0	0	0	0	0	0	0	0
Norway, million NOK										
Contribution under 2000 heading	2 009	28 205	79 362	132 170	204 473	243 002	325 130	381 231	401 990	428 463
Other taxes	1 305	4 256	0	0	0	0	0	0	0	0
Voluntary contributions to government	0	0	0	0	0	0	0	0	0	0
Compulsory contributions to private sector	0	242	339	0	0	0	0	0	0	0
Total	3 314	32 703	79 701	132 170	204 473	243 002	325 130	381 231	401 990	428 463
Poland, million PLN										
Contribution under 2000 heading	..	..	..	97 411	141 457	157 432	225 711	318 636	344 720	396 507
Other taxes	..	..	..	0	0	0	0	0	1421	1 975
Voluntary contributions to government	..	..	..	0	0	0	49	48	48	50
Compulsory contributions to private sector	..	..	..	0	0	0	0	0	0	0
Total	..	..	..	97 411	141 457	157 432	225 760	318 684	346 189	398 532

	1965	1980	1990	2000	2007	2010	2015	2020	2021	2022
Portugal, million EUR										
Contribution under 2000 heading	22	531	4 026	10 168	14 305	15 462	16 182	20 943	22 471	24 734
Other taxes	0	1	29	434	658	698	994	883	915	970
Voluntary contributions to government	0	0	0	0	0	0	0	0	0	0
Compulsory contributions to private sector	0	0	0	0	0	0	0	0	0	0
Total	22	532	4 055	10 602	14 932	16 154	17 176	21 826	23 386	25 705
Slovak Republic, million EUR										
Contribution under 2000 heading	..	..	..	4 409	7 244	8 154	10 897	14 229	15 261	15 968
Other taxes	..	..	..	0	0	0	0	0	0	0
Voluntary contributions to government	..	..	..	0	22	31	11	12	29	28
Compulsory contributions to private sector	..	..	..	0	701	719	413	717	940	1093
Total	..	..	..	4 409	7 968	8 904	11 321	14 958	16 230	17 088
Slovenia, million EUR										
Contribution under 2000 heading	..	..	..	2 820	5 046	5 761	5 983	7 908	8 561	9 134
Other taxes	..	..	..	0	0	0	0	0	0	0
Voluntary contributions to government	..	..	..	0	0	0	0	0	0	0
Compulsory contributions to private sector	..	..	..	0	0	0	0	0	0	0
Total	..	..	..	2 820	5 046	5 761	5 983	7 908	8 561	9 134
Spain, million EUR										
Contribution under 2000 heading	350	10 682	36 722	74 683	127 088	127 235	122 835	154 315	163 824	172 438
Other taxes	0	49	0	0	0	0	0	0	0	0
Voluntary contributions to government	0	0	0	447	937	1 155	1 170	891	931	930
Compulsory contributions to private sector	0	0	0	0	0	0	0	0	0	0
Total	350	10 731	36 722	75 130	128 025	128 390	124 005	155 206	164 755	173 368
Sweden, million SEK										
Contribution under 2000 heading	4 851	74 647	205 867	306 974	388 505	384 668	404 851	455 396	489 876	518 438
Other taxes	1 407	0	0	0	0	0	0	0	0	0
Voluntary contributions to government	0	0	0	7 951	12 376	13 167	16 726	24 731	30 070	30 421
Compulsory contributions to private sector	0	0	0	0	0	0	0	0	0	0
Total	6 258	74 647	205 867	314 925	400 881	397 835	421 577	480 127	519 946	548 859
Switzerland, million CHF										
Contribution under 2000 heading	1 670	10 844	19 952	30 961	34 974	38 385	44 285	49 056	50 655	52 285
Other taxes	336	778	1 176	4 509	6 342	6 644	7 590	3 357	3 428	3 446
Voluntary contributions to government	95	431	0	0	0	0	0	0	0	0
Compulsory contributions to private sector	2 505	9 674	20 797	29 532	42 219	45 974	52 890	60 122	61 308	63 336
Total	4 606	21 727	41 924	65 002	83 535	91 004	104 765	112 535	115 391	119 067
Türkiye, million TRY										
Contribution under 2000 heading	0	0	15	7 543	44 052	71 696	170 282	357 677	481 163	767 544
Other taxes	0	0	0	0	0	0	0	0	0	0
Voluntary contributions to government	0	0	0	0	0	0	0	0	0	0
Compulsory contributions to private sector	0	0	0	0	0	0	0	0	0	0
Total	0	0	15	7 543	44 052	71 696	170 282	357 677	481 163	767 544
United Kingdom, million GBP										
Contribution under 2000 heading	1 685	13 531	34 457	60 252	93 210	97 346	114 173	143 608	156 208	176 951
Other taxes	0	0	0	0	0	0	0	0	0	0
Voluntary contributions to government	0	11	3 288	8 103	18 629	21 217	25 025	38 013	40 449	42 616
Compulsory contributions to private sector	1 148	13 350	7 945	8 308	9 969	9 656	5 495	0	0	0
Total	2 833	26 892	45 690	76 663	121 808	128 219	144 693	181 621	196 657	219 567
United States, million USD										
Contribution under 2000 heading	22 192	159 763	396 972	683 104	907 357	917 409	1 125 493	1 327 683	1 430 254	1 556 656
Other taxes	0	0	0	0	0	0	0	0	0	0
Voluntary contributions to government	488	3 407	11 719	22 562	51 635	61 833	74 886	118 059	124 053	141 377
Compulsory contributions to private sector	0	0	0	0	0	0	0	0	0	0
Total	22 680	163 170	408 691	705 666	958 992	979 242	1 200 379	1 445 742	1 554 307	1 698 033

.. Not available

Table 5.40. Social security contributions and payroll taxes paid by government, national currency

	1965	1980	1990	2000	2007	2010	2015	2020	2021	2022
Australia, million AUD										
2000 Social security contributions										
Federal or Central government	..	..	..	..	..	..	..	..	..	..
State/Regional	..	..	..	..	..	..	..	..	..	..
Local government	..	..	..	..	..	..	..	..	..	..
Social Security Funds	..	..	..	..	..	..	..	..	..	..
Total	0	0	0	0	0	0	0	0	0	0
3000 Taxes on payroll and workforce										
Federal or Central government	0	4	0	0	0	0	0	0	0	0
State/Regional	15	302	0	0	0	0	0	0	0	0
Local government	0	0	2	19	41	31	38	45	42	49
Social Security Funds	0	0	0	0	0	0	0	0	0	0
Multi-jurisdictional (University) sector[1]	..	..	..	..	..	..	..	..	..	..
Total	15	306	92	301	496	579	765	959	889	993
2000+3000 Total	15	306	92	301	496	579	765	959	889	993
Austria, million EUR[2]										
2000 Social security contributions										
Federal or Central government	48	230	337	620	1 244	1 532	1 825	2 261	2 388	2 506
State/Regional	13	166	337	692	988	1 179	1 376	1 800	2 035	2 187
Local government	17	145	292	699	1 036	1 277	1 515	1 908	2 033	2 132
Social Security Funds	11	79	48	176	203	226	264	303	309	325
Total	88	619	1015	2186	3471	4213	4980	6272	6764	7150
3000 Taxes on payroll and workforce										
Federal or Central government	0	49	134	186	337	533	624	658	676	667
State/Regional	0	48	74	232	351	458	492	507	539	585
Local government	1	29	79	301	262	359	428	456	487	503
Social Security Funds	0	0	39	44	51	55	65	73	74	78
Total	1	125	326	763	1 000	1 405	1 609	1 693	1 776	1 834
2000+3000 Total	89	745	1 341	2 949	4 471	5 618	6 589	7 965	8 540	8 984
Belgium, million EUR										
2000 Social security contributions										
Federal or Central government	..	536	211	259	434	493	859	908	945	1028
State/Regional	..	0	614	1 218	1 600	1 873	2 440	2 878	3 027	3 294
Local government	..	434	768	1 376	2 151	2 655	3 973	4 618	4 738	4 945
Social Security Funds	..	89	176	252	308	360	415	420	449	474
Total	..	1 059	1 769	3 105	4 493	5 381	7 686	8 824	9 158	9 741
3000 Taxes on payroll and workforce										
Federal or Central government	..	..	..	..	..	..	..	..	..	..
State/Regional	..	..	..	..	..	..	..	..	..	..
Local government	..	..	..	..	..	..	..	..	..	..
Social Security Funds	..	..	..	..	..	..	..	..	..	..
Total	..	0	0	0	0	0	0	0	0	0
2000+3000 Total	..	1 059	1 769	3 105	4 493	5 381	7 686	8 824	9 158	9 741
Canada, million CAD										
2000 Social security contributions										
Federal or Central government	..	..	..	944	1 198	1 397	1 515	2 150	2 108	2 111
State/Regional	..	..	..	3 023	4 269	5 071	6 349	7 487	7 958	8 030
Local government	..	..	..	2 225	2 806	3 390	4 205	4 793	5 250	5 297
Social Security Funds	..	..	..	0	0	0	0	0	0	0
Total	..	..	..	6 192	8 273	9 857	12 070	14 430	15 316	15 438
3000 Taxes on payroll andworkforce										
Federal or Central government	..	..	..	0	0	0	0	0	0	0
State/Regional	..	..	..	173	234	328	362	413	439	472
Local government	..	..	..	0	0	0	0	0	0	0
Social Security Funds	..	..	..	0	0	0	0	0	0	0
Total	..	..	..	173	234	328	362	413	439	472
2000+3000 Total	..	..	..	6 365	8 507	10 185	12 432	14 843	15 755	15 910

	1965	1980	1990	2000	2007	2010	2015	2020	2021	2022
Chile, million CLP										
2000 Social security contributions										
Federal or Central government	..	..	..	43 210	107 911	148 006	205 125	269 335	251 721	210 316
State/Regional	..	..	..	..	..	..	..	..	..	..
Local government	..	..	..	11 317	30 218	41 518	63 603	110 058	103 689	84 953
Social Security Funds	..	..	..	106	263	449	600	872	798	650
Total	..	..	..	54 633	138 392	189 974	269 328	380 265	356 208	295 920
3000 Taxes on payroll and workforce										
Federal or Central government	..	..	..	..	..	..	..	..	..	..
State/Regional	..	..	..	..	..	..	..	..	..	..
Local government	..	..	..	..	..	..	..	..	..	..
Social Security Funds	..	..	..	..	..	..	..	..	..	..
Total	..	..	..	..	..	..	..	..	..	..
2000+3000 Total	..	..	..	54 633	138 392	189 974	269 328	380 265	356 208	295 920
Colombia, million COP										
2000 Social security contributions										
Federal or Central government	..	..	..	..	..	..	0	0	0	0
State/Regional	..	..	..	..	..	..	0	0	0	0
Local government	..	..	..	..	..	..	0	0	0	0
Social Security Funds	..	..	..	..	..	..	1 255 666	1 937 898	2 114 229	2 318 852
Total	..	..	..	..	..	..	1 255 666	1 937 898	2 114 229	2 318 852
3000 Taxes on payroll and workforce										
Federal or Central government	..	..	..	..	..	..	436 646	614 683	654 006	723 535
State/Regional	..	..	..	..	..	..	0	0	0	0
Local government	..	..	..	..	..	..	0	0	0	0
Social Security Funds	..	..	..	..	..	..	0	0	0	0
Total	..	..	..	..	..	..	436 646	614 683	654 006	723 535
2000+3000 Total	..	..	..	..	..	..	1 692 312	2 552 581	2 768 235	3 042 387
Costa Rica, million CRC										
2000 Social security contributions										
Federal or Central government	..	..	3 219	35 099	102 041	197 340	301 475	364 628	365 341	388 821
State/Regional	..	..	0	0	0	0	0	0	0	0
Local government	..	..	228	2 214	5 357	9 866	17 177	23 212	23 842	24 031
Social Security Funds	..	..	0	0	0	0	0	0	0	0
Total	..	..	3 447	37 313	107 398	207 206	318 652	387 840	389 183	412 852
3000 Taxes on payroll and workforce										
Federal or Central government	..	..	91	2 666	5 320	12 405	17 321	22 030	23 077	23 233
State/Regional	..	..	0	0	0	0	0	0	0	0
Local government	..	..	0	0	0	0	0	0	0	0
Social Security Funds	..	..	0	0	0	0	0	0	0	0
Total	..	..	91	2 666	5 320	12 405	17 321	22 030	23 077	23 233
2000+3000 Total	..	..	3 538	39 979	112 718	219 611	335 973	409 870	412 260	436 085
Czechia, million CZK										
2000 Social security contributions										
Federal or Central government	..	..	..	28 050	44 437	45 439	37 553	56 141	58 645	57 997
State/Regional	..	..	..	..	..	..	..	..	..	..
Local government	..	..	..	5 660	8 253	9 394	41 954	68 981	74 834	76 842
Social Security Funds	..	..	..	510	791	938	975	1 310	1 360	1 447
Total	..	..	..	34 220	53 481	55 771	80 482	126 432	134 839	136 286
3000 Taxes on payroll and workforce										
Federal or Central government	..	..	..	..	..	..	..	..	..	..
State/Regional	..	..	..	..	..	..	..	..	..	..
Local government	..	..	..	..	..	..	..	..	..	..
Social Security Funds	..	..	..	..	..	..	..	..	..	..
Total	..	..	..	0	0	0	0	0	0	0
2000+3000 Total	..	..	..	34 220	53 481	55 771	80 482	126 432	134 839	136 286
Denmark, million DKK										
2000 Social security contributions										
Federal or Central government	..	179	..	..	..	..	..	..	..	..
State/Regional	..	..	..	..	..	..	..	..	..	..
Local government	..	0	..	..	..	..	..	..	..	..
Social Security Funds	..	0	..	..	..	..	..	..	..	..
Total	..	179	0	0	0	0	0	0	0	0
3000 Taxes on payroll and workforce										
Federal or Central government	..	..	..	..	..	..	..	..	..	..
State/Regional	..	..	..	..	..	..	..	..	..	..
Local government	..	..	..	..	..	..	..	..	..	..
Social Security Funds	..	..	..	..	..	..	..	..	..	..

	1965	1980	1990	2000	2007	2010	2015	2020	2021	2022
Total	..	0	0	0	0	0	0	0	0	0
2000+3000 Total	..	179	0	0	0	0	0	0	0	0
Estonia, million EUR										
2000 Social security contributions										
Federal or Central government	..	..	..	115	230	258	359	514	553	603
State/Regional	..	..	..	..	..	..	..	..	..	..
Local government	..	..	..	48	155	173	232	354	372	410
Social Security Funds	..	..	..	0	1	3	4	9	10	11
Total	..	..	..	163	386	434	596	876	935	1023
3000 Taxes on payroll and workforce										
Federal or Central government	..	..	..	..	..	..	..	..	..	..
State/Regional	..	..	..	..	..	..	..	..	..	..
Local government	..	..	..	..	..	..	..	..	..	..
Social Security Funds	..	..	..	..	..	..	..	..	..	..
Total	..	..	..	0	0	0	0	0	0	0
2000+3000 Total	..	..	..	163	386	434	596	876	935	1023
Finland, million EUR										
2000 Social security contributions										
Federal or Central government	..	61	196	908	1 057	1 138	1 229	1 138	1 213	1 282
State/Regional	..	..	..	..	..	..	..	..	..	..
Local government	..	170	1 709	2 786	4 061	4 352	4 868	4 315	4 575	4 677
Social Security Funds	..	9	34	75	88	89	109	109	126	131
Total	..	239	1 939	3 769	5 206	5 579	6 206	5 562	5 914	6 090
3000 Taxes on payroll and workforce										
Federal or Central government	..	1	..	..	..	..	..	..	..	..
State/Regional	..	..	..	..	..	..	..	..	..	..
Local government	..	4	..	..	..	..	..	..	..	..
Social Security Funds	..	0	..	..	..	..	..	..	..	..
Total	..	5	0	0	0	0	0	0	0	0
2000+3000 Total	..	245	1 939	3 769	5 206	5 579	6 206	5 562	5 914	6 090
France, million EUR										
2000 Social security contributions										
Federal or Central government	..	3 834	7 919	10 876	13 023	13 656	14 199	15 706	15 992	16 642
State/Regional	..	..	..	..	..	..	..	..	..	..
Local government	..	1 683	5 419	10 053	15 435	17 509	20 815	21 831	22 435	23 529
Social Security Funds	..	2 761	6 979	10 827	14 035	15 427	17 344	18 183	19 714	20 367
Total	..	8 279	20 317	31 756	42 492	46 592	52 358	55 720	58 141	60 538
3000 Taxes on payroll and workforce										
Federal or Central government	..	920	581	1016	1 856	1 896	2 117	2 420	2 485	2 591
State/Regional	..	..	..	..	..	..	..	..	..	..
Local government	..	23	103	308	522	656	814	950	994	1 061
Social Security Funds	..	703	2 204	3 344	4 437	4 871	5 437	5 945	6 540	6 862
Total	..	1 646	2 889	4 669	6 815	7 424	8 368	9 315	10 019	10 514
2000+3000 Total	..	9 925	23 206	36 425	49 307	54 016	60 726	65 035	68 160	71 052
Germany, million EUR										
2000 Social security contributions										
Federal or Central government	775	1 324	2 376	1 554	1 377	1 649	1 766	2 507	2 768	2 995
State/Regional	293	2 611	4 647	5 664	6 045	6 781	7 749	9 981	10 250	10 514
Local government	325	3 140	5 791	6 920	8 296	9 499	10 767	14 568	15 067	15 748
Social Security Funds	1 495	456	767	1 806	2 131	2 446	2 840	3 570	3 677	3 748
Total	2 887	7 531	13 581	15 945	17 849	20 374	23 123	30 626	31 762	33 005
3000 Taxes on payroll and workforce										
Federal or Central government	..	..	..	..	..	..	..	..	..	..
State/Regional	..	..	..	..	..	..	..	..	..	..
Local government	..	..	..	..	..	..	..	..	..	..
Social Security Funds	..	..	..	..	..	..	..	..	..	..
Total	0	0	0	0	0	0	0	0	0	0
2000+3000 Total	2 887	7 531	13 581	15 945	17 849	20 374	23 123	30 626	31 762	33 005

	1965	1980	1990	2000	2007	2010	2015	2020	2021	2022
Greece, million EUR										
2000 Social security contributions										
Federal or Central government	..	..	124	510	1 045	1 176	1 160	2 324	2 374	2 397
State/Regional	..	..	..	..	..	..	..	..	..	..
Local government	..	..	0	124	286	341	339	401	442	421
Social Security Funds	..	..	0	99	268	200	74	61	60	62
Total	..	..	124	733	1 599	1 717	1 573	2 786	2 876	2 880
3000 Taxes on payroll and workforce										
Federal or Central government	..	..	..	..	..	..	..	..	..	..
State/Regional	..	..	..	..	..	..	..	..	..	..
Local government	..	..	..	..	..	..	..	..	..	..
Social Security Funds	..	..	..	..	..	..	..	..	..	..
Total	..	..	0	0	0	0	0	0	0	0
2000+3000 Total	..	..	124	733	1 599	1 717	1 573	2 786	2 876	2 880
Hungary, million HUF										
2000 Social security contributions										
Federal or Central government	..	..	..	148 251	293 684	352 354	539 106	511 362	491 643	476 172
State/Regional	..	..	..	..	..	..	..	..	..	..
Local government	..	..	..	173 475	343 306	291 375	152 189	136 697	129 333	133 251
Social Security Funds	..	..	..	4 936	8 052	6 763	2 977	709	755	702
Total	..	..	..	326 661	645 042	650 492	694 272	648 768	621 731	610 125
3000 Taxes on payroll and workforce										
Federal or Central government	..	..	..	13 901	7 287	5 419	12 876	20 850	21 296	21 446
State/Regional	..	..	..	..	..	..	..	..	..	..
Local government	..	..	..	25 990	11 928	9 275	3 357	4 978	5 346	6 612
Social Security Funds	..	..	..	406	162	194	110	45	0	0
Total	..	..	..	40 297	19 377	14 888	16 342	25 873	26 642	28 058
2000+3000 Total	..	..	..	366 958	664 420	665 380	710 614	674 641	648 373	638 183
Iceland, million ISK										
2000 Social security contributions										
Federal or Central government	..	..	..	..	..	..	..	..	..	..
State/Regional	..	..	..	..	..	..	..	..	..	..
Local government	..	..	..	..	..	..	..	..	..	..
Social Security Funds	..	..	..	..	..	..	..	..	..	..
Total	..	..	..	..	..	..	..	..	..	..
3000 Taxes on payroll and workforce										
Federal or Central government	..	..	..	..	..	..	..	..	..	..
State/Regional	..	..	..	..	..	..	..	..	..	..
Local government	..	..	..	..	..	..	..	..	..	..
Social Security Funds	..	..	..	..	..	..	..	..	..	..
Total	..	..	..	..	..	..	..	..	..	..
2000+3000 Total	..	..	..	..	..	..	..	..	..	..
Ireland, million EUR										
2000 Social security contributions										
Federal or Central government	..	21	65	166	460	395	497	629	695	695
State/Regional	..	..	..	..	..	..	..	..	..	..
Local government	..	25	83	277	862	740	932	1 180	1 304	1 304
Social Security Funds	..	0	1	4	6	6	6	6	6	7
Total	..	46	149	447	1 328	1 140	1 435	1 816	2 005	2 006
3000 Taxes on payroll and workforce										
Federal or Central government	..	..	..	..	..	..	..	..	..	..
State/Regional	..	..	..	..	..	..	..	..	..	..
Local government	..	..	..	..	..	..	..	..	..	..
Social Security Funds	..	..	..	..	..	..	..	..	..	..
Total	..	0	0	0	0	0	0	0	0	0
2000+3000 Total	..	46	149	447	1 328	1 140	1 435	1 816	2 005	2 006
Israel, million ILS										
2000 Social security contributions										
Federal or Central government	..	..	..	840	1 030	1 180	1 780	2 320	2 540	2 870
State/Regional	..	..	..	..	..	..	..	..	..	..
Local government	..	..	..	280	340	390	590	770	840	950
Social Security Funds	..	..	..	5	12	15	0	0	0	0
Total	..	..	..	1 120	1 370	1 570	2 370	3 090	3 380	3 820
3000 Taxes on payroll and workforce										
Federal or Central government	..	..	..	2 330	3 600	4 180	5 650	6 950	7 240	7 430
State/Regional	..	..	..	..	..	..	..	..	..	..
Local government	..	..	..	780	1 120	960	1 290	1 590	1 650	1 700
Social Security Funds	..	..	..	5	12	15	0	0	0	0

	1965	1980	1990	2000	2007	2010	2015	2020	2021	2022
Total	..	..	..	3 110	4 720	5 140	6 940	8 540	8 890	9 130
2000+3000 Total	..	..	..	4 230	6 090	6 710	9 310	11 630	12 270	12 950
Italy, million EUR										
2000 Social security contributions										
Federal or Central government	..	..	..	0	0	0	0	0	0	0
State/Regional	..	..	..	..	..	..	..	..	..	..
Local government	..	..	..	0	0	0	0	0	0	0
Social Security Funds	..	..	..	36 679	47 394	50 627	49 251	52 493	53 896	56 535
Total	..	..	..	36 679	47 394	50 627	49 251	52 493	53 896	56 535
3000 Taxes on payroll and workforce										
Federal or Central government	..	..	..	..	..	..	..	..	..	..
State/Regional	..	..	..	..	..	..	..	..	..	..
Local government	..	..	..	..	..	..	..	..	..	..
Social Security Funds	..	..	..	..	..	..	..	..	..	..
Total	..	..	..	0	0	0	0	0	0	0
2000+3000 Total	..	..	..	36 679	47 394	50 627	49 251	52 493	53 896	56 535
Japan, billion JPY										
2000 Social security contributions										
Federal or Central government	..	..	507	732	766	758	881	928	927	940
State/Regional	..	..	..	..	..	..	..	0	0	0
Local government	..	..	1 510	2 168	2 216	2 223	2 524	2 606	2 651	2 682
Social Security Funds	..	..	0	0	0	0	0	0	0	0
Total	..	..	2 017	2 900	2 982	2 981	3 405	3 533	3 578	3 622
3000 Taxes on payroll and workforce										
Federal or Central government	..	..	..	..	..	..	..	..	..	..
State/Regional	..	..	..	..	..	..	..	..	..	..
Local government	..	..	..	..	..	..	..	..	..	..
Social Security Funds	..	..	..	..	..	..	..	..	..	..
Total	..	..	0	0	0	0	0	0	0	0
2000+3000 Total	..	..	2 017	2 900	2 982	2 981	3 405	3 533	3 578	3 622
Korea, billion KRW										
2000 Social security contributions										
Federal or Central government	..	..	..	..	..	..	..	..	..	..
State/Regional	..	..	..	..	..	..	..	..	..	..
Local government	..	..	..	..	..	..	..	..	..	..
Social Security Funds	..	..	..	..	..	..	..	..	..	..
Total	..	..	..	..	..	..	..	..	..	..
3000 Taxes on payroll and workforce										
Federal or Central government	..	..	..	..	..	..	..	..	..	..
State/Regional	..	..	..	..	..	..	..	..	..	..
Local government	..	..	..	..	..	..	..	..	..	..
Social Security Funds	..	..	..	..	..	..	..	..	..	..
Total	..	..	..	..	..	..	..	..	..	..
2000+3000 Total	..	..	..	..	..	..	..	..	..	..
Latvia, million EUR										
2000 Social security contributions										
Federal or Central government	..	..	..	..	..	..	..	..	..	..
State/Regional	..	..	..	..	..	..	..	..	..	..
Local government	..	..	..	..	..	..	..	..	..	..
Social Security Funds	..	..	..	..	..	..	..	..	..	..
Total	..	..	..	40	156	174	262	326	354	418
3000 Taxes on payroll and workforce										
Federal or Central government	..	..	..	..	..	..	..	..	..	..
State/Regional	..	..	..	..	..	..	..	..	..	..
Local government	..	..	..	..	..	..	..	..	..	..
Social Security Funds	..	..	..	..	..	..	..	..	..	..
Total	..	..	..	0	0	0	0	0	0	0
2000+3000 Total	..	..	..	40	156	174	262	326	354	418
Lithuania, million EUR										
2000 Social security contributions										
Federal or Central government	..	..	..	179	327	335	426	51	54	59
State/Regional	..	..	..	..	..	..	..	..	..	..
Local government	..	..	..	174	294	351	375	46	52	57
Social Security Funds	..	..	..	5	14	16	16	1	1	1
Total	..	..	..	358	635	701	818	98	107	117
3000 Taxes on payroll and workforce										
Federal or Central government	..	..	..	..	..	..	..	..	..	..

	1965	1980	1990	2000	2007	2010	2015	2020	2021	2022
State/Regional	..	..	..	..	..	..	..	..	..	..
Local government	..	..	..	..	..	..	..	..	..	..
Social Security Funds	..	..	..	..	..	..	..	..	..	..
Total	..	..	..	0	0	0	0	0	0	0
2000+3000 Total	..	..	..	358	635	701	818	98	107	117
Luxembourg, million EUR										
2000 Social security contributions										
Federal or Central government	..	..	257	273	413	488	648	828	864	917
State/Regional	..	..	..	..	..	..	..	..	..	..
Local government	..	..	2	4	4	4	4	4	4	4
Social Security Funds	..	..	7	11	12	13	17	23	24	26
Total	..	..	267	288	429	505	669	855	891	947
3000 Taxes on payroll and workforce										
Federal or Central government	..	..	..	..	..	..	..	..	..	..
State/Regional	..	..	..	..	..	..	..	..	..	..
Local government	..	..	..	..	..	..	..	..	..	..
Social Security Funds	..	..	..	..	..	..	..	..	..	..
Total	..	..	0	0	0	0	0	0	0	0
2000+3000 Total	..	..	267	288	429	505	669	855	891	947
Mexico, million MXN										
2000 Social security contributions										
Federal or Central government	..	25	2 952	44 879	94 251	103 440	145 329	196 039	197 668	209 353
State/Regional	..	0	0	0	0	0	0	0	0	0
Local government	..	0	0	0	0	0	0	0	0	0
Social Security Funds	..	0	0	0	0	0	0	0	0	0
Total	..	25	2 952	44 879	94 251	103 440	145 329	196 039	197 668	209 353
3000 Taxes on payroll and workforce										
Federal or Central government	..	..	..	..	..	..	..	..	..	..
State/Regional	..	..	..	..	..	..	..	..	..	..
Local government	..	..	..	..	..	..	..	..	..	..
Social Security Funds	..	..	..	..	..	..	..	..	..	..
Total	..	0	0	0	0	0	0	0	0	0
2000+3000 Total	..	25	2 952	44 879	94 251	103 440	145 329	196 039	197 668	209 353
Netherlands, million EUR										
2000 Social security contributions										
Federal or Central government	63	1 366	286	..	..	..	..	..	..	..
State/Regional	..	..	..	..	..	..	..	..	..	..
Local government	0	0	0	..	..	..	..	..	..	..
Social Security Funds	7	91	59	..	..	..	..	..	..	..
Total	70	1 457	345	2 006	4 310	..	..	..	..	..
3000 Taxes on payroll and workforce										
Federal or Central government	..	..	..	..	..	..	..	..	..	..
State/Regional	..	..	..	..	..	..	..	..	..	..
Local government	..	..	..	..	..	..	..	..	..	..
Social Security Funds	..	..	..	..	..	..	..	..	..	..
Total	0	0	0	0	0	0	0	0	0	0
2000+3000 Total	70	1 457	345	2 006	4 310	0	0	0	0	0
New Zealand, million NZD										
2000 Social security contributions										
Federal or Central government	..	..	..	..	..	..	..	..	..	..
State/Regional	..	..	..	..	..	..	..	..	..	..
Local government	..	..	..	..	..	..	..	..	..	..
Social Security Funds	..	..	..	..	..	..	..	..	..	..
Total	0	0	0	0	0	0	0	0	0	0
3000 Taxes on payroll and workforce										
Federal or Central government	..	..	..	..	..	..	..	..	..	..
State/Regional	..	..	..	..	..	..	..	..	..	..
Local government	..	..	..	..	..	..	..	..	..	..
Social Security Funds	..	..	..	..	..	..	..	..	..	..
Total	0	0	0	0	0	0	0	0	0	0
2000+3000 Total	0	0	0	0	0	0	0	0	0	0
Norway, million NOK										
2000 Social security contributions										
Federal or Central government	..	1 242	2 859	11 895	28 233	33 746	46 487	53 465	57 123	60 204
State/Regional	..	..	..	..	..	..	..	..	..	..
Local government	..	4 538	11 964	24 831	32 110	41 024	59 556	68 072	70 982	75 024
Social Security Funds	..	1 222	3 064	0	0	0	0	0	0	0

	1965	1980	1990	2000	2007	2010	2015	2020	2021	2022
Total	..	7 002	17 887	36 726	60 343	74 770	106 043	121 537	128 105	135 228
3000 Taxes on payroll and workforce										
Federal or Central government	..	..	..	..	..	..	..	..	..	..
State/Regional	..	..	..	..	..	..	..	..	..	..
Local government	..	..	..	..	..	..	..	..	..	..
Social Security Funds	..	..	..	..	..	..	..	..	..	..
Total	..	0	0	0	0	0	0	0	0	0
2000+3000 Total	..	7 002	17 887	36 726	60 343	74 770	106 043	121 537	128 105	135 228
Poland, million PLN										
2000 Social security contributions										
Federal or Central government	..	..	..	4 566	6 023	6 643	9 840	13 328	13 857	15 209
State/Regional	..	..	..	..	..	..	..	..	..	..
Local government	..	..	..	6 756	9 856	11 411	14 796	20 025	20 642	22 654
Social Security Funds	..	..	..	279	426	499	518	712	810	919
Total	..	..	..	11 601	16 305	18 553	25 154	34 065	35 309	38 782
3000 Taxes on payroll and workforce										
Federal or Central government	..	..	..	..	..	..	..	..	..	..
State/Regional	..	..	..	..	..	..	..	..	..	..
Local government	..	..	..	..	..	..	..	..	..	..
Social Security Funds	..	..	..	..	..	..	..	..	..	..
Total	..	..	..	0	0	0	0	0	0	0
2000+3000 Total	..	..	..	11 601	16 305	18 553	25 154	34 065	35 309	38 782
Portugal, million EUR										
2000 Social security contributions										
Federal or Central government	..	0	0	0	..	..	..	..	..	..
State/Regional	..	..	..	..	..	..	..	..	..	..
Local government	..	0	33	197	..	..	..	..	..	..
Social Security Funds	..	4	0	0	..	..	..	..	..	..
Total	..	4	33	197	0	0	0	0	0	0
3000 Taxes on payroll and workforce										
Federal or Central government	..	..	..	..	..	..	..	..	..	..
State/Regional	..	..	..	..	..	..	..	..	..	..
Local government	..	..	..	..	..	..	..	..	..	..
Social Security Funds	..	..	..	..	..	..	..	..	..	..
Total	..	0	0	0	0	0	0	0	0	0
2000+3000 Total	..	4	33	197	0	0	0	0	0	0
Slovak Republic, million EUR										
2000 Social security contributions										
Federal or Central government	..	..	..	489	602	791	1 069	1 439	1 645	1 521
State/Regional	..	..	..	..	..	..	..	..	..	..
Local government	..	..	..	130	427	515	658	1002	1 070	1 105
Social Security Funds	..	..	..	22	26	43	36	49	52	56
Total	..	..	..	642	1 056	1 348	1 763	2 490	2 766	2 683
3000 Taxes on payroll and workforce										
Federal or Central government	..	..	..	..	..	..	..	..	..	..
State/Regional	..	..	..	..	..	..	..	..	..	..
Local government	..	..	..	..	..	..	..	..	..	..
Social Security Funds	..	..	..	..	..	..	..	..	..	..
Total	..	..	..	0	0	0	0	0	0	0
2000+3000 Total	..	..	..	642	1 056	1 348	1 763	2 490	2 766	2 683
Slovenia, million EUR										
2000 Social security contributions										
Federal or Central government	..	..	..	178	339	409	375	539	577	557
State/Regional	..	..	..	..	..	..	..	..	..	..
Local government	..	..	..	94	175	195	189	268	303	289
Social Security Funds	..	..	..	3	7	8	6	8	9	9
Total	..	..	..	275	521	612	571	815	889	855
3000 Taxes on payroll and workforce										
Federal or Central government	..	..	..	56	77	6	7	9	14	12
State/Regional	..	..	..	..	..	..	..	..	..	..
Local government	..	..	..	29	36	3	4	4	5	5
Social Security Funds	..	..	..	1	2	0	0	0	0	0
Total	..	..	..	86	114	9	11	14	20	18
2000+3000 Total	..	..	..	361	636	621	582	829	909	873

	1965	1980	1990	2000	2007	2010	2015	2020	2021	2022
Spain, million EUR										
2000 Social security contributions										
Federal or Central government	..	387	989	1 408	1 966	2 201	2 239	2 830	3 001	3 267
State/Regional	..	2	0	4 411	9 426	10 996	11 245	14 951	16 420	17 444
Local government	..	252	1 819	2 524	4 098	4 781	4 797	5 688	6 172	6 267
Social Security Funds	..	396	1 202	1 284	484	527	496	535	549	543
Total	..	1 037	4 010	9 627	15 974	18 505	18 777	24 004	26 142	27 521
3000 Taxes on payroll and workforce										
Federal or Central government	..	..	..	..	..	..	..	..	..	..
State/Regional	..	..	..	..	..	..	..	..	..	..
Local government	..	..	..	..	..	..	..	..	..	..
Social Security Funds	..	..	..	..	..	..	..	..	..	..
Total	..	0	0	0	0	0	0	0	0	0
2000+3000 Total	..	1 037	4 010	9 627	15 974	18 505	18 777	24 004	26 142	27 521
Sweden, million SEK										
2000 Social security contributions										
Federal or Central government	..	7 543	12 430	21 153	25 164	24 729	25 707	29 039	30 750	32 156
State/Regional	..	..	..	..	..	..	..	..	..	..
Local government	..	18 149	49 298	66 215	83 877	82 141	85 373	96 810	102 794	105 564
Social Security Funds	..	0	0	0	0	0	0	0	0	0
Total	..	25 692	61 728	87 367	109 040	106 870	111 079	125 849	133 543	137 720
3000 Taxes on payroll and workforce										
Federal or Central government	..	..	1 527	3 453	5 394	6 912	12 326	16 317	17 624	18 688
State/Regional	..	..	..	..	..	..	..	..	..	..
Local government	..	..	6 060	10 808	17 980	22 958	40 935	54 398	58 915	61 352
Social Security Funds	..	..	0	0	0	0	0	0	0	0
Total	..	0	7 587	14 261	23 374	29 870	53 261	70 715	76 539	80 040
2000+3000 Total	..	25 692	69 315	101 628	132 414	136 740	164 340	196 564	210 082	217 760
Switzerland, million CHF										
2000 Social security contributions										
Federal or Central government	13	91	224	293	381	448	530	606	616	621
State/Regional	34	380	770	971	1 269	1 520	1 766	2 013	2 079	2 114
Local government	22	270	460	595	745	823	911	1020	1 042	1 052
Social Security Funds	2	21	4	14	18	23	26	28	29	31
Total	71	762	1 458	1 873	2 413	2 813	3 234	3 667	3 766	3 818
3000 Taxes on payroll and workforce										
Federal or Central government	..	..	..	..	..	..	..	..	..	..
State/Regional	..	..	..	..	..	..	..	..	..	..
Local government	..	..	..	..	..	..	..	..	..	..
Social Security Funds	..	..	..	..	..	..	..	..	..	..
Total	0	0	0	0	0	0	0	0	0	0
2000+3000 Total	71	762	1 458	1 873	2 413	2 813	3 234	3 667	3 766	3 818
Türkiye, million TRY										
2000 Social security contributions										
Federal or Central government	..	..	9	3 619	20 442	39 363	95 067	204 045	272 370	440 551
State/Regional	..	..	..	..	..	..	..	..	..	..
Local government	..	..	0	0	0	0	0	0	0	0
Social Security Funds	..	..	0	0	0	0	0	0	0	0
Total	..	..	9	3 619	20 442	39 363	95 067	204 045	272 370	440 551
3000 Taxes on payroll and workforce										
Federal or Central government	..	..	..	..	..	..	..	..	..	..
State/Regional	..	..	..	..	..	..	..	..	..	..
Local government	..	..	..	..	..	..	..	..	..	..
Social Security Funds	..	..	..	..	..	..	..	..	..	..
Total	..	..	0	0	0	0	0	0	0	0
2000+3000 Total	..	..	9	3 619	20 442	39 363	95 067	204 045	272 370	440 551

	1965	1980	1990	2000	2007	2010	2015	2020	2021	2022
United Kingdom, million GBP										
2000 Social security contributions										
Federal or Central government	87	920	2 134	3 164	5 886	6 488	7 862	11 298	12 608	14 519
State/Regional	..	..	..	..	..	..	..	..	..	..
Local government	83	926	1 957	2 956	4 896	5 375	4 623	5 170	5 538	6 388
Social Security Funds	0	0	0	0	0	0	0	0	0	0
Total	170	1 846	4 091	6 120	10 782	11 863	12 485	16 468	18 146	20 907
3000 Taxes on payroll and workforce										
Federal or Central government	..	360	..	..	..	..	..	..	..	..
State/Regional	..	..	..	..	..	..	..	..	..	..
Local government	..	410	..	..	..	..	..	..	..	..
Social Security Funds	..	0	..	..	..	..	..	..	..	..
Total	0	770	0	0	0	0	0	0	0	0
2000+3000 Total	170	2 616	4 091	6 120	10 782	11 863	12 485	16 468	18 146	20 907
United States, million USD										
2000 Social security contributions										
Federal or Central government	301	2 053	9 059	11 323	19 628	25 434	26 803	29 892	30 662	31 420
State/Regional	699	7 585	19 802	32 814	44 061	45 936	49 105	61 894	61 472	63 676
Local government	0	0	0	0	0	0	0	0	0	0
Social Security Funds	0	0	0	0	0	0	0	0	0	0
Total	1 000	9 638	28 861	44 137	63 689	71 370	75 908	91 786	92 134	95 096
3000 Taxes on payroll and workforce										
Federal or Central government	..	..	..	..	..	..	..	..	..	..
State/Regional	..	..	..	..	..	..	..	..	..	..
Local government	..	..	..	..	..	..	..	..	..	..
Social Security Funds	..	..	..	..	..	..	..	..	..	..
Total	0	0	0	0	0	0	0	0	0	0
2000+3000 Total	1 000	9 638	28 861	44 137	63 689	71 370	75 908	91 786	92 134	95 096

.. Not available

1. The multi-jurisdictional sector contains units where jurisdiction is shared between two or more governments, or classification of a unit to a jurisdiction is otherwise unclear. The main type of units currently falling into this category is public universities.
2. There is a break in the series in 1990. The data are based on ESA 2010 from that year onwards.

6 Tax revenues by subsectors of general government

Chapter 6 provides information on tax revenues by subsectors of general government for each OECD country.

Country tables 1975, 1995, 2005, 2015 and 2022

This chapter presents detailed country information on tax revenues by level of government. The data have been attributed to the sub-sectors of general government identified in section A.12 of the Interpretative Guide (see Annex A) and the attribution criteria used are those set out in that guide.

Table 6.1. Australia, tax revenues by sub-sectors of government

Million AUD

	Federal government					State/Regional				
	1975	1995	2005	2015	2022	1975	1995	2005	2015	2022
1000 Taxes on income, profits and capital gains	11 831	82 615	175 695	261 345	468 871	0	0	0	0	0
1100 Of individuals	9 213	60 602	118 239	191 720	304 566	..	..	..	..	..
1200 Corporate	2 618	22 013	57 456	69 625	164 305	..	..	..	..	..
1300 Unallocable between 1100 and 1200	0	0	0	0	0	0	..	..	..	..
2000 Social security contributions	0	0	0	0	0	0	0	0	0	0
2100 Employees	0	0	0	0	0	0	0	0	0	0
2200 Employers	0	0	0	0	0	0	0	0	0	0
2300 Self-employed or non-employed	0	0	0	0	0	0	0	0	0	0
2400 Unallocable between 2100, 2200 and 2300	0	0	0	0	0	0	0	0	0	0
3000 Taxes on payroll and workforce	54	3 065	369	670	1 243	1 171	7 120	13 095	22 684	34 066
4000 Taxes on property	103	8	14	15	15	883	7 988	16 940	32 533	48 067
4100 Recurrent taxes on immovable property	12	0	0	0	0	217	1 840	4 559	10 029	18 366
4200 Recurrent taxes on net wealth	0	0	0	0	0	0	0	0	0	0
4300 Estate, inheritance and gift taxes	87	0	0	0	0	227	0	0	0	0
4400 Taxes on financial and capital transactions	4	8	14	15	15	439	6 148	12 381	22 504	29 701
4500 Non-recurrent taxes	0	0	0	0	0	0	0	0	0	0
4600 Other recurrent taxes on property	0	0	0	0	0	0	0	0	0	0
5000 Taxes on goods and services	4 932	30 004	68 710	103 455	144 366	1 262	13 295	14 479	23 407	34 743
5100 Taxes on production, sale, transfer, etc	4 919	29 613	67 172	97 166	134 673	532	4 923	8 188	11 884	17 748
5110 General taxes	1 408	12 970	39 436	60 680	88 602	0	0	0	0	0
5120 Taxes on specific goods and services	3 511	16 643	27 736	36 486	46 071	532	4 923	8 188	11 884	17 748
5130 Unallocable between 5110 and 5120	0	0	0	0	0	0	0	0	0	0
5200 Taxes on use of goods and perform activities	13	391	1 538	6 289	9 693	730	8 372	6 291	11 523	16 995
5300 Unallocable between 5100 and 5200	0	0	0	0	0	0	0	0	0	0
6000 Other taxes	0	0	0	0	0	0	0	0	0	0
6100 Paid solely by business	..	..	..	..	..	..	..	..	..	..
6200 Other	..	..	..	..	..	..	..	..	..	..
Total tax revenue	16 920	115 692	244 788	365 485	614 495	3 316	28 403	44 514	78 624	116 876

	Local government					Social Security Funds				
	1975	1995	2005	2015	2022	1975	1995	2005	2015	2022
1000 Taxes on income, profits and capital gains	0	0	0	0	0	0	0	0	0	0
1100 Of individuals	..	..	..	..	..	..	..	..	..	..
1200 Corporate	..	..	..	..	..	..	..	..	..	..
1300 Unallocable between 1100 and 1200	0	..	..	..	..	0	..	..	..	..
2000 Social security contributions	0	0	0	0	0	0	0	0	0	0
2100 Employees	0	0	0	0	0	0	0	0	0	0
2200 Employers	0	0	0	0	0	0	0	0	0	0
2300 Self-employed or non-employed	0	0	0	0	0	0	0	0	0	0
2400 Unallocable between 2100, 2200 and 2300	0	0	0	0	0	0	0	0	0	0
3000 Taxes on payroll and workforce	0	0	0	0	0	0	0	0	0	0
4000 Taxes on property	883	5 134	8 726	16 620	21 822	0	0	0	0	0
4100 Recurrent taxes on immovable property	883	5 134	8 726	16 620	21 822	..	..	..	..	..
4200 Recurrent taxes on net wealth	0	0	0	0	0	..	..	..	..	..
4300 Estate, inheritance and gift taxes	0	0	0	0	0	..	..	..	..	..
4400 Taxes on financial and capital transactions	0	0	0	0	0	..	..	..	..	..
4500 Non-recurrent taxes	0	0	0	0	0	..	..	..	..	..
4600 Other recurrent taxes on property	0	0	0	0	0	..	..	..	..	..
5000 Taxes on goods and services	0	0	0	0	0	0	0	0	0	0
5100 Taxes on production, sale, transfer, etc	0	0	0	0	0	0	0	0	0	0
5110 General taxes	0	0	0	0	0	0	0	0	0	0
5120 Taxes on specific goods and services	0	0	0	0	0	0	0	0	0	0
5130 Unallocable between 5110 and 5120	0	0	0	0	0	0	0	0	0	0
5200 Taxes on use of goods and perform activities	0	0	0	0	0	0	0	0	0	0
5300 Unallocable between 5100 and 5200	0	0	0	0	0	0	0	0	0	0
6000 Other taxes	0	0	0	0	0	0	0	0	0	0
6100 Paid solely by business	..	..	..	..	..	..	..	..	..	..
6200 Other	..	..	..	..	..	..	..	..	..	..
Total tax revenue	883	5 134	8 726	16 620	21 822	0	0	0	0	0

.. Not available

Table 6.2. Austria, tax revenues by sub-sectors of government

Million EUR

	Federal government					State/Regional				
	1975	1995	2005	2015	2022	1975	1995	2005	2015	2022
1000 Taxes on income, profits and capital gains	3 064	18 452	28 781	43 714	58 282	865	547	742	1 081	1 450
1100 Of individuals	2 381	14 649	22 126	34 901	41 758	834	459	637	941	1 282
1200 Corporate	655	2 267	5 341	7 519	15 157	31	88	104	141	169
1300 Unallocable between 1100 and 1200	27	1 536	1 313	1 295	1 367	0	0	0	0	0
2000 Social security contributions	352	4 243	5 720	7 547	9 337	34	311	409	496	412
2100 Employees	225	2 379	2 978	3 911	4 783	34	310	395	465	378
2200 Employers	127	1 830	2 498	3 350	4 283	0	0	0	0	0
2300 Self-employed or non-employed	0	34	243	286	271	0	1	14	31	33
2400 Unallocable between 2100, 2200 and 2300	0	0	0	0	0	0	0	0	0	0
3000 Taxes on payroll and workforce	1 217	3 394	4 384	6 861	6 631	0	132	156	203	1 213
4000 Taxes on property	282	655	801	1 247	1 778	35	31	36	44	49
4100 Recurrent taxes on immovable property	18	32	32	43	41	15	31	36	44	49
4200 Recurrent taxes on net wealth	226	58	0	0	0	10	0	0	0	0
4300 Estate, inheritance and gift taxes	24	82	140	12	0	10	0	0	0	0
4400 Taxes on financial and capital transactions	14	483	629	1 116	1 694	0	0	0	0	0
4500 Non-recurrent taxes	0	0	0	0	0	0	0	0	0	0
4600 Other recurrent taxes on property	0	0	0	0	0	0	0	0	0	0
5000 Taxes on goods and services	4 554	19 894	29 646	39 720	50 138	1 013	222	234	362	469
5100 Taxes on production, sale, transfer, etc	4 549	18 639	27 613	36 693	46 216	926	158	139	216	299
5110 General taxes	2 545	13 436	19 421	26 282	35 802	662	0	0	0	0
5120 Taxes on specific goods and services	1 991	5 159	8 148	10 408	10 408	264	158	139	216	299
5130 Unallocable between 5110 and 5120	14	44	45	4	6	0	0	0	0	0
5200 Taxes on use of goods and perform activities	5	1 255	2 033	3 027	3 922	87	64	95	146	170
5300 Unallocable between 5100 and 5200	0	0	0	0	0	0	0	0	0	0
6000 Other taxes	52	486	699	517	588	8	50	61	91	104
6100 Paid solely by business	..	..	..	..	..	..	..	..	..	..
6200 Other	..	..	..	..	..	..	..	..	..	..
Total tax revenue	9 521	47 124	70 031	99 606	126 753	1 955	1 294	1 638	2 277	3 697

	Local government					Social Security Funds				
	1975	1995	2005	2015	2022	1975	1995	2005	2015	2022
1000 Taxes on income, profits and capital gains	887	46	0	0	0	0	0	0	0	0
1100 Of individuals	771	19	0	0	..	..	..	..	..	..
1200 Corporate	115	26	0	0	..	..	..	..	..	..
1300 Unallocable between 1100 and 1200	0	0	0	0	..	..	..	..	..	..
2000 Social security contributions	29	258	267	266	222	4 667	21 173	28 912	41 557	55 922
2100 Employees	29	207	240	241	206	1 840	8 110	10 751	15 499	21 233
2200 Employers	0	50	27	26	15	2 375	10 912	14 037	19 906	26 781
2300 Self-employed or non-employed	0	0	0	0	0	453	2 151	4 125	6 153	7 908
2400 Unallocable between 2100, 2200 and 2300	0	0	0	0	0	0	0	0	0	0
3000 Taxes on payroll and workforce	262	1 492	2 035	2 977	4 267	0	0	0	0	0
4000 Taxes on property	254	395	539	675	807	0	0	0	0	0
4100 Recurrent taxes on immovable property	139	395	539	675	807	..	..	..	..	..
4200 Recurrent taxes on net wealth	35	0	0	0	0	..	..	..	..	..
4300 Estate, inheritance and gift taxes	0	0	0	0	0	..	..	..	..	..
4400 Taxes on financial and capital transactions	81	0	0	0	0	..	..	..	..	..
4500 Non-recurrent taxes	0	0	0	0	0	..	..	..	..	..
4600 Other recurrent taxes on property	0	0	0	0	0	..	..	..	..	..
5000 Taxes on goods and services	792	738	302	353	408	0	0	0	0	0
5100 Taxes on production, sale, transfer, etc	769	582	134	96	91	..	..	..	..	..
5110 General taxes	448	0	0	0	0	..	..	..	..	..
5120 Taxes on specific goods and services	321	582	134	96	91	..	..	..	..	..
5130 Unallocable between 5110 and 5120	0	0	0	0	0	..	..	..	..	..
5200 Taxes on use of goods and perform activities	24	155	168	258	317	..	..	..	..	..
5300 Unallocable between 5100 and 5200	0	0	0	0	0	..	..	..	..	..
6000 Other taxes	55	60	103	129	89	0	0	0	0	0
6100 Paid solely by business	..	..	..	..	..	..	..	..	..	..
6200 Other	..	..	..	..	..	..	..	..	..	..
Total tax revenue	2 279	2 987	3 246	4 400	5 792	4 667	21 173	28 912	41 557	55 922

.. Not available

Note: Including taxes collected on behalf of the European Union.

Table 6.3. Belgium, tax revenues by sub-sectors of government

Million EUR

	Federal government					State/Regional				
	1975	1995	2005	2015	2022	1975	1995	2005	2015	2022
1000 Taxes on income, profits and capital gains	8 534	30 905	45 859	57 131	71 807	..	79	0	4 283	11 119
1100 Of individuals	6 929	25 997	36 007	43 436	50 046	..	79	..	4 283	11 119
1200 Corporate	1 596	4 867	9 811	13 644	21 679	..	0	..	0	0
1300 Unallocable between 1100 and 1200	10	41	42	51	81	..	0	..	0	0
2000 Social security contributions	299	1 181	1 904	2 336	58	..	0	34	11	280
2100 Employees	264	854	1 125	1 372	0	..	..	7	2	270
2200 Employers	36	228	608	715	58	..	..	27	9	10
2300 Self-employed or non-employed	0	99	171	249	0	..	..	0	0	0
2400 Unallocable between 2100, 2200 and 2300	0	0	0	0	0	..	..	0	0	0
3000 Taxes on payroll and workforce	0	0	0	0	0	..	0	0	0	0
4000 Taxes on property	583	1 340	873	1 861	2 541	..	1 168	4 669	7 087	8 988
4100 Recurrent taxes on immovable property	12	25	41	41	54	..	83	192	249	449
4200 Recurrent taxes on net wealth	0	8	189	661	1 096	..	0	0	0	0
4300 Estate, inheritance and gift taxes	178	42	0	0	0	..	647	1 749	2 996	3 578
4400 Taxes on financial and capital transactions	393	1 193	521	596	660	..	438	2 728	3 763	4 956
4500 Non-recurrent taxes	0	73	123	563	320	..	0	0	79	5
4600 Other recurrent taxes on property	0	0	0	0	410	..	0	0	0	0
5000 Taxes on goods and services	5 813	20 951	29 984	39 004	49 273	..	412	2 044	2 678	3 434
5100 Taxes on production, sale, transfer, etc	5 562	19 767	29 742	38 985	49 187	..	58	76	227	386
5110 General taxes	3 776	13 894	21 533	27 952	36 442	..	0	0	0	0
5120 Taxes on specific goods and services	1 785	5 872	8 208	11 034	12 745	..	58	76	227	386
5130 Unallocable between 5110 and 5120	0	0	0	0	0	..	0	0	0	0
5200 Taxes on use of goods and perform activities	249	1 178	234	10	73	..	355	1 968	2 451	3 047
5300 Unallocable between 5100 and 5200	3	6	8	9	13	..	0	0	0	0
6000 Other taxes	0	0	0	0	0	..	0	68	40	0
6100 Paid solely by business	..	..	..	..	..	..	..	0	0	0
6200 Other	..	..	..	..	..	..	..	68	40	0
Total tax revenue	15 230	54 377	78 621	100 332	123 678	..	1 659	6 816	14 099	23 820

	Local government					Social Security Funds				
	1975	1995	2005	2015	2022	1975	1995	2005	2015	2022
1000 Taxes on income, profits and capital gains	683	3 058	2 249	3 052	3 684	0	335	825	1 106	1 347
1100 Of individuals	675	3 058	2 249	3 052	3 684	..	335	825	1 106	1 347
1200 Corporate	8	0	0	0	0	..	0	0	0	0
1300 Unallocable between 1100 and 1200	0	0	0	0	0	..	0	0	0	0
2000 Social security contributions	27	80	20	27	19	6 709	28 479	39 537	56 438	71 163
2100 Employees	27	80	18	21	19	1 749	8 268	11 558	15 640	21 356
2200 Employers	0	0	3	6	0	4 347	17 746	24 613	35 510	43 070
2300 Self-employed or non-employed	0	0	0	0	0	612	2 465	3 366	5 289	6 738
2400 Unallocable between 2100, 2200 and 2300	0	0	0	0	0	0	0	0	0	0
3000 Taxes on payroll and workforce	0	0	0	0	0	0	0	5	8	5
4000 Taxes on property	154	815	3 599	5 142	6 160	0	121	229	318	343
4100 Recurrent taxes on immovable property	154	815	3 599	5 142	6 160	..	0	0	0	0
4200 Recurrent taxes on net wealth	0	0	0	0	0	..	0	0	0	0
4300 Estate, inheritance and gift taxes	0	0	0	0	0	..	0	0	0	0
4400 Taxes on financial and capital transactions	0	0	0	0	0	..	0	0	0	0
4500 Non-recurrent taxes	0	0	0	0	0	..	0	0	0	0
4600 Other recurrent taxes on property	0	0	0	0	0	..	121	229	318	343
5000 Taxes on goods and services	166	332	523	715	747	14	330	1 237	1 520	1 705
5100 Taxes on production, sale, transfer, etc	150	295	437	694	723	14	330	1 237	1 520	1 705
5110 General taxes	0	0	0	0	0	0	29	373	219	272
5120 Taxes on specific goods and services	150	295	437	694	723	14	301	865	1 302	1 433
5130 Unallocable between 5110 and 5120	0	0	0	0	0	0	0	0	0	0
5200 Taxes on use of goods and perform activities	16	37	87	22	25	0	0	0	0	0
5300 Unallocable between 5100 and 5200	0	0	0	0	0	0	0	0	0	0
6000 Other taxes	0	0	0	0	0	0	0	0	0	0
6100 Paid solely by business	..	..	..	..	..	..	..	..	..	..
6200 Other	..	..	..	..	..	..	..	..	..	..
Total tax revenue	1 029	4 284	6 392	8 937	10 610	6 723	29 265	41 833	59 391	74 563

.. Not available

Note: Including taxes collected on behalf of the European Union.

Table 6.4. Canada, tax revenues by sub-sectors of government

Million CAD

	Federal government					State/Regional				
	1975	1995	2005	2015	2022	1975	1995	2005	2015	2022
1000 Taxes on income, profits and capital gains	19 047	82 237	140 013	191 684	303 505	8 165	52 373	78 331	123 157	187 442
1100 Of individuals	12 822	65 384	102 366	143 315	207 161	6 074	43 428	62 435	96 989	139 008
1200 Corporate	5 741	14 739	32 197	41 726	83 597	2 091	8 944	15 896	26 168	48 435
1300 Unallocable between 1100 and 1200	484	2 114	5 450	6 643	12 747	0	0	0	0	0
2000 Social security contributions	0	0	17 936	23 603	26 413	0	0	11 759	13 892	15 904
2100 Employees	..	..	7 429	9 772	10 922	..	..	1 858	1 128	1 749
2200 Employers	..	..	10 507	13 831	15 491	..	..	9 901	12 764	14 155
2300 Self-employed or non-employed	..	..	0	0	0	..	..	0	0	0
2400 Unallocable between 2100, 2200 and 2300	..	..	0	0	0	..	..	0	0	0
3000 Taxes on payroll and workforce	0	0	0	0	0	0	6 498	9 230	13 256	20 697
4000 Taxes on property	13	0	0	0	0	428	6 492	9 298	11 809	19 049
4100 Recurrent taxes on immovable property	0	..	..	..	..	85	2 960	2 934	5 410	7 791
4200 Recurrent taxes on net wealth	0	..	..	..	..	200	2 914	3 456	372	561
4300 Estate, inheritance and gift taxes	13	..	..	..	..	143	3	0	268	489
4400 Taxes on financial and capital transactions	0	..	..	..	..	0	0	1 965	3 912	8 331
4500 Non-recurrent taxes	0	..	..	..	..	0	0	0	0	0
4600 Other recurrent taxes on property	0	..	..	..	..	0	0	0	0	0
5000 Taxes on goods and services	8 180	31 160	48 551	53 837	77 995	10 128	42 076	67 537	95 289	127 445
5100 Taxes on production, sale, transfer, etc	8 180	31 136	48 506	53 797	77 956	6 800	37 961	61 316	86 827	114 572
5110 General taxes	3 504	19 167	35 069	36 958	51 705	3 664	21 328	33 353	53 577	77 359
5120 Taxes on specific goods and services	4 676	11 969	13 437	16 839	26 251	3 136	16 633	27 963	33 250	37 213
5130 Unallocable between 5110 and 5120	0	0	0	0	0	0	0	0	0	0
5200 Taxes on use of goods and perform activities	0	24	45	40	39	3 328	4 115	6 221	8 462	12 873
5300 Unallocable between 5100 and 5200	0	0	0	0	0	0	0	0	0	0
6000 Other taxes	198	0	0	0	0	0	0	0	0	0
6100 Paid solely by business	0	..	..	..	..	..	..	..	..	..
6200 Other	198	..	..	..	..	..	..	..	..	..
Total tax revenue	27 438	113 397	206 500	269 124	407 912	18 721	107 439	176 156	257 403	370 538

	Local government					Social Security Funds				
	1975	1995	2005	2015	2022	1975	1995	2005	2015	2022
1000 Taxes on income, profits and capital gains	0	0	0	0	0	0	0	0	0	0
1100 Of individuals	..	..	..	..	..	..	..	..	..	..
1200 Corporate	..	..	..	..	..	..	..	..	..	..
1300 Unallocable between 1100 and 1200	..	..	..	..	..	..	..	..	..	..
2000 Social security contributions	0	0	0	0	0	5 787	40 559	38 834	58 876	91 261
2100 Employees	..	..	..	..	..	2 142	15 028	18 328	27 785	43 091
2200 Employers	..	..	..	..	..	3 527	24 765	18 328	27 785	43 091
2300 Self-employed or non-employed	..	..	..	..	..	118	766	2 177	3 307	5 079
2400 Unallocable between 2100, 2200 and 2300	..	..	..	..	..	0	0	0	0	0
3000 Taxes on payroll and workforce	0	0	0	0	0	0	0	0	0	0
4000 Taxes on property	5 018	24 415	40 495	65 969	79 491	0	0	0	0	0
4100 Recurrent taxes on immovable property	4 770	23 150	37 409	57 241	66 909	..	..	..	..	..
4200 Recurrent taxes on net wealth	0	0	0	0	0	..	..	..	..	..
4300 Estate, inheritance and gift taxes	0	0	0	0	0	..	..	..	..	..
4400 Taxes on financial and capital transactions	0	0	375	1 063	2 487	..	..	..	..	..
4500 Non-recurrent taxes	248	0	0	0	0	..	..	..	..	..
4600 Other recurrent taxes on property	0	0	0	0	0	..	..	..	..	..
5000 Taxes on goods and services	142	406	833	1 149	1 524	0	0	0	0	0
5100 Taxes on production, sale, transfer, etc	22	51	104	126	338	..	..	..	..	..
5110 General taxes	10	40	88	63	75	..	..	..	..	..
5120 Taxes on specific goods and services	12	11	16	63	263	..	..	..	..	..
5130 Unallocable between 5110 and 5120	0	0	0	0	0	..	..	..	..	..
5200 Taxes on use of goods and perform activities	120	355	729	1 023	1 186	..	..	..	..	..
5300 Unallocable between 5100 and 5200	0	0	0	0	0	..	..	..	..	..
6000 Other taxes	525	3 662	1 483	748	1053	0	0	0	0	0
6100 Paid solely by business	437	2 946	541	0	0	..	..	..	..	..
6200 Other	88	716	942	748	1053	..	..	..	..	..
Total tax revenue	5 685	28 483	42 811	67 866	82 068	5 787	40 559	38 834	58 876	91 261

.. Not available

Table 6.5. Chile, tax revenues by sub-sectors of government

Million CLP

	Central government					State/Regional				
	1975	1995	2005	2015	2022	1975	1995	2005	2015	2022
1000 Taxes on income, profits and capital gains	..	1 359 694	5 171 293	11 840 521	27 491 879	..	..	..	..	..
1100 Of individuals	..	281 293	738 620	3 199 876	6 626 617	..	..	..	..	..
1200 Corporate	..	836 725	3 155 480	6 839 133	14 900 568	..	..	..	..	..
1300 Unallocable between 1100 and 1200	..	241 676	1 277 193	1 801 512	5 964 694	..	..	..	..	..
2000 Social security contributions	..	155 855	287 422	434 659	548 558	..	..	..	..	..
2100 Employees	..	142 001	249 526	370 745	398 535	..	..	..	..	..
2200 Employers	..	13 854	37 896	63 914	150 023	..	..	..	..	..
2300 Self-employed or non-employed	..	0	0	0	0	..	..	..	..	..
2400 Unallocable between 2100, 2200 and 2300	..	0	0	0	0	..	..	..	..	..
3000 Taxes on payroll and workforce	..	0	0	0	0	..	..	..	..	..
4000 Taxes on property	..	181 432	490 120	377 667	1456 756	..	..	..	..	..
4100 Recurrent taxes on immovable property	..	13 044	4 909	13 313	274 828	..	..	..	..	..
4200 Recurrent taxes on net wealth	..	0	0	0	0	..	..	..	..	..
4300 Estate, inheritance and gift taxes	..	13 245	23 184	92 236	416 219	..	..	..	..	..
4400 Taxes on financial and capital transactions	..	155 143	462 027	272 118	765 709	..	..	..	..	..
4500 Non-recurrent taxes	..	0	0	0	0	..	..	..	..	..
4600 Other recurrent taxes on property	..	0	0	0	0	..	..	..	..	..
5000 Taxes on goods and services	..	3 179 304	6 831 482	16 182 428	27 754 579	..	..	..	..	..
5100 Taxes on production, sale, transfer, etc	..	3 169 645	6 811 389	16 130 662	27 543 004	..	..	..	..	..
5110 General taxes	..	2 187 602	5 391 285	13 273 958	24 515 246	..	..	..	..	..
5120 Taxes on specific goods and services	..	982 043	1 420 104	2 856 704	3 027 758	..	..	..	..	..
5130 Unallocable between 5110 and 5120	..	0	0	0	0	..	..	..	..	..
5200 Taxes on use of goods and perform activities	..	9 659	20 094	51 767	211 576	..	..	..	..	..
5300 Unallocable between 5100 and 5200	..	0	0	0	0	..	..	..	..	..
6000 Other taxes	..	-29 554	-85 954	-576 893	-722 555	..	..	..	..	..
6100 Paid solely by business	..	0	0	0	0	..	..	..	..	..
6200 Other	..	-29 554	-85 954	-576 893	-722 555	..	..	..	..	..
Total tax revenue	..	4 846 730	12 694 362	28 258 382	56 529 218	..	..	..	..	..

	Local government					Social Security Funds				
	1975	1995	2005	2015	2022	1975	1995	2005	2015	2022
1000 Taxes on income, profits and capital gains	..	0	0	0	0	..	0	0	0	0
1100 Of individuals	..	..	..	..	..	..	..	..	..	..
1200 Corporate	..	..	..	..	..	..	..	..	..	..
1300 Unallocable between 1100 and 1200	..	..	..	..	..	..	..	..	..	..
2000 Social security contributions	..	0	0	0	0	..	193 269	644 295	1 817 831	2 036 863
2100 Employees	..	..	..	..	..	..	193 269	644 295	1 817 831	2 036 863
2200 Employers	..	..	..	..	..	..	0	0	0	0
2300 Self-employed or non-employed	..	..	..	..	..	..	0	0	0	0
2400 Unallocable between 2100, 2200 and 2300	..	..	..	..	..	..	0	0	0	0
3000 Taxes on payroll and workforce	..	0	0	0	0	..	0	0	0	0
4000 Taxes on property	..	157 193	411 656	1 041 671	2 009 425	..	0	0	0	0
4100 Recurrent taxes on immovable property	..	157 193	411 656	1 041 671	2 009 425	..	..	..	..	..
4200 Recurrent taxes on net wealth	..	0	0	0	0	..	..	..	..	..
4300 Estate, inheritance and gift taxes	..	0	0	0	0	..	..	..	..	..
4400 Taxes on financial and capital transactions	..	0	0	0	0	..	..	..	..	..
4500 Non-recurrent taxes	..	0	0	0	0	..	..	..	..	..
4600 Other recurrent taxes on property	..	0	0	0	0	..	..	..	..	..
5000 Taxes on goods and services	..	192 325	514 952	1 415 658	2 325 932	..	0	0	0	0
5100 Taxes on production, sale, transfer, etc	..	52 690	140 703	385 532	535 676	..	..	..	..	..
5110 General taxes	..	0	0	0	0	..	..	..	..	..
5120 Taxes on specific goods and services	..	52 690	140 703	385 532	535 676	..	..	..	..	..
5130 Unallocable between 5110 and 5120	..	0	0	0	0	..	..	..	..	..
5200 Taxes on use of goods and perform activities	..	139 635	374 249	1 030 126	1 790 256	..	..	..	..	..
5300 Unallocable between 5100 and 5200	..	0	0	0	0	..	..	..	..	..
6000 Other taxes	..	0	0	0	0	..	0	0	0	0
6100 Paid solely by business	..	..	..	..	..	..	..	..	..	..
6200 Other	..	..	..	..	..	..	..	..	..	..
Total tax revenue	..	349 518	926 608	2 457 329	4 335 357	..	193 269	644 295	1 817 831	2 036 863

.. Not available

Table 6.6. Colombia, tax revenues by sub-sectors of government

Million COP

	Federal government					State/Regional				
	1975	1995	2005	2015	2022	1975	1995	2005	2015	2022
1000 Taxes on income, profits and capital gains	..	3 393 700	17 348 618	52 656 876	95 911 106	..	0	0	0	0
1100 Of individuals	..	131 405	3 594 441	9 218 735	20 356 452	..	..	..	..	..
1200 Corporate	..	988 082	13 044 361	41 406 848	73 300 918	..	..	..	..	..
1300 Unallocable between 1100 and 1200	..	2 274 213	709 816	2 031 293	2 253 735	..	..	..	..	..
2000 Social security contributions	..	0	0	0	0	..	0	0	0	0
2100 Employees	..	..	..	..	..	..	..	..	..	..
2200 Employers	..	..	..	..	..	..	..	..	..	..
2300 Self-employed or non-employed	..	..	..	..	..	..	..	..	..	..
2400 Unallocable between 2100, 2200 and 2300	..	..	..	..	..	..	..	..	..	..
3000 Taxes on payroll and workforce	..	599 198	2 179 842	2 797 308	4 421 997	..	0	0	0	0
4000 Taxes on property	..	0	2 863 946	12 094 140	12 588 105	..	0	0	0	0
4100 Recurrent taxes on immovable property	..	..	0	0	0	..	..	..	..	..
4200 Recurrent taxes on net wealth	..	..	462 720	5 352 940	73 113	..	..	..	..	..
4300 Estate, inheritance and gift taxes	..	..	0	0	0	..	..	..	..	..
4400 Taxes on financial and capital transactions	..	..	2 401 226	6 741 200	12 281 751	..	..	..	..	..
4500 Non-recurrent taxes	..	..	0	0	233 241	..	..	..	..	..
4600 Other recurrent taxes on property	..	..	0	0	0	..	..	..	..	..
5000 Taxes on goods and services	..	4 773 500	21 645 318	51 831 190	103 231 251	..	771 560	2 507 423	4 986 314	9 817 124
5100 Taxes on production, sale, transfer, etc	..	4 773 500	21 645 318	51 831 190	103 231 251	..	771 560	2 228 909	4 456 650	8 365 348
5110 General taxes	..	3 427 600	17 427 948	41 659 696	91 723 278	..	0	0	0	0
5120 Taxes on specific goods and services	..	1 345 900	4 217 370	10 171 494	11 507 974	..	771 560	2 228 909	4 456 650	8 365 348
5130 Unallocable between 5110 and 5120	..	0	0	0	0	..	0	0	0	0
5200 Taxes on use of goods and perform activities	..	0	0	0	0	..	0	278 514	529 665	1 451 776
5300 Unallocable between 5100 and 5200	..	0	0	0	0	..	0	0	0	0
6000 Other taxes	..	17 900	682 084	419 939	923 110	..	0	575 919	2 624 769	4 053 893
6100 Paid solely by business	..	0	0	0	0	..	..	0	0	0
6200 Other	..	17 900	682 084	419 939	923 110	..	..	575 919	2 624 769	4 053 893
Total tax revenue	..	8 784 297	44 719 808	119 799 453	217 075 569	..	771 560	3 083 342	7 611 084	13 871 017

	Local government					Social Security Funds				
	1975	1995	2005	2015	2022	1975	1995	2005	2015	2022
1000 Taxes on income, profits and capital gains	..	0	0	0	0	..	0	0	0	0
1100 Of individuals	..	..	..	..	..	..	..	..	..	..
1200 Corporate	..	..	..	..	..	..	..	..	..	..
1300 Unallocable between 1100 and 1200	..	..	..	..	..	..	..	..	..	..
2000 Social security contributions	..	0	0	0	0	..	3 159 328	7 845 000	13 585 138	23 908 538
2100 Employees	..	..	..	..	..	..	..	..	..	..
2200 Employers	..	..	..	..	..	..	..	..	..	..
2300 Self-employed or non-employed	..	..	..	..	..	..	..	..	..	..
2400 Unallocable between 2100, 2200 and 2300	..	..	..	..	..	..	3 159 328	7 845 000	13 585 138	23 908 538
3000 Taxes on payroll and workforce	..	0	0	0	0	..	0	0	0	0
4000 Taxes on property	..	365 051	1 974 213	6 061 965	9 937 041	..	0	0	0	0
4100 Recurrent taxes on immovable property	..	365 051	1 974 213	6 061 965	9 937 041	..	..	..	..	..
4200 Recurrent taxes on net wealth	..	0	0	0	0	..	..	..	..	..
4300 Estate, inheritance and gift taxes	..	0	0	0	0	..	..	..	..	..
4400 Taxes on financial and capital transactions	..	0	0	0	0	..	..	..	..	..
4500 Non-recurrent taxes	..	0	0	0	0	..	..	..	..	..
4600 Other recurrent taxes on property	..	0	0	0	0	..	..	..	..	..
5000 Taxes on goods and services	..	471 710	3 496 411	8 899 062	16 283 558	..	0	0	0	0
5100 Taxes on production, sale, transfer, etc	..	471 710	3 496 411	8 400 241	15 449 777	..	..	..	..	..
5110 General taxes	..	471 710	2 506 452	7 025 204	13 360 841	..	..	..	..	..
5120 Taxes on specific goods and services	..	0	989 959	1 375 037	2 088 936	..	..	..	..	..
5130 Unallocable between 5110 and 5120	..	0	0	0	0	..	..	..	..	..
5200 Taxes on use of goods and perform activities	..	0	0	498 821	833 781	..	..	..	..	..
5300 Unallocable between 5100 and 5200	..	0	0	0	0	..	..	..	..	..
6000 Other taxes	..	355 943	588 614	4 200 992	7 766 603	..	0	0	0	0
6100 Paid solely by business	..	0	0	0	0	..	..	..	..	..
6200 Other	..	355 943	588 614	4 200 992	7 766 603	..	..	..	..	..
Total tax revenue	..	1 192 705	6 059 238	19 162 019	33 987 202	..	3 159 328	7 845 000	13 585 138	23 908 538

.. Not available

Table 6.7. Costa Rica, tax revenues by sub-sectors of government

Million CRC

	Central government					State/Regional				
	1975	1995	2005	2015	2022	1975	1995	2005	2015	2022
1000 Taxes on income, profits and capital gains	..	47 678	324 224	1 247 308	2 430 200	..	..	..	..	..
1100 Of individuals	..	..	16 438	386 241	691 305	..	..	..	..	..
1200 Corporate	..	..	288 355	659 951	1188 835	..	..	..	..	..
1300 Unallocable between 1100 and 1200	..	47 678	19 430	201 116	550 059	..	..	..	..	..
2000 Social security contributions	..	11 096	30 854	63 458	515 732	..	..	..	..	..
2100 Employees	..	..	..	..	..	..	..	..	..	..
2200 Employers	..	0	0	0	0	..	..	..	..	..
2300 Self-employed or non-employed	..	..	..	..	..	..	..	..	..	..
2400 Unallocable between 2100, 2200 and 2300	..	11 096	30 854	63 458	515 732	..	..	..	..	..
3000 Taxes on payroll and workforce	..	0	0	0	0	..	..	..	..	..
4000 Taxes on property	..	2 023	10 846	37 334	71 009	..	..	..	..	..
4100 Recurrent taxes on immovable property	..	440	0	4 076	5 206	..	..	..	..	..
4200 Recurrent taxes on net wealth	..	0	0	0	0	..	..	..	..	..
4300 Estate, inheritance and gift taxes	..	0	0	0	0	..	..	..	..	..
4400 Taxes on financial and capital transactions	..	1 583	10 846	33 258	65 802	..	..	..	..	..
4500 Non-recurrent taxes	..	0	0	0	0	..	..	..	..	..
4600 Other recurrent taxes on property	..	0	0	0	0	..	..	..	..	..
5000 Taxes on goods and services	..	185 943	917 118	2 536 562	3 519 484	..	..	..	..	..
5100 Taxes on production, sale, transfer, etc	..	177 808	884 359	2 385 807	3 326 853	..	..	..	..	..
5110 General taxes	..	84 034	485 168	1 368 601	2 217 743	..	..	..	..	..
5120 Taxes on specific goods and services	..	93 774	399 192	1 017 206	1 109 110	..	..	..	..	..
5130 Unallocable between 5110 and 5120	..	0	0	0	0	..	..	..	..	..
5200 Taxes on use of goods and perform activities	..	8 135	32 758	150 755	192 631	..	..	..	..	..
5300 Unallocable between 5100 and 5200	..	0	0	0	0	..	..	..	..	..
6000 Other taxes	..	11 010	54 338	162 200	394 676	..	..	..	..	..
6100 Paid solely by business	..	0	0	0	0	..	..	..	..	..
6200 Other	..	11 010	54 338	162 200	394 676	..	..	..	..	..
Total tax revenue	..	257 751	1 337 380	4 046 862	6 931 100	..	..	..	..	..

	Local government					Social Security Funds				
	1975	1995	2005	2015	2022	1975	1995	2005	2015	2022
1000 Taxes on income, profits and capital gains	..	0	0	0	0	..	0	0	0	0
1100 Of individuals	..	..	..	..	..	..	..	..	..	..
1200 Corporate	..	..	..	..	..	..	..	..	..	..
1300 Unallocable between 1100 and 1200	..	..	..	..	..	..	..	..	..	..
2000 Social security contributions	..	0	0	0	0	..	106 727	586 829	2 241 674	3 409 960
2100 Employees	..	..	..	..	..	..	..	..	..	..
2200 Employers	..	..	..	..	..	..	14 654	84 988	318 652	412 852
2300 Self-employed or non-employed	..	..	..	..	..	..	..	..	..	..
2400 Unallocable between 2100, 2200 and 2300	..	..	..	..	..	..	92 073	501 841	1 923 022	2 997 108
3000 Taxes on payroll and workforce	..	0	0	0	0	..	22 992	115 730	423 616	639 737
4000 Taxes on property	..	2 037	14 264	85 927	149 733	..	0	0	0	0
4100 Recurrent taxes on immovable property	..	2 037	14 264	85 927	149 724	..	..	..	..	..
4200 Recurrent taxes on net wealth	..	0	0	0	0	..	..	..	..	..
4300 Estate, inheritance and gift taxes	..	0	0	0	0	..	..	..	..	..
4400 Taxes on financial and capital transactions	..	0	0	0	0	..	..	..	..	..
4500 Non-recurrent taxes	..	0	0	0	0	..	..	..	..	..
4600 Other recurrent taxes on property	..	0	0	0	0	..	..	..	..	..
5000 Taxes on goods and services	..	1 214	27 506	125 341	155 239	..	0	0	0	0
5100 Taxes on production, sale, transfer, etc	..	0	94	3 093	3 919	..	..	..	..	..
5110 General taxes	..	..	0	0	0	..	..	..	..	..
5120 Taxes on specific goods and services	..	..	94	3 093	3 919	..	..	..	..	..
5130 Unallocable between 5110 and 5120	..	..	0	0	0	..	..	..	..	..
5200 Taxes on use of goods and perform activities	..	1 214	27 411	122 248	151 320	..	..	..	..	..
5300 Unallocable between 5100 and 5200	..	0	0	0	0	..	..	..	..	..
6000 Other taxes	..	2 935	3 207	155	198	..	0	0	0	0
6100 Paid solely by business	..	0	0	0	0	..	..	..	..	..
6200 Other	..	2 935	3 207	155	198	..	..	..	..	..
Total tax revenue	..	6 185	44 976	211 422	305 170	..	129 718	702 559	2 665 291	4 049 697

.. Not available

Table 6.8. Czechia, tax revenues by sub-sectors of government

Million CZK

	Central government (1)					State/Regional				
	1975	1995	2005	2015	2022	1975	1995	2005	2015	2022
1000 Taxes on income, profits and capital gains	..	137 616	273 549	329 768	515 371	..	..	..	..	..
1100 Of individuals	..	70 361	137 937	164 678	214 131	..	..	..	..	..
1200 Corporate	..	67 255	135 611	165 090	301 240	..	..	..	..	..
1300 Unallocable between 1100 and 1200	..	0	0	0	0	..	..	..	..	..
2000 Social security contributions	..	0	0	0	0	..	..	..	..	..
2100 Employees	..	..	..	..	..	..	..	..	..	..
2200 Employers	..	..	..	..	..	..	..	..	..	..
2300 Self-employed or non-employed	..	..	..	..	..	..	..	..	..	..
2400 Unallocable between 2100, 2200 and 2300	..	..	..	..	..	..	..	..	..	..
3000 Taxes on payroll and workforce	..	0	0	0	0	..	..	..	..	..
4000 Taxes on property	..	3 857	8 050	11 607	82	..	..	..	..	..
4100 Recurrent taxes on immovable property	..	0	5	20	27	..	..	..	..	..
4200 Recurrent taxes on net wealth	..	0	0	0	0	..	..	..	..	..
4300 Estate, inheritance and gift taxes	..	393	728	20	0	..	..	..	..	..
4400 Taxes on financial and capital transactions	..	3 464	7 317	11 566	55	..	..	..	..	..
4500 Non-recurrent taxes	..	0	0	0	0	..	..	..	..	..
4600 Other recurrent taxes on property	..	0	0	0	0	..	..	..	..	..
5000 Taxes on goods and services	..	175 869	343 554	505 085	713 103	..	..	..	..	..
5100 Taxes on production, sale, transfer, etc	..	162 913	325 662	487 086	695 801	..	..	..	..	..
5110 General taxes	..	91 673	215 118	333 274	536 896	..	..	..	..	..
5120 Taxes on specific goods and services	..	71 240	110 544	153 812	158 905	..	..	..	..	..
5130 Unallocable between 5110 and 5120	..	0	0	0	0	..	..	..	..	..
5200 Taxes on use of goods and perform activities	..	12 956	17 892	17 999	17 303	..	..	..	..	..
5300 Unallocable between 5100 and 5200	..	0	0	0	0	..	..	..	..	..
6000 Other taxes	..	545	55	387	232	..	..	..	..	..
6100 Paid solely by business	..	0	0	0	0	..	..	..	..	..
6200 Other	..	545	55	387	232	..	..	..	..	..
Total tax revenue	..	317 887	625 207	846 847	1 228 789	..	..	..	..	..

	Local government					Social Security Funds				
	1975	1995	2005	2015	2022	1975	1995	2005	2015	2022
1000 Taxes on income, profits and capital gains	..	0	0	0	0	..	0	0	0	0
1100 Of individuals	..	..	..	..	..	..	..	..	..	..
1200 Corporate	..	..	..	..	..	..	..	..	..	..
1300 Unallocable between 1100 and 1200	..	..	..	..	..	..	..	..	..	..
2000 Social security contributions	..	0	0	0	0	..	227 871	481 626	659 743	1 074 201
2100 Employees	..	..	..	..	..	..	54 536	108 316	133 878	215 214
2200 Employers	..	..	..	..	..	..	148 342	307 618	417 778	661 335
2300 Self-employed or non-employed	..	..	..	..	..	..	24 993	65 692	108 088	197 653
2400 Unallocable between 2100, 2200 and 2300	..	..	..	..	..	..	0	0	0	0
3000 Taxes on payroll and workforce	..	0	0	0	0	..	0	0	0	0
4000 Taxes on property	..	3 778	4 987	10 313	12 419	..	0	0	0	0
4100 Recurrent taxes on immovable property	..	3 778	4 987	10 313	12 419	..	..	..	..	..
4200 Recurrent taxes on net wealth	..	0	0	0	0	..	..	..	..	..
4300 Estate, inheritance and gift taxes	..	0	0	0	0	..	..	..	..	..
4400 Taxes on financial and capital transactions	..	0	0	0	0	..	..	..	..	..
4500 Non-recurrent taxes	..	0	0	0	0	..	..	..	..	..
4600 Other recurrent taxes on property	..	0	0	0	0	..	..	..	..	..
5000 Taxes on goods and services	..	1 150	7 395	7 749	11 500	..	0	0	0	0
5100 Taxes on production, sale, transfer, etc	..	124	199	292	138	..	..	..	..	..
5110 General taxes	..	0	0	0	0	..	..	..	..	..
5120 Taxes on specific goods and services	..	124	199	292	138	..	..	..	..	..
5130 Unallocable between 5110 and 5120	..	0	0	0	0	..	..	..	..	..
5200 Taxes on use of goods and perform activities	..	1 026	7 196	7 457	11 362	..	..	..	..	..
5300 Unallocable between 5100 and 5200	..	0	0	0	0	..	..	..	..	..
6000 Other taxes	..	0	0	0	0	..	0	0	0	0
6100 Paid solely by business	..	..	..	..	..	..	..	..	..	..
6200 Other	..	..	..	..	..	..	..	..	..	..
Total tax revenue	..	4 928	12 382	18 063	23 919	..	227 871	481 626	659 743	1 074 201

.. Not available

Note: Including taxes collected on behalf of the European Union.

1. Tax revenues of the regions are reported under the heading of central government up to and including 1995 and under local government thereafter.

Table 6.9. Denmark, tax revenues by sub-sectors of government

Million DKK

	Central government					State/Regional				
	1975	1995	2005	2015	2022	1975	1995	2005	2015	2022
1000 Taxes on income, profits and capital gains	29 912	166 881	259 789	388 660	493 652	..	..	..	..	..
1100 Of individuals	25 904	126 557	167 192	304 084	388 198	..	..	..	..	..
1200 Corporate	4 008	23 778	55 559	61 854	94 281	..	..	..	..	..
1300 Unallocable between 1100 and 1200	0	16 546	37 038	22 721	11 173	..	..	..	..	..
2000 Social security contributions	143	562	1 180	1332	1797	..	..	..	..	..
2100 Employees	1	559	1 177	826	697	..	..	..	..	..
2200 Employers	142	3	3	506	1100	..	..	..	..	..
2300 Self-employed or non-employed	0	0	0	0	0	..	..	..	..	..
2400 Unallocable between 2100, 2200 and 2300	0	0	0	0	0	..	..	..	..	..
3000 Taxes on payroll and workforce	0	2 262	2 907	5 894	7 150	..	..	..	..	..
4000 Taxes on property	1 786	6 962	11 801	11 276	15 395	..	..	..	..	..
4100 Recurrent taxes on immovable property	16	0	0	0	0	..	..	..	..	..
4200 Recurrent taxes on net wealth	414	968	0	0	0	..	..	..	..	..
4300 Estate, inheritance and gift taxes	336	2 372	3 154	5 177	7 444	..	..	..	..	..
4400 Taxes on financial and capital transactions	943	3 583	8 613	6 099	7 951	..	..	..	..	..
4500 Non-recurrent taxes	0	0	0	0	0	..	..	..	..	..
4600 Other recurrent taxes on property	0	0	0	0	0	..	..	..	..	..
5000 Taxes on goods and services	29 013	156 308	253 271	301 263	362 120	..	..	..	..	..
5100 Taxes on production, sale, transfer, etc	27 337	149 123	239 870	277 556	337 992	..	..	..	..	..
5110 General taxes	15 117	94 008	154 654	191 328	266 040	..	..	..	..	..
5120 Taxes on specific goods and services	12 220	55 116	85 216	86 228	71 952	..	..	..	..	..
5130 Unallocable between 5110 and 5120	0	0	0	0	0	..	..	..	..	..
5200 Taxes on use of goods and perform activities	1 676	4 739	9 379	16 530	13 546	..	..	..	..	..
5300 Unallocable between 5100 and 5200	0	2 446	4 021	7 177	10 582	..	..	..	..	..
6000 Other taxes	0	0	203	2781	1382	..	..	..	..	..
6100 Paid solely by business	..	..	203	2781	1382	..	..	..	..	..
6200 Other	..	..	0	0	0	..	..	..	..	..
Total tax revenue	60 854	332 973	529 151	711 204	881 495	..	..	..	..	..

	Local government					Social Security Funds				
	1975	1995	2005	2015	2022	1975	1995	2005	2015	2022
1000 Taxes on income, profits and capital gains	22 171	140 762	214 586	221 084	282 574	0	0	0	0	0
1100 Of individuals	22 170	140 757	214 586	221 084	282 574	..	..	..	..	..
1200 Corporate	1	5	0	0	0	..	..	..	..	..
1300 Unallocable between 1100 and 1200	0	0	0	0	0	..	..	..	..	..
2000 Social security contributions	0	0	0	0	0	58	0	529	542	544
2100 Employees	..	..	..	..	..	0	..	0	0	0
2200 Employers	..	..	..	..	..	58	..	529	542	544
2300 Self-employed or non-employed	..	..	..	..	..	0	..	0	0	0
2400 Unallocable between 2100, 2200 and 2300	..	..	..	..	..	0	..	0	0	0
3000 Taxes on payroll and workforce	0	0	0	0	0	0	0	0	0	0
4000 Taxes on property	3 518	10 325	17 485	28 085	33 080	0	0	0	0	0
4100 Recurrent taxes on immovable property	3 518	10 325	17 485	28 085	33 080	..	..	..	..	..
4200 Recurrent taxes on net wealth	0	0	0	0	0	..	..	..	..	..
4300 Estate, inheritance and gift taxes	0	0	0	0	0	..	..	..	..	..
4400 Taxes on financial and capital transactions	0	0	0	0	0	..	..	..	..	..
4500 Non-recurrent taxes	0	0	0	0	0	..	..	..	..	..
4600 Other recurrent taxes on property	0	0	0	0	0	..	..	..	..	..
5000 Taxes on goods and services	0	0	0	0	0	0	0	0	0	0
5100 Taxes on production, sale, transfer, etc	0	..	..	..	..	..	..	..	..	..
5110 General taxes	0	..	..	..	..	..	..	..	..	..
5120 Taxes on specific goods and services	0	..	..	..	..	..	..	..	..	..
5130 Unallocable between 5110 and 5120	0	..	..	..	..	..	..	..	..	..
5200 Taxes on use of goods and perform activities	..	..	..	..	..	..	..	..	..	..
5300 Unallocable between 5100 and 5200	0	..	..	..	..	..	..	..	..	..
6000 Other taxes	0	0	0	0	0	0	0	0	0	0
6100 Paid solely by business	..	..	..	..	..	..	..	..	..	..
6200 Other	..	..	..	..	..	..	..	..	..	..
Total tax revenue	25 689	151 087	232 071	249 169	315 653	58	0	529	542	544

.. Not available

Note: Including taxes collected on behalf of the European Union.

Table 6.10. Estonia, tax revenues by sub-sectors of government

Million EUR

	Central government					State/Regional				
	1975	1995	2005	2015	2022	1975	1995	2005	2015	2022
1000 Taxes on income, profits and capital gains	..	301	782	1 607	2 876	..	..	..	..	..
1100 Of individuals	..	234	622	1 182	2 279	..	..	..	..	..
1200 Corporate	..	67	160	424	596	..	..	..	..	..
1300 Unallocable between 1100 and 1200	..	0	0	0	0	..	..	..	..	..
2000 Social security contributions	..	191	636	1 191	2 226	..	..	..	..	..
2100 Employees	..	0	0	0	0	..	..	..	..	..
2200 Employers	..	191	636	1 179	2 117	..	..	..	..	..
2300 Self-employed or non-employed	..	0	0	12	109	..	..	..	..	..
2400 Unallocable between 2100, 2200 and 2300	..	0	0	0	0	..	..	..	..	..
3000 Taxes on payroll and workforce	..	0	0	0	0	..	..	..	..	..
4000 Taxes on property	..	3	0	0	0	..	..	..	..	..
4100 Recurrent taxes on immovable property	..	3	..	..	..	..	..	..	..	..
4200 Recurrent taxes on net wealth	..	0	..	..	..	..	..	..	..	..
4300 Estate, inheritance and gift taxes	..	0	..	..	..	..	..	..	..	..
4400 Taxes on financial and capital transactions	..	0	..	..	..	..	..	..	..	..
4500 Non-recurrent taxes	..	0	..	..	..	..	..	..	..	..
4600 Other recurrent taxes on property	..	0	..	..	..	..	..	..	..	..
5000 Taxes on goods and services	..	350	1 385	2 864	4 689	..	..	..	..	..
5100 Taxes on production, sale, transfer, etc	..	345	1 348	2 790	4 374	..	..	..	..	..
5110 General taxes	..	266	908	1 873	3 309	..	..	..	..	..
5120 Taxes on specific goods and services	..	79	440	917	1 065	..	..	..	..	..
5130 Unallocable between 5110 and 5120	..	0	0	0	0	..	..	..	..	..
5200 Taxes on use of goods and perform activities	..	5	37	74	316	..	..	..	..	..
5300 Unallocable between 5100 and 5200	..	0	0	0	0	..	..	..	..	..
6000 Other taxes	..	0	0	0	0	..	..	..	..	..
6100 Paid solely by business	..	..	..	..	..	..	..	..	..	..
6200 Other	..	..	..	..	..	..	..	..	..	..
Total tax revenue	..	845	2 803	5 662	9 791	..	..	..	..	..

	Local government					Social Security Funds				
	1975	1995	2005	2015	2022	1975	1995	2005	2015	2022
1000 Taxes on income, profits and capital gains	..	0	0	0	0	..	0	0	0	0
1100 Of individuals	..	0	0	0	0	..	0	0	0	0
1200 Corporate	..	0	0	0	0	..	0	0	0	0
1300 Unallocable between 1100 and 1200	..	0	0	0	0	..	0	0	0	0
2000 Social security contributions	..	0	0	0	0	..	149	511	1 110	1 896
2100 Employees	..	..	..	..	..	..	0	31	99	171
2200 Employers	..	..	..	..	..	..	143	466	1 002	1 654
2300 Self-employed or non-employed	..	..	..	..	..	..	6	14	8	71
2400 Unallocable between 2100, 2200 and 2300	..	..	..	..	..	..	0	0	0	0
3000 Taxes on payroll and workforce	..	0	0	0	0	..	0	0	0	0
4000 Taxes on property	..	7	32	58	59	..	0	0	0	0
4100 Recurrent taxes on immovable property	..	7	32	58	59	..	..	..	..	..
4200 Recurrent taxes on net wealth	..	0	0	0	0	..	..	..	..	..
4300 Estate, inheritance and gift taxes	..	0	0	0	0	..	..	..	..	..
4400 Taxes on financial and capital transactions	..	0	0	0	0	..	..	..	..	..
4500 Non-recurrent taxes	..	0	0	0	0	..	..	..	..	..
4600 Other recurrent taxes on property	..	0	0	0	0	..	..	..	..	..
5000 Taxes on goods and services	..	1	7	11	15	..	0	0	0	0
5100 Taxes on production, sale, transfer, etc	..	0	2	4	7	..	..	..	..	..
5110 General taxes	..	0	0	0	0	..	..	..	..	..
5120 Taxes on specific goods and services	..	0	2	4	7	..	..	..	..	..
5130 Unallocable between 5110 and 5120	..	0	0	0	0	..	..	..	..	..
5200 Taxes on use of goods and perform activities	..	1	5	7	7	..	..	..	..	..
5300 Unallocable between 5100 and 5200	..	0	0	0	0	..	..	..	..	..
6000 Other taxes	..	0	0	0	0	..	0	0	0	0
6100 Paid solely by business	..	..	..	..	..	..	..	..	..	..
6200 Other	..	..	..	..	..	..	..	..	..	..
Total tax revenue	..	8	40	69	74	..	149	511	1 110	1 896

.. Not available

Note: Including taxes collected on behalf of the European Union.

Table 6.11. Finland, tax revenues by sub-sectors of government

Million EUR

	Central government					State/Regional				
	1975	1995	2005	2015	2022	1975	1995	2005	2015	2022
1000 Taxes on income, profits and capital gains	1 304	6 538	12 885	12 127	18 122	..	..	..	..	..
1100 Of individuals	1 146	5 320	8 791	9 248	12 843	..	..	..	..	..
1200 Corporate	157	1 218	4 094	2 879	5 279	..	..	..	..	..
1300 Unallocable between 1100 and 1200	0	0	0	0	0	..	..	..	..	..
2000 Social security contributions	0	25	0	0	0	..	..	..	..	..
2100 Employees	..	0	..	..	..	..	..	..	..	..
2200 Employers	..	25	..	..	..	..	..	..	..	..
2300 Self-employed or non-employed	..	0	..	..	..	..	..	..	..	..
2400 Unallocable between 2100, 2200 and 2300	..	0	..	..	..	..	..	..	..	..
3000 Taxes on payroll and workforce	153	0	0	0	0	..	..	..	..	..
4000 Taxes on property	127	533	1 169	1 414	1 818	..	..	..	..	..
4100 Recurrent taxes on immovable property	0	0	0	0	0	..	..	..	..	..
4200 Recurrent taxes on net wealth	33	35	129	0	0	..	..	..	..	..
4300 Estate, inheritance and gift taxes	14	167	486	631	901	..	..	..	..	..
4400 Taxes on financial and capital transactions	80	331	554	783	917	..	..	..	..	..
4500 Non-recurrent taxes	0	0	0	0	0	..	..	..	..	..
4600 Other recurrent taxes on property	0	0	0	0	0	..	..	..	..	..
5000 Taxes on goods and services	2 099	13 241	21 768	29 650	36 392	..	..	..	..	..
5100 Taxes on production, sale, transfer, etc	2 082	12 937	21 178	28 592	34 715	..	..	..	..	..
5110 General taxes	1 030	7 621	13 748	18 974	25 061	..	..	..	..	..
5120 Taxes on specific goods and services	1 052	5 316	7 430	9 618	9 654	..	..	..	..	..
5130 Unallocable between 5110 and 5120	0	0	0	0	0	..	..	..	..	..
5200 Taxes on use of goods and perform activities	16	304	590	1 058	1 677	..	..	..	..	..
5300 Unallocable between 5100 and 5200	0	0	0	0	0	..	..	..	..	..
6000 Other taxes	10	90	68	81	87	..	..	..	..	..
6100 Paid solely by business	0	0	0	0	0	..	..	..	..	..
6200 Other	10	90	68	81	87	..	..	..	..	..
Total tax revenue	3 693	20 427	35 890	43 272	56 419	..	..	..	..	..

	Local government					Social Security Funds				
	1975	1995	2005	2015	2022	1975	1995	2005	2015	2022
1000 Taxes on income, profits and capital gains	1 547	9 313	13 574	20 244	24 538	0	0	0	0	0
1100 Of individuals	1 393	8 319	12 420	18 576	21 761	..	..	..	..	..
1200 Corporate	154	994	1 154	1 668	2 777	..	..	..	..	..
1300 Unallocable between 1100 and 1200	0	0	0	0	0	..	..	..	..	..
2000 Social security contributions	0	0	0	0	0	1 347	13 493	18 879	26 639	31 954
2100 Employees	..	..	..	..	..	278	2 537	3 464	6 364	9 580
2200 Employers	..	..	..	..	..	990	9 447	14 127	18 232	20 283
2300 Self-employed or non-employed	..	..	..	..	..	79	1 509	1 288	2 043	2 091
2400 Unallocable between 2100, 2200 and 2300	..	..	..	..	..	0	0	0	0	0
3000 Taxes on payroll and workforce	0	0	0	0	0	0	0	0	0	0
4000 Taxes on property	0	441	725	1 603	2 046	0	0	0	0	0
4100 Recurrent taxes on immovable property	0	441	725	1 603	2 046	..	..	..	..	..
4200 Recurrent taxes on net wealth	0	0	0	0	0	..	..	..	..	..
4300 Estate, inheritance and gift taxes	0	0	0	0	0	..	..	..	..	..
4400 Taxes on financial and capital transactions	0	0	0	0	0	..	..	..	..	..
4500 Non-recurrent taxes	0	0	0	0	0	..	..	..	..	..
4600 Other recurrent taxes on property	0	0	0	0	0	..	..	..	..	..
5000 Taxes on goods and services	3	7	8	2	1	0	0	0	0	0
5100 Taxes on production, sale, transfer, etc	1	1	4	1	1	..	..	..	..	..
5110 General taxes	0	0	0	0	0	..	..	..	..	..
5120 Taxes on specific goods and services	1	1	4	1	1	..	..	..	..	..
5130 Unallocable between 5110 and 5120	0	0	0	0	0	..	..	..	..	..
5200 Taxes on use of goods and perform activities	2	6	4	1	0	..	..	..	..	..
5300 Unallocable between 5100 and 5200	0	0	0	0	0	..	..	..	..	..
6000 Other taxes	0	0	0	0	0	0	0	0	0	0
6100 Paid solely by business	..	..	..	..	..	..	..	..	..	..
6200 Other	..	..	..	..	..	..	..	..	..	..
Total tax revenue	1 550	9 761	14 307	21 849	26 585	1 347	13 493	18 879	26 639	31 954

.. Not available

Note: Including taxes collected on behalf of the European Union.

Table 6.12. France, tax revenues by sub-sectors of government

Million EUR

	Central government					State/Regional				
	1975	1995	2005	2015	2022	1975	1995	2005	2015	2022
1000 Taxes on income, profits and capital gains	13 106	69 433	101 392	123 790	183 873	..	..	..	..	..
1100 Of individuals	8 743	46 087	61 341	80 773	108 271	..	..	..	..	..
1200 Corporate	4 282	23 347	40 052	43 017	75 602	..	..	..	..	..
1300 Unallocable between 1100 and 1200	80	0	0	0	0	..	..	..	..	..
2000 Social security contributions	419	3 733	5 796	7 941	7 855	..	..	..	..	..
2100 Employees	419	3 733	4 812	6 048	7 237	..	..	..	..	..
2200 Employers	0	0	984	1 893	618	..	..	..	..	..
2300 Self-employed or non-employed	0	0	0	0	0	..	..	..	..	..
2400 Unallocable between 2100, 2200 and 2300	0	0	0	0	0	..	..	..	..	..
3000 Taxes on payroll and workforce	1 194	11 167	14 329	5 946	15 735	..	..	..	..	..
4000 Taxes on property	1 372	7 356	13 945	20 522	27 852	..	..	..	..	..
4100 Recurrent taxes on immovable property	26	9	30	100	2 953	..	..	..	..	..
4200 Recurrent taxes on net wealth	0	1 309	3 053	5 224	2 283	..	..	..	..	..
4300 Estate, inheritance and gift taxes	616	4 261	9 006	12 477	18 981	..	..	..	..	..
4400 Taxes on financial and capital transactions	731	1 777	1 856	2 721	3 635	..	..	..	..	..
4500 Non-recurrent taxes	0	0	0	0	0	..	..	..	..	..
4600 Other recurrent taxes on property	0	0	0	0	0	..	..	..	..	..
5000 Taxes on goods and services	26 154	129 278	167 349	178 978	138 182	..	..	..	..	..
5100 Taxes on production, sale, transfer, etc	25 618	126 568	163 492	174 082	134 993	..	..	..	..	..
5110 General taxes	19 077	89 630	126 866	140 988	101 906	..	..	..	..	..
5120 Taxes on specific goods and services	6 540	36 939	36 626	33 094	33 087	..	..	..	..	..
5130 Unallocable between 5110 and 5120	0	0	0	0	0	..	..	..	..	..
5200 Taxes on use of goods and perform activities	536	2 710	3 857	4 896	3 189	..	..	..	..	..
5300 Unallocable between 5100 and 5200	..	0	0	0	0	..	..	..	..	..
6000 Other taxes	49	924	3 522	1 683	4444	..	..	..	..	..
6100 Paid solely by business	32	871	3 502	1 677	4425	..	..	..	..	..
6200 Other	17	53	21	6	19	..	..	..	..	..
Total tax revenue	42 294	221 892	306 335	338 860	377 941	..	..	..	..	..

	Local government					Social Security Funds				
	1975	1995	2005	2015	2022	1975	1995	2005	2015	2022
1000 Taxes on income, profits and capital gains	0	0	0	20	35	0	14 805	78 892	111 270	150 262
1100 Of individuals	0	0	0	13	13	0	14 805	78 892	111 265	150 258
1200 Corporate	0	0	0	7	22	0	-0	0	5	4
1300 Unallocable between 1100 and 1200	0	0	0	0	0	0	0	0	0	0
2000 Social security contributions	0	0	0	0	0	33 089	217 907	273 765	360 719	387 634
2100 Employees	..	..	..	..	..	6 683	65 964	64 598	86 805	88 298
2200 Employers	..	..	..	..	..	24 236	135 804	189 192	245 479	267 431
2300 Self-employed or non-employed	..	..	..	..	..	2 170	16 139	19 975	28 435	31 905
2400 Unallocable between 2100, 2200 and 2300	..	..	..	..	..	0	0	0	0	0
3000 Taxes on payroll and workforce	299	2 529	5 437	9 278	10 505	107	186	1 957	21 130	25 795
4000 Taxes on property	2 876	27 132	44 633	69 361	70 481	0	0	0	0	0
4100 Recurrent taxes on immovable property	2 626	23 144	36 034	57 427	48 853	..	..	..	..	..
4200 Recurrent taxes on net wealth	..	0	0	0	0	..	..	..	..	..
4300 Estate, inheritance and gift taxes	0	0	0	0	0	..	..	..	..	..
4400 Taxes on financial and capital transactions	250	3 988	8 599	11 934	21 628	..	..	..	..	..
4500 Non-recurrent taxes	0	0	0	0	0	..	..	..	..	..
4600 Other recurrent taxes on property	..	0	0	0	0	..	..	..	..	..
5000 Taxes on goods and services	496	7 936	14 452	43 282	82 943	301	5 778	13 686	37 103	89 836
5100 Taxes on production, sale, transfer, etc	297	4 168	12 178	39 533	78 924	301	5 758	13 649	36 456	89 131
5110 General taxes	0	0	0	12 973	49 792	248	1 810	4 271	15 569	61 561
5120 Taxes on specific goods and services	297	4 168	12 178	26 560	29 132	53	3 948	9 378	20 887	27 570
5130 Unallocable between 5110 and 5120	..	0	0	0	0	..	0	0	0	0
5200 Taxes on use of goods and perform activities	198	3 768	2 274	3 749	4 019	0	20	37	647	705
5300 Unallocable between 5100 and 5200	..	0	0	0	0	..	0	0	0	0
6000 Other taxes	2 577	19 065	22 490	9 520	10 634	0	122	370	907	6764
6100 Paid solely by business	2 577	19 064	22 490	9 520	10 634	..	..	..	907	6764
6200 Other	0	1	0	0	0	..	..	..	0	0
Total tax revenue	6 248	56 662	87 011	131 461	174 598	33 497	238 797	368 671	531 129	660 291

.. Not available

Note: Including taxes collected on behalf of the European Union.

Table 6.13. Germany, tax revenues by sub-sectors of government

Million EUR

	Federal government					State/Regional				
	1975	1995	2005	2015	2022	1975	1995	2005	2015	2022
1000 Taxes on income, profits and capital gains	26 782	90 688	89 383	143 652	200 649	26 428	77 258	83 503	133 852	192 826
1100 Of individuals	23 469	83 710	77 468	129 730	172 038	23 267	71 598	70 916	118 871	166 240
1200 Corporate	3 314	6 978	11 915	13 922	28 611	3 160	5 659	12 587	14 981	26 586
1300 Unallocable between 1100 and 1200	0	0	0	0	0	0	0	0	0	0
2000 Social security contributions	0	0	0	0	0	0	0	0	0	0
2100 Employees	..	..	..	..	..	..	..	..	..	..
2200 Employers	..	..	..	..	..	..	..	..	..	..
2300 Self-employed or non-employed	..	..	..	..	..	..	..	..	..	..
2400 Unallocable between 2100, 2200 and 2300	..	..	..	..	..	..	..	..	..	..
3000 Taxes on payroll and workforce	0	0	0	0	0	0	0	0	0	0
4000 Taxes on property	1 225	175	0	1 688	1 614	2 606	9 080	10 102	18 926	27 913
4100 Recurrent taxes on immovable property	0	0	..	0	0	0	0	1117	1389	1 565
4200 Recurrent taxes on net wealth	920	147	..	1 688	1 614	1 993	4 163	97	-2	0
4300 Estate, inheritance and gift taxes	0	0	..	0	0	271	1 815	4 097	6 290	9 226
4400 Taxes on financial and capital transactions	305	28	..	0	0	342	3 102	4 791	11 249	17 122
4500 Non-recurrent taxes	0	0	..	0	0	0	0	0	0	0
4600 Other recurrent taxes on property	0	0	..	0	0	0	0	0	0	0
5000 Taxes on goods and services	35 370	125 377	153 240	222 221	242 072	13 082	62 564	82 093	107 685	158 677
5100 Taxes on production, sale, transfer, etc	35 370	125 377	153 240	211 649	219 610	10 371	55 506	66 406	99 805	150 373
5110 General taxes	18 458	67 178	74 361	110 451	135 518	9 194	52 783	62 851	96 751	146 223
5120 Taxes on specific goods and services	16 913	58 200	78 443	100 906	83 832	1 177	2 723	3 555	3 054	4 150
5130 Unallocable between 5110 and 5120	0	0	436	292	260	0	0	0	0	0
5200 Taxes on use of goods and perform activities	0	0	0	10 572	22 462	2 711	7 058	15 687	7 880	8 304
5300 Unallocable between 5100 and 5200	0	0	0	0	0	0	0	0	0	0
6000 Other taxes	0	0	-1	0	0	0	0	0	0	0
6100 Paid solely by business	..	..	0	..	..	..	..	..	..	..
6200 Other	..	..	-1	..	..	..	..	..	..	..
Total tax revenue	63 378	216 240	242 622	367 561	444 335	42 116	148 902	175 698	260 463	379 416

	Local government					Social Security Funds				
	1975	1995	2005	2015	2022	1975	1995	2005	2015	2022
1000 Taxes on income, profits and capital gains	11 819	40 295	46 725	73 882	112 539	0	0	0	0	0
1100 Of individuals	9 931	33 761	31 261	50 761	75 108	..	..	..	..	..
1200 Corporate	1 888	6 534	15 464	23 121	37 431	..	..	..	..	..
1300 Unallocable between 1100 and 1200	0	0	0	0	0	..	..	..	..	..
2000 Social security contributions	0	0	0	0	0	64 290	268 052	311 530	424 842	567 083
2100 Employees	..	..	..	..	..	28 106	117 916	134 939	186 307	246 434
2200 Employers	..	..	..	..	..	34 609	133 120	148 507	196 665	266 727
2300 Self-employed or non-employed	..	..	..	..	..	1 575	17 016	28 084	41 870	53 922
2400 Unallocable between 2100, 2200 and 2300	..	..	..	..	..	0	0	0	0	0
3000 Taxes on payroll and workforce	1 533	0	0	0	0	0	0	0	0	0
4000 Taxes on property	3 461	9 794	9 130	11 825	13 717	0	0	0	0	0
4100 Recurrent taxes on immovable property	2 122	7 027	9 130	11 825	13 717	..	..	..	..	..
4200 Recurrent taxes on net wealth	911	2 615	0	0	0	..	..	..	..	..
4300 Estate, inheritance and gift taxes	0	0	0	0	0	..	..	..	..	..
4400 Taxes on financial and capital transactions	428	151	0	0	0	..	..	..	..	..
4500 Non-recurrent taxes	0	0	0	0	0	..	..	..	..	..
4600 Other recurrent taxes on property	0	0	0	0	0	..	..	..	..	..
5000 Taxes on goods and services	162	448	3 395	5 947	9 514	0	0	0	0	0
5100 Taxes on production, sale, transfer, etc	94	271	3 136	5 615	9 093	..	..	..	..	..
5110 General taxes	0	0	2 909	4 734	8 221	..	..	..	..	..
5120 Taxes on specific goods and services	94	271	227	881	872	..	..	..	..	..
5130 Unallocable between 5110 and 5120	0	0	0	0	0	..	..	..	..	..
5200 Taxes on use of goods and perform activities	68	176	259	332	421	..	..	..	..	..
5300 Unallocable between 5100 and 5200	0	0	0	0	0	..	..	..	..	..
6000 Other taxes	67	130	79	216	358	0	0	0	0	0
6100 Paid solely by business	0	0	0	0	0	..	..	..	..	..
6200 Other	67	130	79	216	358	..	..	..	..	..
Total tax revenue	17 042	50 666	59 329	91 870	136 128	64 290	268 052	311 530	424 842	567 083

.. Not available

Note: Including taxes collected on behalf of the European Union.

Table 6.14. Greece, tax revenues by sub-sectors of government

Million EUR

	Central government					State/Regional				
	1975	1995	2005	2015	2022	1975	1995	2005	2015	2022
1000 Taxes on income, profits and capital gains	64	5 456	16 101	14 577	17 452	..	..	..	..	..
1100 Of individuals	43	3 011	8 719	10 146	11 540	..	..	..	..	..
1200 Corporate	17	2 067	6 487	3 800	5 127	..	..	..	..	..
1300 Unallocable between 1100 and 1200	4	378	895	631	785	..	..	..	..	..
2000 Social security contributions	0	380	1 048	745	61	..	..	..	..	..
2100 Employees	..	380	1 031	744	61	..	..	..	..	..
2200 Employers	..	0	17	1	0	..	..	..	..	..
2300 Self-employed or non-employed	..	0	0	0	0	..	..	..	..	..
2400 Unallocable between 2100, 2200 and 2300	..	0	0	0	0	..	..	..	..	..
3000 Taxes on payroll and workforce	1	0	0	0	0	..	..	..	..	..
4000 Taxes on property	47	1 060	2 263	3 931	3 835	..	..	..	..	..
4100 Recurrent taxes on immovable property	1	0	0	3 046	2 452	..	..	..	..	..
4200 Recurrent taxes on net wealth	0	138	284	180	191	..	..	..	..	..
4300 Estate, inheritance and gift taxes	5	274	258	134	232	..	..	..	..	..
4400 Taxes on financial and capital transactions	41	641	1 469	509	945	..	..	..	..	..
4500 Non-recurrent taxes	0	0	0	0	0	..	..	..	..	..
4600 Other recurrent taxes on property	0	7	179	62	15	..	..	..	..	..
5000 Taxes on goods and services	224	10 586	21 526	25 740	35 892	..	..	..	..	..
5100 Taxes on production, sale, transfer, etc	205	9 953	19 454	21 550	31 273	..	..	..	..	..
5110 General taxes	90	5 504	13 605	12 904	18 628	..	..	..	..	..
5120 Taxes on specific goods and services	114	4 413	5 772	8 552	12 606	..	..	..	..	..
5130 Unallocable between 5110 and 5120	0	36	77	94	39	..	..	..	..	..
5200 Taxes on use of goods and perform activities	20	385	1 780	3 188	3 916	..	..	..	..	..
5300 Unallocable between 5100 and 5200	0	248	292	1 002	703	..	..	..	..	..
6000 Other taxes	0	0	0	0	0	..	..	..	..	..
6100 Paid solely by business	..	..	..	..	..	..	..	..	..	..
6200 Other	..	..	..	..	..	..	..	..	..	..
Total tax revenue	337	17 482	40 938	44 993	57 240	..	..	..	..	..

	Local government					Social Security Funds				
	1975	1995	2005	2015	2022	1975	1995	2005	2015	2022
1000 Taxes on income, profits and capital gains	3	0	0	0	0	0	0	0	9	9
1100 Of individuals	2	..	..	..	..	0	..	..	9	9
1200 Corporate	0	..	..	..	..	0	..	..	0	0
1300 Unallocable between 1100 and 1200	1	..	..	..	..	0	..	..	0	0
2000 Social security contributions	0	0	0	0	0	148	7 991	20 288	18 062	25 125
2100 Employees	..	..	..	..	..	62	4 181	10 206	10 351	13 558
2200 Employers	..	..	..	..	..	62	3 810	10 082	7 711	11 567
2300 Self-employed or non-employed	..	..	..	..	..	0	0	0	0	0
2400 Unallocable between 2100, 2200 and 2300	..	..	..	..	..	24	0	0	0	0
3000 Taxes on payroll and workforce	0	0	0	0	0	0	0	0	0	0
4000 Taxes on property	1	447	1 208	1 449	1 824	0	66	361	38	0
4100 Recurrent taxes on immovable property	0	180	420	546	721	..	32	83	0	..
4200 Recurrent taxes on net wealth	0	267	788	903	1103	..	0	0	0	..
4300 Estate, inheritance and gift taxes	0	0	0	0	0	..	0	0	0	..
4400 Taxes on financial and capital transactions	0	0	0	0	0	..	34	278	38	..
4500 Non-recurrent taxes	0	0	0	0	0	..	0	0	0	..
4600 Other recurrent taxes on property	0	0	0	0	0	..	0	0	0	..
5000 Taxes on goods and services	10	89	197	96	138	0	124	248	240	267
5100 Taxes on production, sale, transfer, etc	7	87	185	82	111	..	102	195	224	260
5110 General taxes	2	32	26	3	2	..	86	85	170	224
5120 Taxes on specific goods and services	6	55	159	79	109	..	16	110	47	31
5130 Unallocable between 5110 and 5120	0	0	0	0	0	..	0	0	7	5
5200 Taxes on use of goods and perform activities	3	2	12	14	27	..	22	53	16	7
5300 Unallocable between 5100 and 5200	0	0	0	0	0	..	0	0	0	0
6000 Other taxes	0	0	0	0	0	0	0	0	0	0
6100 Paid solely by business	..	..	..	..	..	..	..	..	..	..
6200 Other	..	..	..	..	..	..	..	..	..	..
Total tax revenue	17	536	1 405	1 545	1 962	148	8 181	20 897	18 349	25 401

.. Not available

Note: Including taxes collected on behalf of the European Union.

Table 6.15. Hungary, tax revenues by sub-sectors of government

Million HUF

	Central government					State/Regional				
	1975	1995	2005	2015	2022	1975	1995	2005	2015	2022
1000 Taxes on income, profits and capital gains	..	498 608	1 915 178	2 299 697	4 618 397	..	..	..	..	..
1100 Of individuals	..	383 744	1 449 552	1 698 410	3 524 450	..	..	..	..	..
1200 Corporate	..	106 259	465 626	601 287	1093 947	..	..	..	..	..
1300 Unallocable between 1100 and 1200	..	8 605	0	0	0	..	..	..	..	..
2000 Social security contributions	..	69 554	235 148	148 044	307 455	..	..	..	..	..
2100 Employees	..	18 468	53 611	144 868	305 231	..	..	..	..	..
2200 Employers	..	51 086	175 013	3 176	2 224	..	..	..	..	..
2300 Self-employed or non-employed	..	0	0	0	0	..	..	..	..	..
2400 Unallocable between 2100, 2200 and 2300	..	0	6 524	0	0	..	..	..	..	..
3000 Taxes on payroll and workforce	..	5 474	39 459	231 467	463 547	..	..	..	..	..
4000 Taxes on property	..	11 463	63 007	292 329	347 324	..	..	..	..	..
4100 Recurrent taxes on immovable property	..	0	0	55 906	53 495	..	..	..	..	..
4200 Recurrent taxes on net wealth	..	0	0	135 661	66 657	..	..	..	..	..
4300 Estate, inheritance and gift taxes	..	1 364	7 678	7 373	11 399	..	..	..	..	..
4400 Taxes on financial and capital transactions	..	10 099	55 329	93 389	215 773	..	..	..	..	..
4500 Non-recurrent taxes	..	0	0	0	0	..	..	..	..	..
4600 Other recurrent taxes on property	..	0	0	0	0	..	..	..	..	..
5000 Taxes on goods and services	..	924 906	2 870 189	5 168 034	9 841 048	..	..	..	..	..
5100 Taxes on production, sale, transfer, etc	..	919 500	2 854 738	5 060 613	9 556 364	..	..	..	..	..
5110 General taxes	..	423 954	1 972 998	3 485 479	6 829 332	..	..	..	..	..
5120 Taxes on specific goods and services	..	495 546	881 740	1 575 134	2 727 032	..	..	..	..	..
5130 Unallocable between 5110 and 5120	..	0	0	0	0	..	..	..	..	..
5200 Taxes on use of goods and perform activities	..	5 406	15 451	107 421	284 684	..	..	..	..	..
5300 Unallocable between 5100 and 5200	..	0	0	0	0	..	..	..	..	..
6000 Other taxes	..	8 901	25 403	30 665	63 975	..	..	..	..	..
6100 Paid solely by business	..	0	4 240	9 156	38700	..	..	..	..	..
6200 Other	..	0	0	0	0	..	..	..	..	..
Total tax revenue	..	1 518 905	5 148 383	8 170 236	15 641 746	..	..	..	..	..

	Local government					Social Security Funds				
	1975	1995	2005	2015	2022	1975	1995	2005	2015	2022
1000 Taxes on income, profits and capital gains	..	0	173	45	38	..	0	26 307	126 216	-9
1100 Of individuals	..	0	173	45	38	..	0	26 307	126 216	-9
1200 Corporate	..	0	0	0	0	..	0	0	0	0
1300 Unallocable between 1100 and 1200	..	0	0	0	0	..	0	0	0	0
2000 Social security contributions	..	0	0	0	0	..	778 467	2 452 562	4 285 420	6 174 390
2100 Employees	..	..	..	..	..	..	116 824	530 098	1 626 055	3 524 582
2200 Employers	..	..	..	..	..	..	632 478	1 894 306	2 634 154	2 617 150
2300 Self-employed or non-employed	..	..	..	..	..	..	27 466	2 080	0	0
2400 Unallocable between 2100, 2200 and 2300	..	..	..	..	..	..	1 699	26 078	25 211	32 658
3000 Taxes on payroll and workforce	..	1 075	1 153	0	0	..	0	44 397	10 283	8 886
4000 Taxes on property	..	17 531	123 929	145 000	184 619	..	0	0	0	0
4100 Recurrent taxes on immovable property	..	6 068	58 836	145 000	184 619	..	..	..	..	..
4200 Recurrent taxes on net wealth	..	0	0	0	0	..	..	..	..	..
4300 Estate, inheritance and gift taxes	..	1 364	7 932	0	0	..	..	..	..	..
4400 Taxes on financial and capital transactions	..	10 099	57 162	0	0	..	..	..	..	..
4500 Non-recurrent taxes	..	0	0	0	0	..	..	..	..	..
4600 Other recurrent taxes on property	..	0	0	0	0	..	..	..	..	..
5000 Taxes on goods and services	..	41 970	388 385	625 571	907 893	..	0	0	103 105	148 251
5100 Taxes on production, sale, transfer, etc	..	39 240	337 935	594 855	906 717	..	..	..	103 105	148 251
5110 General taxes	..	38 472	334 077	584 380	890 118	..	..	..	29 882	77 272
5120 Taxes on specific goods and services	..	768	3 858	10 475	16 599	..	..	..	73 223	70 979
5130 Unallocable between 5110 and 5120	..	0	0	0	0	..	..	..	0	0
5200 Taxes on use of goods and perform activities	..	2 730	50 450	30 716	1 176	..	..	..	0	0
5300 Unallocable between 5100 and 5200	..	0	0	0	0	..	..	..	0	0
6000 Other taxes	..	0	0	0	0	..	21 605	9 616	14 021	10 635
6100 Paid solely by business	..	..	..	..	..	..	0	0	0	0
6200 Other	..	..	..	..	..	..	0	0	0	0
Total tax revenue	..	60 576	513 641	770 616	1092 550	..	800 072	2 532 882	4 539 045	6 342 153

.. Not available

Note: Including taxes collected on behalf of the European Union.

Table 6.16. Iceland, tax revenues by sub-sectors of government

Million ISK

	Central government					State/Regional				
	1975	1995	2005	2015	2022	1975	1995	2005	2015	2022
1000 Taxes on income, profits and capital gains	68	27 156	105 705	210 536	400 070	..	..	..	..	..
1100 Of individuals	55	22 914	70 944	127 535	242 249	..	..	..	..	..
1200 Corporate	13	4 242	20 297	52 544	100 909	..	..	..	..	..
1300 Unallocable between 1100 and 1200	0	0	14 464	30 457	56 911	..	..	..	..	..
2000 Social security contributions	17	11 452	32 777	79 707	115 564	..	..	..	..	..
2100 Employees	0	460	..	..	..	..	..	..	..	..
2200 Employers	17	10 992	..	..	..	..	..	..	..	..
2300 Self-employed or non-employed	0	0	..	..	..	..	..	..	..	..
2400 Unallocable between 2100, 2200 and 2300	0	0	32 777	79 707	115 564	..	..	..	..	..
3000 Taxes on payroll and workforce	27	0	324	6 638	10 003	..	..	..	..	..
4000 Taxes on property	15	7 198	4 267	4 459	14 046	..	..	..	..	..
4100 Recurrent taxes on immovable property	0	47	0	178	323	..	..	..	..	..
4200 Recurrent taxes on net wealth	5	3 191	2 887	657	0	..	..	..	..	..
4300 Estate, inheritance and gift taxes	0	389	866	2 919	12 154	..	..	..	..	..
4400 Taxes on financial and capital transactions	9	3 571	0	0	0	..	..	..	..	..
4500 Non-recurrent taxes	0	0	0	0	0	..	..	..	..	..
4600 Other recurrent taxes on property	0	0	266	343	767	..	..	..	..	..
5000 Taxes on goods and services	392	66 356	177 366	264 323	436 139	..	..	..	..	..
5100 Taxes on production, sale, transfer, etc	387	62 140	167 012	254 422	419 446	..	..	..	..	..
5110 General taxes	182	42 358	122 968	188 001	329 554	..	..	..	..	..
5120 Taxes on specific goods and services	205	19 782	44 044	66 421	89 892	..	..	..	..	..
5130 Unallocable between 5110 and 5120	0	0	0	0	0	..	..	..	..	..
5200 Taxes on use of goods and perform activities	5	4 216	10 354	9 901	16 693	..	..	..	..	..
5300 Unallocable between 5100 and 5200	0	0	0	0	0	..	..	..	..	..
6000 Other taxes	0	0	1 504	38 364	14 223	..	..	..	..	..
6100 Paid solely by business	..	..	565	32 477	6 228	..	..	..	..	..
6200 Other	..	..	939	5 887	7 995	..	..	..	..	..
Total tax revenue	519	112 162	321 941	604 026	990 044	..	..	..	..	..

	Local government					Social Security Funds				
	1975	1995	2005	2015	2022	1975	1995	2005	2015	2022
1000 Taxes on income, profits and capital gains	78	21 170	74 465	170 443	302 885	0	0	0	0	0
1100 Of individuals	74	21 170	74 455	170 443	302 885	..	..	..	..	..
1200 Corporate	4	0	10	0	0	..	..	..	..	..
1300 Unallocable between 1100 and 1200	0	0	0	0	0	..	..	..	..	..
2000 Social security contributions	0	0	0	0	0	0	0	0	0	0
2100 Employees	..	..	..	..	..	..	..	..	..	..
2200 Employers	..	..	..	..	..	..	..	..	..	..
2300 Self-employed or non-employed	..	..	..	..	..	..	..	..	..	..
2400 Unallocable between 2100, 2200 and 2300	..	..	..	..	..	..	..	..	..	..
3000 Taxes on payroll and workforce	0	0	0	0	0	0	0	0	0	0
4000 Taxes on property	18	5 674	13 931	34 701	62 115	0	0	0	0	0
4100 Recurrent taxes on immovable property	18	5 674	13 931	34 701	62 115	..	..	..	..	..
4200 Recurrent taxes on net wealth	0	0	0	0	0	..	..	..	..	..
4300 Estate, inheritance and gift taxes	0	0	0	0	0	..	..	..	..	..
4400 Taxes on financial and capital transactions	0	0	0	0	0	..	..	..	..	..
4500 Non-recurrent taxes	0	0	0	0	0	..	..	..	..	..
4600 Other recurrent taxes on property	0	0	0	0	0	..	..	..	..	..
5000 Taxes on goods and services	9	2 585	6 904	2 832	10 369	0	0	0	0	0
5100 Taxes on production, sale, transfer, etc	9	2 585	0	0	0	..	..	..	..	..
5110 General taxes	0	2 585	..	..	..	..	..	..	..	..
5120 Taxes on specific goods and services	9	0	..	..	..	..	..	..	..	..
5130 Unallocable between 5110 and 5120	0	0	..	..	..	..	..	..	..	..
5200 Taxes on use of goods and perform activities	0	0	6 904	2 832	10 369	..	..	..	..	..
5300 Unallocable between 5100 and 5200	0	0	0	0	0	..	..	..	..	..
6000 Other taxes	14	0	93	0	0	0	0	0	0	0
6100 Paid solely by business	14	..	93	..	..	..	..	..	..	..
6200 Other	0	..	0	..	..	..	..	..	..	..
Total tax revenue	119	29 429	95 393	207 976	375 369	0	0	0	0	0

.. Not available

Table 6.17. Ireland, tax revenues by sub-sectors of government

Million EUR

	Central government					State/Regional				
	1975	1995	2005	2015	2022	1975	1995	2005	2015	2022
1000 Taxes on income, profits and capital gains	456	7 022	21 186	26 599	55 679	..	..	..	..	..
1100 Of individuals	382	5 563	15 674	19 722	33 033	..	..	..	..	..
1200 Corporate	73	1 458	5 511	6 873	22 646	..	..	..	..	..
1300 Unallocable between 1100 and 1200	0	0	0	4	0	..	..	..	..	..
2000 Social security contributions	11	87	217	1 351	1 639	..	..	..	..	..
2100 Employees	10	87	217	1 351	1 639	..	..	..	..	..
2200 Employers	0	0	0	0	0	..	..	..	..	..
2300 Self-employed or non-employed	1	0	0	0	0	..	..	..	..	..
2400 Unallocable between 2100, 2200 and 2300	0	0	0	0	0	..	..	..	..	..
3000 Taxes on payroll and workforce	0	209	332	357	951	..	..	..	..	..
4000 Taxes on property	37	370	2 741	2 530	3 458	..	..	..	..	..
4100 Recurrent taxes on immovable property	0	15	0	475	500	..	..	..	..	..
4200 Recurrent taxes on net wealth	5	0	0	169	0	..	..	..	..	..
4300 Estate, inheritance and gift taxes	17	76	255	401	615	..	..	..	..	..
4400 Taxes on financial and capital transactions	15	279	2 486	1 484	2 344	..	..	..	..	..
4500 Non-recurrent taxes	0	0	0	0	0	..	..	..	..	..
4600 Other recurrent taxes on property	0	0	0	0	0	..	..	..	..	..
5000 Taxes on goods and services	671	6 763	19 122	19 686	27 020	..	..	..	..	..
5100 Taxes on production, sale, transfer, etc	639	6 419	18 106	17 709	25 318	..	..	..	..	..
5110 General taxes	223	3 666	12 373	11 831	19 176	..	..	..	..	..
5120 Taxes on specific goods and services	416	2 753	5 733	5 878	6 142	..	..	..	..	..
5130 Unallocable between 5110 and 5120	0	0	0	0	0	..	..	..	..	..
5200 Taxes on use of goods and perform activities	33	344	1 015	1 977	1 702	..	..	..	..	..
5300 Unallocable between 5100 and 5200	0	0	0	0	0	..	..	..	..	..
6000 Other taxes	0	0	0	12	13	..	..	..	..	..
6100 Paid solely by business	..	..	..	0	0	..	..	..	..	..
6200 Other	..	..	..	12	13	..	..	..	..	..
Total tax revenue	1 175	14 451	43 598	50 535	88 761	..	..	..	..	..

	Local government					Social Security Funds				
	1975	1995	2005	2015	2022	1975	1995	2005	2015	2022
1000 Taxes on income, profits and capital gains	0	0	0	0	0	0	0	0	0	0
1100 Of individuals	..	..	..	..	..	..	..	..	..	..
1200 Corporate	..	..	..	..	..	..	..	..	..	..
1300 Unallocable between 1100 and 1200	0	..	..	..	..	0	..	..	..	..
2000 Social security contributions	0	56	90	121	94	198	2 215	6 230	8 527	14 233
2100 Employees	..	56	90	121	..	73	576	1 415	1 856	3 686
2200 Employers	..	0	0	0	..	125	1 528	4 427	6 211	9 917
2300 Self-employed or non-employed	..	0	0	0	..	0	111	388	460	631
2400 Unallocable between 2100, 2200 and 2300	..	0	0	0	..	0	0	0	0	0
3000 Taxes on payroll and workforce	0	0	0	0	0	0	0	0	0	0
4000 Taxes on property	110	408	1 020	1 389	1 551	..	0	0	0	0
4100 Recurrent taxes on immovable property	110	408	1 020	1 389	1 551	..	..	..	..	..
4200 Recurrent taxes on net wealth	0	0	0	0	0	..	..	..	..	..
4300 Estate, inheritance and gift taxes	0	0	0	0	0	..	..	..	..	..
4400 Taxes on financial and capital transactions	0	0	0	0	0	..	..	..	..	..
4500 Non-recurrent taxes	0	0	0	0	0	..	..	..	..	..
4600 Other recurrent taxes on property	0	0	0	0	0	..	..	..	..	..
5000 Taxes on goods and services	0	0	0	0	0	0	0	0	0	0
5100 Taxes on production, sale, transfer, etc	..	..	..	..	..	..	..	..	..	..
5110 General taxes	..	..	..	..	..	..	..	..	..	..
5120 Taxes on specific goods and services	..	..	..	..	..	..	..	..	..	..
5130 Unallocable between 5110 and 5120	0	..	..	..	..	0	..	..	..	..
5200 Taxes on use of goods and perform activities	..	..	..	..	..	0	..	..	..	..
5300 Unallocable between 5100 and 5200	0	..	..	..	..	0	..	..	..	..
6000 Other taxes	0	0	0	0	0	0	0	0	0	0
6100 Paid solely by business	..	..	..	..	..	..	..	..	..	..
6200 Other	..	..	..	..	..	..	..	..	..	..
Total tax revenue	110	464	1 110	1 510	1 645	198	2 215	6 230	8 527	14 233

.. Not available

Note: Including taxes collected on behalf of the European Union. The personal income tax data shown for the country table for Ireland is different to the ESA2010 presentation as the expenditure component of the payable tax credits are excluded in accordance with the OECD Interpretative Guide.

Table 6.18. Israel, tax revenues by sub-sectors of government

Million ILS

	Central government					State/Regional				
	1975	1995	2005	2015	2022	1975	1995	2005	2015	2022
1000 Taxes on income, profits and capital gains	..	37 422	73 082	113 976	216 384	..	..	..	..	..
1100 Of individuals	..	28 399	47 062	70 895	127 900	..	..	..	..	..
1200 Corporate	..	8 514	21 909	34 676	76 187	..	..	..	..	..
1300 Unallocable between 1100 and 1200	..	509	4 111	8 405	12 297	..	..	..	..	..
2000 Social security contributions	..	0	0	0	0	..	..	..	..	..
2100 Employees	..	..	..	..	..	..	..	..	..	..
2200 Employers	..	..	..	..	..	..	..	..	..	..
2300 Self-employed or non-employed	..	..	..	..	..	..	..	..	..	..
2400 Unallocable between 2100, 2200 and 2300	..	..	..	..	..	..	..	..	..	..
3000 Taxes on payroll and workforce	..	5 007	9 920	13 760	16 253	..	..	..	..	..
4000 Taxes on property	..	4 122	5 547	10 593	25 349	..	..	..	..	..
4100 Recurrent taxes on immovable property	..	786	322	44	22	..	..	..	..	..
4200 Recurrent taxes on net wealth	..	0	0	0	0	..	..	..	..	..
4300 Estate, inheritance and gift taxes	..	0	0	0	0	..	..	..	..	..
4400 Taxes on financial and capital transactions	..	2 049	3 591	6 732	14 438	..	..	..	..	..
4500 Non-recurrent taxes	..	0	0	0	0	..	..	..	..	..
4600 Other recurrent taxes on property	..	0	0	0	0	..	..	..	..	..
5000 Taxes on goods and services	..	38 673	75 932	136 848	186 618	..	..	..	..	..
5100 Taxes on production, sale, transfer, etc	..	36 637	70 741	128 277	176 388	..	..	..	..	..
5110 General taxes	..	24 900	48 143	90 824	130 757	..	..	..	..	..
5120 Taxes on specific goods and services	..	11 737	22 598	37 453	45 631	..	..	..	..	..
5130 Unallocable between 5110 and 5120	..	0	0	0	0	..	..	..	..	..
5200 Taxes on use of goods and perform activities	..	2 036	5 191	8 571	10 230	..	..	..	..	..
5300 Unallocable between 5100 and 5200	..	0	0	0	0	..	..	..	..	..
6000 Other taxes	..	0	0	0	0	..	..	..	..	..
6100 Paid solely by business	..	..	..	..	..	..	..	..	..	..
6200 Other	..	..	..	..	..	..	..	..	..	..
Total tax revenue	..	85 224	164 481	275 177	444 604	..	..	..	..	..

	Local government					Social Security Funds				
	1975	1995	2005	2015	2022	1975	1995	2005	2015	2022
1000 Taxes on income, profits and capital gains	..	0	0	0	0	..	0	0	0	0
1100 Of individuals	..	0	0	0	0	..	0	0	0	0
1200 Corporate	..	..	..	..	..	..	..	..	..	..
1300 Unallocable between 1100 and 1200	..	0	0	0	0	..	0	0	0	0
2000 Social security contributions	..	0	0	0	0	..	14 958	34 597	59 561	88 775
2100 Employees	..	..	..	..	..	..	7 953	19 720	34 692	49 880
2200 Employers	..	..	..	..	..	..	4 672	10 679	17 247	27 845
2300 Self-employed or non-employed	..	..	..	..	..	..	2 334	4 198	7 622	11 050
2400 Unallocable between 2100, 2200 and 2300	..	..	..	..	..	..	0	0	0	0
3000 Taxes on payroll and workforce	..	0	0	0	0	..	0	0	0	0
4000 Taxes on property	..	7 363	16 435	30 016	46 029	..	0	0	0	0
4100 Recurrent taxes on immovable property	..	5 592	13 962	23 658	31 494	..	..	..	..	..
4200 Recurrent taxes on net wealth	..	0	0	0	0	..	..	..	..	..
4300 Estate, inheritance and gift taxes	..	0	0	0	0	..	..	..	..	..
4400 Taxes on financial and capital transactions	..	0	0	0	0	..	..	..	..	..
4500 Non-recurrent taxes	..	0	0	0	0	..	..	..	..	..
4600 Other recurrent taxes on property	..	0	0	0	0	..	..	..	..	..
5000 Taxes on goods and services	..	298	748	1 309	1 724	..	0	0	0	0
5100 Taxes on production, sale, transfer, etc	..	0	0	0	0	..	..	..	..	..
5110 General taxes	..	0	0	0	0	..	..	..	..	..
5120 Taxes on specific goods and services	..	0	0	0	0	..	..	..	..	..
5130 Unallocable between 5110 and 5120	..	0	0	0	0	..	..	..	..	..
5200 Taxes on use of goods and perform activities	..	298	748	1 309	1 724	..	..	..	..	..
5300 Unallocable between 5100 and 5200	..	0	0	0	0	..	..	..	..	..
6000 Other taxes	..	0	0	0	0	..	0	0	0	0
6100 Paid solely by business	..	..	..	..	..	..	..	..	..	..
6200 Other	..	..	..	..	..	..	..	..	..	..
Total tax revenue	..	7 661	17 182	31 325	47 752	..	14 958	34 597	59 561	88 775

.. Not available

Table 6.19. Italy, tax revenues by sub-sectors of government

Million EUR

	Central government					State/Regional				
	1975	1995	2005	2015	2022	1975	1995	2005	2015	2022
1000 Taxes on income, profits and capital gains	3 897	128 458	165 580	195 451	257 742	..	..	..	..	..
1100 Of individuals	2 767	98 695	131 047	156 320	196 542	..	..	..	..	..
1200 Corporate	1 131	32 890	31 969	31 421	56 319	..	..	..	..	..
1300 Unallocable between 1100 and 1200	0	-3 127	2 564	7 710	4 881	..	..	..	..	..
2000 Social security contributions	0	0	0	0	0	..	..	..	..	..
2100 Employees	..	..	..	..	..	..	..	..	..	..
2200 Employers	..	..	..	..	..	..	..	..	..	..
2300 Self-employed or non-employed	..	..	..	..	..	..	..	..	..	..
2400 Unallocable between 2100, 2200 and 2300	..	..	..	..	..	..	..	..	..	..
3000 Taxes on payroll and workforce	0	1 136	0	0	0	..	..	..	..	..
4000 Taxes on property	587	13 546	15 717	22 226	29 370	..	..	..	..	..
4100 Recurrent taxes on immovable property	4	0	0	3 892	4 181	..	..	..	..	..
4200 Recurrent taxes on net wealth	0	4 494	0	231	447	..	..	..	..	..
4300 Estate, inheritance and gift taxes	39	587	56	638	1067	..	..	..	..	..
4400 Taxes on financial and capital transactions	544	8 464	13 794	16 310	21 230	..	..	..	..	..
4500 Non-recurrent taxes	0	0	1 322	303	118	..	..	..	..	..
4600 Other recurrent taxes on property	0	0	545	852	2 327	..	..	..	..	..
5000 Taxes on goods and services	5 506	95 323	123 870	157 330	200 333	..	..	..	..	..
5100 Taxes on production, sale, transfer, etc	5 306	92 042	121 824	154 713	191 575	..	..	..	..	..
5110 General taxes	2 685	52 531	80 619	93 282	138 925	..	..	..	..	..
5120 Taxes on specific goods and services	2 621	39 245	41 205	61 431	52 650	..	..	..	..	..
5130 Unallocable between 5110 and 5120	0	323	0	0	0	..	..	..	..	..
5200 Taxes on use of goods and perform activities	200	2 802	1 535	2 191	6 678	..	..	..	..	..
5300 Unallocable between 5100 and 5200	0	479	511	426	2 080	..	..	..	..	..
6000 Other taxes	1	0	0	0	0	..	..	..	..	..
6100 Paid solely by business	0	..	..	..	..	..	..	..	..	..
6200 Other	1	..	..	..	..	..	..	..	..	..
Total tax revenue	9 991	238 462	305 167	375 007	487 445	..	..	..	..	..

	Local government					Social Security Funds				
	1975	1995	2005	2015	2022	1975	1995	2005	2015	2022
1000 Taxes on income, profits and capital gains	134	5 658	18 494	30 483	17 919	0	0	0	0	0
1100 Of individuals	81	145	16 995	28 302	17 919	..	..	..	..	..
1200 Corporate	54	97	1 491	2 109	0	..	..	..	..	..
1300 Unallocable between 1100 and 1200	0	5 416	8	72	0	..	..	..	..	..
2000 Social security contributions	0	0	0	0	0	8 607	119 612	179 362	214 376	256 430
2100 Employees	..	..	..	..	..	1 692	23 036	31 998	39 805	46 967
2200 Employers	..	..	..	..	..	6 915	79 716	125 099	143 273	171 799
2300 Self-employed or non-employed	..	..	..	..	..	0	16 860	22 265	31 298	37 664
2400 Unallocable between 2100, 2200 and 2300	..	..	..	..	..	0	0	0	0	0
3000 Taxes on payroll and workforce	0	0	0	0	0	0	0	0	0	0
4000 Taxes on property	29	7 915	13 484	24 033	18 787	0	0	0	0	0
4100 Recurrent taxes on immovable property	29	7 449	11 736	21 666	18 495	..	..	..	..	..
4200 Recurrent taxes on net wealth	0	0	0	0	0	..	..	..	..	..
4300 Estate, inheritance and gift taxes	0	0	5	36	0	..	..	..	..	..
4400 Taxes on financial and capital transactions	0	466	904	935	0	..	..	..	..	..
4500 Non-recurrent taxes	0	0	481	6	75	..	..	..	..	..
4600 Other recurrent taxes on property	0	0	358	1 390	217	..	..	..	..	..
5000 Taxes on goods and services	4	6 941	30 231	34 551	27 042	0	0	0	0	0
5100 Taxes on production, sale, transfer, etc	0	1 505	17 114	15 138	5 167	..	..	..	..	..
5110 General taxes	..	0	4 698	7 410	0	..	..	..	..	..
5120 Taxes on specific goods and services	..	1 505	12 416	7 728	5 167	..	..	..	..	..
5130 Unallocable between 5110 and 5120	..	0	0	0	0	..	..	..	..	..
5200 Taxes on use of goods and perform activities	4	2 838	7 512	8 939	9 299	..	..	..	..	..
5300 Unallocable between 5100 and 5200	0	2 597	5 605	10 474	12 576	..	..	..	..	..
6000 Other taxes	0	0	34 690	28 072	28 111	0	0	0	0	0
6100 Paid solely by business	..	..	34 690	28 072	28 111	..	..	..	..	..
6200 Other	..	..	0	0	0	..	..	..	..	..
Total tax revenue	168	20 514	96 899	117 139	91 859	8 607	119 612	179 362	214 376	256 430

.. Not available

Note: Including taxes collected on behalf of the European Union.

Table 6.20. Japan, tax revenues by sub-sectors of government

Billion JPY

	Central government					State/Regional				
	1975	1995	2005	2015	2022	1975	1995	2005	2015	2022
1000 Taxes on income, profits and capital gains	9 747	33 255	29 975	31 607	41 989	..	..	..	..	..
1100 Of individuals	5 482	19 515	16 702	18 178	22 992	..	..	..	..	..
1200 Corporate	4 265	13 740	13 274	13 429	18 996	..	..	..	..	..
1300 Unallocable between 1100 and 1200	0	0	0	0	0	..	..	..	..	..
2000 Social security contributions	0	0	0	0	0	..	..	..	..	..
2100 Employees	..	..	..	..	..	..	..	..	..	..
2200 Employers	..	..	..	..	..	..	..	..	..	..
2300 Self-employed or non-employed	..	..	..	..	..	..	..	..	..	..
2400 Unallocable between 2100, 2200 and 2300	..	..	..	..	..	..	..	..	..	..
3000 Taxes on payroll and workforce	0	0	0	0	0	..	..	..	..	..
4000 Taxes on property	871	5 561	2 735	3 018	3 952	..	..	..	..	..
4100 Recurrent taxes on immovable property	0	406	0	0	0	..	..	..	..	..
4200 Recurrent taxes on net wealth	0	0	0	0	0	..	..	..	..	..
4300 Estate, inheritance and gift taxes	310	2 690	1 566	1 968	2 969	..	..	..	..	..
4400 Taxes on financial and capital transactions	561	2 464	1 169	1 050	982	..	..	..	..	..
4500 Non-recurrent taxes	0	0	0	0	0	..	..	..	..	..
4600 Other recurrent taxes on property	0	0	0	0	0	..	..	..	..	..
5000 Taxes on goods and services	3 888	16 147	19 580	25 345	30 390	..	..	..	..	..
5100 Taxes on production, sale, transfer, etc	3 579	15 083	18 424	24 673	29 677	..	..	..	..	..
5110 General taxes	0	7 238	10 583	17 426	23 079	..	..	..	..	..
5120 Taxes on specific goods and services	3 579	7 845	7 840	7 247	6 598	..	..	..	..	..
5130 Unallocable between 5110 and 5120	0	0	0	0	0	..	..	..	..	..
5200 Taxes on use of goods and perform activities	309	1 065	1 157	671	713	..	..	..	..	..
5300 Unallocable between 5100 and 5200	0	0	0	0	0	..	..	..	..	..
6000 Other taxes	0	0	0	0	8	..	..	..	..	..
6100 Paid solely by business	..	..	..	..	0	..	..	..	..	..
6200 Other	..	..	..	..	8	..	..	..	..	..
Total tax revenue	14 506	54 963	52 290	59 969	76 338	..	..	..	..	..

	Local government					Social Security Funds				
	1975	1995	2005	2015	2022	1975	1995	2005	2015	2022
1000 Taxes on income, profits and capital gains	4 472	17 752	16 655	19 362	21 681	0	0	0	0	0
1100 Of individuals	2 147	10 283	8 520	12 669	13 843	..	..	..	..	..
1200 Corporate	2 325	7 470	8 135	6 693	7 837	..	..	..	..	..
1300 Unallocable between 1100 and 1200	0	0	0	0	0	..	..	..	..	..
2000 Social security contributions	0	0	0	0	0	9 253	44 794	50 848	64 464	75 458
2100 Employees	..	..	..	..	..	3 436	18 404	20 982	27 139	32 194
2200 Employers	..	..	..	..	..	4 825	21 432	23 154	29 494	35 265
2300 Self-employed or non-employed	..	..	..	..	..	992	4 958	6 712	7 832	7 999
2400 Unallocable between 2100, 2200 and 2300	..	..	..	..	..	0	0	0	0	0
3000 Taxes on payroll and workforce	0	0	0	0	0	0	0	0	0	0
4000 Taxes on property	2 029	10 653	10 593	10 382	11 463	0	0	0	0	0
4100 Recurrent taxes on immovable property	1 848	9 865	10 116	10 005	11 044	..	..	..	..	..
4200 Recurrent taxes on net wealth	0	0	0	0	0	..	..	..	..	..
4300 Estate, inheritance and gift taxes	0	0	0	0	0	..	..	..	..	..
4400 Taxes on financial and capital transactions	181	788	477	377	418	..	..	..	..	..
4500 Non-recurrent taxes	0	0	0	0	0	..	..	..	..	..
4600 Other recurrent taxes on property	0	0	0	0	0	..	..	..	..	..
5000 Taxes on goods and services	1 636	4 941	7 206	8 942	10 437	0	0	0	0	0
5100 Taxes on production, sale, transfer, etc	1 234	3 245	5 299	7 198	8 472	..	..	..	..	..
5110 General taxes	0	0	2 551	4 974	6 415	..	..	..	..	..
5120 Taxes on specific goods and services	1 234	3 245	2 747	2 223	2 057	..	..	..	..	..
5130 Unallocable between 5110 and 5120	0	0	0	0	0	..	..	..	..	..
5200 Taxes on use of goods and perform activities	402	1 697	1 907	1 744	1 965	..	..	..	..	..
5300 Unallocable between 5100 and 5200	0	0	0	0	0	..	..	..	..	..
6000 Other taxes	20	329	351	413	472	0	0	0	0	0
6100 Paid solely by business	15	307	297	361	398	..	..	..	..	..
6200 Other	5	22	54	52	74	..	..	..	..	..
Total tax revenue	8 157	33 675	34 805	39 099	44 052	9 253	44 794	50 848	64 464	75 458

.. Not available

Table 6.21. Korea, tax revenues by sub-sectors of government

Billion KRW

	Central government					State/Regional				
	1975	1995	2005	2015	2022	1975	1995	2005	2015	2022
1000 Taxes on income, profits and capital gains	344	23 000	55 109	106 162	233 535	..	..	..	..	..
1100 Of individuals	134	13 713	24 766	60 828	129 096	..	..	..	..	..
1200 Corporate	139	8 988	30 343	45 334	104 439	..	..	..	..	..
1300 Unallocable between 1100 and 1200	71	300	0	0	0	..	..	..	..	..
2000 Social security contributions	0	0	0	0	0	..	..	..	..	..
2100 Employees	..	..	..	..	..	..	..	..	..	..
2200 Employers	..	..	..	..	..	..	..	..	..	..
2300 Self-employed or non-employed	..	..	..	..	..	..	..	..	..	..
2400 Unallocable between 2100, 2200 and 2300	..	..	..	..	..	..	..	..	..	..
3000 Taxes on payroll and workforce	0	0	0	0	0	..	..	..	..	..
4000 Taxes on property	65	2 482	6 769	15 164	34 042	..	..	..	..	..
4100 Recurrent taxes on immovable property	0	106	535	1 666	8 099	..	..	..	..	..
4200 Recurrent taxes on net wealth	0	0	0	0	0	..	..	..	..	..
4300 Estate, inheritance and gift taxes	11	1 029	1 873	5 044	14 594	..	..	..	..	..
4400 Taxes on financial and capital transactions	49	1 258	4 363	8 454	11 349	..	..	..	..	..
4500 Non-recurrent taxes	5	0	0	0	0	..	..	..	..	..
4600 Other recurrent taxes on property	0	0	0	0	0	..	..	..	..	..
5000 Taxes on goods and services	920	29 170	63 480	93 127	121 046	..	..	..	..	..
5100 Taxes on production, sale, transfer, etc	920	29 170	63 480	93 127	121 046	..	..	..	..	..
5110 General taxes	198	14 637	36 118	54 159	81 627	..	..	..	..	..
5120 Taxes on specific goods and services	722	14 533	27 362	38 968	39 419	..	..	..	..	..
5130 Unallocable between 5110 and 5120	0	0	0	0	0	..	..	..	..	..
5200 Taxes on use of goods and perform activities	0	0	0	0	0	..	..	..	..	..
5300 Unallocable between 5100 and 5200	0	0	0	0	0	..	..	..	..	..
6000 Other taxes	64	2 121	2 108	3 435	7 316	..	..	..	..	..
6100 Paid solely by business	0	0	0	0	0	..	..	..	..	..
6200 Other	64	2 121	2 108	3 435	7 316	..	..	..	..	..
Total tax revenue	1 393	56 774	127 466	217 888	395 939	..	..	..	..	..

	Local government					Social Security Funds				
	1975	1995	2005	2015	2022	1975	1995	2005	2015	2022
1000 Taxes on income, profits and capital gains	36	1 704	5 500	12 989	24 658	0	0	0	0	0
1100 Of individuals	0	1 137	2 804	6 772	12 830	..	..	..	..	..
1200 Corporate	0	565	2 696	6 217	11 828	..	..	..	..	..
1300 Unallocable between 1100 and 1200	36	3	0	0	0	..	..	..	..	..
2000 Social security contributions	0	0	0	0	0	13	9 913	43 902	104 693	176 747
2100 Employees	..	..	..	..	..	0	4 539	17 632	44 281	77 530
2200 Employers	..	..	..	..	..	13	3 918	18 486	47 846	80 600
2300 Self-employed or non-employed	..	..	..	..	..	0	1 456	7 784	12 566	18 617
2400 Unallocable between 2100, 2200 and 2300	..	..	..	..	..	0	0	0	0	0
3000 Taxes on payroll and workforce	0	237	514	1 122	1 982	0	0	0	0	0
4000 Taxes on property	87	8 960	17 928	33 461	48 023	0	0	0	0	0
4100 Recurrent taxes on immovable property	45	2 636	4 495	10 820	18 411	..	..	..	..	..
4200 Recurrent taxes on net wealth	0	0	0	0	0	..	..	..	..	..
4300 Estate, inheritance and gift taxes	0	0	0	0	0	..	..	..	..	..
4400 Taxes on financial and capital transactions	42	6 324	13 433	22 641	29 612	..	..	..	..	..
4500 Non-recurrent taxes	0	0	0	0	0	..	..	..	..	..
4600 Other recurrent taxes on property	0	0	0	0	0	..	..	..	..	..
5000 Taxes on goods and services	36	4 218	7 561	17 199	35 732	0	0	0	0	0
5100 Taxes on production, sale, transfer, etc	19	2 464	5 589	10 127	28 402	..	..	..	..	..
5110 General taxes	0	0	0	6 003	23 931	..	..	..	..	..
5120 Taxes on specific goods and services	19	2 464	5 589	4 124	4 471	..	..	..	..	..
5130 Unallocable between 5110 and 5120	0	0	0	0	0	..	..	..	..	..
5200 Taxes on use of goods and perform activities	17	1 754	1 972	7 072	7 330	..	..	..	..	..
5300 Unallocable between 5100 and 5200	0	0	0	0	0	..	..	..	..	..
6000 Other taxes	0	198	4 474	6 207	8 176	0	0	0	0	0
6100 Paid solely by business	..	0	0	0	0	..	..	..	..	..
6200 Other	..	198	4 474	6 207	8 176	..	..	..	..	..
Total tax revenue	159	15 316	35 977	70 978	118 571	13	9 913	43 902	104 693	176 747

.. Not available

Table 6.22. Latvia, tax revenues by sub-sectors of government

Million EUR

	Central government					State/Regional				
	1975	1995	2005	2015	2022	1975	1995	2005	2015	2022
1000 Taxes on income, profits and capital gains	..	68	453	677	953	..	..	..	..	..
1100 Of individuals	..	0	195	289	565	..	..	..	..	..
1200 Corporate	..	68	258	389	388	..	..	..	..	..
1300 Unallocable between 1100 and 1200	..	0	0	0	0	..	..	..	..	..
2000 Social security contributions	..	0	0	0	127	..	..	..	..	..
2100 Employees	..	..	..	..	127	..	..	..	..	..
2200 Employers	..	..	..	..	0	..	..	..	..	..
2300 Self-employed or non-employed	..	..	..	..	0	..	..	..	..	..
2400 Unallocable between 2100, 2200 and 2300	..	..	..	..	0	..	..	..	..	..
3000 Taxes on payroll and workforce	..	0	4	3	3	..	..	..	..	..
4000 Taxes on property	..	4	48	47	55	..	..	..	..	..
4100 Recurrent taxes on immovable property	..	0	0	0	-0	..	..	..	..	..
4200 Recurrent taxes on net wealth	..	0	0	0	0	..	..	..	..	..
4300 Estate, inheritance and gift taxes	..	0	0	3	4	..	..	..	..	..
4400 Taxes on financial and capital transactions	..	4	48	42	47	..	..	..	..	..
4500 Non-recurrent taxes	..	0	0	3	4	..	..	..	..	..
4600 Other recurrent taxes on property	..	0	0	0	0	..	..	..	..	..
5000 Taxes on goods and services	..	453	1 553	3 139	5 144	..	..	..	..	..
5100 Taxes on production, sale, transfer, etc	..	453	1 510	2 997	4 868	..	..	..	..	..
5110 General taxes	..	343	1 002	2 130	3 657	..	..	..	..	..
5120 Taxes on specific goods and services	..	110	508	867	1 211	..	..	..	..	..
5130 Unallocable between 5110 and 5120	..	0	0	0	0	..	..	..	..	..
5200 Taxes on use of goods and perform activities	..	1	43	142	276	..	..	..	..	..
5300 Unallocable between 5100 and 5200	..	0	0	0	0	..	..	..	..	..
6000 Other taxes	..	0	0	0	0	..	..	..	..	..
6100 Paid solely by business	..	..	..	..	..	..	..	..	..	..
6200 Other	..	..	..	..	..	..	..	..	..	..
Total tax revenue	..	525	2 058	3 867	6 281	..	..	..	..	..

	Local government					Social Security Funds				
	1975	1995	2005	2015	2022	1975	1995	2005	2015	2022
1000 Taxes on income, profits and capital gains	..	197	538	1 156	1 700	..	0	0	0	0
1100 Of individuals	..	197	538	1 156	1 700	..	..	..	..	..
1200 Corporate	..	0	0	0	0	..	..	..	..	..
1300 Unallocable between 1100 and 1200	..	0	0	0	0	..	..	..	..	..
2000 Social security contributions	..	0	0	0	0	..	445	1 079	2 030	3 483
2100 Employees	..	..	..	..	..	..	12	292	585	1057
2200 Employers	..	..	..	..	..	..	433	781	1 432	2 374
2300 Self-employed or non-employed	..	..	..	..	..	..	1	7	12	53
2400 Unallocable between 2100, 2200 and 2300	..	..	..	..	..	..	0	0	0	0
3000 Taxes on payroll and workforce	..	0	0	0	0	..	0	0	0	0
4000 Taxes on property	..	37	88	197	231	..	0	0	4	9
4100 Recurrent taxes on immovable property	..	37	88	197	231	..	..	..	..	..
4200 Recurrent taxes on net wealth	..	0	0	0	0	..	..	..	..	..
4300 Estate, inheritance and gift taxes	..	0	0	0	0	..	..	0	4	9
4400 Taxes on financial and capital transactions	..	0	0	0	0	..	..	..	..	..
4500 Non-recurrent taxes	..	0	0	0	0	..	..	..	..	..
4600 Other recurrent taxes on property	..	0	0	0	0	..	..	..	..	..
5000 Taxes on goods and services	..	2	8	18	11	..	0	0	0	0
5100 Taxes on production, sale, transfer, etc	..	0	5	7	1	..	..	..	..	..
5110 General taxes	..	0	0	0	0	..	..	..	..	..
5120 Taxes on specific goods and services	..	0	5	7	1	..	..	..	..	..
5130 Unallocable between 5110 and 5120	..	0	0	0	0	..	..	..	..	..
5200 Taxes on use of goods and perform activities	..	2	3	11	10	..	..	..	..	..
5300 Unallocable between 5100 and 5200	..	0	0	0	0	..	..	..	..	..
6000 Other taxes	..	0	0	0	0	..	0	0	0	0
6100 Paid solely by business	..	..	..	..	..	..	..	..	..	..
6200 Other	..	..	..	..	..	..	..	..	..	..
Total tax revenue	..	236	634	1 371	1 942	..	445	1 079	2 034	3 493

.. Not available

Note: Including taxes collected on behalf of the European Union.

Table 6.23. Lithuania, tax revenues by sub-sectors of government

Million EUR

	Central government					State/Regional				
	1975	1995	2005	2015	2022	1975	1995	2005	2015	2022
1000 Taxes on income, profits and capital gains	..	646	1 871	2 013	6 678	..	..	..	..	..
1100 Of individuals	..	487	1 435	1 439	5 105	..	..	..	..	..
1200 Corporate	..	160	437	574	1 573	..	..	..	..	..
1300 Unallocable between 1100 and 1200	..	0	0	0	0	..	..	..	..	..
2000 Social security contributions	..	0	0	0	0	..	..	..	..	..
2100 Employees	..	..	..	..	..	..	..	..	..	..
2200 Employers	..	..	..	..	..	..	..	..	..	..
2300 Self-employed or non-employed	..	..	..	..	..	..	..	..	..	..
2400 Unallocable between 2100, 2200 and 2300	..	..	..	..	..	..	..	..	..	..
3000 Taxes on payroll and workforce	..	0	0	0	0	..	..	..	..	..
4000 Taxes on property	..	0	0	1	14	..	..	..	..	..
4100 Recurrent taxes on immovable property	..	..	..	1	14	..	..	..	..	..
4200 Recurrent taxes on net wealth	..	..	..	0	0	..	..	..	..	..
4300 Estate, inheritance and gift taxes	..	..	..	0	0	..	..	..	..	..
4400 Taxes on financial and capital transactions	..	..	..	0	0	..	..	..	..	..
4500 Non-recurrent taxes	..	..	..	0	0	..	..	..	..	..
4600 Other recurrent taxes on property	..	..	..	0	0	..	..	..	..	..
5000 Taxes on goods and services	..	892	2 273	4 220	7 534	..	..	..	..	..
5100 Taxes on production, sale, transfer, etc	..	869	2 235	4 164	7 414	..	..	..	..	..
5110 General taxes	..	635	1 584	2 913	5 693	..	..	..	..	..
5120 Taxes on specific goods and services	..	234	651	1 252	1 720	..	..	..	..	..
5130 Unallocable between 5110 and 5120	..	0	0	0	0	..	..	..	..	..
5200 Taxes on use of goods and perform activities	..	24	38	56	121	..	..	..	..	..
5300 Unallocable between 5100 and 5200	..	0	0	0	0	..	..	..	..	..
6000 Other taxes	..	0	0	0	0	..	..	..	..	..
6100 Paid solely by business	..	..	..	..	..	..	..	..	..	..
6200 Other	..	..	..	..	..	..	..	..	..	..
Total tax revenue	..	1 539	4 145	6 235	14 226	..	..	..	..	..
	Local government					**Social Security Funds**				
	1975	1995	2005	2015	2022	1975	1995	2005	2015	2022
1000 Taxes on income, profits and capital gains	..	0	0	0	0	..	0	0	0	0
1100 Of individuals	..	..	..	..	..	..	..	..	..	..
1200 Corporate	..	..	..	..	..	..	..	..	..	..
1300 Unallocable between 1100 and 1200	..	..	..	..	..	..	..	..	..	..
2000 Social security contributions	..	0	0	0	0	..	559	1 864	4 338	6 656
2100 Employees	..	..	..	..	..	..	17	154	873	5 091
2200 Employers	..	..	..	..	..	..	537	1 522	2 916	503
2300 Self-employed or non-employed	..	..	..	..	..	..	4	188	549	1062
2400 Unallocable between 2100, 2200 and 2300	..	..	..	..	..	..	0	0	0	0
3000 Taxes on payroll and workforce	..	0	0	0	0	..	0	0	0	0
4000 Taxes on property	..	25	72	125	180	..	0	0	0	0
4100 Recurrent taxes on immovable property	..	25	71	124	177	..	..	..	..	..
4200 Recurrent taxes on net wealth	..	0	0	0	0	..	..	..	..	..
4300 Estate, inheritance and gift taxes	..	0	1	1	3	..	..	..	..	..
4400 Taxes on financial and capital transactions	..	0	0	0	0	..	..	..	..	..
4500 Non-recurrent taxes	..	0	0	0	0	..	..	..	..	..
4600 Other recurrent taxes on property	..	0	0	0	0	..	..	..	..	..
5000 Taxes on goods and services	..	23	17	18	40	..	0	0	0	6
5100 Taxes on production, sale, transfer, etc	..	0	0	0	0	..	..	..	..	..
5110 General taxes	..	..	..	..	..	..	..	..	..	..
5120 Taxes on specific goods and services	..	..	..	..	..	..	..	..	..	..
5130 Unallocable between 5110 and 5120	..	..	..	..	..	..	..	..	..	..
5200 Taxes on use of goods and perform activities	..	23	17	18	40	..	..	..	..	..
5300 Unallocable between 5100 and 5200	..	0	0	0	0	..	..	..	..	..
6000 Other taxes	..	0	0	0	0	..	0	0	0	0
6100 Paid solely by business	..	..	..	..	..	..	..	..	..	..
6200 Other	..	..	..	..	..	..	..	..	..	..
Total tax revenue	..	48	89	143	220	..	559	1 864	4 338	6 661

.. Not available

Note: Including taxes collected on behalf of the European Union.

Table 6.24. Luxembourg, tax revenues by sub-sectors of government

Million EUR

	Central government					State/Regional				
	1975	1995	2005	2015	2022	1975	1995	2005	2015	2022
1000 Taxes on income, profits and capital gains	353	1 873	3 454	6 405	10 435	..	..	..	..	..
1100 Of individuals	254	1 214	2 161	4 716	8 028	..	..	..	..	..
1200 Corporate	99	659	1 293	1 689	2 407	..	..	..	..	..
1300 Unallocable between 1100 and 1200	0	0	0	0	0	..	..	..	..	..
2000 Social security contributions	4	20	89	150	229	..	..	..	..	..
2100 Employees	3	15	89	150	229	..	..	..	..	..
2200 Employers	0	0	0	0	0	..	..	..	..	..
2300 Self-employed or non-employed	1	5	0	0	0	..	..	..	..	..
2400 Unallocable between 2100, 2200 and 2300	0	0	0	0	0	..	..	..	..	..
3000 Taxes on payroll and workforce	0	0	0	0	0	..	..	..	..	..
4000 Taxes on property	42	371	928	1 661	2 796	..	..	..	..	..
4100 Recurrent taxes on immovable property	0	0	0	0	0	..	..	..	..	..
4200 Recurrent taxes on net wealth	21	268	698	1 318	2 101	..	..	..	..	..
4300 Estate, inheritance and gift taxes	3	15	44	74	145	..	..	..	..	..
4400 Taxes on financial and capital transactions	18	88	186	269	550	..	..	..	..	..
4500 Non-recurrent taxes	0	0	0	0	0	..	..	..	..	..
4600 Other recurrent taxes on property	0	0	0	0	0	..	..	..	..	..
5000 Taxes on goods and services	189	1 374	3 241	4 466	6 731	..	..	..	..	..
5100 Taxes on production, sale, transfer, etc	182	1 350	3 202	4 381	6 638	..	..	..	..	..
5110 General taxes	112	670	1 812	2 946	4 692	..	..	..	..	..
5120 Taxes on specific goods and services	70	680	1 390	1 435	1 947	..	..	..	..	..
5130 Unallocable between 5110 and 5120	0	0	0	0	0	..	..	..	..	..
5200 Taxes on use of goods and perform activities	7	23	39	85	93	..	..	..	..	..
5300 Unallocable between 5100 and 5200	0	0	0	0	0	..	..	..	..	..
6000 Other taxes	0	6	11	27	28	..	..	..	..	..
6100 Paid solely by business	..	6	10	27	28	..	..	..	..	..
6200 Other	..	0	0	0	0	..	..	..	..	..
Total tax revenue	588	3 644	7 722	12 708	20 219	..	..	..	..	..

	Local government					Social Security Funds				
	1975	1995	2005	2015	2022	1975	1995	2005	2015	2022
1000 Taxes on income, profits and capital gains	46	331	460	606	1 001	0	0	0	0	0
1100 Of individuals	0	0	0	0	0	..	..	..	..	..
1200 Corporate	46	331	460	606	1 001	..	..	..	..	..
1300 Unallocable between 1100 and 1200	0	0	0	0	0	..	..	..	..	..
2000 Social security contributions	0	0	0	0	0	268	1 460	3 086	5 399	8 057
2100 Employees	..	..	..	..	..	102	577	1 321	2 348	3 613
2200 Employers	..	..	..	..	..	150	684	1 378	2 335	3 417
2300 Self-employed or non-employed	..	..	..	..	..	16	200	387	715	1028
2400 Unallocable between 2100, 2200 and 2300	..	..	..	..	..	0	0	0	0	0
3000 Taxes on payroll and workforce	9	0	0	0	0	0	0	0	0	0
4000 Taxes on property	6	21	35	54	67	0	0	0	0	0
4100 Recurrent taxes on immovable property	6	17	26	36	44	..	..	..	..	..
4200 Recurrent taxes on net wealth	0	0	0	0	0	..	..	..	..	..
4300 Estate, inheritance and gift taxes	0	0	0	0	0	..	..	..	..	..
4400 Taxes on financial and capital transactions	0	4	10	18	23	..	..	..	..	..
4500 Non-recurrent taxes	0	0	0	0	0	..	..	..	..	..
4600 Other recurrent taxes on property	0	0	0	0	0	..	..	..	..	..
5000 Taxes on goods and services	1	4	8	10	9	0	0	0	0	0
5100 Taxes on production, sale, transfer, etc	1	3	7	8	8	..	..	..	..	..
5110 General taxes	0	0	0	0	0	..	..	..	..	..
5120 Taxes on specific goods and services	1	3	7	8	8	..	..	..	..	..
5130 Unallocable between 5110 and 5120	0	0	0	0	0	..	..	..	..	..
5200 Taxes on use of goods and perform activities	0	1	1	1	1	..	..	..	..	..
5300 Unallocable between 5100 and 5200	0	0	0	0	0	..	..	..	..	..
6000 Other taxes	0	1	2	1	1	0	0	0	0	0
6100 Paid solely by business	..	1	2	1	1	..	..	..	..	..
6200 Other	..	0	0	0	0	..	..	..	..	..
Total tax revenue	62	357	505	671	1 079	268	1 460	3 086	5 399	8 057

.. Not available

Note: Including taxes collected on behalf of the European Union.

Table 6.25. Mexico, tax revenues by sub-sectors of government

Million MXN

	Federal government					State/Regional				
	1975	1995	2005	2015	2022	1975	1995	2005	2015	2022
1000 Taxes on income, profits and capital gains	..	76 148	402 036	1 230 555	2 280 791	..	1	0	0	0
1100 Of individuals	..	..	195 869	609 384	1066 965	..	..	..	..	..
1200 Corporate	..	..	135 840	592 443	1136 636	..	..	..	..	..
1300 Unallocable between 1100 and 1200	..	76 148	70 327	28 728	77 190	..	1	..	..	..
2000 Social security contributions	..	0	0	0	0	..	0	0	0	0
2100 Employees	..	..	..	..	..	..	..	..	..	..
2200 Employers	..	..	..	..	..	..	..	..	..	..
2300 Self-employed or non-employed	..	..	..	..	..	..	..	..	..	..
2400 Unallocable between 2100, 2200 and 2300	..	..	..	..	..	..	..	..	..	..
3000 Taxes on payroll and workforce	..	0	0	0	0	..	2 976	20 429	70 221	141 159
4000 Taxes on property	..	0	0	0	0	..	2 927	10 905	22 481	33 683
4100 Recurrent taxes on immovable property	..	..	..	..	..	..	2 198	6 544	14 245	21 898
4200 Recurrent taxes on net wealth	..	..	..	..	..	..	0	0	0	0
4300 Estate, inheritance and gift taxes	..	..	..	..	..	..	2	0	0	0
4400 Taxes on financial and capital transactions	..	..	..	..	..	..	727	4 361	8 235	11 785
4500 Non-recurrent taxes	..	..	..	..	..	..	0	0	0	0
4600 Other recurrent taxes on property	..	..	..	..	..	..	0	0	0	0
5000 Taxes on goods and services	..	91 452	416 533	1 116 026	1 592 921	..	441	2 124	24 355	29 364
5100 Taxes on production, sale, transfer, etc	..	88 372	401 580	1 115 525	1 592 129	..	22	1 364	4 357	12 784
5110 General taxes	..	51 785	318 432	707 213	1 221 803	..	0	0	0	0
5120 Taxes on specific goods and services	..	36 587	83 148	408 312	370 327	..	22	1 364	4 357	12 784
5130 Unallocable between 5110 and 5120	..	0	0	0	0	..	0	0	0	0
5200 Taxes on use of goods and perform activities	..	3 080	14 954	501	792	..	419	760	19 998	16 581
5300 Unallocable between 5100 and 5200	..	0	0	0	0	..	0	0	0	0
6000 Other taxes	..	5 149	8 616	27 379	83 919	..	228	1 537	6 489	14 477
6100 Paid solely by business	..	0	0	0	0	..	0	0	0	0
6200 Other	..	5 149	8 616	27 379	83 919	..	228	1 537	6 489	14 477
Total tax revenue (collecting government)	..	172 749	827 186	2 373 960	3 957 631	..	6 573	34 995	123 545	218 683
Adjustment[1]	..	-49 115	-278 892	-629 130	0	..	39 225	218 291	494 239	814 017
Total tax revenue (beneficiary government)	..	123 634	548 294	1 744 830	3 957 631	..	45 798	253 286	617 784	1032 700

	Local government					Social Security Funds				
	1975	1995	2005	2015	2022	1975	1995	2005	2015	2022
1000 Taxes on income, profits and capital gains	..	16	0	0	0	..	0	0	0	0
1100 Of individuals	..	..	..	..	..	..	..	..	..	..
1200 Corporate	..	..	..	..	..	..	..	..	..	..
1300 Unallocable between 1100 and 1200	..	16	..	..	..	..	..	..	..	..
2000 Social security contributions	..	0	0	0	0	..	50 871	206 551	409 249	681 672
2100 Employees	..	..	..	..	..	..	..	..	..	..
2200 Employers	..	..	..	..	..	..	..	..	..	..
2300 Self-employed or non-employed	..	..	..	..	..	..	..	..	..	..
2400 Unallocable between 2100, 2200 and 2300	..	..	..	..	..	..	50 871	206 551	409 249	681 672
3000 Taxes on payroll and workforce	..	6	32	1	2	..	0	0	0	0
4000 Taxes on property	..	2 702	15 891	35 193	71 562	..	0	0	0	0
4100 Recurrent taxes on immovable property	..	1 854	10 098	23 715	43 005	..	..	..	..	..
4200 Recurrent taxes on net wealth	..	0	0	0	0	..	..	..	..	..
4300 Estate, inheritance and gift taxes	..	0	0	0	0	..	..	..	..	..
4400 Taxes on financial and capital transactions	..	848	5 793	11 477	28 557	..	..	..	..	..
4500 Non-recurrent taxes	..	0	0	0	0	..	..	..	..	..
4600 Other recurrent taxes on property	..	0	0	0	0	..	..	..	..	..
5000 Taxes on goods and services	..	582	288	789	1320	..	0	0	0	0
5100 Taxes on production, sale, transfer, etc	..	575	214	728	1231	..	..	..	..	..
5110 General taxes	..	0	0	0	0	..	..	..	..	..
5120 Taxes on specific goods and services	..	572	214	728	1231	..	..	..	..	..
5130 Unallocable between 5110 and 5120	..	3	0	0	0	..	..	..	..	..
5200 Taxes on use of goods and perform activities	..	7	74	61	89	..	..	..	..	..
5300 Unallocable between 5100 and 5200	..	0	0	0	0	..	..	..	..	..
6000 Other taxes	..	179	1 539	10 743	17 449	..	0	0	0	0
6100 Paid solely by business	..	0	0	0	0	..	..	..	..	..
6200 Other	..	179	1 539	10 743	17 449	..	..	..	..	..
Total tax revenue (collecting government)	..	3 485	17 750	46 726	90 332	..	50 871	206 551	409 249	681 672
Adjustment[1]	..	9 890	60 601	134 892	248 417	..	0	0	0	0
Total tax revenue (beneficiary government)	..	13 375	78 351	181 617	338 749	..	50 871	206 551	409 249	681 672

.. Not available

1. This adjustment is for taxes collected by Federal government in which States and Local governments have a share. Sub-central government's shares cannot be identified by type of tax.

Table 6.26. Netherlands, tax revenues by sub-sectors of government

Million EUR

	Central government					State/Regional				
	1975	1995	2005	2015	2022	1975	1995	2005	2015	2022
1000 Taxes on income, profits and capital gains	15 075	33 520	52 640	70 849	123 828	..	..	..	..	..
1100 Of individuals	11 713	23 557	33 905	52 405	76 656	..	..	..	..	..
1200 Corporate	3 361	9 963	18 735	18 444	47 172	..	..	..	..	..
1300 Unallocable between 1100 and 1200	0	0	0	0	0	..	..	..	..	..
2000 Social security contributions	0	0	0	0	0	..	..	..	..	..
2100 Employees	..	..	..	..	..	..	..	..	..	..
2200 Employers	..	..	..	..	..	..	..	..	..	..
2300 Self-employed or non-employed	..	..	..	..	..	..	..	..	..	..
2400 Unallocable between 2100, 2200 and 2300	..	..	..	..	..	..	..	..	..	..
3000 Taxes on payroll and workforce	0	0	0	0	0	..	..	..	..	..
4000 Taxes on property	767	2 880	6 235	4 731	8 134	..	..	..	..	..
4100 Recurrent taxes on immovable property	50	0	0	1 345	918	..	..	..	..	..
4200 Recurrent taxes on net wealth	231	671	60	0	0	..	..	..	..	..
4300 Estate, inheritance and gift taxes	163	773	1 709	1 614	2 614	..	..	..	..	..
4400 Taxes on financial and capital transactions	323	1 436	4 466	1 772	4 602	..	..	..	..	..
4500 Non-recurrent taxes	0	0	0	0	0	..	..	..	..	..
4600 Other recurrent taxes on property	0	0	0	0	0	..	..	..	..	..
5000 Taxes on goods and services	9 716	31 892	57 116	70 161	103 513	..	..	..	..	..
5100 Taxes on production, sale, transfer, etc	9 113	29 728	54 658	65 990	98 091	..	..	..	..	..
5110 General taxes	6 257	19 832	36 950	44 879	70 458	..	..	..	..	..
5120 Taxes on specific goods and services	2 856	9 896	17 708	21 111	27 633	..	..	..	..	..
5130 Unallocable between 5110 and 5120	0	0	0	0	0	..	..	..	..	..
5200 Taxes on use of goods and perform activities	604	2 164	2 458	4 171	5 422	..	..	..	..	..
5300 Unallocable between 5100 and 5200	0	0	0	0	0	..	..	..	..	..
6000 Other taxes	109	491	989	416	1 156	..	..	..	..	..
6100 Paid solely by business	109	448	372	0	15	..	..	..	..	..
6200 Other	0	43	617	416	1 141	..	..	..	..	..
Total tax revenue	25 667	68 783	116 980	146 157	236 631	..	..	..	..	..

	Local government					Social Security Funds				
	1975	1995	2005	2015	2022	1975	1995	2005	2015	2022
1000 Taxes on income, profits and capital gains	77	0	0	0	0	0	0	0	0	0
1100 Of individuals	77	0	0	0	0	0	0	0	0	0
1200 Corporate	0	0	0	0	0	0	0	0	0	0
1300 Unallocable between 1100 and 1200	0	0	0	0	0	0	0	0	0	0
2000 Social security contributions	0	0	0	0	0	16 732	48 532	66 547	96 426	124 463
2100 Employees	..	..	..	..	..	7 139	32 795	35 383	48 213	46 899
2200 Employers	..	..	..	..	..	7 687	5 941	20 595	34 614	49 303
2300 Self-employed or non-employed	..	..	..	..	..	1 905	9 796	10 569	13 599	28 261
2400 Unallocable between 2100, 2200 and 2300	..	..	..	..	..	0	0	0	0	0
3000 Taxes on payroll and workforce	0	0	0	0	0	0	0	0	0	0
4000 Taxes on property	272	2 287	4 341	5 037	6 644	0	0	0	0	0
4100 Recurrent taxes on immovable property	272	2 287	4 341	5 037	6 644	..	..	..	..	..
4200 Recurrent taxes on net wealth	0	0	0	0	0	..	..	..	..	..
4300 Estate, inheritance and gift taxes	0	0	0	0	0	..	..	..	..	..
4400 Taxes on financial and capital transactions	0	0	0	0	0	..	..	..	..	..
4500 Non-recurrent taxes	0	0	0	0	0	..	..	..	..	..
4600 Other recurrent taxes on property	0	0	0	0	0	..	..	..	..	..
5000 Taxes on goods and services	153	1 533	3 330	4 652	5 439	0	0	0	0	0
5100 Taxes on production, sale, transfer, etc	14	59	118	249	396	..	..	..	..	..
5110 General taxes	0	6	10	43	0	..	..	..	..	..
5120 Taxes on specific goods and services	14	53	108	206	396	..	..	..	..	..
5130 Unallocable between 5110 and 5120	0	0	0	0	0	..	..	..	..	..
5200 Taxes on use of goods and perform activities	139	1 474	3 212	4 403	5 043	..	..	..	..	..
5300 Unallocable between 5100 and 5200	0	0	0	0	0	..	..	..	..	..
6000 Other taxes	0	0	0	0	43	0	0	0	0	0
6100 Paid solely by business	..	..	..	..	..	..	..	..	..	..
6200 Other	..	..	..	..	..	..	..	..	..	..
Total tax revenue	502	3 820	7 671	9 689	12 126	16 732	48 532	66 547	96 426	124 463

.. Not available

Note: Including taxes collected on behalf of the European Union.

Table 6.27. New Zealand, tax revenues by sub-sectors of government

Million NZD

	Central government					State/Regional				
	1975	1995	2005	2015	2022	1975	1995	2005	2015	2022
1000 Taxes on income, profits and capital gains	2 296	21 253	37 379	44 723	76 139	..	..	..	..	..
1100 Of individuals	1 874	15 626	24 373	30 297	54 402	..	..	..	..	..
1200 Corporate	407	4 122	9 957	11 407	17 905	..	..	..	..	..
1300 Unallocable between 1100 and 1200	16	1 505	3 049	3 019	3 832	..	..	..	..	..
2000 Social security contributions	0	0	0	0	0	..	..	..	..	..
2100 Employees	..	0	0	0	0	..	..	..	..	..
2200 Employers	..	0	0	0	0	..	..	..	..	..
2300 Self-employed or non-employed	..	0	0	0	0	..	..	..	..	..
2400 Unallocable between 2100, 2200 and 2300	..	0	0	0	0	..	..	..	..	..
3000 Taxes on payroll and workforce	0	0	0	0	0	..	..	..	..	..
4000 Taxes on property	83	218	86	84	153	..	..	..	..	..
4100 Recurrent taxes on immovable property	3	-1	0	0	0	..	..	..	..	..
4200 Recurrent taxes on net wealth	0	0	0	0	0	..	..	..	..	..
4300 Estate, inheritance and gift taxes	54	3	3	0	0	..	..	..	..	..
4400 Taxes on financial and capital transactions	25	216	83	84	153	..	..	..	..	..
4500 Non-recurrent taxes	0	0	0	0	0	..	..	..	..	..
4600 Other recurrent taxes on property	0	0	0	0	0	..	..	..	..	..
5000 Taxes on goods and services	807	11 395	18 744	31 146	46 145	..	..	..	..	..
5100 Taxes on production, sale, transfer, etc	770	10 833	17 792	29 551	44 495	..	..	..	..	..
5110 General taxes	311	7 895	14 133	24 587	39 661	..	..	..	..	..
5120 Taxes on specific goods and services	459	2 938	3 659	4 964	4 834	..	..	..	..	..
5130 Unallocable between 5110 and 5120	0	0	0	0	0	..	..	..	..	..
5200 Taxes on use of goods and perform activities	37	562	952	1 595	1 650	..	..	..	..	..
5300 Unallocable between 5100 and 5200	0	0	0	0	0	..	..	..	..	..
6000 Other taxes	0	0	14	2	0	..	..	..	..	..
6100 Paid solely by business	..	..	0	0	0	..	..	..	..	..
6200 Other	..	..	14	2	0	..	..	..	..	..
Total tax revenue	3 186	32 866	56 223	75 955	122 437	..	..	..	..	..

	Local government					Social Security Funds				
	1975	1995	2005	2015	2022	1975	1995	2005	2015	2022
1000 Taxes on income, profits and capital gains	0	0	0	0	0	0	0	0	0	0
1100 Of individuals	0	0	0	0	0	0	0	0	0	0
1200 Corporate	0	0	0	0	0	0	0	0	0	0
1300 Unallocable between 1100 and 1200	0	0	0	0	0	0	0	0	0	0
2000 Social security contributions	0	0	0	0	0	0	0	0	0	0
2100 Employees	..	0	0	0	0	..	0	0	0	0
2200 Employers	..	0	0	0	0	..	0	0	0	0
2300 Self-employed or non-employed	..	0	0	0	0	..	0	0	0	0
2400 Unallocable between 2100, 2200 and 2300	..	0	0	0	0	..	0	0	0	0
3000 Taxes on payroll and workforce	0	0	0	0	0	0	0	0	0	0
4000 Taxes on property	237	1 646	2 825	4 962	7 420	0	0	0	0	0
4100 Recurrent taxes on immovable property	237	1 646	2 825	4 962	7 420	..	..	..	..	..
4200 Recurrent taxes on net wealth	0	0	0	0	0	..	..	..	..	..
4300 Estate, inheritance and gift taxes	0	0	0	0	0	..	..	..	..	..
4400 Taxes on financial and capital transactions	0	0	0	0	0	..	..	..	..	..
4500 Non-recurrent taxes	0	0	0	0	0	..	..	..	..	..
4600 Other recurrent taxes on property	0	0	0	0	0	..	..	..	..	..
5000 Taxes on goods and services	29	184	310	582	929	0	0	0	0	0
5100 Taxes on production, sale, transfer, etc	18	33	30	33	176	..	..	..	..	..
5110 General taxes	0	0	0	0	0	..	..	..	..	..
5120 Taxes on specific goods and services	18	33	30	33	176	..	..	..	..	..
5130 Unallocable between 5110 and 5120	0	0	0	0	0	..	..	..	..	..
5200 Taxes on use of goods and perform activities	11	151	280	549	753	..	..	..	..	..
5300 Unallocable between 5100 and 5200	0	0	0	0	0	..	..	..	..	..
6000 Other taxes	0	0	0	0	0	0	0	0	0	0
6100 Paid solely by business	..	..	..	..	..	..	..	..	..	..
6200 Other	..	..	..	..	..	..	..	..	..	..
Total tax revenue	266	1 830	3 135	5 544	8 349	0	0	0	0	0

.. Not available

Table 6.28. Norway, tax revenues by sub-sectors of government

Million NOK

	Central government (1)					State/Regional				
	1975	1995	2005	2015	2022	1975	1995	2005	2015	2022
1000 Taxes on income, profits and capital gains	6 495	67 402	318 701	315 719	1291 767	..	..	..	..	..
1100 Of individuals	5 424	38 059	89 353	175 544	244 077	..	..	..	..	..
1200 Corporate	1 071	29 343	229 348	140 175	1047 690	..	..	..	..	..
1300 Unallocable between 1100 and 1200	0	0	0	0	0	..	..	..	..	..
2000 Social security contributions	1 341	6 013	173 151	325 130	428 463	..	..	..	..	..
2100 Employees	331	1 233	58 320	112 662	148 315	..	..	..	..	..
2200 Employers	1 010	4 780	104 794	190 923	251 048	..	..	..	..	..
2300 Self-employed or non-employed	0	0	0	0	0	..	..	..	..	..
2400 Unallocable between 2100, 2200 and 2300	0	0	0	0	0	..	..	..	..	..
3000 Taxes on payroll and workforce	0	0	0	0	2 415	..	..	..	..	..
4000 Taxes on property	771	3 497	9 328	11 282	20 937	..	..	..	..	..
4100 Recurrent taxes on immovable property	0	0	0	0	0	..	..	..	..	..
4200 Recurrent taxes on net wealth	490	1 172	2 891	2 561	8 724	..	..	..	..	..
4300 Estate, inheritance and gift taxes	146	975	1 768	295	32	..	..	..	..	..
4400 Taxes on financial and capital transactions	135	1 350	4 669	8 426	12 181	..	..	..	..	..
4500 Non-recurrent taxes	0	0	0	0	0	..	..	..	..	..
4600 Other recurrent taxes on property	0	0	0	0	0	..	..	..	..	..
5000 Taxes on goods and services	25 056	143 726	235 529	363 929	481 038	..	..	..	..	..
5100 Taxes on production, sale, transfer, etc	24 367	134 965	220 898	342 410	458 093	..	..	..	..	..
5110 General taxes	13 670	81 772	153 820	256 029	373 515	..	..	..	..	..
5120 Taxes on specific goods and services	10 697	53 193	67 078	86 381	84 578	..	..	..	..	..
5130 Unallocable between 5110 and 5120	0	0	0	0	0	..	..	..	..	..
5200 Taxes on use of goods and perform activities	689	8 761	14 631	21 519	22 945	..	..	..	..	..
5300 Unallocable between 5100 and 5200	0	0	0	0	0	..	..	..	..	..
6000 Other taxes	130	15	0	0	0	..	..	..	..	..
6100 Paid solely by business	124	1	..	..	..	..	..	..	..	..
6200 Other	6	14	..	..	..	..	..	..	..	..
Total tax revenue	33 793	220 653	736 709	1 016 060	2 224 620	..	..	..	..	..

	Local government					Social Security Funds				
	1975	1995	2005	2015	2022	1975	1995	2005	2015	2022
1000 Taxes on income, profits and capital gains	13 725	67 978	100 512	160 582	218 900	2 728	0	0	0	0
1100 Of individuals	12 877	61 784	100 512	160 582	218 900	2 728	..	..	..	..
1200 Corporate	848	6 194	0	0	0	0	..	..	..	..
1300 Unallocable between 1100 and 1200	0	0	0	0	0	0	..	..	..	..
2000 Social security contributions	0	0	0	0	0	15 224	84 563	0	0	0
2100 Employees	..	..	..	..	..	2 949	30 417	..	..	..
2200 Employers	..	..	..	..	..	11 315	48 396	..	..	..
2300 Self-employed or non-employed	..	..	..	..	..	960	5 750	..	..	..
2400 Unallocable between 2100, 2200 and 2300	..	..	..	..	..	0	0	..	..	..
3000 Taxes on payroll and workforce	0	0	0	0	0	0	0	0	0	0
4000 Taxes on property	772	7 352	10 283	21 812	34 291	0	0	0	0	0
4100 Recurrent taxes on immovable property	278	2 792	4 324	11 177	16 091	..	..	..	..	..
4200 Recurrent taxes on net wealth	494	4 560	5 959	10 635	18 200	..	..	..	..	..
4300 Estate, inheritance and gift taxes	0	0	0	0	0	..	..	..	..	..
4400 Taxes on financial and capital transactions	0	0	0	0	0	..	..	..	..	..
4500 Non-recurrent taxes	0	0	0	0	0	..	..	..	..	..
4600 Other recurrent taxes on property	0	0	0	0	0	..	..	..	..	..
5000 Taxes on goods and services	0	431	2 281	1 574	1 672	51	267	0	0	0
5100 Taxes on production, sale, transfer, etc	0	0	0	0	0	51	267	..	..	..
5110 General taxes	0	0	0	0	0	0	0	..	..	..
5120 Taxes on specific goods and services	0	0	0	0	0	51	267	..	..	..
5130 Unallocable between 5110 and 5120	0	0	0	0	0	0	0	..	..	..
5200 Taxes on use of goods and perform activities	0	431	2 281	1 574	1 672	0	0	..	..	..
5300 Unallocable between 5100 and 5200	0	0	0	0	0	0	0	..	..	..
6000 Other taxes	432	0	0	0	0	0	0	0	0	0
6100 Paid solely by business	0	..	..	..	..	..	..	..	..	..
6200 Other	432	..	..	..	..	..	..	..	..	..
Total tax revenue	14 929	75 761	113 076	183 968	254 863	18 003	84 830	0	0	0

.. Not available

1. The Norwegian National Insurance has been integrated into the Central government sector from the year 2000 onwards.

Table 6.29. Poland, tax revenues by sub-sectors of government

Million PLN

	Central government					State/Regional				
	1975	1995	2005	2015	2022	1975	1995	2005	2015	2022
1000 Taxes on income, profits and capital gains	..	32 774	40 398	71 381	140 494	..	..	..	..	..
1100 Of individuals	..	23 937	24 518	45 462	70 452	..	..	..	..	..
1200 Corporate	..	8 837	15 880	25 919	70 042	..	..	..	..	..
1300 Unallocable between 1100 and 1200	..	0	0	0	0	..	..	..	..	..
2000 Social security contributions	..	0	0	0	0	..	..	..	..	..
2100 Employees	..	..	..	..	..	..	..	..	..	..
2200 Employers	..	..	..	..	..	..	..	..	..	..
2300 Self-employed or non-employed	..	..	..	..	..	..	..	..	..	..
2400 Unallocable between 2100, 2200 and 2300	..	..	..	..	..	..	..	..	..	..
3000 Taxes on payroll and workforce	..	831	2 555	4 028	17 154	..	..	..	..	..
4000 Taxes on property	..	0	0	0	3	..	..	..	..	..
4100 Recurrent taxes on immovable property	..	..	..	..	..	..	..	..	..	..
4200 Recurrent taxes on net wealth	..	..	..	..	..	..	..	..	..	..
4300 Estate, inheritance and gift taxes	..	..	..	..	..	..	..	..	..	..
4400 Taxes on financial and capital transactions	..	..	..	..	..	..	..	..	..	..
4500 Non-recurrent taxes	..	..	..	..	..	..	..	..	..	..
4600 Other recurrent taxes on property	..	..	..	..	..	..	..	..	..	..
5000 Taxes on goods and services	..	43 483	120 207	207 129	371 347	..	..	..	..	..
5100 Taxes on production, sale, transfer, etc	..	42 863	119 805	203 303	341 121	..	..	..	..	..
5110 General taxes	..	21 051	75 783	125 895	226 721	..	..	..	..	..
5120 Taxes on specific goods and services	..	21 812	44 022	77 408	114 400	..	..	..	..	..
5130 Unallocable between 5110 and 5120	..	0	0	0	0	..	..	..	..	..
5200 Taxes on use of goods and perform activities	..	620	402	3 826	30 226	..	..	..	..	..
5300 Unallocable between 5100 and 5200	..	0	0	0	0	..	..	..	..	..
6000 Other taxes	..	99	18	0	0	..	..	..	..	..
6100 Paid solely by business	..	0	0	..	..	..	..	..	..	..
6200 Other	..	99	18	..	..	..	..	..	..	..
Total tax revenue	..	77 187	163 178	282 538	528 998	..	..	..	..	..

	Local government					Social Security Funds				
	1975	1995	2005	2015	2022	1975	1995	2005	2015	2022
1000 Taxes on income, profits and capital gains	..	4 896	23 093	45 697	83 529	..	0	0	0	0
1100 Of individuals	..	4 427	17 916	38 512	67 806	..	..	..	..	..
1200 Corporate	..	469	5 177	7 185	15 723	..	..	..	..	..
1300 Unallocable between 1100 and 1200	..	0	0	0	0	..	..	..	..	..
2000 Social security contributions	..	0	0	0	0	..	38 808	121 522	225 711	396 507
2100 Employees	..	..	..	..	..	..	16 727	49 469	92 607	173 427
2200 Employers	..	..	..	..	..	..	19 364	47 753	88 749	144 069
2300 Self-employed or non-employed	..	..	..	..	..	..	2 717	24 300	44 355	79 011
2400 Unallocable between 2100, 2200 and 2300	..	..	..	..	..	..	0	0	0	0
3000 Taxes on payroll and workforce	..	0	0	0	0	..	0	0	0	0
4000 Taxes on property	..	4 370	14 723	24 637	35 792	..	0	0	0	0
4100 Recurrent taxes on immovable property	..	3 579	12 718	22 206	30 084	..	..	..	..	..
4200 Recurrent taxes on net wealth	..	0	0	0	0	..	..	..	..	..
4300 Estate, inheritance and gift taxes	..	44	242	246	552	..	..	..	..	..
4400 Taxes on financial and capital transactions	..	747	1 763	2 185	5 156	..	..	..	..	..
4500 Non-recurrent taxes	..	0	0	0	0	..	..	..	..	..
4600 Other recurrent taxes on property	..	0	0	0	0	..	..	..	..	..
5000 Taxes on goods and services	..	1 340	3 492	4 139	4 335	..	0	0	0	1 975
5100 Taxes on production, sale, transfer, etc	..	0	0	0	0	..	..	..	..	1 975
5110 General taxes	..	..	..	..	..	..	..	..	..	0
5120 Taxes on specific goods and services	..	..	..	..	..	..	..	..	..	1 975
5130 Unallocable between 5110 and 5120	..	..	..	..	..	..	..	..	..	0
5200 Taxes on use of goods and perform activities	..	1 340	3 492	4 139	4 335	..	..	..	..	0
5300 Unallocable between 5100 and 5200	..	0	0	0	0	..	..	..	..	0
6000 Other taxes	..	158	278	647	1 519	..	0	0	0	0
6100 Paid solely by business	..	0	0	0	0	..	..	..	..	..
6200 Other	..	158	278	647	1 519	..	..	..	..	..
Total tax revenue	..	10 764	41 586	75 120	125 175	..	38 808	121 522	225 711	398 482

.. Not available

Note: Including taxes collected on behalf of the European Union.

Table 6.30. Portugal, tax revenues by sub-sectors of government

Million EUR

	Central government					State/Regional				
	1975	1995	2005	2015	2022	1975	1995	2005	2015	2022
1000 Taxes on income, profits and capital gains	81	6 557	11 576	17 516	23 518	..	..	..	..	..
1100 Of individuals	..	4 547	7 694	12 316	15 960	..	..	..	..	..
1200 Corporate	..	1 866	3 761	5 199	7 559	..	..	..	..	..
1300 Unallocable between 1100 and 1200	81	144	121	0	0	..	..	..	..	..
2000 Social security contributions	0	621	265	217	2 204	..	..	..	..	..
2100 Employees	..	2	7	19	2 040	..	..	..	..	..
2200 Employers	..	619	259	198	164	..	..	..	..	..
2300 Self-employed or non-employed	..	0	0	0	0	..	..	..	..	..
2400 Unallocable between 2100, 2200 and 2300	..	0	0	0	0	..	..	..	..	..
3000 Taxes on payroll and workforce	12	0	0	0	0	..	..	..	..	..
4000 Taxes on property	12	226	308	202	572	..	..	..	..	..
4100 Recurrent taxes on immovable property	0	0	0	6	161	..	..	..	..	..
4200 Recurrent taxes on net wealth	0	0	0	0	0	..	..	..	..	..
4300 Estate, inheritance and gift taxes	4	57	25	0	0	..	..	..	..	..
4400 Taxes on financial and capital transactions	7	169	283	196	411	..	..	..	..	..
4500 Non-recurrent taxes	0	0	0	0	0	..	..	..	..	..
4600 Other recurrent taxes on property	0	0	0	0	0	..	..	..	..	..
5000 Taxes on goods and services	198	10 407	19 782	21 725	30 156	..	..	..	..	..
5100 Taxes on production, sale, transfer, etc	187	10 198	19 374	20 899	28 535	..	..	..	..	..
5110 General taxes	52	5 481	11 846	13 745	20 886	..	..	..	..	..
5120 Taxes on specific goods and services	135	4 717	7 529	7 154	7 648	..	..	..	..	..
5130 Unallocable between 5110 and 5120	0	0	141	18	5	..	..	..	..	..
5200 Taxes on use of goods and perform activities	12	179	381	814	1 612	..	..	..	..	..
5300 Unallocable between 5100 and 5200	0	30	27	13	9	..	..	..	..	..
6000 Other taxes	2	9	143	333	407	..	..	..	..	..
6100 Paid solely by business	1	9	143	333	405	..	..	..	..	..
6200 Other	0	0	0	0	2	..	..	..	..	..
Total tax revenue	304	17 820	32 075	39 992	56 858	..	..	..	..	..
	Local government					Social Security Funds				
	1975	1995	2005	2015	2022	1975	1995	2005	2015	2022
1000 Taxes on income, profits and capital gains	0	307	725	1 246	1 475	0	0	0	0	0
1100 Of individuals	..	156	298	832	952	..	..	..	..	..
1200 Corporate	..	151	427	414	523	..	..	..	..	..
1300 Unallocable between 1100 and 1200	0	0	0	0	0	..	..	..	..	..
2000 Social security contributions	0	941	1 629	1 867	0	161	5 267	11 133	14 099	22 530
2100 Employees	..	941	1 629	1 867	..	62	2 100	4 053	5 106	7 649
2200 Employers	..	0	0	0	..	97	3 167	7 080	8 993	14 881
2300 Self-employed or non-employed	..	0	0	0	..	2	0	0	0	0
2400 Unallocable between 2100, 2200 and 2300	..	0	0	0	..	0	0	0	0	0
3000 Taxes on payroll and workforce	0	0	0	0	0	0	0	0	0	0
4000 Taxes on property	0	599	1 541	2 105	3 159	0	0	0	0	0
4100 Recurrent taxes on immovable property	..	310	827	1 529	1 478	..	..	..	..	..
4200 Recurrent taxes on net wealth	..	0	0	0	0	..	..	..	..	..
4300 Estate, inheritance and gift taxes	..	0	1	0	0	..	..	..	..	..
4400 Taxes on financial and capital transactions	..	289	713	576	1 682	..	..	..	..	..
4500 Non-recurrent taxes	..	0	0	0	0	..	..	..	..	..
4600 Other recurrent taxes on property	..	0	0	0	0	..	..	..	..	..
5000 Taxes on goods and services	0	499	962	1 132	1 521	0	335	823	1 179	1 200
5100 Taxes on production, sale, transfer, etc	0	442	827	876	1 196	..	335	823	1 179	1 181
5110 General taxes	0	318	563	629	855	..	276	592	994	970
5120 Taxes on specific goods and services	0	124	264	247	341	..	59	231	184	211
5130 Unallocable between 5110 and 5120	0	0	0	0	0	..	0	0	0	0
5200 Taxes on use of goods and perform activities	0	57	133	256	325	..	0	0	0	19
5300 Unallocable between 5100 and 5200	0	0	1	0	0	..	0	0	0	0
6000 Other taxes	0	3	28	10	11	0	0	0	0	0
6100 Paid solely by business	..	0	25	8	9	..	..	..	..	..
6200 Other	..	3	3	1	2	..	..	..	..	..
Total tax revenue	0	2 349	4 884	6 360	6 165	161	5 602	11 956	15 278	23 730

.. Not available

Note: Including taxes collected on behalf of the European Union.

Table 6.31. Slovak Republic, tax revenues by sub-sectors of government

Million EUR

	Central government					State/Regional				
	1975	1995	2005	2015	2022	1975	1995	2005	2015	2022
1000 Taxes on income, profits and capital gains	..	1 993	2 968	5 542	8 453	..	..	..	..	..
1100 Of individuals	..	695	1 496	2 464	4 126	..	..	..	..	..
1200 Corporate	..	1 166	1 345	2 917	4 012	..	..	..	..	..
1300 Unallocable between 1100 and 1200	..	132	128	162	315	..	..	..	..	..
2000 Social security contributions	..	85	240	253	438	..	..	..	..	..
2100 Employees	..	10	104	58	135	..	..	..	..	..
2200 Employers	..	75	136	195	302	..	..	..	..	..
2300 Self-employed or non-employed	..	0	0	0	1	..	..	..	..	..
2400 Unallocable between 2100, 2200 and 2300	..	0	0	0	0	..	..	..	..	..
3000 Taxes on payroll and workforce	..	0	0	0	0	..	..	..	..	..
4000 Taxes on property	..	27	28	-0	0	..	..	..	..	..
4100 Recurrent taxes on immovable property	..	8	9	-0	0	..	..	..	..	..
4200 Recurrent taxes on net wealth	..	0	0	0	0	..	..	..	..	..
4300 Estate, inheritance and gift taxes	..	2	1	-0	0	..	..	..	..	..
4400 Taxes on financial and capital transactions	..	16	18	-0	0	..	..	..	..	..
4500 Non-recurrent taxes	..	0	0	0	0	..	..	..	..	..
4600 Other recurrent taxes on property	..	0	0	0	0	..	..	..	..	..
5000 Taxes on goods and services	..	2 782	6 031	8 974	13 108	..	..	..	..	..
5100 Taxes on production, sale, transfer, etc	..	2 594	5 773	8 442	12 319	..	..	..	..	..
5110 General taxes	..	1 616	3 880	5 423	8 441	..	..	..	..	..
5120 Taxes on specific goods and services	..	978	1 893	3 020	3 878	..	..	..	..	..
5130 Unallocable between 5110 and 5120	..	0	0	0	0	..	..	..	..	..
5200 Taxes on use of goods and perform activities	..	189	256	532	758	..	..	..	..	..
5300 Unallocable between 5100 and 5200	..	0	2	0	30	..	..	..	..	..
6000 Other taxes	..	0	0	0	0	..	..	..	..	..
6100 Paid solely by business	..	..	..	..	..	..	..	..	..	..
6200 Other	..	..	..	..	..	..	..	..	..	..
Total tax revenue	..	4 887	9 267	14 770	21 999	..	..	..	..	..

	Local government					Social Security Funds				
	1975	1995	2005	2015	2022	1975	1995	2005	2015	2022
1000 Taxes on income, profits and capital gains	..	0	0	0	0	..	0	0	0	0
1100 Of individuals	..	..	..	..	..	..	..	..	..	..
1200 Corporate	..	..	..	..	..	..	..	..	..	..
1300 Unallocable between 1100 and 1200	..	..	..	..	..	..	..	..	..	..
2000 Social security contributions	..	0	0	0	0	..	2 817	6 037	10 643	15 529
2100 Employees	..	..	..	0	..	..	540	1 377	2 352	3 874
2200 Employers	..	..	..	0	..	..	1 774	3 356	6 124	9 163
2300 Self-employed or non-employed	..	..	..	0	..	..	503	1 304	2 168	2 491
2400 Unallocable between 2100, 2200 and 2300	..	..	..	0	..	..	0	0	0	0
3000 Taxes on payroll and workforce	..	0	0	0	0	..	0	0	0	0
4000 Taxes on property	..	84	220	335	469	..	0	0	0	0
4100 Recurrent taxes on immovable property	..	72	220	335	469	..	..	..	..	..
4200 Recurrent taxes on net wealth	..	0	0	0	0	..	..	..	..	..
4300 Estate, inheritance and gift taxes	..	0	0	0	0	..	..	..	..	..
4400 Taxes on financial and capital transactions	..	12	0	0	0	..	..	..	..	..
4500 Non-recurrent taxes	..	0	0	0	0	..	..	..	..	..
4600 Other recurrent taxes on property	..	0	0	0	0	..	..	..	..	..
5000 Taxes on goods and services	..	17	198	182	243	..	0	0	0	0
5100 Taxes on production, sale, transfer, etc	..	10	9	12	15	..	..	..	..	..
5110 General taxes	..	0	0	-0	0	..	..	..	..	..
5120 Taxes on specific goods and services	..	10	9	12	15	..	..	..	..	..
5130 Unallocable between 5110 and 5120	..	0	0	0	0	..	..	..	..	..
5200 Taxes on use of goods and perform activities	..	1	94	17	33	..	..	..	..	..
5300 Unallocable between 5100 and 5200	..	6	95	153	194	..	..	..	..	..
6000 Other taxes	..	0	0	0	0	..	0	0	0	0
6100 Paid solely by business	..	..	..	..	..	..	..	..	..	..
6200 Other	..	..	..	..	..	..	..	..	..	..
Total tax revenue	..	101	418	517	712	..	2 817	6 037	10 643	15 529

.. Not available

Note: Including taxes collected on behalf of the European Union.

Table 6.32. Slovenia, tax revenues by sub-sectors of government

Million EUR

	Central government					State/Regional				
	1975	1995	2005	2015	2022	1975	1995	2005	2015	2022
1000 Taxes on income, profits and capital gains	..	479	1 828	1 528	2 923	..	..	..	..	..
1100 Of individuals	..	413	1 029	958	1 588	..	..	..	..	..
1200 Corporate	..	54	795	568	1 332	..	..	..	..	..
1300 Unallocable between 1100 and 1200	..	12	5	2	3	..	..	..	..	..
2000 Social security contributions	..	38	42	59	93	..	..	..	..	..
2100 Employees	..	20	24	31	49	..	..	..	..	..
2200 Employers	..	17	15	23	37	..	..	..	..	..
2300 Self-employed or non-employed	..	1	3	5	7	..	..	..	..	..
2400 Unallocable between 2100, 2200 and 2300	..	0	0	0	0	..	..	..	..	..
3000 Taxes on payroll and workforce	..	14	521	20	27	..	..	..	..	..
4000 Taxes on property	..	5	3	2	3	..	..	..	..	..
4100 Recurrent taxes on immovable property	..	0	0	0	0	..	..	..	..	..
4200 Recurrent taxes on net wealth	..	0	3	0	0	..	..	..	..	..
4300 Estate, inheritance and gift taxes	..	0	0	0	0	..	..	..	..	..
4400 Taxes on financial and capital transactions	..	0	0	0	0	..	..	..	..	..
4500 Non-recurrent taxes	..	0	0	0	0	..	..	..	..	..
4600 Other recurrent taxes on property	..	0	0	0	0	..	..	..	..	..
5000 Taxes on goods and services	..	1 554	3 826	5 543	7 321	..	..	..	..	..
5100 Taxes on production, sale, transfer, etc	..	1 524	3 645	5 205	6 860	..	..	..	..	..
5110 General taxes	..	1 192	2 489	3 224	4 681	..	..	..	..	..
5120 Taxes on specific goods and services	..	332	1 156	1 981	2 179	..	..	..	..	..
5130 Unallocable between 5110 and 5120	..	0	0	0	0	..	..	..	..	..
5200 Taxes on use of goods and perform activities	..	31	181	338	462	..	..	..	..	..
5300 Unallocable between 5100 and 5200	..	0	0	0	0	..	..	..	..	..
6000 Other taxes	..	0	0	0	0	..	..	..	..	..
6100 Paid solely by business	..	..	..	..	..	..	..	..	..	..
6200 Other	..	..	..	..	..	..	..	..	..	..
Total tax revenue	..	2 090	6 221	7 152	10 368	..	..	..	..	..

	Local government					Social Security Funds				
	1975	1995	2005	2015	2022	1975	1995	2005	2015	2022
1000 Taxes on income, profits and capital gains	..	194	559	1 019	1 365	..	0	0	0	0
1100 Of individuals	..	192	556	1 019	1 365	..	..	..	..	..
1200 Corporate	..	0	0	0	0	..	..	..	..	..
1300 Unallocable between 1100 and 1200	..	2	2	0	0	..	..	..	..	..
2000 Social security contributions	..	0	0	0	0	..	1 793	4 354	5 924	9 041
2100 Employees	..	..	..	..	..	..	812	2 124	2 879	4 511
2200 Employers	..	..	..	..	..	..	806	1 579	2 112	3 311
2300 Self-employed or non-employed	..	..	..	..	..	..	175	652	933	1 219
2400 Unallocable between 2100, 2200 and 2300	..	..	..	..	..	..	0	0	0	0
3000 Taxes on payroll and workforce	..	2	0	0	0	..	0	0	0	0
4000 Taxes on property	..	53	167	239	344	..	0	0	0	0
4100 Recurrent taxes on immovable property	..	37	122	199	260	..	..	..	..	..
4200 Recurrent taxes on net wealth	..	0	0	0	0	..	..	..	..	..
4300 Estate, inheritance and gift taxes	..	1	5	8	17	..	..	..	..	..
4400 Taxes on financial and capital transactions	..	12	40	29	55	..	..	..	..	..
4500 Non-recurrent taxes	..	0	0	0	0	..	..	..	..	..
4600 Other recurrent taxes on property	..	0	0	0	0	..	..	..	..	..
5000 Taxes on goods and services	..	7	91	96	101	..	0	0	0	0
5100 Taxes on production, sale, transfer, etc	..	7	43	57	72	..	..	..	..	..
5110 General taxes	..	0	0	0	0	..	..	..	..	..
5120 Taxes on specific goods and services	..	7	43	57	72	..	..	..	..	..
5130 Unallocable between 5110 and 5120	..	0	0	0	0	..	..	..	..	..
5200 Taxes on use of goods and perform activities	..	0	48	39	29	..	..	..	..	..
5300 Unallocable between 5100 and 5200	..	0	0	0	0	..	..	..	..	..
6000 Other taxes	..	0	0	0	0	..	0	0	0	0
6100 Paid solely by business	..	..	..	..	..	..	..	..	..	..
6200 Other	..	..	..	..	..	..	..	..	..	..
Total tax revenue	..	256	817	1 354	1 811	..	1 793	4 354	5 924	9 041

.. Not available

Note: Including taxes collected on behalf of the European Union.

Table 6.33. Spain, tax revenues by sub-sectors of government

Million EUR

	Federal government					State/Regional				
	1975	1995	2005	2015	2022	1975	1995	2005	2015	2022
1000 Taxes on income, profits and capital gains	1 388	38 846	71 598	62 198	98 614	..	588	19 503	34 814	52 134
1100 Of individuals	897	31 789	38 219	39 659	63 874	..	457	19 104	34 600	51 758
1200 Corporate	490	7 057	33 379	22 539	34 740	..	131	399	214	376
1300 Unallocable between 1100 and 1200	1	0	0	0	0	..	0	0	0	0
2000 Social security contributions	0	2 027	3 027	3 505	3 610	..	0	0	0	0
2100 Employees	..	1 017	1 369	1 541	1 318	..	..	..	..	..
2200 Employers	..	1 010	1 658	1 964	2 292	..	..	..	..	..
2300 Self-employed or non-employed	..	0	0	0	0	..	..	..	..	..
2400 Unallocable between 2100, 2200 and 2300	..	0	0	0	0	..	..	..	..	..
3000 Taxes on payroll and workforce	0	0	0	0	0	..	0	0	0	0
4000 Taxes on property	421	405	77	1 197	820	..	4 050	19 031	10 286	16 874
4100 Recurrent taxes on immovable property	1	3	5	4	5	..	0	2	38	25
4200 Recurrent taxes on net wealth	0	166	38	32	118	..	419	1 246	961	1 475
4300 Estate, inheritance and gift taxes	56	1	24	222	256	..	835	2 315	2 454	3 253
4400 Taxes on financial and capital transactions	364	235	10	6	207	..	2 796	15 468	6 833	12 121
4500 Non-recurrent taxes	0	0	0	0	0	..	0	0	0	0
4600 Other recurrent taxes on property	0	0	0	0	0	..	0	0	0	0
5000 Taxes on goods and services	1 609	32 388	71 536	89 031	112 014	..	2 556	7 956	6 553	7 573
5100 Taxes on production, sale, transfer, etc	1 599	32 206	70 895	87 536	108 854	..	2 387	7 637	6 022	6 803
5110 General taxes	990	20 331	51 583	61 839	84 231	..	786	1 980	2 571	3 521
5120 Taxes on specific goods and services	608	11 875	19 312	25 697	24 623	..	1 601	5 657	3 451	3 282
5130 Unallocable between 5110 and 5120	0	0	0	0	0	..	0	0	0	0
5200 Taxes on use of goods and perform activities	10	182	641	1 495	3 160	..	169	319	531	770
5300 Unallocable between 5100 and 5200	0	0	0	0	0	..	0	0	0	0
6000 Other taxes	0	0	0	101	193	..	0	1	19	10
6100 Paid solely by business	0	..	..	0	0	..	..	0	0	0
6200 Other	0	..	..	101	193	..	..	1	19	10
Total tax revenue	3 418	73 666	146 238	156 032	215 251	..	7 194	46 491	51 672	76 591

	Local government					Social Security Funds				
	1975	1995	2005	2015	2022	1975	1995	2005	2015	2022
1000 Taxes on income, profits and capital gains	175	2 514	4 892	5 633	7 957	0	0	0	0	0
1100 Of individuals	131	2 137	3 426	4 637	6 519	..	..	..	..	..
1200 Corporate	0	377	1 466	996	1 438	..	..	..	..	..
1300 Unallocable between 1100 and 1200	44	0	0	0	0	..	..	..	..	..
2000 Social security contributions	0	0	0	0	0	3 367	49 851	106 040	119 330	168 828
2100 Employees	..	..	..	..	..	645	7 372	15 332	17 242	24 945
2200 Employers	..	..	..	..	..	2 722	35 137	77 989	86 024	125 351
2300 Self-employed or non-employed	..	..	..	..	..	0	7 342	12 719	16 064	18 532
2400 Unallocable between 2100, 2200 and 2300	..	..	..	..	..	0	0	0	0	0
3000 Taxes on payroll and workforce	0	0	0	0	0	0	0	0	0	0
4000 Taxes on property	26	3 759	8 869	16 372	17 245	0	0	0	0	0
4100 Recurrent taxes on immovable property	26	2 754	6 038	12 581	14 052	..	..	..	..	..
4200 Recurrent taxes on net wealth	0	177	431	911	1020	..	..	..	..	..
4300 Estate, inheritance and gift taxes	0	19	79	114	153	..	..	..	..	..
4400 Taxes on financial and capital transactions	0	166	423	145	333	..	..	..	..	..
4500 Non-recurrent taxes	0	0	0	0	0	..	..	..	..	..
4600 Other recurrent taxes on property	0	0	0	0	0	..	..	..	..	..
5000 Taxes on goods and services	104	6 072	12 810	13 067	16 299	0	0	0	0	0
5100 Taxes on production, sale, transfer, etc	104	1 976	5 946	6 846	8 699	..	..	..	..	..
5110 General taxes	95	1 805	4 186	5 068	6 938	..	..	..	..	..
5120 Taxes on specific goods and services	10	171	1 760	1 778	1 761	..	..	..	..	..
5130 Unallocable between 5110 and 5120	0	0	0	0	0	..	..	..	..	..
5200 Taxes on use of goods and perform activities	0	4 096	6 864	6 221	7 600	..	..	..	..	..
5300 Unallocable between 5100 and 5200	0	0	0	0	0	..	..	..	..	..
6000 Other taxes	0	8	6	69	12	0	0	0	0	0
6100 Paid solely by business	..	0	0	0	0	..	..	..	..	..
6200 Other	..	8	6	69	12	..	..	..	..	..
Total tax revenue	305	12 353	26 577	35 141	41 513	3 367	49 851	106 040	119 330	168 828

.. Not available

Note: Including taxes collected on behalf of the European Union.

Table 6.34. Sweden, tax revenues by sub-sectors of government

Million SEK

	Central government					State/Regional				
	1975	1995	2005	2015	2022	1975	1995	2005	2015	2022
1000 Taxes on income, profits and capital gains	28 216	72 342	123 698	21 820	45 369	..	..	..	..	..
1100 Of individuals	25 626	22 541	21 708	-102 059	-155 324	..	..	..	..	..
1200 Corporate	2 590	49 801	101 989	123 878	200 693	..	..	..	..	..
1300 Unallocable between 1100 and 1200	0	0	0	0	0	..	..	..	..	..
2000 Social security contributions[1]	0	0	0	0	0	..	..	..	..	..
2100 Employees	..	0	0	0	0	..	..	..	..	..
2200 Employers	..	49 222	209 370	179 056	218 355	..	..	..	..	..
2300 Self-employed or non-employed	..	1 338	4 639	1 875	1 523	..	..	..	..	..
2400 Unallocable between 2100, 2200 and 2300	..	0	-1 044	-209	-1988	..	..	..	..	..
3000 Taxes on payroll and workforce	5 723	17 800	62 432	194 121	301 306	..	..	..	..	..
4000 Taxes on property	1 469	23 260	40 116	27 917	33 577	..	..	..	..	..
4100 Recurrent taxes on immovable property	11	15 263	25 139	16 509	17 185	..	..	..	..	..
4200 Recurrent taxes on net wealth	647	3 583	4 998	0	0	..	..	..	..	..
4300 Estate, inheritance and gift taxes	335	1 388	1 092	-0	0	..	..	..	..	..
4400 Taxes on financial and capital transactions	476	3 026	8 887	11 408	16 391	..	..	..	..	..
4500 Non-recurrent taxes	0	0	0	0	0	..	..	..	..	..
4600 Other recurrent taxes on property	0	0	0	0	0	..	..	..	..	..
5000 Taxes on goods and services	31 985	237 720	354 724	508 172	708 157	..	..	..	..	..
5100 Taxes on production, sale, transfer, etc	29 820	233 671	343 704	489 420	685 630	..	..	..	..	..
5110 General taxes	15 806	166 557	250 470	383 002	552 379	..	..	..	..	..
5120 Taxes on specific goods and services	14 014	67 114	93 234	106 418	133 251	..	..	..	..	..
5130 Unallocable between 5110 and 5120	0	0	0	0	0	..	..	..	..	..
5200 Taxes on use of goods and perform activities	2 165	4 049	11 019	18 752	22 527	..	..	..	..	..
5300 Unallocable between 5100 and 5200	0	0	0	0	0	..	..	..	..	..
6000 Other taxes	260	1 438	1 347	1 356	3 294	..	..	..	..	..
6100 Paid solely by business	0	0	0	0	0	..	..	..	..	..
6200 Other	260	1 438	1 347	1 356	3 294	..	..	..	..	..
Total tax revenue	67 653	403 120	795 281	934 108	1 309 593	..	..	..	..	..
	Local government					**Social Security Funds**				
	1975	1995	2005	2015	2022	1975	1995	2005	2015	2022
1000 Taxes on income, profits and capital gains	38 415	265 068	435 577	635 719	852 510	0	0	0	0	0
1100 Of individuals	35 269	265 068	435 577	635 719	852 510	..	..	..	..	..
1200 Corporate	3 146	0	0	0	0	..	..	..	..	..
1300 Unallocable between 1100 and 1200	0	0	0	0	0	..	..	..	..	..
2000 Social security contributions[1]	0	0	0	0	0	25 756	0	0	0	0
2100 Employees	..	..	..	..	..	0	28 989	74 178	108 356	145 337
2200 Employers	..	..	..	..	..	24 203	154 154	74 438	112 589	152 020
2300 Self-employed or non-employed	..	..	..	..	..	1 553	3 849	2 403	3 183	3 191
2400 Unallocable between 2100, 2200 and 2300	..	..	..	..	..	0	0	0	0	0
3000 Taxes on payroll and workforce	0	0	0	0	0	0	0	0	0	0
4000 Taxes on property	0	0	0	15 935	21 430	0	0	0	0	0
4100 Recurrent taxes on immovable property	..	..	..	15 935	21 430	..	..	..	..	..
4200 Recurrent taxes on net wealth	..	..	..	0	0	..	..	..	..	..
4300 Estate, inheritance and gift taxes	..	..	..	0	0	..	..	..	..	..
4400 Taxes on financial and capital transactions	..	..	..	0	0	..	..	..	..	..
4500 Non-recurrent taxes	..	..	..	0	0	..	..	..	..	..
4600 Other recurrent taxes on property	..	..	..	0	0	..	..	..	..	..
5000 Taxes on goods and services	149	786	0	0	0	0	0	0	0	0
5100 Taxes on production, sale, transfer, etc	119	732	0	0	0	..	..	..	..	..
5110 General taxes	0	0	0	0	0	..	..	..	..	..
5120 Taxes on specific goods and services	119	732	0	0	0	..	..	..	..	..
5130 Unallocable between 5110 and 5120	0	0	0	0	0	..	..	..	..	..
5200 Taxes on use of goods and perform activities	30	54	0	0	0	..	..	..	..	..
5300 Unallocable between 5100 and 5200	0	0	0	0	0	..	..	..	..	..
6000 Other taxes	0	0	0	0	0	0	0	0	0	0
6100 Paid solely by business	..	..	..	..	..	..	..	..	..	..
6200 Other	..	..	..	..	..	..	..	..	..	..
Total tax revenue	38 564	265 854	435 577	651 654	873 941	25 756	186 992	151 019	224 129	300 548

.. Not available

Note: Including taxes collected on behalf of the European Union.

1. From 1985, social security contributions are classified using the SNA definition of Social security Funds which means that a proportion of these payments are shown under the heading of Central Government. Prior to that year, all such payments were classified under the heading of Social Security.

Table 6.35. Switzerland, tax revenues by sub-sectors of government

Million CHF

	Federal government					State/Regional				
	1975	1995	2005	2015	2022	1975	1995	2005	2015	2022
1000 Taxes on income, profits and capital gains	3 422	10 468	16 341	26 841	30 886	7 756	19 408	26 544	34 657	41 100
1100 Of individuals	2 712	5 699	7 823	10 567	12 897	6 342	16 182	21 289	27 156	31 756
1200 Corporate	710	2 678	4 519	9 731	13 601	1 414	2 628	4 627	6 294	7 329
1300 Unallocable between 1100 and 1200	0	2 092	4 000	6 543	4 388	0	598	628	1 207	2 015
2000 Social security contributions	0	0	0	0	0	0	0	0	0	0
2100 Employees	..	..	..	..	..	..	..	..	..	..
2200 Employers	..	..	..	..	..	..	..	..	..	..
2300 Self-employed or non-employed	..	..	..	..	..	..	..	..	..	..
2400 Unallocable between 2100, 2200 and 2300	..	..	..	..	..	..	..	..	..	..
3000 Taxes on payroll and workforce	0	0	0	0	0	0	0	0	0	0
4000 Taxes on property	463	1 703	2 703	1 674	1 713	1 428	4 116	5 523	7 191	9 521
4100 Recurrent taxes on immovable property	0	0	0	0	0	60	162	230	349	440
4200 Recurrent taxes on net wealth	89	0	0	0	0	988	2 467	3 683	4 992	6 496
4300 Estate, inheritance and gift taxes	0	0	0	0	0	270	974	824	964	1 292
4400 Taxes on financial and capital transactions	374	1 703	2 703	1 674	1 713	110	103	157	177	259
4500 Non-recurrent taxes	0	0	0	0	0	0	0	0	0	0
4600 Other recurrent taxes on property	0	0	0	0	0	0	411	629	709	1 035
5000 Taxes on goods and services	7 431	20 854	28 489	35 508	38 600	795	1 706	2 373	2 901	3 192
5100 Taxes on production, sale, transfer, etc	7 431	19 763	27 114	33 093	35 706	154	266	447	615	702
5110 General taxes	3 205	12 428	18 429	22 791	24 920	0	0	0	0	0
5120 Taxes on specific goods and services	4 226	7 335	8 685	10 302	10 786	154	236	410	594	686
5130 Unallocable between 5110 and 5120	0	0	0	0	0	0	29	37	20	16
5200 Taxes on use of goods and perform activities	0	1 092	1 375	2 415	2 894	641	1 440	1 927	2 286	2 490
5300 Unallocable between 5100 and 5200	0	0	0	0	0	0	0	0	0	0
6000 Other taxes	0	0	0	0	68	0	19	23	230	445
6100 Paid solely by business	..	..	..	..	0	..	6	7	64	108
6200 Other	..	..	..	..	68	..	13	16	165	337
Total tax revenue	11 316	33 026	47 533	64 023	71 267	9 979	25 249	34 462	44 979	54 257

	Local government					Social Security Funds				
	1975	1995	2005	2015	2022	1975	1995	2005	2015	2022
1000 Taxes on income, profits and capital gains	6 403	15 575	18 091	22 865	26 786	0	0	0	0	0
1100 Of individuals	5 398	13 340	15 326	18 651	21 024	..	..	..	..	..
1200 Corporate	1 005	1 624	2 316	3 407	4 178	..	..	..	..	..
1300 Unallocable between 1100 and 1200	0	611	450	806	1 585	..	..	..	..	..
2000 Social security contributions	0	0	0	0	0	8 111	28 019	32 332	44 285	52 285
2100 Employees	..	..	..	..	..	3 589	13 115	15 133	20 542	24 623
2200 Employers	..	..	..	..	..	3 618	13 126	15 146	20 574	24 512
2300 Self-employed or non-employed	..	..	..	..	..	840	1 778	2 053	3 169	3 149
2400 Unallocable between 2100, 2200 and 2300	..	..	..	..	..	64	0	0	0	0
3000 Taxes on payroll and workforce	0	0	0	0	0	0	0	0	0	0
4000 Taxes on property	1 068	2 614	3 251	4 275	5 757	0	0	0	0	0
4100 Recurrent taxes on immovable property	182	443	588	789	1059	..	..	..	..	..
4200 Recurrent taxes on net wealth	809	1 873	2 393	3 104	4 086	..	..	..	..	..
4300 Estate, inheritance and gift taxes	27	89	79	124	187	..	..	..	..	..
4400 Taxes on financial and capital transactions	50	42	38	52	85	..	..	..	..	..
4500 Non-recurrent taxes	0	0	0	0	0	..	..	..	..	..
4600 Other recurrent taxes on property	0	168	153	206	340	..	..	..	..	..
5000 Taxes on goods and services	22	97	78	132	256	0	0	0	0	0
5100 Taxes on production, sale, transfer, etc	17	55	26	63	127	..	..	..	..	..
5110 General taxes	0	0	0	0	0	..	..	..	..	..
5120 Taxes on specific goods and services	17	29	20	15	9	..	..	..	..	..
5130 Unallocable between 5110 and 5120	0	25	6	48	117	..	..	..	..	..
5200 Taxes on use of goods and perform activities	5	42	52	70	129	..	..	..	..	..
5300 Unallocable between 5100 and 5200	0	0	0	0	0	..	..	..	..	..
6000 Other taxes	0	164	223	569	646	0	0	0	0	0
6100 Paid solely by business	..	49	67	277	316	..	..	..	..	..
6200 Other	..	115	156	292	330	..	..	..	..	..
Total tax revenue	7 493	18 451	21 643	27 841	33 445	8 111	28 019	32 332	44 285	52 285

.. Not available

Table 6.36. Türkiye, tax revenues by sub-sectors of government

Million TRY

	Central government					State/Regional				
	1975	1995	2005	2015	2022	1975	1995	2005	2015	2022
1000 Taxes on income, profits and capital gains	..	433	30 324	104 699	761 245	..	..	..	..	..
1100 Of individuals	..	330	20 458	75 426	315 141	..	..	..	..	..
1200 Corporate	..	103	9 866	29 272	446 104	..	..	..	..	..
1300 Unallocable between 1100 and 1200	..	0	0	0	0	..	..	..	..	..
2000 Social security contributions	..	0	0	0	0	..	..	..	..	..
2100 Employees	..	..	..	..	..	..	..	..	..	..
2200 Employers	..	..	..	..	..	..	..	..	..	..
2300 Self-employed or non-employed	..	..	..	..	..	..	..	..	..	..
2400 Unallocable between 2100, 2200 and 2300	..	..	..	..	..	..	..	..	..	..
3000 Taxes on payroll and workforce	..	0	0	0	0	..	..	..	..	..
4000 Taxes on property	..	49	3 626	20 211	80 340	..	..	..	..	..
4100 Recurrent taxes on immovable property	..	0	0	0	0	..	..	..	..	..
4200 Recurrent taxes on net wealth	..	0	0	0	35	..	..	..	..	..
4300 Estate, inheritance and gift taxes	..	1	78	379	2 547	..	..	..	..	..
4400 Taxes on financial and capital transactions	..	29	3 548	19 832	77 758	..	..	..	..	..
4500 Non-recurrent taxes	..	0	0	0	0	..	..	..	..	..
4600 Other recurrent taxes on property	..	0	0	0	0	..	..	..	..	..
5000 Taxes on goods and services	..	574	71 956	231 227	1215 353	..	..	..	..	..
5100 Taxes on production, sale, transfer, etc	..	567	69 266	222 702	1192 588	..	..	..	..	..
5110 General taxes	..	475	30 343	107 451	665 388	..	..	..	..	..
5120 Taxes on specific goods and services	..	92	38 923	115 251	527 200	..	..	..	..	..
5130 Unallocable between 5110 and 5120	..	0	0	0	0	..	..	..	..	..
5200 Taxes on use of goods and perform activities	..	8	2 691	8 526	22 764	..	..	..	..	..
5300 Unallocable between 5100 and 5200	..	0	0	0	0	..	..	..	..	..
6000 Other taxes	..	259	4 181	3 779	13 559	..	..	..	..	..
6100 Paid solely by business	..	0	0	0	0	..	..	..	..	..
6200 Other	..	259	4 181	3 779	13 559	..	..	..	..	..
Total tax revenue	..	1 316	110 088	359 915	2 070 497	..	..	..	..	..

	Local government					Social Security Funds				
	1975	1995	2005	2015	2022	1975	1995	2005	2015	2022
1000 Taxes on income, profits and capital gains	..	63	4 011	14 445	102 673	..	0	0	0	0
1100 Of individuals	..	48	2 706	10 330	41 324	..	..	..	..	..
1200 Corporate	..	15	1 305	4 116	61 349	..	..	..	..	..
1300 Unallocable between 1100 and 1200	..	0	0	0	0	..	..	..	..	..
2000 Social security contributions	..	0	0	0	0	..	212	35 321	170 282	767 544
2100 Employees	..	..	..	..	..	..	82	12 128	64 214	296 029
2200 Employers	..	..	..	..	..	..	110	16 132	95 067	440 551
2300 Self-employed or non-employed	..	..	..	..	..	..	19	7 061	11 001	30 965
2400 Unallocable between 2100, 2200 and 2300	..	..	..	..	..	..	0	0	0	0
3000 Taxes on payroll and workforce	..	0	0	0	0	..	0	0	0	0
4000 Taxes on property	..	4	1 627	8 371	29 132	..	0	0	0	0
4100 Recurrent taxes on immovable property	..	0	1 148	5 882	18 633	..	..	..	..	..
4200 Recurrent taxes on net wealth	..	0	0	0	5	..	..	..	..	..
4300 Estate, inheritance and gift taxes	..	0	10	56	339	..	..	..	..	..
4400 Taxes on financial and capital transactions	..	4	469	2 433	10 156	..	..	..	..	..
4500 Non-recurrent taxes	..	0	0	0	0	..	..	..	..	..
4600 Other recurrent taxes on property	..	0	0	0	0	..	..	..	..	..
5000 Taxes on goods and services	..	84	5 649	28 737	154 778	..	0	0	0	0
5100 Taxes on production, sale, transfer, etc	..	82	5 295	27 560	151 659	..	..	..	..	..
5110 General taxes	..	69	4 014	13 619	88 721	..	..	..	..	..
5120 Taxes on specific goods and services	..	13	1 281	13 940	62 939	..	..	..	..	..
5130 Unallocable between 5110 and 5120	..	0	0	0	0	..	..	..	..	..
5200 Taxes on use of goods and perform activities	..	1	354	1 177	3 118	..	..	..	..	..
5300 Unallocable between 5100 and 5200	..	0	0	0	0	..	..	..	..	..
6000 Other taxes	..	73	721	4 971	19 642	..	0	0	0	0
6100 Paid solely by business	..	0	0	0	0	..	..	..	..	..
6200 Other	..	73	721	4 971	19 642	..	..	..	..	..
Total tax revenue	..	224	12 008	56 525	306 226	..	212	35 321	170 282	767 544

.. Not available

Table 6.37. United Kingdom, tax revenues by sub-sectors of government

Million GBP

	Central government					State/Regional				
	1975	1995	2005	2015	2022	1975	1995	2005	2015	2022
1000 Taxes on income, profits and capital gains	16 716	92 147	177 149	212 726	335 214	..	..	..	..	..
1100 Of individuals	14 936	71 973	130 135	168 901	253 612	..	..	..	..	..
1200 Corporate	2 310	20 174	47 014	43 825	81 601	..	..	..	..	..
1300 Unallocable between 1100 and 1200	-530	0	0	0	0	..	..	..	..	..
2000 Social security contributions	0	0	0	0	0	..	..	..	..	..
2100 Employees	..	..	..	..	..	..	..	..	..	..
2200 Employers	..	..	..	..	..	..	..	..	..	..
2300 Self-employed or non-employed	..	..	..	..	..	..	..	..	..	..
2400 Unallocable between 2100, 2200 and 2300	..	..	..	..	..	..	..	..	..	..
3000 Taxes on payroll and workforce	-1	0	0	0	3 520	..	..	..	..	..
4000 Taxes on property	619	15 730	32 583	46 498	57 537	..	..	..	..	..
4100 Recurrent taxes on immovable property	44	12 369	19 523	28 265	29 059	..	..	..	..	..
4200 Recurrent taxes on net wealth	0	0	0	0	0	..	..	..	..	..
4300 Estate, inheritance and gift taxes	307	1 441	3 150	4 442	6 808	..	..	..	..	..
4400 Taxes on financial and capital transactions	266	1 920	9 910	13 791	21 670	..	..	..	..	..
4500 Non-recurrent taxes	2	0	0	0	0	..	..	..	..	..
4600 Other recurrent taxes on property	0	0	0	0	0	..	..	..	..	..
5000 Taxes on goods and services	8 982	85 507	136 863	205 106	271 347	..	..	..	..	..
5100 Taxes on production, sale, transfer, etc	8 502	81 175	131 467	197 663	257 624	..	..	..	..	..
5110 General taxes	3 515	47 539	84 649	132 906	184 258	..	..	..	..	..
5120 Taxes on specific goods and services	4 987	33 636	46 818	64 757	73 366	..	..	..	..	..
5130 Unallocable between 5110 and 5120	0	0	0	0	0	..	..	..	..	..
5200 Taxes on use of goods and perform activities	698	4 332	5 396	7 443	13 723	..	..	..	..	..
5300 Unallocable between 5100 and 5200	-218	0	0	0	0	..	..	..	..	..
6000 Other taxes	0	0	0	0	0	..	..	..	..	..
6100 Paid solely by business	..	..	..	..	..	..	..	..	..	..
6200 Other	..	..	..	..	..	..	..	..	..	..
Total tax revenue	26 316	193 384	346 595	464 330	667 618	..	..	..	..	..

	Local government					Social Security Funds				
	1975	1995	2005	2015	2022	1975	1995	2005	2015	2022
1000 Taxes on income, profits and capital gains	0	0	0	0	0	0	0	0	0	0
1100 Of individuals	0	..	0	0	0	0	..	0	0	0
1200 Corporate	0	..	0	0	0	0	..	0	0	0
1300 Unallocable between 1100 and 1200	0	..	0	0	0	0	..	0	0	0
2000 Social security contributions	0	0	0	0	0	6 540	44 397	84 459	114 173	176 951
2100 Employees	..	..	..	..	..	2 562	18 646	35 159	44 488	65 337
2200 Employers	..	..	..	..	..	4 068	24 210	46 475	66 491	105 980
2300 Self-employed or non-employed	..	..	..	..	..	195	1 541	2 825	3 194	5 634
2400 Unallocable between 2100, 2200 and 2300	..	..	..	..	..	-285	0	0	0	0
3000 Taxes on payroll and workforce	0	0	0	0	0	0	0	0	0	0
4000 Taxes on property	4 127	9 303	21 255	29 901	43 054	0	0	0	0	0
4100 Recurrent taxes on immovable property	3 978	9 303	21 255	29 754	42 624	..	..	..	..	..
4200 Recurrent taxes on net wealth	0	0	0	0	0	..	..	..	..	..
4300 Estate, inheritance and gift taxes	0	0	0	0	0	..	..	..	..	..
4400 Taxes on financial and capital transactions	0	0	0	0	0	..	..	..	..	..
4500 Non-recurrent taxes	0	0	0	0	0	..	..	..	..	..
4600 Other recurrent taxes on property	149	0	0	0	0	..	..	..	..	..
5000 Taxes on goods and services	0	0	0	0	0	0	0	0	0	0
5100 Taxes on production, sale, transfer, etc	..	..	..	..	..	..	..	..	..	..
5110 General taxes	..	..	..	..	..	..	..	..	..	..
5120 Taxes on specific goods and services	..	..	..	..	..	..	..	..	..	..
5130 Unallocable between 5110 and 5120	..	..	..	..	..	..	..	..	..	..
5200 Taxes on use of goods and perform activities	..	..	..	..	..	..	..	..	..	..
5300 Unallocable between 5100 and 5200	..	..	..	..	..	..	..	..	..	..
6000 Other taxes	0	0	0	0	0	0	0	0	0	0
6100 Paid solely by business	..	..	..	..	..	..	..	..	..	..
6200 Other	..	..	..	..	..	..	..	..	..	..
Total tax revenue	4 127	9 303	21 255	29 901	43 054	6 540	44 397	84 459	114 173	176 951

.. Not available

Note: Including taxes collected on behalf of the European Union.

Table 6.38. United States, tax revenues by sub-sectors of government

Million USD

	Federal government					State/Regional				
	1975	1995	2005	2015	2022	1975	1995	2005	2015	2022
1000 Taxes on income, profits and capital gains	163 072	750 144	1 268 412	1 883 845	2 908 068	25 509	157 598	275 728	390 957	685 940
1100 Of individuals	122 386	594 213	948 921	1 554 757	2 539 126	..	128 429	226 576	343 101	539 976
1200 Corporate	40 686	155 931	319 490	329 088	368 943	..	29 169	49 152	47 855	145 964
1300 Unallocable between 1100 and 1200	0	0	0	0	0	..	0	0	0	0
2000 Social security contributions	0	0	0	0	0	0	0	0	0	0
2100 Employees	..	..	..	..	..	..	..	..	..	..
2200 Employers	..	..	..	..	..	..	..	..	..	..
2300 Self-employed or non-employed	..	..	..	..	..	..	..	..	..	..
2400 Unallocable between 2100, 2200 and 2300	..	..	..	..	..	..	..	..	..	..
3000 Taxes on payroll and workforce	0	0	0	0	0	0	0	0	1 774	3 634
4000 Taxes on property	4 613	14 948	24 989	20 191	32 830	3 284	16 880	28 808	29 193	47 393
4100 Recurrent taxes on immovable property	0	0	0	0	0	1 451	7 240	9 037	12 039	16 825
4200 Recurrent taxes on net wealth	0	0	0	0	0	0	0	0	0	0
4300 Estate, inheritance and gift taxes	4 611	14 948	24 989	20 191	32 830	1 418	5 061	5 322	5 115	7 498
4400 Taxes on financial and capital transactions	2	0	0	0	0	415	2 386	11 711	8 392	17 973
4500 Non-recurrent taxes	0	0	0	0	0	0	0	0	0	0
4600 Other recurrent taxes on property	0	0	0	0	0	0	2 193	2 738	3 647	5 097
5000 Taxes on goods and services	20 773	75 553	99 411	141 864	194 189	52 032	232 033	377 795	499 158	746 193
5100 Taxes on production, sale, transfer, etc	20 442	75 553	99 411	141 864	194 189	43 960	200 495	323 137	434 664	644 217
5110 General taxes	0	0	0	0	0	24 916	135 132	218 917	287 681	447 763
5120 Taxes on specific goods and services	20 442	75 553	99 411	141 864	194 189	19 044	65 363	104 220	146 984	196 453
5130 Unallocable between 5110 and 5120	0	0	0	0	0	0	0	0	0	0
5200 Taxes on use of goods and perform activities	331	0	0	0	0	8 072	31 538	54 658	64 494	101 976
5300 Unallocable between 5100 and 5200	0	0	0	0	0	0	0	0	0	0
6000 Other taxes	0	0	0	0	0	0	0	0	0	0
6100 Paid solely by business	..	..	..	..	..	..	..	..	..	..
6200 Other	..	..	..	..	..	..	..	..	..	..
Total tax revenue	188 458	840 645	1 392 812	2 045 901	3 135 087	80 825	406 511	682 331	921 083	1 483 160

	Local government					Social Security Funds				
	1975	1995	2005	2015	2022	1975	1995	2005	2015	2022
1000 Taxes on income, profits and capital gains	2 635	15 795	28 272	40 426	60 861	0	0	0	0	0
1100 Of individuals	..	13 308	22 481	32 220	48 231	..	..	..	..	..
1200 Corporate	..	2 487	5 791	8 206	12 630	..	..	..	..	..
1300 Unallocable between 1100 and 1200	..	0	0	0	0	..	..	..	..	..
2000 Social security contributions	0	0	0	0	0	85 039	510 476	831 410	1 125 493	1 556 656
2100 Employees	..	..	..	..	..	36 382	221 800	362 829	502 103	716 437
2200 Employers	..	..	..	..	..	45 241	261 805	423 936	561 936	757 071
2300 Self-employed or non-employed	..	..	..	..	..	3 416	26 871	44 645	61 454	83 148
2400 Unallocable between 2100, 2200 and 2300	..	..	..	..	..	0	0	0	0	0
3000 Taxes on payroll and workforce	0	0	0	0	0	0	0	0	0	0
4000 Taxes on property	50 040	197 392	359 344	488 579	656 624	0	0	0	0	0
4100 Recurrent taxes on immovable property	50 040	195 339	342 203	477 293	643 201	..	..	..	..	..
4200 Recurrent taxes on net wealth	0	0	0	0	0	..	..	..	..	..
4300 Estate, inheritance and gift taxes	0	30	114	243	306	..	..	..	..	..
4400 Taxes on financial and capital transactions	0	50	13 570	6 223	6 621	..	..	..	..	..
4500 Non-recurrent taxes	0	0	0	0	0	..	..	..	..	..
4600 Other recurrent taxes on property	0	1 973	3 457	4 821	6 497	..	..	..	..	..
5000 Taxes on goods and services	8 389	57 507	108 696	151 229	214 724	0	0	0	0	0
5100 Taxes on production, sale, transfer, etc	6 518	42 269	76 976	118 436	167 253	..	..	..	..	..
5110 General taxes	4 322	29 316	53 842	85 569	123 031	..	..	..	..	..
5120 Taxes on specific goods and services	2 196	12 953	23 134	32 867	44 222	..	..	..	..	..
5130 Unallocable between 5110 and 5120	0	0	0	0	0	..	..	..	..	..
5200 Taxes on use of goods and perform activities	1 871	15 238	31 720	32 793	47 471	..	..	..	..	..
5300 Unallocable between 5100 and 5200	0	0	0	0	0	..	..	..	..	..
6000 Other taxes	0	0	0	0	0	0	0	0	0	0
6100 Paid solely by business	..	..	..	..	..	..	..	..	..	..
6200 Other	..	..	..	..	..	..	..	..	..	..
Total tax revenue	61 064	270 695	496 313	680 234	932 209	85 039	510 476	831 410	1 125 493	1 556 656

.. Not available

Annex A. The OECD classification of taxes and interpretative guide

Table of Contents

A.1 The OECD Classification of Taxes

1. **1000. Taxes on income, profits and capital gains**

    1100. Taxes on income, profits and capital gains of individuals

        1110. On income and profits

        1120. On capital gains

    1200. Corporate taxes on income, profits and capital gains

        1210. On income and profits

        1220. On capital gains

    1300. Unallocable as between 1100 and 1200

2. **2000. Social security contributions**

    2100. Employees

        2110. On a payroll basis

        2120. On an income tax basis

    2200. Employers

        2210. On a payroll basis

        2220. On an income tax basis

    2300. Self-employed or non-employed

        2310. On a payroll basis

        2320. On an income tax basis

    2400 Unallocable as between 2100, 2200 and 2300

        2410. On a payroll basis

        2420. On an income tax basis

3. **3000. Taxes on payroll and workforce**

4. **4000. Taxes on property**

    4100. Recurrent taxes on immovable property

        4110. Households

        4120. Other

    4200 Recurrent taxes on net wealth

        4210. Individual

        4220. Corporate

    4300. Estate, inheritance and gift taxes

        4310. Estate and inheritance taxes

        4320. Gift taxes

    4400. Taxes on financial and capital transactions

4500. Other non-recurrent taxes on property

4510. On net wealth

4520. Other non-recurrent taxes

4600. Other recurrent taxes on property

5. **5000. Taxes on goods and services**

5100. Taxes on production, sale, transfer, leasing and delivery of goods and rendering of services

5110. General taxes

5111. Value added taxes

5112. Sales taxes

5113. Turnover and other general taxes on goods and services

5120. Taxes on specific goods and services

5121. Excises

5122. Profits of fiscal monopolies

5123. Customs and import duties

5124. Taxes on exports

5125. Taxes on investment goods

5126 . Taxes on specific services

5127. Other taxes on international trade and transactions

5128. Other taxes on specific goods and services

5130. Unallocable as between 5110 and 5120

5200. Taxes on use of goods, or on permission to use goods or perform activities

5210. Recurrent taxes

5211. Paid by households in respect of motor vehicles

5212. Paid by others in respect of motor vehicles

5213. Other recurrent taxes

5220. Non-recurrent taxes

5300. Unallocable as between 5100 and 5200

6. **6000. Other taxes**

6100. Paid solely by business

6200. Paid by other than business or unidentifiable

A.2 Coverage

General criteria

1. In the OECD classification, the term "taxes" is confined to compulsory unrequited payments to the general government or to a supranational authority. Taxes are unrequited in the sense that benefits provided by government to taxpayers are not normally in proportion to their payments.

2. The term "tax" does not include fines, penalties and compulsory loans paid to government. Borderline cases between tax and non-tax revenues in relation to certain fees and charges are discussed in §12–15.

3. General government consists of the central administration, agencies whose operations are under its effective control, state and local governments and their administrations, certain social security schemes and autonomous governmental entities, excluding public enterprises. This definition of government follows that of the 2008 *System of National Accounts* (SNA).[1] In that publication, the general government sector and its sub-sectors are defined in Chapter 4, paragraphs 4.117 to 4.165.

4. Extra-budgetary units are part of the general government system. These are general government entities with individual budgets that are not fully covered by the main or general budget. These entities operate under the authority or control of a central, state, or local government. Extra-budgetary entities may have their own revenue sources, which may be supplemented by grants (transfers) from the general budget or from other sources. Even though their budgets may be subject to approval by the legislature, similar to that of budgetary accounts, they have discretion over the volume and composition of their spending. Such entities may be established to carry out specific government functions, such as road construction, or the nonmarket production of health or education services. Budgetary arrangements vary widely across countries, and various terms are used to describe these entities, but they are often referred to as "extra-budgetary funds" or "decentralised agencies."

5. Compulsory, unrequited payments collected by national governments and paid to supranational authorities are also included as taxes under the definition in paragraph 1. Taxes that are collected by national governments and paid to a supranational authority are included as tax revenues at the level of the supranational authority in the SNA2008 (paragraphs 22.60-61, 22.88 and 22.99 refer) and the ESA2010 (paragraph 20.165 refers). In Revenue Statistics, these taxes include customs duties, contributions to the EU Single Resolution Fund, and any other taxes collected by EU member states on behalf of the European Union. They are included in the tax revenue amounts in the country tables (Chapter 5) of the country in which they are collected and are attributed to the supranational level of government (see §102).

6. In countries where the church forms part of general government, church taxes are included, provided they meet the criteria set out in §1 above. As the data refer to receipts of general government and to supranational authorities, levies paid to non-government bodies, welfare agencies or social insurance schemes outside general government, trade unions or trade associations, even where such levies are compulsory, are excluded. Compulsory payments to general government earmarked for such bodies are, however, included, provided that the government is not simply acting in an agency capacity.[2] Profits from fiscal monopolies are distinguished from those of other public enterprises and are treated as taxes because they reflect the exercise of the taxing power of the state by the use of monopoly powers (see §66–68), as are profits received by the government from the purchase and sale of foreign exchange at different rates (see §76).

7. Taxes paid by governments (e.g., social security contributions and payroll taxes paid by governments in their capacity as an employer, consumption taxes on their purchases or taxes on their property) are not excluded from the data provided. However, where it is possible to identify the amounts of revenue involved,[3] they are shown in Table 5.40 of this Report.

8. The relationship between this classification and that of the System of National Accounts (SNA) is set out in Sections A.9 and A.11 below. Because of the differences between the two classifications, the data shown in national accounts are sometimes calculated or classified differently from the practice set out in this guide. These and other differences are mentioned where appropriate (e.g., in §31 below) but it is not possible to refer to all of them. There may also be some differences between this classification and that employed domestically by certain national administrations (e.g., see §13 below), so that OECD and national statistics data may not always be consistent: any such differences, however, are likely to be very slight in terms of amounts of revenues involved.

Social security contributions

9. Compulsory social security contributions, as defined in §40, and paid to general government, are treated here as tax revenues. They may, however, differ from other taxes in that the receipt of social security benefits depends, in most countries, upon appropriate contributions having been made, although the size of the benefits is not necessarily related to the amount of the contributions. Better comparability between countries is obtained by treating social security contributions as taxes, but they are listed under a separate heading so that they can be distinguished in any analysis.

10. The strict dividing line between tax revenues (compulsory unrequited payments to general government or a supranational authority) and non-tax compulsory payments (NTCPs) (payments that are either requited or made to other institutions) is clearly defined. However, within the range of different compulsory payments to governments existing across countries, it is not always straightforward in practice to decide whether specific payments are either taxes or NTCPs. For example, compulsory pension savings that are controlled by general government and that accumulate on an individual account earning a market return or a rate that compensates for inflation would at first sight be categorised as NTCPs as opposed to taxes. However, even these payments might still be 'unrequited' and therefore classify as taxes instead of NTCPs (for example if these pension savings are not paid out when the taxpayer dies before reaching the pension age and the funds are then used to provide a minimum pension to all taxpayers that are insured). These issues result in the social security revenue figures reported for most countries being based on the premise that all types of compulsory payments to general government are judged to some extent to have a re-distributional element. It should be noted that this conclusion is based on a typically broad interpretation of the term 'unrequited' in the tax definition.

11. Social security contributions which are either voluntary or not payable to general government (see §1) are not treated as taxes, though in some countries, as indicated in the country footnotes, there are difficulties in completely eliminating voluntary contributions and certain compulsory payments to the private sector from the revenue figures. Imputed social security contributions are also not treated as taxes.

Fees, user charges and licence fees

12. Apart from vehicle licence fees, which are universally regarded as taxes, it is not easy to distinguish between those fees and user charges which are to be treated as taxes and those which are not, since, whilst a fee or charge is levied in connection with a specific service or activity, the strength of the link between the fee and the service provided may vary considerably, as may the relation between the amount of the fee and the cost of providing the service. Where the recipient of a service pays a fee clearly related to the cost of providing the service, the levy may be regarded as requited and under the definition of §1 would not be considered as a tax. In the following cases, however, a levy could be considered as 'unrequited':

- *a)* where the charge greatly exceeds the cost of providing the service;
- *b)* where the payer of the levy is not the receiver of the benefit (e.g., a fee collected from slaughterhouses to finance a service which is provided to farmers);

c) where government is not providing a specific service in return for the levy which it receives even though a licence may be issued to the payer (e.g., where the government grants a hunting, fishing or shooting licence which is not accompanied by the right to use a specific area of government land);

d) where benefits are received only by those paying the levy but the benefits received by each individual are not necessarily in proportion to his payments (e.g., a milk marketing levy paid by dairy farmers and used to promote the consumption of milk).

e) where the payer of the levy cannot opt out from making payments when not using the service (e.g. public broadcast fees where the payer is obliged to pay the levy even if not consuming public broadcast service).

13. In marginal cases, however, the application of the criteria set out in §1 can be particularly difficult. The solution adopted — given the desirability of international uniformity and the relatively small amounts of revenue usually involved — is to follow the predominant practice among tax administrations rather than to allow each country to adopt its own view as to whether such levies are regarded as taxes or as non-tax revenue.[4]

14. A list of the main fees and charges in question and their normal[5] treatment in this publication is as follows:

Non-tax revenues:	court fees; driving licence fees; harbour fees; passport fees
Taxes within heading 5200	permission to perform such activities as distributing films; hunting, fishing and shooting; providing entertainment or gambling facilities; selling alcohol or tobacco; permission to own dogs or to use or own motor vehicles or guns; severance taxes

15. In practice, it may not always be possible to isolate tax receipts from non-tax revenue receipts when they are recorded together. If it is estimated that the bulk of the receipts derive from non-tax revenues, the whole amount involved is treated as a non-tax revenue; otherwise, such government receipts are included and classified according to the rules provided in §33 below.

Royalties

16. The ownership of subsoil assets in the form of deposits of minerals or fossil fuels (coal, oil, or natural gas) depends upon the way in which property rights are defined by law and also on international agreements in the case of deposits below international waters. In some cases, either the ground below which the mineral deposits are located, the deposits themselves or both may belong to a local or central government unit.

17. In such cases, these general government units may grant leases to other institutional units that permit them to extract these deposits over a specified period of time in return for a payment or series of payments. These payments are often described as 'royalties' but they are essentially rent that accrues to owners of natural resources in return for putting these assets at the disposal of other units for specified periods of time. The rent may take the form of periodic payments of fixed amounts, irrespective of the rate of extraction, or, more commonly, they may be a function of the quantity, volume, or value of the asset extracted. Enterprises engaged in exploration on government land may make payments to general government units in exchange for the right to undertake test drilling or otherwise investigate the existence and location of subsoil assets. Such payments are also recorded as rents even though no extraction may take place. These payments are therefore classified as non-tax revenues.

18. The same principles apply when other institutional units are granted leases that permit them to fell timber in natural forests on land owned by general government units. These payments are also classified as non-tax revenues.

19. These rents or royalties paid to general government should not be confused with taxes on income and profits, severance taxes, business licenses, or other taxes. If the payments are levied on the profits from the extraction activity, then they should be classified as taxes on incomes, profits and gains (1000). In addition, any severance payments that are imposed on the extraction of minerals and fossil fuels from reserves owned privately or by another government should be classified as taxes. Payments related to the gross value of production should be classified as other taxes on goods and services (5128). Payments for a license or permit to conduct extraction operations should be classified as taxes on use of goods and on permission to use goods or perform activities (5213).

Fines and penalties

20. In principle, fines and penalties charged on overdue taxes or penalties imposed for the attempted evasion of taxes should not be recorded as tax revenues. However, it may not be possible to separate payments of fines or other penalties from the revenues from the taxes to which they relate. In this case, the fines and penalties relating to a particular tax are recorded together with the revenues from that tax and fines and penalties paid with revenue from unidentifiable taxes are classified as other taxes in Category 6000. Fines not relating to tax offences (e.g., for parking offences), or not identifiable as relating to tax offences, are also not treated as tax revenues.

A.3 Basis of reporting

Accrual or cash reporting

21. The data reported in the *Revenue Statistics* publications for recent years are predominantly recorded on an accrual basis for OECD countries, i.e. recorded at the time that the tax liability was created. Further information is provided in the footnotes to the country table in Chapter 5 of the Report.

22. However, data for earlier years and for non-OECD countries are still predominantly recorded on a cash basis, i.e. at the time at which the payment was received by government. Thus, for example, taxes withheld by employers in one year but paid to the government in the following year and taxes due in one year but actually paid in the following year are both included in the receipts of the second year. Corrective transactions, such as refunds, repayments and drawbacks, are deducted from gross revenues of the period in which they are made.

23. Data on tax revenues are recorded without offsets for the administrative expenses connected with tax collection. Similarly, where the proceeds of tax are used to subsidise particular members of the community, the subsidy is not deducted from the yield of the tax, though the tax may be shown net of subsidies in the national records of some countries.

24. As regards fiscal monopolies (heading 5122), only the amount actually transferred to the government is included in government revenues. However, if any expenditures of fiscal monopolies are considered to be government expenditures (e.g., social expenditures undertaken by fiscal monopolies at the direction of the government) they are added back for the purpose of arriving at tax revenue figures (see §66 below).

The distinction between tax and expenditure provisions[6]

25. Because this publication is concerned only with the revenue side of government operations, no account being taken of the expenditure side, a distinction has to be made between tax and expenditure provisions. Normally there is no difficulty in making this distinction as expenditures are made outside the tax system and the tax accounts and under legislation separate from the tax legislation. In borderline cases, cash flow is used to distinguish between tax provisions and expenditure provisions. Insofar as a provision

affects the flow of tax payments from the taxpayer to the government, it is regarded as a tax provision and is taken into account in the data shown in this publication. A provision which does not affect this flow is seen as an expenditure provision and is disregarded in the data recorded in this publication.

26. Tax allowances, exemptions and deductions against the tax base clearly affect the amount of tax paid to the government and are therefore considered as tax provisions. At the other extreme, those subsidies which cannot be offset against tax liability and which are clearly not connected with the assessment process, do not reduce tax revenues as recorded in this publication. Tax credits are amounts deductible from tax payable (as distinct from deductions from the tax base). Two types of tax credits are distinguished, those (referred to here as wastable tax credits) which are limited to the amount of the tax liability and therefore cannot give rise to a payment by the authorities to the taxpayer, and those (referred to as non-wastable tax credits) which are not so limited, so that the excess of the credit over the tax liability can be paid to the taxpayer.[7] A wastable tax credit, like a tax allowance, clearly affects the amount of tax paid to the government, and is therefore considered as a tax provision. The practice followed for non-wastable tax credits[8] is to distinguish between the 'tax expenditure component',[9] which is that portion of the credit that is used to reduce or eliminate a taxpayer's liability, and the 'transfer component', which is the portion that exceeds the taxpayer's liability and is paid to that taxpayer. Reported tax revenues should be reduced by the amount of the tax expenditure component but not by the amount of the transfer component. In addition, the amounts of the tax expenditure and transfer components should be reported as memorandum items in the country tables. Countries that are unable to distinguish between the tax expenditure and transfer components should indicate whether or not the tax revenues have been reduced by the total of these components, and provide any available estimates of the amounts of the two components. Further information is given in Chapter 1 of the Report, which illustrates the effect of alternative treatments of non-wastable tax credits on tax to GDP.

Calendar and fiscal years

27. National authorities whose fiscal years do not correspond to the calendar year show data, where possible, on a calendar year basis to permit maximum comparability with the data of other countries. There remain a few countries where data refer to fiscal years. For these the GDP data used in the comparative tables also correspond to the fiscal years.

A.4 General classification criteria

The main classification criteria

28. The classification of receipts among the main headings (1000, 2000, 3000, 4000, 5000 and 6000) is generally governed by the base on which the tax is levied: 1000 income, profits and capital gains; 2000 and 3000 earnings, payroll or number of employees; 4000 property; 5000 goods and services; 6000 multiple bases, other bases or unidentifiable bases. Where a tax is calculated on more than one base, the receipts are, where possible, split among the various headings (see §33 and §84). The headings 4000 and 5000 cover not only taxes where the tax base is the property, goods or services themselves but also certain related taxes. Thus, taxes on the transfer of property are included in 4400[10] and taxes on the use of goods or on permission to perform activities in 5200. In headings 4000 and 5000 a distinction is made in certain sub-headings between recurrent and non-recurrent taxes: recurrent taxes are defined as those levied at regular intervals (usually annually) and non-recurrent taxes are levied once and for all (see also §48 to §51, §54, §55 and §81 for particular applications of this distinction).

29. Earmarking of a tax for specific purposes does not affect the classification of tax receipts. However, as explained in §40 on the classification of social security contributions, the conferment of an entitlement to social benefits is crucial to the definition of the 2000 main heading.

30. The way that a tax is levied or collected (e.g., by use of stamps) does not affect classification.

Classification of taxpayers

31. In certain sub-headings, distinctions are made between different categories of taxpayers. These distinctions vary from tax to tax:

a) *Between individuals and corporations in relation to income and net wealth taxes*

The basic distinction is that corporation income taxes, as distinct from individual income taxes, are levied on the corporation as an entity, not on the individuals who own it, and without regard to the personal circumstances of these individuals. The same distinction applies to net wealth taxes on corporations and those on individuals. Taxes paid on the profits of partnerships and the income of institutions, such as life insurance or pension funds, are classified according to the same rule. They are classified as corporate taxes (1200) if they are charged on the partnership or institution as an entity without regard to the personal circumstances of the owners. Otherwise, they are treated as individual taxes (1100). Usually, there is different legislation for the corporation taxes and for the individual taxes.[11] The distinction made here between individuals and corporations does not follow the sector classification between households, enterprises, and so on of the System of National Accounts for income and outlay accounts. The SNA classification requires certain unincorporated businesses[12] to be excluded from the household sector and included with non-financial enterprises and financial institutions. The tax on the profits of these businesses, however, cannot always be separated from the tax on the other income of their owners, or can be separated only on an arbitrary basis. No attempt at this separation is made here and the whole of the individual income tax is shown together without regard to the nature of the income chargeable.

b) *Between households and others in relation to taxes on immovable property*

Here the distinction is that adopted by the SNA for the production and consumption expenditure accounts. The distinction is between households as consumers (i.e. excluding non-incorporated business) on the one hand and producers on the other hand. However, taxes on dwellings occupied by households, whether paid by owner-occupiers, tenants or landlords, are classified under households. This follows the common distinction made between taxes on domestic property versus taxes on business property. Some countries are not, however, in a position to make this distinction.

c) *Between households and others in relation to motor vehicle licences*

Here the distinction is between households as consumers on the one hand and producers on the other, as in the production and consumption expenditure accounts of the SNA.

d) *Between business and others in relation to the residual taxes (6000)*

The distinction is the same as in c) above between producers on the one hand and households as consumers on the other hand. Taxes which are included under the heading 6000 because they involve more than one tax base or because the tax base does not fall within any of the previous categories but which are identifiable as levyable only on producers and not on households are included under 'business'. The rest of the taxes which are included under the heading 6000 are shown as 'other' or non-identified.

Surcharges

32. Receipts from surcharges in respect of particular taxes are usually classified with the receipts from the relevant tax whether or not the surcharge is temporary. If, however, the surcharge has a characteristic which would render it classifiable in a different heading of the OECD list, receipts from the surcharge are classified under that heading separately from the relevant tax.

Unidentifiable tax receipts and residual sub-headings

33. A number of cases arise where taxes cannot be identified as belonging entirely to a heading or sub-heading of the OECD classification and the following practices are applied in such cases:

a) The heading is known, but it is not known how receipts should be allocated between sub-headings: receipts are classified in the appropriate residual sub-heading (1300, 2400, 4520, 4600, 5128, 5130, 5300 or 6200).

b) It is known that the bulk of receipts from a group of taxes (usually local taxes) is derived from taxes within a particular heading or sub-heading, but some of the taxes in the group whose amount cannot be precisely ascertained may be classifiable in other headings or sub-headings: receipts are shown in the heading or sub-heading under which most of the receipts fall.

c) Neither the heading nor sub-heading of a tax (usually local) can be identified: the tax is classified in 6200 unless it is known that it is a tax on business in which case it is classified in 6100.

A.5 Commentaries on items of the list

1000 — Taxes on income, profits and capital gains

34. This heading covers taxes levied on the net income or profits (i.e. gross income minus allowable tax reliefs) of individuals and enterprises. Also covered are taxes levied on the capital gains of individuals and enterprises, and gains from gambling.

35. Included in the heading are:

a) taxes levied predominantly on income or profits, though partially on other bases. Taxes on various bases which are not predominantly income or profits are classified according to the principles laid down in §33 and §84;

b) taxes on property, which are levied on a presumed or estimated income as part of an income tax (see also §48(a), (c) and (d));

c) compulsory payments to social security fund contributions that are levied on income but do not confer an entitlement to social benefits. When such contributions do confer an entitlement to social benefits, they are included in heading 2000 (see §40);

d) receipts from integrated scheduler income tax systems are classified as a whole in this heading, even though certain of the scheduler taxes may be based upon gross income and may not take into account the personal circumstances of the taxpayer.

36. The main subdivision of this heading is between levies on individuals (1100) and those on corporate enterprises (1200). Under each subdivision a distinction is made between taxes on income and profits (1110 and 1210), and taxes on capital gains (1120 and 1220). If certain receipts cannot be identified as appropriate to either 1100 or 1200, or if in practice this distinction cannot be made (e.g., because there are no reliable data on the recipients of payments from which withholding taxes are deducted) they are classified in 1300 as not-allocable.

Treatment of credits under imputation systems

37. Under imputation systems of corporate income tax, a company's shareholders are wholly or partly relieved of their liability to income tax on dividends paid by the company out of income or profits liable to corporate income tax. In countries with such systems,[13] part of the tax on the company's profits is available

to provide relief against the shareholders' own tax liability. The relief to the shareholder takes the form of a tax credit, the amount of which may be less than, equal to, or more than the shareholder's overall tax liability. If the tax credit exceeds this tax liability the excess may be payable to the shareholder. As this type of tax credit is an integral part of the imputation system of corporate income tax, any payment to the shareholders is treated as a repayment of tax and not as expenditure (compare the treatment of other tax credits described in §26).

38. As the tax credit under imputation systems (even when exceeding tax liability) is to be regarded as a tax provision, the question arises whether it should be deducted from individual income tax receipts (1110) or corporate income tax receipts (1210). In this Report, the full amount of corporate income tax paid is shown under 1210 and no imputed tax is included under 1110. Thus, the full amount of the credit reduces the amount of 1110 whether the credit results in a reduction of personal income tax liability or whether an actual refund is made because the credit exceeds the income tax liability. (Where, however, such tax credits are deducted from corporation tax in respect of dividends paid to corporations the amounts are deducted from the receipts of 1210).

1120 and 1220 — Taxes on capital gains

39. These sub-headings comprise taxes imposed on capital gains, 1120 covering those levied on the gains of individuals and 1220 those levied on the gains of corporate enterprises, where receipts from such taxes can be separately identified. In many countries, this is not the case and the receipts from such taxes are then classified with those from the income tax. Heading 1120 also includes taxes on gains from gambling.

2000 — Social security contributions

40. Classified here are all compulsory payments to general government that confer an entitlement to receive a (contingent) future social benefit. Such payments are usually earmarked to finance social benefits and are often paid to institutions of general government that provide such benefits. However, such earmarking is not part of the definition of social security contributions and is not required for a tax to be classified here. However, conferment of an entitlement is required for a tax to be classified under this heading. So, levies on income or payroll that are earmarked for social security funds but do not confer an entitlement to benefit are excluded from this heading and shown under personal income taxes (1100) or taxes on payroll and workforce (3000). Taxes on other bases, such as goods and services, which are earmarked for social security benefits are not shown here but are classified according to their respective bases because they generally confer no entitlement to social security benefits.

41. Contributions for the following types of social security benefits would, *inter alia*, be included: unemployment insurance benefits and supplements, accident, injury and sickness benefits, old-age, disability and survivors' pensions, family allowances, reimbursements for medical and hospital expenses or provision of hospital or medical services. Contributions may be levied on both employees and employers.

42. Contributions may be based on earnings or payroll ('on a payroll basis') or on net income after deductions and exemptions for personal circumstances ('on an income tax basis'), and the revenues from the two bases should be separately identified if possible. However, where contributions to a general social security scheme are on a payroll basis, but the contributions of particular groups (such as the self-employed) cannot be assessed on this basis and net income is used as a proxy for gross earnings, the receipts may still be classified as being on a payroll basis. In principle, this heading excludes voluntary contributions paid to social security schemes. When separately identifiable these are shown in the memorandum item on the financing of social security benefits. In practice, however, they cannot always be separately identified from compulsory contributions, in which case they are included in this heading.

43. Contributions to social insurance schemes which are not institutions of general government and to other types of insurance schemes, provident funds, pension funds, friendly societies or other saving schemes are not considered as social security contributions. Provident funds are arrangements under which the contributions of each employee and of the corresponding employer on his/her behalf are kept in a separate account earning interest and withdrawable under specific circumstances. Pension funds are separately organised schemes negotiated between employees and employers and carry provisions for different contributions and benefits, sometimes more directly tied to salary levels and length of service than under social security schemes. When contributions to these schemes are compulsory or quasi-compulsory (e.g., by virtue of agreement with professional and union organisations) they are shown in the memorandum item (refer to Table 5.39 of the Report).

44. Contributions by government employees and by governments in respect of their employees, to social security schemes classified within general government are included in this heading. Contributions to separate schemes for government employees, which can be regarded as replacing general social security schemes, are also regarded as taxes.[14] Where, however, a separate scheme is not seen as replacing a general scheme and has been negotiated between the government, in its role as an employer, and its employees, it is not regarded as social security and contributions to it are not regarded as taxes, even though the scheme may have been established by legislation.

45. This heading excludes 'imputed' contributions, which correspond to social benefits paid directly by employers to their employees or former employees or to their representatives (e.g., when employers are legally obliged to pay sickness benefits for a certain period).

46. Contributions are divided into those of employees (2100), employers (2200), and self-employed or non-employed (2300), and then further sub-divided according to the basis on which they are levied. Employees are defined for this purpose as all persons engaged in activities of business units, government bodies, private non-profit institutions, or other paid employment, except the proprietors and their unpaid family members in the case of unincorporated businesses. Members of the armed forces are included, irrespective of the duration and type of their service, if they contribute to social security schemes. The contributions of employers are defined as their payments on account of their employees to social security schemes. Where employees or employers are required to continue the payment of social security contributions when the employee becomes unemployed these contributions, data permitting, are shown in 2100 and 2200 respectively. Accordingly, the sub-heading 2300 is confined to contributions paid by the self-employed and by those outside of the labour force (e.g., disabled or retired individuals).

3000 — Taxes on payroll and workforce

47. These consist of taxes payable by enterprises assessed either as a proportion of the wages or salaries paid or as a fixed amount per person employed. They do not include compulsory social security contributions paid by employers or any taxes paid by employees themselves out of their wages or salaries

4000 — Taxes on property

48. This heading covers recurrent and non-recurrent taxes on the use, ownership or transfer of property. These include taxes on immovable property or net wealth, taxes on the change of ownership of property through inheritance or gift and taxes on financial and capital transactions. The following kinds of tax are excluded from this heading:

- *a)* taxes on capital gains resulting from the sale of a property (1120 or 1220);
- *b)* taxes on the use of goods or on permission to use goods or perform activities (5200); see §78;

c) taxes on immovable property levied on the basis of a presumed net income which take into account the personal circumstances of the taxpayer. They are classified as income taxes along with taxes on income and capital gains derived from property (1100);

d) taxes on the use of property for residence, where the tax is payable by either proprietor or tenant and the amount payable is a function of the user's personal circumstances (pay, dependants, and so on). They are classified as taxes on income (1100);

e) taxes on building in excess of permitted maximum density, taxes on the enlargement, construction or alteration of certain buildings beyond a permitted value and taxes on building construction. They are classified as taxes on permission to perform activities (5200);

f) taxes on the use of one's own property for special trading purposes like selling alcohol, tobacco, meat or for exploitation of land resources (e.g., United States severance taxes). They are classified as taxes on permission to perform activities (5200).

4100 — Recurrent taxes on immovable property

49. This sub-heading covers taxes levied regularly in respect of the use or ownership of immovable property.

- these taxes are levied on land and buildings;
- they can be in the form of a percentage of an assessed property value based on a national rental income, sales price, or capitalised yield; or in terms of other characteristics of real property, (for example size or location) from which a presumed rent or capital value can be derived.
- such taxes can be levied on proprietors, tenants, or both. They can also be paid by one level of government to another level of government in respect of property under the jurisdiction of the latter.
- debts are not taken into account in the assessment of these taxes, and they differ from taxes on net wealth in this respect.

50. Taxes on immovable property are further sub-divided into those paid by households (4110) and those paid by other entities (4120), according to the criteria set out in §31(*b*) above.

4200 — Recurrent taxes on net wealth

51. This sub-heading covers taxes levied regularly (in most cases annually) on net wealth, i.e. taxes on a wide range of movable and immovable property, net of debt. It is sub-divided into taxes paid by individuals (4210) and taxes paid by corporate enterprises (4220) according to the criteria set out in §31(*a*) above. If separate figures exist for receipts paid by institutions, the tax payments involved are added to those paid by corporations.

4300 — Estate, inheritance and gift taxes

52. This sub-heading is divided into taxes on estates and inheritances (4310) and taxes on gifts (4320).[15] Estate taxes are charged on the amount of the total estate whereas inheritance taxes are charged on the shares of the individual recipients; in addition the latter may take into account the relationship of the individual recipients to the deceased.

4400 — Taxes on financial and capital transactions

53. This sub-heading comprises, *inter alia*, taxes on the issue, transfer, purchase and sale of non-financial and financial assets (including foreign exchange or securities), taxes on cheques and other forms of payment, and taxes levied on specific legal transactions such as validation of contracts and the sale of immovable property. The heading does not include:

a) taxes on the use of goods or property or permission to perform certain activities (5200);

b) fees paid to cover court charges, charges for birth, marriage or death certificates, which are normally regarded as non-tax revenues (see §12);

c) taxes on capital gains (1000);

d) recurrent taxes on immovable property (4100);

e) recurrent taxes on net wealth (4200);

f) once-and-for-all levies on property or wealth (4500);

g) stamp taxes not related to financial and capital transactions

  i. Stamp taxes on the sale of specific products, such as alcoholic beverages or tobacco (5121);

  ii. Stamp taxes restricted by law to imported products (5123) or to exported products (5124); or

  iii. Stamp taxes not falling exclusively on a single category of transaction (6000).

4500 — Other non-recurrent taxes on property

54. This sub-heading covers once-and-for-all, as distinct from recurrent, levies on property. It is divided into taxes on net wealth (4510) and other non-recurrent taxes on property (4520). Heading 4510 would include taxes levied to meet emergency expenditures, or for redistribution purposes. Heading 4520 would cover taxes levied to take account of increases in land value due to permission given to develop or provision of additional local facilities by general government, any taxes on the revaluation of capital and once-and-for-all taxes on particular items of property.

4600 — Other recurrent taxes on property

55. These rarely exist in OECD member countries, but the heading would include taxes on goods such as cattle, jewellery, windows, and other external signs of wealth.

5000 — Taxes on goods and services

56. All taxes and duties levied on the production, extraction, sale, transfer, leasing or delivery of goods, and the rendering of services (5100), or in respect of the use of goods or permission to use goods or to perform activities (5200) are included here. The heading thus covers:

a) multi-stage cumulative taxes;

b) general sales taxes — whether levied at manufacture/production, wholesale or retail level;

c) value-added taxes;

d) excises;

e) taxes levied on the import and export of goods;

f) taxes levied in respect of the use of goods and taxes on permission to use goods, or perform certain activities;

g) taxes on the extraction, processing or production of minerals and other products.

57. Borderline cases between this heading and heading 4000 (taxes on property) and 6100 (other taxes on business) are referred to in §48, §53 and §80. Residual sub-headings (5300) and (5130) cover tax receipts which cannot be allocated between 5100 and 5200 and between 5110 and 5120, respectively; see §33.

5100 — Taxes on the production, sale, transfer, leasing and delivery of goods and rendering of services

58. This sub-heading consists of all taxes, levied on transactions in goods and services on the basis of their intrinsic characteristics (e.g., value, weight of tobacco, strength of alcohol, and so on) as distinct from taxes imposed on the use of goods, or permission to use goods or perform activities, which fall under 5200.

5110 — General taxes on goods and services

59. This sub-heading includes all taxes, other than import and export duties (5123 and 5124), levied on the production, leasing, transfer, delivery or sales of a wide range of goods and/or the rendering of a wide range of services, irrespective of whether they are domestically produced or imported and irrespective of the stage of production or distribution at which they are levied. It thus covers value-added taxes, sales taxes and multi-stage cumulative taxes. Receipts from border adjustments in respect of such taxes when goods are imported are added to gross receipts for this category, and repayments of such taxes when goods are exported are deducted. These taxes are subdivided into 5111 value-added taxes, 5112 sales taxes, 5113 turnover and other general taxes on goods and services.

60. Borderline cases arise between this heading and taxes on specific goods (5120) when taxes are levied on a large number of goods, for example, the United Kingdom purchase tax (repealed in 1973) and the Japanese commodity tax (repealed in 1988). In conformity with national views, the former United Kingdom purchase tax is classified as a general tax (5112) and the former Japanese commodity tax as excises (5121).

5111 — Value-added taxes

61. All general consumption taxes charged on value-added are classified in this sub-heading, irrespective of the method of deduction and the stages at which the taxes are levied. In practice, all OECD countries with value-added taxes normally allow immediate deduction of taxes on purchases by all but the final consumer and impose tax at all stages. In some countries the heading may include certain taxes, such as those on financial and insurance activities, either because receipts from them cannot be identified separately from those from the value-added tax, or because they are regarded as an integral part of the value-added tax, even though similar taxes in other countries might be classified elsewhere (e.g., 5126 as taxes on services or 4400 as taxes on financial and capital transactions).

5112 — Sales taxes

62. All general taxes levied at one stage only, whether at manufacturing or production, wholesale or retail stage are classified here.

5113 — Turnover and other general taxes on goods and services

63. These are multi-stage cumulative taxes and taxes where elements of consumption taxes are combined with multistage taxes. These taxes are levied each time a transaction takes place without deduction for taxes paid on inputs. Multi-stage taxes can be combined with elements of value-added or sales taxes.

5120 — Taxes on specific goods and services

64. Excises, profits generated and transferred from fiscal monopolies, and customs and imports duties as well as taxes on exports, foreign exchange transactions, investment goods and betting stakes and special taxes on services, which do not form part of a general tax of 5110, are included in this category.

5121 — Excises

65. Excises are taxes levied as a product specific unit tax on a predefined limited range of goods. Excises are usually levied at differentiated rates on nonessential or luxury goods, alcoholic beverages, tobacco, and energy. Excises may be imposed at any stage of production or distribution and are usually assessed as a specific charge per unit based on characteristics by reference to the value, weight, strength, or quantity of the product. Included are special taxes on individual products such as sugar, sugar beets, matches, and chocolates; taxes levied at varying rates on a certain range of goods; and taxes levied on tobacco goods, alcoholic drinks, motor fuels, and hydrocarbon oils. If a tax collected principally on imported goods also applies, or would apply, under the same law to comparable domestically produced goods, then the revenue from this tax is classified as arising from excises rather than from import duties. This principle applies even if there is no comparable domestic production or no possibility of such production. Taxes on the use of utilities such as water, electricity, gas, and energy are regarded as excises rather than taxes on specific services (5126). Excises exclude those taxes that are levied as general taxes on goods and services (5110); profits of fiscal monopolies (5122); customs and other import duties (5123); or taxes on exports (5124).

5122 — Profits of fiscal monopolies

66. This sub-heading covers that part of the profits of fiscal monopolies which is transferred to general government or which is used to finance any expenditures considered to be government expenditures (see §24). Amounts are shown when they are transferred to general government or used to make expenditures considered to be government expenditures.

67. Fiscal monopolies reflect the exercise of the taxing power of government by the use of monopoly powers. Fiscal monopolies are non-financial public enterprises exercising a monopoly in most cases over the production or distribution of tobacco, alcoholic beverages, salt, matches, playing cards and petroleum or agricultural products (i.e. on the kind of products which are likely to be, alternatively or additionally, subject to the excises of 5121), to raise the government revenues which in other countries are gathered through taxes on dealings in such commodities by private business units. The government monopoly may be at the production stage or, as in the case of government-owned and controlled liquor stores, at the distribution stage.

68. Fiscal monopolies are distinguished from public utilities such as rail transport, electricity, post offices, and other communications, which may enjoy a monopoly or quasi-monopoly position but where the primary purpose is normally to provide basic services rather than to raise revenue for government. Transfers from such other public enterprises to the government are considered as non-tax revenues. The traditional concept of fiscal monopoly is not generally extended to include state lotteries, the profits of which are usually accordingly regarded as non-tax revenues. However, they can be included as tax revenues if the prime reason for their operation is to raise revenues to finance government expenditure. Fiscal monopoly profits are distinguished from export and import monopoly profits (5127) transferred from marketing boards or other enterprises dealing with international trade.

5123 — Customs and other import duties

69. Taxes, stamp duties and surcharges restricted by law to imported products are included here. Also included are levies on imported agricultural products which are imposed in member countries of the European Union and amounts paid by certain of these countries under the Monetary Compensation Accounts (MCA) system.[16] Customs duties collected by European Union member states on behalf of the European Union are reported under this heading at the supranational level of government in the country tables (in Chapter 5 of the Report). Excluded here are taxes collected on imports as part of a general tax on goods and services, or an excise applicable to both imported and domestically produced goods.

5124 — Taxes on exports

70. In the 1970s, export duties were levied in Australia, Canada and Portugal as a regular measure and they have been used in Finland for counter-cyclical purposes. Some member countries of the European Union pay, as part of the MCA system, a levy on exports (see note 16 to §69). Where these amounts are identifiable, they are shown in this heading. This heading does not include repayments of general consumption taxes or excises or customs duties on exported goods, which should be deducted from the gross receipts under 5110, 5121 or 5123, as appropriate.

5125 — Taxes on investment goods

71. This sub-heading covers taxes on investment goods, such as machinery. These taxes may be imposed for a number of years or temporarily for counter-cyclical purposes. Taxes on industrial inputs which are also levied on consumers [e.g., the Swedish energy tax which is classified under (5121)] are not included here.

5126 — Taxes on specific services

72. All taxes assessed on the payment for specific services, such as taxes on insurance premiums, banking services, gambling and betting stakes (e.g., from horse races, football pools, lottery tickets), transport, entertainment, restaurant and advertising charges, fall into this category. Taxes on entry to casinos, races, other similar events or venues as well as stamp taxes on specific services are also classified under this heading. Taxes levied on the gross income of companies providing a specific service (e.g. transportation [including airport and other passenger taxes] insurance, banking, entertainment, restaurants, and advertising) are also classified under this heading.

73. Tax revenues from bank levies and payments to deposit insurance and financial stability schemes are also included here:

- Compulsory payments of stability fees, bank levies and deposit insurance should generally be treated as tax revenues where the payments are made to general government or supranational authorities and are allocated to the governments' consolidated or general funds so that the government is free to make immediate use of the money for the purposes that it chooses. This principle would apply regardless of whether the government is promising to make payments to guarantee the banks' customer deposits in some future contingency.
- If the compulsory payments are made to general government and placed in funds that are earmarked to be entirely channelled back to the sector of the economy that comprises the companies that are subject to the payment, they would still generally be treated as tax revenues on the grounds that the funds would be available for the government and would reduce its budget deficit, the fee is unrequited for an individual entity and the amounts raised could be unrelated to any eventual pay out to depositors or expenditure on wider support for the financial sector.

- Payments to made to the smaller long-standing schemes for insuring 'retail' deposits, where the payment levels are consistent with the costs of insurance should be classified as fee for service.
- Any payments which involve governments realising the assets of a failed institution or receiving a priority claim on its assets in liquidation in order to fund payments of compensation to customers for their lost deposits would be treated as a fee for a service as opposed to tax revenues.
- Compulsory payments that are made to funds operated outside the government sector and non-state institutions backed by the deposit takers and all payments to voluntary schemes should not be treated as tax revenues.
- Contributions made to the EU Single Resolution Fund are also included here and recorded under the supranational level of government in the country tables.

74. Excluded from this sub-heading are:

a) taxes on services forming part of a general tax on goods and services (5110);

b) taxes on electricity, gas and energy (5121 as excises);

c) taxes on individual gains from gambling (1120 as taxes on capital gains of individuals and non-corporate enterprises) and lump-sum taxes on the transfer of private lotteries or on the permission to set up lotteries (5200);[17]

d) taxes on cheques and on the issue, transfer or redemption of securities (4400 as taxes on financial and capital transactions);

e) general taxes on turnover (5113).

5127 — Other taxes on international trade and transactions

75. This sub-heading covers revenue received by the government from the purchase and sale of foreign exchange at different rates. When the government exercises monopoly powers to extract a margin between the purchase and sales price of foreign exchange, other than to cover administrative costs, the revenue derived constitutes a compulsory levy exacted in indeterminate proportions from both purchaser and seller of foreign exchange. It is the common equivalent of an import duty and export duty levied in a single exchange rate system or of a tax on the sale or purchase of foreign exchange. Like the profits of fiscal monopolies and import or export monopolies transferred to government, it represents the exercise of monopoly powers for tax purposes and is included in tax revenues.

76. The sub-heading covers also the profits of export or import monopolies, which do not however exist in OECD countries, taxes on purchase or sale of foreign exchange, and any other taxes levied specifically on international trade or transactions.

5128 — Other taxes on specific goods and services

77. This item includes taxes on the extraction of minerals, fossil fuels and other exhaustible resources from deposits owned privately or by another government together with any other unallocable receipts from taxes on specific goods and services. Taxes on the extraction of exhaustible resources are usually a fixed amount per unit of quality or weight, but can be a percentage of value. The taxes are recorded when the resources are extracted. Payments from the extraction of exhaustible resources from deposits owned by the government unit receiving the payment are classified as rent.

5200 — Taxes on use of goods or on permission to use goods or perform activities

78. This sub-heading covers taxes which are levied in respect of the use of goods as distinct from taxes on the goods themselves. Unlike the latter taxes – reported under 5100 –, they are not assessed on the value of the goods but usually as fixed amounts. Taxes on permission to use goods or to perform activities are also included here, as are pollution taxes not based upon the value of particular goods. It is

sometimes difficult to distinguish between compulsory user charges and licence fees which are regarded as taxes and those which are excluded as non-tax revenues. The criteria which are employed are noted in §12–13.

79. Although the sub-heading refers to the 'use' of goods, registration of ownership rather than use may be what generates liability to tax, so that the taxes of this heading may apply to the ownership of animals or goods rather than their use (e.g., race horses, dogs and motor vehicles) and may apply even to unusable goods (e.g., unusable motor vehicles or guns).

80. Borderline cases arise with:

a) taxes on the permission to perform business activities which are levied on a combined income, payroll or turnover base and, accordingly, are classified following the rules in §84;

b) taxes on the ownership or use of property of headings 4100, 4200 and 4600. The heading 4100 is confined to taxes on the ownership or tenancy of immovable property and – unlike the taxes of 5200 – they are related to the value of the property. The net wealth taxes and taxes on chattels of 4200 and 4600 respectively are confined to the ownership rather than the use of assets, apply to groups of assets rather than particular goods and again are related to the value of the assets,

5210 — Recurrent taxes on use of goods and on permission to use goods or perform activities

81. The principal characteristic of taxes classified here is that they are levied at regular intervals and that they are usually fixed amounts. The most important item in terms of revenue receipts is vehicle licence taxes. This sub-heading also covers taxes on permission to hunt, shoot, fish or to sell certain products and taxes on the ownership of dogs, broadcast licence fees and taxes on the performance of certain services, provided that they meet the criteria set out in §12–13. The sub-divisions of 5210 are:

- user taxes on motor vehicles paid by households (5211);
- taxes on motor vehicles paid by others (5212); and
- other recurrent taxes (5213). This sub-heading covers business and professional licences paid by enterprises in order to obtain a licence to carry on a particular kind of business or profession when the levies are on a recurring basis. Licences such as taxi and casino licences are included. Dog licences and recurrent general licences for hunting, shooting and fishing where the right to carry out these activities is not granted as part of a normal commercial transaction are also included under this heading. Broadcast licence fees are included when the payer of the levy cannot opt out from making payments for public broadcast if they do not wish to watch or listen to public broadcast services (e.g. by declaring that one does not consume public broadcast services). Specific exemptions (for example, for elderly people) do not change the compulsory nature of the payment.

82. Excluded from sub-heading 5213 are:

a) licences where the right to carry out such activities is granted as part of a normal commercial transaction (e.g., the granting of the licence is accompanied by the right to use a specific area which is owned by government);

b) payments relating to the checks carried out by the government on the suitability and or safety of the business premises or equipment, or on the quality or standard of goods or services produced as a condition for granting such a licence. These payments are not unrequited and should be treated as payments for services rendered, unless the amounts charged for the licences are out of all proportion to the costs of the checks carried out by governments.

c) broadcast licence fees if users can opt out from paying broadcast licence fees in cases where they do not wish to consume these services without affecting their ability to consume private broadcast services.

5220 — Non-recurrent taxes on use of goods and on permission to use goods or perform activities

83. This section covers non-recurrent taxes levied on the use of goods or on permission to use goods or perform activities and taxes levied each time goods are used. It includes taxes levied on the emission or discharge into the environment of noxious gases, liquids or other harmful substances.

- Payments for tradable emission permits issued by governments under cap and trade schemes should be recorded here at the time the emissions occur. No revenue should be recorded for permits that governments issue free of charge. The accrual basis of recording means that there can be a timing difference between the cash being received by government for the permits and the time the emission occurs. In the national accounts, this timing gives rise to a financial liability for government during the period.
- Payments made for the collection and disposal of waste or noxious substances by public authorities should be excluded as they constitute a sale of services to enterprises.

84. Other taxes falling under heading 5200 that are not levied recurrently are also included here. Thus, once-and-for-all payments for permission to sell liquor or tobacco or to set up betting shops are included provided they meet the criteria set out in §12–13.

6000 — Other taxes

85. Taxes levied on a base, or bases, other than those described under headings 1000, 3000, 4000 and 5000, or on bases of which cannot be considered to be related to any one of these headings, are included here. Where taxes are levied on a multiple base and it is possible to estimate the receipts related to each base the separate amounts are included under the appropriate headings. If separate amounts cannot be estimated and it is known that most of the receipts are derived from one base, the whole of the receipts are classified according to that base. Otherwise, they are classified here. Other revenues included here are presumptive taxes not included elsewhere in the classification system, taxes on individuals in the form of a poll tax or capitation tax, stamp taxes not related to financial and capital transactions nor falling exclusively on a single category of transaction, expenditure taxes where personal deductions or exemptions are applied and unidentifiable tax receipts. A subdivision is made between taxes levied wholly or predominantly on business (6100) and those levied on others (6200).

A.6 Conciliation with National Accounts

86. This section of the tables provides a re-conciliation between the OECD calculation of total tax revenues and the total of all taxes and social contributions paid to general government as recorded in the country's National Accounts. Where the country is a member of the European Union (EU), the comparison is between the OECD calculation of total tax revenues and the sum of tax revenues and social contributions recorded in the combination of the general government and the institutions of the EU sectors of the National Accounts.

A.7 Memorandum item on the financing of social security benefits

87. In view of the varying relationship between taxation and social security contributions and the cases referred to in §40 to §46, a memorandum item collects together all payments earmarked for social security-

type benefits, other than voluntary payments to the private sector. Data are presented as follows (refer Table 5.39 of the Report):

a) Taxes of 2000 series.

b) Taxes earmarked for social security benefits.

c) Voluntary contributions to the government.

d) Compulsory contributions to the private sector.

Guidance on the breakdown of (a) to (d) above is provided in §40 to §46.

A.8 Memorandum item on identifiable taxes paid by government

88. Identifiable taxes actually paid by government are presented in a memorandum item classified by the main headings of the OECD classification of taxes. In the vast majority of countries, only social security contributions and payroll taxes paid by government can be identified. These are, however, usually the most important taxes paid by governments (refer to Table 5.40 of the Report).

A.9 Relation of OECD classification of taxes to national accounting systems

89. A system of national accounts (SNA) seeks to provide a coherent framework for recording and presenting the main flows relating respectively to production, consumption, accumulation and external transactions of a given economic area, usually a country or a major region within a country. Government revenues are an important part of the transactions recorded in SNA. The final version of the 2008 SNA was jointly published by five international organisations: the United Nations, the International Monetary Fund, the European Union, the Organisation for Economic Co-operation and Development, and the World Bank in August 2009. The *System* is a comprehensive, consistent and flexible set of macroeconomic accounts. It is designed for use in countries with market economies, whatever their stage of economic development, and also in countries in transition to market economies. The important parts of the SNA's conceptual framework and its definitions of the various sectors of the economy have been reflected in the OECD's classification of taxes.

90. There are, however, some differences between the OECD classification of taxes and SNA concepts that are listed below. They arise because the aim of the former is to provide the maximum disaggregation of statistical data on what are generally regarded as taxes by tax administrations.

a) OECD includes compulsory social security contributions paid to general government in total tax revenues. Imputed and voluntary contributions plus those paid to private funds are not treated as taxes (§9 and §11 above);

b) there are different points of view on whether or not some levies and fees are classified as taxes (§12 and §13 above);

c) OECD excludes imputed taxes or subsidies resulting from the operation of official multiple exchange rates or from the central bank paying a rate of interest on required reserves that is different from other market rates;

d) there are differences in the treatment of non-wastable tax credits

91. As noted in §1 and §2, headings 1000 to 6000 of the OECD list of taxes cover all unrequited payments to general government or to a supranational authority, other than compulsory loans and fines. Such unrequited payments including fines, but excluding compulsory loans can be obtained from adding together the following figures in the 2008 SNA

- value-added type taxes (D.211);

- taxes and duties on imports, excluding VAT (D.212);
- export taxes (D.213);
- taxes on products, excluding VAT, import and export taxes (D.214);
- other taxes on production (D.29);
- taxes on income (D.51);
- other current taxes (D.59);
- actual social contributions (D.611 and D613), excluding voluntary contributions and payments to employment-related schemes that are not social security schemes
- capital taxes (D.91).

A.10 The OECD classification of taxes and the International Monetary Fund (GFS) system

92. The coverage and valuation of tax revenues in the GFS system and the 2008 SNA are very similar. Therefore, the differences between the OECD classification and that of the 2008 SNA (see §90 above) also apply to the GFS. In addition, the International Monetary Fund subdivides the OECD 5000 heading into section IV (Domestic Taxes on Goods and Services) and section V (Taxes on International Trade and Transactions). This reflects the fact that while the latter usually yield insignificant amounts of revenue in OECD countries, this is not the case in many non-OECD countries.

A.11 Comparison of the OECD classification of taxes with other international classifications

93. The table below describes an item by item comparison of the OECD classification of taxes and the classifications used in the following:

a) System of National Accounts (2008 SNA);

b) European System of Accounts (2010 ESA);

c) IMF Government Finance Statistics Manual (GFSM2014).

94. These comparisons represent those that would be expected to apply in the majority of cases. However in practice some flexibility should be used in their application. This is because in particular cases, countries can adopt varying approaches to the classification of revenues in National Accounts.

			OECD Classification	2008 SNA	2010 ESA	GFSM2014
1000			Taxes on income, profits and capital gains			
	1100		Individuals			
		1110	Income and profits	D51-8.61a	D51A	1111
		1120	Capital gains	D51-8.61c, d	D51C, D	1111
	1200		Corporations			
		1210	Income and profits	D51-8.61b	D51B	1112
		1220	Capital gains	D51-8.61c	D51C	1112
	1300		Unallocable as between 1100 and 1200			1113
2000			Social security contributions			
	2100		Employees	D613-8.85	D613	1211
	2200		Employers	D611-8.83	D611	1212
	2300		Self-employed, non-employed	D613-8.85	D613	1213
	2400		Unallocable as between 2100, 2200 and 2300			1214

3000				Taxes on payroll and workforce	D29-7.97a	D29C	112
4000				Taxes on property			
	4100			Recurrent taxes on immovable property			
		4110		Households	D59-8.63a	D59A	1131
		4120		Other	D29-7.97b	D29A	1131
	4200			Recurrent net wealth taxes			
		4210		Individual	D59-8.63b	D59A	1132
		4220		Corporations	D59-8.63b	D59A	1132
	4300			Estate, inheritance and gift taxes			
		4310		Estate and inheritance taxes	D91-10.207b	D91A	1133
		4320		Gift taxes	D91-10.207b	D91A	1133
	4400			Taxes on financial and capital transactions	D59-7.96d; D29-7.97e	D214B, C	11414; 1161
	4500			Other non-recurrent taxes on property	D91-10.207a	D91B	1135
	4600			Other recurrent taxes on property	D59-8.63c	D59A	1136
5000				Taxes on goods and services			
	5100			Taxes on production, sale and transfer of goods and services			
		5110		General taxes on goods and services			
			5111	Value-added taxes	D211-7.89	D211; D29G	11411
			5112	Sales taxes	D2122-7.94a; D214-7.96a	D21224; D214I	11412
			5113	Turnover and other general taxes on goods and services	D214-7.96a	D214I	11413
		5120		Taxes on specific goods and services			
			5121	Excises	D2122-7.94b; D214-7.96b	D21223; D214A, B, D	1142
			5122	Profits of fiscal monopolies	D214-7.96e	D214J	1143
			5123	Customs and other import duties	D2121-7.93	D2121; D21221, 2	1151
			5124	On exports	D213-7.95a	D214K	1152-4
			5125	On investment goods			
			5126	On specific services	D2122-7.94c; D214-7.96c	D21225; D214E, F, G, H; D29F	1144; 1156
			5127	Other taxes on international trade and transactions	D2122-7.94d D29-7.95b D29-7.97g D59-8.64d	D21226; D29D; D59E	1153; 1155-6
			5128	Other taxes on specific goods and services			1146
		5130		Unallocable between 5110 and 5120			
	5200			Taxes on use of goods and on permission to use goods or perform activities			
		5210		Recurrent taxes on use of goods and on permission to use goods or perform activities			
			5211	Motor vehicle taxes households	D59-8.64c	D59D	11451
			5212	Motor vehicles taxes others	D29-7.97d	D214D; D29B	11451
			5213	Other recurrent taxes on use of goods and on permission to use goods or perform activities	D29-7.97c, d, f D59-8.64c	D29B, E, F; D59D	11452
		5220		Non-recurrent taxes on permission to use goods or perform activities			11452
	5300			Unallocable as between 5100 and 5200			
6000				Other taxes			
	6100			Payable solely by business			1161
	6200			Payable by other than business, or unidentifiable	D59-8.64a, b	D59B, C	1162

A.12 Attribution of tax revenues by sub-sectors of general government

95. The OECD classification requires a breakdown of tax revenues by sub-sectors of government. The definition of each sub-sector and the criteria to be used to attribute tax revenues between these sub-sectors are set out below. They follow the guidance of the 2008 SNA and GFSM 2014.

Sub-sectors of general government to be identified

a) *Central government*

96. The central government sub-sector includes all governmental departments, offices, establishments and other bodies which are agencies or instruments of the central authority whose competence extends over the whole territory, with the exception of the administration of social security funds. Central government therefore has the authority to impose taxes on all resident and non-resident units engaged in economic activities within the country.

b) *State, provincial or regional government*

97. This sub-sector consists of intermediate units of government exercising a competence at a level below that of central government. It includes all such units operating independently of central government in a part of a country's territory encompassing a number of smaller localities, with the exception of the administration of social security funds. In unitary countries, regional governments may be considered to have a separate existence where they have substantial autonomy to raise a significant proportion of their revenues from sources within their control and their officers are independent of external administrative control in the actual operation of the unit's activities.

98. At present, federal countries comprise the majority of cases where revenues attributed to intermediate units of government are identified separately. Colombia and Spain are the only two unitary countries in this position. In the remaining unitary countries, regional revenues are included with those of local governments.

c) *Local* government

99. This sub-sector includes all other units of government exercising an independent competence in part of the territory of a country, with the exception of the administration of social security funds. It encompasses various urban and/or rural jurisdictions (e.g., local authorities, municipalities, cities, boroughs, districts).

d) *Social security funds*

100. Social security funds form a separate sub-sector of general government. The social security sub-sector is defined in the 2008 SNA by the following extracts from paragraphs 4.124 to 4.126 and 4.147:

"Social security schemes are social insurance schemes covering the community as a whole or large section of the community that are imposed and controlled by government units. The schemes cover a wide variety of programmes, providing benefits in cash or in kind for old age, invalidity or death, survivors, sickness and maternity, work injury, unemployment, family allowance, health care, etc. There is not necessarily a direct link between the amount of the contribution paid by an individual and the benefits he or she may receive." (Paragraph 4.124).

"When social security schemes are separately organised from the other activities of government units and hold their assets and liabilities separately from the latter and engage in financial transactions on their own account they qualify as institutional units that are described as social security funds." (Paragraph 4.125).

"The amounts raised, and paid out, in social security contributions and benefits may be deliberately varied in order to achieve objectives of government policy that have no direct connection with the concept of social security as a scheme to provide social benefits to members of the community. They may be raised or lowered in order to influence the level of aggregate demand in the economy, for example. Nevertheless, so long as they remain separately constituted funds, they must be treated as separate institutional units in the SNA. (Paragraph 4.126).

"The social security funds sub-sector (of general government) consists of the social security funds operating at all levels of government. Such funds are social insurance schemes covering the community as a whole or large section of the community that are imposed by government units." (Paragraph 4.147).

101. This definition of social security funds is followed in the OECD classification with the two following exceptions which are excluded

- Schemes imposed by government and operated by bodies outside the general government sector, as defined in §3 of this manual; and
- Schemes to which all contributions are voluntary.

Supranational Authorities

102. This sub-sector covers the revenue-raising operations of supra-national authorities within a country. In practice, the only relevant supranational authority in the OECD area is that of the institutions of the European Union (EU). Tax revenues collected by member countries and paid to the EU are included in the *Revenue Statistics* at the supranational level of government. Income taxes and social security contributions collected by European Institutions and paid by European civil servants who are resident of EU member countries should not be included.

Criteria to be used for the attribution of tax revenues

103. When a government collects taxes and pays them over in whole or in part to other governments, it is necessary to determine whether the revenues should be considered to be those of the collecting government which it distributes to others as grants, or those of the beneficiary governments which the collecting government receives and passes on only as their agent. The criteria to be used in the attribution of revenues are set out in §104 to §107 which replicate paragraphs 3.70 to 3.73 from the 2008 SNA.

104. In general, a tax is attributed to the government unit that

a) exercises the authority to impose the tax (either as a principal or through the delegated authority of the principal),

b) has final discretion to set and vary the rate of the tax

105. Where an amount is collected by one government for and on behalf of another government, and the latter government has the authority to impose the tax, and set and vary its rate, then the former is acting as an agent for the latter and the tax is reassigned. Any amount retained by the collecting government as a collection charge should be treated as a payment for a service. Any other amount retained by the collecting government, such as under a tax-sharing arrangement, should be treated as a current grant. If the collecting government was delegated the authority to set and vary the rate, then the amount collected should be treated as tax revenue of this government.

106. Where different governments jointly and equally set the rate of a tax and jointly and equally decide on the distribution of the proceeds, with no individual government having ultimate overriding authority, then the tax revenues are attributed to each government according to its respective share of the proceeds. If an arrangement allows one government unit to exercise ultimate overriding authority, then all of the tax revenue is attributed to that unit.

107. There may also be the circumstance where a tax is imposed under the constitutional or other authority of one government, but other governments individually set the tax rate in their jurisdictions. The proceeds of the tax generated in each respective government's jurisdiction are attributed as tax revenues of that government.

108. The levies paid by the member states of the EU take the form specific levies which include

a) custom duties and levies on agricultural goods (5123),

b) gross monetary compensation accounts (5123 if relating to imports and 5124 if relating to exports);

c) contributions to the Single Resolution Fund (5126); and

d) Steel, coal, sugar and milk levies (5128).

109. The custom duties collected by member states on behalf of the EU are recorded

- on a gross of collection fee basis;
- using figures adjusted so that duties are shown on a 'final destination' as opposed to a 'country of first entry' basis where such adjustments can be made. These adjustments concern in particular duties collected at important (sea) ports. Although the EU duties are collected by the authorities of the country of first entry, when possible these duties should be excluded from the revenue of the collecting country and be included in the revenue of the country of final destination

110. These are the specific EU levies that most clearly conform to the attribution criterion described in §102 above. Consequently, these amounts are footnoted as a memorandum item to the EU member state country tables (in Chapter 5) and are shown as supranational revenues against each of the tax headings identified in §108.

Notes

1. All references to SNA are to the 2008 edition.

2. See section A.12 of this guide for a discussion of the concept of agency capacity.

3. It is usually possible to identify amounts of social security contributions and payroll taxes, but not other taxes paid by government.

4. If, however, a levy which is considered as non-tax revenue by most countries is regarded as a tax — or raises substantial revenue — in one or more countries, the amounts collected are footnoted at the end of the relevant country tables, even though the amounts are not included in total tax revenues.

5. Names, however, can frequently be misleading. For example, though a passport fee would normally be considered a non-tax revenue, if a supplementary levy on passports (as is the case in Portugal) were imposed in order to raise substantial amounts of revenue relative to the cost of providing the passport, the levy would be regarded as a tax under 5200.

6. A more detailed explanation of this distinction can be found in the special feature, 'Current issues in reporting tax revenues', in the 2001 edition of *Revenue Statistics*.

7. Sometimes the terms 'non-refundable' and 'refundable' are used, but it may be considered illogical to talk of 'refundable' when nothing has been paid.

8. A different treatment, however, is accorded to non-wastable tax credits under imputation systems of corporate income tax (§37–39).

9. This is not strictly a true tax expenditure in the formal sense. Such tax expenditures require identification of a benchmark tax system for each country or, preferably, a common international benchmark. In practice it has not been possible to reach agreement on a common international benchmark.

10. Unless based on the profit made on a sale, in which case they would be classified as capital gains taxes under 1120 or 1220.

11. In some countries the same legislation applies to both individual and corporate enterprises for particular taxes on income. However, the receipts from such taxes are usually allocable between individuals and enterprises and can therefore be shown in the appropriate sub-heading.

12. For example, "... sufficiently self-contained and independent that they behave in the same way as corporations... (including) keeping a complete set of accounts" (2008 SNA, section 4.44).

13. In Canada — a country also referred to as having an imputation system — the (wastable) tax credit for the shareholder is in respect of domestic corporation tax deemed to have been paid whether or not a corporation tax liability has arisen. As there is no integral connection between the corporation tax liability and the credit given against income tax under such systems, these credits for dividends are treated, along with other tax credits, on the lines described in §26.

14. This may also apply where a scheme for government employees existed prior to the introduction of a general social security scheme.

15. In the 2008 SNA, these are regarded as capital transfers and not as taxes (see section A.8).

16. This is the system by which the European Union adjusts for differences between the exchange rates used to determine prices under the Common Market Agricultural Policy and actual exchange rates. Payments under the system may relate to imports or exports and where these amounts are separately identifiable they are shown under the appropriate heading (5123 or 5124). In this Report, these amounts are shown gross (i.e. without deducting any subsidies paid out under the MCA system).

17. Transfers of profits of State lotteries are regarded as non-tax revenues (see also §68).

www.ingramcontent.com/pod-product-compliance
Lightning Source LLC
Chambersburg PA
CBHW061158240926
51846CB00006B/1047
* 9 7 8 9 2 6 4 4 2 2 1 8 6 *